Power and the People:

Essays on Russian History

Power and the People: Essays on Russian History

John L. H. Keep

EAST EUROPEAN MONOGRAPHS, BOULDER
DISTRIBUTED BY COLUMBIA UNIVERSITY PRESS, NEW YORK

1995

EAST EUROPEAN MONOGRAPHS, NO. CDXV

Copyright © 1995 by John Keep
ISBN 0–88033–312–X
Library of Congress Catalog Card Number 95–60899

Printed in the United States of America

CONTENTS

Acknowledgements   7

Foreword   9

List of Abbreviations   19

Part I: MUSCOVITE RUSSIA

1. The Muscovite Elite and the Approach to Pluralism   23
2. The Decline of the Zemsky Sobor   51
   Afterword   73
3. Bandits and the Law in Muscovy   87
4. The Regime of Filaret, 1619–1633   109

Part II: ARMY AND SOCIETY IN IMPERIAL RUSSIA

5. The Secret Chancellery, the Guards and the Dynastic Crisis of 1740–1741   135
6. Catherine's Veterans   163
7. Paul I and the Militarization of Government   175
8. The Military Style of the Romanov Rulers   189
9. The Russian Army's Response to the French Revolution   211
10. From the Pistol to the Pen: the Military Memoir as a Source on the Social History of Pre-reform Russia   239
11. Chernyshevsky and the *Military Miscellany*   267

Part III: THE RUSSIAN REVOLUTION

12. Emancipation by the Ax: Peasant Revolts in Russian Thought and Literature   295
13. Russian Social Democracy and the First State Duma   311
14. Russia 1917: the Tyranny of Paris over Petrograd   329
15. Lenin as Tactician   341
16. Lenin's Letters as a Historical Source   357

Part IV: SOVIET HISTORIOGRAPHY

17. The Rehabilitation of M. N. Pokrovskii   383
18. Soviet Historians on "Great October"   405
19. The Agrarian Revolution of 1917–18 in Soviet Historiography   425

Bibliography   441

ACKNOWLEDGEMENTS

The author and publishers gratefully acknowledge kind permission to reprint material which previously appeared in the following books and journals:

1. *Slavonic and East European Review,* 48 (London, 1970), 201–31.
2. Ibid., 36 (1957), 100–22. Also in *Readings in Russian History,* vol. I, ed. S. Harcave (New York: Crowell, 1962), 195–211. (Afterword: not previously published.)
3. Ibid., 35 (1956), 201–22.
4. Ibid., 38 (1960), 334–60.
5. *Forschungen zur osteuropäischen Geschichte,* 25 (Berlin/Wiesbaden, 1978), 169–93.
6. *Slavonic and East European Review,* 59 (London, 1981), 385–96.
7. *Canadian-American Slavic Studies,* 7 (Philadelphia [now Irvine CA], 1973), 1–14. Also in *Paul I: a Reassessment of his Life and Reign,* ed. S. Ragsdale (Pittsburgh, 1979), 91–103.
8. *War and Society,* 1 (Duntroon, Australia, 1983/4), 61–84.
9. *Jahrbücher für Geschichte Osteuropas,* 28 (Munich/Stuttgart, 1981), 500–23.
10. *Cahiers du monde russe et soviétique,* 21 (Paris, 1981), 295–320.
11. *Felder und Vorfelder russischer Geschichte: Studien zu Ehren von Peter Scheibert,* ed. I. Auerbach et al. (Freiburg i. Br.: Rombach, 1985), 111–33.
12. *Cahiers du monde russe et soviétique,* 22 (1982), 45–61. (Also in *Peasants in History and Literature* (Canberra: Australian Academy of the Humanities, 1981), 27–52.)
13. *Slavonic and East European Review,* 34 (1955), 180–99.
14. *Soviet Studies,* 20 (Glasgow, 1968), 22–35.
15. *Lenin: the Man, the Theorist, the Leader: a Reappraisal,* ed. L. B. Schapiro and P. Reddaway (London: Pall Mall, 1968, reprinted Boulder CO: Westview, 1987), 135–58.
16. *Lenin and Leninism: State, Law and Society,* ed. B. W. Eissenstat (Lexington MA: Heath, 1971), 245–68.
17. *Windows on the Russian Past: Essays on Soviet Historiography,* ed. S. H. Baron and N. W. Heer (Columbus OH: American Association for the Advancement of Slavic Studies, 1977), 139–56.
18. *Russian Review,* 36 (Cambridge MA, 1977), 405–23.
19. *Revolution and Politics in Russia: Essays in Memory of B. I. Nicolaevsky,* ed. A. and J. Rabinowitch (Bloomington IN, Indiana University Press, 1972), 293–313.

FOREWORD

Collections of essays such as this are not unfairly considered as vanities. They give an author an opportunity to reflect, with satisfaction or chagrin as the case may be, on his handiwork. For the reader their modest utility lies in the convenience of saving him or her one of those searches through the mustier recesses of the library that often yield unexpected delights. To the scholarly book reviewer a set of articles by a single individual is only a little less offputting than that other academic bogy, the *Festschrift*. On behalf of the present volume, which has come into being thanks to Professor Stephen Fischer-Galati, and marks my entry into the seventh decade of life, it may be at least claimed that the pieces it contains are all concerned with a single theme: the often painful relationship that has existed over the centuries between the Russians and their rulers, between the people (*narod*) and the central power (*vlast'*), whether that power was an autocratic monarchy or a self-styled proletarian dictatorship.

I hope it will not be thought presumptuous or old-fashioned to suggest that this relationship ought to be a major issue for those of us who are professionally engaged in the study of Russian history and are lucky enough to live in better ordered polities. Undeniably, there is much of value to be learned about demographic processes, economic development, popular beliefs, and many other matters that today are the preferred stamping ground of the social historian, but all the resources of computer technology will not help us much in trying to answer the layman's simple question: why has Russia's historical experience been so different from ours? Or, a little less naively: what is peculiar about Russia's institutional development? For surely the most signal characteristic of this historical experience has been the remarkable paramountcy of the state. It is not easy to explain either its staying power or its indifference to its subjects' basic human rights.

These are legitimate questions, if scarcely novel ones. They were asked, in different terms, by the first Western travelers to what, in the sixteenth and seventeenth centuries, was known as the Tsardom of Muscovy. It is with that period—less distant from ours than many suppose—that the first section of this book deals. We begin with a look at the faint initial stirrings of independent thought among three categories of the privileged servitor class (*sluzhilye liudi*). The argument is that none of these groups succeeded in acquiring a consciousness of their identity, still less in imposing their will on the central power. Such concessions as they won rested on unstable foundations and could without much difficulty be countermanded by a resolute ruler like Peter the Great, whose reign (1682/89–1725) forms the watershed between the "old" medieval Rus', isolated and self sufficient, and the "new" Europeanized Russian empire. It was only later, after Western influences had percolated into the ruling élite during the eighteenth century, that the gentry (*dvoriane*) could take up where their predecessors had left off. The problem in both eras was the lack of autonomous social institutions that might have served the privileged groups as strongholds from which to press their claims.

This is evident from an examination of the body which for a hundred years or more (approximately 1550–1653) did duty for a parliament. The Zemskii Sobor, or "Assembly of [All] the Land," did have some features in common with more familiar representative assemblies in Western and Central Europe; whether it belonged to the same genus (as I still believe) or not is perhaps an insoluble metaphysical problem. The Sobor is no longer *terra incognita*. The Soviet historian L. B. Cherepnin in particular has written a monograph on the subject, of which some account is taken here in a postscript to the original article.

"Bandits and the Law in Muscovy" draws attention to another Muscovite institution, less well known, which was entrusted with responsibilities in the field of criminal justice. The so-called *guba* authorities were elected by the local inhabitants, but were not for that reason "democratic" in the modern understanding of the term. They lost much of their popular quality as agents of the central power strengthened their hold over the provinces. This is a chapter in the development of early Russian public law—an area of study that is happily no longer as neglected as it used to be.[1]

The fourth essay looks at a period that again has been generally disregarded: the years when Muscovy was under the scepter of Patriarch Filaret (1619–33). The father of the first Romanov tsar, it should be acknowledged, still remains a murky figure. He is far less well known, for instance, than Tsar Alexis Mikhailovich (1645–76), whose biography has recently appeared in English.[2] Like Alexis, and so many other Russian rulers since, Filaret was a convinced believer in the benefits of absolute power. He sought to concentrate authority at the summit of the political structure, in order to harness the nation's resources more effectively in accomplishing those tasks he deemed important. Overriding priority was given to fighting a war of revenge against Poland-Lithuania, then still a formidable foe. Although he was no reformer, Filaret made a start on the modernization of Muscovy's ramshackle armed forces, a development that brought other unscheduled changes in its wake.

Military concerns loomed large throughout the Imperial period of Russian history (1721–1917), when the army was the principal mainstay of the autocratic regime. We have examined elsewhere some of the social consequences which this effort had,

---

1 The two leading American specialists, H. W. Dewey and Ann Kleimola, have produced, in tandem or independently, a plethora of valuable studies. R. Hellie edited the principal legal document, the code (*Ulozhenie*) of 1649: Richard Hellie, trans. and ed., *The Muscovite Law Code* (Ulozhenie) *of 1649*. 2 vols. (Irvine, CA: Charles Schlacks Jr., 1988–89). In German, the work by H.-J. Torke, referred to on note 19, is fundamental.

2 P. Longworth, *Alexis, Tsar of All the Russias* (London: Watts, 1984).

particularly in regard to the soldiers themselves.[3] The second section of the present volume contains seven pieces with a bearing on this theme. We begin with politics: with the role played by the élite guards regiments during one of the several interregna or periods of ineffectual government that characterized the immediate post-Petrine era. The development of "Praetorian" tendencies in the Russian empire is an intriguing problem that may well preoccupy the writer of these lines until his dotage. What the reader may gain here is an insight into the relationship between two key elements in the early eighteenth-century "establishment": the guards and the "security apparatus" (as we might call it today). The procedures of the Secret Chancellery, as it was then termed, were archaic and inefficient, even by contemporary standards; nevertheless it had a sinister reputation and was greatly feared. Its activities can be investigated only on the basis of archival materials in the USSR. Fortunately I was able to pay three visits to Moscow (1962, 1978, 1984) under the invaluable Anglo-Soviet cultural exchange agreement, and on the first of these was allowed to see some of the relevant documents.

On the second of these trips the designated theme was the condition of the common soldiers in the late eighteenth century—a field which Elise Kimerling-Wirtschafter has since made her own.[4] This resulted *inter alia* in some findings with regard to "Catherine's Veterans"—a title that does not, one hastens to add, refer to any of the dignitaries at the empress's court.

With "Paul I and the Militarization of Government" we pass on to consider the army's role in the civil administration of the empire during the brief but trend-setting reign of Catherine's successor (1796–1801). Paul, who like his father Peter III (1762) was the victim of a *coup d'état* carried out by elements of the guards, was followed on the Romanov throne by two of his sons: Alexander I (1801–25) and Nicholas I (1825–55). All three rulers, and several of their relatives, practiced what we have ventured to call "the Romanov military style." It emphasized the virtues of the parade ground, respect for the hierarchy of *chin* (rank), observance of bureaucratic formalities, and the maintenance of strict discipline—the latter founded on a particularly brutal code of military law.[5] There was a great deal more to this style than a simple emulation of Prussian ways, as some nationally conscious Russian officers thought.

Already by the 1790s the Imperial armed forces were facing up to the challenge of the French Revolution. We examine here its economic and more especially intellectual impact. The latter was indirect and delayed, being most evident in the two armed insurrections which took place in December 1825—four years after Napoleon's demise and more than thirty years after Thermidor. Since the insurgents and their sympathizers were mainly officers who may be seen, at least in part, as incipient "Praetorians,"

---

3 *Soldiers of the Tsar: Army and Society in Russia, 1462–1874* (Oxford: Clarendon Press, 1985).

4 *From* Serf to Russian Soldier, Princeton, 1990.

5 Military law is another neglected area of study which throws much light on the relationship between the Power and the People. See Bibliography, items 54, 56, 57 and 68.

this theme follows on that of the eighteenth-century *coups d'état* considered earlier, and also on our first topic, the emergence of potentially opposition-minded interest groups within the élite. The hundred years or so that lay between the "Muscovite baroque" (ca. 1680) and the reign of Alexander I saw the emergence of a *dvorianstvo* which from 1775/85 enjoyed important privileges, at least on paper—notably freedom from corporal punishment. They had now also acquired, in the provincial and county noble assemblies, organs that might have served as an arena for political action. But Russian *dvoriane* were slow to develop the "corporate consciousness" of their West or Central European counterparts. As for *political* consciousness, this likewise was still embryonic, which no doubt helps to explain the Decembrists' failure. In the eyes of later generations of Russian intellectuals (Colonel) P. I. Pestel' and his comrades were martyrs for the sacred cause of freedom. The halo which surrounds them even today makes it hard to examine their conduct and *mentalité* dispassionately, nevertheless the task is worth undertaking. The first step, we have argued, is to place them firmly in the military context to which they rightfully belong.

Memoirs, for all their defects, are an important source of information on the Russian officers' material and moral-intellectual world during this era. About eighty of those that have been published form the basis of the essay entitled "From the Pistol to the Pen." It extends chronologically from the post-Petrine era, when the first such autobiographical writings saw the light, to the Crimean War. The shock produced by defeat in this conflict (1854–55) caused Tsar Alexander II (1855–81) reluctantly to embark on several reforms, not the least important of which were in the military domain. One early step, taken in 1858, was to authorize the publication of a journal that would reflect opinion within the army yet be loyal to the government. For a few months the *Military Miscellany* was edited, quite successfully, by none other than N. G. Chernyshevskii, already a well-known radical journalist. Although the censor soon stepped in and forced him to resign his post, the incident was something of a landmark in the long struggle for freedom of opinion in Russia. It showed that junior officers responded readily enough to the new gospel of progress that was preached by the intelligentsia.

Returning to the civilian world, in Part III we consider some themes from the history (and prehistory) of the Russian Revolution—a topic on which a large literature now exists in English and other languages. Alain Besançon has suggested that the Russian radical intelligentsia, like its emulators in other lands, was "structured around ideology" and condemned to commit suicide in the social turmoil it helped to engender.[6] There is much justice in this criticism, although one must beware of attributing to the "fathers" responsibility for the errors of their "sons." Certainly their idealism today often seems mere naiveté, their penchant for utopian system-building a tragic mistake, their elaborate sociological theories unscientific. Now that Russia is abandoning Soviet perceptions, the "heroic deeds" of the Populists (*narodniki*) cannot but appear menacing. And yet: we can appreciate that the dream of a just social order,

---

6 A. Besançon, *Les Origines intellectuelles du léninisme* (Paris: Calmann-Lévy, 1977), 99–118.

to be brought about by violence, was a source of psychological solace to men and women who had deliberately broken with the conventions of their milieu and had entered upon the dangerous road of revolutionary conspiracy. The revolutionaries' inability to make much of a dent in the apparently impregnable armor of the autocratic-bureaucratic regime naturally fostered extremism and a sense of alienation; the greater the credit that attaches to those who resisted the lure of terror and remained true to their democratic convictions.

The paradox of the Russian Revolution was that, in destroying the *ancien régime*, it paved the way for a new *vlast'* that represented a far more formidable threat to human liberties than its predecessor. In Russia "emancipation by the ax"—that is, by mass violence—was an ancient notion, or more correctly a myth. It can be traced back to the great cossack and peasant rebellions of the seventeenth and eighteenth centuries. These popular uprisings were regarded by many later intellectuals as "progressive" and therefore laudable. Not that they seriously advocated a repetition of such acts of blind vengeance (although the anarchist thinker Mikhail Bakunin came close to this); rather they shut their eyes to the destructive forces inseparable from any violent upheaval, assuming that, if handled "scientifically," it would have a cleansing moral effect. (The error was not, incidentally, confined to the left: some contemporary ideologists expected the same beneficent results to flow from *international* armed conflict.) Social myths, we suggest here, may have an extraordinarily long life and change their nature as they "migrate" from one milieu to another.

The civil violence that broke out in Russia in 1905–06, and again in 1917, had many affinities with earlier "troubles." Popular energies were unleashed which swept aside the self-confident assumptions of those who had hoped to tame and direct them against targets of their own choosing. In the terminology favored by the socialists of the day, "spontaneity" triumphed over "consciousness" in 1905: the revolutionary tide temporarily swept all before it, only to ebb just as suddenly the following year. At the moment of greatest danger to the autocracy Nicholas II (1894–1917) was obliged to act contrary to his deepest beliefs and to promise that in future he would rule with the consent of the people's elected representatives. Imperial Russia entered, formally at least, on a brief era of constitutional government (1906–17). We examine here the tense situation in the spring and summer of 1906, when the revolutionary Marxists of the Russian Social Democratic Labor Party (RSDRP) unexpectedly had to define their attitude to the new State Duma, the lower house in the bicameral legislature. The premature dissolution of the first session of this body[7]—and of the second (1907), followed by Prime Minister P. A. Stolypin's *coup de force* of June 3—spared the Social Democrats the necessity of rethinking their fundamental ideas on the proper place of civil violence in their political credo. Nor did they do so during

---

7 There are curious parallels between the fate of three representative assemblies in Russian history: the *Zemskii Sobor* (see item 2), the *Duma*, and the Constituent Assembly of January 1918. On the latter, see our *The Debate on Soviet Power: Minutes of the Central Executive Committee of Soviets, Second Convocation, October 1917–January 1918* (Oxford: Clarendon Press, 1979), 401–04, 419–20.

the years that followed which, although they may look peaceful in retrospect, were in reality wracked by one crisis after another. The expediency of the "June 3 system" could be justified: but its legitimacy stood in doubt. Although the Russian economy prospered in the last prewar years, the political climate remained unpropitious for the development of that spirit of consensus, tolerance, and self-restraint that were essential if Russia were to solve her problems peacefully. Instead ancient bitternesses continued to fester and the general malaise worsened after 1914, when the empire became involved in a great war it could not win. The wonder is that the crisis did not break until February 1917.

We have examined elsewhere the ways in which, during that revolutionary year, the "maximalists" (Bolsheviks and others) sooner or later won control of the soviets and other mass organizations that sprang up once the tsarist state had collapsed, so that contrary to most of their members' expectations they became the infrastructure of a single-party dictatorship.[8] These political developments took place against a backdrop of near-starvation in the cities, strikes and agrarian disturbances, the dissolution of the armed forces, and the growth of separatist feeling among the national minorities. These would have been problems enough even for the most stable of regimes. They were far beyond the competence of the feeble Provisional Government, a series of uneasy coalitions between inexperienced liberal and moderate socialist politicians. Their commitment to democratic values (and thus to Russia's Western allies, who claimed to be defending them) was praiseworthy—but ultimately self-defeating. In these pages we offer some reflections on "The Tyranny of Paris over Petrograd"— that is, on the remarkable hold exercised over men of the center and moderate left by a limited and conventional understanding of the way in which earlier European revolutions had developed—assumptions that up to a point help to account for their actions, or inaction, in the face of redoubtable enemies.

Lenin was among those least inhibited in his thinking by such models from the past. The Bolshevik victory in October 1917, in so far as it was not simply the product of other leaders' failures, may be explained in large measure by the tactical skill which the party's acknowledged chief displayed in handling rival political formations as well as dissidents within the "maximalist" camp. In "Lenin as Tactician" we consider his debt to Clausewitz and his record up to the seizure of power, but suggest that these skills were less than adequate for one who aspired to govern the new Soviet state on socialist principles—supposedly in a manner far more democratic than that of the *bourgeoisie*. This notion, which one might have thought fairly noncontroversial, provoked an angry retort from the Marxist ranks when it was first put forward. This was in 1967, when the Western academic world was in the throes of a quasi-revolutionary upsurge; it was also the fiftieth anniversary of the October Revolution. In 1970 devotees of the Marxist-Leninist faith had another historical landmark to celebrate: the centennial of Lenin's birth. Even UNESCO, following the intellectual fashion of the day, joined in the paeans of praise that were sung to

---

8 *The Russian Revolution: A Study in Mass Mobilization* (London: Weidenfeld & Nicolson, 1976 and New York: Norton, 1977).

the Soviet dictator as an outstanding "humanist" and friend of all oppressed peoples. As a mere historian with a professional bias toward ascertaining the facts, I thought it right to offer a modest corrective to these effusions. "Lenin's Letters as a Historical Source" looks at the Bolshevik leader's published correspondence during the first three years after October. It reveals a normal flesh-and-blood individual, not a plaster cast saint: a man, moreover, prey to the doubts and contradictions that beset any politician, a leader who found the nascent Soviet bureaucracy baffling—and also whose formidable intellect was accompanied by an unusual blindness to the moral responsibilities incumbent on a statesman. Lenin's onesidedly political perception of his role explains his readiness to use terroristic measures against real or suspected foes to bolster his regime.[9] The cruel streak in his character is more evident in the correspondence than in his more public theoretical writings. On occasion it even embarrassed his Soviet editors, who for this or other reasons have yet to produce a complete unexpurgated text of his letters.

In the fourth and last section we turn to the way in which historians in the USSR have dealt with Russia's past. For a decade or so after the civil war ended the leading figure in Soviet Marxist historiography was M. N. Pokrovskii, an industrious propagandist for the internationalist credo of the early Bolsheviks. Shortly after his death in 1932 Pokrovskii's intellectual legacy was repudiated, and he himself "unpersoned," as part of J. V. Stalin's campaign to bring the historians to heel. Stalinism was much more than a strategy for rapid industrialization and the forcing of peasant smallholders into collective farms: it also meant the total subordination of Soviet cultural life to the requirements of "socialist construction" as these were defined by the new Leader. "Toilers on the historical front" had to strain every nerve to produce work that justified, by implication, the party's current policies. In this propaganda the nationalist motif sounded ever more strongly. This emphasis contrasted with the internationalism of the first generation revolutionaries; nevertheless, Stalinism had its roots in Leninism, intellectually as well as organizationally.

It was not until Stalin died (March 1953) and was laid to rest in Lenin's tomb, that Soviet historians could begin to grapple with his grim legacy. Political exigencies still set narrow limits to what they could achieve. It was impossible to raise matters—notably, the millions who had died without cause during the Terror—that might cast doubt on the Party's fitness to govern. Nevertheless during N. S. Khrushchev's tenure of the Party leadership (1953–64), especially in the early 1960s, there were many welcome signs of renewed intellectual vitality among historians, as there were among writers, social scientists, and others. Discussions were held and ideas ventilated with a degree of freedom that gradually diminished once L. I. Brezhnev took the helm, whereupon a gray conformity once again became the watchword.

---

9 "Lawlessness is the cornerstone of Leninism," writes a historian of Poland: N. Davies, *Heart of Europe: A Short History of Poland* (London and New York: Oxford Univ. Press, 1984), 40. The few pages that follow this statement offer the best summary I have seen of the nature of the Soviet dictatorship and the problems encountered by Westerners in understanding it.

Soviet historians rarely show their hand clearly, and any attempt to fathom their hidden controversies in the post-Stalin era is necessarily a somewhat speculative enterprise. Yet the attempt is worth making, for it is only when historians are allowed to come to terms with the past, even within the confines of Marxist methodology, that a way will be found out of the present political impasse.

Three aspects of their predicament are considered here. The first essay deals with the partial rehabilitation of Pokrovskii in 1959–61. This did not have the effect, which at the time seemed possible, of stimulating or facilitating a fundamental revision of the old clichés. The overall political situation in the USSR was not favorable to such a bold departure. The second and third essays are concerned with the way historians have handled a particular issue, namely the October Revolution—both as a general phenomenon and with special reference to developments in the countryside.

This is not a field where they could afford to give free rein to their fancy, since the controls were perhaps even tighter here than in any other. The significance of the agrarian revolt is plain. Peasants constituted the bulk of the Russian population in 1917. Any urban-based regime would have found it hard to devise an effective way of getting rural producers to part with their harvest on equitable terms. The injection into this situation of Marxist ideology, with its proletarian bias, made the problem more difficult to solve than it might otherwise have been. The peasant could be cajoled, but he could not be coerced beyond a certain point without putting the regime's credibility and security at considerable risk. Peasant resistance to Bolshevik forced requisitioning was instrumental in forcing the Party to undertake the "strategic retreat" of 1921. Seven years later the "New Economic Policy" (NEP) had failed, or at least was deemed by Stalin to have failed. His solution to the dilemma was punitive terror on a still more drastic scale than in 1918–20. Millions of country-dwellers were deported from their homes and perished, but the grain was secured for the state and the basis thereby established for Stalinist "socialism" and the political order that, with some modifications, survived its creator for over thirty years after his death. It follows that any questioning of Soviet agrarian policy would awaken specters whose memory those in authority preferred to keep in oblivion.

* * * * *

The essays in this volume are reprinted as they appeared on first publication except for a few very minor changes. Thanks are due to the original publishers for their kind cession of copyright, as well as to many colleagues and friends who have given advice and encouragement. A few additions have been made to the footnotes (in square brackets) in order to draw attention to major recent work of relevance to the various topics discussed, but bibliographical comprehensiveness has not been the aim. Spelling, punctuation, transliteration, and so on have been Americanized: if the attentive reader still detects one or two "Britishisms," one may hope these will be forgiven in the interest of Anglo-Saxon harmony; errors of fact and judgement, of course, should get all the criticism they deserve. Today one can hope that Russians, at last freed from the historic tutelage of their *vlast'*, will do most of the criticizing.

LIST OF ABBREVIATIONS

AAE   *Akty sobrannye v bibliotekakh . . . Arkheograficheskoi ekspeditsiei Imperatorskoi Akademii Nauk,* 4 vols., Spb., 1836.

AI   *Aktv istoricheskie sobrannye i izdannye Arkheograficheskoi ekspeditsiei Imp. Akademii Nauk,* 5 vols., Spb., 1841–2.

AIu   *Akty iuridicheskie ili sobranie form starinnogo deloizprodstva,* izd. Arkheograficheskoi komissiei, Spb., 1838.

AIuB   *Akty otnosiashchiesia do iuridicheskogo byta drevnei Rusi,* ed. N. Kalachev, 3 vols., Spb., 1857–84.

AKV   *Arkhiv kniazia Vorontsova,* 40 vols., M., 1870–95.

AMG   *Akty Moskovskogo gosudarstva: Razriadnyi prikaz, Moskovskii stol, 1571–1664,* ed. N. A. Popov and D. Ia. Samokvasov, 3 vols., Spb., 1890–1901.

Chernyshevsky, *PSS*   N. G. Chernyschevskii, *Polnoe sobranie sochinenii v 15 tt.,* M., 1939–53.

ChIOIDR   *Chteniia v Imperatorskom Obschchestve istorii i drevnostei rossiiskikh,* 256 vols., M., 1846–1916.

CSP   *Canadian Slavonic Papers,* Ottawa/Toronto, 1959–.

DAI   *Dopolneniia k Aktam istoricheskim. . . ,* 12 vols., Spb., 1846–72.

DRV   *Drevniaia rossiiskaia vivliofika,* 2nd series, ed. N. N. Novikov, 20 vols., M. 1788–91, reprinted The Hague, 1970.

FOEG   *Forschungen zur osteuropäischen Geschichte,* Berlin, 1954–.

GDSO   Russia. State Duma. *Stenograficheskie otchety, sessiia I,* 2 vols., Spb., 1906.

IA   *Istoricheskii arkhiv,* 8 vols., M., 1955–62.

IOIDR   see *ChIOIDR.*

IV   *Istoricheskii vestnik,* 150 vols., Spb./Pg., 1880–1917.

IZ   *Istoricheskii zapiskii,* 112 vols. to date, M., 1937–.

JGOE   *Jahrbücher für Geschichte Osteuropas,* Stuttgart/Wiesbaden, 1953–.

Lenin, *Sochineniia*   V. I. Lenin, *Sobranie sochinenii,* 3rd ed., 30 vols., M., 1930–2.

Lenin, *PSS*   V. I. Lenin, *Polnoe sobranie sochinenii,* 5th ed., 56 vols., M., 1958–66.

PSS   see Chernyschevsky, Lenin

I PSZ   *Polnoe sobranie zakonov Rossiiskoi Imperii,* 1st coll., 45 vols., Spb., 1830.

II PSZ   *Polnoe sobranie zakonov Rossiiskoi Imperii,* 2nd coll., 55 vols., Spb., 1830–84.

III PSZ   *Polnoe sobranie zakonov Rossiiskoi Imperii,* 3rd coll., 28 vols., Spb./Pg., 1884–1916.

RA   *Russkii arkhiv,* ed. P. I. Bartenev, 55 vols., M., 1863–1917.

RBS   *Russkii biograficheskii slovar,* 25 vols. (incomplete), Spb./Pg., 1896–1918, reprinted N. Y., 1962.

RIB   *Russkaia istoricheskaia biblioteka,* 35 vols., Spb./Pg., 1872–1917.

RS   *Russkaia starina,* 176 vols., Spb./Pg., 1870–1918.

SEER   *Slavonic and East European Review,* London, 1922–.

SGGD   *Sbornik gosudarstvennykh gramot i dogovorov,* 4 vols., Spb., 1813–28.

SIRIO   *Sbornik Imperatorskogo Rossiiskogo istoricheskogo obshchestva*, 148 vols.,
         Spb./Pg., 1867–1916, reprinted Nendeln, 1971.
SR   *Slavic Review: American Quarterly of Soviet and East European Studies*,
         Seattle/Columbus/Stanford, 1945–.
TP   *The Trotsky Papers, 1917–1919*, ed. J. M. Meier, The Hague, 1964, vol. I.
TsGVIA   Tsentral'nyi gosudarstvennyi voenno-isotoricheskii arkhiv, Moscow.
VD   *Vosstanie dekabristov*, ed. M. N. Pokrovskii et al., Moscow, 1925–76.
VE   *Voennaia entsiklopediia*, ed. K. I. Velichko et al., 18 vols., Spb./Pg., 1911–
         15.
VS   *Voennyi sbornik*, 254 vols., Spb./Pg., 1858–1916.
ZhMNP   *Zhurnal Ministerstva narodnogo prosveshcheniia*, Spb./Pg., 1834–1917.

PART I:

MUSCOVITE RUSSIA

CHAPTER 1

The Muscovite Élite
and the Approach to Pluralism

I

Western visitors to Muscovite Russia were greatly impressed by two phenomena in the country's political and social life: first, the extravagant powers claimed, and to some extent exercised, by the autocratic sovereign: second, the material poverty and inferior status of the élite. The nearest equivalent to the nobility of the West, the serving men (*sluzhilye liudi*), lacked the corporate rights or traditions that elsewhere served to counterbalance the power of the crown; on the contrary, they assumed an attitude of exaggerated humility towards the tsar, willingly calling themselves his slaves (*kholopy*). Some contemporary travelers made speculative efforts to explain the connection between these two phenomena. Giles Fletcher, who considered the Muscovite government's "state and form . . . plain tyranicall, . . . much after the Turkish fashion," suggested that the nobles were deliberately "kept in an underproportion and far uneven balance in their several degrees" to prevent them from challenging the central power.[1] Writing almost a century later, the Dutchman Koenraad van Klenk detected a political purpose behind the requirement that the great lords should attend daily at court: "this is done lest, living on their possessions among their subjects, they might plot against his tsarist majesty."[2]

A more profound and sympathetic witness, Jakob Reitenfels, considered that for the same reason "members of the most prominent families are usually separated or sent off to [posts in] distant regions in the guise of rendering them honor."[3] These observations raise an interesting problem. If the Russian nobles were so subservient,

---

1 L. E. Berry and R. O. Crummey, eds., *Rude and Barbarous Kingdom: Russia in the Accounts of Sixteenth-Century English Voyagers* (Madison, Wisc.-Milwaukee-London, 1968), 132.

2 *Posol'stvo Kunraada fan-Klenka k tsariam Alekseiu Mikhailovichu i Fedoru Alekseevichu* (St. Petersburg, 1900), 491.

3 J. Reitenfels, *Skazaniia svetleishemu gertsogu toskanskomu Koz'me III o Moskovii, Chteniia IOIDR* (1905), III, 101–102; on Reitenfels see F.-K. Proehl, "Eine Beschreibung Moskaus durch den Kurländer Jakob Reintenfels," H. Weczerka, ed., *Rossica externa: Studien zum 15.–17. Jahrhundert. Festgabe für Paul Johansen zum 60. Geburtstag* (Marburg, 1963), 157–177.

how could they be thought to pose a potential threat to the monarch? Can it be that beneath the outward calm of seventeenth-century Muscovy the leading groups in society were bestirring themselves to autonomous political activity? If so, what impact did their pressure have upon governmental policies?

For answers to such questions one naturally turns to the historians. Those in the classical tradition, as one might call it, have stressed the absolute nature of the autocratic *vlast'* and the dependence upon it of all categories of noble serving men.[4] In their view any political movement by elements of the social élite can have been of only negligible proportions, if it existed at all; in any case it deserves to be considered as basically egoistic, reactionary, and injurious to the national interest. The conventional wisdom among prerevolutionary Russian historians is neatly summarized by A. E. Presniakov: "A class such as this could not display any real social independence; in its very existence it was but a function of the governmental system."[5] While the cultural impact on Muscovy of western ideas was generally recognized, the political implications of these contacts were scarcely considered—especially where Catholic countries were concerned. This bias stemmed partly from the intellectual climate in Imperial Russia and partly from the nature of the available source materials. The latter consisted mainly of dry official records: the edicts and other state documents published in the great collections[6] and the (incomplete) service registers known as *knigi razriadnye*.[7] Successive historians of repute in the "juridical school," from K. A. Nevolin to A. N. Filippov, did valuable work in establishing the basic principles of the state service system, and drew attention to the fluctuations in government policy,[8] but their studies were inadequately related to the general history of

---

4 The terms gentry and nobility, although not strictly accurate for the ancestors of the post-Petrine *dvorianstvo*, will be used here for the sake of convenience. Serving men still referred to themselves as *dvoriane* or *deti boiarskie*, although the historic distinction between the two groups had become obscured by the seventeenth century, and the main social divisions were determined by administrative practice (see below, 34).

5 A. E. Presniakov, *Moskovskoe tsarstvo* (Petrograd, 1918), 93.

6 I *PSZ* I–III; *AI*, IV–V.

7 On these, once incorrectly termed *dvortsovye razriady*, see the important recent studies by V. I. Buganov, especially " 'Gosudarev razriad' I-oi poloviny XVII v." *Problemy istochnikovedeniia*, VIII (Moscow, 1959), 361–71; [*Razriadnye knigi poslednei chetverti XV—nachala XVII v.* (Moscow, 1962); *Razriadnaia kniga 1475–1598 gg.* (Moscow, 1966); *Razriadnye knigi 1598–1638 gg.* (Moscow, 1974); *Razriadnaia kniga 1475–1605 gg.*, vol. I (Moscow, 1977).]

8 M. F. Vladimirskii-Budanov, *Obzor istorii russkogo prava*[6] (St. Petersburg-Kiev, 1909), 115–27; M. D'iakonov, *Skizzen zur Gesellschafts- und Staatsordnung des alten Russlands*, tr. E. Goluboff (Berlin, 1931), 219–56. V. O. Kliuchevskii's youthful work, *Istoriia soslovii v Rossii* (1886) (Petrograd, 1918) is outdated, whereas A. I. Markevich, *Istoriia mestnichestva v Moskovskom gosudarstve v XV–XVII v.* (Odessa, 1888), has not yet been superseded. [Recent work by A. Kleimola includes "Boris Godunov and the Politics of Mestnichestvo," *SEER*, 53 (1975), 355–69; "Military Service and Élite Status in Muscovy in the Second Quarter of the Sixteenth Century," *RH*, 7 (1980), 47–64; "Status, Place and Politics: the Rise of Mestnichestvo During the Boiarskoe Pravlenie," *FOEG*, 27 (1980), 195–214.]

the period. S. M. Solov'ev and several late nineteenth-century scholars expanded significantly our knowledge of political events.[9] Writers on the Russian nobility[10] were naturally concerned primarily with the post-Petrine period, although N. P. Pavlov-Silvanskii broke new ground by analyzing the process whereby seventeenth-century serving men strengthened their rights to landed property.[11] At the same time interest developed in the regional history of the gentry[12] and in genealogy.[13]

After the 1917 revolution A. A. Novosel'skii, perhaps the most able scholar in the field, published several important articles.[14] Most Soviet historians, however, have confined their interest in the nobles to their economic role, laying particular stress on landlord-serf relationships.[15] Even the *strel'tsy*, who were non-noble serving men, were regarded with some suspicion, especially once they had been roundly categorized as reactionary by J. V. Stalin—a verdict modified by present-day Soviet specialists.[16] On the other hand, opposition movements among the urban population have been well studied,[17] and professional military historians, building on a prerevolutionary tradition of independent scholarship, have investigated certain questions relating to Russia's armed forces in the seventeenth century.[18]

As this brief review suggests, research in this field has been more than usually

---

9 S. M. Solov'ev, *Istoriia Rossii s drevneishikh vremen* (Moscow, 1961–2), vols. VI–VII (XII–XIV); E. A. Belov, "Moskovskie smuty v kontse XVII v.," *Zhurnal Ministerstva narodnogo prosvescheniia*, pts. 249–250 (St. Petersburg, 1887), 99–146, 319–66; E. F. Shmurlo, "Padenie tsarevny Sof'i," *ibid.*, pt. 303 (1896), 38–95.

10 A. V. Romanovich-Slavatinskii, *Dvorianstvo v Rossii ot nachala XVIII v. do otmeny krepostnogo prava* (Kiev, 1912).

11 N. P. Pavlov-Silvanskii, *Gosudarevy sluzhilye liudi. Proiskhozhdenie russkogo dvorianstva* (St. Petersburg, 1898).

12 V. N. Storozhev, *Tverskoe dvorianstvo XVII v.*, 4 pts. (Tver', 1891–5); idem, *Materialy dlia istorii deloproizvodstva Pomestnogo Prikaza po Vologodskomu uezdu v XVII v., Zapiski Rossiiskoi Akademii Nauk po ist.-filolog. otdeleniiu* vol. IX (St. Petersburg, 1906–18). A valuable study of landowning is Iu. V. Got'e, *Zamoskovnyi krai v XVIII v.: opyt issledovaniia po istorii ekonomicheskogo byta*² (Moscow, 1937).

13 Under the energetic guidance of N. P. Likhachev the Russian Genealogical Society published 4 volumes of *Izvestiia* between 1900 and 1911.

14 A. A. Novosel'skii, "Pobegi krest'ian i kholopov i ikh sysk v Moskovskom gosudarstve vo II-oi polovine XVII v.," *Trudy Rossiiskoi Assotsiatsii nauchno-issledovatel'skikh institutov*, pt. I (Moscow, 1926), 327–56; "Kollektivnye dvorianskie chelobit'ia po voprosam mezhevaniia i opisaniia zemel'" v 80–kh gg. XVII v.," *Uchenye zapiski RANIONa*, pt. IV (Moscow, 1929), 103–8; "Praviashchie gruppy v sluzhilom 'gorode' XVII v.," *ibid*, pt. V (1929), 315–35; *Votchinnik i ego khoziaistvo v XVII v.* (Moscow-Leningrad, 1929).

15 A. I. Iakovlev, ed., *Akty khoziaistva boiarina V. I. Morozova*, 2 vols. (Moscow-Leningrad, 1940–5).

16 V. I. Buganov, "Moskovskie vosstaniia poslednei chetverti XVII v. v dorevoliutsionnoi i sovetskoi istoriografii," *Istoriia SSSR*, X (Moscow, 1966), 2, 105–15.

17 Idem, *Moskovskoe vosstanie 1662 g.* (Moscow, 1964) with an accompanying volume of documents.

18 A. V.Chernov, *Vooruzhennye sily Russkogo gosudarstva v XV–XVII vv. . . .* (Moscow, 1954); F. I. Kalinychev, *Pravovye voprosy voennoi organizatsii Russkogo gosudarstva II-oi poloviny*

fragmentary. Ideally, the work done by political, economic, military and legal historians needs to be co-ordinated and interpreted with keen sociological and psychological insight.[19] Such a task would, however, require ample space and rich sources of a non-official character. This article will attempt to show that by the late seventeenth century certain elements in Muscovite society were beginning to shake off their accustomed political passivity, and that the country stood on the threshold of "pluralism." This latter term is admittedly an anachronism. It is open to the objection that in the early modern era no political structure, however absolute, attained the monolithic character associated with some modern governmental systems. Pluralism is used here to mean an order having not just one central focus of power but several, able to compete for the allegiance of the public, which is deemed capable of independent thought and action designed to ensure that policy takes some account of group interests. It will be contended that Muscovite Russia did not actually cross this threshold, and was indeed forcibly turned away from it by the "tsar-reformer," who imposed new shackles upon the Russian élite. The first stages in the *raskreposhchenie* of Russian society are important in that they anticipate the better-known developments of the post-Petrine era.

II

We may first consider the nature of the traditional political order in seventeenth-century Muscovy. The old term "patrimonial (*votchinnaia*) monarchy" hardly satisfies modern requirements. If an anthropologist would at once recognize the lineaments of "sacral monarchy" (*Gottkönigtum*), a political scientist might prefer to designate it as an "oriental despotism."[20] Such a term does not, of course, imply any adverse inferences about Russia's "rightful place in the world"; it must also be said that Muscovy did not reproduce this political system *in toto*, in its classic oriental form. Her nearest equivalent to the "hydraulic" works of ancient Egypt or China was the *zagranichnaia cherta*: the extensive system of defensive fortifications along her exposed southern border. This certainly required a considerable input of manpower and material resources, but did not have a comparable all-encompassing "mass mobilization" function. Moreover, Russia was never wholly isolated from her more pluralistic neighbors, but (despite confessional antagonisms) shared in a common Christian civilization which to some degree mitigated the rigors of absolutism.

XVII v. (Moscow, 1954).

19 As displayed by Marc Raeff in his stimulating analysis of the eighteenth-century nobility: *Origins of the Russian Intelligentsia: the Eighteenth-Century Nobility* (New York, 1966). [This has now been done by R. O. Crummey, *Aristocrats and Servitors: the Boiar Elite in Russia, 1613–1689* (Princeton, 1983). Cf. also R. Hellie, *Enserfment and Military Change in Muscovy* (Chicago and London, 1971); H.-J. Torke, *Die staatsbedingte Gesellschaft im Moskauer Reich: Zar und Zemlja in der altrussischen Herrschaftsverfassung* (Leiden, 1974); and, for the fifteenth and sixteenth centuries, H. Rüss, *Adel und Adelsoppositionen im Moskauer Staat* (Wiesbaden, 1975).]

20 C.-A. Wittfogel, *Oriental Despotism: a Comparative Study of Total Power* (New Haven-London, 1963).

For all this contemporaries had good reason to compare the tsar's government with that of the sultan. The parallels were most evident in the lavish ostentation of the court, the close ties between the central religious and political authority, the low cultural level and the roughness of social *mores*, and above all the neglect of legal norms in public administration, carried on by predominantly irresponsible and corrupt functionaries. Looked at through modern eyes, the political system of seventeenth-century Russia might be said to have had three basic characteristics:

a) The attribution to the sacrosanct ruler of an absolute power which, whatever the theory, was in practice restricted by material limitations (primitive communications, lack of trained executives, etc.) as well as by customary sanctions which, if infringed, could imperil stability;

b) the legitimation of this power primarily in terms of "transcendental myth," i.e. a framework of ideas articulated by a priestly caste largely dependent upon the state power but which were generally accepted by the populace;

c) the physical maintenance of this power by a military-bureaucratic apparatus of state servitors—in Wittfogel's terminology, an "agrobureaucracy."[21]

In such a society political activity will necessarily conform to laws different from those pertaining in a more pluralistic environment. Social conflict may occur, and even be endemic, but there can be no class struggle, since there are no autonomous classes;[22] a man's status or outlook is primarily determined by his relationship, not to the means of production, but to the source of political power. The court (*dvor*) dispenses favors and patronage that are keenly valued, especially by the more highly-placed elements in society. At moments of crisis inter-group competition for favors may be utilized by the state to reinforce its own prerogatives, although normally it does not interfere, since there is as yet little sign of a conscious "social policy" in the modern sense. Many executive decisions on domestic affairs are taken in response to pressure from below. This may be expressed either formally, through petitions (*chelobit'ia*), or informally, by what one loosely calls "connections" (*sviazi*) or "court intrigue."

Such public pressure can acquire a political content irrespective of the intentions of the petitioners, who may quite sincerely regard their conduct as legitimate. In an "oriental despotism" the modern distinction between social and political action is not really relevant. It is more illuminating to ascertain the source from which pressure is brought to bear—i.e., whether by underprivileged elements or by interest groups within the élite. The cossack-peasant revolts led by Bolotnikov and Razin are obvious examples of the former. They were essentially uprisings against oppressive functionaries and landowners, with anarchistic or chiliastic ideological overtones that doomed them to failure.[23] The movements of the latter type have received very little attention, although their historical significance is probably greater. They were of

---

21 Ibid., 299.

22 "Class struggle is a luxury of multi-centered and open societies" (Ibid., 331).

23 These movements have been extensively studied by Soviet scholars, whose approach, however, suffers from modernistic bias. S. P. Mel'gunov, a perceptive and sympathetic historian,

course "conservative" in the sense that all members of the élite sought to maintain (and even extend) their privileges over the enserfed masses. Nevertheless the prospect existed that such pressure, especially where it reflected the impact of western ideas, might achieve some modification of the political structure.

In particular, a positive role could be played by court factions which, although originally concerned to press the claims of a particular favorite in regard to precedence, spoils of office, or similar matters of limited import, might as time passed come to differ over questions of state policy—notably where it was a matter of peace or war. It is probably true to say that most Muscovite serving men were interested in warfare, as a source of prestige and material reward; however, their zeal was bound to vary in accordance with differing estimates of the risks and opportunities involved. The great question was whether these factional groupings could maintain pressure in a given direction over a number of years, and even acquire some kind of institutional base.

It would be wrong to exaggerate the scope of opposition from within the élite. Feelings of religious and national solidarity might outweigh the sense of group allegiance. All Orthodox believers had a mystic reverence for the sacrosanct ruler and for the symbols of his power—and even for his residence;[24] any deviation from prescribed norms of conduct exposed a man to the indignation of his fellows. Thus normally the tsar had little to fear from his subjects. However, during the seventeenth century the regime's prestige and authority were periodically weakened. The most serious of these crises followed the extinction of the old ruling dynasty in 1598. Others resulted from the assumption of military commitments that strained the country's slender resources. In any centralized political system there is an obvious relationship between warfare and socio-political change. The government must tighten controls if it is to make the new burdens palatable; military setbacks will invite speculation about the quality of the leadership; finally, enemy occupation may confront the population with an alien value system, which may appeal to those beginning to question the legitimacy of their own government.

All these phenomena are to be found in seventeenth-century Muscovy, and we may take account of them in attempting to periodize its history afresh.[25] There are three periods during which state authority is weakened, opening the way to autonomous political activity, between which lie two epochs of centralization. We might speak of eras of "thaw" and "freeze." The *Smutnoe vremia* (1598–1613) leads to the complete breakdown of government and the emergence of several competing centers of loyalty: some boiars (and even provincial gentry) favor a quasi-constitutional regime

---

takes the view that "of course [Razin's] rising bore a spontaneous anarchic character and its failure was a foregone conclusion" Mel'gunov, *Religiozno-obshchestvennye dvizheniia XVII–XVIII vv.* (1911–12) (Moscow, 1922), 65.

24 Moscow was holy, the Kremlin holier still. Entry to it was governed by elaborate ceremonial. Kotoshikhin records that horsemen had to dismount at a certain distance from the inner sanctum, which was precisely calculated according to their rank. G. Kotoshikhin, *O Rossii v tsarstvovanii Alekseia Mikhailovicha*⁴ (St. Petersburg, 1906), 29–31.

25 G. V. Vernadskii, *The Tsardom of Moscow, 1547–1682*, vol. II (New Haven-London, 1969), 752, offers an interesting "periodicity chart" based on somewhat different criteria.

under a foreign prince; the main body of serving men, however, opt for a restored national monarchy; their lower-grade associates press the merits of cossack "military democracy."[26] In a formal sense this period ends with Michael Romanov's election, but chaos and uncertainty continue until the peace settlement of 1618–19. There follows an era of centralization under Filaret, who exercises effective power until his death in 1633, in the midst of an unsuccessful war.[27] During the next twenty years of ineffectual clique government, burdensome ventures in foreign policy are generally avoided, lest they provoke internal dissension—especially among the provincial serving men, who (with the townspeople) submit several collective petitions backed by a threat of force.[28] This pressure reaches its climax in 1648, when the inexperienced Alexis is compelled to summon a representative zemskii sobor.[29] A new "freeze" era begins in 1653 when Alexis, aided by Patriarch Nikon, takes the helm in earnest: his decision to embark on a major war with Poland necessitates a tightening up of the administration; the Sobor is suppressed; opposition by the underprivileged elements is ruthlessly put down.[30] It is with the fifth and last period that we shall be concerned. Alexis's remarriage leads to dynastic schism, the effects of which are manifest after his death in 1676. The rival factions embroil different groups of the service élite in their political activities, and in the 1680s there are no less than three attempted *coups d'état*. The duumivirate established in 1682 is clearly a provisional expedient; the government vacillates on important matters of policy and loses prestige by two unsuccessful military campaigns.[31] This period extends beyond the downfall of the regent Sophia in 1689, which alters little, and ends only nine years later when Peter I takes firm control of affairs, plans a major war in the Baltic, and suppresses the incipient *fronde*. An enfeebled "oriental despotism" gives way to a "rational" bureaucratic absolutism on the western model.

III

A few general points about the service élite may be made before examining more

---

26 In his standard work *Ocherki po istorii Smuty v moskovskom gosudarstve XVI–XVII vv.*, new ed. (Moscow, 1937), S. F. Platonov offers a conventionally hostile interpretation of the boiars' motives. Cf. the more penetrating analysis by H. Fleischhacker, *Russland zwischen zwei Dynastien: eine Untersuchung über die Krise in der obersten Gewalt* (Baden bei Wien, 1933).

27 Cf. below, 109–34.

28 P. P. Smirnov, "Chelobitnye dvorian i detei boiarskikh vsekh gorodov v I-oi polovine XVII v.," *Chteniia IOIDR*, CCLIII (1915), pt. I.

29 Cf. below, pp. 51–86; [and P. Longworth, *Alexis, Tsar of All the Russias* (London, 1984), 47–50.]

30 Cf. H. Neubauer, *Car und Selbstherrscher: Beiträge zur Geschichte der Autokratie in Russland.* Veröffentlichungen des Osteuropa-Instituts München, vol. 22 (Wiesbaden, 1964), 87 ff.

31 A useful study of this period is C. B. O'Brien, *Russia under Two Tsars, 1682–9: The Regency of Sophia Alekseevna*, California University Publications in History, vol. 42 (Berkeley-Los Angeles, 1952).

closely its social position and political attitudes.

The first relates to the continuing significance of family connections—a factor that was correctly appreciated by Solov'ev but seems to have been overlooked until recently. For most Great Russians, whatever their rank or status, the kin relationship was undoubtedly the primary one in this period. Among nobles the survival of the traditional extended family (*rod*) was favored by *mestnichestvo*, a ritualized system of determining precedence, at ceremonial occasions or on appointment to office, by reference to the genealogical seniority and service record of one's immediate ancestors.[32] This institution gained ground during the seventeenth century in the sense that even medium-ranking serving men began to engage in such precedence disputes. Élite families were large and tended to expand rapidly. It is true that the customary practice of dividing property equally among one's progeny often led to rapid dissipation of accumulated wealth; but against this must be set the fact that the law gave other branches of a family a prior claim on property liable to alienation. The more successful *rod* members would extend assistance (sometimes on harsh terms) to their poorer relations: hence the frequency of such terms as *plemiannik* (nephew), *derzhal'nik* (retainer), *klevret* (companion), *khleboiazhets* (one who eats another's bread)—such persons usually although not invariably being kinsmen. Muscovite serving men had ample opportunities to rise socially, so that at least one branch of a family could be expected to prosper and keep its name prominent. This explains why, despite the rapid turnover among senior office-holders, many old families withstood the test of time remarkably well. The existence of a secular tendency towards upward movement within the élite can be shown by data for the Arsen'ev family of Tula. Fedor Makar'evich Arsen'ev (d. 1556) had four sons and twenty-one grandsons; following the senior line, of his six grandsons two reached metropolitan rank; of the great-grandsons at least six out of twelve did so; from the next generation we know of eight metropolitan nobles and four others.[33]

A closely related point is the existence of a well-developed patronage system. In Muscovite Russia, as elsewhere, an aspiring young nobleman would initiate his career by invoking the good offices of a senior kinsman or neighbor, to whom he would subsequently be indebted morally and/or financially. The most junior rank (*chin*) in the metropolitan hierarchy, that of *zhilets*, comprised ambitious young men from both metropolitan and provincial families.[34] Their chief functions seem to have

---

32 Markevich, *Mestnichestvo*; S. O. Shmidt, "Mestnichestvo i absoliutizm: postanovka voprosa," N. M. Druzhinin et al., eds., *Absoliutizm v Rossii XVII–XVIII vv.: sbornik statei k 70-letiiu . . . B. B. Kafengauza* (Moscow, 1964), 168–205.

33 V. S. Arsen'ev, *Rod dvorian Arsen'evykh 1389–1901gg.* (Tula, 1903), *passim.* Similar conclusions are suggested by information on the Volynskii family published by G. A. Vlas'ev, "Rod dvorian Volynskikh," *Izvestiia Russkogo genealogicheskogo obshchestva*, pt. IV (ii) (1911), 127–201. The more extensive data from the Likhachev family in *ibid.*, pt. II (i) (1903), 149–64, do not reveal much about the ranks and offices held, but the family was of fairly humble origin and among its late seventeenth-century members were many metropolitan nobles.

34 Novosel'skii, "Pobegi," 332; idem, "Gruppy," 317.

been honorary (although in an emergency they would be mobilized along with their fellows); in any case this was a sought-after appointment which conferred prestige upon the holder and also enabled him to make contacts useful in his later career. It would be interesting to know which prominent persons were most active in extending patronage, and whether this practice was increasing or decreasing; but information on this is scanty. One leader with a large following was V. V. Golitsyn. In 1676, when he was rising to power, he received several letters (which have survived) from kinsmen of persons under his command invoking his protection.[35] One of his clients was *stol'nik* A. I. Bezobrazov (1621/2–1690), who paid with his life for loyalty to his patron: after Golitsyn's fall he declined a service assignment, whereupon he was arrested and executed.[36]

In this patronage system territorial as well as kinship ties played their part. Many historians have assumed too readily that with the consolidation of Muscovite absolutism in the late fifteenth and sixteenth centuries all consciousness of regional identity was expunged, and that serving men saw themselves solely as agents of the central *vlast'*. In fact the various regions of the tsardom continued to differ widely in their socio-economic pattern and in what might be called their "style of life." The Soviet scholar M. N. Tikhomirov has drawn attention to this fact in a valuable work on sixteenth-century Russia.[37] By and large his observations apply to the next century as well. Not only was service landowning (or landholding) more widespread in some regions than in others, but the very conditions of existence in a rough frontier district such as Belev or Tula differed radically from those in an area close to Moscow.

Varieties of interest and experience naturally affected men's public attitudes. It is true that Muscovite nobles lacked that sense of attachment to their *terroir* characteristic of most western European aristocrats, with their feudal heritage;[38] that they had been brought into being by the state and held much of their land as *pomest'ia*. Nevertheless the view of state service held by those who had to bear its burdens was bound to be ambivalent. On one hand it offered opportunities for social progress and material enrichment; on the other it involved them in disturbance and risk. The latter aspect evidently weighed most heavily with those who were beginning to appreciate the economic advantages to be derived from working their estates. Such men were more likely to be found among higher-ranking nobles and those with land in the more fertile south. These two groups were not identical, but increasingly tended to overlap as the wealthier men shifted the center of gravity of their holdings southwards; they were also better able to strengthen their proprietary rights by converting from conditional to patrimonial tenure. Thus a problem familiar to students of post-Petrine Russia made itself felt already in the seventeenth century.

---

35 *Vremennik IOIDR*, XIII (1852), 26–9.

36 This had the happy consequence that his papers were confiscated and preserved; he is thus one of the few senior noblemen whose activities are relatively well documented. Novosel'skii, *Votchinnik*, 1–10, 28.

37 M. N. Tikhomirov, *Rossiia v XVI v.* (Moscow, 1962).

38 Raeff, *Origins*, 30.

This growing interest in economic gain was closely linked to another development which has only recently begun to attract attention: the impact of advances in
military technology, which led to major changes in the structure of the armed forces.
Traditionally, the backbone of Muscovy's military might was the levy (*opolchenie*)
of noble serving men who, accompanied by their retainers, formed a sizeable but
untrained cavalry force. In 1632, during the war with Poland-Lithuania, these men
(excluding followers) numbered 26,185, of whom 11,688 served in the field army.
They showed themselves much inferior to the recently formed, trained "new model
forces" (*polki novogo stroia*). In the relatively trouble-free years that followed, the
number of noble serving men grew, no doubt largely for demographic reasons, until
by 1651 it reached 39,408 (30% of total effectives).[39] In the second Russo-Polish
war the government was obliged to expand rapidly the new model forces. In some
cases noble serving men not otherwise assigned to duty were simply enrolled as infantrymen (*soldaty*).[40] According to the military budget for 1662/3 the total number
of nobles had sunk to 21,850, of whom 14,598 seem to have been mobilized in the
traditional way.[41] By 1681 a military roster listed only 13,473 men in the gentry levy,
whereas the new model forces could muster over 80,000 men. In the two campaigns
of 1687 and 1689 the gentry supplied only a small part of the forces engaged: 8,712
and 10,173 men respectively.[42] The total number of enrolled serving men at this
time must, however, have been at least 50,000. In brief, by the end of the century a
smaller proportion of this group, probably less than one man in five, was required to
render active military service.[43]

IV

Three groups within the service élite will be discussed here: the musketeers, provincial
gentry and metropolitan nobility.

The musketeers (*strel'tsy*), Russia's first professional soldiers, had been formed
in the sixteenth century.[44] Like the new model forces that came into being later,
they were not noblemen; administratively, they were classified as *sluzhilye liudi po*

39 Chernov, *Vooruzh. sily*, 167, citing unpublished Razriad materials; cf. also *Vremennik IOIDR*, IV (1849), iii, 18–20.

40 *AI* IV, no. 70 (1653); [*AMG* III, 170 (1660).]

41 Chernov, *Vooruzh. sily*, 161, 168, citing S. B. Veselovskii, in *Chteniia v IOIDR* III (i) (1911), 1–60. A count of the number of *dvoriane* or *deti boiarskie* listed in this source shows a much higher figure: 37, 217. Evidently the bulk of them were serving in other formations. [E. D. Stashevskii, "Smeta voennykh sil Moskovskogo gosudarstva na 1663 g.," *Voenno-istoricheskii vestnik*, nos. 9–10 (Kiev, 1910).]

42 Kalinychev, *Pravovye voprosy*, 46: Chernov, *Vooruzh. sily*, 195. [See now our *Soldiers of the Tsar: Army and Society in Russia, 1462–1874* (Oxford, 1985), 49–53.]

43 The total population in 1678 has been put at 11.5 million. B. Ts. Urlanis, *Rost naseleniia v Evrope: opyt ischisleniia* (Moscow-Leningrad, 1941), 193.

44 N. I. Shpakovskii, "Strel'tsy," *Zhurnal Ministerstva narodnogo prosveshcheniia*, pt. 318 (1898), 137–51; [A. V. Chernov, "Obrazovanie streletskogo voiska," *IZ*, 38 (1950), 281–90.]

priboru, as distinct from *sluzhilye liudi po otechestvu*. The distinction arose from the method of recruitment. In principle a senior-grade man rendered service on an individual basis. He was awarded, or inherited, land for his maintenance, and it was from this land that he served.[45] Lower-grade serving men were generally recruited *en bloc*, i.e. by assignment, from various unattached segments of the population.[46] This act was termed *pribor* or *nabor*; the latter carried a stronger overtone of compulsion, but there was little difference in practice.

The musketeers constituted a separate rank (*chin*) or community of state bondsmen—one might almost say a caste, since service tended to be hereditary and they could not of their own volition legally leave their community. In their mode of life the *strel'tsy* anticipated the military colonists of a later age. When not actually performing service duties, they resided in their settlements (*slobody*) and earned their living by trade or handicrafts, enjoying certain privileges *vis-à-vis* the rest of the urban population; they also had small plots of land which they could farm. In principle they received an annual salary, although the government sought to commute this to a land allotment.[47] They were organized into companies (*sotni*) and regiments (*polki, prikazy*), named after their commanders or the town where they were stationed. The regimental chief (*streletskii golova*) had below him centurions (*sotniki*), quinquagenarians (*piatidesiatniki*) and decurions (*desiatniki*). Overall control lay with the Streletskii prikaz, one of the more important central executive organs, which exercised police as well as military functions (as did the musketeers themselves). Most of these soldiers served in the provincial towns. Those in Moscow formed a kind of *corps d'élite*; they included the Stremiannoi polk, which acted as the tsar's bodyguard. In 1632 there were 19,540 *strel'tsy*, of whom about 4,000 belonged to the Moscow group; by 1662/3 the figure had risen to 29,048, of whom 15,878 fell in this category; by 1681 the numbers were 55,000 and 22,500 respectively.[48] The élite element thus tended to acquire increased weight. A feature of some political importance was the existence of a "promotion bloc." Ordinary musketeers could rise to become decurions or quinquagenarians, the appointments being made by their commanders; but the regimental chiefs, who were centrally appointed, and some of the centurions were drawn from the gentry—i.e., were men extraneous to the community. Given the fact that *strel'tsy* could not normally enter higher grades of the service class,[49] this was bound to create tension, however honorably the commanders acquitted themselves.

---

45 Cf. the idiom "sluzhit' s pomest'ia."

46 E.g. *AI*, V, no. 13 (1676).

47 Shpakovskii, "Strel'tsy," 149.

48 *Vremennik IOIDR*, IV (1849), iii, 20–24. Chernov, *Vooruzh. sily*, 162, citing Razriad materials, gives a figure of 33,775 and 8,000 for the Moscow *strel'tsy*. Kalinychev, *Pravovye voprosy*, 44, gives a figure of 16,955 for the Moscow *strel'tsy* in 1681. For the 1662/3 figures, see *ChIOIDR* (1911), III, i, 26–30.

49 An *ukaz* of September 1652 (*PSZ*, I, no. 82) ordained that fugitive *strel'tsy* who had enrolled as *deti boiarskie* were to be returned to their communities, suggesting that hitherto there had been greater flexibility in this respect.

Among noble serving men, the major distinction was between the relatively privileged metropolitan or court nobility and the mass of provincial gentry: in contemporary administrative terms, between those who served "from the Moscow roll" (*s
moskovskogo spisku*) and those who served "from the [provincial] towns" (*s gorodov*).
We may consider the latter group first.

From a juridical point of view the gentry resident in each town—that is, the
area (normally an *uezd*) of which the town was the administrative center—formed a
community with the right to run its own affairs to the extent judged compatible with
the interests of the central *vlast'*. The term *gorod* denoted this community and/or
the administrative organization which regulated the service of its members. Some
later historians called it a "corporation," rather misleadingly implying that the *gorod*
was more institutionalized than was the case and that its members had a modern
consciousness of their legal rights. The *gorod* had no office staff and kept no records.
All adult male members were periodically summoned for inspection by the local
voivode or by a representative of the Razriad (the central executive organ concerned
with administration of the service class). He would call the muster, note the absentees,
and compile three rolls: those present and fit to serve, those awaiting enrollment,
and those who had been retired or despatched on service elsewhere. Thereupon the
members would elect from among themselves assessors (*okladchiki*) "of the first and
the middle and the least grade, good and honest and well-informed men, as many
as may be suitable." Their task was to help the government agent to determine,
by questioning their fellows and examining any statements (*skazki*) they submitted,
how much land they should receive as an allotment (*oklad*) and to what extent this
norm should be met. The first act was known as *verstanie*, the second as *razbor*.
The elected assessors would also help distribute any monetary rewards and check the
qualifications of men claiming exemption from service on grounds of disability.[50]

It was not within the assessors' formal competence to determine the grade (*stat'ia*)
to which a man belonged: this function was reserved to the Razriad. Nevertheless it
seems clear that decisions taken on the spot could indirectly affect this classification.
What criteria, one may ask, were employed? The inspectors' instructions stated that
a man's service record (*sluzhby*), material circumstances (*prozhitki*) and genealogical
seniority (*otechestvo*) should be taken into account. This left plenty of latitude.
Novosel'skii believes that a man's service record mattered most,[51] but the evidence
in support of this view is inconclusive. Most historians have assumed that the chief
criterion was genealogical seniority, but again there is no hard proof that this was
so. The instruction of 1678 suggests that in the official view material wealth was
given the greatest weight. This would have accorded with the general principle
in Muscovite administration that increased prosperity should confer correspondingly
greater responsibilities. A kind of automatic levelling tendency existed within the
provincial service organization, as it did within the *posad* or the rural *mir*, but it was

---

50 Kalinychev, *Pravovye voprosy*, 55–6; for instructions to inspectors, see [*DRV*, XVI (1791),
    345–66 (1676);] *PSZ*, II, nos. 744–5 (1678).

51 Novosel'skii, "Gruppy," 318.

offset by informal factors. In practise much depended on the local balance of power; the distance of the locality from Moscow; the relative venality of the authorities concerned; and the ability of any group of members, especially the wealthier and best-connected men, to act together as a faction.

If one takes account of such variables, it seems that on balance the *gorod* system favored élitist trends within the provincial gentry. Members of the three grades were known as *vybornye, dvorovye* and *gorodovye*. The very name given to the senior men is suggestive: "the elect"—or more accurately "the selected ones." The first *vybornye* were men summoned to Moscow for a limited term of service, who then returned to their localities laden with prestige.[52] When the practice of periodical summonses died out in the early seventeenth century, men were simply ascribed to this grade after inspection. Alternatively, they could petition the Razriad for inclusion in it. Surviving documents indicate that such requests were not always granted; that applicants normally had to have served in the second grade; and that one could be demoted for evading service[53]—or as a matter of routine, if one's means had seriously deteriorated since the previous inspection. Data for Kashira, an old border town southeast of Moscow, show that the proportion of *vybornye* increased from 9% to 25% between 1599 and 1648.[54]

Senior-grade men normally received larger land allotments and were more likely to have these allocations covered by actual grants.[55] The main reason for this was that the wealthier members could be expected to serve more effectively. But in part this will have resulted from gentry pressure. For the assessors were usually *vybornye* (and men from large families). This again was predictable, given the Muscovite administrative practice whereby elected persons were bound to their electors by a mutual guarantee (*krugovaia poruka*) so that they could be held responsible for any malfeasance.[56] Yet an informal element was involved here as well. Senior-grade men coveted the office of assessor because it enabled them to wield power over their fellows and to influence the authorities' decisions. One need not exclude *a priori*, as many historians have done, all altruistic motives; nevertheless an element of enlightened self-interest was undoubtedly prominent. In some districts certain families monopolized the office of assessor for several years. In the Derevskaia *piatina* of Novgorod, for example,

---

52 V. I. Novitskii, *Vybornoye i bol'shoe dvorianstvo XVI–XVII vv.* (Kiev, 1915), *passim*.

53 Ibid., 79–80, quoting *AMG*, vol. II, nos. 51, 185, 556, 578; cf. *PSZ*, I, no. 260 (October 5, 1659).

54 Ibid., 149. The figures are: 18 out of 206 in 1599, 26 out of 219 in 1622, and 67 out of 263 in 1648. No information is available for the latter half of the century, and this example may be untypical.

55 Novosel'skii, "Gruppy," 321–2, selects five of the 16 towns for which land distribution registers (*desiatni*) have been preserved for 1622, and shows that in each *vybornye* owned more dependents than *dvorovye*, who in turn owned more than *gorodovye*. It is not clear, however, whether this situation was characteristic of all sixteen towns, let alone of the country as a whole. In Novgorod there were no *vybornye* until the mid-seventeenth century.

56 For the operation of this principle in regard to elected *guba* officials, see below, pp. 87–108.

between 1606 and 1665 it was held by thirty-five families out of a possible 110.[57] At Tula in 1631 there was conflict between some serving men, led by the Pisarev family, who wanted new assessors appointed, and another group, comprising the Aleksandrovs and Il'ins, evidently local potentates; the latter rejected a compromise proposed by the Razriad and went in a body to Moscow, where the decision went in their favor.[58] More evidence of such informal oligarchic associations has recently come to light. At Elets, also on the southern border, in the 1630s the voivode entered into collusion with a coterie of *vybornye* led by one Dmitrii Snetin, who not only arbitrarily altered revenue assessments to their own benefit (*v iashchik*, as the document expressively puts it), but even resorted to such crude expedients as using a false-bottomed bucket when issuing grain allocations to their comrades.[59]

Such transactions expose the social reality behind the rigid façade of the service system. Whatever the moral or legal implications of this activity, from the standpoint of Russia's social and political advance its effects were by no means wholly negative. It could lead to the emergence of a local élite with roots in the life of the area and a capacity for leadership. As Novosel'skii rightly observes, elected assessors often "took the initiative in petitioning the central government on all manner of questions in which the *gorod* had an interest."[60] It was they who, for example, represented the serving men of their district at the Zemskii Sobor.

Moreover, senior-grade men could acquire land in districts other than that where they were enrolled. In Tula between 1622 and 1678 the proportion of serving men with such land rose from 36% to 75%.[61] This is clear evidence that the *gorod* service organization was in decline. In the central areas around Moscow assessors would report that they had lost touch with men now resident "in various distant towns," whose land had been appropriated by persons outside the jurisdiction of the local *gorod*; the latter "are growing rich and building stone houses, but not serving the Sovereign."[62] For the state this development meant that the gentry of such areas could no longer be readily mobilized if the need arose. For the provincial serving men themselves, on the contrary, it meant greater freedom from military duties and the opportunity to widen their mental horizons. They could shake off the constraining influences of the local milieu and see themselves as part of a wider entity, regional and even national in scope. It also offered them a chance of escaping from the grinding

---

57 Novosel'skii, "Gruppy," 325.

58 Ibid., 326.

59 E. V. Chistiakova, "Volneniia sluzhilykh liudei v iuzhnykh gorodakh Rossii v seredine XVII v.," N. V. Ustiugov et al., eds., *Russkoe gosudarstvo v XVII v. Novye iavleniia v sotsial'no-ekonomicheskoi, politicheskoi i kul'turnoi zhizni. Sbornik statei* (Moscow, 1961), 254–71, esp. 258–9.

60 Novosel'skii, "Gruppy," 323.

61 A. A. Novosel'skii, "Raspad zemlevladeniia sluzhilogo 'goroda' v XVII v.: po desiatnam," Ustyugov et al., eds., *Russkoe gosudarstvo,* 231–54, at 252.

62 Novosel'skii, "Gruppy," 328 (Iaroslavl', 1676).

poverty that had hitherto been their general lot,[63] by expanding and diversifying their holdings. The rise of the gentry had begun.

Let us now turn to the metropolitan nobles. At the summit of the social pyramid ideas of hierarchy and status were naturally stronger than they were elsewhere. The court ranks (*chiny*), in order of precedence, were as follows: *boiarin, okol'nichii, stol'nik, striapchii, moskovskii dvorianin, zhilets*. All but the first and the fifth of these had originally designated court functions, of which the memory lingered on; tenure of a *chin* might well be combined with that of some court appointment that now carried wide administrative responsibilities as well. The confusion between rank and office in Muscovite thought and practice was a source of puzzlement to contemporary observers, as it has been to historians since. In fact the seventeenth-century system of *chin* was not very different from that established by Peter I. Rank was conferred (*pozhalovan*) upon the holder by the tsar, acting upon the formal or informal advice of his counselors, with appropriate ceremony. The view that it was awarded simply on grounds of birth, or length of service in a junior grade, needs modification. In practice ever greater attention was paid to the quality of the service rendered.[64] It is true that sons of boiars could start to climb the ladder at the rung of *stol'nik*, and that sixteen leading families enjoyed accelerated promotion to boiar rank.[65] But undistinguished highborn men often failed to make a career, and normally intermediate grades could not be bypassed. The real fault of the Muscovite court was not that non-aristocrats had poor promotion prospects, but that senior officials did not need to display much professional expertise: in other words, that the Russian state was still basically traditionalist. This, however, is a problem of a very different order.

The institution of mestnichestvo, which has given rise to these misunderstandings, was less a political than a cultural phenomenon, derived from ingrained notions of family honor (*chest'*). It is true that in the sixteenth century it had been utilized by Ivan IV to bolster his absolute power. Seventeenth-century rulers, however, did not follow his example; instead, they tried to reduce mestnichestvo contestations by exempting particularly important appointments (e.g. military commands in wartime).[66] Thus although the number of such disputes increased, as lesser men emulated their betters, their social impact lessened. As a means of preventing infiltration of senior appointments by non-aristocrats it was a failure. The rapidly expanding bureaucratic and military apparatus could not be filled solely by men from leading families.

---

63 At Elets, for instance, at an unspecified date early in the seventeenth century 415 serving men owned between them 190 peasants; the wealthiest had only ten, and most worked their land with the labor of their family (Chistiakova, *op. cit.*, 256). The Soviet historian reporting this fact nevertheless refers to such persons as "lords" (*feodaly*). They were in fact among the first *odnodvortsy*, or single-homesteaders.

64 Markevich, *Mestnichestvo*, 525. This could be demonstrated by a detailed investigation into career patterns, as has been done by G. Alef for the fifteenth-century boiars: "Reflections on the Boiar Duma in the Reign of Ivan III," *Slavonic and East European Review*, XLV (1967), 76–123.

65 Kotoshikhin, *O Rossii*, 41.

66 Shmidt, "Mestnichestvo," 194 ff.

Numerous outsiders entered the metropolitan nobility through service, while others achieved prominence as kinsmen or favorites of the tsar. Indeed, when working their way up the ladder, newcomers sometimes successfully invoked mestnichestvo precedents against "dishonored" aristocrats who stood in their way. As Kliuchevskii noted long ago, the genealogical order whereby precedence disputes were decided did not coincide with the *chin* order taken into account when making state appointments.[67] By 1682 mestnichestvo had become little more than an embarrassment and could be abolished with relative ease.

It might be supposed that mestnichestvo encouraged aristocratic feeling, but this was not so: it perpetuated a practical interest in one's ancestors' service record, but otherwise kept the leading families divided. On the contrary, true aristocratic feeling could only develop once it had been abolished. The official invitation to compile family genealogies and register them with the authorities nourished prominent nobles' self-esteem.[68] They began to justify their privileged status in terms similar to those employed by European aristocrats of the day, and to assume the features characteristic of the "old nobility" of eighteenth-century Russia.

Some of them already behaved like *grands seigneurs*. Johann-Georg Korb, passing through Mozhaisk on his way to Moscow in 1698, noted that the boiar Ivanov "has a fine *dacha*; the land there is well tilled; in his garden are many flower beds and a wood with little artificial mounds, skillfully arranged."[69] The *stol'nik* Bezobrazov found his service duties onerous and evaded them by exploiting personal contacts in the Razriad; some officials there complained that, when sent to muster recruits, he went hunting instead.[70] He pursued a consistent policy of territorial aggrandizement, extending his *votchiny* into the more fertile southern border region, and expropriating unfortunate lesser nobles whose land he coveted. After twenty years of effort Bezobrazov accumulated 239 dependent peasant households and a large amount of movable property, meticulously recorded by the officials who confiscated it.[71]

All metropolitan nobles possessed land in the Moscow region, without which they could not have performed their duties at court. This is evident from a list of 54 such holdings compiled in 1647, which also shows that 13 of them owned at least one thousand peasant homesteads.[72] The tendency for successful families

---

67 *Istoriia soslovii v Rossii* (Petrograd, 1918), 214–21.

68 These documents were, however, not published and remained in the archives until, in the late nineteenth century, they attracted the attention of genealogists.

69 J.-G. Korb, *Dnevnik poiezdki v Moskovskoe gosudarstvo . . . 1698 g.*, tr. V. Zhenev and M. I. Semevskii (St. Petersburg, 1866), 43. (The English edition of this work, *Diary of an Austrian Secretary of Legation at the Court of Czar Peter the Great*, tr. and ed. The Count Mac Donnell, 2 vols. (London, 1863), re-issued London, 1968, is unsatisfactory.)

70 Novosel'skii, *Votchinnik*, 9, 41. He sweetened the *d'iaki* by gifts of apples, watermelons and (curiously) onions.

71 Ibid., 31, 24.

72 S. V. Rozhdestvenskii, "Rospis' zemel'nykh vladenii moskovskogo boiarstva 1647–8 gg.," *Drevnosti. Trudy Arkheograficheskoi komissii Imperatorskogo Moskovskogo arkheologicheskogo obshchestva*, vol. III (Moscow, 1913), 193–238.

to accumulate property is borne out by data for the Cherkasskiis. In the 1620s
I. B. Cherkasskii (d. 1642) had 2,582 male peasants on his estates; when his cousin
and heir, Ia. K. Cherkasskii, died in 1666, he bequeathed a veritable empire of 24,946
such persons; ten years later, under the administration of his son, M. Ia. Cherkasskii,
the figure had risen to approximately 28,000.[73] Yet the Cherkasskiis seem to have been
less entrepreneurially minded than Bezobrazov, or the better known (but untypical!)
Morozov family. Like many nobles, they owed their wealth mainly to grants from
the state. To generalize: in Muscovite conditions it was not economic interest that
stimulated political activity, but rather the reverse.

V

How did these three élite groups react to the political opportunities opened up during
the seventeenth century's last "thaw" period?

In regard to the musketeers one is still treading shaky ground. With some justice
Buganov reproaches earlier writers for assuming that they were just a passive tool of
court factions;[74] yet without access to Streletskii Prikaz records it is difficult to reconstruct their political physiognomy. When the dramatist depicted them invoking the Almighty to preserve their young sovereigns he was probably close to the truth.[75] Their
deeply rooted legitimism went hand in hand with a deep distrust of their social superiors,
particularly the metropolitan nobles and officials who stood between throne and people.
Their outlook was close to that of other townsmen, and no doubt of many peasants as
well. More specifically, it was colored by Old Believer teachings. These seem to have
won more support in some *strel'tsy* units than in others, but the extent of their dissemina-
tion is hard to judge. Thirty-three musketeers were implicated in the 1662 "copper revolt," of whom half came from one detachment (I. Monastyrev's *prikaz*).[76] During the
Razin rising some *strel'tsy* at Astrakhan' went over to the rebels (who characteristically
formed their *own* musketeer units), and there was disaffection in contingents stationed
elsewhere along the Volga; but other units, particularly the Moscow *strel'tsy*, took an energetic part in suppressing the rising, and suffered 165 casualties in the process.[77]

73 K. N. Shchepetov, "Pomeshchich'e predprinimatel'stvo v XVII v. Po materialam khoziaistva
kn. Cherkasskikh," Ustyugov et al., *Russkoe gosudarstvo*, 18–22. The *krest'iane* and *bobyli*
have here been grouped together.

74 Buganov, "Moskovskie vosstaniia," 105.

75 "From evil foes, arrogant boiars, wrongdoers and embezzlers," A. P. Mussorgskii, *Kho-
vanshchina*, Act I. The great composer was a connoisseur of seventeenth-century Russian
history.

76 V. I. Buganov, "O sotsial'nom sostave uchastnikov Moskovskogo vosstaniia 1662 g.," *Istoricheskie zapiski*, 66 (1960), 313–17.

77 E. A. Shvestov (comp.), A. A. Novosel'skii and V. I. Lebedev, eds., *Krest'ianskaia voina*

During the 1670s, if not before, the musketeers appear to have acquired a sense of corporate identity. Four developments may have facilitated this: first, the emergence of the new model forces, which were better trained and competed successfully with the *strel'tsy* for official favors; second, the difficulties experienced in collecting the special impost assigned to their upkeep (*streletskie den'gi*), which taxpayers found burdensome; third, the frustrations engendered by the "promotion bloc"; fourth, rivalry between musketeers and gentry over fugitive peasants. In regard to the last point, parties of *strel'tsy* guarded the special investigators (*syshchiki*) sent out to ensure the return of runaways, and serving men complained that musketeer communities sometimes offered sanctuary to such fugitives.[78] The collection of *streletskie den'gi* was in 1679 entrusted to the Streletskii Prikaz, instead of to various central organs as hitherto[79]; but this does not seem to have improved the flow of revenue, or at least the distribution of funds to the men concerned. The elderly and inefficient boiar in charge of this office, Iu. A. Dolgorukii, left affairs to his son, M. Iu. Dolgorukii, who seems to have been equally incompetent.[80] As a result the officers in charge of certain musketeer units had ample opportunity to engage in corrupt practices, such as appropriating their men's pay or forcing them to work on their own properties. Morale was further weakened by a decree of March 25, 1680 giving the Moscow *strel'tsy* chiefs western titles (colonel etc.) to bring them into line with foreigners in Muscovite service.[81] This move will certainly have been unpopular, if not with the officers concerned, at least with the rank and file, who were distrustful of alien influences. Finally, when V. V. Golitsyn called a consultative commission in November 1681 to consider important military reforms, the musketeers do not appear to have been invited.[82]

It is therefore not surprising that, when the dynastic power struggle broke out in earnest a few months later, the musketeers should have become involved, although no one foresaw that they would help to determine its outcome.[83] The first sign of trouble came in February, when men in Pyzhov's contingent complained of abuses

pod predvoditel'stvom Stepana Razina. Sbornik dokumentov, 3 vols. (Moscow, 1954–62), III, nos. 187, 209, 248, 274–6; for the casualties, see no. 237.

78 A. G. Man'kov, *Razvitie krepostnogo prava v Rossii vo II-oi polovine XVII v.* (Moscow-Leningrad, 1962), 53.

79 *AI*, V, no. 48, October 21, 1679.

80 V. A. Miakotin, *Istoriia Rossii v kontse XVII i v I-oi polovine XVIII st.* (Sofia, 1938); (*Godishnik na Sofiskaia Universitet,* XXXIV, 4), 19; *RBS,* vol. *Dabelov-Diad'kovskii,* 569.

81 *PSZ*, II, no. 812.

82 The official record (*PSZ*, II, no. 905 (January 12, 1682), "Sobornoe deianie ob unichtozhenii mestnichestva") mentions *polkovniki reitarskie i pekhotnye,* which might be taken as including the *strel'tsy* chiefs, but in any case no delegates were elected by the units, as would have been customary practice.

83 This reconstruction of events is based mainly on data in Belov, "Smuty"; Solov'ev, *Istoriia,* VII (XIII), 266–302; N. G. Ustrialov, *Istoriia tsartvovaniia Petra Velikogo,* I (1858), 12–45. Vernadskii (*The Tsardom of Moscow, 1547–1682,* vol. II, 711 ff.) represents the musketeers as motivated wholly by religious considerations. [A full account is given by V. I. Buganov, *Moskovskie vosstaniia kontsa XVII v.* (Moscow, 1969); see also our translation of Heinrich

by their chiefs. On April 23 Griboedov's regiment followed suit. Dolgorukii ordered the ringleader to be seized and punished, but his comrades freed him from arrest and assaulted several officials of the Streletskii Prikaz. By the following day all 16 regiments in Moscow were in uproar. The authorities were unable to pursue a consistent policy, either of appeasement or of repression, as Tsar Theodore II was fatally ill. When he died (April 27), the patriarch quickly attempted to settle the succession issue by installing the ten-year-old Peter as tsar, and this solution was endorsed by an *ad hoc* public gathering. Three days later some *strel'tsy* marched peacefully to the Kremlin, evidently in the hope that the new Naryshkin regime would satisfy their service grievances. Two weeks later their movement assumed a political character. The chief reason for this was that A. S. Matveev, of whom they had high expectations, did nothing to help them when he returned from exile on May 12; instead he conferred secretly with the hated Dolgorukii. This became known and naturally aroused fear of reprisals. The disaffected *strel'tsy* accordingly turned to partisans of the Miloslavskii faction, who had been spreading propaganda in the city against their opponents. On May 15 a three-day *pogrom* began. It cost the lives of eighteen noblemen, including six boiars; the two Dolgorukiis were among the victims; several foreign officers were attacked or threatened. A variety of charges were leveled against their enemies, most related to administrative abuses; G. G. Romodanovskii was blamed for ineffectual leadership in battle against the Turks; the Naryshkins were accused of trespassing upon the sovereign power.

The musketeers' political outlook may therefore be described as legitimist and chauvinistic. An element of social radicalism is also evident in their destruction of two government offices closely concerned with peasant bondage. It seems unlikely that they had any positive ideas for a solution to the succession crisis. The quaint idea of a duumvirate, which they are known to have discussed from May 23 onwards, must have been suggested to them from above—probably by the Miloslavskiis, who were now stepping into the seats of power. Ivan Miloslavskii secured the invaluable services of I. A. Khovanskii, an ambitious but popular figure sympathetic to the Old Believers, in restraining the *strel'tsy*. While he took over the Streletskii Prikaz, the Miloslavskiis extended official hospitality to the rebel troops for three days in succession, during which time they first proclaimed the duumvirate (May 26) and then tsarevna Sophia's regency (May 29).

With the political issue out of the way, the *strel'tsy* leaders turned their attention to religious problems. This was a great mistake, for the "old faith" did not command general support among their followers: it was popular in Titov's regiment, but not in the privileged Stremiannoi polk. The Miloslavskiis could exploit this division. After a public confrontation on religious matters (July 5), some Old Believer leaders were arrested and exiled; others were assaulted by hostile *strel'tsy*, whose passions had been inflamed by alcohol dispensed from the Kremlin cellars. These events disrupted Ivan Miloslavskii's alliance with Khovanskii. The latter sought to maintain

Butenant's memoir: "Mutiny in Moscow, 1682: A Contemporary Account," *CSP*, 23 (1981), 410–42.]

his position by demanding a large monetary grant for his men, which was formally considered by the government but rejected (August 16). It was now increasingly clear that Sophia and her advisors, relying on the noble serving men, were preparing to crush the musketeers. The court withdrew from the capital to a secure suburban base, whence it prepared and executed a successful "counter-revolution." On August 29 the Stremiannoi polk was summoned from Moscow; on September 14 "men of all [noble] ranks" were instructed to assemble "for their majesties' affairs"; three days later Khovanskii was arrested, charged with treason, and hurriedly put to death. The patriarch solemnized an act of reconciliation, but discontent simmered for some time to come.

It may confidently be asserted that the musketeers were not just the pliant instruments of a Miloslavskii or a Khovanskii. Their movement was basically autonomous and developed a wide spectrum of interests and motives—professional, political, social and religious—which were, however, not readily compatible. Isolated from other groups, such as the cossacks, which might have lent them support, they could hope to exercise only a temporary influence on state policy. The Streletskii Prikaz, now headed by F. F. Shaklovitii, a confidant of the regent, regained control by granting landed estates on favorable terms to loyal *strel'tsy* officers.[84] Nevertheless the metropolitan nobles remained afraid of a new outbreak.[85] In 1687 Sophia seems to have sounded them out with a view to possible action against Tsar Peter and his menacing *poteshnye* regiments, but found them reluctant to assist her.[86] It was Peter who provoked the next crisis in August 1689. He and his counselors followed faithfully the tactics employed by the Miloslavskiis seven years earlier. From his stronghold in the Trinity monastery he summoned to his presence successive military units, until he felt strong enough to depose the regent; it was now Shaklovitii's turn to be cast as a conspirator and to face the supreme penalty, although there is no trustworthy evidence of his guilt.[87]

The *strel'tsy* regiments did not play an active part in these events. Those of Sukharev and Tsykler were loyal to Peter; the Stremiannoi, Efimov and Zhukov regiments, which favored Sophia, were paralyzed by her chronic indecisiveness.[88]

---

84 *PSZ*, II, nos. 940, 1046; for later concessions see *AI*, V, nos. 148, 170, and for evidence of continuing discontent, no. 130.

85 The Jesuit Jiři David, who lived in Moscow from 1686 to 1689, reflected this alarm: He described the *strel'tsy* as "insolentissimi dum occasionem nanciscuntur, maximum timorem Moscuae incutiunt," Georgius David S. J., *Status modernus Magnae Russiae seu Moscoviae* (1690), ed. . . . A. V. Florovskij, (The Hague and Paris, 1965), 86–7.

86 Shmurlo, "Padenie," citing *Rozysknoe delo o F. Shaklovitom i ego soobshchnikakh*, 3 vols. (St. Petersburg, 1884), I, 117, 128. Shmurlo places more confidence than seems warranted in the evidence of this inquiry, obtained under severe physical duress.

87 Shmurlo demonstrates that each party misinterpreted the other's purposes, yet contradictorily asserts ("Padenie," 80–1) that Sophia planned a *coup* against Peter. Her conduct is, however, explicable only on the assumption that she consistently tried to avoid bringing the conflict to a head.

88 *AI*, V, no. 189 (i); Shmurlo, "Padenie," 87–8; B. I. Kurakin, "Gistoriia o tsare Petre Alek-

Nevertheless Peter suspected the entire *chin* of disloyalty, and in 1698 a relatively minor affray, touched off by service grievances and quickly suppressed, gave him a pretext to launch a massacre; at least 800 men were put to death with appalling cruelty.[89] Thereby he not only liquidated an emergent interest group which might in other circumstances have asserted itself against the central *vlast'*, but made a clear breach with previous juridical assumptions, so clearing the way for the new state order.

In accomplishing this feat both the Miloslavskiis and the Naryshkins relied principally upon noble serving men. The provincial gentry had become a force to be reckoned with in any political crisis. Its practice of submitting collective petitions, on a local, regional or even nationwide basis, continued in the latter half of the seventeenth century. Most of these petitions evidently concerned the enforcement of peasant bondage, which had become law under their pressure in the 1649 code;[90] a secondary demand related to land surveys. It may be that gentry spokesmen also raised other professional questions (e.g. terms of service), but these documents have not yet been published *in extenso*, and only the bondage petitions have been properly studied.[91] They arose from the fact that without state assistance owners of fugitive bondsmen found it extremely difficult to secure their return: this required ample leisure, an executive force, and good contacts with authorities in other areas. Moreover, those harboring runaways were often other noble serving men, so that the gentry did not speak with one voice on this issue. A similar ambivalence affected the state authorities: in principle they sought to maintain bondage right, but were sometimes compelled by colonial or military considerations to adopt a more permissive attitude. Government policy was also influenced by different social or regional pressure groups within the service class.

An attempt may be made here to sketch the main fluctuations in this policy. In 1653 the outbreak of war over the Ukraine obliged the government to treat the border

seeviche i blizhnikh k nemu liudiakh 1682–94 gg." (on 39–78 of *Arkhiv kn. F. A. Kurakina*, ed. M. I. Semevskii, vol. I (St. Petersburg, 1890), 57). The latter account (cited hereafter as Kurakin, "Gistoriia") was written in 1723–7; it is not always reliable.

89 Korb, *Dnevnik, passim*. M. M. Bogoslovskii, *Petr I: Materialy dlia biografii* (Moscow, 1946), III, 5–126, provides a thorough account of this affair. [Several hundred more were killed a few weeks later. See now V. I. Buanov and N. G. Savich, comps., *Vosstanie moskovskikh strel'tsov, 1698 god: materialy sledstvennogo dela: sbornik dokumentov* (Moscow, 1980).]

90 M. N. Tikhomirov and P. P. Epifanov, eds., *Sobornoe ulozhenie 1649 g.: posobie dlia vysshey shkoly* (Moscow, 1961); for an English translation of the relevant chapter of the Code, see R. E. F. Smith, *The Enserfment of the Russian Peasantry* (Cambridge, 1968), 141–52.

91 The relatively sophisticated interpretation offered by Novosel'skii, "Pobegi," has recently been challenged by Man'kov, *Razvitie*. This work, although based on an extensive reading of the primary sources, suffers from ideological rigidity. Man'kov assumes a basic community of interest between all elements of what he calls "the noble class" (35, 82), plays down regional differences, and neglects the non-socioeconomic factors that entered into government decision-making.

population relatively gently, and the same attitude was adopted three years later.[92] Subsequently, after petitions from the gentry of Zamoskov'e and the border region, and as the intensity of the war increased, its line hardened. Special investigators (*syshchiki*) were dispatched to return fugitives, mainly from wealthy owners (including Patriarch Nikon, now in disgrace).[93] Runaways themselves, as distinct from those harboring them, were for the first time made liable to penal sanctions.[94] In 1660 a strongly-worded petition for tougher legislation was submitted by several gentry service organizations. A decree of September 13, 1661, ostensibly granted their requests, but characteristically the main innovation was a measure that originated with the government: harborers of runaways were to make compensation by handing over a specified number of their own peasants (*naddatochnye*).[95] This order was confirmed on March 31, 1663. In the years that followed investigators were sent out more and more frequently, a climax being reached during the struggle against Razin.[96]

In the 1670s this practice was temporarily suspended and the number of special investigators fell significantly.[97] The government now gave more attention to the actual content of the petitions submitted. In 1675 a "soft" policy was once again adopted on fugitives in the border region owing to "the impending war with the Turks."[98] The serving men complained *en masse* and in 1676 the status quo was restored[99]—on paper, at least. The authorities seemed to have dragged their feet, probably for military reasons, so that in April-May 1677, before the second Chigirin campaign, two further general petitions were submitted.[100] The despatch of investigators and the levying of *naddatochnye* were resumed.

In August 1681 policy veered once again to the detriment of the smaller owners. This may have owed something to boiar pressure, as Novosel'skii argues[101]; but it should also be seen in the context of the recently concluded peace of Bāghče Saräy. The 1682 crisis strengthened the hand of the provincial men. There have survived numerous petitions submitted by those summoned to help crush Khovanskii. On December 1 Sophia's government entrusted the task of searching for runaways to regular census clerks (*pistsy*), but one month later was obliged to rescind this decision and to send out special investigators instead.[102] This is clear evidence of a divergence of interest between the southern gentry and the men of the center. The former wanted searches to be carried out either by local voivodes or by relatively

---

92 Novosel'skii, "Pobegi," 342; Man'kov, *Razvitie*, 25.

93 Ibid., 27–8; Novosel'skii, "Pobegi," 334, 337.

94 Man'kov, *Razvitie*, 34 (August 8, 1659).

95 Ibid., 41, 55.

96 Ibid., 47–52.

97 Sixteen in the 1670s, as against 42 in the previous decade. Ibid., 53, 90.

98 Novosel'skii, "Pobegi," 343; Man'kov fails to mention this.

99 Man'kov, *Razvitie*, 129.

100 Ibid., 54.

101 Ibid., 55; Novosel'skii, "Pobegi," 344.

102 Ibid., 345; Man'kov, *Razvitie*, 56–60.

humble census clerks, whom they could influence in their own favor, whereas the latter put their trust in investigators responsible to the central authorities.[103] The southerners won, for in October 1683 the *syshchiki* were recalled, and it was now the turn of the nobles in the central districts to complain (February 22, 1687).[104] But with war imminent against the Tatars, Golitsyn was disinclined to humor them. Not until the Naryshkins had acceded to power was policy reversed. The despatch of investigators was resumed (March 1691), and the number sent before the end of the century rose to forty-seven, as against nine in the 1680s.[105] The new government did not as yet dare to annul its predecessor's reform whereby monetary compensation was substituted for the provision of *naddatochnye*[106]—the latter one of the most cruel features of bondage right.

Similar fluctuations occurred in official policy over penetration of the southern border regions by high-ranking metropolitan nobles. Their activities were naturally unpopular with the local men, not only on economic grounds (competition for scarce peasant labor, forced transfers of land), but also for professional reasons: the newcomers, having land elsewhere, could avoid enrollment in the local service organization. In 1681 the government sought to ease the tension by introducing a zoning arrangement, whereby twenty-nine districts were opened and sixteen (in the "deep south") closed to such settlement.[107] This evidently did not satisfy the provincial men, who wanted nothing less than a general survey. Their demands for this became particularly vociferous in 1682–4.[108]

The survey question was also discussed at the general commission of serving men convoked in the autumn of 1681 "to equalize all manner of services and dues." Unfortunately no record of these debates has survived; they were probably animated, since we know that delegates were free to speak as individuals.[109] The chief result of these deliberations, the abolition of mestnichestvo, was certainly to the advantage of the lesser gentry, but they did not get their way over the survey. As soon as Theodore died their deputies were sent back to their respective districts.[110] Since Russia was at peace in 1682 and there was no general spring mobilization, they were hindered from playing an active role in the succession crisis until September. Seven years later matters were somewhat different. The gentry resented the government's tergiversations on matters they considered vital, and the unfamiliar burdens placed upon them by the unsuccessful campaigns into the steppe. Golitsyn was ideally cast for the role of scapegoat. Many lesser noblemen had joined the *poteshnye* regiments,

---

103 Ibid., 73, 101; Novosel'skii, "Pobegi," 346–51.

104 Man'kov, *Razvitie*, 74.

105 Ibid., 75, 84, 90.

106 Ibid., 76.

107 *PSZ*, II, no. 884; for earlier legislation, see I, nos. 516, 521–2, II, nos. 690, 856.

108 Novosel'skii, "Chelobit'ia."

109 See the documents on the census, published by S. B. Veselovskii in 300–96 of *Istoricheskii arkhiv*, VII (Moscow, 1951), 301.

110 *AI*, V, no. 93.

and Peter's court, with its marked military ethos, afforded a viable alternative focus of loyalty.[111] The tsar was to prove a harder taskmaster than they expected.

The outlook of the higher-ranking metropolitan nobles was in many ways similar, but they were of course much better placed to give their demands political expression. The conventional picture of the Muscovite boiars as ignorant conformists[112] needs refinement, at any rate for the last third of the century. The leading families were the most exposed to the new cultural influences seeping in from the west; what remains obscure is the extent to which these influences affected their political views and behavior. It seems that this was by no means negligible.

Some courtiers came to realize the need to reform the machinery of state. In the 1670s the dynastic schism led to conflict among the monarch's counselors (*dumnye liudi*). Under Theodore II the Miloslavskiis exercised a dominant influence. The office-holders who came to the fore with their protection included A. T. and M. T. Likhachev, I. M. and S. I. Iazykov, and V. V. Golitsyn; the first four were active in the capital, while the latter saw active service against the Turks. Golitsyn fought and eventually won a protracted struggle against his fellow-commander G. G. Romodanovskii, an "old warrior" who enjoyed the support of most other notables (e.g. M. A. Cherkasskii, B. P. Sheremetev, I. B. Troekurov), although M. Iu. Dolgorukii backed Golitsyn.[113] This seems to have been basically a straightforward factional dispute, although some policy differences were also involved. In 1681 the Likhachev-Iazykov group, fore-seeing the likelihood of Theodore's early demise, transferred their allegiance to the Naryshkins, to whom most boiar families already inclined. But in the events of April-May 1682 this party was unexpectedly worsted by the Miloslavskiis. Precisely their weakness among the court nobles led the latter to look for support to the *strel'tsy*. The Likhachevs and the Iazykovs fell from power, and the old boiar families nervously sought to make their peace with the new regime.[114] They could not entirely trust Sophia or her counselors, among whom (after Khovanskii's fall) Golitsyn was clearly paramount. The previous factional struggle continued, and now acquired overtly political and even ideological overtones.

The omnipotent "minister of the temporal state"[115] had long favored closer relations with Poland and other Catholic countries, mainly for the aid they could render

111 Kurakin, ("Gistoriia," 57) states that Sophia was supported by "some of the middling gentry"; he may, however, mean metropolitan nobles.
112 Cf. the well-known description of them nodding their beards in silent assent to the tsar's commands in Kotoshikhin, *O Rossii*, 24.
113 N. N. [Danilov], "V. V. Golitsyn bis zum Staatsstreich vom Mai 1682," *JGOE*, I (1936), 13, 17–21.
114 Kurakin, ("Gistoriia," 44) mentions Ia. N. Odoevskii as apparently the only boiar who favored the Miloslavskii cause before April; his kinsmen, characteristically, disapproved of this.
115 Foy de la Neuville, *Relation curieuse et nouvelle de Moscovie* . . . (The Hague, 1699), 55. Hövel, the Austrian envoy in 1683, called Golitsyn "premier Minister und Direktor aller Geschäfte": N. N. Danilov, "Vasilii Vasil'evič Golicyn (1682–1714)," *JGOE*, II (1937), 552.

against the Turks and Tatars, but also from a vague sympathy for their cultural attain-
ments. Somewhat dilatorily, as was his wont, he endeavored to implement these ideas.
In May and June 1684 talks were held with envoys from King Jan Sobieski. Golitsyn demanded the conclusion of a "permanent peace," with territorial concessions in
Russia's favor, as the price of her adhesion to the anti-Turkish coalition.[116] This new
orientation in foreign policy was unpopular. Kurakin states that in discussions of the
April 1686 treaty "there were two contrary opinions: to wit, Tsarevna Sophia and
Prince Golitsyn and his party were for ratifying the peace with the Poles and beginning
war with the Crimea, but another party of boiars, including Prince P. Prozorovskii,
F. R. Saltykov and others, wanted to fight the Poles."[117] Golitsyn was dangerously
isolated. Many of his critics, formerly identified with the Naryshkins, continued to
hold high office, since Sophia did not dare take action against them.[118] During the
favorite's absence on his ill-starred campaigns these men had ample opportunity to
undermine him.

The issue was fundamentally political. Golitsyn's opponents also objected to the
tolerance he extended to foreigners, particularly Catholics, resident in Moscow, but
interestingly enough this charge was not among those made against him after his
fall; the expulsion of the Jesuits and the execution of the humanist writer Silvester
Medved'ev were the work of Patriarch Ioakhim rather than the Naryshkins.[119] For
members of the anti-Golitsyn faction the cultural question was but a means to an end.
Many of them (e.g. his cousin Boris, or M. A. Cherkasskii) were attracted to western
ways; conversely, Golitsyn's client Bezobrazov was in his mode of life an extreme
traditionalist.

If the reformist group was to achieve any lasting gains, basic institutional changes
were essential. Contrary to what is generally thought, they seem to have appreciated
this point. In the winter of 1681–2, as the dynastic crisis loomed, ideas were mooted
which, had they been implemented, would have significantly altered the Muscovite
governmental system. Like many nineteenth-century constitutional plans, they were
the indirect consequence of a military setback. While the commission of serving men
was discussing the professional aspects of the problem (and the clergy were debating
their own affairs), the basic political questions were tackled in a document which was
apparently prepared in quarters close to Golitsyn.[120] This proposed the introduction
of an elaborate hierarchy of 34 ranks and dignities in court, military and civilian

116 Ibid., 554 ff.; O'Brien, *Regency*, 127.
117 Kurakin, "Gistoriia," 52. Their positions were more subtle than Kurakin suggests. One may
   also doubt whether the aging Prozorovskii was a formidable foe; more important may have
   been Golitsyn's loss of support from the Dolgorukiis.
118 Ibid., 49. Foy de la Neuville exaggerated in stating that Golitsyn distributed *all* the important
   offices among his partisans, who were not from high-born families but men of proven service
   experience (*Relation curieuse*, 56).
119 Shmurlo, "Padenie," 93 ff.; A. Prozorovskii, *Silvestr Medved'ev. Ego zhizn' i deiatel'nost'*
   (Moscow, 1896), 338.
120 G. Ostrogorskii, "Das Projekt einer Rangtabelle aus der Zeit des Caren Fedor Alekseevič,"
   Jahrbuch für Kultur und Geschichte der Slawen, IX (Breslau, 1933), 86–138 at 106. (This

service; the three branches were clearly distinguished, and the civilian officials given precedence. For this reason alone, as Ostrogorskii rightly points out, the plan marks "very considerable progress in Muscovite political thought."[121] In some respects it anticipates Peter's Table of Ranks, although it was socially more restrictive.

But it contains another proposal that is even more remarkable: a provision that the chief office-holder in the state should head a consultative body to be known as the Palata (chamber), to consist of twelve members (*zasedateli*), drawn from the sovereign's counselors. "And all those twelve members are to remain permanently in our tsarist majesty's chamber established for that purpose, and are to watch diligently that every judge (*sud'ia*) fulfills our tsarist majesty's command and [exercises] civil justice conscientiously and discerningly." The language suggests a supreme court of appeal, but the ambiguity of the term *sud'ia* in Muscovite practice meant that general administrative as well as judicial matters would fall within its purview. It would have been a forerunner of those eighteenth-century advisory bodies which, whatever their founders' intentions, endeavored to subject the sovereign to the constraints of legality.

The limited membership of the prospective Palata, far from being a reactionary feature, was a point in its favor. By 1682, owing to demographic and other factors, more than one hundred men had attained *dumnyi* rank[122]—too many to operate effectively. A quasi-cabinet of thirteen would have been better suited to perform an advisory function. It must be emphasized that the so-called "Boiar Duma" (the very name is a figment of the historians' imagination) was never an institution in the proper sense: that is to say, it had no corporate existence independently of the monarch, even though its members enjoyed fairly wide decision-making powers. The establishment of a Palata, referred to by name in official documents as the Duma never was, would therefore have signified considerable progress towards institutionalization.

At this point it is necessary to consider the body bearing this name (Raspravnaia Palata) that actually existed from 1681 until 1700.[123] It confined itself largely to

---

document was first published in N. Kalachov, ed., *Arkhiv istoriko-iuridicheskikh svedenii otnosiashchikhsia do Rossii* (Moscow, 1850), I (ii), 21–44.) Ostrogorskii provides a German translation (94–102). He argues, with Miliukov, that it should be carefully distinguished from another document, published in extract by E. E. Zamyslovskii, *Tsar Fedor Alekseevich* (St. Petersburg, 1871), appendix, 34 ff. and taken from an MS of *c.* 1700, "Ikona ili izobrazhenie del Patriarshego prikaza." He believes that the former was a moderate counterproposal stimulated by the strongly marked decentralizing tendencies of the latter. However, there are close parallels between the two plans, and it seems more probable that the "Ikona" scheme was a garbled version, prepared in hostile clerical circles some time later, of the plan put forward by Golitsyn's circle. This is consonant with the statement in the former that the plan, having been approved by the tsar, was stifled by Patriarch Ioakhim. The latter is known as an active opponent of Golitsyn, and is most unlikely to have been a sponsor of the draft, as Ostrogorskii suggests (105).

121 Ibid., 103.

122 I.e. boiars, *okol'nichie,* those *stol'niki* etc. who held certain major appointments, and the all-important secretaries (*d'iaki*); not all of them were present in Moscow at any one time.

123 S. Bogoiavlenskii, "Raspravnaia Palata pri Boiarskoi Dume", *Sbornik statei posviashchen-*

appeals in civil suits, and did not play any policy-making role. Why, one may ask, did the reformers not extend its powers to the limits originally envisaged? On this the sources are silent. The reason may lie partly in Golitsyn's temperament and partly in his political isolation. Kliuchevskii describes him as a courageous dreamer.[124] He was certainly short of reliable supporters who might have helped him achieve his broader purposes. He seems to have contented himself with keeping the Raspravnaia Palata under his own control, by appointing a kinsman, M. A. Golitsyn, as its chief. In any case he knew that his rivals would oppose any major institutional innovations on his part, and so allowed the opportunity to slip.

What was the source of the reformist ideas put forward in Golitsyn's circle? Ostrogorskii points out that the 1681 scheme gives the Byzantine equivalents of many of the ranks and offices listed.[125] However, it does not necessarily follow from this that the framers of the document were inspired by such precedents; they may have invoked them simply as a tactical device to lull the suspicions of the conservatives. It seems far more probable that they were looking westwards—to the Rzeczpospolita. They were doubtless familiar with the institution of *senatorowie-rezydenci*, which originally was a 16-man body,[126] and one might draw a parallel between the principal office-holder ("the boiar with the twelve") and the chancellor in Poland-Lithuania. The Russian reformers were attracted less by constitutional particulars than by the general atmosphere of public life across the border, above all by the status and prestige which leading functionaries enjoyed. They stood in the tradition of the incipient constitutionalists of 1610, whose ideas, as has recently been shown, owed much to the Lithuanian Statute of 1588.[127] In neither case was it a question of thorough-going "polonization," as prejudiced Russian nationalists might think, but of borrowing from the Commonwealth certain features of its more advanced political culture. Such ventures aroused distrust and hostility among the conservatives. The result was that, when the Russian governmental structure was modernized, the driving force came from the autocracy and the intellectual inspiration from a different quarter of Europe.

Peter the Great drastically curbed these hesitant approaches to pluralism by the Muscovite élite. Absolutism, in its new western dress, emerged triumphant and forced society back into its straitjacket. The task was not very difficult. If even the metropolitan nobility could not institutionalize its informal gains, how could its provincial cousins be expected to do so? The gentry made use of their service organizations for

---

nykh V. O. Kliuchevskomu ego uchenikami . . . (Moscow, 1909), 409–27.

124 V. O. Kliuchevskii, *Sochineniia*, 8 vols. (Moscow, 1957–9), III, 352–7. Kliuchevskii's sketch of Golitsyn is based upon an imaginative reading of Foy de la Neuville; he does not mention in this connection the 1681 project, although he had discussed it briefly in his *Istoriia soslovii v Rossii*.

125 Ostrogorskii, "Das Projekt. . . ," 132–8.

126 J. Bardach et al., eds., *Historia państwa i prawa Polski*³ (Warsaw, 1968), II, 126–8.

127 G. Stökl, "Gab es im Moskauer Staat 'Stände'?" *Jahrbücher für Geschichte Osteuropas*, XI (1963), 321–42.

limited purposes only; less affected by external cultural influences, they felt that their professional and economic interests required them to seek the protection of the central *vlast'*. The musketeers gained least of all, and were driven back upon chiliastic longings for a "just tsardom." Yet each group had acquired a new sense of identity and had played its part in weakening the traditional political order.

1970

CHAPTER 2

The Decline of the Zemskii Sobor

I

The seventeenth century was a time of severe trial for the representative institutions of Europe. In the north and northwest of the continent, and also in Poland, they weathered the storm; in most countries, however, they were destroyed or reduced to insignificance by the powerful new absolute monarchies. Even in remote Muscovite Russia the same general process was at work. The national assembly, or Zemskii Sobor, which elected Michael Romanov to the throne in 1613, lost its authority in the years that followed; reviving triumphantly in 1648, it again failed to establish itself and ceased to be convoked after 1653.

Can the Sobor properly be compared with other European parliaments? The Western student's first reaction, on discovering a representative institution in such apparently incongruous surroundings, is one of astonishment.[1] Nor are Russian historians agreed upon the nature of the Sobor. The slavophil K. S. Aksakov had no doubts as to its "originality" (*samobytnost'*): unlike the parliaments of the militant West, the Russian assembly had collaborated harmoniously with the monarchy for the common good.[2] This idealized picture was soon shattered by Solov'ev's methodical criticism.[3] The sharpest reaction came from the liberal B. N. Chicherin, who emphasized the worthlessness of the Sobor as an institution in comparison with its early equivalents elsewhere: with its inadequate system of representation and slavish loyalty to the government, it had played no important role in Russian history.[4] Paradoxically, the westerners thus came to share the slavophil view of the Sobor's "originality."

This outlook, although undergoing modification, proved remarkably virile. As early as 1875 the jurist V. I. Sergeevich pointed to the similarities between the Russian assembly and the early representative institutions of Western Europe,[5] but his

---

1 G. Stökl, "Recent Work and Present Views on the Origins and Development of Representative Assemblies," *X Congresso Internazionale di Scienze Storiche: Relazioni*, 7 vols. (Florence, 1955), I, 94.

2 K. S. Aksakov, *Polnoe sobranie sochinenii*, 3 vols. (Moscow, 1861–80), I (1861), 296.

3 S. M. Solov'ev, "Shletser i anti-istoricheskoe napravlenie," *Russkii vestnik*, VIII (1857).

4 B. N. Chicherin, *O narodnom predstavitel'stve* (Moscow, 1866), 355–82.

5 V. I. Sergeevich, "Zemskie sobory v Moskovskom gosudarstve," *Sbornik gosudarstvennykh*

conclusions did not go unchallenged.[6] Even the great historian Kliuchevskii, who showed in a brilliant but somewhat discursive study the limited nature of representation at the sixteenth-century Sobors, inclined towards this point of view.[7] The twentieth century brought a number of new studies, mostly of particular aspects of the Sobor's activity.[8] The most notable work has been done by P. P. Smirnov, who has shown that the assembly was by no means so subservient to the government as earlier historians had supposed.[9] Although Sergeevich's basic assumption have not been explicitly contested, the prevailing tendency has been to stress the idiosyncrasies of the Sobor rather than the parallels with Western European institutions. In this respect Soviet historians have by and large remained in the Kliuchevskii tradition,[10] for which they have been criticized by a leading Soviet jurist, S. V. Iushkov.[11] His argument that the Sobor is an institution typical of "monarchies based upon class representation," although unacceptably dogmatic, is a sign of a healthy reaction against the limited national outlook that has dominated the literature on the subject over the past 60 years.

The Sobor has hitherto received little attention from non-Russian historians.[12]

---

znanii, 8 vols. (St. Petersburg, 1874–80), II (1875), 1–60. His views were shared by V. N. Latkin, whose *Zemskie sobory drevnei Rusi* (St. Petersburg, 1885), although outdated in some respects, remains the best and fullest account of these assemblies.

6 Cf. N. P. Zagoskin, *Istoriia prava Moskovskogo gosudarstva*, 2 vols. (Kazan', 1877–9), I, 337 ff.; M. F. Vladimirskii-Budanov, *Obzor istorii russkogo prava*[6] (St. Petersburg-Kiev, 1909), 183–5.

7 He criticized those who searched for parallels with western Europe, and, pointing to the system of "mutual guarantee" (*krugovaia poruka*), argued that Russia had possessed "a specific type of popular representation different from Western representative assemblies." V. O. Kliuchevskii, "Sostav predstavitel'stva na zemskikh soborakh drevnei Rusi," *Opyty i issledovaniia* (Moscow, 1912), 424, 428.

8 A general survey of the history of the Sobor is given by S. F. Platonov, "K istorii Moskovskikh zemskikh soborov," *Sochineniia*, 2 vols. (St. Petersburg, 1912–13), I, 279–338. Some of the important primary sources have been reprinted by Iu. V. Got'e, *Akty otnosiashchiesia k istorii zemskikh soborov* (Moscow, 1909). Of the specialist studies the following are particularly worthy of note: A. Kabanov, "Organizatsiia vyborov na zemskikh soborakh XVII v.," *Zhurnal Ministerstva narodnogo prosveshcheniia*, XXIX (St. Petersburg, 1910); A. Zaozerskii, " K voprosu o sostave i znachenii zemskikh soborov," ibid., XXI (1909); G. Shmelev, "Otnosheniia naseleniia i oblastnoi administratsii k vyboram na zemskikh soborakh v XVII v.," *Sbornik statei posviashchennykh . . . V. O. Kliuchevskomu* (Moscow, 1909).

9 Smirnov's view, first developed before the Russian revolution, were later given a Marxist-Leninist twist in his *Posadskie liudi i ikh klassovaia bor'ba do serediny XVII v.*, 2 vols. (Moscow-Leningrad, 1947–8), but retain their fundamental validity.

10 Cf. *Istoriia Moskvy*, 6 vols. (Moscow, 1952–9), I, 536 ff.; *Ocherki istorii SSSR; period feodalizma XVII v.* (Moscow, 1955), 360–6.

11 "K voprosu o soslovno-predstavitel'noi monarkhii v Rossii," *Sovetskoe gosudarstvo i pravo* (1950), no. 10, 39–51.

12 The posthumous work of F. de Rocca, *Les zemskié sobors; étude historique* (Paris, 1899), is apparently unknown to Russian scholars.

G. Stökl has recently taken the slavophil position to a new extreme, drawing a sharp dividing line between the assemblies in the Roman Catholic and Greek Orthodox lands of Eastern Europe, the implication being that they were essentially different in type.[13] This line of approach, based upon an apparently arbitrary division into religio-cultural "spheres," cannot be considered particularly fruitful. On balance the similarities between the Russian Sobor and the early representative assemblies of other European countries are far more striking than the differences. It is of course undeniable that the Sobor as an institution was still at a primitive stage of development. It was remarkably formless in that it did not work out any fixed procedural rules, let alone any rights vis-à-vis the monarch, who retained full autocratic powers. Even the name Zemskii Sobor is merely a convenient invention by later historians. The basic reason for this difference was that in Russia the state power developed earlier and more rapidly that the social "estates" (*sosloviia*); indeed, when these did develop, they were largely the product of state action. Thus we cannot expect to find any clearly defined division into chambers, each with its spirit of corporate solidarity. Nevertheless, the election of deputies took place separately, by estates: "in this respect," wrote Latkin, "there exists between our Sobors and the European assemblies not only an analogy but even complete identity."[14] As in the West, the higher ranking members attended *ex officio*, while others were elected. The parallels, especially with regard to procedure at elections and in the assembly itself, are numerous and often impressive. A full comparative analysis is beyond the scope of this study, which is confined to an examination of the checkered history of the Sobor in the seventeenth century and the reasons for its decline and eventual extinction.

II

It was during the revolutionary period conventionally known as the "Time of Troubles" that there arose a new conception of the nature and role of the Sobor as a "council of the whole land," expressing the will of the entire nation and composed of popularly elected representatives instead of mere official members.[15] The various

---

13 Stökl, "Recent Work," 75–99.

14 Latkin, *Zemskie sobory*, 407.

15 Kliuchevskii was the first to point out, correctly, the qualitative difference between the sixteenth-century Sobors (1566 and 1598) and those of the seventeenth century, at which elected deputies were present ("Sostav", 430)—although, as will be shown, many of the Sobors under the new dynasty were in fact, to use Kliuchevskii's phrase referring to the sixteenth-century assemblies, "consultations of the government with its own agents" (474).

As regards the composition of the Sobors in the sixteenth century, Kliuchevskii's views have not been shaken by the arguments of M. N. Pokrovskii, "Zemskii sobor i parlament," *Konstitutsionnoe gosudarstvo; sbornik statei* . . . (St. Petersburg, [? 1906]), 322–4, but they are open to objection on other grounds. Kliuchevskii argued that, although the category of so-called "chosen men" (*vybornye*) present in 1566 were members of the élite corps within the gentry class, nominated by the government because of their administrative position (546), some 34 of the *vybornye* mentioned as present in 1598 were indeed elected by local "corporations" of gentry. He hails these elected deputies as "the most outstanding new

pretenders sought to give an aura of popular sanction to their claims by appealing to
the authority of a Zemskii Sobor.[16] The idea fell upon soil fertilized by traditions of
local selfgovernment, particularly strong in the north and east of the country. The
local communities were galvanized into political action by the tumultuous course of
events: councils, comprising representatives of all important social groups, sprang up
spontaneously and rapidly established contact with one another. In 1611, largely as a
result of their activities, a popular levy (*opolchenie*) was formed to liberate the country from the invader. Authority in this body rested less with its three acknowledged
leaders, Trubetskoi, Liapunov, and Zarutskii, than with an elected council, which
declared menacingly that, should the triumvirate govern badly, "we shall freely exchange our boiars and generals, and elect others, consulting with the whole land."[17]
The membership of this "campaign council" was limited to deputies from the various military contingents; neither the boiars (at that time in the enemy camp) nor the
clergy were present, and the townspeople were represented only indirectly, in so far
as they served in the levy. But since the contingents were formed on a territorial
basis and thus were, broadly speaking, "representative" of their areas of origin, the
council deserves to be considered as the first imperfect example of a new type of
Sobor, which aspired to give effect to the popular will.

The levy of 1611 soon fell apart. Its successor in the following year, however,
enjoyed better fortune, and correspondingly the council by which it was governed
exercised greater authority.[18] Pozharskii summoned a Sobor "to elect a Sovereign
by the whole land, whomsoever the merciful God . . . shall grant us."[19] Ironically
enough, his ambitious plans were frustrated by his own military success: once in the
capital, the prevailing political situation did not allow the levy to impose its own will
on the country. The assembly by which it was led now comprised townspeople as
well as serving men,[20] but it still lacked boiars or clergy; a more representative body
was required. In November, 1612, it accordingly proclaimed its own liquidation and
called for elections to a new assembly "to take counsel for the nation and to elect a

element present" (494), but at the same time admits that they "do not alter the general
physiognomy of representation" (499). Since Kliuchevskii himself points out that the two
sources of authority, nomination and election, cannot be opposed to one another (543), the
whole argument loses point. One may therefore agree with Zaozerskii ("K voprosu," 304)
that both the sixteenth-century Sobors should be regarded as entirely nonelective.

16 Latkin, *Zemskie sobory*, 105–11; Platonov, "K istorii," 301–7.

17 Latkin, *op. cit.*, 113–15; Zagoskin, *Istoriia*, 236. According to the chronicle, the initiative
in this move came from "the gentry and all the serving men, after having consulted with
the cossacks." Students of the Sobor have not yet considered the possible influence exerted
by the cossack political system on the elective Sobor of the seventeenth century. Although
it is no doubt true that the cossacks' contribution to Russian political life at this time was
largely destructive, it must be remembered that they were a major factor in the politics of
this crucial formative period, and that their democratic practices (election of the *ataman* by
the *krug*, etc.) appealed to a large part of the Muscovite population.

18 Latkin, *op. cit.*, 118 ff.; *Chteniia IOIDR*, CCXV (1905), IV, 65.

19 *SGGD*, II, no. 281; cf. *AAE*, II, no. 203.

20 Latkin, *op. cit.*, 121.

Sovereign."[21]

This great assembly was flooded by deputies from the provinces. The electoral deed contains 277 names, but the total number present has been put as high as 700. Deputies came from some fifty towns scattered over all European Russia; even peasants appear to have been represented;[22] so great was the concourse that the meetings took place, not in a chamber of the Kremlin, but in the spacious Cathedral of the Assumption.[23] But numbers did not necessarily signify political power. Even the official electoral act could not conceal that the new tsar was elected only after "people of every rank . . . had spoken at the Sobor for many days without hesitation"; the chronicle, more honestly, records that "there was much excitement, everyone wanting to act according to his own ideas, everyone advocating someone else."[24] The guiding spirit behind Michael's candidature, Prince Sheremetev, to whom are ascribed the incriminating words "Misha Romanov is still young, has not yet reached the age of reason and will be amenable to us,"[25] manipulated the assembly with the skill of an experienced parliamentarian. The atmosphere was one of forgiveness and reconciliation. Far from undertaking a purge of the boiars who had acted treacherously during the Troubles, the Sobor was more than considerate about allowing them to participate in its deliberations.[26] The liberation forces failed to secure their military victory in the political field. Their defeat was symbolized by the fact that their leader Pozharskii signed the electoral deed in the tenth place among the boiars, after those senior to him in status.[27]

The Sobor loyally carried on the work of day-to-day administration pending Michael's arrival in Moscow. The tsar made no haste to leave his retreat—partly, it seems, through fear of the assembly's intentions: although they had elected him, might not the fickle deputies all too easily change their allegiance? The Sobor in its present form was the child of chaos, a stranger to the Muscovite political scene, and a phenomenon that accorded ill with absolutist traditions. This suspicion is evident in the complaints by Michael at the assembly's failure to clear the road to Moscow

---

21 *DAI*, I, no. 166; cf. *Chteniia IOIDR*, CCXXXIX (1911), no. 82.

22 The deed was signed by 11 or 12 "rural people" (*uezdnye liudi*). Platonov ("K istorii," 316) considers that, except for two who came from northern Russia, they were probably lower-grade members of the servitor class. Of course, the peasantry was not an "estate" in Muscovy—this was rare even in western Europe. Some who were actually peasants may have attended this and later Sobors as representatives of urban communities (*posady*), for there was no clearly marked division between town and country.

23 Platonov, "Zametki po istorii moskovskikh zemskikh soborov," *Sochineniia*, I, 12.

24 Text of electoral deed in *SGGD*, I, no. 203, more readily in *Chteniia IOIDR*, CCXVIII (1906), I; "Novyi Letopisets," *PSRL* (St. Petersburg/Leningrad, 1841–1949), XIV (i)^2 (St. Petersburg, 1910), 129.

25 N. I. Kostomarov, *Sobranie sochinenii*, 8 vols. (St. Petersburg, 1903–5), II (1904), 621.

26 *Chteniaa IOIDR*, CCXXXIX (1911), no. 80; E. D. Stashevskii, *Ocherki po istorii tsarstvo- vaniia Mikhaila Fedorovicha* (Kiev, 1913), 68–9.

27 *Chteniia IOIDR*, CCXVIII (1906), I, 77.

of bandits:[28] "bandits" at that juncture meant primarily marauding cossack bands, whose violent and egalitarian tendencies were notorious; was not collusion possible between them and the radical elements of the Sobor? In any case, Michael took the precaution of dealing directly with Miloslavskii and the boiars in Moscow as well as with the Sobor[29]—a dualism full of significance for the future. Events were soon to show that the threat to the monarchy came, not from the Sobor, which continued to act in the most loyal manner, but from the leading boiar families.

Whatever the truth about the obligations supposedly undertaken by Michael on his accession,[30] it is indisputable that for the next few years the affairs of the country were in the hands of an unscrupulous clique, bound to the throne by dynastic links and political interest. To speak of these years as the "golden age" of the Sobor, or as a period of "joint rule" by the government and the assembly, is thoroughly misleading.[31] True, the Sobor continued to exist for some time. In 1613 it negotiated with the Polish invaders and, when the talks broke down, advised the tsar on the conduct of military operations.[32] In the following year it called on Zarutskii's cossacks to transfer their loyalty to the tsar, and sent a commission, backed by force, to persuade the cossack bands in northern Russia to cease their plundering.[33] The Sobor also assisted the government in raising revenue: its first act after Michael's accession was to appeal to the wealthy Stroganov family; in 1614 the voivode of Belozersk was ordered to hand over the revenue he had collected to an official dispatched for the purpose "by the tsar's decree and with the assent of the land."[34]

But on closer examination the Sobor's role is seen to be less executive than exhortative. There is nothing to indicate that the assembly played any active part in initiating policy; once a decision had been taken by the government, the Sobor's function was to invest it with an aura of popular approval, in order to render it more palatable to a population still partly in rebellious mood and loath to recognize the authority of the government's agents. Thus the recalcitrant cossacks were expected to be convinced by the Sobor's appeal that tsar Michael enjoyed nationwide support. Possibly the government also calculated that this move would serve to counteract any sympathy for cossack radicalism within the assembly, and to identify it more

---

28 P. I. Ivanov, *Opisanie Gosudarstvennogo Razriadnogo arkhiva* (Moscow, 1842), 217–53.

29 Latkin, *Zemskie sobory*, 140–1; Ivanov, *passim.*

30 This involved question is fully discussed by Stashevskii (*Ocherki*, 62–78), who, following Kliuchevskii, argues convincingly that the undertaking, if given at all, was to a clique of intimates, rather than to the Boiarskaia Duma as such, and in any case certainly not to the Zemskii Sobor.

31 Zagoskin, *Istoriia*, 246; M. D'iakonov, *Ocherki obshchestvennogo i gosudarstvennogo stroia drevnei Rusi*[4] (Moscow-Leningrad, 1926), 396.

32 Latkin, *op. cit.*, 136–7, 148.

33 *AAE*, III, nos. 26, 29; *SGGD*, III, no. 22.

34 *AAE*, III, no. 3, cf. nos. 5, 31–2. The formula used here would seem significant to a contemporary, for the usual wording in decrees ran: "by the tsar's decree and with the assent of the boiars," i.e. the Boiarskaia Duma.

closely with the government's policies. The fact that the Church hierarchy also sent such exhortatory appeals[35] suggests that in the government's eyes both played the same moral-propagandist role. From the history of the collection of "fifths" (*piataia den'ga*), levied on the urban population annually from 1614 to 1618, it is clear that the government avoided consultation with the assembly whenever possible: while the first levy was raised with its consent, the second was ordered on the authority of the government alone; it was probably only the accumulation of arrears that caused the Sobor to be consulted over the third levy, to which it evidently agreed with some reluctance: in the laconic words of the official deed, "they consulted with one another and thought about this for many days." The Sobor collaborated in raising the fourth levy, but not the fifth.[36] Zaozerskii considers that the deputies merely played the role of experts on local conditions, while Veselovskii inclines to the view that they could influence the size of the assessments;[37] in either case, their role was secondary and largely formal.

Another puzzling question is the composition of the Sobor in these years. It is hard to believe that at this time of national emergency the Moscow authorities, always so concerned to prevent evasion of service obligations, would have kept the members of the electoral assembly in the capital with no other function than to proffer occasional advice to the government. Most of those present for Michael's election must surely have returned to their homes or duties shortly afterwards. The generally accepted view is that there was a full "session" of the Sobor from 1613 to 1615, which was followed by another from 1616 to 1618. Although it is now reasonably certain that something in the nature of a "general election" took place early in 1616,[38] it does not necessarily follow that the sittings were continuous. If the Sobor was a permanent institution at all, which seems doubtful, it is more likely to have been a commission of selected deputies, whose membership of the assembly was secondary to the other duties which they performed in the capital.[39]

The day-to-day government of the country was carried on, not by the tsar and

---

35 *AAE*, III, nos. 23, 25; cf. the latter with no. 26, from the Sobor.

36 S. B. Veselovskii, "Sem' sborov zaprosnykh i piatinnykh deneg v pervye gody tsarstvovaniia Mikhaila Fedorovicha," *Chteniia IOIDR*, CCXXVII (1909), III, 26, 58, 65, 67, 69, and documents nos. 4–7, 52, 56, 62, 63; *AAE*, III, nos. 68, 70, 79–81.

37 Zaozerskii, "K voprosu," 350; Veselovskii, *op. cit.*, 66.

38 This assumption previously rested upon the evidence of three elections ordered to be held in certain towns in northeastern Russia (*AAE*, III, no. 77 (Iu. V. Got'e, *op. cit.*, no. 4) in Perm'; *Chteniia IOIDR*, CCXXVIII (1909), III, nos. 52, 54, in Sol'vychegodsk and Tot'ma). But later an account of part of the proceedings at the 1616 Sobor was discovered, from which it is apparent that it was attended by deputies from all towns, who were presented by the tsar's spokesman with a remarkably frank and detailed picture of the budgetary situation. N. I. Likhachev, "Novye dannye o zemskom sobore 1616 g.," *Russkii istoricheskii zhurnal* (Petrograd, 1922), VIII, 60–87.

39 This view is supported by the document recording the Sobor which endorsed the fourth collection of "fifths": after relating the sorry plight of the Russian army, faced by a superior Polish force, it lists in the usual way the classes which the tsar consulted on the means of obtaining funds for its relief (Veselovskii, "Sem' sborov," no. 63). In this list the gentry are conspicuous by their absence. Presumably all those members of the gentry in Moscow who normally provided deputies for a Sobor were now at the front. In contrast, the gentry

the Sobor, as was fondly supposed by earlier historians eager to stress the allegedly "popular" nature of the new dynasty, but by the boiars and clerks (*d'iaki*), whose corrupt malpractices were shocking even by Muscovite standards.[40] A matter of such importance as the peace of Stolbovo, concluded with Sweden in February, 1617, was decided without the participation of the assembly. Prince Władysław of Poland was doubtless well aware of the real nature of the government of the country when, on his advance to Moscow, he reiterated his undertaking of 1610 to rule in conjunction with the boiars and the Sobor.[41] Whether this propaganda was effective we do not know; it was the seriousness of the military situation, above all else, that caused Michael to summon a Sobor shortly afterwards.[42] The speed with which it assembled showed clearly that, like its immediate predecessors, it was attended only by those representatives who were already in Moscow at the time.[43] All classes stood together against the invader; the deputies left the chamber straight for their battle stations on the city ramparts. Had the Sobor sought to convince the government of its usefulness, it could hardly have acted more efficiently. But the clumsy Muscovite autocracy could not collaborate with any representative institution, even one of such proven loyalty.

An ominous new figure now appeared on the scene—Filaret, father of the tsar, and the most powerful man in the land from 1619, when he returned from Polish captivity, until his death in 1633. Filaret had an almost oriental conception of absolute monarchy. By skillfully taking advantage of the rivalry between various factions and pressure groups, he contrived to elevate the throne to a position of great power and prestige. His policy was one of stabilization rather than reform. It was progressive in that he attempted to deal with the worst administrative abuses, but reactionary in that he looked to the past for inspiration and sought to resurrect the pattern of a bygone age. The key role in effecting this program fell to the bureaucrats of the central "offices" (*prikazy*), not to the Boiarskaia Duma—and still less to the Sobor, which was speedily consigned to limbo.[44]

A few days after Filaret's return, "men of all classes" petitioned the tsar to appoint him patriarch.[45] We have no means of ascertaining whether this meeting was a fully representative Sobor or merely an *ad hoc* gathering; as is evident from the foregoing, such a distinction would in any case be unreal. One may presume that the petition was submitted in response to promptings from above. Filaret lost no time in working out a program—not in collaboration with the Sobor, as generally supposed, but by consulting first the clergy (and, presumably, the bureaucrats) and then the tsar; the

---

figure most prominently in the Sobor of 1618, when the bulk of the Russian army was concentrated in the capital for its defence. *SGGD*, III, no. 40.

40 Cf. Platonov, "Moskovskoe pravitel'stvo pri pervykh Romanovykh," *Sochineniia*, I, 339–406.

41 *SGGD*, III, no. 39.

42 *SGGD*, III, no. 40.

43 Zagoskin, *Istoriia*, 251; Latkin, *Zemskie sobory*, 162–3.

44 See below, 109–33.

45 Latkin, *Zemskie sobory*, 164.

fruit of these deliberations was then presented to the Sobor. A comparison of the government's draft with the assembly's final decision reveals important differences on policy: the assembly showed greater zeal in advocating measures on behalf of the townspeople, and apparently added a provision for the convocation of a new Sobor to elaborate the plan.[46] But this Sobor, as can be inferred from the official summonses, was to play a slighter role than its predecessors: whereas in 1613 the deputies had been convoked "to take counsel for the nation," and a similar phrase had been used three years later, they were now "to relate their grievances, their sufferings and their losses," so that, on the basis of the information thus provided, "We, the Great Sovereign, with the Patriarch [title], acting upon their petition, may begin to . . . carry out such reforms in all matters as may be best for the Muscovite state."[47] There is no hint of the deputies being expected to play any part in the elaboration of policy; they seem to have lost even their earlier "exhortatory" function.

Significantly enough, it was only in foreign affairs that the Sobor was henceforth invited to act. When the government thought of launching an attack upon Poland in 1621, it turned to the assembly for support. As in 1618, the deputies eagerly endorsed the government's policy. Since a virtual ultimatum had already been dispatched, they had in any case no opportunity to do otherwise. War was averted only through a sudden change in the international situation. It was symptomatic of later developments that the gentry deputies should have used the opportunity to request a general redistribution of estates to enable them to meet their service obligations, a request to which the government promptly acceded, nominating the appropriate officials in the presence of the assembly.[48] But the government's response to this initiative from below did not signify any readiness to allow the assembly any scope in determining internal policy. From the government's point of view, the Sobor had outlived what limited usefulness it had once possessed. It was not only a question of the govern-

---

46 *SGGD*, III, no. 47 (in Iu. V. Got'e, *op. cit.*, no. 6). P. P. Smirnov (*Posadskie liudi*, I, 363 ff.) shows that, with regard to those townspeople who had fled from their communities and had entered into engagements as debtor serfs (*zakladchiki*) with powerful landowners, Filaret's draft only mentioned cases affecting secular owners, whereas the assembly included ecclesiastical estates (except, tactfully, those of the patriarch himself!). On the other burning question, the forcible return of townspeople who had fled to Moscow and elsewhere from the devastated regions of the Ukraine and Zamoskov'e, Smirnov is less convincing. There does not appear to be any difference of principle between Filaret's proposal, which included both regions, and that of the assembly, which omitted Zamoskov'e. It is more reasonable to assume that Filaret had the interests of the treasury in view, which, he misguidedly conceived, would be served by such a general reshuffle of taxpayers, rather than to attribute the idea to the desire of corrupt officials for profit and vengeance. On the other hand, there is an evident difference between the two policies in that the Sobor urged the need to grant tax relief to those who were compulsorily resettled, whereas Filaret's draft only mooted this as a vague possibility. But we must remember that the government had invited the assembly to express its views on its draft, and beware of unnecessarily inflating the differences between them.

47 *SGGD*, *loc. cit.*,; cf. *AAE*, III, no. 105; Stashevskii, *Ocherki*, 86–7.

48 *SGGD*, III, no. 57.

ment no longer *needing* the assembly, as the earlier historians maintained; it did not *want* it. If, as Filaret considered, the sole purpose of the deputies to the Sobor was to provide information, it was clear that this task could best be performed, not through an institution, but through informal consultations. It is therefore highly significant that, as Smirnov has shown, shortly after the Sobor of 1621 the tsar and the patriarch should resort to the practise of holding daily receptions at their respective courts to which favored representatives of all important social groups were invited.[49] Although direct evidence is lacking, we may assume that political questions were discussed at such meetings, and that they provided an adequate substitute for the Sobor, at least in the eyes of the government.

But with the first major crisis in foreign relations, the government was obliged to abandon this expedient and to call a Sobor. The death of Sigismund III in April, 1632, gave Filaret his long awaited opportunity. The decision to intervene in Polish affairs was taken on the government's own responsibility; the assembly, which met in November, after hostilities had begun, was concerned only with the provision of funds, which were promised with apparent enthusiasm.[50] Fifteen months later, when the government again came to the Sobor with a demand for aid, the deputies were less acquiescent. The Russian general, Shein, forced to acknowledge defeat by laying down his standards at Wladyslaw's feet, paid for his humiliating failure with his life. The government was anxious to divert popular disaffection by laying the blame on others. Shein was one scapegoat; another was Urban VIII, "the accursed Pope of Rome" as he was called, in terms of unusual militancy, in the remarkably insincere official address the Sobor. By recalling age-old grievances against the Poles and raising the cry that the holy faith was once more in danger, the government hoped to secure yet another "fifth" from the hard-pressed townspeople. Now that the country had recovered, it declared, there was no excuse for delay or deficiency; compliance with its demands would earn the taxpayer the gratitude of both the tsar and the Almighty. After such highflown eloquence, the deputies' reply that "they will give money according to their belongings, as much as each can afford" sounded cool in the extreme.[51] Their attitude reflected the mood of the country: The archimandrite of the Pecherskii monastery at Nizhnii Novgorod, entrusted with the collection of the levy in his locality, was punished for failing to show sufficient zeal.[52]

---

49 Smirnov, *Posadskie liudi*, I, 357–61. Filaret, who went further in this practice than the tsar, brought to his table even cossack chiefs and humble craftsmen from the *posady*. Previously, only the most senior nobles had received such invitations. After Filaret's death the gentry, if invited at all, attended as servitors rather than as guests.

50 As no official deed has been preserved, we know of this assembly only from casual references, in particular the "speech from the throne" at the next Sobor: "the last year, 7139 [Sept. 1632–Aug. 1633] the Sovereign Tsar [title], having taken counsel with his father [title], made known unto you *at the first Sobor* the many injustices of the former king of Poland, Sigismund. . . ." *SGGD*, III, no. 99 (our italics); cf. *AAE*, III, no. 211; *Knigi razriadnye*, 2 vols. (St. Petersburg, 1853–5), II, 480.

51 *SGGD*, III, no. 99 (Iu. V. Got'e, *Akty*, no. 9); cf. Pokrovskii, "Zemskii sobor," 334.

52 *SGGD*, III, no. 101.

The next Sobors met in similar circumstances, although the threat of foreign attack now came from the south. In September, 1637, on hearing that the Turks and Tatars were planning to invade, as an act of retaliation for the cossacks' seizure of Azov, the government convoked an assembly, which took the necessary military and financial measures; the attack however did not materialize.[53] Two years later, as recent research has shown, another Sobor was held to discuss the action to be taken after the grievous maltreatment of two Russian envoys by the Crimean Tatars.[54] It throws much new light on the role and composition of all four Sobors known to have been held during the 1630s.

The decision to call the Sobor was taken at a meeting of the Boiarskaia Duma a few days earlier, which discussed the whole affair and decided to take a strong line on the main outstanding issue, the counterclaim put forward by a Tatar embassy then in Moscow. The purpose of the assembly was merely to register popular indignation at the incident and thus to strengthen the government's hand in dealing with the envoys; in the ensuing talks the Russians did in fact refer to the Sobor's proceedings in this way.[55] It was called, not to take a decision, but to make a demonstration. But there is also no doubt that the assembly did genuinely express the popular mood: some deputies were anxious to go further than the government thought desirable; naturally enough, their views were disregarded.

As regards the composition of these Sobors, it appears that representation was of an even more limited nature than in the early years of Michael's reign. At none of them do we find deputies from the provincial townspeople. The government doubtless considered that they were adequately "represented" by members of the urban community (*posad*) of the capital.[56] The provincial gentry were represented only at the last two of these four Sobors;[57] they were definitely away on active service in 1634 and apparently also in 1632.[58] Only once do we hear of elections being held in the provinces. Late in 1636 provincial voivodes were ordered to elect six members

---

53 *AAE*, III, no. 275; Latkin, *Zemskie sobory*, 183–4.

54 A. A. Novosel'skii, "Zemskii sobor 1639 g.," *IZ*, XXIV (1947), 14–29. His discovery of nearly all the relevant materials invalidates the earlier hypotheses of Latkin, *Zemskie sobory*, 182–3, Platonov, "Zametki," 15 n., and A. N. Zertsalov, *Chteniia IOIDR*, CLXX (1894), IV, 35–8, which were based on the sole document then extant, the "opinion" (*skazka*) submitted by the clergy.

55 Novosel'skii, "Zemskii sobor 1639 g.," 28.

56 In 1639, 31 merchants (*gosti*) and traders from one commercial organization (the *gostinnaia sotnia*) submitted one "opinion"; 14 traders from the other main commercial organization (the *sukhonnaia sotnia*) submitted another. The "men of all ranks" (presumably craftsmen from the *posad*, and possibly also from the settlements (*slobody*) outside the city) asked for more time to consider the matter, but their opinion, if given, has not been preserved. Unfortunately no such details are available for the other Sobors: in 1632 the urban element was composed of "*gosti* and [men of] the *gostinnaia* and *sukhonnaia* hundreds and the black hundreds and men of all ranks." *AAE*, III, no. 211; cf. similar list for 1634 in *SGGD*, III, no. 99.

57 *AAE*, III, no. 275; Novosel'skii, *op. cit.*, 25–6.

58 Cf. *SGGD*, III, no. 99, where they are omitted from the catalog of groups present. The

of the gentry "for the affairs of the Sovereign and the land."[59]

Latkin took this to indicate that some meeting must have been held early in 1637, of which no record has been preserved, and which then reassembled in September to deal with the Crimean threat.[60] But the number of deputies to be elected, six, is unusually large; it seems more likely that they were required for some military or administrative task. No doubt it was these men who sponsored the first of the series of remarkable petitions, submitted in the name of the whole gentry class, to which Smirnov has since drawn attention.[61] The whole perspective changes when we consider the Sobors, not as regularly constituted assemblies of deputies specially elected for the purpose, but as *ad hoc* consultations between the government, the ecclesiastical and secular hierarchy, and men chosen by such provincial gentry as chanced to be in the capital at the time, and by the Moscow townspeople. The gentry would congregate in Moscow before the three dates during the year appointed for the hearing of their lawsuits in the *prikazy*; and in spring they would generally be required to assemble, either in Tula or in Moscow, before moving off in a great cavalcade to guard the southern border against Tatar incursions.[62] These meetings gave the gentry an opportunity for social and political organization. In their petition of 1637 they sharply attacked the privileged boiars and bureaucrats, demanded a decentralization of judicial procedure, and—on a less enlightened note—called for the lifting of all restrictions on the return of fugitive peasants to their owners. Simultaneously the townspeople, acting separately, but presumably in liaison with the gentry, petitioned for the return of fugitive *zakladchiki* to the towns.[63] One of the tragic paradoxes of Russian history—and a factor that was to determine the fate of the Sobors—was that, when the independent voice of the "middle classes" first made itself heard, their cry should have been for the imposition of bondage on their fellow-men.

It was not long before these active elements came to realize the opportunities which the Sobors presented for the exertion of pressure upon the government. The celebrated assembly of 1642, attended by no less than 195 elected representatives, 115 of whom were deputies of the provincial gentry,[64] was occasioned by the Don

---

government spokesman's statement, "we made known unto you at the first Sobor," implies that the membership was much the same in both instances.

59 *RIB*, X (1886), 39, 54–5; cf. a report by the voivode of Galich on the elections there in Got'e, *op. cit.*, 39.

60 Latkin, *Zemskie sobory*, 184 n.

61 Smirnov, "Chelobitnye dvorian i detei boiarskikh vsekh gorodov v pervoi polovine XVII v.," *Chteniia IOIDR*, CCLIII (1915), I, 4–5.

62 *RIB*, X (1886), 62 [1637], 151–7 [1639], 244–6 [1641], 348, 355 [1646].

63 Smirnov, "Chelobitnye dvorian. . . ," 7–9; *Posadskie liudi*, I, 425–9.

64 *SGGD*, III, no. 113; Latkin, *Zemskie sobory*, 196. As in the preceding Sobors, the provincial townspeople were not represented. S. V. Rozhdestvenskii pointed out that, since the elections did not take place until some days after the first session, the provincial gentry representatives must have already been called to Moscow for some other reason: "O zemskom sobore 1642 g.," *Sbornik statei posviashchennykh V. I. Lamanskomu*, 2 vols. (St. Petersburg, 1907), I, 100—a view which Smirnov's discoveries later confirmed. This is made clear in

cossacks' request for military aid to enable them to hold the vital strongpoint of Azov against a renewed Turkish onslaught. Although the government had virtually committed itself to support them,[65] it dared not risk a major war with Turkey on its own responsibility: the stakes were now too high. The relative weakness at the top—I. B. Cherkasskii, now the chief figure in the government, was no Filaret—gave the deputies their chance to speak their minds.

Chicherin considered that the Sobor did no honor to the Russian society of the day, for the deputies' "opinions" (*skazki*) showed them to be egoistic, irrational and irresponsible.[66] But behind their archaic Byzantine protestations of loyalty there lay a lively comprehension of their own interests—and, indeed, those of the country as a whole. Two of the Moscow gentry, dissenting from their colleagues, presented views broadly in line with government policy. Others wanted Azov to be retained, but suggested that volunteers should be recruited for the purpose. Most provincial gentry urged the sending of musketeers and other trained state-maintained troops; the *strel'tsy* themselves returned a formal and colorless reply. The merchants rhetorically proclaimed their readiness to lay down their lives for the faith, although they were doubtless well aware that it was their money, not their lives, which the government required; here, they made it plain, they had nothing to spare. The clergy were equally devious, pretending that military matters were beyond their competence; their failure to promise their prayers for victory—eagerly given, for example, at the Sobor of 1621—implied that they condemned the proposed enterprise. Many groups of deputies loudly protested against the prevailing abuses. The merchants called for a return to local self-government. The craftsmen complained of their onerous service obligations. The gentry violently criticized the boiars, who were excused from providing the recruits they could well afford to spare, and the officials, whose ill-gotten fortunes enabled them to build stone mansions of unparalleled luxury; "we, thy slaves," they concluded, "are worse ruined by the bureaucratic delays (*volokita*), injustices and corrupt judges of Moscow than by the infidels of Turkey and the Crimea."[67] The theme running through the whole proceedings was that internal reform must have precedence over any forward foreign policy. The government wisely ordered the cossacks to evacuate; less wisely, the idea of reform was stifled at birth, and the country continued to be administered with the customary appalling ineptitude.

This neglect was to have fateful consequences in the reign of Alexis, who, unlike his father, acceded to the throne without a Sobor being called.[68] The policy of his chief minister B. I. Morozov, although more consistent, was no more popular than that

some of the *skazki*: "and the gentry of Vladimir, *who are in Moscow*, have set down their opinion as follows . . . " [our italics]. Smirnov considers that many of them had been in the capital in July, 1641, when the submission of a petition modeled on that of 1637 was accompanied by disturbances: "Chelobitnye dvorian. . . ,"18.

65 *SGGD*, III, no. 112.

66 Chicherin, *O narodnom predstavitel'stve*, 378; for a detailed criticism of his views, see Sergeevich, "Zemskie sobory," 44.

67 *SGGD*, III, no. 113.

68 Some earlier historians (e.g. Vladimirskii-Budanov, *Obzor*, 177; Zagoskin, *Istoriia*, 280–1)

of the preceding government;[69] on the contrary, his clumsy efforts at reform served to accentuate the general discontent, which the boiar faction led by N. I. Romanov was only too eager to exploit. A favorable moment came in the spring of 1648, when several thousand troops congregated in the capital. After a petition for redress of their grievances had been summarily rejected, the urban population rioted (June 2); the city was set ablaze; Alexis, terrified, handed over unpopular officials to be lynched by the mob. On June 10, at a joint meeting, the gentry and townspeople petitioned the tsar to call a fully representative Sobor at which they might state their grievances. According to the Swedish resident in Moscow, "the common people were promised that their advice would be sought when the affairs of the whole country were discussed."[70] Morozov was compelled to leave the city and was succeeded by Ia. K. Cherkasskii, who promptly proceeded to purge the administration of Morozov's supporters. This reshuffle, and the necessity of repressing a slave revolt, delayed the fulfillment of the government's promise until July 16. The meeting of that date was attended by those present on June 10, by delegates from certain army units, and by the tsar, the clergy, and the boiars; it therefore deserves to be called a Sobor.[71] As well as presenting petitions with regard to their immediate needs, the deputies put forward comprehensive new demands in the sphere of justice, requesting "that the Sovereign should order the compilation of a Code of Laws. . . , according to which all cases should henceforth be conducted and decided." The tsar yielded and, after consulting further with the clergy and boiars, set up a commission, headed by N. I. Odoevskii, to work through the old laws; the gaps were to be filled "by joint consultations, so that men of all the ranks in the Muscovite state, from the highest to the lowest, should have justice equally in all matters." At the same time elections were ordered in the provinces; the deputies were to arrive by September 1. The initiative in convoking

---

were misled by the evidence of Kotoshikhin (*O Rossii v tsarstvovanie Alekseia Mikhailovicha*[4] (St. Petersburg, 1906), 4, 126) and Olearius (*Vermehrte newe Beschreibung der Muscowitischen und Persischen Reyse . . .* (Schleswig, 1656), 245). It now seems clear that their references are to the gathering of notables in Moscow for Alexis's coronation, which had no political significance. Even if Morozov, the power behind the throne, had thought it in his interests to convoke a Sobor, which is doubtful, he could scarcely have done so, because by July, 1645, when Michael died, the gentry had already left the capital for the south to repel an expected Crimean attack. Smirnov, "Chelobitnye dvorian. . . ," 19; *Posadskie liudi*, II, 10.

69 The Morozov government has recently been "rehabilitated" by Smirnov, who argues cogently that historians have hitherto placed excessive reliance on the evidence of Olearius, whose information was derived from sources hostile to Morozov: *Posadskie liudi*, II, 68 ff.

70 K. Iakubov, "Rossiia i Shvetsiia v pervoi polovine XVII v.," *Chteniia IOIDR*, CLXXXVI (1898), I, 420.

71 This is the name given to it in Odoevskii's memorandum of that date, published by Smirnov: "Neskol'ko dokumentov k istorii Sobornogo Ulozheniia i zemskogo sobora 1648-9 gg.," *Chteniia IOIDR*, CCXLVII (1913), IV, 6; cf. also his "O nachale Ulozheniia i zemskogo sobora 1648-9 gg.," *Zhurnal Ministerstva narodnogo prosveshcheniia*, XLVII (1913), 41, which has forced a revision of previously accepted notions of the course of events leading up to the 1648 Sobor.

the Sobor thus clearly came from below, although this was carefully concealed in the official preamble to the Code.[72]

The Odoevskii commission began work at once. From the start elected representatives took part in its deliberations, since the army deputies automatically had their mandates reendorsed for this purpose. In a manner of speaking, therefore, it already functioned as a Sobor, although its functions were unlike those of any Sobor to date. As deputies from the provinces arrived in the capital, they were assigned to work in the commission.[73] By October 3, when Alexis returned to Moscow from a pilgrimage, they had already completed several chapters of the new Code. It was now that the Sobor formed itself into two chambers: an "upper house" of clergy and boiars (including Odoevskii) presided over by the tsar, and a "lower house" of elected delegates under Iu. A. Dolgorukii. This was a sign that the Sobor was maturing as an institution. The system worked well, for it allowed the elected deputies to express their views without being overpowered by the presence of the tsar and boiars.[74] Their proposals were submitted in the form of petitions to the "upper house" and enacted into law without undue conflict or difficulty. By January 29, 1649,[75] their work was completed, and after an official dinner the deputies dispersed. The Code was published in April.

The great Sobor of 1648–9 marks the climax in the history of that institution. It deserves to be called great for two reasons: its broad representative character, and the influence which it exerted. It cannot be sufficiently emphasized that the "general election" in August, 1648, was the first to be held since the beginning of Michael's reign and marked a radical breach with recent practise. The gentry of each district elected one deputy (two in larger "towns"),[76] as did each *posad*; in contrast, the nobility of the capital and the Moscow merchants and craftsmen had only a handful of representatives, who were swamped by the wave of provincial deputies.[77] The early hypotheses of the slavophil writer A. P. Shchapov[78] as to the extent of popular influence in framing the Code have since been amply confirmed. Zagoskin found that 82 articles were enacted as a direct result of the deputies' petitions;[79] subsequent

---

72 *SGGD*, III, no. 129.

73 Latkin, ed., *Materialy dlia istorii zemskikh soborov XVII stoletiia* (St. Petersburg, 1884), 54–5, 57, 69.

74 Zagoskin, *Istoriia*, 287.

75 This date, given in the preamble to the Code, was queried by Platonov, "Zametki," 19–20, but is confirmed by the document published by Iu. V. Got'e, *Akty*, 66.

76 Despite their relative insignificance in Muscovy, towns were the normal administrative centers for the surrounding districts (*uezdy*), and the term as used here denoted a constituency. Novgorod, which was divided into "fifths" (*piatiny*), had its own arrangements.

77 For the townspeople the figures were 15 and 80 respectively, for the nobility 6 and 150. The ecclesiastical and secular hierarchy (the official part of the Sobor) numbered only 48. The Code has 315 signatures, and we know of 25 other deputies present, and 5 clerks, who did not sign it. Latkin, *Zemskie sobory*, 217.

78 A. P. Shchapov, *Sochineniia*, 4 vols. (St. Petersburg-Irkutsk, 1906–37), I (1906), 720.

79 Zagoskin, "Ulozhenie tsaria Alekseia Mikhailovicha i zemskii sobor 1648–9 gg.: rech' na

research has amended the figure to 89.[80] This may seem a small proportion of the total of over 900 articles, but it included legislation on the burning questions of the day. The Code ceded the townspeople's longstanding demand for the expropriation of tax-exempt settlements (*slobody*) and the ascription to the *posad* of all persons engaged in crafts or commerce.[81] The gentry failed to secure the expropriation of all lands acquired by the Church since the ban of 1580,[82] but were amply compensated by the laws binding the peasants to their owners, which finally established the ugly edifice of Russian serfdom.

The Sobor did not consolidate its position of authority, and its moment of greatness was followed by rapid decline. At the next assembly in 1650 representation was apparently on the same limited scale as at the Sobors of 1632–42.[83] Two meetings were held, July 4 and 26: the first elected a number of representatives to accompany Bishop Rafail on his mission to intercede with the Pskov rebels; the second discussed what action should be taken in the light of the discouraging reports sent by Rafail on his way to the city.[84] Here again the Sobor was called, not to take a decision on policy, but mainly for propagandist effect—to pacify the population in Moscow, where the government feared new riots in sympathy with the outbreak in Pskov. Characteristically, the government sought to exploit the prestige acquired by elected deputies: of the nine clergy and gentry on Rafail's mission, five, including Rafail himself, had attended the Sobor of 1648–9.[85] The moderate line taken by the assembly in 1650 may well have added to the government's distrust of the Sobor, particularly when it dealt with domestic affairs.

It was a new crisis in foreign relations that caused the convocation of another

godichnom sobranii Kazanskogo universiteta 5 noiabria 1879 g." cited by Latkin, *Zemskie sobory*, 225.

80 Platonov, "Zametki," 17–18; cf. N. Novombergskii, "K voprosu o vneshnei istorii Sobornogo Ulozheniia 1649 g.," *IZ*, XXI (1947), 43–50.

81 *Sobornoe Ulozhenie tsaria Alekseia Mikhailovicha 1649 g.* (Moscow, 1907), Ch. XIX. The government's initial reply to the townsmen's petition submitted by the "lower house" on October 30 did not envisage any noteworthy departure from previous practise; the deputies then politely asked for the "mistake" to be corrected, in a second petition (November 25) which contained the thinly veiled threat that, unless their full demands were granted, there would be a repetition of the June riots. *AAE*, IV, no. 32; Smirnov, *Posadskie liudi*, II, 234–9.

82 Smirnov, *op. cit.*, II, 232–3; Zertsalov, "Novye dannye o zemskom sobore 1648–9 gg.," *Chteniia IOIDR*, CXLII (1887), IV, 1–80.

83 A Soviet historian has stated that it was as broadly representative as that of 1648–9, but he brings no evidence to support his contention: *Ocherki istorii SSSR; period feodalizma XVII v.* (Moscow, 1955), 365. There is no record of any elections having been held in the provinces; the only townspeople known to have attended were from Moscow, and the provincial gentry present were presumably also chosen from those in the capital at the time.

84 S. M. Solov'ev, *Istoriia Rossii s drevneishikh vremen*[2], 6 vols. (St. Petersburg, 1896), II, 1547 [15 vols. (Moscow, 1959–66), V (1961), 512–16]; M. N. Tikhomirov, *Pskovskoe vosstanie 1650 g.* (Moscow-Leningrad, 1935), 138.

85 Tikhomirov, *op. cit.*, 142.

assembly six months later. This was a much more representative gathering, with nationwide election of deputies as in 1648.[86] They were informed that, unless Russia accepted suzerainty over the Ukraine, the *hetman* would seek the protection of the Turks. It was obvious that this would involve the country in war with Poland, but the issue was not presented squarely to the assembly. The "speech from the throne" related the familiar catalog of grievances against the Poles, evidently with the aim of putting the deputies into a warlike mood, but the really vital question of Russo-Ukrainian relations was dealt with summarily in a single concluding paragraph. As in 1648, the Sobor met in two chambers, although the "upper house" on this occasion was composed of the clergy alone. They heard the tsar's address on February 19 and replied on February 27; on the following day the remaining deputies were consulted.[87]

Why should the government resort to such unusual procedure? Possibly because it hoped that the clergy, as the class most likely to be moved by a call for an anti-Latin crusade, would pronounce a formal breach with Poland, and thus make it difficult for the secular deputies, who as soldiers or taxpayers can hardly have relished the idea of a major war, not to follow their lead.[88] But the ruse, if such it was, misfired. The clergy agreed to hostilities if the Poles rejected the latest Moscow ultimatum, but issued no flaming appeal for a holy war. Latkin assumes that the other deputies returned similar replies.[89] But is it not more likely that they made known their reluctance to fight? (This may possibly explain why their replies have not been preserved.) For in fact Moscow raised no finger to aid Khmel'nitskii (Khmelnyts'kyj) when the Poles attacked; defeated at Berestechko, he was forced to conclude a disadvantageous peace at Belaia Tserkov' in September. During the spring of 1651 Russo-Polish relations were still fairly amicable; not until June did Moscow's line become sharper. It is not unreasonable to infer that this moderation was forced on the government by the attitude of the Sobor.

As the crisis matured, so we learn from Tsar Alexis himself, a number of assemblies were held.[90] The court records mention only one session, in June 1653.

---

86 Documents have been preserved relating to the elections in no less than 44 towns: Latkin, ed., *Materialy*, 92–128. In view of its more representative character, it is especially unfortunate that we should not know more about the proceedings at this Sobor. Its existence was apparently unknown to earlier historians such as Solov'ev or Zagoskin; the official deed, first published by Latkin (*Materialy*, 81–7), is reproduced in Iu. V. Got'e, *Akty*, 68–72, and in *Vossoedinenie Ukrainy s Rossiei; dokumenty i materialy v 3 tt.* (Moscow, 1954), III, 7–11, but we lack the replies submitted by "estates" other than the clergy.

87 Got'e, *Akty*, 68.

88 In this connection it is worth noting that in 1650 the Russian envoy G. Pushkin threatened the Poles that, if his demands were not conceded, the tsar would call a Sobor and proceed solemnly to the cathedral, where an anathema would be pronounced against Wladyslaw for allegedly infringing the treaty of 1634. Solov'ev, *Istoriia*, II, 1596. Here the clergy were clearly envisaged as playing a leading part in rallying the people for war.

89 Latkin, *Zemskie sobory*, 235.

90 Addressing his army in April, 1654, he said: "Last year there were several Sobors (*byli sobory ne raz*), to which you sent two elected men from each town; at these meetings we

We know nothing of its composition; no doubt, judging by Alexis's remarks, it was dominated by the army, with the deputies being chosen in the usual *ad hoc* way. This activity culminated in the famous Sobor which, October 1, 1653, formally accepted suzerainty over the Ukraine, thereby involving Muscovy in the fateful war with Poland. Buturlin was dispatched directly from the assembly to swear in the tsar's newly acquired subjects. Another envoy, R. Streshnev, had been dispatched already on September 6 with news of the crucial decision. In a polemic with the slavophil Aksakov, Solov'ev argued that this showed that the Sobor, which merely played a formal role, was already in decline; the blame for its liquidation could not therefore be placed on Peter the Great.[91] Aksakov replied with the surmise that the decision contained in Streshnev's instructions had been taken at some previous Sobor.[92] When later research showed the existence of such meetings, it was assumed that Aksakov had been proved right.[93] But we do not know what decisions were taken at the earlier meetings; moreover, the very fact that the Sobor of October 1 played such a purely ceremonial role is in itself a sign of the assembly's loss of authority.

This was the last consultation with popular representatives to which the title of Zemskii Sobor can properly be attached. After 1653 the government restricted itself to taking the advice of individual social groups. These "bureaucratic commissions," as they have rightly been termed, were no innovation; already in 1617 and 1620 the Moscow merchants had been consulted on problems of commercial policy.[94] In 1660, and again two years later, the government held similar conferences about the reasons for, and the measures advisable to deal with, the prevailing high price of grain, which was causing serious and widespread distress. At the first meeting the deputies did not mention the real cause of the crisis, the debasement of the coinage.[95] But in 1662 a sharper note of criticism was sounded; in particular, all the groups present called for a Zemskii Sobor: "we ask the Great Sovereign graciously to order the election of the best men of every rank, also from the [provincial] towns, for without such men we do not know what to say about copper coins, because that it is a matter for the whole state, for all towns and men of every degree"; some even

---

told you of the Polish king's unjust deeds." Solov'ev, *op. cit.*, II, 1661–2. [1959–66 ed., V (1961), 621 f.] Latkin refers to them as taking place in 1653, although it is clear from the document he prints (*op. cit.*, 434), as well as from Alexis's speech, that he is referring to the year 7161 in the Russian calendar, i.e. the period September 1652–August 1653. Although the existence of such meetings was already known to Solov'ev, they appear to have escaped the notice of recent Soviet writers: both A. I. Zaozerskii (*Ocherki istorii SSSR. . .* , 365) and E. N. Kusheva (*Istoriia Moskvy*, I, 543) mention the assembly of October 1 as the only Sobor held in 1653.

91 Solov'ev, "Shletser," as cited by Latkin, *Zemskie sobory*, 240.

92 Aksakov, *Polnoe sobranie sochinenii*, I, 207.

93 Latkin, *op. cit.*, 241; Zagoskin, *Istoriia*, 296.

94 Solov'ev, *Istoriia*, II, 1128. [1959–66 ed., V (1961), 139–40.]

95 K. V. Bazilevich, *Denezhnaia reforma Alekseia Mikhailovicha i vosstanie v Moskve v 1662 g.* (Moscow and Leningrad, 1936), 46.

specified the number of deputies who ought to be chosen.[96] The government, probably fearing that a Sobor would expose and condemn its financial policies, remained deaf to these appeals. The riots in Moscow six months later, which were ruthlessly suppressed, must have strengthened Alexis's conviction that he had acted rightly, and his determination to avoid a Sobor in the future. In 1681 V. V. Golitsyn discussed plans of military and fiscal reform with elected representatives of the gentry and the townspeople respectively; at about the same time an ecclesiastical council met. But, characteristically, the three assemblies were kept strictly apart. The days of the Zemskii Sobor were now very decidedly over.

III

The foregoing account shows that in the early years of Michael's reign, and again in 1648–9, the Sobor had the chance to assert itself against the weakened autocratic power. But although the deputies understood how to utilize the assembly as a means of exerting pressure on the government, they could not proceed from a consciousness of their *interests* to a consciousness of their *rights*: that is to say, they were unable to consolidate their political gains in constitutional form by securing definite legal guarantees for the institution through which those gains had been won. Hence the Sobor remained an administrative convenience rather than an organ of state authority: the tsar was entirely free to decide when a Sobor should be called, how it should be composed, and what role it should play, and, of course, was quite within his rights in ceasing to call the Sobor altogether.

Broadly speaking, there are two schools of thought on the question of the reasons for the extinction of the assembly. Some earlier writers emphasized the part played by its own natural internal weaknesses—its "worthlessness," as Chicherin put it. They pointed out that Russia remained scarcely touched by Roman law, which in the West provided the basis for the age-long struggle for political rights; the very idea that an assembly of popular delegates should seek to obtain, say, the right of legislative initiative was fundamentally alien to Russian thought, with its Byzantine tradition of passive acceptance of the God-given authority. There is a germ of truth in this view, although so far as the Sobors are concerned the theme of native Russian passivity has been greatly overworked. To evaluate this view satisfactorily, we should need to know much more about the attitude of the electors and the deputies themselves to the assembly. Did they regard attendance at the Sobor as an onerous obligation, on a par with the other miscellaneous duties they were compelled to render to the state? Kabanov's arguments to this effect are unconvincing, and are not borne out by the evidence of the personal service records of deputies who belonged to the gentry.[97] The deputies received payment for their work from the government,[98] but the main

---

96 Zertsalov, "O miatezhakh v gorode Moskve . . . v 1648, 1662, i 1671 gg.," *Chteniia IOIDR*, CLIV (1890), 260, 264–5.

97 Kabanov, "Organizatsiia vyborov," 114; cf. record of Prince V. Z. Ukhtomskii in Zertsalov, "Novye dannye," 66.

98 Kabanov, *op. cit.*, 111 ff.; Latkin, *Zemskie sobory*, 268–9. In addition to a monetary salary,

burden of their upkeep fell on the communities that elected them. This burden was sometimes no doubt a heavy one, but there is no evidence to suggest that reluctance to bear it played any part in the Sobor's decline. On the contrary, it may possibly have enhanced the voters' interest in the elections. It has been argued that they participated only in response to pressure from local agents of the administration.[99] But it is dangerous to generalize from isolated instances of electors' disinclination to appear when summoned;[100] on other occasions they sent more than the prescribed number of deputies. The detailed evidence that has been preserved of the elections at Novgorod in 1648 shows that the townspeople took a lively interest in the selection of their representatives; at Elets they resisted efforts by the voivode to force the election of his own nominee.[101] At Kursk in 1649 the electors threatened violence against their deputy, on his return from the Sobor, for having failed to frustrate an unpopular edict, in contravention of the instructions given him by the electors.[102] (Such instructions (*nakazy*), reminiscent of the *cahiers* brought to the French States-General, were a feature of the more representative Sobors.)[103] One can agree with Pokrovskii that this shows progress from a medieval to a modern conception of the nature and functions of popular representation.[104]

Nor can it be maintained that during the actual proceedings the deputies manifested either apathetic indifference or uncritical concurrence with the government's viewpoint. The various groups of deputies were not simply called upon individually to answer set questions, as was once thought, but there was a free debate within each group.[105] Although decisions were arrived at unanimously, it was possible at certain Sobors for deputies to submit independent opinions.[106] One gains an exaggerated impression of unanimity from the official deeds, which were compiled after the proceedings by government clerks. The authorities were not above "editing" such documents to suit their own purposes, as was shown by an incident at the ecclesiastical Sobor of 1667.[107]

The decline of the Sobor may thus confidently be attributed to external rather

---

the deputies frequently obtained the privilege, which was greatly sought after, of exemption from the strict ban on the distillation of liquor for personal consumption. Cf. the illuminating data in Got'e, *Akty*, 66–8.

99 Shmelev, "Otnosheniia naseleniia," 496.

100 D'iakonov, *Ocherki*, 385–6.

101 Smirnov, "Neskol'ko dokumentov. . . ," 8–20; Got'e, *op. cit.*, no. 14.

102 V. P. Alekseev, "Novyi dokument k istorii zemskogo sobora 1648–9 gg.," *Drevnosti: Trudy arkheograficheskoi komissii Imperatorskogo moskovskogo arkheologicheskogo obshchestva*, 3 vols. (Moscow, 1899–1913), II (i) (1900), 79–86.

103 D'iakonov, *op. cit.*, 385.

104 Pokrovskii, *op. cit.*, 327.

105 Sergeevich, *Zemskie sobory*, 30; D'iakonov, *op. cit.*, 387.

106 D'iakonov, *loc. cit.* The "opinion" presented by N. Beklemyshev and T. Zheliabuzhskii at the Sobor of 1642 is the most striking example of this.

107 N. F. Kapterev, *Patriarkh Nikon i tsar' Aleksei Mikhailovich*, 2 vols., Sergiev posad, 1909–12, II (1912), 99–100.

than to internal factors. Sergeevich laid the blame on those boiars who had personal influence over Alexis in the fateful years after 1649, when the Sobor had caused laws to be enacted that were prejudicial to their interests.[108] Zagoskin challenged his search for "hidden causes," preferring to regard the dying out of the Sobor as a natural spontaneous process, rendered historically inevitable by the strengthening of the monarchy.[109] This was a statement of fact rather than an explanation. Platonov followed Sergeevich, but singled out Patriarch Nikon as the "chief culprit."[110] Nikon, who had attended the 1648–9 Sobor as a deputy, later bitterly attacked the Code as "an accursed book," compiled by men of low birth who were ignorant of the law of God.[111] One wonders whether these views, expressed in the heat of a polemic many years afterwards, can be taken as reliable evidence of his opinions at the time: in 1650 Nikon was urging the same policy on the tsar as was advocated by the Sobor. But substantially the indictment of vested interests, both secular and ecclesiastical, remains valid.

The relations between the government and the assembly, it is now clear, were characterized by suspicion rather than confidence, by conflict rather than collaboration. The great Sobor of 1648 was an almost revolutionary body; in 1650, and apparently also in 1651, the Sobors' recommendations did not accord with official policy. From the government's point of view, it was time to put a stop to the assembly before it became too dangerous.

The tsar and his close associates now had the means to enforce their will—a constantly expanding phalanx of loyal bureaucrats and trained regular troops. If, even in countries where representative assemblies had the weight of accumulated custom behind them, those who tried to maintain them were unsuccessful, it is obvious that no effective opposition to the suspension of the Sobor could be expected on the part of the amorphous Russian society of the day. Moreover, the groups which might have been capable of reacting, the provincial gentry and the townspeople, now went separate ways. The Code of 1649 established rigid barriers between the various "estates." Having achieved their immediate social aims, the gentry had no major grievance against the regime, and in the conflicts of the 1650s and 1660s they remained, by and large, loyal to the government. The townspeople's call for an assembly in 1662 evoked no sympathetic echo among them.

The new absolutism, based upon serfdom, that developed in Russia during the seventeenth century differed in many essential respects from the absolute monarchies of western Europe. Similarly, the Zemskii Sobor was a much more primitive institution than its contemporaries in other countries. Yet in its way it represented a threat

108 Sergeevich, "Zemskie sobory," 58–9.
109 Zagoskin, *Istoriia*, 338. A similar standpoint was taken by Latkin, *Zemskie sobory*, 286.
110 Platonov, "K istorii," 334.
111 *Zapiski otdeleniia russkoi i slavianskoi arkheologii Imperatorskogo arkheologicheskogo obshchestva*, II (1861), cited by Smirnov, "O nachale," 38. [V. M. Undol'skii, "Otzyv patriarkha Nikona ob Ulozhenii tsaria Alekseia Mikhailovicha: novye materialy dlia istorii zakonodatel'stva v Rossii," *RA* (1886), 2, 605–20.]

to the absolutist order. Fundamentally the same historical process was at work.

1957

The Decline of the Zemskii Sobor:
An Afterword

I

Since this article was written some thirty years ago the Muscovite "assembly of [all] the land" has received a good deal of scholarly attention both in the USSR and in the West. Some new documents have appeared in print;[1] more important, the Sobor has been thoroughly studied by L. V. Cherepnin (1905–77), a leading Soviet historian, in a posthumously published monograph, and by Hans-Joachim Torke, professor of Russian history at the Free University of Berlin, who devotes to it a substantial section (119–215) of his major reassessment of Muscovite Russia's social and political institutions.[2] Each of these two volumes in its way may be regarded as a standard work, and it is to them that students of the problem will now first turn. Cherepnin benefits from his proximity to and close familiarity with the archival sources; Torke's strong points are his willingness to question and discard traditional but fallacious concepts, his gift for keen analysis, and his grounding in continental European *Ver-*

---

1 *Sobor of 1639*: V. N. Shumilov, "Delo zemskogo sobora 1639 g.," in N. I. Pavlenko *et al.*, eds., *Dvorianstvo i krepostnoi stroi Rossii XVI–XVIII vv.* (Moscow, 1975), 295–302 (6 documents). *Sobor of 1650*: M. N. Tikhomirov, "Dokumenty zemskogo sobora 1650 g.," *IA*, no. 4 (1958), 141–56, no. 5, 129–45, no. 6, 139–54; reprinted with additions in *idem*, *Klassovaia bor'ba v Rossii XVII v.* (Moscow, 1969), 234–332 (40 documents). *Sobor of 1653*: A. I. Kozachenko, "K istorii zemskogo sobora 1653 g.," *IA*, no. 4 (1957), 223–7 (1 document); cf. his article, "Zemskii sobor 1653 g.," *VI*, no. 5 (1957), 151–58.

2 Cherepnin's book, *Zemskie sobory russkogo gosudarstva v XVI–XVII vv.* (Moscow, 1978), has been reviewed by E. L. Keenan in *Kritika*, 16 (1980), 82–94 and by Torke in *JGOE*, 27 (1979), 580–81. Torke's work, *Die staatsbedingte Gesellschaft im Moskauer Reich: Zar und Zemlia in der altrussischen Herrschaftsverfassung, 1613–1689* (Leiden, 1974), was reviewed by C. Goehrke in *JGOE*, 26 (1978), 414–18, by R. O. Crummey in *SR*, 35 (1976), 529–30, and by the present writer in *SEER*, 55 (1977), 112–14. G. Stökl expanded his 1955 conference report (see note 1) in "Der Moskauer Zemskii Sobor: Forschungsproblem und politisches Leitbild," *JGOE*, 8 (1960), 149–70; this article is mainly concerned with the sixteenth-century assemblies. Cherepnin gave a preliminary exposition of his views in "Zemskii sobor i utverzhdenie absoliutizma v Rossii," in B. B. Kafengauz *et al.*, eds., *Absoliutizm v Rossii, XVII–XVIII vv.* (Moscow, 1964), 92–133. He had almost completed his book when Torke's work appeared: *Zemskie sobory*, 47.

fassungsgeschichte. If Torke proceeds, perhaps unwittingly, from an awareness of the considerable achievements of the early modern *Ständestaat*, Cherepnin is hampered in his exposition by a commitment to orthodox Marxist-Leninist dogmas: to the belief that the "centralized multinational Russian state"—that is, Muscovite absolutism—was "objectively" a "progressive" force in the country's development; that the society of this era should be characterized as "feudal"; and above all that the form of government, for a century or so after 1584, was that of an "estate-representative monarchy." This term has a respectable ancestry in Marxist historical writing, but needs to be handled carefully if it is not to become an impediment to clarity of thought. It implies that Orthodox Rus' had, in its *chiny* (service ranks), an equivalent to the "estates of the realm" (*états, Stände, sosloviia*) that existed at the time in the rest of Christian Europe. Most non-Marxists, and some Marxists too, would challenge this assumption. The question is a most important one for students of Russian history, but it cannot be considered further here.[3]

Our aim in "The Decline of the Zemskii Sobor" was a relatively modest one: to show, within the compass of a mere twenty pages, that the Sobor was more than just a pliant instrument in the hands of an omnipotent autocrat, and that from time to time it served as a forum for the articulation of social demands and even as a channel through which pressure could be exerted upon the central *vlast'*; furthermore, to suggest— although without following up the parallels in detail—that the relationship between the crown and the assembly in Rus', marked as this was by tension as well as cooperation, had something in common with that in other European lands during the period, when absolutist rule was becoming the norm. It was not argued that the Sobor was, or could have become, a Western-style parliament, although it was certainly implied that the Sobor's inadequacies, its failure to develop into a viable legislative institution with clearly defined juridical powers, were a misfortune for Russia. I still believe this to be true, and consider that a full scale comparative analysis would be useful. This view is closer to that of many pre-revolutionary Russian historians, and indeed also to that of Cherepnin, than it is to Torke's, whose methodological approach is more congenial to me than Cherepnin's. Torke's austere professional standards would—if I have understood him correctly—oblige him to dismiss this reasoning as unhistorical. But before asking the reader to judge whether the argument in "The Decline of the Zemskii Sobor" still holds good, we must pause to examine certain particulars of successive meetings of the assembly, and then some more general questions. It is only to be expected that some comments and revisions should be called for in the light of the research carried out by these two eminent historians, who have given more thorough attention to the matter than I was able to do and have also been granted

---

3 See G. Stökl, "Gab es im Moskauer Staat 'Stande'?," *JGOE*, 11 (1963), 321–42 and Torke, *Gesellschaft*, eps. 129–31, 271–83. The interesting discussion on Russian and European absolutism conducted by Soviet historians in the late 1960s and early 1970s is reviewed by Torke in "Die neuere Sowjethistoriographie zum Problem des russischen Absolutismus," *FOEG*, 20 (1973), 113–33 and, in more popular vein, by the present writer in "The Current Scene in Soviet Historiography," *Survey* (London, 1973).

a more generous allowance of space in which to develop their views. These points, taken chronologically, are as follows.

1) *Sobor of 1612.* This assembly, as we stated (54), included representatives of the townspeople as well as gentry servitors, and was therefore more "popular" than its predecessor. Cherepnin points out (183) that the townspeople were not mentioned in *all* the instructions sent out by the Sobor after June 1612, when the levy (*opolchenie*) which it directed left Iaroslavl' for Moscow, so that their role in its affairs may have declined during the latter part of the year. However incomplete its representation may have been, this "campaign" assembly had a broader range of functions than any of its forerunners. It became a vehicle for the political activism which the Troubles engendered among certain groups of the population, especially in the provinces. This expanded role, one might add, was forced on the Sobor by external events (the eclipse of the monarchy, an unprecedented social catastrophe including mass famine and civil strife, foreign intervention) rather than by conscious choice of the deputies or their electors, who saw the levy as a means of reconstituting the traditional sociopolitical order. There is no hard evidence whether or not they expected the Sobor to continue in being once the monarchy had been restored.

2) *Sobor of 1612–13.* The same is true of the deputies to the great Sobor which chose Michael Romanov as tsar. Torke remarks justly (162) that February 1613 was the key moment, when they had an opportunity to consolidate "the upsurge of social life" (of which the Sobor was both the symbol and the expression), but that this opportunity was missed (*verspielt*). He is also right to take Cherepnin to task for his belief, inadequately supported by the documents and disproved by such pre-revolutionary historians as Stashevskii, that the Sobor may have imposed conditions on the first of the Romanovs: for he does not try to refute Stashevskii's elaborate analysis of this question. On the other hand, in our view Torke exaggerates in stating (164) that to have advanced such a demand would have been "senseless" (*widersinnig*) in view of the general desire for a return to the old ways, to *starina*. Had the deputies been such staid traditionalists, they would not have participated in a lively intrigue over the choice of a candidate for the throne; it is reasonable to conclude that the young Michael's reluctance to assume the powers thrust on him by the Sobor was not just feigned for effect, but reflected genuine doubts as to the Sobor's loyalty (or malleability), which will have been suggested to him by his entourage; and finally, G. Stökl has argued cogently that the Polish-Lithuanian model of government had some influence on Muscovite thought at this time—admittedly, mainly within the *boiarstvo*, but then Torke points out (158) that the boiars played a greater role at the Sobor than used to be thought. He is also justified in questioning (154) the high figures (700 to 800) advanced by earlier historians (whom we followed) for the number of deputies to this assembly.

3) *Sobor of February-March 1616.* The "general election" should be dated to late 1615, rather than to early 1616, as stated on 57 (Cherepnin, 221; cf. Torke, 171). The latter suggests plausibly (172) that the government, which had sent the previous deputies home several months earlier, may at first have planned to do without the

Sobor's advice but then have changed its mind once it realized the gravity of the
country's financial situation.

Cherepnin also makes the point, based on an unpublished (and unidentified!)
document,[4] that some peasants participated in the vote. They were presumably "black"
(that is, non-seignorial, taxpaying) peasants in the northern forest zone; they will not
have been perceived, or perceived themselves, as falling into a different category
from the townspeople (cf. our note 22), and their addition to the throng will not have
affected the deliberations in any material way. Nevertheless the fact deserves to be
recorded—as does their participation in the 1619 election, noted by Torke.[5]

4) *Sobor of September 1616.* Cherepnin (221, note 61), citing a source unavailable
to me,[6] shows that the deputies discussed the terms of the forthcoming compromise
peace with Sweden. It is therefore incorrect to say, as we did (58), that the assembly
had no part at all in this matter. It was not, indeed—as Torke notes (173–74)—asked
to approve the Treaty of Stolbovo once this had been signed in February 1617; what
it did on the earlier occasion was to tell the government that the country could not
afford the alternative option. This would have been to pay Sweden a large indemnity
for the recovery of Russian sovereignty over the Baltic littoral, which the Swedes had
taken during the Troubles. It seems highly likely that this was also the prevailing
opinion at court and in the administration, and that in this matter, as in so many
others at this time, the ruling group was simply asking the deputies (who were not
specially elected for the session) for an endorsement of its own position. The Sobor
was thus, as we suggested (56), "invest[ing the goverenment's decision] with an aura
of popular approval" rather than initiating policy—an interpretation with which Torke
agrees (168). As he notes, the Sobor was important to the government primarily for
its "informative" role, since the central authorities were poorly acquainted with the
situation in the provinces. This is not to say that the consultations of these years were
purely fictitious, or that the Sobor's cooperation in raising revenue and so on was not
valued.

5) *Sobor of February-March 1622.* Both Cherepnin (239) and Torke (180) mention
an order sent by the tsar on March 14, 1622 to Novgorod,[7] which the former interprets
as evidence that a consultation was held at this time (between February 11 and March
14) to discuss the tension with Poland-Lithuania in the light of a report brought back to
Moscow by the envoy G. Borniakov. Unfortunately nothing is known of its decision,

---

4 TsGADA, f. 1107, op. 1, d. 175, 1. 42; cf. Veselovskii, "Sem' sborov," no. 54, 165.

5 *Gesellschaft*, 178, n. 3, citing a communication from the tsar to the voivode of Tot'ma,
November 2, 1619; Veselovskii, "Sem' sborov," no. 74; cf. 139, where peasant participation
is mentioned as being officially sanctioned in 1613 and 1682.

6 G. A. Zamiatin, "Dva dokumenta k istorii zemskogo sobora 1616 g.," *Trudy Voronezhskogo
gosudarstvennogo universiteta*, 1 (1925), 302; cf. Torke, *Gesellschaft*, 173–4. Torke cites
(327) another work published by Zamiatin at Voronezh in 1926: *K istorii zemskogo sobora
1613 g.*

7 *Knigi razriadnye po ofitsial'nym onykh spiskam, 1614–1679 gg.*, 2 vols. (St. Petersburg,
1853–55), I, cols. 830–31.

or indeed whether any decision was called for. Torke doubts that a Sobor met at all; if it did, it may be regarded as a sequel to that of October 1621, and the assembly's composition was probably similar.

6) *Sobor of November 1632.* Cherepnin adduces (246–48) a hitherto unexploited Razriad document[8] which throws fresh light on this gathering. We may now safely assume that Tsar Michael and his father addressed it—no doubt indirectly, through an official, as was the custom—since we have both the draft and the fair copy their (joint) speech. Since there are slight differences in the form of address to the various *chiny*, copies of the declaration were evidently issued to them. The government gave in effect five reasons for going to war. They were as follows: "for the honor of the tsar"; "for the true Orthodox faith"; "for the liberation (*izbavlenie*) of Orthodox peasants" [in White Russia]; "for the extension and freedom of the entire Muscovite state"; and "revenge for previous Polish-Lithuanian wrongs and spilling of [Orthodox] Christian blood"—that is, respectively, motives of a dynastic, religious, social, political, and psychological character. None of them is particularly surprising, but it is good to have them listed so clearly. The irony in our statement that the deputies gave their support to the offensive "with apparent enthusiasm" (60) is reinforced by Cherepnin's observation (248): "it is clear from the materials on the collection of the fifth money that the tax gatherers encountered resistance from the population"—a sentiment that would be expressed openly at the next assembly.

7) *Sobor of January 1634.* Our statement that "the deputies were less acquiescent" than they had been in 1632 holds good—but on reconsideration perhaps they should not have been called "deputies," since this term suggests election and we do not really know whether any *vybornye* were present (cf. our note 58; Cherepnin, 251; Torke, 182). The servitors at least were probably "represented" only by those who happened to be in the capital at the time, as in the case of the other Sobors held in this period. The meeting was attended by a superabundance of clerical dignitaries, and this no doubt helps to explain the vehemence of the anti-Catholic rhetoric in the official declaration.

8) *Sobor of January (?) 1642.* It has long been known (see our note 64) that the elections did not take place until several days after the assembly first met; therefore once again those provincial gentrymen who attended had to come to Moscow for some other reason. Cherepnin has now adduced archival evidence (265)[9] which confirms that, on the very day when the degree convoking the Sobor was issued (January 3), the Razriad prepared a list, for the benefit of the Posol'skii prikaz, of the servitor representatives who were to attend; the names in this list correspond by and large with those of the signatories to the Sobor's final act. It is thus clearer than ever that these men at least, if not all the servitor deputies, were nominated instead of being chosen by their fellows—and so that "representation" did not mean to seventeenth-century Muscovites what it does to us today.

---

8 TsGADA, f. 210, stolbtsy raznykh stolov, stb. 33.

9 TsGADA, f. 210, Moskovskii stol [of the Razriad], d. 173.

Torke offers (186–89)—as does Cherepnin (268–70)—an extensive summary of the deputies' opinions, so far as these can be reconstructed from their formal statements (*skazki*), and notes justly that the official record of this assembly is far more revealing than the *Utverzhdennaia gramota* compiled after the 1613 Sobor, which endeavored to suppress unpalatable facts. It is hard to agree, though, with Torke's suggestion (189–90) that those who "voted" against Muscovy's retention of Azov, and thus against the prospect of hostilities with the Turks, did so only because they did not want to provide the men or money, and not because they questioned the need for a war—a decision which, he contends, they were prepared to leave to the authorities. This takes us back to Chicherin's unduly negative evaluation of their motives. After all, they had been asked for an opinion on this specific issue and were quite capable of making up their minds about it, the more so since defense of the steppe border was the service gentry's *raison d'être*. Torke vacillates as to whether the various groups pursued their own egoistic "personal" or group interests: after stating that they displayed only a "personal interest" and only an "unconscious" political sense (since their own interests coincided with those of the country), he concludes that "the land and the army were becoming more selfconscious" (190–91). This is surely where the significance of the 1642 Sobor lies. It gave the gentry and townspeople a better opportunity than they usually had, when the levy assembled in the spring, to formulate their grievances and desiderata; it was precisely their loud (but reasonable) demands for internal reform as the first priority that the ruling clique found unacceptable, and which led it to abstain from engaging in a major war. The same "program" would be articulated still more stridently a few years later at the great assembly of 1648–49, which Torke places—in our view rather too schematically—into a completely different category from its predecessors (192; see also below, 82). Nevertheless his interpretation of the deputies' intentions is certainly nearer the mark than Cherepnin's dogmatic view (271) that the 1642 Sobor took a step toward the development of "class conflict" and was thus *ipso facto* "progressive."

9) *Sobors of 1650.* The documents published by Tikhomirov on the Pskov revolt (only few of which relate directly to the Sobor) include a list of the delegates chosen on July 4 to accompany Bishop Rafail on his mission of conciliation to the rebels, and the record of the second meeting on July 26, which contains the official declaration.[10] These materials make it quite clear that the government, as we suggested, convoked the Sobor "mainly for propagandist effect—to pacify the population in Moscow," where it was feared that the townspeople might rise in sympathy. Characteristically, after the second meeting, the authorities summoned the "hundredsmen" (*sotskie*) who had charge of the plebeian quarters of the capital and reminded them that it was their duty to denounce anyone who engaged in seditious talk.[11] We went too far in stating that "the moderate line taken by the assembly in 1650 may well have added to the government's distrust of the Sobor," since no one knows what, if anything, the

---

10 Tikhomirov, *Klassovaia bor'ba*, nos. 7, 12, 258, 266–70.

11 Ibid., 270. This episode, it should be added, was already referred to by Solov'ev: *Istoriia Rossii*, V (1961), 514.

deputies actually *said.* Nevertheless we do know that their delegates to Pskov did not favor stronger measures against the rebels, as some of Alexis's senior advisors seem to have done, but rather the opposite course. We now have another scrap of evidence which reinforces Cherepnin's view—a view we share—that the government's attitude to the assembly was ambiguous: as he puts it (317), "it relied on the Sobor but at the same time distrusted it." In September 1650 the senior member of the delegation to Pskov, *stol'nik* I. V. Olfer'ev, was denounced by the Pskov voivode, Prince V. P. L'vov, for having taken too sympathetic an approach toward the rebels. The evidence against Olfer'ev was strong, but in the end Tsar Alexis forgave him—as he did also the men of Pskov—in what deserves to be called an act of statesmanship. With all the anachronistic talk of "class struggle" in some of the literature we should not lose sight of the fact that this revolt was quelled with a minimum of violence, compared with the repression that followed the outbreaks in 1662 and 1670–71.[12] The Olfer'ev episode seems to weaken Torke's assumption (197) that there was no tension in 1650 between government and assembly, and that the former had already decided on an appeasement policy in which the deputies meekly concurred; he is correct, however, in stating that the Sobor was not *in itself* responsible for the relatively peaceful liquidation of the Pskov conflict.

Both authors (Torke, 198; Cherepnin, 317; cf. Tikhomirov, *Klassovaia bor'ba*, no. 30, 317–18) correctly draw attention to the fact that a third meeting of the Sobor was held on October 8, at which the government formally announced this reconciliation. No action seems to have been required of the deputies, who did not even discuss the matter. This is clear evidence of the assembly's slight importance; and we would see it as a further hint of official distrust: after all, how many more Olfer'evs could Alexis risk?

10) *Sobors of 1653.* Kozachenko's work has removed the basis for our strictures (note 90) on Soviet historians for omitting to mention the first gatherings held in this year. The tercentenary of the so-called "reunification of the Ukraine with Russia," celebrated with great pomp in 1954, sponsored some fruitful archival research.[13] Previously we had the contradictory evidence of the "Palace registers" (*dvortsovye razriady*) that the first Sobor was summoned for May 20, but that on May 15 the arrival of provincial servitor representatives was postponed to June 5. Cherepnin now maintains that the assembly met on May 25—a Wednesday, he adds for good measure—and not on May 20 as Kozachenko had argued.[14] The precise date does not matter very much, since the real decision had already been taken elsewhere— by the tsar and boiars, in late February and early March (Torke, 198). Was this

---

12 On this see now P. Longworth, *Alexis, Tsar of All the Russias* (London, 1984), 66.

13 *Inter alia,* the Sobor's decision of October 1, previously published in *SGGD,* III, no. 157, and in *Akty Iuzhnoi i Zapadnoi Rossii,* 15 vols. (St. Petersburg, 1863–92), X, no. 2, was reprinted with photographic reproductions of sections of the text in *Vossoedinenie Ukrainy s Rossiei: materialy i dokumenty,* 3 vols. (Moscow, 1954), III, no. 197, 406–14.

14 Cherepnin, *Zemskie sobory,* 328–31; cf. Kozachenko, "Zemskii sobor," 157; *idem,* "K istorii," 224. Torke (199) follows Kozachenko.

meeting followed by others? Alexis's subsequent remark to this effect (note 90) may have referred to an official dinner staged on June 5, which was attended by "pairs (*dvoiniki*) of provincial gentry representatives."[15] Cherepnin may well be right in thinking that such meetings were held as and when the servitors trickled into the capital and reported for duty. But he has overlooked what is surely the most important implication of this recent Soviet research: namely, that these gatherings were highly casual affairs. We might almost call them "morale-raising sessions" at which the dynamic young ruler sought to inspire his officers with his own zeal for combat. This informality is underlined by the fact that, directly after the May 25 meeting, Alexis went on to consult with men whom the source discovered by Kozachenko refers to as *ploshchadnye liudi*—presumably, servitors who had foregathered in the square (*ploshchad'*) outside the tsar's palace; like the "men of all ranks" at the Sobor, they "unanimously stated that the Cherkassians should be accepted."[16] One could scarcely have a more graphic indication of the low status to which the Sobor had fallen, a mere four years after it had registered its maximum impact.

Cherepnin also shows that there is clear documentary evidence of the connection between the spring assemblies of 1653 (and also that of 1651) and the ceremonial session of the Sobor on October 1, at which the Cossack host's submission to the tsar's scepter was accepted (for this was how the Muscovites interpreted Khmel'nits'kyi's decision, whatever the cossacks or other Ukranians might feel about the matter). The litany of charges against the Poles read out on the later occasion was an expanded version of that presented at the earlier meetings, the only major difference being that now greater attention was paid, reasonably enough, to the Ukrainian angle of the conflict. It is significant that the very word *vybornye* (elected men) was omitted from the text of the decision which the assembly took on October 1.[17] The boiars are the only group of representatives whose opinion has been preserved, and so we can only speculate as to what may have been in the minds of the other *chiny* who attended. Were they perhaps apprehensive about the impending hostilities, which were destined to last for thirteen years and cost both Muscovy and the Ukraine incalculable losses? At any rate one may doubt that, if they had been able to look further into the future, they would have endorsed Cherepnin's interpretation that the Sobor's decision "corresponded objectively to the interests of the people, to the needs of national development" (337).

II

Was this the last Sobor? Torke thinks so, and so do we, that it was the last complete one. Cherepnin, however, pleads for inclusion of the various consultations held

15 Cherepnin, *Zemskie sobory*, 333, citing *Dvortsovye razriady*, III, col. 354.

16 Kozachenko, "Zemskii sobor," 153; Cherepnin, *Zemskie sobory*, 331.

17 Cherepnin, *Zemskie sobory*, 334. Torke, *Gesellschaft*, 200, following Latkin, thinks the composition was the same as at the spring session; Cherepnin, *Zemskie sobory*, 334–35, that the provincial gentry was absent. The latter view seems more plausible, since they will have been needed at the front.

between the government and specific interest groups, particularly the merchants and townspeople (1660, 1662, 1667, 1672, 1676), and also the gatherings held concurrently under V. V. Golitsyn's chairmanship in 1681–82, the two assemblies which tried to resolve dynastic issues after Theodore II's death (April, May 1682), and even the summons of active and retired servitors to Moscow in December 1683 to approve a "perpetual peace" treaty with Poland-Lithuania—which failed to materialize, whereupon the deputies were sent home again, having accomplished nothing. Torke (208) regards the latter as little more than a charade which took the practice of holding "acclamatory" Sobors *ad absurdum*. Clearly a decision on this matter depends on one's answer to the question: what *was* the Zemskii Sobor?

Earlier historians took the view that a "proper" or fully representative Sobor required the presence of the "black" clergy ("Sacred Synod"), boiars (Duma), state servitors—both metropolitan and provincial—and townspeople. But if such a criterion were to be applied strictly, we would be left with only a handful of assemblies, since most of them do not measure up to such requirements and the representatives who attended were not specially elected for the purpose; hence the talk of "incomplete" or "partial" Sobors.

Both Cherepnin and Torke recognize that this distinction is untenable. The former is inconsistent. Having decided that *any* meeting between the ruler or his officials and public representatives was a Sobor, and that one should discard the notion of "sessions," "commissions," and the like, he nevertheless calls the 1550 meeting a *soveshchanie* (89) and speaks of others as "military" or "ecclesiastical" assemblies: in which case, why not call the 1662 gathering a "merchant" or "urban" Sobor? His romantic inclinations lead him even to qualify as a Sobor the emergency town council set up by the Pskov rebels, and so to present the talks held under Bishop Rafail's auspices as a negotiation between *two* Sobors—a pleasing but fanciful notion that makes the Russia of 1650 sound much like the Russia of 1917! He offers a list of forty-four assemblies (three of them "doubtful") after 1611, and assigns them to four groups (382–85); but it must be said that the last, analytical, chapter of his book is far inferior in quality to the rest. The case for Muscovite Russia as an "estate-representative monarchy" remains to be made.

With Torke we have a breath of fresh air that dispels the confusion that has long befuddled discussion of the Sobor. He shows that, since its status lacked juridical definition and there were no fixed principles for representation, it is unreasonable (and anachronistic) to insist on typological distinctions that exist only in the mind of the beholder. This is why he lists the post-1653 gatherings as Sobors (269 ff.). He further reminds us that the very title "Zemskii Sobor" is an artificial construct, invented in the mid-nineteenth century. He suggests the term "Moscow assemblies" (*Moskauer Versammlugen*) as a practical alternative to the more appropriate *Reichsversammlungen*, which one might translate as "assemblies of the realm"—for they were convoked to deal with the affairs of the sovereign (*Gosudar'*) as well as those of "the land" (*zemlia*) (137). The latter term, Torke maintains, had not yet acquired its modern meaning of "countrywide" but (after 1612 at least) referred only to *local* affairs as distinct from those of the entire realm (135). Whether this fine distinction is tenable or not,[18] it is certainly desirable, though not at all easy, to consider the Sobor in its contemporary sociopolitical context, and to free one's mind of concepts that were developed later or in other lands. This error of Aksakov's seems to have beset all subsequent researchers, the present writer not excepted.

It follows that the Sobors were not visualized at the time as popular representative bodies (*Volksvertretungen*) but as "forums to ease the government's task by securing the participation of society" (140). The *chiny* were convoked in order to inform and advise the tsar and his officials on specific issues; their obligations were directed toward higher authority rather than toward their electors; the job of representation was seen as official service, for which the deputy was entitled to an appropriate reward; and the electors took "no great interest" in the proceedings, since they concerned them only indirectly (147), as the voivodes' frequent reports of poor turnout at electoral meetings suggest. Last but not least, Muscovy lacked the local assemblies that characterized institutional life in more developed polities, notably the *seimiki* in Poland-Lithuania.

The present writer shares this reasoning and would, if pressed, acknowledge that he may have inflated the Sobor's importance and the degree of resonance it acquired among the public of the day: evidence on this point is notoriously thin. Nevertheless lingering doubts remain as to whether Torke's schema represents fully actual realities, as distinct from what was supposed to occur. In the course of his study the author seems to modify the rather austere principles from which he sets out and to take a more flexible view. If the Sobor consisted of "representatives of (various) interests," as the term *Interessenvertretungen* (141) seems to suggest, this surely implies that the *chiny* were expected a) to know and articulate their own respective interests (if not those of others); and b) to convey them accurately to the authorities. If this was so, then the way was open for them legitimately to influence the shaping of policy if the circumstances of the moment permitted. This is precisely our modest point: that at certain epochs the official, traditional view of what the Sobor was and should do could not in practice be sustained; that relationships became less hierarchical and more fluid whenever a power vacuum appeared, and that such situations could be exploited by advocates of special interests, to which pressures the government, forced on the defensive, was obliged to respond. We need not seek to press all the assemblies into a single typological mold, but should rather view them as acquiring and forfeiting a more active role in policy formation which never became institutionalized.

We further maintain that the "gray eras" when political realities no longer corresponded to the image held of them by right-thinking Muscovites were not brief episodes but of considerable duration. The "high points" of public activity that occurred in 1611–13 and 1648–49 should not be seen as exceptions, radically different from the norm, but rather as occupying one extreme in a continuum, at the other end of which lies the decade (1622–32) when no Sobors were held.

At this point we need to introduce personalities: the tsars, patriarchs, and other *sil'nye liudi* who for some reason both Cherepnin and Torke are reluctant to incorpo-

---

18 Goehrke, *JGOE*, 416, accepts it, but Crummey is more sceptical.

rate into their accounts. Yet in any autocracy the personal attributes of the autocrat, and of the favorites at his court, cannot but play a decisive role in affairs, and it is not mere antiquarianism to recognize this. According to the consensus view Tsar Michael was a nonentity, a cipher whose rule was nominal at least for the first twenty years of his reign, whereas his father Filaret was an experienced politician with *idées fixes*, not to say solid prejudices; later Alexis, who like his father acceded to the throne at a tender age, was at first the tool of powerful courtiers (Morozov, Nikon) but by 1652–53 had acquired a clear idea of the "good order" he was determined to impose on his subjects, and of his objectives in military and foreign policy.[19] It is no accident that in periods of relatively strong government the "assembly of the realm" should have been eclipsed and royal consultations confined to boiars and occasional *ad hoc* gatherings of special interest groups.

Torke agrees that Filaret owed his election as patriarch in 1619 to an act of spontaneous acclamation, not to any regular body (*geordnetes Gremium*, 176), and that he put over his ideas first to the clergy and then to an assembly (perhaps the same one) which again had an "acclamatory" character; only then did he call elections to a more representative body. About its proceedings unfortunately nothing is known, but in all likelihood the Sobor did not meet continuously until 1622, as earlier historians thought. Cherepnin (235) takes issue with Stashevskii's views (which we accepted: 59) of a decline in the Sobor's role after 1619, as reflected in the wording of the summonses; he argues that one should go by its actions, not words. But these actions, alas, seem to have been important only in October 1621—and that meeting was a simple *odnodnevka*, a one-day affair. The ten-year "suspension" of the Sobor after March 1622 (or October 1621), Torke contends, was not due to the new ruler's preference for limited, "private" consultations, but to the fact that until 1632 no emergency occurred that would have required convocation of a Sobor, since the assembly's purpose, after all, was "just to render reports and sanction government initiatives" (181: "blossen Berichterstttung und Sanktion von Regierungsvorlagen"). Furthermore, prior to 1622 Filaret did summon several consultative gatherings which included two Sobors, and in 1632 he summoned a third. Now there is certainly something to this explanation, but it seems strained. Of problems there surely were plenty (the cadaster, for example); in the first three years after his return the patriarch was still finding his feet (customs could not be dispensed with overnight); and by 1632 his anti-Polish belligerence was arousing misgivings among élite servitors. The 1619 Sobor, moreover, took a line subtly different from that of the government, as Torke himself agrees (177), following P. P. Smirnov and ourselves, which can scarcely have endeared it to the new men now at the helm.

Similarly, the more frequent convocation of assemblies after 1633 needs to be seen in the light of the post-Filaret government's internal strains and its tendency to drift as major domestic and foreign problems mounted (administrative abuses, peasant flights, Tatar attacks). Cherepnin fails even to mention Filaret's death. It was in these years that the practice of collective petitioning by gentry servitors and townspeople

---

19 Longworth, *Alexis*, 47–91.

took root (a matter which Torke investigates elsewhere in his volume), so preparing
the ground for the resurgence of public activity that culminated in the open dissidence
of 1648.

The same "dynamic" can be observed in Alexis's reign, with postwar disillusionment (1667) and the emergence of rival court factions (1672) leading to a new period
of political instability, which lasted until the end of the century. But now the bureaucracy and the "new formation" army gave the autocracy fresh sources of strength; the
Sobors were just a memory.

The last public call for a Sobor was by the merchants and Moscow townspeople
in 1662. Torke offers (203) an interpretation of this episode which upholds nicely
the symmetry of his thesis and is in itself not implausible: that the petitioners may
simply have wanted other groups to share with them the responsibility for endorsing
the government's ruinous monetary policy, so as not to be made the scapegoats for it.
This explanation still appears less likely than the obvious one: that they valued such
occasions for their own sake, since they offered an opportunity to win the support
of other groups for their sectional demands. Admittedly, neither hypothesis can be
verified.

The assumption that the Sobor was deliberately suppressed by the government,
with the tacit support of its officials, gentry servitors, and the Church, which we
upheld in "The Decline of the Zemskii Sobor," certainly needs to be filled out:
as Torke notes (208), it leaves many questions open. If the Sobor enjoyed popular
support, why was there not more resistance to its demise? Why did not the authorities
replace it by regular gatherings of a more limited composition? On the other hand, if
the assembly had been totally devoid of independent spirit, its enforced disappearance
would have been counterproductive and thus even harder to explain.

One way out of the dilemma is to assume, with Cherepnin, that it did not really die
anyway,[20] but continued in a modified form until the 1680s: this puts the responsibility
on Peter I, who reconstituted the entire political order. But this argument is not
available to those who think that the Sobor faded out already in 1650–53.

To the reasons we gave should be added the government's growing international
self-confidence after its initial successes in the Thirteen Years' War; the heavy domestic stresses imposed by this conflict, which necessitated a tightening of the reins;
and possibly the influence of an enfeebled Poland-Lithuania as a "negative exemplar"
of parliamentarianism—an example that lay much closer at hand than that of England
under the Commonwealth!

Torke's solution to the riddle is subtly nuanced and on the whole persuasive. He
contends that there was no latent conflict between the administration and the assembly (as we suppose), for this is to transfer the West European estate concept to Rus',
where it could have no place since there were no *Stände*. No one saw the ruler's
failure to convoke the assembly as a breach of privilege, for the very idea that so-

---

20 "The Zemskii Sobors lasted . . . up to Peter I" (346). Curiously enough, this formulation is
   identical with Cherepnin's summary of the Slavophile view (8)! So far as we know Peter
   never referred to the Sobor.

cial groups bore some joint responsibility for the "Sovereign's affairs" appeared only episodically, in 1611–13 and 1648–49. Yet, Torke concedes, Muscovite Russia's "state-conditioned" society was not *wholly* passive, amorphous, and concerned with the defense of narrow group interests. There was a "spirit of resistance" (*Widerstandsgeist*), best evidenced by the joint action of servitors and townspeople in 1648, which *did* alarm the government (212).

But is this not to have one's cake and eat it too? If it is conceded that the Sobor could be "turned" in this way by action from below, it is hard to see why such an absolute, qualitative distinction should be drawn between Russia's sociopolitical structure and that of countries to the west. Why should it be "senseless" (*sinnlos*: a harsh epithet!)[21] to compare the Sobor's "external forms, internal organization and tasks" (132) with those of Western states-general in their earliest phases? After all, to compare is not necessarily to equate. We see the Sobor as an embryonic states-general—a "poor relation," so to speak, which does not deserve on account of its indigence to be excluded from the family. If a conflict situation could arise even in Muscovy's "state-conditioned" society, may not this antagonism be viewed as a milder variant of the conflicts which elsewhere took the form of mature constitutional struggles? In this case the inability of Muscovite Russia's *chiny* to institutionalize the political influence they acquired at the "high points" of social activism appears, not as some irredeemable congenital defect, but rather as a reflection of the country's cultural backwardness, of its centuries-long isolation from the rest of Europe. It was a historic lag that with time could be made good—just as the *chiny* of servitors eventually, after 1775/1785, became an authentic "estate" of *dvoriane*, comparable (but by no means identical!) with the gentry of Western and Central Europe.

To the pessimist, they say, the wine-glass appears half-empty, to the optimist half-full. The scientific way of finding out the truth is to measure the amount of wine in the glass. Now that Professors Cherepnin and Torke, each according to his lights, have accomplished this task for the Zemskii Sobor, so far as the sparse sources permit, it is surely time for the full scale comparative study on which the liberal historian B. N. Chicherin embarked over a century ago. The last words of the late Cherepnin's monograph may stand as a challenge: "the comparative method of historical analysis promises a great deal" (401)—provided, of course, that future researchers avoid the perceptual errors that his colleague has masterfully identified.

1985

---

21 In a letter to the present writer (March 1, 1985), Torke says that by the epithet "senseless" he meant only that "it leads nowhere, or only to false hopes, if one applies the West European model."

CHAPTER 3

Bandits and the Law in Muscovy

I

One of the most striking features of the domestic scene in Muscovite Russia was the prevalence of crime, and in particular of banditry. A tradition of lawlessness had existed from the earliest times, and the growing power of the state and the landowning gentry gave ample cause for popular grievances. The peasant who sought to evade oppression, if he did not join in the mass exodus to the unsettled border lands, would commonly associate with one of the numerous gangs of outcasts which roamed the country, living off the land and wreaking violence on those in authority who ventured to resist them. Such bands were sometimes more than a hundred strong and organized on a paramilitary basis under an *ataman*. They planned their operations methodically, ambushing traveling merchants or peasants bringing their taxes to the capital, or descending suddenly on an estate to reap the crops as they stood awaiting the harvesters. The extensive forests of northern Russia provided excellent possibilities for concealment, and bandits might continue to exist unmolested for several years.[1]

To the government, banditry was a menace to internal security which had to be suppressed by every possible means. The attitude of the people was more equivocal: at times they might refuse to cooperate with the authorities, or give positive support to the bandits by acting as guides and lookouts, affording them shelter, or receiving stolen property. In extreme cases the *ataman* might become a popular hero whose exploits were celebrated in song and legend.[2]

Brigandage was particularly rife in the years following the Time of Troubles, when the authority of the state was temporarily disrupted. Companies of marauding cossacks and Tatars roamed as far as the shores of the White Sea, where according to a local account they killed over two thousand people.[3] In the Beloozero area regular

---

1 S. M. Solov'ev, *Istoriia Rossii s drevneishikh vremen*[2], 6 vols. (St. Petersburg, 1896), II, 487, 637, III, 732; N. V. Kalachov, *Arteli v drevnei i nyneshnei Rossii* (St. Petersburg, 1864), 16; *Chteniia IOIDR*, LXXI (1869), V, 36.

2 *Pesni sobrannye P. V. Kireevskim; izd. Obshchestva liubitelei rossiiskoi slovesnosti*, 10 parts (Moscow, 1860–74), VI (1864), 199.

3 *AAE*, III, no. 64.

engagements took place between such bands and troops, and Novgorod province was
also severely affected.[4] The troops themselves sometimes joined in the looting.[5] The
German traveler Olearius, who visited Moscow in 1636, states that bands of nocturnal
marauders caused the death of 15 people in the city during 11 successive nights.[6] The
eventual complete enserfment of the peasants, and subsequently the persecution of
the *raskol'niki*, swelled the flow of recruits to the bandits' lairs. A guarded offer of
an amnesty by the patriarch was apparently ineffective.[7] Documents relating to the
years 1658 and 1659 show that attacks were proceeding in all parts of the country.[8]
On the troubled southern frontier and along the lower reaches of the Volga violence
never ceased. In the last decade of the century the problem remained as intractable
as ever, with clashes between troops and robber bands in several areas.[9] As the
independent-minded Pososhkov commented

> For many years great efforts have been made to eliminate bandits . . . but all in vain;
> everywhere, except in Pomor'e and Zaonezh'e, there is always a large number of them,
> committing many robberies, destroying many large villages and killing people. And
> there will never be an end to these bandits unless the present administration of justice is
> changed and the thing that causes them to exist is abolished.[10]

Let us now consider the system which aroused such scornful and well-merited criticism.

II

It was an indication of the seriousness of the bandit problem in Russia that special
institutions were evolved to deal with it. For the greater part of the Muscovite period
the task of suppressing brigandage and other crimes was performed by elected local
authorities. The creation of a comprehensive centrally maintained police apparatus
was obviously impracticable in such primitive economic and political conditions.
Willy-nilly, the government had to rely largely on local initiative and resources. In
spite of their manifold limitations, and the vicissitudes which they underwent during
the century and a half that they existed, the so-called *guba*[11] institutions were the

---

4 *Op. cit.*, nos. 44, 50, 53, 57–61; *DAI*, II, no. 23.

5 *AAE*, III, nos. 34, 167; *AIuB*, II, no. 193.

6 Adam Olearius, *Vermehrte newe Beschreibung der Muscowitischen und Persischen Reyse . . .*
   (Schleswig, 1656), 199; [S. H. Baron, tr. and ed., *The Travels of Olearius in Seventeenth-
   Century Russia* (Stanford, 1967), 150.]

7 *PSZ*, I, no. 163 (1655).

8 *Dela Tainogo Prikaza*, I, (*RIB*, XXI) (St. Petersburg, 1907), 658–64.

9 *AI*, V, nos. 219–254.

10 I. T. Pososhkov, *Kniga o skudosti i bogatstve i drugie sochineniia*, ed. B. B. Kafengauz
   (Moscow, 1951), 151. His own proposals for reform, however, were remarkable neither for
   consistency nor for originality.

11 The origin of the term *guba* is not clear. Tatishchev's derivation from *gubiti* "to destroy,"

most adequate representative bodies in pre-Petrine Russia. A study of their fate throws considerable light upon the crucial problem of the relations between the local communities and the bureaucratic state.[12]

Guba authorities were first introduced by charters granted individually to certain districts in response to a petition by the inhabitants. Fourteen such charters, most of them dated between 1539 and the mid-1550s, are extant.[13] The petitioners referred to the frequency of bandit attacks and complained that the special agents sent out by the government had oppressed them, adding that they did not dare to take action themselves without permission. They were now ordered to consult together and elect suitable persons to put down banditry.[14]

The significance of this reform is not entirely clear. Earlier historians, regard-

---

although challenged long ago, is still adhered to by K. Kadlec, *Introduction à l'étude comparative de l'histoire du droit public des peuples slaves* (Paris, 1933), 185. The view that it derives from Germanic *huopa, huba* "an area of cultivated land" is more convincing. The *guba* was an ancient administrative-territorial unit in northwestern Russia, and the term was still current in the nineteenth century. (Cf. §76 of the fifteenth century *Pskovskaia sudnaia gramota* (*PRP*, II (1953), 296); F. M. Dmitriev, *Istoriia sudebnykh instantsii i grazhdansskogo appelliatsionnogo sudoproizvodstva ot Sudebnika do Uchrezhdeniia o Guberniakh* (Moscow, 1859), 52; N. P. Retvikh, "Termin 'guba', opredelenie 'gubnoi gramoty', prichiny vozniknoveniia 'gubnogo instituta' . . . ," *Vestnik arkheologii i istorii*, IX (St. Petersburg, 1892), 185–6). The name probably spread from there to central Russia, where it was applied to indigenous local institutions, and ultimately throughout the country: S. Shumakov, *Gubnye i zemskie gramoty Moskovskogo gosudarstva* (Moscow, 1895), 15. The idea advanced by some early writers that the institution itself was Germanic may be disregarded in the light of modern research into the parallel development of judicial institutions and practises: cf. especially A. S. Diamond, *The Evolution of Law and Order* (London, 1951). Retvikh breaks new ground in pointing to similarities between the Russian *gubnoe pravo* and the Swedish *hauld* law, but hedges on the vital question of a direct link. After referring to "a certain kinship" he says the similarities were only "coincidental": *op. cit.*, 183–4.

12 The principal documents, the *guba* charters and the Statute Book of the Banditry Office, have been competently analyzed by Shumakov, *op. cit.*, N. Shalfeev, *Ob ustavnoi knige Razboinogo Prikaza* (St. Petersburg, 1868), and M. F. Vladimirskii-Budanov, annotated text of the Statute Book, *Khrestomatiia po istorii russkogo prava*[4], 3 parts (St. Petersburg-Kiev, 1908). The pioneer work of B. N. Chicherin, *Oblastnye uchrezhdeniia Rossii v XVII veke* (St. Petersburg, 1856), is still an indispensable guide to Muscovite local institutions. N. P. Retvikh's study of the *guba* system, "Organy gubnogo upravleniia v XVI i XVII vekakh," *Sbornik pravovedeniia i obshchestvennykh znanii*, VI (St. Petersburg, 1896) is valuable, although like many nineteenth-century writers his approach is juridical rather than historical. Soviet historians have hitherto devoted little attention to Muscovite administrative structure.

13 Shumakov, *Gubnye gramoty*, 18 ff.; "Novye gubnye i zemskie gramoty," *Zhurnal Ministerstva Narodnogo Prosveshcheniia*, XXIII (St. Petersburg, 1909), 329 ff. They are conveniently reproduced in A. I. Iakovlev, ed., *Namestnich'i, gubnye i zemskie ustavnye gramoty Moskovskogo gosudarstva* (Moscow, 1909), and references are to this edition. With the compilation of the Statute Book of the Banditry Office, the provisions of which were valid for the whole country, individual charters were issued only in exceptional circumstances (e.g. to replace or confirm a charter granted before the 1550s).

14 Iakovlev, *Namestnich'i . . . gramoty*, nos. 1, 2, 3, 6.

ing it primarily as a prelude to the "territorial" reform (*zemskaia reforma*) of the 1550s, which substituted a form of local self-government for the tyrannical rule of the prince's lieutenants (*namestniki*), tended to interpret it as a deliberate concession to popular aspirations.[15] But it seems clear that the government was building on a sound foundation of existing custom. The privilege of jurisdiction over criminal matters sometimes granted to monasteries in the fifteenth century[16] can be regarded as a precedent for the subsequent granting of such privileges to entire communities. Shumakov may perhaps be correct in contending that the *guba* system had in fact already evolved spontaneously by the beginning of the sixteenth century, although there is no sound evidence to support his theory.[17] Pokrovskii also pleads for its spontaneous origin, but dates this only from the 1530s.[18] If this view be accepted, the significance of the reform lies in the fact that it gave a semiofficial character to a practice that already existed *de facto* in some parts of the country and extended it to new areas as an act of state policy. The government was not concerned with advancing the rights of the communities, and regarded these institutions from the standpoint of state interest. Its motives were utilitarian, not ideological: the power to deal with bandits was given to the local population only because the situation had become critical and the state lacked agents of its own capable of performing this task.[19] However, the real question is not the motives of the government, but the opportunities which were opened up by the reform: could it be a starting point for a development of popular rights? Of course, in yielding to popular demands, the government was imposing an obligation on the communities as much as conceding them a privilege. But it would be wrong to assume that the communities regarded their new duties merely as a burden: in its initial phase the *guba* system had a certain popular flavor which it lost when it later became bureaucratized.

The compiler of the First Pskov Chronicle, with healthy democratic bias, welcomed the reform as a victory in the struggle against Muscovite rule:

> The men of Pskov received such a charter, and the wardens and "centurions" of Pskov began to try evildoers in the prince's court, in the court-room by the Velikaia river, and to put them to death . . . And there was, as lieutenant in Pskov, only Prince Vasilii Repnin-Obolenskii, and he greatly hated the men of Pskov, because they had a charter

---

15 An extreme statement of this view was made by the slavophil I. D. Beliaev, who argued that the reform represented a conscious attempt to return to the old democratic communal ways of government instead of relying upon the bureaucratic state administration. Cf. I. M. Sobest'ianskii, *Krugovaia poruka u slavian po drevnim pamiatnikam ikh zakonodatel'stva* (Khar'kov, 1888), 129.

16 *AAE*, I, no. 35.

17 Shumakov, *Gubnye gramoty*, 41.

18 M. N. Pokrovskii, "Mestnoe samoupravlenie v drevnei Rusi," *Melkaia zemskaia edinitsa; sbornik statei K. K. Arsen'eva* (St. Petersburg, [1903]), 211 note. Cf. V. Sergeevich, *Lektsii i issledovaniia po drevnei istorii russkogo prava*[3] (St. Petersburg, 1903), 302.

19 Chicherin, *Oblastnye uchrezhdeniia*, 450; Retvikh, "Termin 'guba,'" 188, 195–6; Sobestianskii, *op. cit.*, 130.

from the Sovereign like a mirror of justice. And the Christians were joyful and had much relief from evildoers . . . and from the lieutenants and their agents, who travel around the district; and the men of Pskov began to pray to God for the Sovereign . . . as he had shown mercy unto his people.[20]

As this account shows, at first new authorities were not established expressly for the purpose of dealing with criminal matters, which were the function of the ordinary local elders. The Belozersk *guba* charter provides for new elections to be held, but the men elected are referred to as "chosen chiefs" (*izliublennye golovy*), and the term *guba* is not used at all.[21] The celebrated charters of self-government granted to the Vaga and Dvina districts in 1552 and 1556 respectively gave the local elders (*zemskie starosty*) authority over matters which were later to become the specific concern of the *guba* authorities. The earliest charter of this kind, which has only recently been discovered, contains a similar provision.[22] In districts which were granted special judicial privileges, criminal matters were dealt with by a joint court in which both the elected popular judges and the *guba* authorities were present.[23] Normally however by this time, the *guba* system had become separated from the regular organs of local self-government, where the latter managed to survive.[24]

Wherever crimes were dealt with either wholly or partly by popular judges, this had the important effect of allowing the community some influence over the proceedings. True, the penalties were doubtless equally harsh, and one need not unduly idealize this early "democratic" phase, which was in any case shortlived. But, to some extent at least, the interests of the community were at first protected against abuse by agents of the state power, so that the election of *guba* authorities was still valued as something advantageous. It would however be misleading to interpret the fact that *guba* authorities were elected in a modern sense, as if it indicated that they were *ipso facto* "democratic." Like all Muscovite popular institutions, the *guba* system was based upon the principle of mutual guarantee (*krugovaia poruka*). The elected authorities were responsible not to the electorate, but to an office of the central government. Election ensured not that the person elected would act in the interests of the population, but that he and they would each fulfill their respective obligations to the state. If they did not do so, the elected person, and ultimately those who had elected him, would be liable to pay the appropriate penalty and to satisfy any private claims against them.

A *guba* charter was granted to any community, irrespective of size, which petitioned for one. Whether the privileged area was an entire district (*uezd*) or a group

---

20 *Pskovskie letopisi*, 2 vols. (Moscow-Leningrad, 1941–55), I, 110.

21 Iakovlev, *Namestnich'i . . . gramoty*, no. 1.

22 Ibid., nos. 2, 8; also A. I. Kopanev, ed., "Ustavnaia gramota krestianam trekh volostei Dvinskogo uezda 25 fevralia 1552 g.," *Istoricheskii arkhiv*, VIII (Moscow, 1953), 8.

23 Iakovlev, *Namestnich'i . . . gramoty*, nos. 7, 9, 12.

24 Ibid., no. 4, 5, 13.

of estates or rural cantons (*volosti*),[25] the *guba* authorities at first existed at the lowest level, each estate or canton having its own elder. Sometimes they would settle among themselves minor cases affecting several cantons and meet in the chief town of the neighborhood to consult on major matters.[26] But in course of time this changed: in the Beloozero area the multiple authorities established in 1539 were in 1571 subordinated to two officials whose writ ran over the whole area, and a similar process of concentration took place on the great private estates.[27] Subsequently *guba* authorities generally existed only at the higher regional level.

This change is of the greatest importance: the adjustment of *guba* institutions to the standard administrative territorial unit, the *uezd* (district), denotes their increasingly official character. It is about this time that they lose the somewhat amorphous nature that they had originally possessed and become distinct institutions, with their own personnel clearly differentiated from the elected judges in the regular local administration. Simultaneously they cease to be the privilege of individual districts and become a national institution, existing generally throughout the country.[28] All these developments, which can be traced back to the mid-1550s, are closely interconnected. The main thread in the subsequent history of the *guba* institutions is the intensification of their bureaucratic features. The process becomes especially marked after the Time of Troubles, until a new and even more centralized apparatus is introduced in the 1660s.

III

Lets us first examine the system as it was established in the time of Ivan the Terrible.

---

25 *Guba* charters nos. 1–4, 7, 8 serve as examples of the former and nos. 5, 6, and 9 of the latter.

26 Iakovlev, *op. cit.*, nos. 6, 10.

27 Ibid., nos. 1 and 8, 5 and 9; Chicherin, *Oblastnye uchrezhdeniia*, 452–3; V. O. Kliuchevskii, *Kurs russkoi istorii*, 5 vols. (Moscow, 1937), II, 382; A. D. Gradovskii, *Sobranie sochinenii*, 5 vols. (St. Petersburg, 1899–1904), II (1899), 209 ff.

28 This does not necessarily mean that they existed universally, either in the sixteenth century or later. The Pskov chronicle and official legislative acts refer to them as existing "in all towns": *AI*, II, no. 355, *AAE*, III, no. 171; cf. *Sudebnik* of 1550, §60 (*Sudebniki XV–XVI vv.* (Moscow-Leningrad, 1952), 160.) But this can be taken as evidence only of an intention to make them universal; in any case uniformity was never a characteristic feature of Muscovite administration. Shumakov alone is inclined to accept these statements at their face value (*op. cit.*, 40); the other authorities do not however examine the evidence in detail. A study of the location of the *guba* institutions mentioned in published documents (cf. in particular the official list, apparently incomplete, compiled *c.* 1628–9, in *Vremennik IOIDR* (1849), III, 6–8) shows that they were concentrated in the center, northwest and northeast of the country. There is no record of any existing south of Voronezh, in Siberia, or in the extreme north (Pomor'e). In this area, where there were no gentry from whom *guba* elders could be recruited, criminal justice was administered partly by the voivodes and partly by local organs of self-government, which survived here long after they had died out elsewhere. Cf. M. M. Bogoslovskii, *Zemskoe samoupravlenie na russkom severe x XVII veke*, 2 vols. (Moscow, 1909–12) II, 225 ff.

Owing to the scarcity of material for this period, it will be necessary to draw upon seventeenth-century documents where appropriate.

The principal figure, the *guba* elder (*gubnoi starosta*), was elected at a meeting attended by all classes of the population: clergy, gentry, townsmen and peasants from "black" as well as private estates.[29] Where any social group was absent, this can be attributed to exceptional local circumstances.[30] The meeting was called by the local voivode (*voevoda*) or equivalent authority, who could compel reluctant gentry to appear by arresting them or their serfs.[31] An election document (*vybor*), signed by all the electors, was compiled and sent to the Banditry Office in Moscow. At first it sufficed for the fact of the election to be reported, but later the elder himself was required to make the journey to the capital. Here his qualifications were verified, and he was sworn in and issued with the official deed by virtue of which he exercised his functions.[32] A unanimous vote was the rule, although strictly speaking it was not essential. The government intervened in the elections at Novotorzhok in 1627, when the richer gentry were attempting to elect a man from the poorer grade, and ordered them all to vote "for the same *guba* elder, and not differently, so that there should be no dispute in future about who should be the elder."[33] But its aim was not to punish the "opposition" for its views, but to obtain the best possible guarantee that the community would fulfill its obligations. Elections were thus never "free" in the modern sense. In some of the later *guba* charters the government actually named the men who were to be elected.[34] The phrase "according to their petition" suggests that they may have been proposed for office by the petitioners, but this can hardly have been the case in the instance when Tsar Theodore I declared: "I . . . have ordered to be elected as *guba* elders and wardens whomsoever our *boiar* Dmitriy Ivanovich [Godunov] shall order to be elected."[35] This apparent contradiction is comprehensible only when it is recalled that the essence of the electoral act is not the choice of a representative but the signing of the *vybor*.

Only members of the gentry were considered reliable enough to occupy this responsible post. They were expected to be "noblemen of wealth and good repute who have been excused service . . . and who are literate."[36] The office of *guba* elder pos-

---

29 *AAE*, II, no. 170; *AI*, III, no. 150; *Ukaznaia kniga Razboinogo Prikaza* [hereafter cited as UKRP], §56; *Sobornoe Ulozhenie tsaria Alekseia Mikhailovicha 1649 g.* [hereafter cited as *Ulozhenie*] (Moscow, 1907), ch. XXI, §4 [also in *Sobornoe Ulozhenie 1649 g.: posobie dlia vysshei shkoly*, ed. M. N. Tikhomirov and P. P. Epifanov (Moscow, 1961).]

30 *AAE*, IV, no. 72; *DAI*, I, no. 176; Retvikh, "Organy," 262.

31 *Drevnie gramoty . . . kasaiushchiesia Voronezhskoi gubernii . . .*, ed. P. Vtorov and K. Alexandrova-Dol'nikov, 3 vols. (Voronezh, 1851–3), I, no. 35, as cited by Retvikh, *op. cit.*, 262; Chicherin, *Oblastnye uchrezhdeniia*, 456.

32 Iakovlev, *Namestnich'i . . . gramoty*, no. 9 (i); UKRP, §59; *Ulozhenie*, ch. XXI, §4; Retvikh, "Termin 'guba,'" 264; Chicherin, *op. cit.*, 459.

33 *AAE*, III, no. 171.

34 Iakovlev, *op. cit.*, nos. 6, 8, 9 (ii).

35 *Ibid.*, no. 10.

36 *Ulozhenie*, ch. XXI, §4.

sessed an attraction for those who sought to evade their onerous service obligations. The literacy requirement was in practice often difficult to comply with, and the authorities were not too exacting if the man chosen was otherwise suitable.[37] The elder was normally a local man. In ruling that he should belong to the wealthiest grade of the gentry, the government was concerned less with social status than with obtaining the best guarantee that he would be able to meet the demands that might be imposed on him. The period for which he was to hold office was not fixed by law; on an average, he served a two-year term, but there were cases of men serving for periods of up to fourteen years.[38] Nor did the law state how many elders were to serve in each district. Their number varied according to time and place: Pereiaslavl'-Riazan', for example, had three in 1647, two in 1666, and one in 1677.[39]

As head of the *guba* apparatus in the area, the elder had full authority over his subordinates, of whom the most important were the wardens (*gubnye tseloval'niki*). These functionaries, who were peasants or townsmen, played a part similar to the popular representatives required to be present in the lieutenants' courts to see that justice was properly done.[40] Originally they acted as a counterweight to the authority of the *guba* elder, but formally their duties were confined to assisting the elder in his work, and in course of time their status declined. Unlike the elder, the wardens were elected only by taxpaying classes. For this purpose the canton was divided into several portions (*kosti*) of varying size, each comprising one or more peasant communities or private estates. The inhabitants of each portion would elect their own warden independently, binding themselves to pay him a certain sum of money for his maintenance, which might be as high as five roubles a year.[41] The obligation to provide a warden was onerous for a poor community, and the government tried to equalize the burden, first by ordering that it should be borne mainly by the larger estates, and eventually by excusing small estates altogether.[42] Here again electors were required to sign an election document, which was sent to the authorities in the

37 Iakovlev, *op. cit.*, no. 9 (ii); Retvikh, "Termin 'guba,'" 261.

38 F. Kishkin was *guba* elder in Shuia from 1622 to 1635, and L. V. Kishkin from 1651 to 1665. V. Borisov, *Opisanie goroda Shui i ego okrestnostei s prilozheniem starinnykh aktov* (Moscow, 1851), nos. 12, 14, 16, 18; cf. the table in N. P. Retvikh, "Termin 'guba,'" Appendix II. F. Epifanov held office at Kashin in 1628–9 and his son, I. Epifanov, in 1659. Cf. I. Ia. Kunkin, "Gorod Kashin: materialy dlia ego istorii," *Chteniia IOIDR*, CCVII (1903), I, nos. 6, 7, 31. But, of course, neither this nor any other office in the Muscovite administration ever became hereditary as of right.

39 N. P. Retvikh, *op. cit.*, 264–5, and Appendix I; Dmitriev, *Istoriia*, 54; Chicherin, *Oblastnye uchrezhdeniia*, 460.

40 Sudebnik of 1497, §38. Cf. Sudebnik of 1550, §62, where the term *tseloval'niki* is used in place of the earlier *lutchie liudi*; the practice of swearing them in testified to their more official status. The rendering "warden" gives a clearer idea of their function than the more literal "juror."

41 *AAE*, II, no. 19; III, no. 163; *DAI*, I, no. 176; *AIuB*, II, no. 246 (v); *AIu*, no. 352; Retvikh, "Termin 'guba,'" 284; Chicherin, *op. cit.*, 462.

42 *AAE*, II, no. 19; *Ulozhenie*, ch. XXI, §98.

capital, but generally wardens were sworn in locally.[43] They were chosen from the "best" section of the taxpaying population; literacy was not obligatory. In spite of the onerous nature of their duties they sometimes held office for as long as ten years. Where the government intervened, it ordered adherence to the rule of annual elections. Generally there seem to have been three or four wardens to each canton, but local custom was the determining factor.[44]

Some cantons had a *guba* clerk (*gubnoi d'iachok*) who was in charge of all the written work. Normally, like the elder, he was elected by all classes in the canton and confirmed in office personally in Moscow. Where he was engaged on contract, a loss of status was indicated, for this was the usual method of obtaining the services of the remaining members of the *guba* personnel: the executioner, the crier, and the prison warders.[45] Collectively, these officials comprised an institution called, after their place of work, the *guba* office (*gubnaia izba*). A contract for the construction of one such building has been preserved and allows us to form an impression of its appearance.[46]

A rudimentary police system, consisting of the "centurion" (*sotskii*) and his subordinate "quinquagenaries" and "tithingmen" (*piatidesiatskie, desiatskie*) already existed when the *guba* authorities were established. They survived the reform as independent bodies, but recognized the authority of the *guba* elder in certain matters.[47] It is difficult to accept Retvikh's view that their titles still bore some relation to the number of people under their authority: here too it seems more likely that the number appointed was determined by local tradition.[48] In practice they often became moribund; if a subsequent increase in crime drew the attention of the government to the fact, it would intervene to re-establish them.[49]

Originally the competence of the *guba* authorities was confined to the prevention and suppression of banditry.[50] But soon they were given jurisdiction over the closely

---

43 *Ulozhenie*, ch. XXI, §4; *AAE*, III, no. 210, IV, no. 22. Citing these sources, Retvikh, *op. cit.*, 282, states that before the Code it was the practise to send wardens to Moscow to be sworn in. But the former document explicitly states that only the election document is to be sent, and in the latter instance the warden was doubtless only required to attend personally because exceptional local circumstances prevented the normal procedure from being followed.

44 *AAE*, II, no. 19; III, nos. 163, 210; IV, no. 22; N. P. Retvikh, *op. cit.*, 283; Chicherin, *Oblastnye uchrezhdeniia*, 464.

45 *Alu*, no. 352; *AluB*, no. 230 (ii); *AAE*, III, no. 163; Borisov, *Opisanie . . . Shui*, nos. 7, 14, 48; *UKRP*, §57.

46 *DAI*, X, no. 43.

47 *AAE*, I, no. 244; IV, no. 92; *AI*, V, no. 111; *Vremennik IOIDR*, XXIV (1856), III, 42.

48 In Shuia, for example, it was the custom to elect four such officials, without regard to fluctuations in the population: Borisov, *Opisanie Shui*, no. 41.

49 *Op. cit.*, nos. 11, 41; *Sbornik kniazia Khilkova* (St. Petersburg, 1879), 265.

50 Iakovlev, *Namestnich'i . . . gramoty*, nos. 1, 2, 4, 5.

related offences of theft[51] and murder.[52] In the seventeenth century their competence was widened still further to include sacrilege, forgery, serious offences against morality, and eventually arson and even heresy, while their police powers were extended to cover the suppression of witchcraft, prostitution and gaming.[53] But measures against banditry remained the core of their activities, and it is worth looking briefly at the procedure which they employed in such cases.

This had two conspicuous elements: the inquest (*poval'nyi obysk*) and interrogation under torture. The form taken by the inquest in Muscovy corresponds closely with that of the *jurée du pays* in ninth-century France.[54] All classes of the local population were summoned, sworn, and required to give information regarding the whereabouts of known bandits in the district.[55] This "police inquest," which was preventive in purpose, can be distinguished from the inquest applied as a means of proof, in which those present were required to return a plain answer to the question whether a certain suspect was known as a bandit.[56] The inquest procedure was based on the assumption that a community always knew the truth about its members; if a man's fellows cleared him of suspicion, they had to stand surety for him.[57]

To be valid, an inquest had to be as comprehensive as possible. Those present had to be of good repute, and in view of the distances involved, inquests must have been to some extent representative; but it is misleading to say that they were attended not by everyone who knew the accused, but "only by those completely reliable from the point of view of the ruling class."[58] The accused was not allowed to be present and therefore could not defend himself against a false indictment. Severe penalties

---

51 *Ibid.*, nos. 3, 6, and all subsequent charters. But cf. *Sudebnik* of 1550, §60, where theft is still reserved to the lieutenants; also *UKRP*, §§1, 37–9; *Ulozhenie*, ch. XXI, §§9 ff.

52 Iakovlev, *op. cit.*, nos. 9 (ii), II; *UKRP*, supplementary article II.

53 Iakovlev, *loc. cit.*; *UKRP*, §40; *Ulozhenie*, ch. XXI, §§11, 14, 15, 90–92; *Novoukaznye stat'i o tatebnykh, razboinykh i ubiistvennykh delakh* [hereafter cited as *Novoukaznye stat'i*], in *PSZ*, I, no. 441 (1669), §§109–110, 128.

54 Cf. E. Brunner, *Die Entstehung der Schwurgerichte* (Berlin, 1871), 106–126, 462. As one would expect, Muscovite practise followed the general custom of returning individual replies instead of the collective reply that in England later formed the point of departure for the development of the trial jury.

55 Iakovlev, *op. cit.*, nos. 8, 9 (ii); *UKRP*, §42; *Ulozhenie*, ch. XXI, §5; *Novoukaznye stat'i*, §§118–20. For a practical application, see Borisov, *op. cit.*, no. 27.

56 The two types of inquest were not necessarily physically distinct, since a "police inquest," at which certain people present were pointed out as bandits, would automatically constitute itself an inquest of the second type.

57 *UKRP*, §§2, 3, 7, 27; *Ulozhenie*, §§36–7, 42, 61; *Novoukaznye stat'i*, §§27, 34, 58.

58 S. I. Shtamm, *Sudebnik 1497 g.* (Moscow, 1955), 70–1. It was only in civil inquests that the law sought to limit attendance to "the best people" (*Ukaznaia kniga vedomstva kaznacheev*, §3); at criminal inquests members of all classes, including serfs (unless, of course, they were themselves under investigation) were required to attend (*Novoukaznye stat'i*, §28). Injustice was more likely to occur through the net being cast too wide, to include persons of doubtful honesty who were prone to the temptation of making a false denunciation (*poklep*)—a common offence in Muscovy.

were fixed for giving vague, contradictory or false testimony, or for falsification by the inquisitor.[59] But abuses were frequent: according to Pososhkov, "the accursed inquests . . . are possessed of the devil, and there is not a trace of divine justice in them. All the witnesses' evidence is written down without their seeing it, and the priests and clerks endorse their statements without having seen or heard the people whom the parties have called upon."[60]

In Muscovy, as in Western Europe, torture was used to obtain a confession, which was regarded as the most convincing proof of guilt.[61] According to Fletcher, it took the form of "scourging with whips made of sinowes or whitleather (called the pudkey [*pytki*]) as bigge as a man's finger, which giveth a sore lash and entreth into the flesh, or by tying to a spit and roasting at the fire; sometimes by breaking and wresting one of their ribbes with a payre of hote tongues, or cutting their flesh under the nayles, and such like."[62] Olearius gives a graphic description of the terrible *dyba*.[63] Torture was supposed to be applied three times, but in practice there was no limit; on the specious grounds that bandits themselves paid no heed to them, no respite was allowed even on Holy Days.[64]

Until the reign of Tsar Theodore I, an incriminated bandit was tortured and put to death even if he did not confess, and this practice was reintroduced by the Code of 1649.[65] Eventually even a confession did not suffice to save the accused from further torture to obtain information about his accomplices. Not even at his place of execution was the convicted criminal spared the inquisitor's threats: "as they are about to die, question them thoroughly about their accomplices, that they should . . . tell the truth, mindful of the awe of God, and that their souls may be saved."[66]

The *guba* authorities thus relied for their information on denunciations in the form of either a common indictment (*oblikhovanie*) or a personal incrimination (*ogovor*).

---

59 *AI*, I, no. 154, §13; Iakovlev, *Namestnich'i . . . gramoty*, nos. 9, 11, 12; *Ukaznaia kniga vedomstva kaznacheev*, §§5–6; *Ulozhenie*, ch. X, §§161–2, 166; *Novoukaznye stat'i*, §28.

60 Pososhkov, *Kniga*, 64. He was referring here to civil inquests, but the procedure was fundamentally the same for both. Cf. *Ulozhenie*, ch. XXI, §85.

61 A confession obtained after simple interrogation was not considered valuable. A judgement of 1689 awarded a lighter penalty to a bandit who *inter alia* had confessed before torture had been applied, but this was exceptional. In any case, the "alleviation" granted, mutilation instead of death, in fact made the penalty more severe (*DAI*, XII, no. 56).

62 G. Fletcher, "Of the Russe Commonwealth" [1591], *Russia at the Close of the Sixteenth Century* (Hakluyt Society, vol. 18), ed. E. A. Bond (London, 1856), 68; [L. E. Berry and R. O. Crummey, eds., *Rude and Barbarous Kingdom: Russia in the Accounts of Sixteenth-Century English Voyagers* (Madison, Milwaukee and London, 1968), 176.]

63 Olearius, *Reise*, 272; [Baron, ed., *Travels*, 229.] Cf. G. Kotoshikhin, *O Rossii v tsarstvovanni Alekseia Mikhailovicha*[2] (St. Petersburg, 1859), 94–5.

64 *Ulozhenie*, ch. XXI, §39; *Novoukaznye stat'i*, §§31, 67.

65 Iakovlev, *op. cit.*, nos. 8, 9 (ii); *UKRP*, §§6, 9; *Ulozhenie*, ch. XXI, §§28, 41; *Novoukaznye stat'i*, §§24, 33.

66 *Novoukaznye stat'i*, §20.

The word of a convicted criminal was normally given full credit.[67] According to Olearius, the prevalence of false incriminations caused the government to have delators tortured to establish the truth of their allegations before proceeding with the case.[68] This is not substantiated from Russian documents, according to which the only safeguard against arbitrary denunciation was public confrontation (*ochnaia stavka*)— and the protection which this afforded was negligible. Suspected bandits would make arrangements with innocent people whereby, if they were unable to bear the torture, they could gain respite by denouncing them as accomplices and obtaining a confrontation, at which they would withdraw their allegation.[69]

A man indicted at an inquest was at once seized, tortured and put to death. If he incriminated an accomplice and confirmed his allegations when confronted, this person could demand an inquest; if this went against him, he would in turn be tortured, confronted with anyone whom he incriminated, and put to death.[70] Thus the law envisaged a constantly expanding web of denunciation. A man incriminated by two or more suspects was at once subjected to torture, an inquest being held only if he did not confess.[71]

Action could also be taken after a complaint to the authorities by a private individual, generally the victim of the attack. From the reign of Tsar Theodore I onwards, the plaintiff was required to bring material evidence (*polichnoe*), failing which the case was heard by the civil courts.[72] Cases brought by this means, a relic of the old accusatory procedure, were less important than those initiated by the authorities themselves, and the law increasingly restricted the circumstances in which they were permitted.[73]

According to the *Sudebniki* and the *guba* charters, bandits and those who actively helped them were invariably put to death. Godunov introduced the concept

---

67 Exception was made only when the accused aroused suspicion, for example, by incriminating the person who had brought him to justice, or withdrawing an incrimination when awaiting execution. *UKRP*, §§19, 36; *Ulozhenie*, ch. XXI, §§8, 93; *Novoukaznye stat'i*, §7, but cf. §69, which prescribed that in the latter instance such testimony should be credited if confirmed in further questioning.

68 Olearius, *op. cit.*, 188.

69 *UKRP*, §12; *Ulozhenie*, ch. XXI, §44; *Novoukaznye stat'i*, §38; *PSZ*, I, no. 195 (1656).

70 *UKRP*, §§1–2; *Ulozhenie*, ch. XXI, §§35–6; *Novoukaznye stat'i*, §§26–7.

71 Iakovlev, *Namestnich'i . . . gramoty*, nos. 1, 2, 4, 5; *UKRP*, §5; *Ulozhenie*, ch. XXI, §40; *Novoukaznye stat'i*, §32.

72 This protection did not however apply to serfs accused of some crime by their owners: *UKRP*, §§18, 16; *Ulozhenie*, ch. XXI, §§49, 48; *Novoukaznye stat'i*, §§72, 42.

73 The Statute Book establishes rules for the submission of material evidence (§§21–3); the Code of 1649 ordained that such pleas must be submitted in writing (ch. XXI, §51; for an example, see Borisov, *Opisanie Shui*, no. 70); and the Articles of 1669 in principle put an end to them by reducing the penalties to those inflicted for theft (§53). But in practice they continued to be brought, particularly by the gentry against their serfs: *DAI*, XII, no. 56; Iu. Arsen'ev, "Iz deloproizvodstva kashirskikh gubnykh starost vo vtoroi polovine XVII v.," *Drevnosti: Trudy Arkheogr. Komissii Imp. Moskovskogo Arkheol. Obshchestva*, ed. M. V. Dovnar-Zapol'skii, 3 vols. (Moscow, 1899–1913), II, Part I (1900), 97.

of recidivism, stipulating that only those convicted of three attacks, or who had also committed murder, should be punished so severely, but the Code of 1649 characteristically took a step backwards by inflicting death for the second offence.[74] In the following years the penalties for banditry, as for most crimes, were subjected to numerous arbitrary changes.[75] The harshness of these penalties shows that their purpose was overwhelmingly deterrent. The argument that Russian law still preserved to some extent a primitive reformatory approach is unconvincing.[76] If offenders were imprisoned only when the surety of their fellow-men was not available, this might be attributed to purely practical considerations: it was easy to escape from the simple wooden structure that served as a jail in the Muscovite village. This, indeed, was the excuse given for the inhuman law that, where several bandits had incriminated a certain person, only one of them should be left alive for confrontation.[77] The prison regime was very harsh: jails were overcrowded with suspects awaiting interrogation, and it was difficult for a prisoner to obtain release after serving his term.[78]

The procedure employed by the *guba* authorities was thus simple, swift and severe. It was "terroristic," in Pokrovskii's phrase, rather than judicial.[79] It was devised for the practical purpose of suppressing crime, and the accused was scarcely acknowledged to have any rights at all. As far as severity was concerned, there was little to choose between the inquisitorial system in Muscovy and in France, once the old safeguards had been whittled away.[80] The most notable difference is the greater role played in Muscovy by the community—a role sanctioned and enhanced by legislation. But any degree of protection which this may have accorded the accused was probably outweighed by the arbitrariness that was the most outstanding characteristic of the

---

74 *UKRP*, §10; *Ulozhenie*, ch. XXI, §§16–18.

75 From 1643 the death penalty was temporarily suspended, offenders instead being knouted, mutilated, and exiled (*PSZ*, I, no. 105). 1663 saw the peak of judicial barbarity, with the introduction of death by mutilation, loss of both legs and an arm; these limbs were to be displayed prominently in the locality (ibid., no. 334). But after three years the normal death penalty was restored (ibid., no. 383; a case reported shortly afterwards (*AIuB*, II, no. 55 (xix)) shows that this law did in fact take effect) and this was confirmed by the Articles of 1669 (§§17–19).

76 M. F. Vladimirskii-Budanov, *Obzor istorii russkogo prava*[6] (St. Petersburg-Kiev, 1909), 355–6; Shumakov, *Gubnye gramoty*, 83.

77 Iakovlev, *op. cit.*, nos. 9 (ii), 12; *Ulozhenie*, ch. XXI, §21; *Novoukaznye stat'i*, §§20, 123.

78 *AAE*, III, no. 272; *PSZ*, I, nos. 126, 527, 815; II, 1271; Arsen'ev, *op. cit.*, 92. In practise many escaped only by becoming personally dependent upon their gaolers, although this was forbidden by law (*Ulozhenie*, ch. XXI, §104; *Novoukaznye stat'i*, §87). Prisoners had to have a landowner or village community to vouch for them if they were to avoid re-arrest as dangerous vagrants, for their mutilations rendered them easily identifiable as former criminals. It was not easy to join a new community, and although the law prescribed that former owners must take ex-prisoners back, this did not apply to those imprisoned in distant regions; these unfortunates were eventually exiled. *PSZ*, I, nos. 669, 1055.

79 Pokrovskii, "Mestnoe samoupravlenie," 214.

80 A. Esmein, *A History of Continental Criminal Procedure with Special Reference to France*, tr. by J. Simpson, Continental Legal History Series, vol. V (Boston, 1913), 118 ff., 160.

Muscovite judicial system.

IV

After the collapse of organized government in the Time of Troubles the state machine was rebuilt and strengthened. In the provinces power came to be concentrated in the hands of the voivode, a high-ranking official appointed by and responsible to the central government, whose competence extended to military matters as well the general civil administration. Except in the extreme north, local organs of self-government disappeared. The *guba* authorities survived longer, but changed their nature and significance, losing the remnants of their popular origin and becoming bureaucratic institutions. This process had three aspects: first, their functions were expanded and became confused with those of the voivodes, so that it eventually ceased to matter to the government or to the people whether power was exercised by an official appointed by Moscow or by an elected local man; secondly, their actions became increasingly subject to direction and control by the central Banditry Office in Moscow; and thirdly, the wardens ceased to be able to exercise any independent control over the elders and degenerated into their mere agents. This resulted in the stagnation of the *guba* system. The breakdown of the inquest procedure was a juridical reflection of a social phenomenon—the refusal of the people to collaborate in a system which did not correspond to their interests.

Normally a town would have both a voivode and a *guba* elder, each with his own staff. In general the government attempted to keep to the rule that the *guba* authorities were responsible directly to the Banditry Office, and that the voivode, while he had general responsibility for suppressing crime in his area, was not to interfere in their work.[81] If he did so, this was regarded as an irregularity. But if an elder committed some abuse, the voivode would be ordered to take over the *guba* apparatus.[82] Correspondingly, a *guba* elder might be instructed to investigate alleged abuses committed by the voivode; and on one occasion all *guba* elders were ordered to fine their local voivodes 50 roubles for failing to submit certain returns.[83] The government could not afford to be over-scrupulous about the limits of competence of its various institutions; when faced with a shortage of manpower, it would use whatever machinery was available. Thus from 1598 onwards *guba* authorities are found verifying registers of debtor slaves and issuing the appropriate documents.[84] As early as 1582 there is a record of the *guba* elder at Poshekhon'e conducting a survey of local land-ownership; and throughout the seventeenth century they were active in establishing boundaries and settling disputes over property.[85] They were likely to be

81 *Ulozhenie*, ch. XXI, §3.

82 Borisov, *Opisanie Shui*, no. 18; Arsen'ev, "Iz deloproizvodstva," 87; N. P. Retvikh, "Termin 'guba,'" 280.

83 Borisov, *op. cit.*, no. 16; Arsen'ev, *op. cit.*, 88–90; *PSZ*, I, no. 51 (1651).

84 *AluB*, II, 131 (i), 127 (i–iii, vii–xi); I, 9, 93; Arsen'ev, *op. cit.*, 98. Cf. *Ulozhenie*, ch. XX, §§72–3; *Alu*, no. 203 (i).

85 *Chteniia IOIDR*, CXXV (1883), IV, 14–15; *Vremennik IOIDR*, XVII (1853), III, 3; *AAE*,

called on to deal with infringements of the important state liquor monopoly and to preside at the election of men to manage the local concessions, and to assist them in their work.[86] In an emergency they might be entrusted with military duties, such as checking the ammunition of a beleaguered garrison, or even leading men into action.[87] They would mobilize the local gentry for service, recruit masons required for work in Moscow, and track down fugitive peasants and deserters.[88] When the English envoy Lea arrived at Rostov in 1600, he was met by the two *guba* elders, who supplied him and his suite with honey and beer.[89]

In performing such duties the *guba* elder was generally acting on behalf of the voivode. But often he would be formally entrusted with the full responsibility of administering a town. The first recorded instance of this practice was at Shuia in 1601.[90] Part of Novgorod province was completely controlled by *guba* elders for at least thirty years from 1624.[91] Beginning as a temporary expedient in the Time of Troubles, this soon became a regular feature. Acting either on its own initiative or in response to a petition from the population, the Banditry Office would instruct the *guba* elder to take command of a town from the voivode, or to surrender his authority to a successor, who might be either a voivode or another *guba* elder. The governorship of a town would often pass with surprising rapidity from an appointed to an elected official and *vice versa*. The history of the township of Kashin is revealing in this respect. In 1628 the citizens petitioned for the withdrawal of all nominated officials and a return to the system that had existed earlier, with I. P. Kashkarov as *guba* elder. Their request was granted in principle, but the candidate evidently did not prove acceptable, for the Razriad, the office responsible for general administrative appointments, ordered the voivode to hand over to a certain F. Epifanov. A few months later Epifanov was summoned to Moscow, and the Banditry Office, in response to a petition, appointed L. Shatilov to succeed him. Within half a year the government received yet another petition from several landowners, declaring that the first petition represented the wishes only of the townsmen and the local monastery, and asking for Shatilov to be dismissed and a voivode to be reappointed. Although their allegation was false, because the first petition had in fact been supported by 25 members of the gentry, the authorities once more yielded, and the two functionaries existed side by side until 1641, when Shatilov was again to be found in full charge as *guba* elder.[92]

III, no. 47; *AI*, I, no. 249, II, no. 328; *AIuB*, I, 55 (xii); II, 232 (i, iii); Arsen'ev, *op. cit.*, 99.

86 *AAE*, III, nos. 146, 295; Arsen'ev, *op. cit.*, 99–100; N. P. Retvikh, *op. cit.*, 271.

87 *AAE*, III, no. 291; *AIuB*, II, no. 230 (v).

88 *AI*, II, no. 304; *AAE*, III, nos. 201, 311, 263; Arsen'ev, *op. cit.*, 99.

89 *SIRIO*, XXXVIII (1883), 372, 381.

90 Retvikh, *op. cit.*, 276. Cf. *Vremennik IOIDR, loc. cit.; AIuB*, I, no. 55 (iv, v).

91 *AAE*, III, nos. 152, 201, 257; IV, nos. 27, 72; *AIu*, no. 233 (ii); 348, all relating to the southern (*nagornyi*) half of the Onega-side "fifth" (*piatina*). In the Shelona "fifth" *guba* elders assumed full control in 1612 (*DAI*, I, no. 176).

92 I. Ia. Kunkin, *op. cit.*, nos. 6, 7, 8, 9, 18. Cf. the sequel in nos. 31, 33, 42, and *Vremennik*

There is neither rhyme nor reason in these changes, which serve to demonstrate the chaotic and arbitrary nature of Muscovite provincial administration. As these examples show, those who felt aggrieved under the rule of a nominated official could elect one themselves and apply to Moscow for confirmation. This was generally granted, as no fundamental principle was at stake. The government was concerned only to ensure that obligations would be carried out. At the same time it thought it perfectly proper to dismiss an elected man without reference to popular wishes and to replace him by a stranger who had no interest in common with those he was ordered to represent. The electoral act was thus emptied of the element of choice. If the government was preoccupied with the attempt to make the system work, the people were concerned to reduce their obligations to a minimum. Both the nominated and the elected systems were oppressive, and a change from one to the other brought little relief.

The tragedy was that, in an age when the concept of public interest was as yet unborn and corruption was a governmental institution, elected officials regularly abused their powers, so that rule by a nominated official might sometimes effect an improvement. In 1635 the citizens of Shuia petitioned the tsar to order the appointment of voivodes to control the authorities they had elected, so "that we, thy orphans . . . might not perish absolutely and be forced to go away."[93] People complained at being forced to supply *guba* elders with victuals (*korm*), the traditional privilege of provincial officials. One elder actually complained to the brethren of the local monastery of their "impoliteness" in refusing to send him the customary offerings.[94] More serious were the abuses that arose directly out of the arbitrary quasi-judicial systems which the *guba* authorities operated. In Shuia on various occasions they were accused of compelling arrested suspects to incriminate innocent people, falsifying statements, and refusing to allow the confrontation of prisoners; elsewhere they arrested people without cause and detained them without investigation.[95] They would also show favor to suspects by omitting to follow up incriminations or by accepting large bribes to secure their release.[96]

Such abuses were facilitated by the lack of any effective control. Originally control had been exercised from below, and the Banditry Office scarcely existed; it is not mentioned under this name until 1571.[97] Elections apart, the *guba* authorities

---

IOIDR, IV (1849), II, 49–50. At Dmitrov there were four changes in six years: *loc. cit.*, 32–8. Cf. also the changes at Voronezh between the 1620s and 1640s chronicled by Chicherin, *Oblastnye uchrezhdeniia*, 460.

93 Borisov, *Opisanie Shui*, no. 18.

94 *Ibid.*, nos. 4, 5; *Chteniia IOIDR*, CXXV (1883), IV, 14–15.

95 Borisov, *op. cit.*, nos. 5, 16, 18; *AIuB*, I, no. 55 (xi); Retvikh, "Termin 'guba,'" 292 ff.; Arsen'ev, *op. cit.*, 93.

96 Borisov, *op. cit.*, no. 18; *Drevnie gramoty . . . kasaiushchiesia Voronezhskoi gubernii. . . ,* III, no. 112, as cited by Retvikh, *op. cit.*, 292.

97 Iakovlev, *Namestnich'i . . . gramoty*, no. 8; K. A. Nevolin, *Polnoe sobranie sochinenii*, 6 vols. VI, (St. Petersburg, 1859), 169–70. Earlier documents refer only to "the boiars who are charged with affairs concerning banditry," clearly illustrating the gradual process by

corresponded with Moscow only to report the carrying out of executions and the amount of stolen property remaining after plaintiffs' claims had been met. It was sufficient to prescribe that the *guba* elders should not accept bribes, without specifying any penalty for those who did so.[98] The Statute Book contained a general statement that *guba* authorities were responsible for their actions to the Banditry Office.[99] But, if popular initiative was excluded, how was the central government to obtain information about the conduct of its officials? At one point it resorted to internal espionage: "and the *guba* elders and wardens are to watch one another that none of them takes bribes or gifts from anyone."[100] This approach to the problem, fortunately enough, was not followed up in later legislation and does not appear to have been widely applied.[101] Instead the central authorities, in so far as they were concerned at all, relied for information on petitions to the tsar, which was necessarily an arbitrary and inefficient procedure. If the petition was favorably received, the allegation was investigated by some other local official,[102] but we have no evidence whether penalties were actually imposed.

Later, the Banditry Office made increased efforts to exercise control. Between 1653 and 1693 three *guba* elders from Kashira were sent to Moscow under escort to answer charges of misconduct.[103] *Guba* authorities were required to submit frequent reports, although they did not always do so; their accounts were audited annually; and the regulations governing the disposal of confiscated loot were tightened.[104] The Banditry Office attempted to coordinate the activities of *guba* authorities in different areas by insisting upon being informed if they corresponded with one another on official business.[105] As a result, local officials were not distinguished by any high degree of initiative. Negligent about essentials, the government kept a strict control over administrative details. When a new *guba* elder arrived in Voronezh to succeed one who had died, he had to await an order from Moscow before he could open a locked cabinet containing his predecessor's official papers.[106] Fearful of exceeding their authority, they would refer even the most trivial matters to Moscow.[107]

This over-centralized system was an increasingly heavy burden on the local population who had to support it. In countless petitions they painted their plight in gloomy

---

which the central *prikazy* were formed.

98 Iakovlev, *op. cit.*, nos. 1–10, 12.

99 *UKRP*, §60; *Ulozhenie*, ch. XXI, §6.

100 Iakovlev, *op. cit.*, nos. 6, 9 (i).

101 The only instance recorded was at Voronezh, when a *guba* clerk denounced his elder for illegally releasing prisoners: Retvikh, *loc. cit.*

102 Borisov, *Opisanie Shui*, no. 18.

103 Arsen'ev, "Iz deloproizvodstva," 87, 100.

104 *AAE*, III, no. 271; *AIuB*, I, no. 55 (xi); Arsen'ev, *loc. cit.*; Iakovlev, *op. cit.*, no. 12.

105 Iakovlev, *op. cit.*, nos. 8, 9 (ii), 12.

106 *Drevnie gramoty . . . kasaiushchiesia Voronezhskoi gubernii. . .* , I, no. 34; III, no. 183 (iii), as cited by Chicherin, *Oblastnye uchrezhdeniia*, 476.

107 *AAE*, IV, no. 72; *AIuB*, I, no. 55 (x); Arsen'ev, *op. cit.*, 88, 90, 95, 96.

colors. Formally they complained only about abuses by individual men in authority, for to have said more would have been disloyal, but their dissatisfaction with the whole arbitrary *guba* procedure was clearly apparent. They found it oppressive to have a *guba* office situated in the immediate neighborhood.[108] Unless they were specially privileged, they were responsible for building it.[109] Payments for office requisites (candles, paper, firewood, etc.) and allowances or fees for the staff were frequently in arrears.[110] To share out the burden, the rural and urban portions might arrange that each in turn should provide the warden, while the other paid his allowance.[111] Discontent naturally made itself felt in the form of unwillingness to collaborate in the operation of this oppressive system. In the years of the final enserfment of the tax-paying population, which were marked by several violent revolutionary outbreaks, culminating in the great rising led by Sten'ka Razin (1668–71), the occasions when the peasant wardens took the side of the bandits rather than of the government must have become increasingly frequent. The Code of 1649 introduced a clause punishing wardens for deliberately or negligently allowing a criminal to escape.[112]

The population as a whole was also uncooperative. A search party sent out in the 1660s reported that "in all villages and cantons of Ustiug district (*uezd*), Sire, they [the inhabitants] have not found any thieves or robbers, and they say that as soon as those thieves and robbers heard the *strel'tsy* and townsmen pursuing them they fled, but whither they have fled they do not know."[113] Without access to the reports submitted by the *guba* authorities, it is not possible to determine the extent of such passive resistance. But evidence that it became more common during this period is provided by the breakdown of the inquest system. Inquests became the scene of bitter factional struggles, and rules had to be elaborated to deal with cases when unanimity could not be achieved. If the majority party favored an indictment, or even if the community was split into equal halves, this was treated as equivalent to a unanimous condemnation.[114] But if a majority declared the accused innocent, could he be given the benefit of the doubt? Although this crucial question was soon enough posed by real life, and the clerks in the Banditry Office submitted it to the Council of Boiars for a decision, it was not until 1669 that the merciless Muscovite legislators dared to allow such men to be considered as if they had been unanimously acquitted.[115] The growing frequency of such conflicts is also shown by the necessity for the government eventually to intervene and prohibit joint testimonies, which were prepared by faction leaders and circulated among likely supporters for their signature.[116] In course of time

108 *AAE*, III, nos. 152, 154; *Alu*, no. 348.

109 *AAE*, II, no. 19; IV, no. 72; *Ulozhenie*, ch. XXI, §97.

110 *AAE*, III, no. 271; *DAI*; I, no. 176; *Alu*, no. 223 (ii–vii).

111 Borisov, *op. cit.*, no. 14.

112 *Ulozhenie*, ch. XXI, §84.

113 *DAI*, V, no. 94.

114 Iakovlev, *Namestnich'i . . . gramoty*, nos. 8, 9 (ii); *UKRP*, §7; *Ulozhenie*, ch. XXI, §42; *Novoukaznye stat'i*, §34.

115 *UKRP*, §§70–1; *Novoukaznye stat'i*, §§28, 34.

it became impossible to maintain the principle that the opinion of the community was not open to an appeal. A ruling of 1631 permitted the holding of a second inquest, covering a wider area and involving more witnesses, if the accused complained that those who had indicted him were biassed.[117] Eventually he was in practice able to obtain what amounted to a second hearing by alleging that the authority conducting the inquest had been prejudiced.[118]

The fundamental assumptions on which the inquest was based had long since been rendered obsolete. The law continued to adhere to the convenient theory that the community acted of its own free will in recognizing the criminal in its midst and surrendering him to the authorities, but at every turn this was exposed as a mere fiction. Increasingly complex regulation failed to preserve the system in the face of mass non-cooperation. In 1669 the prohibition of hearsay evidence theoretically equated testimony given at an inquest with that of ordinary witnesses.[119] In 1688 the government virtually admitted failure, ordering the refusal of requests for the holding of inquests, because they had led to the conviction of innocent people.[120]

Another aspect of the breakdown of the *guba* system was the inability of the authorities to act against robber bands enjoying the support of powerful local vested interests. In 1688 Prince Lobanov-Rostovskii and an associate were convicted of organizing highway robberies.[121] Olearius has recorded that men working on estates bordering roads near the capital, who attacked passing travelers, were protected by their masters if the victims took the matter to court.[122] Already in the sixteenth century the lawgivers had been faced with the problem of dealing with gentry who refused to surrender men suspected of banditry. But no criminal penalty was imposed and no provision was made for nobles who personally committed such offences.[123] Tsar Theodore I closed this loophole by making the gentry liable to the same penalties as members of other classes, although they were to enjoy the notable privilege of being subjected to torture only if they were incriminated by their serfs, who were tortured first, even though they were personally under no suspicion.[124] Their class privileges were still further increased by the Code of 1649.[125] Proceedings against gentry accused of banditry were sometimes suspended while they were on active

---

116 *PSZ*, II, no. 1412 (1691); Dmitriev, *Istoriia*, 416.

117 *UKRP*, §72, supp. art. VI; *Ulozhenie*, ch. XXI, §76; *Novoukaznye stat'i*, §36.

118 *PSZ*, I, nos. 195, 527 (1656, 1672). Previously such charges had been summarily disposed of by appointing an additional *guba* elder to conduct the inquest: *UKRP*, §61; *Ulozhenie*, ch. XXI, §7.

119 *Novoukaznye stat'i*, §28.

120 *PSZ*, II, no. 1294. Cf. a similar confession made earlier, cited in *Ocherki istorii SSSR; period feodalizma XVII v.* (Moscow, 1955), 408.

121 Solov'ev, *Istoriia*, III, 1039–40.

122 Olearius, *op. cit.*, 200.

123 Iakovlev, *Namestnich'i . . . gramoty*, nos. 8, 9 (ii); *UKRP*, §§13–15.

124 *UKRP*, §15; *Ulozhenie*, ch. XXI, §47; *Novoukaznye stat'i*, §41.

125 *Ulozhenie*, ch. XXI, §39; *Novoukaznye stat'i*, §31.

service.[126] Eventually a fifty-rouble fine was introduced for those who shielded their men, allowed them to escape, or rescued them from their escorts after arrest.[127] But the government's policy was throughout weak and hesitant. In these circumstances provincial authorities could hardly be expected to take a firmer line against recalcitrant gentry than the government itself, and although direct evidence regarding the conduct of *guba* elders in this matter is lacking, one may assume that in practise they swam with the tide. However, in patriarchal Muscovy the service gentry had no clearly formulated class consciousness, and it would be a mistake to depict the *guba* elders as actively propagating the interests of the local gentry against the people;[128] emphasis should rather be laid on the inability of the gentry to use local institutions to protect their interests from the demands of the state.

By the 1660s the government seems to have become conscious that new measures were called for. Given the spirit of the time, the change could be only in the direction of greater centralization and the virtual extinction of the popular elective element. Henceforward the pivot of the system was the inquisitor (*syshchik*), an omnipotent agent of the central government who was specially dispatched to the provinces to suppress banditry. Such officials had often been sent out earlier to certain badly afflicted areas,[129] but only in 1667 did they become a national institution.[130] One inquisitor, usually a high-ranking nobleman with previous experience as a provincial administrator, was appointed to an area comprising several *guba* districts.[131] From the moment of his arrival he exercised virtually dictatorial powers. The local voivode had to furnish him with an office, fully staffed and maintained, a body of soldiers, and as many men as he required, equipped for fighting. His main strength was a force of locally recruited gentry, usually about one hundred strong.[132] The *guba* elder had to present for inspection his accounts and papers and the prisoners under detention; he would be dispatched on minor operations against bandits while the inquisitor led the major campaigns personally. In 1669 the *guba* elders were formally placed under the authority of the inquisitors.[133] The inquisitor himself was strictly responsible to the

---

126 *PSZ*, I, no. 337 (1663). Cf. II, no. 1239 (1687).

127 *Ulozhenie*, ch. XXI, §§77–8, 81; *Novoukaznye stat'i*, §§45–7; *DAI*, V, no. 62; Iakovlev, *op. cit.*, nos. 11, 12.

128 This is the tenor of the observations on the *guba* system in *Ocherki istorii SSSR: period feodalizma XVII v.*, 384.

129 Inquisitors were frequently in operation in the Shuia-Suzdal' area from 1614 onwards (Borisov, *op. cit.*, nos. 4, 11, 27, 28; *AAE*, III, nos. 311, 325; IV, no. 54), in Murom in 1625 (*AAE*, III, no. 163), in the Perm' area in 1636 (*AI*, III, no. 194), in the Ust'iana districts in 1637 (Bogoslovskii, *Zemskoe samoupravlenie*, II, 228), in Pereiaslavl' in 1651 (*Sbornik kniazia Khilkova* (St. Petersburg, 1879), 255–69), and in Kashin in 1656, 1664 and 1665 (*AAE*, IV, no. 92; Kunkin, *op. cit.*, nos. 45, 50).

130 *AAE*, IV, no. 159; cf. *DAI*, V, no. 62.

131 *AI*, III, no. 194; Borisov, *op. cit.*, no. 28.

132 *Vremennik IOIDR*, XXIV (1856), III, 41–7; *Sbornik kniazia Khilkova*, 256; *AI*, III, no. 194; Arsen'ev, "Iz deloproizvodstva," 90.

133 *Novoukaznye stat'i*, §§121–2, 2, 3, 5, 6.

central government, and had to report on all matters. Elected wardens were abolished; the prisons were put in the charge, first of *strel'tsy*, and later of hired warders who were paid by the voivode instead of being maintained directly by the community; and other financial burdens on the people were eased.[134]

These changes could not of themselves solve the problem. But the government fought shy of the idea of reforming the whole arbitrary criminal procedure and contented itself with further bureaucratic manipulations. In 1679 all provincial officials other than the voivode, including both *guba* elders and inquisitors, were abolished.[135] This attempt to anticipate Peter the Great's centralization of the provincial administrative apparatus was premature, and the office of *guba* elder was restored a few years later.[136] But towards the end of the century the main role in suppressing bandits seems to have fallen to local units of *strel'tsy*.[137] The Banditry Office[138] was abolished in 1701, and the inquisitors and *guba* elders finally disappeared early in the following year.[139]

As the only local representative institution embracing all classes of the population, the *guba* authorities might have become the nucleus of a genuine system of local self-government. But with the general consolidation of serfdom in the seventeenth century social antagonisms were greatly accentuated. Peasants and gentry now had few interests in common—least of all in the suppression of bandits, who very often enjoyed popular sympathy and support. The powers of the *guba* authorities increased, but it was an increase of duties rather than of rights. The gentry could not be enthusiastic about serving as mere tools of the central government. Russia was now congealing into a bureaucratic despotism, in which each social class had a fixed status and rendered service in its own way to an omnipotent state. The *guba* reform, like many other promising beginnings in Russian history, had to be sacrificed on the altar of this Moloch.

1956

---

134 *Ibid.*, §4; Iakovlev, *op. cit.*, no. 12; *PSZ*, I, nos. 384, 779; *AIuB*, II, no. 262 (vii); Retvikh, "Termin 'guba,'" 288; Iu. Arsen'ev, "Iz deloproizvodstva," 92.

135 *PSZ*, I, no. 779; cf. Iakovlev, *Namestnich'i . . . gramoty*, no. 12; V. Borisov, *op. cit.*, no. 59. This decree seems to have taken effect as far as the *guba* elders were concerned, for there is no trace of them in the documents for the years immediately following. But it was apparently less effective with regard to the inquisitors, since four years later another decree was issued ordering their abolition (*PSZ*, no. 1011).

136 *PSZ*, no. 1062 (1684).

137 *AI*, V, nos. 219, 254. Cf. also the role allotted to the Streletskii Prikaz by two decrees of 1695: (*PSZ*, III, nos. 1510, 1515).

138 It had been renamed the *Sysknoi Prikaz* in 1683 (ibid., no. 1052), but the new title was not uniformly observed (cf. ibid., no. 1345).

139 Ibid., nos. 1874, 1900.

CHAPTER 4

The Regime of Filaret, 1619–1633

I

On June 14 (O.S.), 1619 an impressive act of oriental ceremonial took place outside the walls of Moscow. Accompanied by representatives of the clergy and a large crowd, the young tsar, Michael Fedorovich, proceeded in state to a point beyond the Tver' gates. A carriage drew up. From it alighted his father, Fedor Nikitich (Filaret) Romanov, who had returned from eight years spent in Polish captivity. The two men greeted each other tearfully, prostrating themselves at full length upon the ground, and then withdrew to the Kremlin. Moscow was in festive mood: the bells pealed, an amnesty was proclaimed, and the general feeling prevailed that a new era in Russian history had begun.[1]

Ten days after his return, Filaret was installed as patriarch of Moscow and All Russia. The appointment was a foregone conclusion: his relationship to the tsar required that, as an ecclesiastic, he should occupy the highest office which the Orthodox Church could offer. In fact he became not only patriarch but the effective master of the country. For the next fourteen years Russia was formally a diarchy, ruled jointly by father and son. Each bore the title of "Great Sovereign" (*Velikii Gosudar'*), hitherto reserved to the tsars alone; they held court together, or, if separately, with identical ceremonial; they normally acted in unison when hearing petitions and reports or issuing decrees. But this elaborate duplication served to conceal the fact that Michael exercised only nominal authority, and that Filaret actually ruled in his name. It was less a partnership than a dictatorship—although Filaret did not usurp power, but merely filled the vacuum left by his son's incapacity. Michael was an unassuming youth with no taste or talent for public affairs. He willingly abdicated his responsibilities in favor of his father, for whom he displayed a touching, if exaggerated, filial respect. Their correspondence shows that no significant disagreement or conflict arose between them.[2]

---

1 *SGGD*, III, no. 43; *Novyi Letopisets, sostavlennyi v tsarstvovanii Mikhaila Fedorovicha, izdan po spisku Kn. Obolenskogo* (Moscow, 1853), 186.

2 *Pis'ma russkikh gosudarei*, vol. I (Moscow, 1848). For an example of this duplication of authority in diplomatic practice, cf. S. Konovalov, "Twenty Russian Royal Letters (1626–1634)," *Oxford Slavonic Papers*, VIII (Oxford, 1958), 142–6.

During Filaret's regime Muscovy regained a measure of stability after the cata-
clysmic upheavals of the civil war known to history as the "Time of Troubles." His
object was to re-establish the authority of the autocratic power and to clamp down
once more upon Russian society the bonds from which it had vainly endeavored to
escape. Filaret, although he never wore the crown, ranks after Alexis Mikhailovich
as the most significant ruler of seventeenth-century Russia, who carried on the centralizing traditions of Ivan Groznyi and Boris Godunov and in a sense prepared the
way for Peter the Great. Yet his policies and achievements still lack adequate critical
assessments.[3]

As is the case with most other figures in pre-Petrine Russia, Filaret's personality
does not emerge clearly from contemporary records. The few references in the official
chronicle, compiled under his own aegis, are naturally couched in hagiographical
terms.[4] The only nonofficial contemporary appraisal of Filaret tells us that he "was
of medium height and build, had a fair knowledge of the scriptures, was of an irascible
and suspicious temperament, and so imperious that even the tsar was afraid of him."[5]
Beneath his ecclesiastical robes there beat the heart of a power-loving boiar. Though
personally pious, he had a fondness for luxury, ostentation and ceremonial display.
Of autocratic mould, proud and stubborn, his strength of will was not matched by
breadth of intellect. It would perhaps be misleading to draw a parallel with his great
contemporary, Cardinal Richelieu, whom he resembles in some external respects.
Filaret had nothing but disdain for western culture; instead, he drew inspiration from
the Byzantine traditions of the Russian past. He could be narrow-minded to the point
of bigotry. In his concern to safeguard the purity of Orthodoxy from contamination by
heretical ideas, he attempted to isolate Muscovy behind an ideological curtain which
retarded the country's intellectual development. The concept of progress had no place
in his thinking. He was, in the literal sense of that overworked word, a "reactionary,"
who sought to solve present problems by applying the formulas of a bygone age.

Filaret's deeply ingrained conservatism was heightened by the sudden changes
of fortune he experienced during the Troubles. His chequered career during this
period reveals him to have been a skillful politician who succeeded in combining
devotion to basic principles with a keen sense of tactical advantage. His ambitions
for supreme personal power were thwarted, first by Godunov—it was as a result of
the latter's savage punitive action against the Romanov family that he was forced to
take monastic vows, thus acquiring the name of Filaret—and later by Shuiskii, who

---

3 The sole biography, by A. Smirnov, "Sviateishii Patriarkh Filaret Nikitich moskovskii i vsea
   Rusi," *Chteniia v obshchestve liubitelei dukhovnogo prosveshcheniia* (Moscow, X, 1873, II–
   V, 1874) is a panegyric, but contains some useful details. E. D. Stashevskii has advanced
   some stimulating ideas in his *Ocherki po istorii tsarstvovaniia Mikhaila Fedorovicha*, pt. I
   (Kiev, 1913), but does not attempt a comprehensive picture. Of Soviet historians only
   P. P. Smirnov has concerned himself with Filaret's policies as such: cf. *Posadskie liudi i
   ikh klassovaia bor'ba do serediny XVII v.*, 2 vols. (Moscow-Leningrad, 1947–8), I, 356 ff.

4 *Novyi Letopisets, loc. cit.*

5 Bishop Pakhomii of Astrakhan', cited by A. Smirnov, *op. cit.*, 823–4, and others from
   A. Popov, *Izbornik russkikh khronografov*, a work which has remained inaccessible to me.

assigned him to the relatively humble post of bishop of Rostov. While serving in this capacity he was seized and taken to the camp of the second pretender, where he was nominated as the rebels' patriarch. The degree to which he identified himself with the pretender's cause is still matter for speculation. The official view, assiduously propagated later by Filaret himself, was that he acted under duress. This is not wholly convincing; on the other hand, he certainly had no sympathy for the rebels' social radicalism, and once it became clear that they were doomed to failure he deserted them. Returning to Moscow, he participated actively in the intrigues that led to Shuiskii's overthrow, and became a prominent figure in the provisional boiar régime which replaced him. With the country torn by dissension, he realized that a Romanov candidature stood no chance of commanding general acceptance, and instead urged that the crown should be offered to Władysław of Poland, subject to his acceptance of certain constitutional limitations on his power. He was subsequently appointed a leader of the delegation which, in the autumn of 1610, made its way to Smolensk to negotiate a settlement with the Poles. Here he distinguished himself by his stubborn insistence upon complete acceptance of the original terms, at a time when the situation in Moscow was deteriorating rapidly. To Sigismund III, bent on intervention, the delegation soon appeared as a tiresome anachronism. In March 1611 the Poles broke off the talks, and Filaret and his companions entered into their long captivity.[6]

He thus played no part in the national revival which led to the liberation of Moscow and the election of his son to the throne. Michael's accession must have given him satisfaction and whetted his ambitions,[7] although it had an adverse effect upon his own position. In Polish eyes Filaret now became an extremely valuable hostage, a means of exerting pressure upon Moscow. His fate depended upon the outcome of the war still in progress between the two countries. The conditions of his confinement in the fortress of Marienburg were not, it seems, unduly harsh (as the Russian public was later led to believe), and he had the opportunity to become acquainted with Polish customs and ideas. But the alien environment apparently held no attraction for him, and the uncertainties of his position served to intensify his scorn for the country and religion of his captors. Thus, when the Deulino armistice (December 1618) allowed him to return to his homeland, he did so as a fervent believer in traditional Muscovite religious and political values. Although already advanced in age and enjoying only indifferent health, he arrived eager to wield the power of which he had so long been

---

6 S. F. Platonov, *Ocherki po istorii Smuty v Moskovskom gosudarstve XVI–XVII vv.*[2] (Moscow, 1937), *passim*; P. G. Vasenko and others, *Nachalo dinastii Romanovykh: istorichskie ocherki* (St. Petersburg, 1912), 46 ff. [For Filaret's early career see now G. B. Bernhard, "F. N. Romanov (Filaret): seine Politik in der Zeit der Smuta, 1598–1613," thesis (Heidelberg, 1977).]

7 In 1615, however, when he was permitted to receive a Russian envoy in the presence of his captors, he protested against the election on the grounds that he had not been consulted in the matter. S. A. Belokurov, ed., *Pamiatniki diplomaticheskikh snoshenii moskovskogo gosudarstva s pol'sko-litovskim gosudarstvom*, in *SIRIO*, CXLII (1913), 563. It may be assumed that this was an effort to dissuade the Polish authorities from taking severer measures against him.

deprived.

II

In Muscovite Russia Church and state co-existed without any clear juridical demarcation of their respective spheres of activity. Their relationship varied according to
changing circumstances and the personal characteristics of those who held highest
office. Filaret played a greater part in secular affairs than almost any Russian prelate
before or since. But this did not imply any paramountcy of Church over state, or
even any significant advance towards an autonomous status for the Church. Filaret
was not born to the cloth; and paradoxically, the period that saw the greatest extension of the patriarchal power was also a stage in that process of secularization and
bureaucratization of the Church which was to call forth the schism.[8]

As patriarch, Filaret faced a situation of some complexity. The Troubles had
shaken Russians out of their lethargic unquestioning acceptance of the authority of
the Orthodox Church and the traditional ideology, a curious compound of piety, obscu-
rantism and nationalistic arrogance. Contact with the outside world had reinforced the
xenophobic prejudices of the clergy and the populace at large, but had also awakened
intellectual curiosity and opened the floodgates to doubt and heresy. Some became
sympathetic to Catholicism; others were influenced by Protestantism—or even, as
the case of Ivan Khvorostinin showed, by Socinian rationalism.[9] Filaret was not
an intellectual; neither by temperament nor by training was he properly equipped to
pronounce on matters of doctrine. His method of solving the problem was essentially
administrative: he sought to stifle dissent and enforce conformity of belief by the
exercise of firm paternalistic control.

As an outsider, his first task was to establish his personal authority over the
hierarchy. He had a rival in Jonah, styled "bishop of Krutitsy," who between 1613
and 1619 had been *locum tenens (mestobliuditel')* of the patriarchal throne. The
conflict came to a head in 1620. While in office Jonah had allowed two Catholic
converts to be admitted to Orthodoxy without undergoing a second baptism. Declaring
roundly that "the Latins are the most impure and ferocious of all heretics, . . . like
unto dogs, known to be enemies of God," Filaret called an ecclesiastical council at
which, with greater resourcefulness than scholarship, he claimed canonical authority
for a ruling that such converts should henceforward be rebaptised. Jonah was asked
whether his action had been prompted by Catholic and Polish sympathies. The sinister

---

8 For a masterly survey of the origins of the *raskol*, cf. P. Pascal, *Avvakum et les débuts
  du raskol* (Paris, 1938). This work makes it possible to discount the views advanced by
  ecclesiastical historians of the official school, such as Bishop Makarii, on the significance of
  Filaret's patriarchate: *Istoriia russkoi tserkvi*, 12 vols. (St. Petersburg, 1857–83), XI (1882),
  67. W. K. Medlin, who does not quote Pascal, erroneously considers that during this period
  there occurred "a shift towards an equilibrium of power between State and Church": *Moscow
  and East Rome: a Political Study of Church and State in Muscovite Russia* (Geneva, 1952).
9 S. F. Platonov, *Moskva i zapad* (Berlin, 1926), 72–80, and *Drevnie russkie skazaniia i povesti
  o Smutnom vremeni XVII v.*, (*Sochineniia*, vol. II) (St. Petersburg, 1913), 230–56; *AAE*, III,
  nos. 147, 149; *SGGD*, III, no. 90.

hint sufficed: he recanted and pleaded for mercy.[10] One year later he was again accused, this time of having unjustly condemned Nektarii, bishop of Vologda, in 1616; Nektarii was rehabilitated, and Jonah's stock suffered a further decline.[11] After three more years had elapsed, by which time Filaret presumably felt more confident of his power, Jonah was dismissed and sent to a monastery at Vologda—"voluntarily or involuntarily," as the church historian Makarii laconically comments.[12]

There is much about this affair that still remains obscure. It is true that Jonah was an unscrupulous man, unworthy of his office; but his fall cannot be attributed purely to the patriarch's repugnance at his moral failings. It is arguable that Jonah may indeed have harbored Catholic sympathies, which Filaret, with his pronounced prejudices, considered harmful. Another explanation, less flattering but possibly more realistic, is that Jonah may have had some support within the hierarchy, that by taking action against him Filaret was warning potential opponents not to attempt to challenge his authority, and that he deliberately inflated the ideological issue to give a cloak of respectability to what was basically a straightforward personal rivalry.

This interpretation is supported by his conduct in the case of Joseph Kurtsevich, a west Russian Orthodox bishop who arrived in Moscow in 1625. According to regulations prescribed in December 1620, at a second session of the council referred to above, such immigrants were required to undergo rebaptism in the same manner as Catholic converts; for although they were Orthodox the purity of their faith was suspect.[13] These rules were applied in practise with the utmost strictness, irrespective of the immigrant's rank. But an exception was made in favor of Kurtsevich. A colorful extrovert and an ardent "Muscophil," he succeeded in ingratiating himself with Filaret, and was soon awarded the lucrative bishopric of Suzdal'. Here he led a life of corruption and debauchery, permitting his followers to behave likewise, while his friendship with the patriarch ensured that complaints against him by members of his flock were disregarded. Only after Filaret's death was the case investigated: Kurtsevich was dismissed and sent to Solovki, in the Arctic, to mend his ways.[14]

Somewhat similar was the career of another of Filaret's intimates, Cyprian, who was elevated from obscurity in 1620 to become the first bishop of Tobol'sk. Shortly after his appointment the patriarch sent him a thundering philippic, in which he drew a vivid picture of the morals of Russian settlers in Siberia and upbraided Cyprian

---

10 Makarii, *Istoriia*, 23–30. His argument that Filaret did not in fact introduce any innovations has been effectively disproved by A. Smirnov, *op. cit.*, 256, 260–2.

11 Smirnov, "Patriarkh Filaret," 653–5.

12 Makarii, *Istoriia*, 39.

13 Ibid., 30–3.

14 *AAE*, III, no. 249; K. V. Kharlampovich, *Malorossiiskoe vliianie na velikorusskuiu tserkovnuiu zhizn'* (Kazan', 1914), 23, 32–9; Pascal, *Avvakum*, 29. N. F. Kapterev mistakenly assumes that Filaret was revolted by Kurtsevich's conduct, although the evidence points the other way (*Patriarkh Nikon i ego protivniki v dele ispravleniia tserkovnykh obriadov: vremia patriarshestva Iosifa*[2], Sergievskii posad (1913), 9). Makarii (*op. cit.*, 79–81) also plays down the connection between him and Filaret. Pascal's views are accepted by A. M. Ammann, *Abriss der ostslawischen Kirchengeschichte* (Vienna, 1950), 255.

for neglecting his duties.[15] But the bishop evidently succeeded in regaining Filaret's confidence. In 1623 he was recalled to Moscow, where he made a rapid ascent up the ladder of promotion: after a few months as successor to Jonah, he was appointed to the most important archbishopric in Russia, that of Novgorod, where he indulged in extortionate practices, though on a less spectacular scale than Kurtsevich, without any action being taken against him during the lifetime of his protector.[16] These two cases, and others besides, indicate that an element of shrewd political calculation was never far from Filaret's mind: by making promotions and demotions dependent upon his estimate of each prelate's personal loyalty, he ensured his own preeminence within the hierarchy.

The same purpose was served by the establishment within the church of a powerful bureaucracy personally dependent upon the patriarch. In May 1625 Filaret secured from the tsar a charter which carved out of the extensive church lands a domain over which he had complete jurisdiction (except as regards the most serious criminal offences) and absolute financial control. All dues from ecclesiastical property in these areas, which included some of the wealthiest commercial centers in Russia, now went directly to swell the patriarchal coffers, instead of being absorbed locally, either at parochial or at diocesan level.[17] To manage this vast empire, which was extended still further by various other grants, bequests and purchases, Filaret set up offices (*prikazy*) modelled upon the principal executive organs in the state administration. One office, the Patriarshii dvortsovyi prikaz, performed general supervisory functions; another, the Kazennyi prikaz, dealt with fiscal matters, while a third, the Razriad, was mainly concerned with the maintenance of discipline; their respective fields of competence were, however, not clearly defined and in practise often overlapped. Most of the officials in these institutions were laymen. To carry out their orders they disposed of a considerable army of serving men. These functionaries, like their secular equivalents, had a strictly regulated hierarchy of ranks and were entitled to possess estates on conditional tenure; the only distinction was that they owed service to the patriarch instead of the tsar. Their significance can be gauged from the fact that in 1627–9 the patriarchal officers with the rank of *stol'nik* actually outnumbered those of the tsar.[18] The amount of revenue which each household or plot of land had to provide was now prescribed, as were the fees which the parochial clergy had to pay to higher authority for each service they rendered their flocks. Bishops as well as humble priests had cause to tremble when these formidable agents of the patriarch arrived to collect dues, or to exact arrears with blows of their whips.

The monasteries were affected especially severely by these centralizing measures, which automatically curtailed the financial and juridical privileges enshrined in the ancient charters which most of them possessed. Filaret set up, on a permanent basis, an "investigating office" in Moscow, to which all charter holders, lay as well as

15 *SGGD*, III, no. 60.

16 Pascal, *Avvakum*, 28–9; Makarii, *Istoriia*, 35 ff.

17 *AAE*, III, no. 164; cf. Smirnov, "Patriarkh Filaret," 634–52; Pascal, *Avvakum*, 25–7.

18 Smirnov, *op. cit.*, 651.

ecclesiastical, were required to submit their documents for confirmation; they were then returned to them with their privileges diminished. From 1623 onwards the restrictions imposed tended to become severer, many monasteries being obliged to resubmit their charters for further changes to be made. Although there were a few foundations which still enjoyed almost total exemption, most were now obliged to pay certain important direct taxes (the *iamskie den'gi* and the *streletskaia podat'*) and to assist when required in construction work for defense purposes; they were permitted duty-free trade only to the extent necessary for subsistence, not for profit; and finally, fixed terms were established for the hearing of cases in which charter holders were involved.[19]

These measures, although serving to consolidate the authority of the patriarch and to give an outward impression of relative order and efficiency, were far from adequate to deal with the real problem that beset the church: how to maintain its hold over Russian society in an age of change. Muscovite Orthodoxy was lamentably ill equipped to face the challenge of rival ideologies. Abuses were legion: genuine piety went hand in hand with primitive superstition; the moral teachings of the church were flagrantly disregarded, even by those meticulous in their observance of religious ritual; the clergy, who for the most part shared the vices of their flocks, lived in abysmal poverty and ignorance.[20] Not only was there no proper schooling; to many obscurantists the very desire for learning appeared fraught with potential heresy. The way for salvation, they held, lay not through reason but through faith; all true knowledge was contained in the ancient liturgical texts and other sacred works cherished by generations of faithful worshippers. But this attitude raised an acute dilemma: as many churchmen were now coming to realize, these traditional works contained innumerable errors and urgently needed correction. However, such work required theological knowledge; and in existing circumstances this necessitated turning to suspect alien sources, to Constantinople or Kiev. The revival of Orthodox learning now under way in western Russia threw into relief the nadir to which it had sunk in Muscovy. In 1616 the abbot of the Trinity monastery, Dionisii, and some of his colleagues had made an attempt to correct certain liturgical works, but the enterprise had ended with the condemnation of Dionisii as a heretic. One of Filaret's first acts on his assumption of office was to reinstate him in his post.[21]

Filaret differed from the obscurantists in several respects, but he shared their mil-

---

19 Stashevskii, *Ocherki*, 305–30; *AAE*, III, nos. 94, 119, 120. For examples of charters with generous exemptions granted by Filaret, cf. *AAE*, III, nos. 175, 178.

20 The situation is vividly and objectively portrayed by P. Pascal in the foreword to his *Avvakum*.

21 The initiative in this matter should be ascribed not to Filaret personally but to the patriarch of Jerusalem, Theophanes, who early in 1619 secured his release from prison and demonstratively identified himself with his cause (Makarii, *op. cit.*, 13). Filaret's attitude towards Dionisii was cooler, and it is perhaps significant that in the years which followed he was not invited to resume his work as a corrector of books. May not the reason for this lie in the fact that Filaret felt some embarrassment at too close an association with a man for whose condemnation his own former wife, the nun Martha, had been partly responsible?

itant chauvinism. He realized the dangers of arousing their hostility, particularly at a time when his centralizing measures were infringing many vested interests, and consequently pursued a religious and cultural policy barely distinguishable from that which they advocated. Not until 1632 did he take any step to promote education, and even so his initiative had no significant result.[22] Prior to this he was content to devote himself stubbornly to the purely negative task of excluding foreign influences. Immigrant ecclesiastics, particularly those from western Russia, were not only subjected to rebaptism but were kept isolated from the local population. Any works which they wrote were minutely examined for heresy. In 1627 L. Z. Tustanevskii, a west Russian monk who on his arrival in Moscow had been commissioned to compile a catechism (a work as yet unknown in Muscovy), was charged with various errors, among them an attempt to explain the movements of heavenly bodies in scientific terms. He admitted his faults, and his work, although printed, was not authorized for public circulation. A few months later sixty copies of a collection of sermons by another west Russian writer, K. T. Stavrovetskii, were publicly burnt in Moscow. Decrees were issued prohibiting the purchase of any "Lithuanian" ecclesiastical literature and ordaining that churches should only be allowed to keep them until they had sufficient books printed in Moscow.[23]

This last qualification graphically illustrates the weakness of the official standpoint. No more than a trickle of printed works issued forth from the Pechatnyi dvor: in the first years of Filaret's patriarchate an average of three volumes appeared annually, only half as many as were printed under his successor Ioasaf (Jehoshaphat).[24] The obstacles to increased output were not so much physical—the Pechatnyi dvor boasted seven printing-presses—as political. When Filaret died, his library was found to contain no less than 124 manuscripts which, though examined and passed by the official censors, he had not sent to be printed.[25] His extreme caution, it seems, stemmed chiefly from the fear that, since printing inevitably raised the problem of the authenticity of the text and the desirability of corrections being made, he would arouse the opposition of the obscurantists. The ideological climate in Moscow was such that any innovation, however slight, exposed its author to the dread charge of heresy. Thus Filaret waited six years, and was careful to obtain the sanction of the other eastern patriarchs, before authorizing the minute change in one of the prayers necessitated by the rehabilitation of Dionisii.[26] He knew the obscurantists' temper; and, rather than stir up a hornet's nest, preferred to follow a purely negative policy.

---

22 Makarii, *Istoriia*, 71–3; cf. Smirnov's unconvincing *apologia* in "Patriarkh Filaret," 615.

23 *SGGD*, III, no. 77; Makarii, *Istoriia*, 48–58; Kapterev, *Patriarkh Nikon*, 6–9. Kharlampovich (*Maloross. vliianie*, 20–1) argues, contrary to all the evidence, that Filaret pursued a pro-Kiev policy.

24 The figures are given by Makarii, *op. cit.*, 44, 89, but the conclusions he draws are unwarrantably favorable to Filaret: he speaks of the "vast number" of books printed under his auspices.

25 Smirnov, *op. cit.*, 250.

26 *AAE*, III, no. 166.

This obstructive approach hardly served the best interests of the Russian Church. Orthodoxy needed a spiritual leader; it obtained an organizer. Filaret's unwillingness to face up to his broader responsibilities and to take reforming action against the notorious abuses in the life of the Church had the result that the function of leadership passed out of the hands of the hierarchy. Where they feared to tread, some laymen did not. Significantly, it was during these years that Ivan Neronov, a future leader of the "zealots" and, ultimately, of the *raskol'niki*, began to raise his voice against the prevailing evils. In 1632 he was exiled to the Arctic by the patriarch for "teaching without authority" and "causing disorder among the people."[27] Unwittingly Filaret, who devoted himself so single-mindedly to maintaining uniformity of belief within the church, did as much as anyone to provoke the schism.

III

As *de facto* ruler of Russia, Filaret was motivated by one constant aim: to restore state authority to its former power and prestige. When he returned in 1619 the new dynasty was still in a most precarious position; when he died 14 years later, it had become firmly integrated into the fabric of Russian society. In the first years of Michael's reign public affairs had been seriously neglected. Fearing to arouse opposition by vigorous action, the government had drifted irresolutely from one expedient to another under pressure from various special interests. Filaret's advent to power did not represent the all-important turning-point suggested by official chroniclers; nevertheless, he did introduce a new consistency and sense of purpose into the conduct of government policy. By steering course skillfully between competing pressures, and presenting the autocratic power as an impartial arbitrator concerned only with the general welfare, he contrived to reestablish it upon a new pinnacle of eminence.[28]

The court soon reverted to its former external splendor and opulence. Internally, it was split between the tsar's paternal and maternal relatives.[29] With the fall of

---

27 *AAE*, III, no. 198; Pascal, *Avvakum*, 45–64.

28 This is broadly the thesis advanced by Stashevskii, *Ocherki*, 190 ff., and *passim*, who is, however, too inclined to put the best possible interpretation on Filaret's policies, characterized as "a dictatorship of the common good." As will be argued here, there was a large gulf between Filaret's principles and his practise.

29 This conflict was not devoid of significance, since it concerned Michael's matrimonial plans and thus, indirectly, the future of the dynasty. Though Martha did not intervene directly in affairs of state, she could influence the course of events (until 1619, at least) through her two nephews, Boris and Mikhail Saltykov, who had an unsavory reputation for court intrigue. They were instrumental in thwarting the tsar's projected marriage to Mariia Khlopova. Filaret, presumably for reasons of personal embarrassment, waited four years before taking action against them. Even after the Khlopova affair had been investigated and the Saltykovs banished, Martha was still successful in obstructing the marriage. Filaret would have preferred his son to conclude a foreign match, but his efforts to bring this about proved unavailing. The tsar's second betrothal, to Mariia Dolgorukova, ended tragically with her sudden death, attributed by suspicious contemporaries to poison. Only with his marriage to Evdokiia Streshneva (1626) and the birth of a male heir three years later was

the Saltykovs in 1623 complete power rested in the hands of Filaret, assisted by a
small group of men, most of whom were linked to him by family ties as well as
by close personal intimacy: I. N. Romanov, I. B. Cherkasskii, F. I. Sheremetev,
B. M. Lykov and others of lesser note.[30] It was they who headed the more important
"offices" (*prikazy*), the main channel through which the country was now governed.
The Boiarskaia Duma played no very significant part during this period; neither did
the Zemskii Sobor, which was not summoned at all between 1621 and 1632. The
assembly's chief function, in Filaret's eyes, was to keep the ruling group in touch
with the popular mood, and his practise of holding frequent informal gatherings at
his court, attended by favored individuals from nearly all social groups, rendered the
Sobor as an institution superfluous.[31] With the mechanism of authority so firmly in his
hands, he had no need to apply measures of political repression, and the few sudden
"disgraces" that took place appear to have been mainly due to disagreements about
foreign policy, over which the patriarch exercised close personal control.[32] As the
years passed, the ruling group became more restricted and isolated from the regular
administration. By 1630 Filaret was lamenting to his son that Cherkasskii, Lykov and
Romanov were his only friends.[33] Even this small coterie was soon split by personal
rivalry: in 1632 Cherkasskii and Lykov became engaged in a dispute over precedence
in the army command, which was given instead to B. M. Shein.

An essential feature of Filaret's conception of absolutist government was the absence of any institutional barrier between the supreme authority and the individual
subject, or group of subjects: in principle, anyone had the right to present a petition
to the tsar or patriarch.[34] Public business was normally conducted in response to such
petitions from below, questions being decided according to the amount of pressure
which each petitioner or counterpetitioner could bring to bear, rather than by the merits of their pleas or abstract principles of justice. Officials were ignorant of the laws,
which were chaotic and often contradictory. Filaret was no systematizer and had little
idea of legality. He made no attempt to codify the law, still less to distinguish judicial

the future of the dynasty assured. Cf. *SGGD*, III, nos. 63, 65, 72; *AAE*, III, no. 156; *AI*, III,
nos. 80, 91; *Pskovskie letopisi*, 2 vols. (Moscow, 1941, 1955), I, 133; A. P. Barsukov, *Rod
Sheremetevykh*, 7 vols. (St. Petersburg, 1881–?), III (1883), 8 ff., 54 ff.

30 S. F. Platonov, *Moskovskoe pravitel'stvo pri pervykh Romanovykh* (St. Petersburg, 1906),
44; cf. data tabulated in S. K. Bogoiavlenskii, *Prikaznye sud'i XVII v.* (Moscow-Leningrad,
1946).

31 Smirnov, *Posadskie liudi*, vol. I, 357; and cf. above, 60. The record of these meetings is in
TsGADA (Moscow), *fond* no. 236.

32 I. T. Gramotin, chief secretary in the Posol'skii prikaz, who was dismissed and exiled in
1626, had adopted a pro-Polish attitude in the Troubles, but had soon been rehabilitated
(Platonov, *op. cit.*, 44–5). It seems a possibility that he ventured to question the patriarch's
policy, or at least his tactics, in the conduct of relations with Poland. He returned to Moscow
after Filaret's death.

33 Cited from *Pis'ma russkikh gosudarey*, I (Moscow, 1848) by E. D. Stashevskii, *Ocherki*,
361.

34 This did not, of course, extend to serfs and other dependent persons, who stood outside the
body politic altogether.

from administrative procedure, and contented himself with ordering each *prikaz* to maintain a register of decrees relevant to its field of activity. These spheres were, however, not properly differentiated. One innovation, designed to obtain more effective coordination of policy on certain problems, was the establishment of so-called "investigating offices" (*sysknye prikazy*) with special powers—a development which foreshadowed the centralizing measures of Alexis Mikhailovich. But in practise these bodies proved disappointingly ineffective, and their work more often than not petered out in bureaucratic routine and confusion. To a large extent they seem to have served the propagandist purpose of giving the impression that energetic efforts were being made to remedy popular grievances which the government was in fact either unwilling or unable to deal with.

This modification of the administrative structure was part of the general program of reconstruction launched a few days after Filaret's installation as patriarch. According to the well-known official account, he led the ecclesiastical hierarchy in approaching the tsar and drawing attention to the prevailing abuses: that fiscal burdens were inequitably apportioned; that many townspeople had fled to escape heavy taxation, some of them having become *zakladchiki*, i.e. persons pledged to serve powerful landowners, who often enjoyed fiscal privileges; and, finally, that some proprietors ("strong men," or *sil'nye liudi*, as they were simply but expressively called) were perpetrating injustices and acts of violence against defenceless humbler folk. The leading groups then apparently formulated definite proposals, which were discussed by the Sobor and approved, although not without some amendment.[35] There was to be a new survey; some (though not all) fugitive townspeople were to be sent back, and granted fiscal relief where necessary; the *zakladchiki* (including those who had taken service with ecclesiastical proprietors) were to be returned and reintegrated into their communities; finally, the complaints against the "strong men" were to be examined in the first of the new "investigating offices."[36]

How was this program translated into action, and what was its ultimate effect upon the various social groups, their relations with each other and with the state? These key questions are crucial for an understanding of the nature of Filaret's regime.

The most important of the measures envisaged was the survey. The task which the government set itself was a formidable one: to reconstruct the national cadaster, the register of land and other sources of wealth on which direct taxes had been assessed before the Troubles. As a consequence of widespread material devastation, great shifts of population, and wholesale changes in landownership, the data contained in the late sixteenth-century registers (where, indeed, these were still in existence) had long since

---

35 How much did this program owe to the patriarch in person? Though official sources naturally stress his responsibility, the details must almost certainly have been the work of *prikaz* officials. The Dutchman Isaac Massa commented that "everything was done by command of the tsar's father, but everything had already been appointed and determined" (cited by Smirnov, *Posadskie liudi*, I, 362–3). He was a perceptive observer—although, as Platonov has shown (*Mosk. pravitel'stvo*, 43), he was mistaken in his assertion that Filaret's return was followed by a general purge of the administration.

36 *AAE*, III, no. 105.

ceased to bear any relation to reality. To add to the chaos, Michael's government, in desperate need of money, had introduced new direct taxes and attempted to levy them on the basis of the old registers. This had imposed excessive burdens upon those communities that had been less severely afflicted by the Troubles, often reducing them to the common level of misery. The dispatch of inspectors (*dozorshchiki*), empowered to grant tax reductions or exemptions, had stimulated, rather than alleviated, popular grievances, since such inspections were made on an individual or local basis without regard to the overall situation; and in practise it had been landowners, not townspeople or free peasants, who had succeeded in securing relief.[37]

The underlying reason for this was the rapid growth of private landowning in the first years of Michael's reign, of which more will be said below. Where this development occurred, it destroyed the traditional system of tax assessment, based upon cooperation between the state surveyors and elected peasant representatives, who had together established a more or less reliable picture of the resources of each community. On private estates the boundaries were generally not coextensive with those of the peasant communities, which were in any case reduced to a shadow of their previous importance. They could therefore play no part in assessing resources, which became a matter for the state surveyor and the landowner alone. Each estate constituted a separate fiscal unit, and it was a comparatively simple matter for the proprietor to persuade or intimidate the visiting official to grant him relief. The most common ruse was to pass off reasonably prosperous peasants as *bobyli*, i.e. persons so impoverished as to merit exemption from taxation. The inspector would find it difficult to check the information given him by the proprietor, for the peasants concerned stood to gain from any relief and had no interest in revealing the truth.[38]

Filaret and his advisers, it appears, greatly underestimated the complexity of their task and failed to take certain steps essential for the new survey's success. Although heralded with loud fanfares as a nationwide operation, there seems at first to have been little improvement in practise over the measures taken prior to 1619. Action was taken only in response to individual petitions, and in the majority of instances the officials sent were not the surveyors (*pistsy*) promised in the government's program, but simple inspectors (*dozorshchiki*) with limited powers.[39] Nor did the authorities appreciate the fundamental importance of speed: the survey dragged on for years and was not finally completed until the early 1640s. No central agency was established to direct the operation. In the peasant north it was conducted by the regional offices (*cheti*), but in the landowning center by various functional *prikazy* until it was transferred, after much interdepartmental friction, to the office of landed estates (Pomestnyi prikaz). The officials in this institution had no experience of the work involved, and in 1626,

37 S. B. Veselovskii, *Soshnoe pis'mo*, 2 vols. (Moscow, 1915–16), II, 186–93, 551. This exhaustive, though somewhat ill-arranged, study has rendered obsolete much of the earlier literature on fiscal policies during this period.

38 Ibid., II, 519, 547–9.

39 Ibid., II, 207, 211. It is impossible to be certain, as the records for these years no longer exist. For the difference between the two types of official, cf. ibid., 197.

after a quarter of the surveys had been completed, a natural catastrophe supervened: one of the fires that periodically swept Moscow destroyed this *prikaz* together with all its laboriously accumulated records.[40] It was only in the late 1620s that the survey really got under way.

The most serious impediment to success, however, was the government's failure to give its surveyors proper guidance and support. They were supposed to evaluate the economic resources of each taxpaying unit (*tiaglo*) in the community to which they were sent, and to establish the proportion of the total assessment for which it should be liable. But this total assessment (calculated in units known as *cheti*, subdivisions of the *sokha*) was fixed in advance by Moscow, for each area individually, in a completely arbitrary manner with little or no regard for economic realities as ascertained by the surveyors. Thus two communities approximately equal in population and prosperity might be required to pay tax at grossly divergent rates.[41] Even the allocations made by surveyors within the communities, after close study of local conditions, were liable to be countermanded by higher authority for no apparent reason.[42] The surveyors might do their best to share out fiscal burdens fairly, but their efforts were nullified by the inequities inherent in the system as a whole. Yet when the government for some reason was willing to admit that an error of assessment had been made, the blame was laid entirely upon the surveyors. In 1621, for example, a number of them were charged with corruption and kept under guard in a room in the Kremlin until they had revised their data to the authorities' satisfaction.[43] In such circumstances, naturally, these officials had little incentive to act honestly, and most of them would normally tailor their assessments to suit the socially dominant elements in the community surveyed.

This was the background to the gradual and haphazard introduction, during the 1620s, of the so-called *dvorovaia chet'*.[44] This was in essence a directive to those surveyors operating in central and southern districts, where private landowning was general, that a *chet'* was henceforward to consist of a certain fixed number of homesteads (*dvory*): as a rule, ten or sixteen on secular estates.[45] This, it was hoped, would

---

40 Ibid., II, 200 ff., 546–7.

41 Ibid., II, 331.

42 Cf. example in ibid., II, 300–2.

43 *AAE*, III, no. 121.

44 This reform, known also as the *zhivushchaia chet'* (or *chetvert'*), was the subject of much confusion among earlier historians, most of whom regarded it as a deliberate attempt by the government to discard the traditional *sokha* in favor of a tax on the homestead (*dvor*): cf. M. Gorchakov, *O zemel'nykh vladeniiakh vserossiiskogo mitropolita, patriarkha i Sv. Sinoda* (St. Petersburg, 1871), 414 ff.; A. Lappo-Danilevskii, *Organizatsiia priamogo oblozheniia v moskovskom gosudarstve* (St. Petersburg, 1890), 243 ff.; P. N. Miliukov, *Gosudarstvennoe khoziaistvo Rossii v I-oi chetverti XVIII v.*[2] (St. Petersburg, 1905), 11–16; Stashevskii, *Ocherki*, 337 ff. Veselovskii has now demonstrated conclusively that it was actually an attempt to maintain the *sokha* by giving it a different content (*Soshnoe pis'mo*, I, 13–14, II, 481–7).

45 Estates of the church in these areas (where they had no fiscal privileges) were taxed at a higher rate, generally 7$\frac{1}{2}$ or 12 homesteads to the *chet'*. For purposes of calculation

bring the *bobyli* within the fiscal net and also ease the surveyors' task in combatting tax evasion by landowners: for they no longer had to try to evaluate their actual resources, but simply to count the number of peasant homesteads on the estate. But although the measure was conceived as a means of increasing fiscal efficiency and speeding up the survey, it was in fact an admission by the state of its impotence to prevent landed proprietors from escaping their obligations. In the years that followed landowners bombarded the government with petitions for their norms to be reduced.[46] With war looming on the horizon, Filaret and his associates could not afford to offer determined resistance to their pressure.

One consequence of this was to accelerate the process whereby Russia was becoming split, geographically as well as socially, into two zones: the "black" peasant communities of the north (together with the urban *posady*), which provided the state with most of its revenue from direct taxation, and the central and southern districts, dominated by landowners who performed military service but provided little in the way of revenue.[47] For in the latter areas the landowners paid no direct taxes personally and could, as we have seen, obtain fiscal advantages for their peasants; what was perhaps still more important, the state refrained from exercising any control over the amount of dues which they imposed upon their dependents, although this obviously affected their capacity as taxpayers. Under these circumstances it was clearly impossible to reestablish a cadaster uniformly applicable to the whole country, which had been the long-term aim behind the new survey. When this was eventually completed, after many years of wearying toil, it proved useless as an instrument for assessing direct taxes on a national basis. The treasury was obliged to rely largely on alternative sources of revenue, which by their very nature fell less equitably. The Smolensk war of 1632–4 had to be financed to a considerable extent by more of the capital levies, known as "fifths" (*piatinnye den'gi*), which had been imposed in the first years of Michael's reign, and which proved particularly ruinous to the townspeople. Much revenue was also derived from various state monopolies, of which the most important, that in alcoholic liquor, had grievous effects on popular wellbeing.[48] It was not until

---

it was assumed that two *bobyli* homesteads equalled one peasant homestead, so that, for example, a village with 12 peasant homesteads and 8 *bobyli* homesteads on secular land would constitute one *chet'*.

46 Veselovskii, *op. cit.*, II, 488–95; Stashevskii, *op. cit.*, 342–4.

47 Unfortunately no reliable estimate can be made of the relative fiscal load in each zone, because the taxes levied varied so greatly from region to region and year to year. One may agree with Veselovskii that Miliukov's estimate (*Ocherki po istorii russkoi kul'tury*[4] (St. Petersburg, 1900), I, 144) that the north paid some 40 times more than the landowning center is exaggerated; nevertheless, the difference seems to have been striking (*Soshnoe pis'mo*, II, 661–3).

48 Miliukov, *Gosudarstvennoe khoziaistvo Rossii. . .* , 18; J. Kulisher, *Russische Wirtschaftsgeschichte* (Jena, 1925), 415–18. For a contemporary account, cf. Adam Olearius, *Vermehrte newe Beschreibung der Muscowitischen und Persischen Reyse . . .* (Schleswig, 1656), 194–7; [S. H. Baron, tr. and ed., *The Travels of Olearius in Seventeenth-Century Russia* (Stanford, 1967), 145.]

the 1650s that a better balance was achieved between direct and indirect taxation.[49] Taken as a whole, Filaret's fiscal policy must be adjudged a failure.

The principal reason for this was the government's unwillingness to consider broader issues and to take decisions on matters of principle—an approach characteristic of Muscovite officialdom throughout the seventeenth century. But it was also partly due to the rise of landowning interests, a factor which the government was obliged to take into account. The landowners did not by any means constitute a homogeneous class. There was a wide gulf between the aristocratic boiars at one extreme and, at the other, the provincial serving men (*sluzhilye liudi*), whose way of life approximated more closely to that of their peasants than of their more fortunate fellow-proprietors. Among those privileged to serve in the capital there were clearly defined gradations of rank and wealth. During the Troubles all groups had acquired a new consciousness of their own importance and interests, but for some twenty years this did not find expression in political form. In the intervening period they were preoccupied with efforts to improve their social and economic status. The first years of Michael's reign witnessed a hectic scramble for landed property, still by far the most important source of wealth in Russia. The government, too feeble to control this process, had actually facilitated it by making generous grants of court estates and, more especially, of the lands of "black" (i.e. free taxpaying) peasant communities. Such grants, particularly extensive after the campaign of 1617–18, continued on a smaller scale until the mid-1620s. By this time there had virtually ceased to be any "black" land in the central districts of the country.[50] But the court estates were rapidly built up again, and by 1627 Filaret felt strong enough to declare a halt to grants from this source.[51]

In this drive for enrichment it was naturally the better-placed elements, with resources in money and labor, or with political influence, which gained most. Among them were the so-called "strong men," who disregarded all legal and moral sanctions in satiating their economic appetites. One of the principal objects of the survey (apart from its fiscal aims) was to verify proprietors' title to their lands, with cuts being made where necessary in favor of the state or other owners. In practise, however, surveyors appear to have paid little attention to the manner in which land had been acquired, and to have automatically authorized the occupier to remain in possession so long as he was "in service" and there was no other claimant to the property.[52] Prominent landowners sometimes received grants of additional land from the tsar, with full rights of ownership,[53] or enlarged their estates by commercial purchases. The wealthiest

49 Veselovskii, *op. cit.*, II, 537–9.

50 Iu. V. Got'e, *Zamoskovnyi krai v XVII v.*[2] (Moscow, 1937), 254; but cf. 223, where the author appears to contradict this statement.

51 *Ibid.*, 210–11; *Ukaznaia kniga Pomestnogo prikaza* [hereafter *UKPP*], in M. F. Vladimir-skii-Budanov, *Khrestomatiia po istorii russkogo prava*[6] (St. Petersburg-Kiev, 1908), pt. III, 164–234, IV, §3.

52 Stashevskii, *Ocherki*, 214.

53 E.g. those to the Cherkasskii family, in *AAE*, III, nos. 159, 215, 218.

secular lords were at the same time those who were most prominent politically, such as I. N. Romanov, I. B. Cherkasskii and F. I. Sheremetev.[54] Figures for the later 1630s show that the first-named possessed over 3,000 peasant homesteads, and the two others more than 2,000.[55]

On a still more impressive scale were the holdings of the great ecclesiastical owners, bishoprics as well as monasteries, which appear to have significantly improved their position during the years of Filaret's rule. Ten of them each possessed more than 10,000 desiatines (approximately 4,000 acres) of land, while the Trinity monastery, with nearly 100,000 desiatines, was the largest proprietor in Russia after the tsar.[56] Monasteries acquired their extensive domains as grants from the tsar or patriarch, by purchase, or from defaulting debtors; but the most important source seems to have been the old custom of bequeathing land to pay for prayers to be said for the souls of the departed. On his accession Michael confirmed an earlier ban on this practice,[57] but it remained a dead letter; indeed, both he and Filaret kept the tradition alive by making such grants themselves, and their example was naturally emulated by other proprietors. The spirit of official policy is also evident from such ordinances as that of 1622, whereby ecclesiastical owners were permitted to keep land acquired prior to 1612 even if the former proprietor or his descendants wished to repurchase it, whereas they normally did not obtain such rights until forty years after the bequest.[58]

Meanwhile the rank-and-file service gentry were complaining about a shortage of land.[59] Though periodical allotments were made of estates on conditional tenure (*pomest'ia*), their actual holdings were as a rule only a fraction of the official entitlement. The *pomest'e* system hindered the development among the gentry of feelings of attachment to their land: occupied for most of the year with military duties, they paid only occasional visits to their homes and tended to look on their property as a source of rapid enrichment. Lacking any strong incentive to manage their estates in a rational economic manner, they thought in terms of obtaining more territory at the expense of others and cast envious eyes at the relatively prosperous and well-populated

---

54 Stashevskii, *op. cit.*, 376. Some details of F. I. Sheremetev's estates are given by A. P. Barsukov, *op. cit.*, *passim*.

55 A. I. Iakovlev, cited by Stashevskii, *loc. cit.* It is interesting to note that economic differentiation corresponded closely to the rank held in the official hierarchy. Thus boiars had an average of 852 homesteads and *okol'nich'i* 263, but the secretaries (*d'iaki*) and "Moscow gentry" only had 30 and 29 homesteads respectively. Actual holdings were probably higher than these figures indicate. [R. O. Crummey, *Aristocrats and Servitors: the Boiar Elite in Russia 1613–1689* (Princeton, 1983), 114–15.]

56 Stashevskii, *Ocherki*, 377. For details of the Trinity properties, cf. Got'e, *Zamosk. krai*, 115 ff. Much of this land was, however, under forest or of poor agricultural quality.

57 Stashevskii, *op. cit.*, 216.

58 *UKPP*, I, §5.

59 Cf. the illuminating petition of one F. F. Uvarov in 1630, in which he drew the patriarch's attention to the "continual great discontent amongst all [serving] people" at the insufficiency of land grants. Stashevskii, *op. cit.*, Appendix, xxiii–xxv and A. I. Iakovlev, *Prikaz Sbora ratnykh liudi 1637–1653 gg.* (Moscow, 1917), 77–8, 162 ff.

lands of the great proprietors.

Filaret, who was concerned to safeguard the integrity of the court and church estates, and no less those of his intimates amongst the boiars, embarked hesitantly upon the only possible alternative policy: to encourage the gentry to develop cultivation within the limits of their existing holdings. Thus in the later 1620s grants would customarily include stretches of untilled land, and a decree of December 1627 allowed such land to be bought from the state at a low price.[60] Of greater moment was another enactment which allowed them to buy from the state full ownership rights over their *pomest'ia*, i.e. to convert them into *votchiny*.[61] The government evidently appreciated the desirability, on economic grounds, of giving the service gentry greater security of tenure. Regulations which hampered their rights over their *pomest'ia* were relaxed: they were, for example, now allowed to exchange them, provided that such transactions were registered with the authorities, and in 1632 an estate was allowed to remain in the *de facto* possession of the widow of a deceased holder instead of automatically reverting to the state for reallocation.[62] The state still retained the ultimate right of ownership and insisted that the land remain "in service"; but important steps had been taken which foreshadowed the eventual rise of the *pomeshchiki* to social preeminence.

From this strengthening of the landowners' position the peasants were the principal sufferers. During the years of Filaret's supremacy they took a long stride down the road to serfdom. For this development the government was not primarily responsible. Filaret sought neither to promote nor to hinder the advance of serfdom, for he had no "peasant policy" as such: certain limited groups apart, the peasants remained, so to speak, outside his field of vision. In so far as the changes that took place were directly facilitated by government policy, they were the by-product of efforts to strengthen the position of the larger lay and ecclesiastical proprietors, whom Filaret regarded as the most reliable bulwark of the throne. But in considering this question, it should be borne in mind that conditions on the larger estates were by and large superior to those on the smaller ones, especially on those *pomest'ia* whose owners thought only of the maximum exploitation of peasant labor. The best evidence of this is the fact that the main stream of fugitives led from smaller estates to larger ones, not *vice versa*.

The drift to serfdom came about basically as a consequence of the economic ruin wrought by the Troubles. Deprived of his slender resources, perhaps driven from his home by hunger, the peasant was often glad to find a proprietor who could offer him an advance in cash or kind, even if this meant that he had to sacrifice his freedom by signing a contract which bound himself, his family, and even his descendants to work for his creditor for an indefinite period. Such documents, sometimes concluded even where no credit was actually given, seem to have become usual by this time in central districts. In the south there was a freer atmosphere owing to the proximity

60 Stashevskii, *Ocherki*, 218; Got'e, *Zamosk. krai*, 254 ff.; *AAE*, III, no. 172.

61 *UKPP*, IV, §§7, 13, 20, 22. It is clear from the *Ukaznaia kniga* that this right was made use of in practise—at least by officials with estates near Moscow.

62 Ibid., IV, §§24, 27; Kulisher, *Russ. Wirtschaftsgeschichte*, 194.

of the open frontier: by holding out the threat of flight, peasants could on occasion turn the general shortage of labor to their own advantage and secure recognition of their ancient right of departure (*vykhod*), which elsewhere had generally become no more than a memory. The *pomeshchiki*, on the other hand, desperately anxious to obtain the labor without which even generous allotments of land were useless, sought to bind their peasants to their estates as firmly as possible.

Flight was, of course, illegal, and owners were entitled to bring back fugitive peasants and demand compensation from those who had sheltered them. But the system was heavily weighted against the smaller proprietors: it was physically difficult for them to undertake a search, and even if they had located a fugitive, a number of bureaucratic formalities had to be complied with before they could obtain his return. Above all, the law specified a limited term, the *urochnye leta*, after the expiry of which claims for return were no longer valid and fugitives became the property of their new masters. During the Troubles the provincial gentry had voiced demands for an extension of the *urochnye leta* from five years to 15, but on Michael's accession the old five-year limit had been confirmed. The Trinity monastery was granted the special favor of a nine-year term and official assistance in tracing and sending back fugitives[63]—a privilege of considerable psychological significance since it stimulated resentment and jealousy among the gentry.

The bitter struggle between the various groups of landowners for peasant labor was the most prominent feature of the Russian social landscape during these years. Under Filaret the government gave the impression of seeking to hold the balance impartially. No changes were made in the law: the time limit remained at five years, and no further individual privileges were granted. But this apparent strict adherence to the *status quo* in fact worked to the advantage of the larger proprietors. Sometimes Filaret would intervene directly on behalf of his intimates. When, for example, some of F. I. Sheremetev's dependants fled, officials were expressly instructed to give his agents all aid in locating and returning them.[64] No action was taken to restrain I. N. Romanov from forcibly abducting peasants from neighboring lesser proprietors (if their complaints are to be believed) and resettling them on extensive new lands which he was developing in southern border areas.[65] Moreover, the larger proprietors also stood to gain automatically from the maintenance of the *status quo*, because the flow of fugitives developed a natural momentum of its own: flights increased the burdens on those left behind, encouraging them to follow the fugitives' example, while on the larger estates, conversely, the influx of manpower led to rising prosperity and enhanced their power of attraction. Filaret's policy thus gave no satisfaction to the bulk of proprietors on the issue in which they were most vitally interested. During his

---

63 *AAE*, III, no. 66; *AI*, III, no. 58; *DAI*, II, no. 35; cf. also S. Rozhdestvenskii, "Iz istorii otmeny 'urochnykh let' dlia sýska beglykh krest'ian v moskovskom gosudarstve XVII v.," *Sbornik statei . . . v.o. Kliuchevskomu* (St. Petersburg, 1909), 154.

64 Barsukov, *Rod Sheremetvykh*, II (1882), 487, III, (1883), 46–9.

65 Kulisher, *Russ. Wirtschaftsgeschichte*, 227, citing a work by E. D. Stashevskii, *K istorii kolonizatsii iuga* (St. Petersburg, 1913) which has remained inaccessible to me.

lifetime they were obliged to moderate their demands, but with his death the political situation became more fluid and they could press for concessions with greater hope of success.

The townspeople constituted another social group with little reason to be grateful to the Filaret regime. The patriarch had no understanding of the significance of commercial activity for the country's economic development, and viewed the urban communities (*posady*) primarily as a source of revenue.[66] The wealthier elements in the provincial towns were siphoned off to Moscow, where they became members of the privileged merchant corporations.[67] The most successful were exempted from taxation, allowed to own estates, and became *personae gratae* at court. They performed arduous, but often lucrative, tasks on behalf of the treasury. Their official standing also gave them an advantage in private business, and they would often act as junior partners to boiars who valued their commercial experience. They soon became wholly assimilated into the ruling élite and lost all sense of affinity with the milieu from which they had sprung.

Meanwhile the mass of provincial townspeople continued to labor under oppressive taxation, not the least of their obligations being the provision of representatives to collect various items of revenue. This might entail long journeys and involve them in losses for which the opportunities of profiteering could not compensate.[68] Still more galling was the task of managing state monopolies in the very commodities in which they themselves dealt privately. They also faced competition from a variety of other sources: from privileged landowners and their dependents, from peasants trading on their own account, and from foreign merchants. It was politically dangerous to protest loudly against state trading, but in complaining about the activities of foreigners they could draw on powerful national and religious emotions. In 1627 merchants from a number of towns joined in petitioning the government to expel foreign traders from the interior of the country, on the grounds that they continually transgressed the restrictions placed upon their activities.[69] These complaints were investigated and foreign merchants reminded of the law; but that was all. Filaret's government could not afford to concede the substance of the petition, partly owing to existing international obligations, and partly because to tighten the restrictions on foreigners would lead to a decline in revenue from customs and possibly deprive the state (and court) of imported goods which they required.

An equally negative attitude was adopted towards the complaints from urban communities about draining away of their members through flight. Like the fugitive peasants, the *zakladchiki* generally (but not always) received credit from their protectors,

---

66 Smirnov, *Posadskie liudi*, I, 400–1.

67 For an example of this practise, cf. *AI*, III, no. 164.

68 In the early 1620s, for example, the government, anxious to reduce the losses caused by corruption on the part of locally elected supervisors of the liquor monopoly, ordained that they should be replaced by men nominated by some other community. *AAE*, III, no. 143; Stashevskii, *Ocherki*, 298–9.

69 S. F. Platonov, *Moskva i zapad* (Berlin, 1926), 102–3; Smirnov, *Posadskie liudi*, I, 394–5.

and in return pledged themselves to work for them as they might prescribe. Most frequently they would be encouraged to continue as traders or artisans, often being settled in settlements (*slobody*) situated in close proximity to the towns. Where their new proprietors, as was generally the case, possessed charters of privilege, the *zakladchiki* had no fiscal obligations to the state. Although they were liable to pay any dues fixed by their masters and were juridically entirely dependent on them, their economic position was nevertheless superior to that of their fellow-citizens. It was this prospect of improved opportunities which led them to sacrifice the liberty they had enjoyed as members of the *posad*, a liberty which the impositions of the tax collectors had rendered meaningless. Their privileged status gave them an advantage in competing commercially with the townspeople. Competition was even keener in the case of those, generally known as *dvorniki* or *zakhrebetniki*, who did not actually leave the *posad* but assumed no share in the obligations of the community.[70]

The townspeople themselves wanted all fugitives to be forcibly returned, and all those in the area who engaged in trade to be ascribed to the *posad*.[71] But Filaret's program of 1619 fell far short of conceding this demand: it provided only for the return of certain fugitives, and then merely in response to petitions by individual communities, which were referred for consideration to one of the *sysknye prikazy*. The fact that I. Ia. Suleshov, the official in charge, was himself accused of harboring *zakladchiki* hardly inspired confidence that the operation would be prosecuted vigorously.[72] Indeed, the *prikaz* effectively sabotaged the government's program. For example, the voivode of one town in northern Russia was instructed to organize the return of fugitives, not from the *posad* itself but from the local *sloboda*; since no such settlement existed there, he could disregard the order.[73] In general, the entrusting of this delicate task, which involved the antagonizing of powerful local vested interests, to the voivode rather than to special agents from Moscow ensured that the matter would be approached with the customary lethargy. It appears that the work was eventually carried out in the main by the surveyors, and that they were more successful in reintegrating those still physically resident in the towns than in return-

---

70 The *dvorniki* originated as watchmen in town houses owned by landed proprietors, who engaged in trade, probably at first on their own account, but later also on their master's behalf, until their commercial activities eventually obscured their other functions. The *zakhrebetniki* were those who sheltered "behind the back (*khrebet*)" of a taxpaying citizen, posing as his dependants, although they in fact carried on business independently and ought to have paid tax themselves. Cf. Stashevskii, *Ocherki*, 236 ff.; Kulisher, *Russ. Wirtschaftsgeschichte*, 288–9.

71 Cf. the petition submitted by the citizens of Novgorod in 1623, in Smirnov, *Posadskie liudi*, I, 396–8.

72 *Ibid.*, 369. Smirnov apparently errs in stating that Suleshov's *prikaz* ceased to operate in 1619. Stashevskii has shown that it continued to exist, although under different chiefs and a different name, until 1624: *Ocherki*, 237. Cf. also I. Ia. Gurland, "Prikaz Sysknykh Del," *Sbornik statei po istorii prava posviashchennyi M. F. Vladimirskomu-Budanovu ego uchenikami i pochitateliami* (Kiev, 1904), 87 ff. and S. K. Bogoiavlenskii, *Prikaznye sud'i XVII v.* (Moscow-Leningrad, 1946), under *"Sysknyi prikaz"*.

73 Smirnov, *Posadskie liudi*, I, 372.

ing fugitives. Often their decisions in favor of the townspeople would be reversed after local landowners had brought pressure to bear in Moscow.[74] The general spirit of the government's policy on this issue under Filaret is shown by a decree of 1621, rescinded only after his death, which permitted privileged landowners to seize the property of town-dwellers who had defaulted on their debts.[75] General decrees were issued prohibiting the practise of *zakladnichestvo*,[76] but their frequency suggests that they were not effective and that they largely served to camouflage the authorities' inactivity.

Thus, here as elsewhere, Filaret steered a course which in effect strongly favored the larger proprietors: while preventing the towns from becoming so drained of manpower as to endanger their revenue-producing capacity, he failed to take energetic action against those who harbored fugitives. This was partly due to his basic social outlook, but partly also because the problem of fugitives, whether urban or rural, was not one amenable to solution by legislative action. Flight was a natural spontaneous reaction to economic adversity which had its own rationale. Those fugitives whom the state forcibly returned to their former owners or communities were liable to flee back once more to their protectors. To some extent those who fled and those who sheltered them were parties to an arrangement of mutual convenience, and they had a common interest in resisting the pretensions of the lesser gentry and townspeople. In Zaraisk in 1625, for example, a landowner joined with his dependents in offering armed violence against an official who attempted to reintegrate them into a taxpaying community.[77]

It was of course regrettable that men should prefer serfdom to freedom, and that the government should passively concur in this mass flight into bondage. But the only practicable alternative before it was to pursue a policy more closely aligned to the wishes of the gentry and townspeople. This was the course which the government followed, with reluctance and under pressure, after Filaret's death. The result, within 15 years, was the *Ulozhenie* of Tsar Alexis, and the bondage of all classes to the state. Filaret cannot legitimately be presented as an enlightened man with the welfare of the masses at heart. He was concerned only to consolidate the new dynasty's position by winning for it the support of the most powerful social elements. This meant acquiescence in a deterioration in the juridical status of their dependents. Nevertheless, judged by its results, such a policy was less injurious to the cause of popular freedom than that advocated by the intermediate social groups. In Russia at this time the tide was flowing strongly towards serfdom, and no government, in existing circumstances, could have swum against it. Filaret's régime did at least temporarily delay the onset of total bondage.

---

74 Stashevskii, *Ocherki*, 257.

75 A. Lappo-Danilevskii, *Organizatsiia*, 72, 146.

76 *Ukaznaia kniga zemskogo prikaza*, in Vladimirskii-Budanov, *op. cit.*, III, 48–163, §§7, 23.

77 Stashevskii, *Ocherki*, 264 n.

IV

Filaret died on October 1, 1633. His death, some contemporaries believed, was expedited by alarming news from the western battlefront: Shein, having failed to take Smolensk, was now himself surrounded and besieged in his camp outside the city.

War with Poland-Lithuania had always been the supreme objective of Filaret's foreign policy. To a certain extent the conflict was inevitable: Deulino had brought an armistice, not a permanent peace, and Władysław still claimed the Russian crown. The general mood in Moscow was one of aggrieved nationalism and religious exclusiveness; memories of the intervention were still fresh, and Poland was commonly seen as the vanguard of militant Catholicism. In pursuing a belligerent policy the government was reflecting popular sentiment, which regarded an attempt to regain the lost territories as fully justified. But this was not the whole truth. Filaret himself, with his intense personal animosity against Poland, did much to stoke the fires of popular resentment. He bears a great deal of the responsibility for the outbreak of the conflict, and to some extent also for its outcome.[78] As has been mentioned above, there is some evidence to show that, even within the select ruling group, not everyone was satisfied with the patriarch's aggressive course. In his indictment (1634) Shein was alleged to have publicly chided his fellow-boiars, before he set out on campaign, for their unwarlike spirit: "they sat about behind their stoves and were nowhere to be found."[79] Their motives may well have owed as much to political calculation as to personal cowardice. There was reason to suppose that the sacrifices which war would involve would jeopardize the work of reconstruction and might even provoke a repetition of the Troubles.

Filaret endeavored to prepare Russia militarily and diplomatically for the impending conflict, but his measures were haphazard and inadequate. New regiments were formed, modelled on the contemporary western European pattern and trained and commanded by foreign officers.[80] But they could not compensate for the abysmally low standard of efficiency of the levy (*opolchenie*) provided by the service gentry, still the backbone of the Russian armed forces. Apparently the government hesitated to take vigorous steps to enforce order and discipline among the gentry for fear of arousing disaffection. It also committed the serious mistake of transferring men to the west from the southern border, leaving the latter virtually defenceless, a tempting target for the Crimean Tatars. Furthermore, at the crucial moment Moscow gave the

---

78 This was a view common at the time in Poland, where the story was current that Filaret forced Michael to go to war against his will, and even on one occasion struck him a blow in irritation: A. Rembowski, ed., *Dyaryusz wojny moskiewskiej 1633 roku* (Warsaw, 1895), 82. It was also put forwarded by Filaret's Russian critic, Archbishop Pakhomii: Smirnov, "Patriarkh Filaret," 824.

79 *AAE*, III, no. 251.

80 S. M. Solov'ev, *Istoriia Rossii s drevneishikh vremen*[2], 6 vols. (St. Petersburg, 1896), II, 1197–9; [ibid., 15 vols. (Moscow, 1959–66), V (1961), 161–3, 281–2]; O. L. Vainshtein, *Rossiia i 30-letniaia voina 1618–1648 gg.* (Moscow, 1947), 92⊥102.

Tatars an additional pretext for attack by refusing to dispatch the "gifts" due for 1633. The disastrous raid which followed that summer led to mass desertions from Shein's army by gentry who rushed back to defend their homes.[81]

In general, it seems, Filaret underestimated the importance of maintaining close alliances with potentially friendly powers. He was not an isolationist, but his policy lacked initiative and flexibility, and in particular he failed to pin other governments down to firm commitments. Admittedly, the situation both in Turkey and in Sweden was unfavorable to Moscow. In addition to her preoccupations in Asia, Turkey was subject to pressure from both warring European camps, which sought, for opposite reasons, to dissuade her from launching an attack on Poland; moreover, she had no real cause to intervene in a Russo-Polish war, which could only serve her interests by weakening both combatants.[82] Sweden, after the death of Gustavus Adolphus, saw little advantage in maintaining the ties with Moscow to which the late king had attached such importance.[83] In these circumstances Filaret showed rashness in attempting to carry out his original plans without modification. Nor did he appreciate sufficiently the role which the Zaporozh'e cossacks could play as auxiliaries in a campaign against Poland. He poured cold water on the idea, mooted by emissaries from Kiev in 1625, that they might accept the sovereignty of the tsar.[84] When the cossacks revolted five years later, Moscow made no move to aid them. Apparently the patriarch feared the cossacks' independent and anti-authoritarian spirit as much as he did the supposedly heretical tendencies within the west Russian Church. Defeated and disillusioned, the cossacks had no alternative but to offer Władysław their loyal support. In his relations with Warsaw, Filaret remained utterly rigid: he made no secret of Russia's bellicose intentions, deliberately inflated minor issues, and ignored possibilities for a negotiated settlement. In 1629 Polish envoys, anxious to forestall invasion, were refused entry into the country.[85] This was shortsighted, even on the assumption that war was inevitable, which is a debatable proposition.

Filaret has no claim to be regarded either as a diplomat or a statesman. Where he should have shown flexibility, he allowed his dogmatic prejudices to obscure his judgement; where firmness of principle was required, he vacillated and temporized.

---

81 Russo-Tatar relations during this period have been closely studied by A. A. Novosel'skii, *Bor'ba moskovskogo gosudarstva s tatarami v I-oi polovine XVII v.* (Moscow-Leningrad, 1948). From his account (167–222) it is clear that the attack was caused by several complex factors of more fundamental significance than the nonpayment of tribute. However, this issue perhaps deserves more attention than he allows. Moscow's action, though understandable in view of the Tatar attacks during 1632, was a serious tactical blunder.

82 Failure to appreciate this last point detracts from the merits of the useful study of Russo-Turkish relations in these years by N. A. Smirnov, *Rossiia i Turtsiia v XVI–XVII vv.*, *Uchenye zapiski Moskovskogo Universiteta*, vol. 94 (Moscow, 1946), II, 22–38.

83 Vainshtein, *op. cit.*, 109–45; M. Roberts, *Gustavus Adolphus: a History of Sweden, 1611–1632*, 2 vols. (London, 1953, 1958), II, 561–4.

84 Kharlampovich, *Maloross. vliianie*, 26–7.

85 E. Wassenbergius, *Gestorum gloriosissimi ac invictissimi Vladislae IV Poloniae et Sveciae regis* (Danzig, 1647), pt. II, 53–4; *AI*, IV, no. 131.

His domestic policies were little more than a succession of expedients, narrowly conceived and inefficiently executed. Never one to refashion a garment where a patch of old material would suffice, he had no conception of the real task which faced the autocracy: to create the conditions that would enable the country to raise itself out of the slough of medievalism. On the contrary, Filaret was himself a medieval figure, for whom stability was the *summum bonum*. He idealized the past and saw himself not as a reformer but as a restorer. He set out to recreate in Russia the political and social conditions that had existed in his early manhood before the outbreak of civil war. Yet if there was any lesson to be learnt from the "Time of Troubles," it was surely that in the long run the old formulas were inadequate. Filaret, however, shared the common clerical view that the Troubles had been but a senseless upsurge of irreligion and anarchy, and he devoted himself with stubborn perseverance to the task of ensuring that they should not recur.

If he succeeded in his immediate aims of consolidating authority in Church and state, this was partly due to his skill in maneuvering between various competing pressures, harnessing some to his purposes, neutralizing others. But chiefly his success is to be attributed to the amorphous state of Muscovite society. He was fortunate in that Russian absolutism faced no vocal opposition, no well-organized social forces or established institutions with which it was obliged to bargain for power. The Troubles, it is true, had stimulated all classes and groups to a hitherto unwonted degree of independent activity; but at the same time they had led to widespread ruin and social disorganization. There was a general desire for a return to normality, for peaceful and orderly reconstruction. For the present the situation was thus admirably suited to the realization of Filaret's own designs. His regime gained time for the absolutist order to become firmly reestablished, so that when, after his death, hidden tensions reasserted themselves, it was able to withstand the shock with relative ease.

1960

PART II

ARMY AND SOCIETY
IN
IMPERIAL RUSSIA

The Secret Chancellery, The Guards
and The Dynastic Crisis of 1740–1741

I

Russia was unique among eighteenth-century European states in having a specific governmental institution for the repression of political crime. Until the 1760s it applied an archaic and brutal procedure which had originated in Muscovite times; the agency itself dated from the reign of Peter the Great. It operated in secret, although the fact of its existence was not concealed; indeed, it relied wholly upon information provided by members of the public—that is to say, by delators. In theory at least it enjoyed unlimited power to investigate any suspicious inhabitant of the Russian empire, whatever his rank or social status, although in practice it was mainly concerned with the unprivileged classes. Fear of becoming embroiled in its clutches was a powerful deterrent to discussions or actions that might be interpreted as disloyal, the more so since physical torture was extensively used against suspects. Penalties were extremely harsh and at least to modern eyes bore little relationship to the gravity of the offences committed. While the security organs' activity may justly be termed "terroristic," one should beware of anachronistic judgments: they did not seek to maintain comprehensive surveillance of the population, and it is probably a matter of coincidence rather than of national tradition that in eighteenth-century Russia these agencies, like their better known twentieth-century successors, underwent several changes of nomenclature.

The first regularly functioning institution of this kind was the Preobrazhenskii Office (*prikaz*), which began its existence as the headquarters of the guards regiment of that name. It acquired a security role as early as 1695, when Peter I returned from his first Azov campaign,1 and expanded its power two years later when the

---

1 N. V. Golikova, *Politicheskie protesessy pri Petre I. Po materialam Preobrazhenskogo prikaza* (Moscow, 1957), 14. Earlier historians, who knew only the first public reference to the fact in a decree of September 25, 1702 (I *PSZ*, III, no. 1918) wrongly dated it to that year. The pioneer study of the police under Peter I was v. I. Semevskii, *Slovo i delo!, 1700–1725* (St. Petersburg, 1884). I should like to thank Mme. Golikova for her kind assistance in the archival research on which this article is partly based; the responsibility for the views

tsar, leaving Russia on his "grand embassy" to Western Europe, entrusted the task of keeping order in the country to his favorite, *stol'nik* F. Iu. Romodanovskii. The latter applied himself to his duties with great zeal. In the early 1700s his office was dealing with about 50 cases a year, and in 1705–06 it punished over 300 individuals implicated in the Astrakhan' *strel'tsy* revolt.[2] On his death in 1717 Fedor Romodanovskii was succeeded by his son Ivan.[3] A few months later, faced with what he considered treachery by the tsarevich Aleksei, Peter set up another organization known as the Secret Chancellery (*Tainaia kantseliariia*). Although conceived as a temporary commission, it remained in being for the rest of the reign. It had responsibility for security matters in the new capital while the Preobrazhenskii Office, which continued to function in Moscow, dealt with offences arising in the rest of the empire.[4] Their relative importance may be gauged from the fact that between 1719 and its dissolution in May 1726 the Secret Chancellery handled 280 cases, whereas the Preobrazhenskii Office dealt with about two thousand.[5]

Shortly before his death Peter seems to have contemplated merging the two agencies and placing them under the Senate.[6] His motive was probably to improve efficiency rather than to introduce greater legality into their operations, although one should not be too dogmatic about this. There is no doubt that many highly-placed personages were keen to curb the arbitrary powers exercised by these bodies, and that their purpose was not merely to safeguard themselves against denunciation but also to revert to less severe methods of ruling the country. In February 1726 the oligarchs who succeeded Peter as *de facto* masters of Russia set up a Supreme Privy Council as a central policy-making body, to which both security organs, along with all other governmental agencies, were made subject.[7] Three months later, as we have noted, the Secret Chancellery was dissolved. Its records and personnel were transferred to Romodanovskii.[8] One reason given for the change was that matters requiring secret investigation were now "less important" than they had been earlier.

expressed lies wholly with the author.

2 Golikova, *Politicheskie protsessy*, 27–8, 249.

3 Ibid., 20; *Zakonodatel'nye akty Petra I*, ed. N. A. Voskresenskii, vol. 1 (Moscow-Leningrad, 1945), 181 ff.

4 N. V. Golikova, "Organy politicheskogo syska i ikh razvitiia v XVII–XVIII vv.," in *Absoliutizm v Rossii (XVII–XVIII vv.). Sbornik statei k semidesiatiletiiu so dnia rozhdeniia i sorokapiatiletiiu nauchnoi i pedagogicheskoi deiatel'nosti B. B. Kafengauza* (Moscow, 1964), 255–8. For a brief summary in English see R. Hingley, *The Russian Secret Police: Muscovite, Imperial Russian and Soviet Political Security Operations, 1565–1970* (London, 1970), 14.

5 Golikova, "Organy," 258.

6 Golikova, "Organy," 262; *Zakonodatel'nye akty Petra I*, 380.

7 *PSZ*, VII, no. 4830; the security organs are not mentioned specifically. The term *tainyi* may be translated either "privy" or "secret"; the first expression seems more appropriate to this body, the second to the *Tainaia kantseliariia*, in view of their very different functions; this also accords with conventional usage.

8 *PSZ*, VII, no. 4892 (28 May 1726).

One may legitimately infer from this an intention to downgrade the security organizations as well as to consolidate them. The move needs to be seen in the context of various measures taken at this time to limit intervention by the military in the regular civil administration.[9] More authority was also given to the local authorities to deal with such matters, and some provision was made to prevent them from abusing these powers.[10] All security cases referred to St. Petersburg or Moscow by provincial governors were to be reported first to the empress's personal cabinet before the Council or Senate were informed.[11] In this way the powers of the Preobrazhenskii Office were being whittled away simultaneously from above and from below. After Catherine I's death and the banishment of P. A. Tolstoi (who had been closely involved in the Secret Chancellery under Peter) the "old boiars" who now ran the country's affairs lost no time in ordering that security offences be first reported to the Supreme Privy Council, which they dominated (the empress's cabinet having been dissolved).[12] At the same time they ruled that cases arising in the northwestern and Baltic area should be dealt with by the Senate, instead of by Romodanovskii in Moscow. Again one may infer that the motives for this reversion to Petrine practice were as much political as practical: the higher nobility (*znat'*) resided in the area excluded from Romodanovskii's domain, and they evidently sought to enhance their personal security.

Thereupon the Preobrazhenskii Office, now often referred to as a mere chancellery, underwent an eclipse. When Romodanovskii, who had been ailing for some time, asked permission to resign, the ruling group took the opportunity to suppress his agency. In future security matters were to be handled solely by the Supreme Privy Council.[13] The reformers, as we call them, took the view that there would be so few such cases that they could be handled without disrupting routine government business. In this, however, they were oversanguine. For reasons that will shortly become apparent, the Senate soon found itself inundated with denunciations—indeed, besieged by wretched convicts and others who, evidently interpreting these changes as harbingers of a less inhuman penal regime, improperly invoked the special procedure on security matters in the hope of easing their lot—for example of being brought from their place of exile to the capital for examination, or of avoiding corporal punishment (*nesterpia poboi*, "unable to bear the blows," as the decree vividly puts it). This, the councillors observed, involved the authorities in unjustifiable expense; accordingly governors and voivodes were ordered to adhere to proper procedure. Before sending delators to the capital they were to check whether their allegations were made in good faith and whether they could be substantiated by evidence.[14]

There was no hint here of any realization on their part that the abuses stemmed

---

9 Ibid., nos. 4872, 4878, 4885, 4886, 4891. Golikova, in her otherwise valuable account, ignores the efforts to limit the security agencies' powers.

10 Ibid., no. 4952 (26 Aug. 1726).

11 Ibid., no. 4954 (7 Sept. 1726).

12 Ibid., no. 5078 (24 May 1727).

13 Ibid., no. 5397 (4 Apr. 1729).

14 Ibid., no. 5434 (June 1729).

from defects inherent in the security system itself, which as we shall see was so constructed as to encourage denunciation of innocent individuals by other innocent individuals, and that the only reasonable course was to abolish it *in toto*. Perhaps the oligarchs might have gone on to consider such a step, but almost at once they were faced with a major political crisis. On the sudden death of Peter II in January 1730 an ill-prepared move was made to introduce a quasi-constitutional regime. This very soon backfired when the partisans of unlimited autocracy, with support from *dvoriane* and others suspicious of the oligarchs' intentions, persuaded Anna Ivanovna, the ruler whom they had invited to succeed, publicly to renounce the "conditions" she had initially signed and to assert her full powers as Sovereign Autocrat.[15]

During the lively but confused informal discussions held in Moscow in February 1730 some gentry servitors favored a more broadly based constitutional order, in which *inter alia* the security authorities should be brought under control of the regular state institutions. In this they were clearly reflecting ideas that had been in the air for some years. Most explicit in this respect was V. N. Tatishchev. He advocated "a system of police or 'overseers' to discourage and prevent intrigue by opportunists"[16] headed by "an honest individual" (*chelovek blagochestivyi*), which should include four members of the Senate, elected for a one-month term, to supervise its activities. He further proposed that a gentry deputy should be present when political suspects (presumably *dvoriane*) were arrested.[17] The signatories to this document no doubt shared Tatishchev's opinion that the present system was unjust and that it gave Russians grounds for shame in the eyes of western Europeans.

Unfortunately for many years nothing was to come of these enlightened ideas. Anna Ivanovna at once acted to bolster her shaky power by tightening up the security

---

15 On the 1730 crisis see D. A. Korsakov, *Votsarenie imperatritsy Anny Ioannovny* (Kazan', 1880); P. N. Miliukov, "Verkhovniki i shliakhetstvo" [1894], in *Iz istorii russkoi intelligentsii. Sbornik statei i etiudov* (St. Petersburg, 1903), 1–51; M. M. Bogoslovskii, *Konstitutsionnoe dvizhenie 1730 g.* (Moscow, 1906) (Biblioteka "Svobodnoi Rossii," no. 18); and the works conveniently listed by M. Raeff, *Plans for Political Reform in Imperial Russia, 1730–1905* (Englewood Cliffs, N.J., 1966), 42 n., to which should be added H. Fleischhacker, "1730. Das Nachspiel der petrinischen Reform," in *Jahrbücher für Geschichte Osteuropas* 6 (1941), 201–74; D. Labelle, "Failure of Dvorianstvo to Establish a Government of Limited Representation in 1730" (Diss. Chicago, 1961); G. A. Protasov, "Zapiska Tatishcheva o 'proizvol'nom rassuzhdenii' dvorianstva v sobytiiakh 1730 g.," in *Problemy istochnikovedeniia*, 11 (1963), 237–65 (based on his dissertation for the Moskovskii oblastnoi pedagogicheskii institut, 1955); B. Meehan-Waters, "The Russian Generalitet of 1730. Towards a Definition of Aristocracy" (Diss. Rochester, 1970); D. L. Ransel, "Political Perceptions of the Russian Nobility. The Constitutional Crisis of 1730," in *Laurentian University Review* 4 (1971/2), 3, 20–38; R. L. Daniels, *V. N. Tatishchev. Guardian of the Petrine Revolution* (Philadelphia, 1973). [See also B. Meehan-Waters, *Autocracy and Aristocracy: the Russian Service Elite of 1730* (New Brunswick, N.J., 1982).]

16 Daniels, *Tatishchev*, 38.

17 Bogoslovskii, *Konstitutsionnoe dvizhenie*, 26. For the text of the project see "Proizvol'noe i soglasnoe rassuzhdenie i mnenie sobravshegosia shliakhetstva russkogo o napravlenii gosudarstvennom," in *Utro* (St. Petersburg, 1859), 369–79.

system, but was at pains to present her motives in the best possible light. In the preamble to an *ukaz* of April 10, 1730 she returned to the problem of excessive numbers of false denunciations. "We, showing mercy toward Our faithful subjects, [and desiring] that in future less blood should be shed in vain, have most graciously ordered the following decree to be printed for general information." The detailed provisions laid down in several respects departed from recent precedents and evoked the terms of Petrine legislation. Delators were positively encouraged to denounce "without fear" (*bez vsiakogo opaseniia i boiazni*), being promised a reward for doing so; in the case of suspected rebels torture was explicitly sanctioned (*bud' doidet do pytki to i pytat'*); and failure to denounce a known traitor was to carry the death penalty, as was false denunciation "out of malice or because of some quarrel."[18] Some attempt was made to define political offences more carefully, and those falsely incriminated were to receive compensation; but on the whole the decree marked a distinct step backward. It was bound to sow alarm among the populace and to accelerate the flow of denunciations, adding to the difficulties of the Senate (to which such matters were now referred, as the Supreme Privy Council had been abolished).

A year later, on March 24, 1731, Anna Ivanovna felt strong enough to draw the obvious inference. Since 1729, when the Preobrazhenskii Office had "been ordered not to exist" [sic], she wrote, there had been "no slight disarray" (*nemaloe pomeshatel'stvo*) in State affairs; "therefore We have ordered the aforementioned important matters to be in charge of Our general Ushakov." The Senate was to provide him with the necessary clerical assistance "and the rest" (a euphemistic reference to those persons skilled in the standard interrogatory practices).[19] On April 6 the new office was formally designated "the Chancellery for Secret Investigatory Affairs" (*Kantseliariia tainykh rozysknyh del*). It was given authority to send memoranda (*promemorii*) to all central governmental institutions and decrees (*ukazy*) to those in the provinces.[20] The Petrine tradition had been restored with a vengeance.

Major-General Andrei Ivanovich Ushakov (1672–1747) was no stranger to his charge, having served in the Secret Chancellery under Peter I and subsequently (1726–7) in the Preobrazhenskii Office; as an associate of Tolstoi he had then fallen into disfavor and had been sent to serve in a field regiment. In the 1730 crisis he had spoken out as a partisan of autocracy and was rewarded by the return of his seat in the Senate. (He also held a lieutenant-colonelcy in the Semenovskii guards regiment and combined military duties with his political and security functions.)[21] As Golikova comments, "obliged to Anna Ivanovna for his future career, he was a man on whom

---

18 *PSZ*, VIII, no. 5528; cf. Golikova, "Organy," 265; V. I. Veretennikov, *Iz istorii Tainoi kantseliarii 1731–1762 gg. Ocherki* (Khar'kov, 1911), 47.

19 *PSZ*, VIII, no. 5727.

20 Ibid., no. 5738.

21 Korsakov, *Votsarenie imperatritsy Anny*, 211; *B & E*, 125. The volume in the *RBS* which would have contained his biography was not published. For his birth date, sometimes given as 1670, see *Azbuchnyi ukazatel' imen russkikh deiatelei dlia Russkogo biograficheskogo slovaria* (St. Petersburg, 1887–8, reprinted Vaduz, 1963).

she could count."[22] This experienced functionary combined ruthlessness with a rare
discretion, steering clear of court intrigue except in so far as was necessary to maintain
the prerogatives of his office. According to D. N. Bantysh-Kamenskii, writing in the
early nineteenth century, "in running the Secret Chancellery he would carry out the
most cruel tortures, while in the salons he distinguished himself by his charm of
manner and a special talent for discerning the thoughts of his conversation partners."[23]
Such a mixture of contrasting psychological traits seems less surprising to us today.

There is no doubt that Ushakov was widely feared and that there was a considerable
increase in the number of political cases during Anna Ivanovna's reign, which many
historians have characterized as a virtual "reign of terror."[24] No large staff was
required for this purpose. In 1736 the KTRD (as we shall call it, although such
abbreviations were of course not in use at the time) had a mere thirteen men in
St. Petersburg and about the same number in Moscow.[25] Some of them had worked
in the Preobrazhenskii Office, whose quarters Ushakov inherited.[26] The source of
his power was his close relationship with the empress, to whom he had the privilege
of reporting directly, either orally or in writing, without having to go through the
Senate. Anna Ivanovna would confirm his decisions without demur and sometimes
took a personal interest in the details of a case. There was in her character a streak
of vindictive cruelty which Ushakov knew how to gratify. This relationship was
somewhat attenuated after 1735, when with the outbreak of war with Turkey greater
power was assumed by the Cabinet (*Kabinet*), a supreme policy-making body in
which A. I. Osterman was the leading figure. Ushakov was not a member of this
three-man organ, although he seems to have attended its sessions frequently.[27] It was

22 Golikova, "Organy," 266.
23 D. N. Bantysh-Kamenskii, *Slovar' dostopamiatnykh liudei Russkoi zemli*, pt. III (St. Petersburg, 1847), 445.
24 Several modern historians (for example V. O. Kliuchevskii, *Kurs russkoi istorii*, pt. IV
(Petrograd, 1918), 380; P. N. Miliukov et al., *Histoire de Russie*, vol. II (Paris, 1932),
464; K. Stählin, *Geschichte Rußlands von den Anfängen bis zur Gegenwart*, Bd. II [1930],
reprinted (Graz, 1961), 231) quote a figure of more than 20,000 persons exiled to Siberia
during Anna Ivanovna's reign; of these 5,000 are said to have disappeared without trace and
some to have been exiled under false names. No evidence is offered in support of these high
figures, which evidently include common criminals as well as political offenders. Shortly
after Anna's death the French ambassador, Marquis de la Chétardie, reported a story that
7,200 persons had been put to death and 30,000 exiled to Siberia during the reign: *SIRIO*,
92 (1894), 197. For a more balanced recent evaluation of the period see A. Lipski, "The
Dark Era of Anna Ivanovna. A Re-examination," in *American Slavic and East European
Review*, 15 (1956), 477–88.
25 Veretennikov, *Iz istorii*, 108, 111. This scarce monograph, although written from a strictly
juridical standpoint, is based upon archival sources and remains the standard work on its
subject.
26 Ibid., 5; Golikova, "Organy," 266.
27 Veretennikov, *Iz istorii*, 14–19, 80. On the Cabinet see A. N. Filippov, in *Istoriia Pravitel'stvuiushchego Senata*, 5 vols. (St. Petersburg, 1911), vol. 1, 500–47, where however the
Secret Chancellery is not mentioned. The Cabinet's papers were printed under Filippov's

presumably at the behest of P. I. Iaguzhinskii, who replaced chancellor G. I. Golovkin in April 1735, that on June 12 of that year the Senate instructed Ushakov to inform it of all verbal commands he received from the empress and to act only on those which the Cabinet confirmed. He at once complained to Anna Ivanovna that this would compromise the secrecy of the KTRD's affairs; she agreed, and the Cabinet had no alternative but to comply with her will.[28] This episode may be regarded as a feeble echo of the efforts made a few years earlier to limit the powers of the security organs. Ushakov continued to report in person to the empress, and was among those responsible for the investigation in 1740 of the would-be reformer A. P. Volynskii, whose "general project" is known to have included measures designed to ensure better observance of the law.[29]

His relations with Anna Ivanovna's favorite, Ernst-Johann von Bühren (Biren), are usually represented as cordial.[30] However, as a Russian and still more as an administrator with considerable political *savoir-faire*, Ushakov could not but be concerned at Bühren's irresponsibility and arrogance. In the autumn of 1740 matters became critical at the Russian court. On October 5 Anna Ivanovna designated as her successor the future Ivan VI, an infant less than two months old. Her health was rapidly failing, and on the very eve of her death (October 17) she confirmed a decision, previously reached at a conclave of her advisers, that Bühren should become regent. Ushakov must have been anxious for the future of the regime he had served with such zeal. An interregnum of indeterminate duration could not be avoided, and the experience of 1730 might well be repeated. How was the KTRD to fulfill its mission of safeguarding state security when the supreme power rested with individuals who were unpopular and unfit to govern?

The troubled year that separates the death of one empress from the accession of another, Elizaveta Petrovna, was to witness two *coups d'état*, intense political maneuvering and diplomatic intrigue, and a brief foreign war. Curiously enough, it has received little attention from historians, largely for political reasons. To partisans of monarchist legitimism the subject seemed embarrassing and distasteful; on the other hand liberal historians, struck by the apparently slight echo of the crisis in Russian "society," have dismissed it as unworthy of serious study. Yet the crisis offers an opportunity to examine the viability of the post-Petrine institutional structure at a time of stress. Of particular interest in this regard is the relationship between two pillars of the regime, distinct yet not unrelated, which were bound to eye one another warily: the KTRD, as the security organ, and the army, or more specifically the guards regiments.

editorship in *SIRIO*, vols. 104, 106, 108, 111, 114, 117, 120, 124, 126, 130, 138, 146 (1898–1915).

28 Veretennikov, *Iz istorii*, 82–5.

29 S. M. Solov'ev, *Istoriia Rossii s drevneishikh vremen v 15 knigakh* (Moscow, 1963), kn. 10 (tom 20), 681.

30 See Veretennikov, *Iz istorii*, 20. The source of this view seems to be the younger Münnich, who was not an unbiased witness: [E. von Münnich], *Ebauche pour donner une idée de la forme du gouvernement de l'Empire de Russie* (Copenhagen, 1774), 130.

II

Before leaving the KTRD for the guards, some explanation must be given of the procedure which the security organs of this period employed in their investigations. It goes without saying that there did not exist any precise legal definition of what constituted a political offence. It did not just extend to treason, mutiny, insurrection, or attempts on the life or health of the monarch—all of which were of course serious crimes throughout Europe.[31] In Russia the distinction between the autocratic sovereign and the state was still imperfectly understood. The ruler's person was popularly regarded with a superstitious awe. This meant that in practise the concept of sedition was broadened to include even the casual utterance of some remark which the listener deemed injurious to the security of the central *vlast'* (authority), regardless of the spirit or circumstances in which it was made—as well as the pilfering of property, corruption by public officials and similar transgressions.

In the seventeenth century anyone having knowledge of such offences was duty bound to bring them to the notice of the authorities.[32] This he could do either by informing them directly or else, if he were in some public place, crying aloud the so-called "Sovereign's words" (*slovo i delo Gosudarevo,* or some similar expression), whereupon it was every bystander's solemn obligation to bring him before the nearest official, who then had at once to forward the person(s) incriminated, the delator, and any witness(es) to the appropriate central government institution. Peter I ordered the regular officials not to interrogate delators themselves,[33] lest they should thereby be tempted to suppress information prejudicial to their own persons; but as we have seen this rule was later relaxed. In 1715 he also made a crude effort to distinguish political offences proper from the many others for which people were being denounced. The former came to be called "the first two [or three] points." They were, respectively: (i) "evil intent against His (Imperial) Majesty's person or treason"; (ii) disturbance or insurrection; (iii) embezzlement of state funds.[34] However, these terms were not defined further, and the tsar simultaneously nullified the positive intentions of this decree by encouraging the spread of delation. Lavish rewards were offered to those whose denunciations were found to be justified, and the notorious fiscals (*fiskaly*) had as their *raison d'être* the task of informing upon their fellow officials.

---

31 C. L. von Bar et al., *A History of Continental Criminal Law,* translated by T. S. Bell et al. (Boston, 1916), esp. 230–2; 240; H. A. Fehr, *Deutsche Rechtsgeschichte* 5 (Lehrbücher und Grundrisse der Rechtswissenschaft, X) (Berlin, 1952), 210–14.

32 For the historical antecedents seenow A. Kleimola, "The Duty to Denounce in Muscovite Russia," *Slavic Review,* 31 (1972), 759–79. The 1649 *Ulozhenie* fixed penalties for what it described as "the great affairs of the Sovereign" (chapter II, §14; cf. also chapter XXI, §103: *Sobornoe Ulozhenie 1649 g. Uchebnoe posobie dlia vysshei shkoly* (Moscow, 1961), 73, 286), but did not regulate the procedure to be employed, which was evidently rooted in custom. The term *slovo i delo,* current in the seventeenth and early eighteenth centuries, was a corruption of *slovo ili delo Gosudarevo* and meant "I know of some utterance (or action) touching the (affairs, interest of the) Sovereign."

33 *PSZ,* III, no. 1918.

34 Ibid., V, no. 2877 (25 Jan. 1715); cf. no. 2756 (23 Dec. 1713).

The result, naturally enough, was to intensify the fear and suspicion that pervaded all classes of the population. On one hand, delation without due cause brought severe penalties; on the other hand, anyone who allowed an offense to go unreported might well, if the affair later came to notice, find himself incriminated as an accomplice of the culprit. In March 1722, in a public place in the town of Penza, a man cried out "many evil words concerning the August honor of His Imperial Majesty," but the crowd of bystanders did nothing about it. The affair was eventually reported and the delator (a shopkeeper named F. Kamenshchik) suitably recompensed; henceforward, the indignant emperor thundered, "culprits shall be handcuffed and fettered and sent under strict guard to the Secret Chancellery or to the Preobrazhenskii Office"; leaving nothing to chance, he attached to the decree a sketch illustrating the size and shape of the fetters.[35]

No such detailed provisions, needless to say, were laid down concerning the treatment which the accused would receive once he was delivered to his interrogators. Here everything was left to the arbitrary judgment of the official concerned. Normally the suspect would be questioned orally and then confronted with the delator; if this failed to clarify the matter the investigator called upon the services of his sinister technician, the *zaplechnyi master*. Torture was referred to in the 1649 law code, but in vague terms.[36] Later legislators, as we have seen in the case of Anna Ivanovna, were less squeamish; and this was of course particularly true of the Tsar-Reformer himself. This is not the place to explore the actual methods employed. Aleksei Tolstoi, in his novel *Petr Pervyi*, gives a graphic description of the barbarous rack (*dyba*).[37] Veretennikov tells us that in the 1730s flogging (with the knout) was first used; if that failed to produce satisfactory results the suspect's head would be placed in a vice and cold water dripped upon his shaven scalp; the ultimate weapons in the investigators' armory were the rack and the branding-iron.[38] There was nothing to stop physical pressure being applied against the delator and the witnesses as well as the suspect. Nor, apparently, was any distinction made in this regard between the first stage of the investigation, designed to establish whether a political offence had indeed been committed, and the second, designed to ascertain the suspect's guilt.

As for the penalties imposed, these likewise increased in cruelty as time went on. For example, the *Ulozhenie* prescribed that a delator who withdrew his allegation under questioning, saying that it had been made when he was intoxicated or under coercion, was to be knouted and returned to his master.[39] The decree of April 10, 1730, added that if his master would not receive him back, and if he were unfit to become a soldier, he should be knouted, have his nostrils torn, and be exiled to

---

35 Ibid., VI, no. 3984 (28 Apr. 1722).

36 *"Pro Gosudarevo delo i pro izmenu syskivat' vsiakimi syski nakrepko"* (chapter II, §16); *"i syshchetsia pro to dopriama"* (§17). On the use of torture against common criminals see above, 97–100.

37 *Petr Pervyi: roman* (Moscow, 1947), 179–84.

38 Veretennikov, *Iz istorii*, 104.

39 Chapter II, §14; see fn. 32.

indefinite hard labor in the silver mines of Siberia.[40]

For offences committed by military personnel, which are of special interest to us here, Peter I substituted for the knout the punishment of running the gauntlet (*shpits-ruten*; German: *Spitzrut[h]en* or *Spiessrut[h]en*), borrowed from western European practise. This was made a standard penalty by the military code of March 30, 1716,[41] which was modeled upon the Prussian *Kriegsartikel* of July 12, 1713.[42] It was the military equivalent of the knout, which Peter thought degrading for a soldier, although the pain and injury inflicted were no less severe. From the authorities' standpoint it had one distinct psychological advantage over the knout, since it isolated the offender morally from his comrades, who were forced to join in administering the penalty. The army unit to which he belonged was drawn up in two facing rows to form a "street" (*ulitsa; Gasse*) through which the offender, stripped to the waist, had to proceed while each man struck him with a thong about one inch in diameter; any indulgence on their part was itself regarded as a punishable offence. The victim could not evade their blows by quickening his pace, since he had to stagger along behind an NCO who held a rifle with fixed bayonet pointed to the rear. It is debatable whether the penalty was administered more brutally in Prussia or in Russia. In both countries the maximum sentence was equivalent to a death penalty. A Prussian officer, J. W. von Archenholz, states that a 30-run sentence was called *auf Leben und Tod* and was spread over three days, "da dann am letzten Tage mit dem Verbrecher auch gleich der Sarg auf die Parade gebracht wurde."[43] In Russia there are reports of the punishment continuing to be exacted upon men who had lost consciousness and were carried through the ranks lying on a board.[44] The chief difference seems to have been that whereas in Prussia the number of men forming the gauntlet was limited (to 200), in Russia it was not clearly specified either in law or in practise.

In considering Russian penal legislation it is the spirit of the law that matters as much as the detailed provisions. The practical effect was to make all those who had anything to do with political offenders treat them with the utmost severity and to repress any humane instincts or even commonsense notions they might have harbored. The procedure was such that even the most trivial incident was automatically inflated out of all proportion to its real significance and brought to the attention of the highest authorities in the land. Moreover, these officials acquired a vested interest in preserving the system as it was. They came to regard it, quite wrongly, as an integral part

---

40 *PSZ*, VIII, no. 5528, §4.

41 *Ustav voinskii*, in *Pamiatniki russkogo prava*, fasc. 8 (*Zakonodatel'nye akty Petra Velikogo*, ed. K. A. Sofronenko) (Moscow, 1961), 319–69, §§1, 6, 26, 37 *et passim*.

42 On the latter see C. Jany, *Geschichte der preußischen Armee vom 15. Jhd. bis 1914*², ed. E. Jany, vol. I. *Von den Anfängen bis 1740*, reprinted (Osnabrück, 1967), 713–14.

43 J. W. von Archenholz, *Gemälde der preußischen Armee vor und in dem Siebenjährigen Kriege* [1791], Zeitgenössische Studien über die altpreußische Armee (Osnabrück, 1974), 28.

44 A. Timofeev, *Shpitsruten*, in *B & E*, 39, 845 f.

of the country's ancient customs and traditions, its *starina*.[45] Inertia and selfinterest combined to thwart moves towards a more rational or enlightened way of protecting the security of the ruler and of the state power which he embodied.

III

It is a curious paradox that the regiments of the Imperial guard (*leib-gvardiia*), which had been so to speak the midwife at the birth of the security organization, should eventually have become one of its major objects of concern. It would be anachronistic to speak at this stage of institutional rivalry, but elements of antagonism certainly existed in embryo.

The Petrine era was followed by a period of dynastic instability in which the élite guards regiments sometimes played a political role, notably at moments of crisis. Guardsmen were the instruments used by powerful personages at court, members of the dynasty as well as so-called "favorites" (*vremenshchiki*), to effect or attempt several *coups d'état*. The whole era has occasionally been referred to as "the age of palace revolutions,"[46] although the term is misleading. Equally inaccurate is the popular notion that the guardsmen acted as "the vanguard of the *dvorianstvo*": while it is true that most guardsmen were nobles, an element of military professionalism is involved in their political interventions as well as an element of social egotism. In any case the advocates of this standard view have yet to explore the modalities whereby the guards regiments articulated such "class consciousness" or political ambition as Russian gentrymen at that time possessed. Another fallacy is that the guardsmen were "Praetorians": although the term was occasionally used in regard to Russia by contemporary western observers, as well as by later historians, it is inapposite and should be discarded. The whole phenomenon deserves critical scrutiny.[47]

What lies beyond all doubt is that the Petrine state rested upon the new regular army and that the guards formed an élite within this élite. Otto Hintze remarked of Prussia that "the entire state acquired a military aspect";[48] the same is true of the Russian empire as well. Both the administration and the society which Peter bequeathed to posterity were heavily militarized.[49] The pressure was eased in some respects during the reigns of his immediate successors, but the army continued to grow and its cost

---

45 W. Philipp, "Altrußland bis zum Ende des 16. Jahrhunderts," in *Propyläen Weltgeschichte*, ed. G. Mann, A. Nitzschke, vol. 5 (Berlin, Frankfurt and Vienna, 1963), 240–63.

46 One who used the cliché term was M. T. Florinsky, *Russia: A History and an Interpretation* (New York, 1953), vol. I, 481.

47 See our *Soldiers of the Tsar . . .* , pp. 232, 247, 269–72.

48 O. Hintze, "Staatsverfassung und Heeresverfassung" [1906], in *Militarismus. Francis Carsten zum 65. Geburtstag*, ed. V. R. Berghahn (Gütersloh, 1975), 76.

49 M. M. Bogoslovskii, *Oblastnaia reforma Petra Velikogo. Provintsiia 1719–1727 gg.* (St. Petersburg, 1902, reprinted The Hague and Paris, 1972) (Slavistic Printings and Reprintings ed. C. H. van Schooneveld, 195), 390–403, 424–43. Guardsmen were used on a variety of essentially civilian errands and tasks, for example helping to construct the celebrated fountains at Petergof, collecting taxes, suppressing banditry etc. Cf. also M. P. Azenchevskii, *Istoriia Preobrazhenskogo polka* (Moscow, 1859), 228; A. P. Kartsov, *Istoriia leib-gvardii Semenovskogo polka, 1683–1854* (St. Petersburg, 1852), 181.

represented a heavy drain upon the state budget. In 1720 total effectives, according to official establishment figures (*shtaty*), were (in round figures) 178,000, excluding the *land-militsiia* and cossack irregulars; of this number guardsmen accounted for a mere 5,817.[50] The *shtaty* for 1731 show an increase in total peacetime effectives, to 199,000 (with an additional 10,000 in wartime), and the number of guardsmen had almost doubled, reaching 9,748—this despite the economy drive instituted by the oligarchic regime of 1725–30. In 1740 the figures for total effectives were little different (203,000) and those for guardsmen identical.[51]

The first infantry guards regiments, the Preobrazhenskii and Semenovskii, formed in 1687, were joined in 1719 by a cavalry unit, the Life Guards (*leib-regiment*). After Peter's death there was formed a so-called Cavalry Guard, a sovereign's honor escort in battalion strength, numbering a mere 73 individuals.[52] A more significant expansion occurred in 1730 with the creation of the Izmailovskii and Cavalry (*Konnyi*) regiments.[53] Political motives were evidently not absent from this decision, for although Anna Ivanovna owed her assumption of autocratic powers to the guards the crisis had shown that the two old regiments were not wholly reliable. There is, however, no hard evidence of this. Shortly afterwards the Cavalry Guard and Life Guards were dissolved.[54] No purge was carried out: some men were transferred from other regiments to the Cavalry regiment,[55] but this was probably just a matter of military routine. On the other hand Anna Ivanovna took care to recruit officers to the Izmailovskii regiment prevailingly from Baltic Germans and foreigners; the NCOs were drawn from line regiments and the privates from the Ukrainian land-militsiia. In the Cavalry regiment non-Russians accounted for 16 out of 38 senior officers whose names are known,[56] but the regimental staff was wholly Russian. The

---

50 F. von Stein, *Geschichte des russischen Heeres vom Ursprunge desselben bis zur Thronbesteigung des Kaisers Nikolai I. Pawlowitsch* (Hanover, 1885), 80–3. L. G. Beskrovnyi, the leading Soviet authority on eighteenth-century Russian military history, gives figures which, when added up, come to approximately 172,000: the difference may be accounted for by the sappers, for whom he offers no estimate. L. G. Beskrovnyi, *Russkaia armiia i flot v XVIII veke. Ocherki* (Moscow, 1958), 40–9. A similar figure (180,000) was given at the time by a well-informed foreign observer: [C. F. Weber], *Das veränderte Rußland* (Frankfurt and Leipzig, 1744), vol. 2, 45.

51 Von Stein, *Geschichte des russischen Heeres*, 99 f., 112 ff. In these calculations we have included the sizeable *Nizovyi korpus* and its successor, which formally speaking were auxiliaries (*nestroevye*), and the artillery, but excluded the land-militsiia, irregulars and the members of the Cadet Corps. See Beskrovnyi, *Russkaia armiia*, 55 for an estimate of strength in 1734, in which the guards regiments number 9,580.

52 *PSZ*, VII, no. 4876 (30 Apr. 1726); increased to 89 in the following year: I. Pushkarev, *Istoriia Imperatorskoi rossiiskoi gvardii* (St. Petersburg, 1844), 11, 137.

53 *PSZ*, VII, nos. 5623 (22 Sept. 1730), 5664 (31 Dec. 1730).

54 *Istoriia kavalergardov i kavalergardskogo E. V. polka s 1724 po 1 iulia 1851 g.* (St. Petersburg, 1851), 16; Pushkarev, *Istoriia*, 178.

55 Pushkarev, *Istoriia*, 149; A. Chicherin, S. Dolgov, A. Afanasev, *Istoriia leib-gvardii Preobrazhenskogo polka, 1683–1853 gg.*, 4 vols. (St. Petersburg, 1883), vol. 2, 548.

56 [I. V.] Annenkov, *Istoriia leib-gvardii Konnogo polka 1731–1848* (St. Petersburg, 1849), 15 ff.

Izmailovskii regiment had exactly the same complement as the Semenovskii: 62 officers, 162 NCOs and 2,437 privates (including 55 auxiliaries (*nestroevye*)). The Preobrazhenskii regiment was considerably larger (85 officers, 194 NCOs and 3,269 + 84 privates) and the Cavalry regiment much smaller (52 officers, 116 NCOs and 1,434 + 169 privates).[57]

In addition to the two new regular guards regiments two companies of retired guardsmen were formed into a "Moscow life-guards battalion" which had no fixed establishment. Anna had assumed the colonelcy of this unit even before she took the throne, and it probably had a political security role as "overseer" of the old capital. She was also colonel of the Preobrazhenskii regiment; later that year she took over the colonelcy of the Semenovskii, and in 1735 that of the Izmailovskii regiments. This concentration of authority could be rationalized as a return to the Petrine tradition, although obviously her role was bound to be more symbolic than Peter's had been. On a practical plane the gesture was designed to secure the officers' personal loyalty and affection. More effective, no doubt, in achieving this purpose was the existence of a central chancellery to administer all guards regiments. This had been set up already before Anna Ivanovna's accession, in December, 1729, by Field-Marshal V. V. Dolgorukii, the most statesmanlike member of the clan which then enjoyed a shortlived paramountcy at court. Anna Ivanovna placed it in the charge of her distant relative and close counselor, S. A. Saltykov, who was also commander-in-chief of the armed forces stationed in Moscow.[58] The general chancellery was directly subordinate to the sovereign and stood on an equal footing with the War College, which administered the remainder of the armed forces.

The effect of these control measures was heightened by a generous pay structure which made guardsmen a privileged élite within the armed forces. During Peter's reign expenditure per head was twice as high for a guardsman than it was for an infantryman in a line regiment.[59] The estimates adopted in 1731 gave certain guards officers and NCOs a significant salary increase,[60] and the differentials between ranks, already vast, were widened still further: for example, a lieutenant-colonel now drew about seven times as much pay as a lieutenant and over 60 times as much as a private. In addition to their regular pay guardsmen sometimes received lavish bonuses. Two of these payments that are documented, relating to 1726 and 1740, were equivalent to one-third of annual salary.[61] Occasionally they received hospitality (such as the almost legendary *riumka* of vodka after a parade in the winter frost) at the hands of the reigning sovereign.[62]

---

57 Pushkarev, *Istoriia*, 153–158.

58 Ibid., 160; *RBS*, vol. 18, 117 f.

59 Von Stein, *Geschichte des russischen Heeres*, 66. This figure, for 1711, refers to direct payments and excludes the cost of equipment, supplies etc.

60 Pushkarev, *Istoriia*, 54, 172 ff. Captains and sergeants received 65–70% more than in the 1716 estimates, lieutenant-colonels and lieutenants 25% more, but privates only 4% more.

61 Ibid., 126, 198.

62 Ibid., 132, 187; D. I. Iazykov, ed., "Zapiski V. A. Nashchokina, . . . ,"

When considering these data two points need to be borne in mind. First, guardsmen had certain obligations that were not shared by officers in line regiments: the provision of resplendent uniforms and mounts, maintenance of expensive residences in the capital, etc. Second, a guards officer's rank had a status two grades higher than that of an officer in a line regiment, so that a lieutenant was the equivalent of an army captain. Nevertheless there is no doubt that guardsmen were the spoiled darlings of the régime. Their privileged status must have aroused a good deal of envy and ill feeling among their fellow soldiers. This sentiment was kept within tolerable bounds by the device of paying the guards regiments from resources allocated specifically to their upkeep, independently of the general military budget.[63] In 1731 the total cost of the guards was estimated at approximately ¼ million roubles, equivalent to 8% of that of the rest of the military establishment (3 million roubles). The approximate average cost per man works out at 24 roubles as against 15 roubles in field and garrison units.[64] This was a narrower differential than in 1711, but the actual cost may well have been higher than these *shtaty* suggest; moreover, budgetary estimates were frequently exceeded in practise.

Generally speaking, in post-Petrine Russia the guards regiments were a noble preserve. However, this rule seems to have been adhered to with some strictness only in the cavalry. Peter had ordered the Life Guards to be recruited from the *dvorianstvo*; but in 1732 of 850 men then in its successor, the Cavalry regiment, only 700 were nobles.[65] The central authorities' policy on this question was necessarily ambiguous, for they were interested in professional efficiency as well as social profile; in any case they could not wholly determine admissions and promotions at unit level so long as such matters were decided, as Peter had laid down, by taking a ballot of the officers concerned.[66] Moreover, the supply of *dvoriane* recruits appears to have fallen behind demand, despite the well-known preference of Russian gentrymen for military rather than civilian service. No figures are available for normal wastage through sickness, postings etc., but the Preobrazhenskii regimental records for 1740–1 suggest that turnover was high.[67] Furthermore, a mixed detachment of guardsmen from various regiments took part in three campaigns against the Turks between 1737 and 1739 in which casualties were heavy.[68] The war forced the authorities to lay more emphasis on merit, rather than length of service, as the criterion for promotion to fill vacancies.

RA, 21 (1883), 2, 286; [C. F. Weber], *Das veränderte Rußland*, vol. 2, 43.

63 Pushkarev, *Istoriia*, 126 f.

64 Calculated from data in von Stein, *Geschichte*, 101 and Pushkarev, *Istoriia*, 173. Curiously Beskrovnyi offers no details on military finance.

65 Annenkov, *Istoriia . . . Konnogo polka*, xix, 18; Pushkarev, *Istoriia*, 137.

66 Pushkarev, *Istoriia*, 59.

67 Chicherin et al., *Istoriia . . . Preobrazhenskogo polka*, vol. II, 266 f. [In the first seven months of 1741 (except for three weeks for which no records have survived), 220 officers or men were retired and 25 posted to other units. TsGVIA, fond 2583, opis' 3, ed. khr. 258 (orders to Preobrazhenskii regimental office, Jan.–Nov. 1741), ll. 1–96.]

68 Pushkarev, *Istoriia*, 189–97; cf. also the "orders of battle" tabulated by V. V. Zvegintsov, *Russkaia armiia*, pt. I (Paris, 1967), 65 ff.

A decree of September 6, 1736, to this effect reached Ushakov, in his capacity as lieutenant-colonel in the Semenovskii regiment.[69] V. A. Nashchokin, who served as a captain-lieutenant in the Izmailovskii regiment, and one of the few officers to have written memoirs, states that in 1740 priority was given to men who had served in the war when making appointments and promotions.[70]

Peter I had conceived the guards regiments as a crack force embodying all the military virtues; better trained and equipped, a model of discipline and morale, they would stiffen the resolve of ordinary soldiers on the battlefield. As the Great Northern War drew to its close they assumed a more explicitly educational role, passing on their experience to men assigned to them for training. From 1733, however, they shared this function with a new pedagogical institution, the Cadet Corps (*Kadetskii skliakhetskii korpus*). By Anna Ivanovna's reign guardsmen were spending more time than before in quasi-military pursuits, only the annual summer maneuvers (and then the Turkish war) reminding them of their *raison d'être*. Permission to retire from the service, or to go on leave, was granted more readily than had been the case under Peter I,[71] although only the wealthier men could take advantage of this privilege. Some officers were temporarily seconded to foreign armies,[72] and disciplinary standards appear to have been relaxed, even if only slightly.[73]

Simultaneously membership of a guards regiment came to be seen as a mark of status, conferring dignity as much as imposing responsibility. In certain circumstances men could retain their guards rank after resigning their commissions and taking up service elsewhere, whether in a line regiment or in the civil bureaucracy.[74] The proportion of such "supernumeraries" (as we may call them) to actual effectives seems to have risen swiftly, although detailed archival research would be necessary to establish this point. It was certainly inflated by the curious practise of enlisting juveniles in guards regiments in order to curtail their term of adult service, although this was less common in this period than in the latter half of the century.[75] We are told by one regimental historian that guardsmen "looked on the regiment as a second family" and preferred to continue to serve in its rank rather than to be posted (with a promotion in rank) to a field unit.[76] The growth of an *esprit de corps* was both a social and a professional phenomenon; it was a significant aspect of this change of role.

By Anna Ivanovna's death in 1740 the military prestige of the guards had declined. The British minister in St. Petersburg reported that they were "fine troops to look at

69 *PSZ*, IX, no. 7049 (6 Sept. 1736); cf. Annenkov, *Istoriia . . . Konnogo polka*, 43; Pushkarev, *Istoriia*, supplement, 15 f.

70 "Zapiski V. A. Nashchokina, . . .", 288.

71 Annenkov, *Istoriia . . . Konnogo polka*, 46.

72 Pushkarev, *Istoriia*, 187.

73 Ibid., 145.

74 Ibid., 185.

75 Chicherin et al., *Istoriia . . . Preobrazhenskogo polka*, vol. II, 265.

76 Ibid., vol. II, 506.

[but] their reputation is not very great among the field regiments."[77] Many officers, and some of the men as well, had acquired familiarity with the social and political life of the capital, where they had long been stationed and had made good careers. Such men could not but entertain ideas of their own about affairs of state, particularly in a time of dynastic uncertainty when gossip and rumor were rife.[78] At the very least they will have been concerned to maintain, and perhaps to extend, their own privileges; a few will have taken a broader view, seeing themselves as upholders of the Petrine absolutist tradition. Any partisan of firm monarchical government, however limited his political culture, could not fail to be apprehensive at the course of events. Others, confusing the symptom with the disease, nourished a quasi- (or proto-) nationalistic resentment against the privileged position enjoyed at court, as well as in their own regiments, by Baltic Germans and other non-Russians. This feeling easily lent itself to exploitation by highly-placed or ambitious personages.

IV

When Peter III abolished the KTRD in 1762 he ordered that its records "are to be taken to the Senate under seal and placed in the archive for eternal oblivion."[79] His command was obeyed and the documents in question are still preserved (and indeed largely forgotten) in the Central Archive of Ancient Acts of Moscow.[80] Even a cursory perusal of the files for the regency period shows that Ushakov's office was kept busy, especially in the months December 1740–February 1741; subsequently the level of activity declined. Several hundred cases were examined, involving persons from all walks of life. Even the Imperial *corps de ballet* was not immune![81] Here we shall restrict ourselves to those in which servicemen, and especially guardsmen, were concerned.

We may take first those cases which did not pass beyond a preliminary stage of investigation since it was ascertained that the "Sovereign's words" had been uttered "falsely" (*lozhno*), i.e. without supporting evidence and/or without due cause. The following document, dated May 21, 1741, is worth citing in full to convey a sense of the manner in which business was handled:

At His Imperial Majesty's command the Chancellery of Secret Investigatory Affairs has heard the case, sent to it with a report from the Preobrazhenskii regiment of lifeguards,

77 Finch to Harrington, 26 January 1741, *SIRIO*, vol. 85 (1893), 431.

78 N. N. Firsov, *Vstuplenie na prestol imperatritsy Elizavety Petrovny* (Kazan', 1887 (1888)), 105. Firsov, whose political views denied him an illustrious academic career, was one of the most percipient early students of eighteenth-century Russia, and his work deserves to be better known. Although he shared the common view that the guards were a noble pressure group, he did allow for professional motives as well.

79 *PSZ*, XV, no. 11445 (21 Feb. 1762).

80 TsGADA, Gosudarstvennyi archiv, fond no. 7, delo no. 266: Protokoly Tainoi kantseliarii. I was kindly permitted to consult the four volumes covering the period September 1740 to December 1741 (chasti [parts] 27–30) and the pertinent dela (fond no. 7, dela nos. 746–811).

81 Pavel Kornoukhov. Protokoly, ch. 27, l. 158.

concerning grenadier Nikita Khvastunov of that regiment, who uttered the Sovereign's words, which, upon his being interrogated in the Secret Chancellery, were not substantiated (*kotorogo . . . za nim neiavilos'*), nor did he bear witness against anyone else, but said that he uttered that word and deed in his drunkenness. It was decided, by virtue of the decree of 10 April [1]730, to punish the aforesaid Khvastunov, for his false utterance of the Sovereign's word and deed, [as follows:] to run the gauntlet through the regiment *three*[82] times; and upon exaction of that punishment, [considering] the impertinences he has committed, which are mentioned by name in the aforesaid report, to have him kept under surveillance (*rassmotrenie uchinit'*) in the regimental office of the aforesaid regiment; and therefore he, Khvastunov, is to be sent from the Secret Chancellery to that regimental office with a written communication.

(signed) Andrei Ushakov
Secretary: Mikhail Guliaev.[83]

An analysis of these 38 cases suggests the following conclusions:

1. *Offenders' particulars.* All but two cases, one of which involves an officer and is exceptional in several respects, and the other a senior NCO,[84] concern men of low rank: soldiers, grenadiers, recruits, clerks and the like. Their unit is invariably identified, as is often its geographical location. All men bear characteristically Russian, not foreign surnames. Eighteen incidents during the whole 14-month period concern guardsmen; and in January and February 1741 these account for one-fifth of the total number of incidents. Of these 18 guardsmen only one belongs to either of the two regiments founded under Anna Ivanovna, and his case was the last to be dealt with during this period.[85] Twelve men belong to the Preobrazhenskii and five to the Semenovskii regiment. All the Semenovskii men get into trouble during the relatively "slack" summer and autumn months of 1741.

2. *Declared motives.* The explanations offered by the men concerned for their utterance of the "Sovereign's words" without due cause are so standardized as to suggest falsification or deliberate distortion. The excuse most frequently proffered, in 21 cases, is that the delator was drunk at the time. The remainder, and some of those who were drunk, plead that they had been involved in a quarrel or brawl with the man whom they denounced. Their purpose, it is implied, was to prevent their adversary from gaining the upper hand over them, since the utterance caused the fight to be broken off immediately. In several instances the offender had been undergoing regular disciplinary chastisement by a superior when he had acted. The two types of situation are not always clearly differentiated in the source; sometimes the motives for the initial

---

82 Added in Ushakov's handwriting.

83 *Protokoly,* ch. 29, 1. 19; [cf. fond 2583, op. 3, ed. khr. 258, 1. 135.]

84 Egor Krotkov, a lieutenant serving under the Admiralty in Simbirsk province, uttered the "Sovereign's words" to prevent himself and members of his family, also serving officials or officers, from being enslaved as *kholopy*: no verdict is recorded (ch. 27, 1. 131). Maksim Krivopliasov was a *profos* (roughly equivalent to a sergeant-major with police functions) in the St. Petersburg arsenal (ch. 28, 1. 23).

85 Leontii Sokovnin, Izmailovskii regiment: delo 790 (6 Oct. 1741).

chastisement (theft, drunkenness) are indicated, but sometimes they are not.[86] One man who claimed that he had uttered the words "from simplicity" (*s prostoty*), i.e. from ignorance of their weighty security connotation, was treated a little less severely than the others.[87]

3. *Penalties imposed.* The punishments, which are out of all proportion to the triviality of the offense, illustrate graphically the arbitrary and brutal nature of the procedure. All these uncalled-for utterances of the "Sovereign's words" are treated as serious crimes, and in practically every case,[88] as prescribed by law, the culprits, as military men, are sentenced to run the gauntlet. The KTRD normally specifies the number of "runs" (passes) to be made—sometimes inserting this, almost as an afterthought, in the document after it has been drawn up. Where it fails to indicate precisely the size of the unit which is to administer the penalty,[89] a further element of arbitrariness is introduced. In one instance alone is a single run imposed: on the last Preobrazhenskii guardsman to be sentenced in this period.[90] The usual number of runs assigned is three; but two men are sentenced to five, one to six, and one to seven runs.[91] None of these four is a guardsman; however, both élite troops and ordinary soldiers are liable to receive "indefinite" sentences, in which the number of runs is left to the discretion (*rassmotrenie*) of the commander concerned. In January and February there are no fewer than nine of these as compared with five three-run sentences. What use the commanders made of their discretionary power is not recorded, since the KTRD takes no interest in execution of the sentence; from its point of view, once the offender has been handed over the case is closed. For the same reason there is some doubt as to the size of the unit actually administering the penalty: could the commander substitute a battalion or company for a regiment?

However this may be—and the climate of the times leads one to suppose that sentences may have been carried out in the most literal manner—age and sex are clearly no barrier to the application of severe physical punishment. Anna Trifanova, a soldier's wife, invokes the procedure while being beaten by her husband; she is sentenced to be knouted (for she is a civilian) and "to be returned to her husband as before."[92] A boy in the St. Petersburg garrison school, Stepan Naumov, plays truant; on his return he is beaten with rods (*batogi*) by a soldier-instructor; "unable to bear his punishment," he utters the "Sovereign's words" and is brought before the KTRD. The penalty: to run a gauntlet formed by his fellow-pupils—and to do so an

---

86 Ch. 28, ll. 56, 171; cf. ch. 28, l. 64, ch. 27, l. 206.

87 Ch. 28, l. 24.

88 For an exception, ch. 28, l. 11.

89 If one takes literally the order to run the gauntlet through the *whole* regiment, two runs would have been the equivalent to a death sentence in the Preobrazhenskii regiment, if we may judge mortality according to von Archenholz's experience in the Prussian army.

90 Petr Koshelev: ch. 29, l. 130 (28 July 1741).

91 Ch. 28, ll. 33, 76, 83; ch. 27, l. 172

92 Ch. 29, l. 36.

incredible seven times.[93] Does Ushakov believe that boy cadets have thicker skins, or that they should become inured at a tender age to the brutalities of the adult world? The sources do not say. To conclude on a milder note, insane persons are usually confined in a monastery until they recover from their "melancholy sickness" instead of being beaten.[94]

Reviewing these data, how may one explain the KTRD's "policy" in such matters? It is clear that it hardened early in December, 1740, and softened early in March, 1741. Not only was the incidence of military cases greater during these three months, reaching a peak of 12 in February, but the penalties imposed were severer: after March we find neither discretionary sentences nor sentences to more than three runs. This period coincides, although not exactly, with the political preeminence of Field-Marshal B. C. von Münnich (Minikh), who overthrew the regent Bühren by a *coup d'état* on November 8/9, 1740, and became chief minister, but was compelled to resign on March 2, 1741.[95] As an experienced professional soldier, Münnich may have feared that the military forces in the capital (which included units under his own personal command) might carry out another *coup d'état* to depose him and/or the new regent, Anna Leopol'dovna, and for this reason, with Ushakov's aid, have kept these forces under closer surveillance than usual.

However this does not take us very far. We may assume that there was a link between the tightening of security controls and the utterance without due cause of the "Sovereign's words": but what was the nature of this link? Why should a soldier have made false allegations against a comrade, or wrongly claimed to possess information about some security matter, when he must have known that the penalties for such action were so harsh? One can scarcely believe that Russian soldiers were so tough, or their conditions so grim, that they could face the gauntlet with equanimity. After all, this penalty was designed, and no doubt felt, as a moral humiliation as well as a physical torture. Nor does it help us very much to remember that soldiers would consume more alcoholic beverages during the winter months, and that when drunk they were naturally given to rowdy and aggressive behavior. Rather more to the point is the fact that in August 1741 Russia found herself at war with Sweden; some troops

---

93 Ch. 28, l. 189 (16 Apr. 1741); some weeks later a three-run sentence was imposed in a similar case: ch. 29, l. 9.

94 Ch. 29, l. 33; cf. l. 78 and ch. 30, l. 23.

95 On Münnich see now the biography by F. Ley, *Le maréchal de Münnich et la Russie au XVIIIe siècle* (Paris, 1958), esp. 179–84; this account does not, however, make full use of the published Russian sources. Münnich's own memoirs, first published in French, were translated into Russian as *Zapiski fel'd-marshala grafa Minikha*, ed. S. N. Shubinskii (St. Petersburg, 1874). Those of his son Ernst (see fn. 30) need to be read in the complete version: *Die Memoiren des Grafen Ernst von Münnich*, ed. A. Jürgensohn (Stuttgart, 1896). According to Jürgensohn, Ernst von Münnich was also the author of a critical commentary on the well-known memoir by C. H. von Manstein, first published in 1771, which he considered too critical of his father. The commentary was published (with an erroneous attribution of authorship) in *RS* (1879), bks. 11–12; cf. ibid. 54 (1887), 309–28, 613–37. [See now D. L. Ransel, "The 'Memoirs' of Count Münnich," *SR*, 30 (1971), 843–52.]

were moved out of the capital and Ushakov will have had to give more attention to his military duties; both these factors must have weakened the vitality of the KTRD.

One hypothesis, however far-fetched it may seem, at least deserves consideration. Has the evidence perhaps been faked to conceal the fact that these were really instances of *political* dissidence? Opposition to the regency existed among guardsmen and others, as we shall see in a moment, and no doubt there was a good deal of loose talk on prohibited matters. Individuals who overheard, or took part in, such conversations may conceivably have invoked the "Sovereign's words" procedure, either from fear of betrayal or from hope of gain, but then, on reaching the KTRD, have discovered to their consternation that their interrogators were far less well disposed to them than they had innocently assumed; and so, instead of their allegations being taken seriously, delators might have been persuaded to withdraw them and to substitute a false and relatively inoffensive standard excuse for their action (e.g. drunkenness); thereupon they would have been effectively silenced by the gauntlet penalty. All offenders, on leaving the KTRD (or its predecessors), were apparently pledged to silence about the treatment they received there,[96] so that they would have been unlikely to divulge the secret compact; even had they done so they would have earned little or no sympathy from their erstwhile comrades, who would hold them in the utmost contempt as "squealers."

The hypothesis is, however, over-subtle and must be discarded. It does not take account of the long tradition of false denunciation, referred to already in the *Ulozhenie*. Only an examination of the records over a number of years could establish whether the wave of such cases early in 1741 was in any way abnormal. Until this is done, may we not turn to social psychology for aid in reaching a more plausible explanation? The increased surveillance over strategically placed army units will have brought soldiers to a high pitch of nervous tension, in which men are liable to behave unpredictably, irrationally, and even suicidally. The acute risk of harsh and unjustified repression, coupled with apocalyptic longings for change, indeed with a vague anticipation that radical improvements might be brought about by arbitrary action, may have produced a mood close to mass hysteria. In such a climate men would have been provoked more easily than usual to utter the "Sovereign's words," even at the risk of bringing nemesis upon themselves as well as upon their innocent comrades. The times were out of joint; who knew what might ensue if one cried out, for all to hear, the magic words: *slovo i delo!*

The soldiers' mood of uncertainty must have been enhanced by knowledge that, if a denunciation were considered proven, the culprit was likely to be treated *more leniently* than those men whose cases we have just considered. If this seems bizarre and paradoxical to us today, with our modern notions of crime and punishment, eighteenth-century Russians may have looked at it differently. In any case it emerges from these records that far fewer allegations were considered by the investigators

---

96 The death penalty was prescribed in such cases: delo no. 746 (Oct. 1740), where a witness had to swear to this effect (*"o tom buduchi v Tainoi kantseliarii pod karaulom i nidge razgovorov nikakikh ni s kem i nigde chto ni pod kakim vidom otniud' ne razglashat'"*).

"clearly with cause" (*iavno po delu*) than those deemed "false," and that the offenders concerned were treated less severely than those who, by making false allegations, brought the security procedures into disrepute. The distinction between the two categories of offence was a good deal less clear-cut than one might suppose. It seems to have rested in part on formal criteria, in the sense that any case which led to sanctions against the person incriminated was adjudged "with cause." (This is why we entertained the hypothesis that even the "false" denunciations may have had some real substance.)

Consider the career of Filip Boboshin, a soldier in the Vyborg garrison. In 1737 he utters the "Sovereign's words" without cause; on grounds of his youth he is treated mildly (by the standards of the time), being sentenced to a whipping with the cat o' nine tails (*koshka*: the principal punishment used in the navy). Three years later he makes another such charge, this time against his regimental clerk, Fedor Miatikhin, whom he accuses of subversive talk. The KTRD record categorizes this as *iavno po delu*, although Boboshin later admits that he had acted from malice and is sentenced to run the gauntlet five times.[97] If we are to credit his confession, the case should surely have been designated as *lozhnoe*. Possibly the clerk merely meant that the KTRD first thought it had been genuine but then changed its mind; in any event this affair shows how arbitrary the classification might be.

Apart from one case of "pretenderism" the *iavno po delu* cases in 1740–1 are concerned with little more prejudicial to the interests of the state than subversive talk. The term for this was (*vazhnye*) *nepristoinye, proderzkie or neprigozhie slova* ([important] indecent, impertinent or unsuitable words). This meant in effect idle gossip about, or criticism of, the infant sovereign, the regent or other prominent court personalities. It may be regarded as the rough equivalent of the *crimen laesae majestatis* of Roman law, familiar to us from contemporary western European practise. Twelve out of twenty offenses affecting servicemen are of this nature. Frequently the grumbling arose from unusually onerous duties imposed on the men, complaints about irregularities in pay, and the like.[98] The normal penalty for such offenses was a whipping, whereupon the miscreant might either be freed for return to his unit or else sent into exile to perform forced labor.[99] The harshest penalty—to be knouted "mercilessly" and committed to life-long forced labor in Siberia—was imposed on a soldier named Ivan Babaevskii. In May 1741, while serving in a battalion working on the Ladoga canal, he and some fellow soldiers were sitting in a forest hut eating a meal of boiled hare. Babaevskii remarked that such food was fit only for dogs, to which a comrade, Andrei Kurbatov, replied that it was eaten even by royalty. Thereupon the first man made a "shameful" reply which has not been recorded (even in the original *delo*), although its purport can readily be guessed. Kurbatov pointed out that Babaevskii had contravened the military code; Babaevskii pleaded that he might be spared; but the conversation was reported by a third soldier, Sevostian Popov,

---

97 Ch. 27, l. 212.

98 Delo no. 808 (19 June 1741): case of Akinfii Perfiliev of Semenovskii regiment, Astrakhan'.

99 Contrast dela nos. 803 (23 Aug. 1741) and 807 (25 Aug. 1741).

who was already known to the KTRD as a delator.[100] Babaevskii's offence would seem slighter than that of Mikhail Kriukov, a hospital orderly who three months later, observing that the road from Petergof to Oranienbaum was being cleared of prisoners to allow Anton Ulbrich of Brunswick, husband of the regent, to pass by in his carriage, compared the prince unfavorably to Peter the Great and added that "these [leaders] are just devouring this Russia of ours" (tol'ko de oni Rossiiu tu nashu iadiat). Kriukov was sentenced to be whipped and to serve for one year in a forced labor battalion.[101] It is tempting to offer a political explanation of this striking difference in treatment, although it should probably be attributed to administrative arbitrariness.

If the KTRD was preoccupied with so many trivial or previous cases of dissent, how did it deal with the very real threats to the security of the unpopular regency government?

As one might expect, the KTRD records contain little direct evidence on major affairs of state. Nevertheless there is enough information on which to base at least a hypothetical interpretation of Ushakov's role in the events of 1740–1 and the relationship between his office and the turbulent guards regiments. Bühren's sudden advent to supreme power touched off a wave of dissatisfaction, notably among the Preobrazhenskii and Semenovskii men. On the morrow of Anna Ivanovna's death (October 18, 1740) all élite units were paraded and the men required to take an oath of allegiance to the new sovereign, Ivan VI. The ceremony was supervised by Bühren, whose appointment as regent came as a complete surprise. His standing was low, partly on account of his personal characteristics and partly because he symbolized the power that had been wielded at Anna Ivanovna's court by non-Russian favorites.[102] Bühren sought to win support by such measures as an amnesty for non-political offences (October 23), which he coupled with a clumsy effort to suppress "malicious discussion of the present government."[103] These gestures only made matters worse. The French ambassador, de la Chétardie, reported to his government two days later that, since the guards could not be trusted, orders had been given to reinforce the garrison in the capital with field regiments. Münnich presented this action as designed to ease the guardsmen's lot, but the argument failed to convince.[104]

100 Protokoly, ch. 29, l. 40 (31 May 1741); delo no. 802, l. 4.

101 Delo no. 807. In two incidents soldiers referred to the reigning monarch as "the little devil" but in both cases the outcome is unknown: dela nos. 785, 803.

102 The national aspect of this sentiment was exaggerated by S. M. Solov'ev, who gives full account of these intrigues in vol. 21 of his Istoriia Rossii s drevneishikh vremen (bk. XI of the Moscow 1963 edition, 7–128). The movement was directed essentially against the arbitrary use of power, for which Russians such as N. Iu. Trubetskoi and A. P. Bestuzhev-Riumin were partly responsible, along with Bühren and other Germans at court.

103 For the former see PSZ, XI, no. 8263, and Solov'ev, Istoriia, XI, 10, who relies in part on the evidence given against Bühren after his fall, which is not wholly credible. The latter decree is in Protokoly, ch. 27, l. 61; it was signed by Ushakov and Trubetskoi and ordered "those discovered in such an important matter to be firmly questioned" (i.e. tortured). The amnesty was applied consistently, as several cases in the KTRD records show.

104 De la Chétardie to Amelot, SIRIO, vol. 92 (1894), 17; previously published in P. Pekarskii,

Within a few days at least three separate cases had come to Ushakov's attention. The most serious involved a lieutenant in the Preobrazhenskii regiment, Petr Khanykov, who carried on a vigorous agitation against Bühren among his fellow officers and NCOs. On October 22, before he could develop his ideas or do anything to put them into effect, he was denounced by a sergeant-major in the Cavalry regiment, Luk'ian Kamynin. Khanykov and three other men from his unit were arrested and on October 31 examined under torture in the KTRD. It seems that they had no definite alternative candidate for the regency in mind but were most sympathetic to the claims of Anna Leopol'dovna, as mother of the infant sovereign.[105]

The second group was based on the Semenovskii regiment. Its adherents preferred the boy's father, Anton Ulbrich, who was also their lieutenant-colonel. The latter aroused Bühren's suspicions and on October 23 was publicly stripped of his offices in a humiliating ceremony. The main activist here was captain Ivan Putiatin, an aristocrat and the regimental adjutant, who for some time had been discussing court affairs with P. Grammatin, Anton Ulrich's personal adjutant. Information on their subversive activities first reached Bühren from A. M. Cherkasskii, who betrayed a confidence; it was confirmed by a confession obtained from Grammatin, who was arrested on October 24. From Putiatin the trail led to two fellow officers, captain Vasilii Semenov and lieutenant-colonel Liubim Pustoshkin. The latter earned his living as a civilian official in the College of Accounts (*Revizionskollegiia*) and was thus evidently a "supernumerary" officer. Also implicated were Andrei Iakovlev, secretary to the Cabinet, and Mikhail Semenov (possibly a relative of Vasilii), Anna Leopol'dovna's secretary. On October 31 Ushakov ordered four of these men to be interrogated. The investigation was still in progress when Bühren was deposed (November 8/9), whereupon they were rehabilitated—only to fall into disgrace once again (along with two of the Preobrazhenskii officers) after Elizaveta Petrovna's accession, as partisans of the Brunswick interest.[106]

These two groups were interconnected, politically if not organizationally, but there was apparently no link between them and the third. This involved one of the new guards units, the Cavalry regiment. On October 18 corporal Aleksandr Khlopov asked some of his comrades to whom they had just sworn allegiance; when they professed not to know he hinted that Elizaveta Petrovna was better suited to govern.[107] He

---

Markiz de-la-Shetardi v Rossii 1740–1742 gg. Perevod rukopisnykh depesh frantsuzskogo posol'stva v Peterburge (St. Petersburg, 1862), 149.

105 Pekarskii, *Markiz de-la-Shetardi*, 154–57; Solov'ev, *Istoriia*, bk. XI, 13–15; also D. P. Strukhov, *Stranitsa istorii gvardii XVIII veka. Doklad (na pravakh rukopisi)* (St. Petersburg, 1898), 19–23. There is a summary record in Protokoly, ch. 27, l. 68. [According to Preobrazhenskii regimental records, Peter Khanykov, a supernumerary, was promoted captain on January 1, 1741 and retired with colonel's rank on March 21, 1741: fond 2583, opis' 3, ed. khr. 258, ll. 13–14, 56, 65.]

106 Pekarskii, *Markiz de-la-Shetardi*, 157–76; Solov'ev, *Istoriia*, XI, 16–18, 142; Protokoly, ch. 27, l. 69.

107 His exact wording was reported differently by witnesses. According to Ivan Dolginskoi Khlopov said "the Emperor of the All-Russian empire Peter I served [his country] but

was reported by a corporal of non-Russian extraction, Karl-Johann Holmström; the matter was taken up at the highest level and on October 24 Khlopov was tortured. At first he imputed the offending words to trooper Semen Shchetinin, and the two men were confronted; but then Khlopov confessed. It emerged that he had previously been presented to Elizaveta Petrovna through his uncle, who had been in her service; a genealogy of the imperial family was found among his possessions when they were impounded. On November 1 Ushakov referred the case to Bühren who decided that Khlopov and Shchetinin, although "deserving the severest penalties," should be pardoned to mark the beginning of the new reign. Khlopov was freed with a warning to exercise more caution in future, and his possessions were returned to him.[108]

It is not difficult to see in this a gesture by Bühren in the direction of Elizaveta Petrovna, whose goodwill would have given him a trump card against the Brunswicks and consolidated his shaky hold on power. But what was Ushakov's role? It would have been in character for him to urge leniency upon Bühren, since he too had everything to gain by a rapprochement with Elizaveta Petrovna. He was evidently playing a double game, for when Anton Ulrich asked him (through Grammatin) for an interview on a false pretext so that he might make known his dissatisfaction with Bühren, he agreed. He must therefore have been acutely embarrassed when the prince, at his confrontation with Bühren before the assembled dignitaries on October 23, broke down and confessed his disloyalty. Ushakov said threateningly that he had the power to treat him in the same way as the humblest commoner—but linked this with a hint that he could earn general respect if he behaved himself well.[109] The scene probably led Ushakov to forsake the Brunswick party and move towards that of Elizaveta Petrovna, and so to plead mercy for Khlopov.

Once Bühren had been deposed and Anna Leopol'dovna named regent the security chief's dilemma became still more delicate. Any obvious disservice to the Brunswicks would incur the wrath of chief minister Münnich, and later of Osterman; yet he had no desire to take strong measures against Elizaveta Petrovna's partisans, who were building up their support abroad and at home, not least among the guards.[110] He maintained discreet surveillance over their activities but carefully abstained from taking any action that would have either embarrassed or encouraged them. This ambiguous position was not lost on the inquisitive de la Chétardie, who on January 6 reported to his government that Elizaveta had suggested to a mutual confidant that Ushakov might be prevailed on to lead her partisans in a *coup d'état*;[111] the interpretation was wide of the mark, since Ushakov would have been debarred from such a

---

that one [Elizaveta] has remained." According to the delator Holmström he nodded in the direction of Elizaveta Petrovna's residence and said: "isn't it shameful?" (*ne obidno-li?*).

108 Delo no. 750, ll. 1–23; summarized in Pekarskii, *Markiz de-la-Shetardi*, 177–8. Solov'ev (bk. XI, 22) fails to connect the pardon with Bühren. There is also some evidence of pro-Elizaveta Petrovna feeling in the Preobrazhenskii regiment at this time.

109 Solov'ev, *Istoriia*, bk. XI, 20–21 (no source given).

110 For a keen analysis of Elizaveta's tactics see Firsov, *Vstuplenie*, 131–5, 142–5.

111 De la Chétardie to Amelot, 6 Jan. 1741, *SIRIO*, vol. 92 (1894), 229.

role by his age and his fearsome past, and he was far more useful to the conspirators indirectly than directly.

Peter I's daughter owed her throne in no small measure to Ushakov's benevolent neutrality. In support of this statement we may adduce two items of evidence from the KTRD records. The first concerns two guardsmen of the Semenovskii regiment, medical orderly Vasilii Ivanov and soldier Fedor Nemtsov, of whom the former allegedly uttered "impertinent words" to the latter. Even the form of the protocol in this case is unusual, for neither the date of the offence nor the source of the information is indicated. Still odder is the verdict. Ivanov is let off, on the grounds of insufficient evidence (the only instance of such leniency to come to light in the records for this year); Nemtsov is held at fault for having repeated and embroidered the phrase uttered by Ivanov, and for this is sentenced to the mildest possible penalty, thrashing with *batogi*, and is returned to his regiment.[112] When one turns to the relevant *delo* one discovers that Nemtsov was denounced by a fellow soldier, Dikarev, for criticizing Münnich and the colonel of his regiment—and that this criticism had originated with none other than Elizaveta Petrovna herself, whose words Nemtsov (and presumably Ivanov) had repeated. Yet the tsarevna's part in the affair has been suppressed from the official record.[113]

The second incident occurred on the night of August 24/25, 1741. Two soldiers of the Preobrazhenskii regiment, Vasilii Buroi and Gerasim Vsevolotskii, on guard duty at the Admiralty, struck up a conversation about the causes of the war with Sweden. Buroi explained that the real reason was not Swedish aggression, as was officially stated, but the denial of Elizaveta Petrovna's rights to the throne, which rights her nephew, the duke of Holstein, was upholding with Swedish support. Buroi said he had obtained his information from his brother, a footman in the tsarevna's household, who had heard it from a guest, and that when he had once visited his brother Elizaveta Petrovna had entered and, struck by his guardsman's uniform, had offered him vodka. All this was duly reported by Vsevolotskii, who wanted the reward since for some reason his pay had been withheld. Now in normal circumstances such denunciations were handled most expeditiously; however, on this occasion Ushakov dawdled until November 27, two days *after* Elizaveta Petrovna's successful *coup*, whereupon the two men were freed.[114]

The *coup* itself has left no trace in the KTRD records. Once hoisted to power the new empress had more need than ever of Ushakov's services. He and procurator-general N. Iu. Trubetskoi were the only prominent politicians of the 1730s to be found in the eleven-man "general assembly," an ad hoc emergency cabinet which met during the first weeks of the reign.[115] In the KTRD itself continuity was the watchword. Ushakov remained its chief until 1744, when he asked to be retired on

---

112 Protokoly, ch. 27, l. 211 (22 Dec. 1740).

113 Delo no. 747, ll. 2, 5.

114 Protokoly, ch. 30, l. 122; delo no. 781.

115 V. I. Veretennikov, *Ocherki istorii general-prokuratury v Rossii do-Ekaterinskogo vremeni* (Khar'kov, 1915), 223.

account of age. As in the past both he and his successor, A. I. Shuvalov, rendered their reports directly to the sovereign and thwarted further efforts by the Senate (and Synod) to limit their office's powers.[116] Nevertheless things were not *exactly* the same as before—if only because Elizaveta Petrovna, for all her obvious failings, was a better ruler than either of the two women who had preceded her. The scale of KTRD operations seems to have declined, particularly in the last decade of her reign. In 1742 a decree substituted the whip for the knout as penalty for those who uttered the "Sovereign's words" without due cause, and from 1745 onwards death sentences were invariably commuted to exile with forced labor, a change duly reflected in the KTRD records.[117] To be sure, these were trivial concessions, and as has often been noted did not necessarily mean more humane treatment of convicts; they were due to political and military expediency rather than to the empress's moral beliefs, still less to the impact of enlightened western ideas on jurisprudence—still fairly modest, one should add, in other European countries at this time.[118]

Thus the KTRD survived, although when judged by any rational criterion its record during the 1740–1 crisis had been one of brutality, inefficiency and above all hypocrisy. While inflicting barbarous tortures on commoners who were victims of ignorance or mass hysteria it had turned a blind eye to actions by certain highly placed individuals that genuinely threatened the government's security. Yet its discreditable performance was ignored. This was due not just to lethargy or self-interest, but also to the fact that the age of rational policy-making had yet to dawn in Russia. Not until the 1760s was the "Sovereign's words" procedure done away with and state security placed on a more modern and intelligent foundation.[119]

Under this bureaucratic system it would become harder for the head of the security agency to pursue a secret political course of its own, as Ushakov was able to do during the regency. His line of conduct was motivated by more than concern for his personal interest. It could be justified up to a point by *raison d'état*. Anna Ivanovna's choice of heir (and of regent) was disastrous, and the second regent was little better than the first. Nevertheless Ivan VI was the legitimate sovereign, since under a law of 1722 the reigning monarch had the right to nominate his or her successor, whereas Elizaveta Petrovna owed her power to a *coup d'état*. It was a misfortune that the crisis of 1740–1, like that of 1730, should have been resolved by a method that did nothing to strengthen regard for legality among the country's leaders. Not until Paul I's reign was the law changed and succession by primogeniture restored.

---

116 Veretennikov, *Iz istorii*, 22, 43, 71, 90.

117 Ibid., 51–52; *PSZ*, XI, no. 8572 (25 June 1742).

118 Although Frederick II of Prussia abolished torture by his edict of June 3, 1740, it was retained for *lèse-majesté* and treason. In the 1730s Moritz August Engel's views justifying the use of torture were "enthusiastically received": J. Heath, *Eighteenth-Century Penal Theory* (London, 1963), 54 n. Beccaria's epoch-making work did not appear until 1764.

119 On the 1762 change see Veretennikov, *Iz istorii*, 111. Many of the old evils persisted, not least reliance on delators, but in our view Hingley, *Russian Secret Police* (see n. 4), 16 f., overstates the case for continuity throughout the eighteenth century.

The crisis also weakened the guards regiments' initially close involvement in matters of state security. One might say that from being the agents of surveillance they had become its objects.[120] They would continue to play an important political role at moments of tension, notably in 1762 and in 1801, and until 1825 would remain a significant element in the empire's "informal constitution." But henceforth command of the security apparatus would be in other hands. In this domain as in many others a process of institutional specialization was under way that was essential if Russia were to become a modern state.

1978

---

120 For this formulation, and for other constructive comments on the draft of this article, I am indebted to Professor Brenda Meehan-Waters.

CHAPTER 6

Catherine's Veterans

Historians of eighteenth-century Russian society have concentrated upon the main élite group, the *dvorianstvo*.[1] It is generally agreed that the gentry succeeded in winning legal emancipation from compulsory military service, but that they continued to provide the armed forces with all the officers they needed; the few officers of non-gentry origin qualified automatically for noble status under the provisions of Peter I's Table of Ranks. Much less familiar is the situation of the "other ranks" in military service. The *nizhnie chiny*, as they were officially called, comprised non-commissioned officers, ranging in rank from sergeant-major to corporal, and private soldiers; here they will be referred to simply as "soldiers" or "men." They were recruited overwhelmingly from the nonprivileged taxpaying (*tiaglye*) classes under a brutal levy system devised by Peter I and only slightly modified by Catherine II.[2] They served for life—"so long as [their] strength and health allow" (*dokole sily i zdorov'e pozvoliat*), as contemporaries put it. Not until the end of Catherine's reign, ostensibly as a mark of recognition for the troops' valorous conduct in the Russo-Turkish war of 1787–91, was a 25-year term introduced.[3] This reform, however, did not make much difference in practise. It was probably more than a coincidence that the term now fixed should have been the same as that first conceded to the gentry, by an edict of December 31, 1736. But whereas the latter had gone on, a quarter-century later, to secure the privilege of not having to serve at all, if they wished and could afford not to do so, in the soldiers' case no such alleviation followed, for the practise of levying recruits by force, usually once a year, as a quota of the male population registered by the census books as resident in each community, proved remarkably durable: it lasted until the 1860s, giving place in 1874 to a system of selective conscription of the entire population.

Some modern historians have argued that the social and national homogeneity

---

1 Three recent studies are R. E. Jones, *The Emancipation of the Russian Nobility, 1762–1785* (New York, 1973); W. Leitsch, "The Russian Nobility in the Eighteenth Century," *East European Quarterly*, 11 (Boulder, Colo., 1977), 317–40; H. A. Bennett, "Evolution of the Meanings of *Chin*. . . ," *California Slavic Studies*, 10 (Berkeley, 1977), 1–43.

2 "General'noe uchrezhdenie o sbore v gosudarstve rekrut," 29 September 1766: *PSZ*, XVII, no. 12748.

3 *PSZ*, XXIII, nos. 17149, §6; 17150, September 2, 1793. A 15-year term was introduced two years later in some southern districts to which the levy was then extended for the first time: ibid., nos. 17393–4, October 6, 1795.

of Russia's largely peasant army was a "progressive" phenomenon and was partly responsible for its effectiveness in battle.[4] However this may be, the social consequences of the levy system were clearly pernicious. It turned the soldiers into a kind of military caste, artificially separated and often emotionally alienated from other commoners. The relationship between peasant and soldier was strained by the practise of quartering troops in rural areas (due to the lack of barracks), by the obligation often imposed on agricultural producers to supply the army with food and fodder, and by the use of military force to exact tax arrears, catch fugitives and quell popular disorders. Since soldiers were hardly ever granted home leave, once they had put on uniform they were unlikely to see their families again. Induction produced something akin to psychological trauma as the recruit was suddenly subjected to unfamiliar and harsh discipline, an inferior diet, and, in the words of one well informed (but none too sympathetic) observer, "perhaps [sic] prolonged grief as he sees himself torn from the arms of his own people, with a very dubious hope of ever returning to them."[5] Even those with the good fortune to survive the manifold perils of their long service with the colors, or who were declared physically unfit before they were due for discharge, might find themselves posted to a garrison unit instead of being sent back to their native village. This practise seems to have been followed not just for the sake of administrative convenience but in order to ensure that the men would be better looked after, or at any rate less badly neglected, if they remained under official supervision. A decree of October, 1795, gave generals in command of large military formations the power to decide whether NCOs who had served 25 years should be sent "to their relatives in their previous [places of] domicile" or to nearby garrisons and invalid companies; should one of the latter unfortunates "find relatives or reliable persons to stand bail for him, to take him and keep him at their own expense until his death," he was to be released and given a passport.[6] Only inadequate provision was made for the care of such persons, who numbered less than 10,000 (mostly officers) in the 1780s.[7]

This note presents some data on veterans of Catherine's army in the year 1795, drawn from records preserved in the Central State Military-Historical Archive (TsGVIA) in Moscow.[8] Unfortunately the statistical sample is very small, so that conclusions drawn from it must remain tentative pending further investigation.

---

4 This is the viewpoint of present-day Soviet scholars, notably of L. G. Beskrovnyi, author of the fundamental study *Russkaia armiia i flot v XVIII v.: ocherki* (Moscow, 1958).

5 A. W. von Hupel, *Beschreibung der Russisch-Kaiserlichen Armee nebst andern kürzern Aufsätzen* ... (Der nordischen Miscellaneen 5. und 6. Stück) (Riga, 1782, reprinted Hanover-Döhren, 1972), 205.

6 *PSZ*, XXIII, no. 17402, §2.

7 A. N. Petrov, ed., *Russkaia voennaia sila. Istoriia razvitiia voennogo dela ot nachala Rusi do nashego vremeni*, 2nd ed. (Moscow, 1892), vol. II, 177.

8 I should like to thank the British Council and the University of Toronto for enabling me to visit this archive, and the Soviet authorities for permitting me to consult certain materials in it.

By 1795 Catherine II might herself be called a veteran in the arts of statecraft.[9] In that year her empire was enjoying a precarious interlude of peace: the campaign against the Persians was on a modest scale; the Poles had been subdued; and the moment had not yet come to take up arms against the French. Among the troops likely to be committed to action in central Europe were those of the First division, stationed in and around Kiev under the command of Lieutenant-General Andrei Iakovlevich Levanidov (1747–?), which, however, were reported in March to be almost one-quarter below their establishment strength.[10] They included an infantry regiment, the Iaroslavl' musketeers, which could trace its origin back to the first years of the eighteenth century and may be taken as fairly typical of the sixty-two such regiments then in the Russian army.[11] It was commanded by a certain Colonel Tauzenberg, who by 1795 had accumulated no less than 35 years of service.[12] Regimental commanders wielded immense power in this period, yet in the matter of discharging ailing veterans neither Tauzenberg nor indeed Levanidov could act at his own discretion; instead authority had to be requested from Field-Marshal P. A. Rumiantsev, the supreme commander of all troops in the southern region. On May 17 Levanidov asked what he should do about three soldiers of the Iaroslavl' regiment who were clearly unfit for further duty since "one has no legs, the others have incurable wounds and hence are continually sick, and of these one is quite disturbed mentally (*vovse pomeshen v razume*)."[13] Presumably they were duly released, although no decision on their fate is reported in this source.

In June and July, 1795, Levanidov received from the Iaroslavl' regiment several lists of invalid and veteran soldiers. These records (*formuliarnye spiski*), compiled on the same principle as those for officers, contain information about the men's civilian background (place of origin and social class), age, dates of enlistment and promotion, literacy and marital status. Other rubrics cover their campaign and battle experience, leave privileges granted, punishments for breaches of military discipline, and (where applicable) physical disabilities. Some data from two of these lists are tabulated below:

---

9 For her biography, see the study by I. de Madariaga, *Russia in the Age of Catherine the Great* (London, 1981 and New Haven, 1982).

10 TsGVIA, fond Voenno-uchenogo arkhiva, 1349, delo no. 300 (Raporty gen. Levanidova o sostoianii voisk), l. 1.

11 Baron V. Shteingeil, comp., *Nastol'nyi khronologicheskii ukazatel' postanovlenii, otnosiashchikhsia do ustroistva voennosukhoputnykh sil Rossii, 1550 do 1890* (St. Petersburg, 1890) (appendix to *Voennyi sbornik*, no. 12 (1890)), 20. The regiment was disbanded in 1798. For the *shtaty*: F. von Stein, *Geschichte des russischen Heeres vom Ursprunge desselben bis zur Thronbesteigung des Kaisers Nikolai I. Pawlowitsch* (Hanover, 1885), 207.

12 TsGVIA, as cited, l. 83.

13 Ibid., l. 87.

Table I.   Educational and Family Status of Veterans*
(NCOs and Men), Iaroslavl' Regiment, 1795

Number of:	Physically fit	Unfit	Total
Bachelors	42	15	57
Married men (no children)	13	6	19
Married men (with children)	2	2	4
Literates	11	2	13
Children	5	2	7
Total:	57	23	80

Source: TsGVIA, fond Voyenno-uchenogo archiva, f. 1349, d. 300, ll. 114 v.–23, 137–60
* Veterans = men who had completed 25 years' service.

Before analyzing this information, let us consider the men's geographical and social origin, confining ourselves for the moment to those who were classified as physically fit. It is striking that of these 57 men only one individual came from the governor-generalship (*namestnichestvo*) of Iaroslavl' (the village of Shakotin). This shows how far the late eighteenth-century Russian army had departed from Peter I's principle of territorially-based recruitment, which the tsar not unreasonably had regarded as a means of promoting *esprit de corps*. The recruiting system now operated in such a way that soldiers of a particular regiment no longer had any necessary connection with the area after which their unit was named. The practise in 1768–70, when these men were enlisted, seems to have been much the same as it was in the First division in 1795: on arrival in the area, in parties of about 200-300, recruits were simply allocated to various units as orders to this effect were received from St. Petersburg; the War College's sole concern evidently was to make good deficiencies reported by the units, so that the men were assigned as convenience dictated, irrespective of their provenance.[14] Indeed it almost seems as if the authorities deliberately sought to avoid accumulations of recruits who might have been drawn together by experiences shared before entering the service;[15] for relatively few veterans of this regiment came from areas located close to Iaroslavl' such as Vladimir governor-generalship (2), Kostroma or Moscow provinces (2, 4), or Suzdal' district (2); on the other hand there was no undue concentration of men from any other region. One should emphasize here that soldiers tended to remain with a single unit throughout their service career, whereas officers could easily transfer from one regiment to another, and did so with inordinate frequency.[16]

As for the men's social origins, a sizeable majority (41 out of 57, or 71.9 percent)

14 Ibid., ll. 59, 78–80, 86, 89, 93, 96–7, 100–1, 162, 168.

15 Such a motive was suggested by a later foreign observer, who, however, offered no evidence to support it: C. von Plotho, *Über die Entstehung, die Fortschritte und die gegenwärtige Verfassung der russischen Armee* . . . (Berlin, 1811), 66.

16 A. A. Kersnovskii, *Istoriia russkoi armii*, pt. I: *Ot Narvy do Parizha, 1700–1814* (Belgrade, 1933), 127. This practise is also mentioned in a contemporary report (undated, but from the 1790s) in the French archives: Ministère des Affaires Etrangères, Notes et Documents, Russie, 14: 1745–1828, Forces militaires, "Observations sur le militaire," l. 124.

were peasants—as one would of course expect. Of these just over half (23 out of 41, or 56.1 percent) had previously been privately-owned serfs, a proportion which accords closely with the latter group's share of the total peasant population (54.2 percent).[17] Seven men had been "economy" peasants, that is dependents of the ecclesiastical institutions whose land had been secularized in 1764, and two were from court estates; nine were not identified more closely, although we learn that one of these came from an Old Believer settlement. The non-peasants included one merchant's son, four from the clerical estate (*iz tserkovnikov*), and 11 "soldiers' children." The latter group is of particular interest since it formed, at any rate potentially, a self-perpetuating warrior class. Already Peter I had ordained that such youths were to be put in the army, and his successors had ruled that they should first receive some training in garrison schools.[18] Catherine II continued the practise, prescribing that *soldatskie deti* should not be permitted to enter the civil service and increasing the number of such schools, which by 1796 had 12,000 pupils.[19] Successive governments seem to have hoped that the *soldatskie deti* might provide them with a means of killing two birds with one stone: obtaining a nucleus of trained NCOs and easing the burden of the recruit levy upon the rest of the population. However, they overlooked one vital consideration: would these men be able to marry and produce enough male heirs to succeed them in their soldierly calling? We shall return to this point presently.

So far as the Iaroslavl' regiment veterans' length of service is concerned, it is immediately apparent that very few of those in the physically fit category had exceeded by a significant margin the recently established 25-year term. Eleven had enlisted during the first five months of 1770, 39 in 1769, and 6 in 1768; only one man had been in the army for a good deal longer—since May 1764, that is for over 31 years, but as the regimental barber (*tsiriul'nik*) his situation was perhaps exceptional. Why should there have been no "old soldiers" who had spent as many years in uniform as, say, Colonel Trauzenberg? Before leaping to the conclusion that this was due to a high mortality rate from battle casualties, epidemic diseases and the strenuous exertions imposed even by peacetime service, one needs to know whether the regimental authorities had not previously eliminated from its ranks men who had served for more than 25 years, and whether they had not perhaps done so regularly even before the decree of 2 September 1793. There is a hint in these records that this may have been the case, for mention is made of a party of men sent to Elizavetgrad

17 V. M. Kabuzan, *Izmeneniia v razmeshchenii naseleniia Rossii v XVIII—pervoi polovine XIX v. Po materialam revizii* (Moscow, 1971), 107–18.

18 *PSZ*, VII, no. 4227, §4; VIII, no. 6188; IX, no. 6639, §2; X, nos. 7544, 7627; XII, no. 8989; XIII, no. 10109; cf. XVII, no. 12723.

19 Ibid., XVI, no. 11816, §1; 12543, §225; 12289, sec. II, §6, sec. XI, §1, 4–6; cf. also J. Hassell, "Implementation of the Russian Table of Ranks during the Eighteenth Century," *Slavic Review*, 29 (Seattle, 1970), 286. For the number of pupils: Stein, *Geschichte*, 224. In 1773 the figure was said to have been 10,313: [Rusinov], *Zapiski sobrannye po poveleniiu imperatora Pavla I* . . . (Sbornik voenno-istoricheskikh materialov, vol. XVI (St. Petersburg, 1904), 166–7.

in May 1792 "without exclusion from the regiment."[20] This rather elementary point could no doubt be established without much difficulty if we had access to a series of documents relating to this regiment over a number of years.

In July 1795 the average age of the fit veterans was 48.1, so that most of them had been 22 or 23 years old when they had enlisted. The 1766 statute specified that recruits should be between the ages of 17 and 35. This rule does not appear to have been observed strictly,[21] for six Iaroslavl' regiment veterans were less than 42 (two aged 41, four aged 40), and another was a sexagenarian of 63, who must have been 37 years old when he enlisted in January 1769. It is of course possible that the men's ages may have been wrongly stated on recruitment: even a century or more later, when the first modern census was taken in 1897, there was a remarkably high degree of inaccuracy in this matter.[22]

When one sets the age data against those for marital status, it is no surprise to find that the married men were older, averaging 52.2 years compared with 46.6 for bachelors (there were no widowers in this group). Nor is it unusual that, where their wives' social origin is stated, the overwhelming majority of them should have been peasants: only one woman was of clerical background. What is remarkable is the low proportion of veterans to have concluded marriages: a mere 15 out of 57, or 26.3 percent—and the even lower number of these marriages that bore fruit. The harsh conditions of military life were clearly prejudicial to raising a family, for only two of the men in our sample had succeeded in having children: one, 51 years old, had a daughter of 30 and a son of 23; another, 52 years old, had two sons of 15 and four, a daughter of two, and also looked after a boy aged 15 from his wife's previous marriage to another soldier. One should add that offspring that had died would not be recorded in these statistics, compiled solely with a view to deciding these veterans' fate; nevertheless our data support Kabuzan's opinion (advanced without evidence) that "from the moment of their enlistment [soldiers] ceased to participate in reproducing the population."[23]

The authorities' concern that the men might be provided for on discharge led them to include information as to whether their wives had accompanied then on service (*zhivet pri nem v polku* was the phrase used) or whether they were still living in their native village, and in the latter case whether the couple had a home of their own. Six of the fifteen married men fell into the first category, nine into the second.

---

20 TsGVIA, as cited, ll. 123v.–126v. All these men were bachelors, which reinforces our point that family status was a major consideration when taking decisions on discharge; they were presumably maintained in Elizavetgrad at public expense.

21 In 1774 an observer stated that boys of 15 or 16 were frequently taken: A. I. Viazemskii, "Zapiska voennaia napisannaia . . . v noiabre 1774 g.," *Arkhiv A. I. Viazemskogo*, ed. S. D. Sheremetev (St. Petersburg, 1881), 6.

22 D. K. Rowney and E. G. Stockwell, "The Russian Census of 1897: Some Observations on the Age Data," *Slavic Review*, 37 (1978), 228–40.

23 Kabuzan, *Izmeneniia*, 6. The proportion of married soldiers (not veterans) was higher in Prussia, but lower in France: see A. Corvisier, *Armées et sociétés en Europe de 1494 à 1789* (Paris, 1976), 160, 189.

Only one veteran, the man with two children, was in the enviable position of having his own homestead; of the other men's wives five lived with the husband's family, two with their own relatives, and one in the house of the village priest. The former arrangement will probably have been considered the more advantageous, since the veteran and his kin could benefit from the wife's labor, but it is not clear whether this was officially encouraged. A. W. von Hupel states that the military authorities did not discourage marriages among soldiers, but rather fostered them, "da immer bei den Compagnien in Quartieren Weibspersonen nötig sind";[24] he adds that wives easily found employment carrying out household tasks, and that those in guards regiments could earn as much as 50 to 70 roubles per annum—about five times a private soldier's annual pay—from this source and from the proceeds of petty trade and handicrafts.[25] This estimate may well be too high—Hupel is keen to present service conditions in the best possible light—and opportunities for extra earnings will have been more limited in the provinces; nevertheless this source of income deserves to be noted, since it will have helped married soldiers to afford the cost of raising a family.

Our sample is too small to permit any meaningful comparison of the birth-rate among couples in the two residential categories. The rarity of home leave—not one of these veterans had ever received it!—meant that most married soldiers with wives at home will have fathered their children before they entered the service; such children were referred to officially as *prizhit pri krest'ianstve* and, if the father had been a serf, were the property of his master.[26]

The moral and demographic implications of the low reproduction rate among soldiers became a matter of public and official concern about this time. Heinrich Storch, whose well-known work on the Russian economy began to appear in 1797, noted that the celibacy of the military represented "a considerable loss" of population which could be reduced by wise government.[27] In the same year Paul I appointed archpriest Pavel Ozeretskovskii as head chaplain to the armed forces. In a report to a senior lay official, D. N. Nepluev, Ozeretskovskii wrote:

> some soldiers' wives, having no information about their husbands, enter into second
> marriages, but when the first husband returns from military service these second marriages
> are dissolved and the children born from them are declared illegitimate and remain

24 Hupel, *Beschreibung*, 109. The law prescribed that they were to earn their livelihood *trudami, rabotoi i remeslom*, and listed as an example of possible occupations sewing, washing and mending clothes, and making tents: *PSZ*, XVII, no. 12543, sec. XXV, §1. Potemkin urged their employment in hospitals: N. [F.] Dubrovin, *A. V. Suvorov sredi preobrazovatelei Ekaterininskoi armii* (St. Petersburg, 1886), 116.

25 Hupel, op. cit., 34.

26 *PSZ*, XVI, no. 12289.

27 H. Storch, *Historisch-statistisches Gemälde des russischen Reiches am Ende des 18. Jahrhunderts*, 8 vols. (Riga, 1797–1803), vol. 1, 459. Cf. S. R. Vorontsov, "Zapiska . . . o russkom voiske, predstavlennaia imperatoru Aleksandru Pavlovichu v 1802 g.," *Arkhiv kniazia Vorontsova*, kn. 10 (Moscow, 1876), 489. [On the whole problem of soldiers' children, see now E. Kimerling(-Wirtschafter), "Soldiers' Children, 1719–1856: a Study of Social Engineering in Imperial Russia," *FOEG*, 30 (1982), 61–136.]

without proper care, while the priest who performed the second marriage loses his rank. Those soldiers' wives who do not conclude second marriages mostly fall into debauchery, and to conceal this mutilate the babies they have conceived or born, and themselves suffer unfortunate consequences. Those who live in moderation until their husbands return from military service are too old to bear children, and for this reason many people are lost.[28]

Nevertheless little was done to remedy these social evils, which were part of a much larger problem: the relatively low reproduction rate among the taxpaying classes generally. This declined during the period 1782–95 in the Great Russian heartland of the empire to 0.61 per annum, as against 1.03 percent in 1762–82 and 0.91 percent between 1795 and 1811—partly, it seems, on account of the increased burden of the recruit levy.[29]

Returning to our source, let us examine the data on the veterans' educational standards. Eleven men in our sample of 57 (19.3 percent) are described as literate (*gramotu umeet*). Of these no less than seven were soldiers' sons who had evidently benefited from the schooling provided for them; three were sons of clergy (*tserkovniki*), and only one was a former peasant. The literacy claimed may have been little more than nominal; nevertheless it definitely conferred an advantage in the competition to win higher rank. Three of these men had reached regimental headquarters staff, serving as "supervisor" (*polkovoi nadziratel'*: this may have had a military-police connotation), baggage-master (*oboznoi*) and locksmith (*slesar'*); four had become sergeants, one a sub-ensign, and another a corporal; only two had failed to rise at all. Of members of the regimental headquarters staff in our list, three out of eight were literate, of sergeants four out of 14, of corporals one out of six, and of private soldiers only one out of 24.

As well as literacy, one needed to display a modicum of professional competence and skill in order to earn promotion to non-commissioned rank. (Officer rank was by this time almost impossible for non-nobles.)[30] It was also important to enjoy the favor of certain influential officers, notably the colonel, whose power in such matters was virtually absolute. Our data suggest that these factors were more important than completion of a specified term of service: that is to say, using the jargon of the Table of Ranks, *zasluga* mattered more than *vysluga*. This was precisely the reverse of the situation by this date among officers. Taking the six corporals, all of whom enlisted in 1769, we find that they reached this rank after serving for the following terms (years and months): 13.1, 15.10, 16.9, 17.0, 17.3 and 22.0. They thus spent a long time (an average of 18 years 3 months) in the ranks, but since they failed to advance beyond

28 TsGVIA, fond 11, opis' VIII, ed. khr. 18 (Reports by Ozeretskovskii to Nepluiev, March 1800–January 1801), ll. 20–21. On the archpriest see I. Smolitsch, *Geschichte der russischen Kirche. 1700–1917*, vol. 1 (Leiden, 1964), 527.

29 Kabuzan, *Izmeneniia*, 10, 13.

30 Hupel, *Beschreibung*, 100. Non-noble NCOs could be put up for promotion to officer rank after four years if they were the sons of (non-noble) officers, eight years if they were of clerical background, and 12 years if they were the sons of recruits: *PSZ*, XVII, no. 12543, sec. 1, §2, note 1.

this humblest *chin* the slow promotion may just reflect a relative lack of merit. Of the 14 sergeants nine had previously served in the rank of corporal. Their promotions to this latter grade occurred after the following intervals (years and months): 1.6, 3.0 (two), 10.6, 10.11, 15.11, 16.3, 17.11 and 21.3 (an average of 11 years and 1 month); and their promotion from corporal to sergeant ensued after the following terms: 0.3, 0.10, 2.0, 4.0, 4.4, 5.0 (two), 7.3 and 19.6 (an average of 5 years 3 months). The four round numbers here suggest that *vysluga* may have been a factor, but the main considerations will surely have been the availability of vacancies. Of the 14 sergeants four reached this rank during the nine-month period June, 1791, to February, 1792, and probably replaced casualties in the war; but the other promotion dates do not reveal any chronological "bunching" of similar significance.

We may now leave this list for the one of 23 veterans categorized as physically unfit. This may best be considered in conjunction with another list, of the same date (June 8, 1795), of 29 invalids who qualified for release on medical groups *before* expiry of their 25-year term of service. In these two groups a higher proportion of the NCOs and men were married: eight and 12 respectively, or 38.5 percent; but the number of offspring was likewise low: two in the first group and 12 in the latter. Two men were widowers; of the others in every case but one, the wife lived as a civilian, and one man alone had a home of his own.

Only seven of these men (13.5 percent) were literate; moreover these included two who claimed knowledge of Polish and German rather than Russian. If one adds the single literate man among those released in 1792, we obtain an aggregate literacy rate in Russian of 13.6 percent.

Table 2.   Educational and Family Status of ex-*Odnodvortsy* Veterans* (NCOs and Men), Iaroslavl' Regiment, 1795

Number of:	Physically fit	Unfit	Total
Bachelors	9	5	14
Married men (no children)	3	2	5
Married men (with children)	2	8	10
Literates	2	0	2
Children	2	17	19
Total	14	15	29

Source: ibid., ll. 126 v.–36
* Veterans = men who (except in one case, not identified) had completed 15 years' service.

Finally, we may look at data from two lists (see Table 2) which relate to veterans who before entering service had belonged to a semi-privileged category of the population, the so-called *odnodvortsy*, many of whose ancestors had once held and who still claimed gentry status, but who were now officially regarded as State peasants.[31] By

31 T. Esper, "The Odnodvortsy and the Russian Nobility," *Slavonic and East European Review*, vol. 45, no. 104 (London, 1967), 124–35; more recently, M. D. Rabinovich, "Sel'skoe

the late eighteenth century perhaps the most important privilege which ex-*odnodvortsy* retained was a shorter term of service, fixed at 15 years instead of 25.

Two curious facts emerge from this table. First, ex-*odnodvortsy* had a literacy rate of 6.9 percent, less than half that of their social inferiors. The probable reason for this is that by family tradition and from economic necessity sons of men in this category went straight into military service on reaching the age of majority, and so did not enjoy even the modest educational facilities provided for *soldatskie deti*; their families were too poor to afford a private school or tutor, an option open to many gentry families. Second, ex-*odnodvortsy* had a much better opportunity than ex-peasants to marry and raise families. Although the ex-peasant veterans were on average some ten years older, only 28.8 percent (23 out of 80) were married, whereas among ex-*odnodvortsy* the figure was 51.7 percent (15 out of 29); and the average number of children per married man was over four times higher among the latter group than among the former: 1.3 as against 0.3. They were less exclusive in their choice of matrimonial partner, whether from choice or necessity it is not clear: only two men took wives from their own social category, while all the others' wives were from the peasantry. Of the 15 wives only one accompanied her husband to his regiment—presumably because they could afford not to do so if they wished. Of the remainder five are recorded as residing in homes owned by their husbands. This was a much higher proportion than among ex-peasant veterans, naturally enough; nevertheless this figure shows that one should not interpret the term *odnodvorets* too literally as implying actual ownership of a homestead. So long as a man's father was alive and he himself was on active service, the incentive and the means to acquire a farm of his own will have been lacking.

Two last points may be made on the basis of these records. As was mentioned *en passant*, not a single individual in the lower ranks of this regiment had been granted leave, although this must have still been a formal possibility since a rubric for this was provided in their *formuliarnye spiski*. Two veterans, one an ex-peasant and the other an ex-*odnodvorets*, had got into trouble with the military authorities during their term of service. Both offences occurred in the same year, 1794; both were of the same nature, namely rape; and both men were punished by being made to run the gauntlet. Characteristically, the ex-*odnodvorets* was sentenced to two passes through one thousand men while the former peasant had to endure three.

On August 27, 1795, the War College decided the fate of the veterans and invalids in the First division. One hundred and thirty men who had served their 25-year term were to be sent back to their "previous domiciles," along with 46 who were sick or prematurely aged; 88 others were posted to garrison units in Kiev and Elizavetgrad. Our Iaroslavl' regiment men will have been among them.[32]

Official records reveal nothing as to the state of mind of these old soldiers as

khoziaistvo i pereselenie odnodvortsev v 30-e–50-e gg. XVIII v.," *Tezisy dokladov i soob-shchenii XIV sessii mezhrespublikanskogo simpoziuma po agrarnoi istorii Vostochnoi Evropy (Minsk-Grodno, 15–29 sentiabria 1972 g.)* (Moscow, 1972), fasc. 1, 141–3.

32 TsGVIA, fond Voenno-uchenogo arkhiva, 1342, delo no. 300, l. 295.

they left the milieu in which they had spent most of their adult lives. One would like to think that they felt relief that their *trudnosti* were at an end and gratitude that they had been numbered among the survivors. Alas, their sentiments will probably have been less joyful: nostalgia for the companionship of former comrades, mixed with foreboding at the uncertain prospects that faced them either in some unfamiliar garrison or in a village where their existence had long since been forgotten.

1981

CHAPTER 7

Paul I and the Militarization of Government

I

The Emperor Paul, leaving his palace one day, ordered a sergeant on guard duty to board his sled, saying "Climb in, lieutenant." The man protested, "Sire, I am but a sergeant." Paul replied: "Climb in, captain." Three days later the newly commissioned officer, by now a lieutenant-colonel, caused the emperor some offense and found himself reduced to the ranks as suddenly as he had risen from them.[1]

The story must, alas, be dismissed as apocryphal, if only because Paul, for all his well-known arbitrariness, showed the utmost solicitude for that rigid hierarchy of rank (*chin*) that was the heart and soul of Imperial Russian officialdom. We have cited it because it illustrates the wealth of myth that for too long has impeded serious historical research into the reign of this unhappy emperor. Throughout the nineteenth century Herzen's view of Paul as "the poet and dialectician of autocracy," who substituted "an orgy of cruelty, pain and brutality" for his mother's sensuality,[2] set the tone for journalists, memoir-writers and belletrists, whether in Russia or abroad. Not until 1916 was an attempt made to probe more deeply into the subject. In that year Mikhail Vasil'evich Klochkov published a magisterial study on certain aspects of the Pauline administration, based on a conscientious study of printed and archival sources.[3] But Klochkov's approach was old-fashionedly institutional—he stood in the tradition of the "historical-juridical school"—and such liberal critics as Baron S. A. Korf justly took him to task for the apologetic tendency evident in his work.[4] Korf himself embodied the tradition of Russian *obshchestvennost'*—those privileged elements in society who sought to defend the autonomous rights of corporate and local institutions against encroachment by the central government. He saw Paul's repression of the nobles' assemblies and elective offices, granted them by Catherine, as a precedent for the later Romanovs' contemptuous treatment of the zemstvo and

---

1 A. Vagts, *A History of Militarism* (New York, 1937), 269.

2 *My Past and Thoughts: The Memoirs of Alexander Herzen*, tr. Constance Garnett, revised by Humphrey Higgins, 4 vols. (London, 1968), 255, 1521.

3 M. V. Klochkov, *Ocherki pravitel'stvennoi deiatel'nosti vremeni Pavla I* (Petrograd, 1916).

4 S. A. Korf, "Pavel I i dvorianstvo," *Golos minuvshego*, 7 (1913), 5–18 (a review of a preliminary sketch by Klochkov).

the Duma.

Neither viewpoint can be considered adequate today. However, modern historians have as yet barely come to grips with the problem of Paul's handling of state affairs. Soviet writers have shown relatively little interest in administrative questions[5] and for this period have tended to adopt and embroider the stock arguments of prerevolutionary "bourgeois" historiography. In the West Marc Raeff, stimulated by Max Weber's concept of the "rationalizing" function of the modern bureaucratic state, since developed by historians like Otto Hintze and Gerhard Ritter with special reference to Prussia, has investigated parallel developments in Russia, and has done much to illuminate the social and psychological ambiguities of the *dvorianstvo*, the service class.[6] Hans-Joachim Torke, in an analysis of Russian officialdom under Alexander I and Nicholas I, has argued plausibly that the bureaucratic abuses rendered so familiar by the literature of the period are largely attributable to the tyranny of the Table of Ranks, the weakness of the legal system, and the immaturity of the country's general social development: notably, the lack of those estates of the realm (*Stände*) which elsewhere resisted the pretensions of the centralized absolutist State.[7]

It was in Paul's reign that Russia first experienced the excesses of bureaucratic rule that were to become so characteristic of the age of Nicholas I. In this sense it deserves to be regarded as a formative period, not a mere aberration. This point was noted by Kliuchevskii, and later by Pokrovskii.[8] However, neither of these eminent historians pursued the line of enquiry which this insight opened up. At the time when they were writing it seemed enough to say that Paul's reign marked a widening of the breach between "government" and "society," dramatically expressed in the *coup d'état* of 11 March 1801—simultaneously the last of the "palace revolutions" and a prelude to the Decembrist revolt. Today we may go further, and assert that Paul's reign witnessed three interrelated processes:

First, the allocation to the military establishment of definite responsibilities in civil administration;

Second, a shift in the locus of executive power away from the aristocratic élite to

---

5 An encouraging exception is N. F. Demidova, "Biurokratizatsiia gosudarstvennogo apparata absoliutizma v XVII–XVIII vv.," *Absoliutizm v Rossii (XVII–XVIII vv.). Sbornik statei k 70-letiiu . . . B. B. Kafengauza* (Moscow, 1964), 206–42. This study is only marginally concerned with the period after 1762.

6 Marc Raeff, *Origins of the Russian Intelligentsia: The Eighteenth-Century Nobility* (New York, 1966).

7 H.-J. Torke, "Das russische Beamtentum in der ersten Hälfte des 19. Jahrhundert," *FOEG*, XIII (1967), 7–346.

8 V. O. Kliuchevskii, *Kurs russkoi istorii*, 5 vols. in *Sochineniia v vos'mi tomakh* (Moscow, 1956), V, 188; M. N. Pokrovskii, "Biurokratiia," *BSE*[1], 65 vols. (Moscow, 1926–1947), VIII, cols. 468–80, tr. by Roman Szporluk, *Russia in World History: Selected Essays by M. N. Pokrovskii* (Ann Arbor, 1970), 66. Another prerevolutionary writer on the period, E. Shumigorskii, noted that Paul "sought to create a new instrument of governmental power, the bureaucracy, which was to stand outside class (*soslovnye*) interests and implement exactly the will of the monarch." *Imperator Pavel Petrovich* (St. Petersburg, 1907), 120.

professional administrators;

Third, a change in the ethos of the public service best expressed by the term "militarization."

We shall speak here of "the militarization of government" as a convenient short-hand term for what was in effect an attempt to achieve greater rationality in the functioning of the administrative machine—a task which preoccupied all the rulers of pre-Reform Russia, from Peter I and Catherine II to Nicholas I.

* * * * *

By way of introduction we may note that Paul's policies of "militarization" implied the conscious adoption of a foreign model. As many contemporaries noted, he greatly admired Frederick the Great of Prussia, in this regard resembling his putative father, Peter III, with whom it became a veritable obsession. Paul hoped to copy Frederick's achievement in building a *Polizeistaat* or "regulated state" in the eighteenth-century understanding of this term: that is to say, he sought to centralize real decision-making power in the autocratic Sovereign, whose will was to be law; to demarcate clearly administrative responsibilities among officials within a hierarchical structure dedicated to the pursuit of efficiency, strict discipline and economy in the use of resources; and to harness all his subjects' energies, within the limits technically possible at the time, to the achievement of certain state-approved tasks. It was a stern and narrow concept of government that left no place for the autonomous individual or social group. Duty, rather than freedom, was to be its watchword. To the modern mind, such an ideal seems inadequate, indeed utopian; but it was one that had a strong appeal for contemporaries all over Europe. (Even the great sceptic Voltaire was not impervious to it.)

Now Russia, one might suggest, was in different ways both peculiarly fitted and peculiarly unfitted for experiments in "Prussianism." On the one hand, the idea of a "service state" had deep roots in the country's history; it had been reinforced by the Petrine reforms, and only slightly weakened by those of Catherine. On the other hand, the Russian élite differed from that of Prussia (or Sweden or France) in its cultural pattern and social ethos. It was more other-worldly, easy-going and individualistic. Its members' principal affinities were to the family group, or even to the locality of residence, rather than to the noble estate (*soslovie*) as such—which after all barely existed in Russia, since corporate institutions were to be found only on the local level. Their political loyalty was given to the autocrat, not to the state, an abstraction they as yet but dimly comprehended; they served in the hope of winning personal advancement, or from economic necessity, not in order to accomplish some distant ideal. The *dvorianstvo* was unpromising material with which to forge a second Prussia. No wonder the attempt failed! Indeed, the "Prussianization" of Russian life which aroused such loud complaints—especially from a later, more articulate generation— existed in men's minds rather than in real life. What offended the critics was not the realization of these goals but the aspiration to reach them. This is a point to which we shall return at the conclusion of this article.

The trouble was that in attempting to emulate foreign experience one could so easily mistake the appearance for the essence, so easily confuse form and substance. The Frederician state certainly had its harsh, cruel and arbitrary aspects, but it had a core of rationality: the means employed bore some rough correlation to the ends in view. In the Russia of Paul this balance was not evident. Discipline became an end in itself, and the original purpose was lost sight of.

Nowhere was this more evident than in the military sphere. Frederick's concern with organizational detail had been combined with strategic flair; Paul, however, was never exposed to the test of battle—not because he lacked courage, but for reasons of high policy. Instead he was given every opportunity to indulge his naive enthusiasm for the external trappings of military glory without being forced to consider too closely the practical functions that soldiers were supposed to perform. Hence what contemporaries called "the Gatchina spirit"—a preoccupation with parades and maneuvers, uniforms and equipment, awards and punishments, in short with the minutiae of army life, and a corresponding neglect of weightier matters likely to prove decisive in war: morale, professional training, technical progress etc. True, such failings were in some degree common to all the *ancien régime* armies, including the Prussian: hence Valmy and Jena. In the Russian case they could be transcended by a brilliant commander like Suvorov, who realized that success in battle demanded more than a capacity for blind obedience. This led him into conflict with Paul, whose ideal was basically a mechanistic one: an army should move like a well-oiled timepiece, each unit responding automatically to the appropriate signal and carrying on smoothly its allotted function. His attitude was also paternalistic: just as he knew his senior officers personally, he wanted relations between officers and men to be simple and direct. This was why he insisted that commanders should report to him at frequent intervals,[9] and why he ordered units to be named after their commanders, not areas of the country. The army seems to have resisted strongly this reactionary move, for the decree had to be repeated on several occasions and was repealed soon after his death.[10]

It should be added that some of Paul's military reforms were reasonable. He centralized the administration in the hands of the War College, which he kept under his close personal control;[11] he did a little to humanize the recruiting system, and tried to keep army strength and expenditure within specified limits. Above all he sought to suppress the venal practices that were so widespread. To this end, as well as to enforce discipline generally, he set up an Auditor-General's department with a hierarchy of judicial officials, some of whom were civilians; their job was to supervise the actions of the military and to hear complaints against them, in much the same

---

9 *PSZ*, XXIV, no. 17865 (5 Mar. 1797).

10 Ibid., nos. 17720 (9 Jan. 1797), XXV, 18470 (8 Apr. 1798), 18725 (31 Oct. 1798), XXVI, 19809 (31 Mar. 1801).

11 Cf. Klochkov, *Ocherki*, 284–93, where the War College is considered in relation to the other colleges rather than to the army.

way as the procuracy supervised the civilian agencies.[12]

Paul has been generally criticized for his harsh disciplinary measures, especially those taken against officers, and beyond question many of his actions were indefensible. Yet it was the means employed rather than the ends pursued that were objectionable. There was a good deal of "slack" in the army as he inherited it: officers surplus to establishment drew high salaries for a minimum of work, while others toiled for a pittance. Paul's rough justice compelled everyone, high and low, to fulfill their service obligations to the letter. This gladdened the hearts of the common soldiers, even though they knew they could not hope to rise to officer rank, since (like Frederick) Paul wanted his officer corps to consist wholly of noblemen. This was certainly reactionary; yet let us note that he also strove to make these noble officers gentlemen, in the Western sense, imbued with notions of chivalry. The introduction into Russia of the Order of St. John of Jerusalem, often seen as pure eccentricity on Paul's part, thus had its rational aspect. Its members, especially those who were officers, were expected to set a pattern for the entire gentry class.

Naturally this aim was scarcely compatible with Paul's exaggerated ideas on discipline. The tension between these objectives, one rational and the other supremely irrational, was inherent not only in his military reforms but also in his policy with regard to the state apparatus, to which we may now turn.

II

Our first point is that the military were given a definite role in the government of the country. The picture is at first sight a rather confused one.

Army garrisons were maintained throughout the empire—infantry in urban and cavalry in rural areas.[13] The number of men involved probably increased, at least in the first, war-free years of Paul's reign. Civil authorities faced with trouble were encouraged to invoke the assistance of these troops without going through time-wasting procedural formalities.[14] In the main centers *voennye gubernatory* (military governors), *komendanty* (commandants) and *plats-maiory* (town-majors) were appointed. As a rule, if not invariably, these were army officers. According to the statute on the administration of St. Petersburg, the military governor had ultimate responsibility for police matters, but his immediate subordinates were civilians.[15] No doubt in the provincial towns, where civilian agencies were notoriously understaffed, the military played an even greater role in urban affairs than they did in the capital cities. In practise the military governors concerned themselves with the construction of barracks, water-supply systems and the like. One typically curt order to General Iu. V. Dolgorukii, when he took over this office in Moscow, reads as follows: "On assuming

---

12 *PSZ*, XXIV, nos. 17719 (9 Jan. 1797), 17757 (24 Jan. 1797), XXV, 18853 (11 Feb. 1799).

13 *Ibid.*, XXIV, no. 17646 (14 Dec. 1796).

14 *Ibid.*, no. 17801 (12 Feb. 1797).

15 *Ibid.*, XXV, no. 18663 (12 Sept. 1798); for the Moscow statute, see no. 18822 (17 Jan. 1799).

responsibility for the Catherine Palace, turn it into barracks."[16] All this reinforces the familiar impression given by memoir literature of a country suddenly placed under the heel of the jackboot.

Yet on closer inspection one finds a number of measures which can only be described as positive in intent, designed to demarcate the respective spheres of military and civilian responsibility and to protect each from encroachment by the other. Thus the Kazan' military governor was told to stop using troops to *maintain* (as distinct from building) the town's water pipeline, since this was the function of the civil police.[17] Army men in the College of Manufactures were told not to refer to themselves as regulars or to wear regular army uniform.[18] All persons with military rank in civil departments were transferred to the appropriate civilian equivalent.[19] A decree of January, 1801, doubtless prompted in part by military exigencies, withdrew all NCOs and soldiers from employment in various government offices and posted them, if they were fit enough, to active service.[20] Even the construction of barracks had a healthy impact on public life, since it got the troops out of private quarters, where their violent behavior often led to conflict with civilians. This was an old problem for eighteenth-century Russian administrators, which Paul tried earnestly to alleviate. One of the functions of the military auditors was to resolve complaints by civilians against the military. The same objective probably inspired his decrees that civilian rather than military agencies should purchase cloth for uniforms, another potential source of friction,[21] and that officers and men on leave should not visit the capital cities without special permission.[22] Military men who incurred debts to civilians were made to pay. A typical order reads: "Dismiss from the service *kornet* Protopopov, of Annenkov's hussar regiment, and proceed according to the law with the suit against him by the merchant Meyer."[23]

Prior to Paul's accession there had been much confusion in the responsibilities of military and civilian functionaries, although one task of the procuracy was to ensure that office-holders did not infringe upon one another's authority. According to the statute on local government of November 7, 1775, the *namestnik* (governor-general) exercised the duties of commander-in-chief; in frontier areas he might be either superior or inferior in authority to the military commander, as the Sovereign

---

16 "Pis'ma Imperatora Pavla Petrovicha k moskovskomu glavnokomanduiushchemu," *RA* (1876), pt. 1, 11 (4 May 1797).

17 *PSZ*, XXIV, no. 17878 (18 Mar. 1797).

18 *Ibid.*, XXIV, no. 17817 (19 Feb. 1797); cf. no. 17951 (2 May 1797).

19 *Ibid.*, no. 17723 (11 Jan. 1797); cf. no. 17876 (11 Mar. 1797) for the special case of surveyors. A decree of 1 Feb. 1797 (no. 17777) ordered all commandants who drew their salary from civil funds to be renamed *gorodnichie* and to come under the civil authorities, instead of the War College as heretofore.

20 *Ibid.*, XXVI, no. 19727 (22 Jan. 1801).

21 *Ibid.*, XXV, no. 18384 (17 Jan. 1798).

22 *Ibid.*, XXIV, no. 17705 (Dec. 1796).

23 "Pis'ma Imperatora Pavla Petrovicha," 22 (Jan. 1798).

directed. Similarly, urban commandants could summon military forces to maintain order in an emergency, but their rights *vis-à-vis* the regular chiefs of these bodies were not prescribed by law.[24]

The emperor's guiding idea, it appears, was that *voennye* and *shtatskie* should keep to their own bailiwicks, but work together amicably on state business. There was to be a kind of "peaceful coexistence" between the two parallel hierarchies. The aim is best exemplified by an ordinance of February, 1798, that civil government departments and provincial governors should send only "communications" (*soobshcheniia*), not decrees (*ukazy*), to military commanders or units, since the latter were not subordinate to the former, but solely to the War College and ultimately to the emperor; each instance, whether military or civilian, was to fulfill the lawful demands of the other, since "the duty of service and mutual effort to advance the Sovereign's affairs requires them to afford [each other] every assistance and satisfaction."[25]

Admittedly, this law seemed more concerned to protect the military from civilian interference than *vice versa*, and in practise no doubt the men with muskets usually got the better of the bargain. But this was not Paul's intention. When Alexander I restored the old order of things, six days after his accession, he (or Count Pahlen, his chief adviser) threw out the baby with the bathwater. Two reasons for the change are given in the decree, only the first of which is plausible: the Senate, it was said, had been unable to communicate directly with the military governors on *civil* matters; if this was indeed the situation in 1801, it clearly had to be remedied. But the second argument blandly declared it "inappropriate" that military commanders should be able to send out memoranda (*vedeniia*), rather than orders, to civilian organs, and so disregarded Paul's objective of achieving equilibrium.[26] Had Alexander gone on to introduce constitutional reforms, this need not have mattered; as it was, the way was open to all manner of abuses by the military, such as those to which the Decembrists vainly drew attention. Nor did Nicholas I redress the balance. On the contrary he went further than Paul in staffing the administration with army officers, who often fulfilled their peaceful tasks in the spirit of the barracks.[27]

III

This brings us to the second point: the nature of the bureaucracy. Paul's reign, we have suggested, sees a shift towards the "professionalization" of the administrative machine—a slight and temporary phenomenon, to be sure, but none the less significant for that. Under Catherine a number of officers had resigned their commissions to enter civilian life and had found their way into the administration; they had been made welcome because this was a major source of recruitment of officials within the

---

24 *PSZ*, XIV, no. 14392 (7 Nov. 1775), §§81, 89, 253, 264, 270.

25 *Ibid.*, XXV, no. 18400 (25 Feb. 1798).

26 *Ibid.*, XXVI, no. 19796 (17 Mar. 1801).

27 Cf. Herzen, *My Past and Thoughts*, 214–15, for a description of the police chief in Perm', who "belonged to a special type of military men turned officials."

service class. Paul, however, considered that all noblemen, unless physically unfit, should perform their duties in the armed forces. The logical corollary would have been to make the civilian bureaucracy a non-noble preserve. This, of course, was politically unfeasible—but Paul's government did take some hesitant steps in this direction, as we shall see in a moment.

A more limited measure that was adopted had the purpose of stemming the drift to civilian jobs by army officers who found the new harsh discipline uncongenial. It did not enforce a total ban on such transfers, but tightened the controls exercised over all appointments by the Heraldmaster's Office (*Gerol'diia*). A department in this agency, the Judicial Desk (*Sudeiskii stol*), issued the necessary documents, among them one stating the applicant's service record and seniority in rank (*starshinstvo*); and this form was now redrafted so as to include more information.[28] In later years these personnel records were to become fuller, although to the modern eye they look naive and perfunctory.

In the Russian official class before the Great Reforms a man's career depended on rank or social status rather than personal merit. His first appointment owed much to his family background and "connections," as well as his educational qualifications; and his gradual ascent up the hierarchical ladder, with its fourteen rungs, might well come about automatically, regardless of his actual performance, since promotion was granted after one had served a certain term in a given rank. This system was obviously harmful to state interests, but it had become so firmly entrenched that even rulers as strong-willed as Paul or Nicholas I could do little to change it. On the contrary, within a few months of his accession Paul issued a stereotyped order to the effect that when making appointments strict attention should be paid to the seniority of applicants and the offices concerned (*starshinstvo mest i chinov*).[29] Later, in December, 1799, he extended the service term for automatic promotion from three years to four in all the junior grades between the fourteenth and the eighth (which conferred noble rank).[30] The object of this was presumably to discourage men from pursuing this leisurely course and to make them work harder, in the hope that their exemplary service would be reported to the emperor, who would then intervene and promote them regardless of their seniority (and regardless of the decree mentioned above). It was consonant with Paul's philosophy of autocratic government that the Sovereign had the sole right to confer rewards of this kind and to punish laggards. Popular legend credits him with many such interventions (as noted at the beginning of this article), but in the absence of a statistical analysis of the archival evidence it is impossible to say how frequently the normal promotion pattern was disturbed.

Another small step towards professionalism was to open up a few limited opportunities to commoners. As we have noted, in the army commoners were rigorously excluded from the officer corps,[31] but in the civil service a rather more broad-minded

---

28 *PSZ*, XXV, no. 18440 (15 Mar. 1798).

29 *Ibid.*, XXIV, no. 17926 (20 Apr. 1797).

30 *Ibid.*, XXV, no. 19219 (9 Dec. 1799), cited by Torke, op. cit., 54.

31 *Ibid.*, XXV, no. 18486 (17 Apr. 1798). In December, 1800, the guards regiments were

policy was adopted. In 1798 the Senate learned that 205 men of non-noble origin (merchants, *meshchane* and even taxpaying peasants) had entered the ranks of officialdom, of whom 29 had reached the eighth grade. It was decided, sensibly enough, that they should be allowed to stay where they were, and that any further such cases should be judged on their individual merits.[32] Paul did not, however, dare to repeal the general prohibition on entry by commoners dating from the 1770s and in May, 1800, he forbade children of clergy to enter the civil service without his express permission.[33]

We now have some statistics on the social composition of the Russian bureaucracy in this period, unearthed and analyzed by Walter Pintner. These show that of those serving in certain central government agencies in the period 1798–1800 16.5 percent were commoners, compared with 11.5 percent for the longer period 1798–1824.[34] The figures for the provincial organs, if available, would doubtless reveal a wider breach in noble prerogatives. Mikhail Speranskii was only the best known of a number of *raznochintsy* who made use of this loophole to pursue a successful career in the bureaucracy—although characteristically he needed protection to overcome the tremendous disadvantages that faced those who sprang from the lower orders.

Commoners, alas, did not write memoirs; but many of them would probably have shared the feelings of N. A. Sablukov, a guards officer who "made good" in Paul's service. (Of 132 officers in his regiment in 1796, he was one of two survivors in 1801.) In his words, "promotion was very rapid for those who had good nerves." In an age of general insecurity those with little to lose must often have looked forward to the prospect of making rapid gains at the expense of their privileged superiors. Life was a lottery, and one might be lucky. This feeling helps to explain Paul's popularity with the masses, or (as Sablukov puts it): "the million, [who] greeted the emperor with such enthusiasm, whenever an occasion offered, that he attributed the coldness and apparent want of affection of the nobility only to moral corruption and jacobinical leanings."[35]

Thus one might say that Paul opened a window and allowed a cool draft of

---

purged of commoners, who were transferred to the category of *odnodvortsy: PSZ,* XXVI, no. 19696 (23 Dec. 1800).

32 Torke, "Das russische Beamtentum," 104.

33 *PSZ,* XXVI, no. 19434 (27 May 1800); cf. Torke, *op. cit.,* 110.

34 Walter M. Pintner, "Social Characteristics of the Early Nineteenth-Century Russian Bureaucracy," *SR,* XXIX (1970), 436. The assumption here is that the higher proportion of commoners in the 1798–1800 reflected deliberate government policy, but in the absence of comparable figures from Catherine's reign it is difficult to be sure; social pressures may have been responsible. [See now Pintner's study, "The Evolution of Civil Officialdom, 1755–1855," in W. McK. Pintner and D. K. Rowney, eds., *Russian Officialdom: the Bureaucratization of Russian Society from the Seventeenth to the Twentieth Century* (Chapel Hill, N. C., 1980), 190–226.]

35 ["Reminiscences of the Court and Times of the Emperor, Paul I of Russia, up to the Period of his Death: from the Papers of a Deceased Russian General Officer [N. A. Sablukov]," *Fraser's Magazine,* 72 (London, 1865), August, 237; for Russian translation cf.] "Iz zapisok N. A. Sablukova," *RA* (1870), col. 1903.

competition to dispel the stifling atmosphere of privilege, precedent and protection which pervaded the official milieu. One can scarcely speak of a "democratization" of government; the emperor's views were unashamedly elitist, but he did appreciate that the martial virtues he cherished were not confined to men of noble birth—much though he may have wished it were otherwise—and he was prepared on occasion to measure a man's worth not by his rank but by his office, provided that his functions served the state interest as the emperor himself understood it.

This indicates a move, albeit a hesitant one, towards greater rationality in the conduct of state affairs. Two developments in the institutional field deserve mention in this context: the decisive role accorded to the Procurator-General and, in the local government sphere, the shift from elected to appointed officials.[36]

The Procurator-General was seen, in the Petrine tradition, as the supreme guardian of legality, and was also entrusted with some vague general authority over policy, the two functions not being clearly distinguished.[37] In practise the Procurator-General became an embryonic prime minister. It is true that in Paul's reign (unlike his predecessor's) the incumbent changed too frequently for consistency, and that he was entrusted with too much power, especially in regard to the Senate, without being provided with any real security against whims of his autocratic master. Nevertheless, taken in conjunction with the ministerial reform (completed in 1802, but prepared during Paul's reign), this marked a step along the road to responsible cabinet government.

The policy of replacing elected officials by appointed ones in the provincial organs of authority[38] was inspired not by any animus against the gentry as such, but by a belief that paid officials who were entirely dependent upon the central power and who had an assured place in the bureaucratic hierarchy would be able to perform their duties in more responsible fashion than men whose allegiance was necessarily divided between their superiors and the electorate. It may of course be objected that this view was too simple, and that Russian "society" was being pressed back into the straitjacket from which Catherine had gingerly begun to free it. But it could also be argued that the officials nominated from the center represented a nucleus of professional administrators in the rural areas, the need for which was felt by Russian rulers and statesmen from Peter I to Stolypin.

Not that Paul himself saw these officials as a professional group: to him they were just servants. But he would surely have acknowledged that they performed certain specialized functions for which they needed to be trained—and this in itself was a step forward. One of his first decrees called for restoration of the so-called "*iunker* schools," originally set up by Peter but closed in 1763, to prepare entrants for the civil branch of the service. These pale copies of the prestigious Cadet Corps offered a two-

---

36 For details see Klochkov, *Ocherki*, 224–70.

37 *PSZ*, XXIV, no. 17652 (16 Dec. 1796). He was to show "vigilance . . . in ensuring exact fulfillment of the laws" and to watch over "the proper flow of the various affairs passing through government offices."

38 See Klochkov, *Ocherki*, 434–80.

year program, divided between general studies (*nauki obshchie*) and professionally-oriented subjects (*nauki zvaniia*). Among the latter jurisprudence was to have pride of place; among the former, as distinct disciplines, were ethics (*nravouchenie*) and logic—for in the words of the decree, "logic is a science which no civil official, and especially a judge, can do without,"[39] Praiseworthy sentiments: alas, in the event only one such school saw the light of day, and its performance was poor; in practise far more emphasis was placed upon general "humanities" than upon the study of jurisprudence. As Torke writes, "the principle of specialized education had not yet won a footing in the government's thinking, but instead, true to the eighteenth-century spirit, priority was given to encyclopedic knowledge."[40]

IV

The assumption in the legislator's mind was that the graduates of this school would set an example to their colleagues, morally as well as intellectually. This brings us to the third aspect of Paul's "militarism": the struggle against corruption. He deplored this vice because it weakened the state and dishonored those who practised it; and he made a sincere effort to eliminate it and to inculcate what one might call the "bureaucratic ethos" by measures derived from military experience. His weapons, in ascending order of priority, were exhortation, control and discipline.

The first of several general hortatory decrees was prompted by the affair of an army doctor who was detained for two days in Saratov by a pair of locally-elected civilian officials who were drunk at the time. Paul characteristically put them in the guardhouse on a diet of bread and water and then issued a philippic against such "violent and insulting behavior towards a neighbor." Officials were called upon to display "goodwill and humanity towards the people. . . , restraint and mildness, without any slacking, and continual vigilance that the established order is universally observed in each locality."[41] Naturally enough, no one took the slightest notice.

Control over official actions in eighteenth-century Russia was a task that fell to the procuracy. A creation of Peter I, its powers had since been eroded, and Paul sought to strengthen it. A steady stream of reports on illegalities and abuses of every kind flowed up through these channels to the Procurator-General and the emperor himself, and usually resulted in administrative or legislative action. When a member of the procuracy appeared in a local government bureau, the officials were obliged to produce forthwith the papers requested—not least those documents relating to prisoners under detention, some of whom might have spent years in the cells before their case was

---

39 *PSZ*, XXIV, nos. 17707 (1 Jan. 1797), 17733 (14 Jan. 1797), 17912 (8 Apr. 1797).

40 Torke, "Das russische Beamtentum," 146. Torke accepts Grech's rather improbable story that when Paul discovered that 4,500 prospective pupils had registered in place of the 50 provided for, those surplus to the norm were sent off to the army as NCOs. [On the development of legal education in early nineteenth-century Russia, see R. S. Wortman, *The Development of a Russian Legal Consciousness* (Chicago and London, 1976), 38–41, 44–50.]

41 *PSZ*, XXV, no. 18964 (15 May 1798).

heard.[42] The Senate was instructed to catch up on its arrears of business and to make its subordinate agencies do likewise.[43] Klochkov has shown that the number of cases settled in the Senate rose from 21,000 in 1797 to 44,000 in 1800—three times as many as in the last years of Catherine's reign.[44] Of course, such statistics do not tell us anything about the quality of the justice dispensed, and it is characteristic of Paul that he should adopt such a crude numerical criterion of success, which even Klochkov, writing a century later, seems to find unobjectionable.

Such action was typical of the emperor's tendency to concentrate on the externals of bureaucratic routine instead of examining the substantive decisions taken by his subordinates. He lavished decrees on such trivia as the need to submit reports regularly, to observe punctual office hours, to return promptly from leave and the like.[45] No less than 48,000 orders were issued by the Emperor in the single year 1797.[46] A reluctance to delegate power is one of the hallmarks of despotism; yet one should not forget the immense obstacles which the authorities faced in enforcing elementary discipline upon officials. For example, it was found necessary to lay down that every state agency which received a Senate ordinance should, when acknowledging the fact, specify the number of copies received: evidently some functionaries, disliking certain decrees, pretended that they had never been informed of them.[47] These petty regulations added to the atmosphere of fear and intrigue that prevailed in government circles during this period. In the hope of escaping or diverting the emperor's wrath, officials would connive with one another to conceal their misdeeds or put the blame on third parties. The humiliations and brutalities inflicted upon them they would avenge upon the populace committed to their charge, convincing themselves that such roughness accorded with the sovereign's own desires—which was by no means the case.

The *excès de zèle* by frightened functionaries sometimes took a ridiculous form. We may dismiss as apocryphal the familiar tale of St. Petersburg policemen ripping off passers-by certain articles of imported clothing deemed to have revolutionary associations. But Sablukov, a reliable witness, tells a hair-raising story about his father, a government contractor, whom the emperor dismissed and banished from the capital for failing to supply uniform cloth in the proper shade of dye. Count Pahlen, the police chief, insisted that the order be carried out immediately, on a cold winter's day, although the elderly Sablukov was confined to bed with a high temperature. When his son protested, Pahlen replied, "if one of us is to go to the devil, I prefer it had to be he"—but promised to do what he could later. After Paul had heard

42 *Ibid.*, XXV, no. 18937 (28 Apr. 1798).

43 *Ibid.*, XXIV, no. 17884 (22 Mar. 1797).

44 Klochkov, *Ocherki*, 219–20.

45 E.g., *PSZ*, XXIV, nos. 17680 (23 Dec. 1796), 17685 (26 Dec. 1796); XXV, 18648 (31 Aug. 1798), 18709 (20 Oct. 1798).

46 R. E. McGrew, "A Political Portrait of Paul I from the Austrian and English Diplomatic Archives," *JGOE*, XVIII (1970), 515 n.

47 *PSZ*, XXV, no. 18357 (31 Jan. 1798).

what had happened, he apologized.[48] The really significant point in this affair is not the emperor's arbitrariness, which so impressed the writer of the memoir, but the unimaginative and irresponsible reaction to it by a leading official.

Servility, formalism, brutality, short-sightedness and sheer stupidity—these were the vices that disfigured the Imperial bureaucracy prior to the "Great Reforms" and imprinted their legacy upon later generations. Of all these faults the most serious was the general indifference to considerations of legality. In this regard Paul's efforts to cure corruption by regimentation served only to make matters worse. He was beset by the dilemma that faced all reforming autocrats: any concession to legality could not but weaken the sacred principle of unlimited autocracy. On the one hand he sincerely wished to encourage respect for the law; on the other he held as stubbornly as any Russian ruler to his sovereign prerogatives, even claiming that his own will constituted the *only* valid source of law—a notion that had no basis in fact. Paul refused to recognize that for any real improvement in public administration to occur it was imperative that officials should be free to state their opinions and to make recommendations without thereby setting themselves at personal risk. In short, Russia needed a modern corpus of administrative law, or *Beamtenrecht*. Paul and his military advisors were of course still more opposed to the notion that persons outside the highest governmental circles might play some part in the policy-making process, or exercise some public control over the workings of the administrative apparatus. In his suspicious mind such ideas smacked of "jacobinism"; indeed, it was partly in order to combat them that he embarked upon measures designed to rationalize the workings of government. Yet militarism was not enough. His reforms were doomed to failure—and may even have cost him his life.

The *coup d'état* of March 11 was not just a palace revolution against an anachronistic tyranny: it was a blow against the increased bureaucratization of Russian society, struck by a small group within the service class, both military and civilian, who enjoyed the tacit support of a much wider segment of élite opinion. In this respect the conspiracy anticipated that of the Decembrists a quarter-century later. The movement had some characteristics of an aristocratic *fronde*, but can scarcely be said to have been motivated by class interest. Far more significant was a nostalgia for a vanished age of easy informality. It was a protest in the name of traditional values against a particularly brutal kind of state-sponsored modernization. As such, it prepared the ground for the growth of Romantic ideology in the 1830s and 1840s. In Nicholas's Russia the struggle between idealistic, individualistic romanticism and unimaginative official conservatism ended—temporarily, at least—in a victory for the latter. Nicholas held to many of his father's ideals and made a more sustained, and no doubt more balanced, attempt to put them into effect. Paul was never able to reconcile the rational and the irrational facets of his policies. Yet his reign is of the utmost significance in the history of Russia: it represented a crucial stage in the emergence of that modern Moloch, the militaristic-bureaucratic state.

1973

48 [Sablukov, "Reminiscences," 239; cf.] "Iz zapisok N. A. Sablukova," col. 1913.

CHAPTER 8

The Military Style of the Romanov Rulers

I

One of the earliest writers on military sociology noted that armies are prey to a curious contradiction. On one hand they are designed as instruments to achieve a supremely rational purpose in the most efficacious manner possible, and so are oriented to the present and future. On the other hand they come to be looked on in peacetime, by romantics inside and outside the officer corps, as embodiments of cherished values and traditions, symbolized and sanctified by ceremonial, which ought to be maintained at all costs. A. Vagts cited a Russian grand duke to the effect that "wars spoil armies."[1] Constantine Pavlovich, of whom more will be said below, was not untypical of a spirit found in many European armies after the bloodletting of the Napoleonic era. It combined a limited respect for humanitarian principles with a renewed emphasis on discipline, smart appearance, and pedantic adherence to every detail of military regulations.

Historians of Imperial Russia have invariably remarked in casual fashion that several of the tsars had a veritable obsession with the paraphernalia of soldiering. They have been indicted for their "paradomania," a term also used by contemporaries. The phenomenon deserves to be examined in its own right, for an undue addiction to ceremonial is one of the hallmarks of militarism, although not the most important one.[2] How did it originate? Should it be attributed to foreign, specifically German, influences? How serious were its effects on Russia's military efficiency? What resistance to it was offered by officers or soldiers with more professional, or at least more imaginative, ideas?

In broaching these questions here we may confine our discussion to three rulers, Paul I (1796–1801), Alexander I (1801–25) and Nicholas I (1825–55), and their immediate kin. There are good reasons for this chronological limitation. During this sixty-year span Russia was still governed by an absolutist regime of a type once general throughout the continent, but one which possessed certain peculiarities

---

1 A. Vagts, *A History of Militarism: Romance and Realities of a Profession* (London, 1938), 13, 26.

2 S. Andreski, "Militarism," in H. F. Reading, ed., *A Dictionary of the Social Sciences* (London and Boston, 1977), 131.

derived from Byzantine and oriental influences that had shaped her political culture in earlier centuries.[3] After the "Eastern" War of 1853–56 the state order underwent a profound transformation, even though elements of the old ways survived. Significant steps were taken toward pluralism in political life; the bureaucracy was demilitarized; economic growth was pursued for its own sake, not just to bolster the empire's war-making capacity; and members of the élite were no longer virtually obliged to enter state service (military or civil) in order to make ends meet, but instead enjoyed a widening range of career options. In the twentieth century tsarism's inability to direct and control this process of "debonding" (*raskreposhchenie*) led to revolution and ultimately to the creation of a new polity which, like its remote predecessor, was based on the old principle of obligatory state service.

It will be contended here that the Romanov rulers developed a particular "military style" which to some extent set them apart from other European sovereigns, to whom they were nevertheless linked by close dynastic and political ties. By "military style" we mean something less than the totality of their actions in regard to the armed forces. The term signifies rather an attitude of mind and a pattern of conduct which reflected a preoccupation with militaria—that is to say, with the externals and minutiae of military life.

First a point may be made in their defense. Historians and biographers, writing mainly from a civilian perspective and with the benefit of hindsight, have too easily overlooked the fact that parade ground skills were essential to the operation of armies in this pretechnological age, when large bodies of infantrymen, mostly illiterate and unmotivated, had to be marched and maneuvered by a complicated system of signals before they could be brought to face the horrors of hand-to-hand combat. A sovereign, whether he appeared on the battlefield or not, needed to know the drillbook, or else he would be a mere plaything of his generals. The more responsible and intelligent rulers saw themselves not just as drillmasters but as strategists, organizers and morale-raisers. Unhappily it was the former type that prevailed in Russia.

One naturally seeks an explanation for this in the education which they received. Richard Wortman, writing of the later nineteenth-century tsars, observes that

> the grand duke's upbringing emphasized the ruler's military calling. The emperor appeared above all as an embodiment of military power. He was an officer, with the appropriate tastes, values and mannerisms. The primacy of the military would be emphasized throughout the childhood and youth of the heir. . . . He watched his father and uncles participate in endless parades, wear military uniforms and speak of military exploits and plans. . . . For the heir to be a man was to be martial.[4]

---

3 R. Pipes, *Russia under the Old Regime* (New York and London, 1974). The history of the service state in its military dimension is examined in my *Soldiers of the Tsar: the Russian Army and Society, 1462–1874* (Oxford, 1985).

4 R. S. Wortman, "Power and Responsibility in the Upbringing of the Nineteenth-Century Tsar," *Newsletter* [of the Group for the Use of Psychology in History], 4,4 (Springfield, Il., March, 1976), 22.

This was even truer of the earlier period, as we shall see. Remarkably, even Alexander I, whose upbringing reflected his mother's "enlightened" principles and cannot really be described as militaristic, fell into the common pattern. This suggests that "paradomania" was fostered as much by environmental factors as by acquired psychological traits. So far as the latter are concerned, Wortman argues suggestively that the ruler-to-be was frequently humiliated, or made to feel inadequate, by his father, the mighty autocrat; that he was expected to be both strong and obedient; and that the intolerable tension set up between these contradictory demands led him to feel ill at ease on assuming his weighty office:

> To these overbearing tasks the Russian emperor preferred those that were within his reach. The drillfield provided a welcome simplification or responsibility and authority. On the drillfield his power was supreme, simple and efficacious. The total control he was supposed to exert was actually possible. [The men] responded quickly, precisely and deferentially. There was neither the danger and gore of combat nor the unmanageable disorder of civil government. . . . The love for drill [was] substituted for a personal dedication to the work of ruling.[5]

To this one may add that the tsarevich measured himself not only against his father but also against the plethora of senior military officers in his entourage. These men inevitably had far more professional experience, yet were obliged to pay him an exaggerated but insincere respect.

This is why Russian rulers generally chose as their intimate counselors—aides-de-camp, for example—men of mediocre military talent. There was often a tense relationship between the autocrat and the more "brilliant" commanders. Paul detested Suvorov; Alexander was loath to appoint Kutuzov to head the Russian armies in 1812; Nicholas distrusted Ermolov, his independent-minded Caucasian viceroy, although he was superior to his successor Paskevich, as well as to Chernyshev, the minister of War. The limited military abilities of Alexander's chief favorite, Arakcheev, are common knowledge.

More generally, the tsars felt insecure on their imperial throne. Although the Russian monarchy was more stable now than it had been in the eighteenth century, since from 1797 the order of succession was determined by law, the threat of *coup d'état* or revolution could not be lightly dismissed, as the events of 1801 and 1825 amply demonstrated; and in 1812 Russia had faced a major foreign invasion. This weakness reinforced the rulers' half-conscious recognition of their own personal limitations and led them to seek support from military men as professional experts in violence. Army officers were regularly appointed to senior positions in the central bureaucracy or to provincial governorships, particularly under Nicholas I.

Another factor was the existence of models, both foreign and domestic, on which the tsars strove to pattern their conduct. The first emperor, Peter I, became the object of a remarkable official cult to which other European monarchies offered no parallel. The empresses who wore the crown for most of the eighteenth century

---

5 Ibid., 27.

were not immune to this, but inevitably saw their role as that of cultural enlightener rather than supreme warlord. The prevailing ideology was patriarchal or matriarchal, according to the ruler's sex. Male sovereigns were portrayed as the "little father" (*tsar'-batiushka*) of their people, and especially of those who bore arms in their service, even though by any objective criterion it was the soldiers who suffered most from the belligerent activities sponsored by the Crown. The myth of autocracy proved astonishingly tenacious, and was invoked by soldiers or peasants who rebelled against their immediate superiors until 1905.

Tsar Peter III (1761–2), who was also duke of Holstein, and his son Paul I both adulated Frederick the Great of Prussia, whose exploits long fascinated élite opinion all over Europe. Russian devotees of *der grosse Fritz* could not hope to militarize their country's resources as thoroughly as he had done, but they tried hard to apply his "secret" in training and equipping the armed forces. On the other hand many officers and others objected to this "aping of the foreigner," considering that Russia's own military traditions were quite adequate, if not actually superior. There was good reason for such beliefs; nevertheless the nationalist reaction against "Prussianism" was exaggerated. It has colored historical writing to this day, for Soviet historians often repeat almost literally the arguments of their forbears in the nineteenth-century military establishment, among whom chauvinistic attitudes were common, and a similar approach has generally been taken in the West. Recently, however, it has been challenged by Christopher Duffy, who dismisses these "sterile controversies" and characterizes both Münnich (commander-in-chief in the 1730s) and Suvorov as "active and creative members of the cosmopolitan European military community."[6] It is fallacious to divide Russian generals neatly into two antagonistic groups: gifted native sons and martinets with an alien cast of mind.[7] The nature of warfare at this time led military leaders everywhere to enforce severe disciplinary codes; some were stricter or crueller than others, but the differences are of degree rather than of kind. One need only mention that in Russia the basis of military justice was a 1716 statute which, although based on Prussian and other western models, was creatively adapted to Russian conditions by Peter I.[8] It would be an idle exercise to try to isolate the Prussian influences in the military style of our three tsars. Each of them relied heavily, as did their predecessors and successors, on Germans, especially from the Baltic provinces of their empire, to fill leading positions in the armed forces and elsewhere. In a prenationalist age this made excellent sense.

Another red herring may be disposed of at this point. Echoing Pushkin, who

6 C. Duffy, *Russia's Military Way to the West: Origins and Nature of Russian Military Power* (London and Boston, 1981), 234.

7 As is done, for example, by A. A. Kersnovskii, *Istoriia russkoi armii*, 3 pts. (Belgrade, 1933–5).

8 "Ustav voinskii, *Pamiatniki russkogo prava*, fasc. 8: *Zakonodatel'nye akty Petra I . . .* , ed. K. A. Sofronenko (Moscow, 1961), 319–69. Soviet historians insist strongly on the code's adaptation to Russian circumstances; see e.g. P. P. Epifanov, "Voinskii ustav Petra Velikogo," in A. I. Andreev, ed., *Petr Velikii: sbornik statei* (Moscow and Leningrad, 1947), 203.

commented on the pronounced family resemblance among male Romanovs, several historians have written as if their militarism could be accounted for genetically. Even Isabel de Madariaga, in her fine recent study of Catherine II, states that her grandson Constantine had "the same underlying streak of violence, . . . even brutality, as . . . Paul (a confirmation perhaps of true Romanov descent from Peter I through Peter III), which none of his tutors was able to tame."[9] There may be something to this in regard to such recurring traits as irascibility or stubbornness; but a preference for one kind of activity over another may be attributed in part to deliberate emulation. Thus Nicholas worshipped Alexander I ("Our Angel," as he was referred to in the royal circle), and his brother Michael is said to have adopted Constantine's tone of voice and phraseology.[10]

Another recent writer, trying hard to find something good to say about Constantine, takes a different tack, assuring us that "it is true that he was a military martinet, but so were many other men of his generation," for instance the duke of Cumberland.[11] Certainly militarism was an all-European phenomenon, not a preserve of the Romanovs; yet it is remarkable that so many of them should have displayed sergeant-major qualities. The explanation, to repeat, lies in the objective situation which they faced as well as in the atmosphere that surrounded them as they grew up.

II

Let us consider their upbringing more closely. The tsarevich Paul was tutored from 1760 to 1773 by Nikita I. Panin, an enlightened diplomat and courtier who had an aversion to the military lifestyle and drew up for his young charge a remarkably modern and balanced pedagogical scheme.[12] However, he may also have helped to turn the boy against his mother and made him look upon his archmilitarist father (Peter III, who had been assassinated) as a martyred warrior hero. On his accession he emulated his father's short-sighted and provocative policies, not least in the military domain, and after four years suffered a similar fate. Earlier, in 1778–79, he carried on a correspondence with his ex-tutor's brother, Petr I. Panin, a successful but brutal general, in which he set out the harsh disciplinarian creed that he would later enforce as sovereign.[13] Denied an active military role by Catherine, the tsarevich set up his own establishment on his estate at Gatchina near the capital. By 1796 this force

---

9 I. de Madariaga, *Russia in the Age of Catherine the Great* (London, 1981), 571; cf. V. Zubow, *Zar Paul I: Mensch und Schicksal* (Stuttgart, 1963), 26.

10 N. Chechulin, "Konstantin Pavlovich," *RBS*, ix, 192.

11 S. W. Jackman, ed., *Romanov Relations: the Private Correspondence of Tsars Alexander I . . . with . . . Anna Pavlovna, 1817–1855* (London, 1969), 9.

12 D. L. Ransel, *The Politics of Catherinian Russia: the Panin Party* (New Haven and London, 1975), 205–14.

13 "Velikii kniaz' Pavel Petrovich: perepiska . . . s grafom Petrom Paninym v 1778 g.," *RS*, 33 (1882), 403–18, 739–64. For an analysis of this and other related documents see Ia. L. Barskov, "Proekty voennykh reform tsesarevicha Pavla," *Russkii istoricheskii zhurnal*, 1 (Petrograd, 1917), 3–4, 104–45.

of some 1,750 men, the *Gatchintsy* as they were contemptuously called, dressed and drilled in the Prussian manner, was poised to take over control of the rest of the army.[14] This threat could have been averted if Catherine had implemented her scheme to exclude Paul from the succession in favor of her grandson Alexander—but the latter would have nothing to do with it.

Alexander was himself an officer in the Gatchina establishment, and although kept away from his father until 1794, took to the Gatchina spirit with a will: its spartan simplicities seem to have offered him a welcome change from the refined cosmopolitanism of Catherine's court.[15] The new tsarevich did guard duty and ran errands with every appearance of enjoyment.[16] "*Wachtparaden* and uniforms became his principal concerns," remarked one contemporary critic, who regretted that the young prince, in behaving like a corporal, was neglecting studies of statecraft more suitable to his future role.[17] Alexander criticized his father's excesses by implication in orders to subordinates, but the view of him chafing under Paul's tyranny rests on one letter of complaint (to Laharpe in 1797)[18] in which he dissembled his true thoughts.

Nicholas I's first biographer claims that Paul's "passion for military drill, which [he] engaged in without interruption . . . at Gatchina . . . must have had a keen impact on [his] future son."[19] Since the Gatchina establishment was disbanded before Nicholas reached the age of two, this genetic explanation for his martial proclivities need not be taken seriously. Fortunately Korf provides ample information to show that environmental influences were important. The grand duke was allotted a "special household staff" of ladies, most of whom were generals' or colonels' wives; his first toy was a wooden rifle; and at the age of three he donned the uniform of the Horse guards.[20] Between 1802 and 1806 no fewer than 76 such outfits were tailored for the growing boy.[21] At seven he was learning how to make bombs out of wax and how to besiege a mock fortress; his lessons in engineering, from a general, then gave way to instruction in strategy. Asked to write an essay on the theme "Military service is

---

14 F. von Stein, *Geschichte des russischen Heeres vom Ursprunge desselben bis zur Thronbesteigung des Kaisers Nikolai I. Pawlowitsch* (Hanover, 1885 reprinted Krefeld, 1975), 199; cf. D. Kobeko, *Tsesarevich Pavel Petrovich (1754–1796); istoricheskoe issledovanie* (St. Petersburg, 1882), 300–1, 366–9.

15 F. Golovkine, *La cour et le règne de Paul Ier: portraits, souvenirs et anecdotes,* introd. S. Bonnet (Paris, 1905), 152–3.

16 Madariaga, *Catherine,* 570.

17 E. R. Dashkova, "Avtobiografiia," *AKV,* xxi (1881), 358.

18 N. K. Shil'der, *Imperator Aleksandr I: ego zhizn' i tsarstvovanie* (St. Petersburg, 1897), i, 162, 280; idem, *Imperator Pavel I: istoriko-biograficheskii ocherk* (St. Petersburg, 1901), 368–70.

19 M. [A.] Korf, "Materialy i cherty k biografii imperatora Nikolaia I-go i k istorii ego tsarstvovaniia," ed. N. F. Dubrovin, *SIRIO,* xcviii (1896), 6.

20 Ibid., 10, 22, 23.

21 Ibid., 32; for the following, cf. also W. B. Lincoln, *Nicholas I, Emperor and Autocrat of All the Russias* (London, 1978), 59.

not the only honorable kind for a nobleman," Nicholas refused, presumably because he disapproved of the topic.[22]

In 1814 he was allowed to join the army in western Europe. His mother, Maria Fedorovna, urged him not to become engrossed by "les bagatelles militaires," but

> to acquire the knowledge . . . which makes a great captain and extends over so many different branches, all of which you should master, especially those that aim at preservation of the soldier, who is very often neglected and sacrificed, for the sake of elegant dress and useless exercises, to the personal ambition and ignorance of his Chief.[23]

Nicholas did not heed this sage advice. When he was 21 he undertook an inspection tour of troops in the provinces, and kept a journal of his experiences. "Almost all the entries," notes his biographer, "pertain solely to the externals of military service: clothing, bearing, marching etc., and do not touch on any essential aspect of military organization, administration, or the men's morale."[24] His actual military duties began in the following year, when he was placed in charge of the engineers, and then appointed commander of a guards brigade. He soon began "to take matters in hand severely," as he put it, which earned him a bad reputation with many senior officers. Those whom he considered "impertinent" or "given to reasoning" were discharged or transferred.[25] It should be added that this mini-purge probably prevented the Decembrist conspiracy of 1825 from having any impact on the division under his nominal command (*shefstvo*), for the regiments affected were subordinate to his younger and less experienced brother Michael.[26]

From 1796 onwards all the grand dukes (i.e., the monarch's closest male relatives) were entrusted with nominal command of a guards regiment. In Nicholas's case this was the Horse guards (*Konnyi polk*); his elder brothers Alexander and Constantine received the Semenovskii and Izmailovskii foot guards respectively.[27] Nicholas was also made colonel of its first battalion, and this was named after him. The idea was that he should rise gradually up the ranks; but whereas Peter I had earned such promotion by zealous deeds as an adult, Nicholas became a general by 1808, when he was only 13. Moreover, at least once he drew his full pay while still in his cradle![28]

---

22 Korf, "Materialy," 73.

23 Mariia Fedorovna to Nikolai Pavlovich, February 5, 1814, in ibid., 79; cf. 82 for a similar letter of May 12, 1815.

24 Ibid., 96; cf. T. Schiemann, *Geschichte Russlands unter Kaiser Nikolaus I* (Berlin), i, (1904), 226.

25 Schiemann, *Geschichte*, i, 227.

26 G. S. Gabaev, "Gvardiia v dekabr'skie dni 1825 g.," in A. E. Presniakov, *14 dekabria 1825 g.* (Moscow and Leningrad, 1926), 162. Nicholas assumed command of the 2nd Guards Division in March, 1825: Schiemann, *Geschichte*, i, 251.

27 Korf, "Materialy," 17; Shil'der, *Pavel*, 289, 377. When Michael was born in 1798 he was appointed head of the artillery; the future Alexander II had to wait a month, until his baptism (May 17, 1818) before he was made chief of the Lifeguards Hussars: Schiemann, *Geschichte*, i, 225.

28 Korf, "Materialy," 17, 58.

From 1797 onwards all the grand dukes qualified automatically for medals (*ordena*) of three designated denominations as soon as they were baptized; other princes of the blood had to await adulthood.[29] Since all cavaliers held the third grade (*chin*) in the Table of Ranks, equivalent to lieutenant-general, the royal children actually occupied two ranks at once.

Such honors could not but help to inflate their self-importance. Their tutors frequently complained that they were lazy or disobedient. Yet senior military appointments were thrust upon them. Constantine became head of the (First) Cadet Corps, the principal officer training establishment, when he was only nineteen, scarcely older than the cadets, and in 1801, aged 22, was made chairman of a military commission to review the army's entire set-up. He did at least gain some active campaign experience later, which strengthened his preference, referred to above, for parade ground armies whose smart turnout would not be spoiled by combat.[30] He did indeed acquire such an army in the Polish kingdom when it was reconstituted in 1815, but his notorious brutality and arbitrariness made him unpopular with the Poles.

Of the youngest of the four brothers, Michael, it is recorded that he "was hated by soldiers and officers alike as a petty and pedantic representative of the most narrow-minded military formalism."[31] He was chosen to head the officer cadet schools on Constantine's death, and when he in turn passed on in 1848 he was succeeded by the current heir, the future Alexander II.[32]

III

Apart from military education (and even so only of officers) the Romanov dynasts paid little attention to those aspects of army life which were most likely to affect battlefield performance. A mechanical view of soldiering was characteristic of all *anciens régimes*, but the Russian military establishment took this further and kept to it for longer. Napoleon reached Moscow, but his ideas made little impact on Russia's "higher spheres."[33] Indeed, the army's success against the "Corsican upstart" in 1812–14 fortified the conservative attitude that came so naturally to the tsars, as it did to most of their advisers. They valued traditional forms for their own sake and insisted pedantically on absolute adherence to orders as if this alone could ensure efficiency. To such leaders the best proof of a unit's soundness was its precision and elegance on the parade ground. As a modern sociologist has put it:

Constant repetition of monotonous movements was designed to make the soldier able to

---

29 *PSZ*, xxiv, 17908 (April 5, 1797), §§5, 8.

30 W. B. Lincoln, "Konstantin Pavlovich," *MERSH*, xvii, 165.

31 Schiemann, *Geschichte*, i, 471; cf. Jackman, *Romanov Relations*, 159.

32 M. Polievktov, *Nikolai I: biografiia i obzor tsarstvovaniia* (Moscow, 1918), 331. An exception to the rule was the statesmanlike Constantine Nikolaevich, whose early training was in the navy: W. B. Lincoln, *In the Vanguard of Reform: Russia's Enlightened Bureaucrats* (De Kalb, Il. 1982), 142.

33 For their effect on Russian society, especially within the officer corps, see below, 211–38.

reproduce individual acts taken from various "packages" and to combine them in several ways to form a composite set of actions . . . His immediate superior used force where necessary in training him to make these movements instinctively. The essential purpose of drill was to get him to handle his weapon correctly and to move to an exactly defined location when he found himself on the battlefield.[34]

At the time a distinction was drawn between maneuvers (*evoliutsii*) and exercises (*eksertsitsii*). The tendency was toward the latter, which took less account of natural landscape features and did not involve any attempt to simulate battlefield conditions.[35] In conventional drill neither officers nor NCOs were expected to display any initiative; the whole object was to keep to predetermined positions and to obey commands unthinkingly. The Russian army was certainly good at this. A Prussian officer invited to St. Petersburg in the mid-1830s noted that "the cavalrymen's knees formed, as it were, a single line" and that the men even seemed to look alike; so, too, did their horses. (Regiments would indeed try to find mounts of identical color, and recruits' height and facial features would be taken into account when they were assigned to units.) Lieutenant-General von Bismarck also admired Nicholas I's assured manner of command. Instead of having the signals sounded by a bugler, he himself would imitate the appropriate notes, which he had memorized; for a sovereign to do this, von Bismarck thought, "verges on the miraculous."[36] When the troops marched past, "if the emperor remains silent, that is a sign that he is dissatisfied."[37] Those who incurred Imperial disfavor might well end up under arrest in the guardroom (*gauptvakhta*), perhaps on a diet of bread and water—as happened to the colonel and two other officers of the Tula chasseurs in Moscow in 1841.[38] On the other hand, if the tsar was content the soldiers could expect a reward. On one occasion each man got "a rouble, a pound [of meat] and a glass [of vodka]."[39]

Nicholas derived psychological satisfaction, indeed an almost sensual pleasure, from the sight of massed formations. From Voznesensk in the Ukraine, where he was attending maneuvers in 1837, he wrote to his wife: "I don't think there has even been anything more splendid, perfect or overwhelming since soldiers first appeared on earth."[40] At one emotional moment during the spectacle "his eyes filled with tears, he placed his hand on his heart, raised his eyes to Heaven and prayed aloud:

---

34 A. Mosen, *Eine Militärsoziologie: technische Entwicklung und Autoritätsprobleme in modernen Armeen* (Berlin and Neuwied, 1967), 33.

35 N. Glinoetskii, "Nekotorye svedeniia ob obuchenii russkogo voiska vo vtoroi polovine proshlogo veka," *VS*, 14 (1871), 11; 9, 26.

36 F. W. von Bismarck, *Die Kaiserlich-Russische Kriegsmacht im Jahre 1835, oder Meine Reise nach St. Petersburg* (Karlsruhe, 1836), 30, 37.

37 Ibid., 96.

38 "Otryvki iz dnevnika rotnogo komandira I. I. Gladilova, 1841 g.," P. I. Shchukin, *Sobranie starykh bumag*, vii (1901), 177.

39 M. A. Markov, "Vospominaniia starogo invalida o sluzhbe leib-gvardii v Pavlovskom polku, 1828–1835," *RS*, 68 (1890), 108.

40 Schiemann, *Geschichte*, iii (1913), 328.

'O God, I thank Thee that Thou hast given me such power. Grant me the strength never to abuse it.' "[41] At a memorial ceremony on the battlefield of Borodino two years later the tsar personally led the cavalry in a marchpast which, to his evident regret, lasted a mere 1¾ hours; the horses kicked up so much dust that the sun's rays were obscured, but the riders displayed "remarkable order and precision."[42]

The officers and men involved had a less euphoric view of such grandiose manifestations. When snow fell in St. Petersburg on the eve of the annual Easter parade soldiers had to spend all night clearing the drifts from the Palace Square, a vast enclosure which reputedly could accommodate 90,000 men.[43] The participants got little sleep. On one occasion in 1841 when the tsar visited Moscow a unit stationed in the city's outskirts was told at 10 p.m. that it would be inspected at 11 a.m. the following day. "The recruits, as usual, swore." They left their quarters at 2 a.m. and reached their destination by 4.30 a.m. Not until 7 o'clock did the brigade commander appear for a dress rehearsal, "in columns, with gunpowder"; he then called the officers together and "cursed us properly"; one man was arrested for talking in the ranks; after an hour's drill the men were marched back to base, where they arrived at 5 p.m. All this was just a preliminary warm-up. After a day's interval the ritual was repeated. During the next week four more parades were held, some in the tsar's presence. According to our informant "the soldiers greeted him with enthusiasm. The air was filled with music and hurrahs. . . . What a miracle of a man he is: so majestic, yet he looks upon the soldiers so kind-heartedly."[44]

Whereas Nicholas only assumed direct command of parades on special occasions, his father, Paul I, did so almost daily. A French diplomat wrote that "he loved soldiers and weapons in the way that some people love dogs and horses; he knew nothing else but drill and drove around in a captain's carriage."[45] Many of the anecdotes recounted about this tsar are exaggerated;[46] nevertheless as soon as he came to the throne he emulated Frederick by introducing the daily *Wachtparade*, which all senior officers were required to attend.[47] The impromptu commands issued at this parade were considered to have the force of the law, equal to decrees (*ukazy*) prepared with more circumspection. This was the most harmful feature of the practise, rather than

---

41 Ibid., 327.

42 Ibid., 374–5.

43 I. I. Venediktov, "Za schestdesiat' let: vospominaniia, 1820–1894," *RS*, 127 (1905), 595; von Bismarck, *Kriegsmacht*, 12 (for the dimensions of Palace Square).

44 "Otryvki . . . Gladilova," 172–85, esp. 174–9.

45 C.-F.-P. Masson, *Mémoires secrets sur la Russie, et particulièrement sur la fin du règne de Catherine II et sur celui de Paul I* (Paris, 1804), i, 218.

46 For an evaluation of the memoir literature, see M. V. Klochkov, *Ocherki pravitel'stvennoi deiatel'nosti vremen Pavla I* (Petrograd, 1916), 1–46; and for a recent review of the reign, H. Ragsdale, ed., *Paul I: a Reassessment of his Life and Reign* (Pittsburgh, 1979).

47 For descriptions: T. von Bernhardi, *Denkwürdigkeiten des kaiserlich-russischen Generals von der Infanterie Carl Friedrich Grafen von Toll* (Leipzig, 1856–8), i, 20–1; Masson, *Mémoires*, i, 197; "Rasskazy kniazia P. M. Volkonskogo, zapisannye s ego slov A. V. Vskovatym v ianvare 1845 g.," *RS*, 16 (1876), 180; Shil'der, *Pavel*, 287.

the obligatory attendance, as the spoiled dignitaries thought. In fact Paul had good reason for insisting that all serving officers should perform regular duty; and since the new tactical regulations were based on the Prussian model it was quite logical that all officers, beginning with the most senior, should familiarize themselves with it quickly.[48] But it was scarcely appropriate for him to supervise this instruction in person, or to upbraid and humiliate those who failed to learn the new evolutions with sufficient promptitude (as happened to the distinguished General Jacobi at Kovno).[49]

This is where the excesses began. Paul did not shrink from drilling men during Holy Week, which scandalized the pious, and once even appeared on parade wearing his Imperial crown, which made him look ridiculous.[50] The Prussian envoy, Count Brühl, commented: "in the main the emperor concerns himself solely with petty details, with ceremonies and parades, and so loses sight of his major ends."[51] Colonel L. N. Engel'gardt, required to hold a parade before the sovereign at Kazan', was more terror-stricken than he had been at the storming of Praga. Fortunately for him Paul was satisfied with the colonel's performance and rewarded him with a medal and a kiss on both cheeks. Engel'gardt expressed gratitude for the honor and characteristically concealed his disrespect for the monarch.[52] Officers learned to dissimulate, or took refuge in gossip and intrigue; a few reacted in more spirited fashion, so that one can see here the beginnings of a "military opposition" to the autocracy at a time when the rest of Russian society was politically quiescent.

Paul was the first ruler to stage great parades involving men from several arms of service. The fashion caught on and reached a climax in 1815, when Alexander is said to have reviewed no less than 150,000 Russian troops on the plain of Vertus, east of Paris.[53] The tsar was worried that his men might become infected with the liberal virus while in France, and saw the parade ground as a convenient means of distracting them. One of the few outspoken officers to have left their memoirs records that "in Paris the soldiers had more work to do than they had had on campaign, since so many parades were held while we were there." He also states that after the battle of Töplitz (Teplice) in 1813 no less than three parades were staged even before the fallen had been buried, so that the ceremonial atmosphere was somewhat spoiled by the stench of rotting corpses.[54] Back in St. Petersburg Alexander maintained his

---

48 For the text, see *PSZ*, xxiv. 17588–90 (November 29, 1796): three regulations for different arms of service.

49 Shil'der, *Pavel*, 356; for an act of mercy, 367.

50 Ibid., 343, 349.

51 Shil'der, *Aleksandr*, i, 365; Golovkine's work (see note 15) is by Paul's master of court ceremonies.

52 L. N. Engel'gardt, *Zapiski. . . , 1766–1836* (Moscow, 1868), 207, 210, 212.

53 M. I. Bogdanovich, *Istoriia tsarstvovaniia imperatora Aleksandra I . . .* (St. Petersburg, 1871 reprinted Ann Arbor and London, 1980), v. 88–92, appx., 5–9; an officer notes that the men had to stand for ten hours in the frost: E. F. fon-Bradke, "Avtobiograficheskie zapiski," *RA* (1875), 1, 28.

54 N. N. Murav'iev-Karskii, "Zapiski," *RA* (1886), 1, 34; 2, 106.

father's daily *Wachtparade*, which even his zealous brother Nicholas found a tiresome and time-wasting formality.[55]

Intelligent senior commanders recognized that this military style made for inefficiency.

> Every day a child [Alexander] dresses and undresses, arms and disarms 300,000 men whom he calls soldiers, makes them dance minuets and *contredanses*. Women and children are exhilarated at the sight, yet for the past three years we haven't been able to make the Turks sue for peace.

This was said in 1810 by a conservative "Baltic baron," Osten-Sacken—which shows that the military opposition was not confined to adherents of the "national school" like Kutuzov, as patriotic mythology would have it.[56] Nationality was less important than professionalism or sheer common sense, a quality which the tsar and his (indubitably Russian) favorite Arakcheev signally lacked. It was they who were responsible for introducing the unpopular and fatiguing "Prussian" slow step of 60 to 70 paces a minute; Constantine, by contrast, was a fan of marching in quick time at 120 to 160 paces a minute.[57] When on parade Alexander used to check whether the men's socks were at regulation height and in 1816 he had three colonels of the Semenovskii guards regiment put under arrest because their men were out of step.[58] In another incident (1815) the tsar had two cavalry officers arrested for losing their footing on parade; ignoring a protest by Ermolov, he declared: "severity is the reason why our army is the bravest and the finest."[59]

"Thank God," wrote the chief of staff, P. M. Volkonskii, to a subordinate from Odessa in 1818, "the inspections and maneuvers went off all right, apart from a few [critical] remarks, which were quite justified."[60] (He was probably referring to discovery of illicit stratagems to maintain equipment up to the required standard, in which all commanders were obliged to engage owing to the inefficiency of the supply system.) Another leading general wrote to the same correspondent in 1821:

> The Russian troops are worn out by the endless drill, equipment changes, inspections etc.,

---

55 Schiemann, *Geschichte*, i, 226.

56 [P. Bartenev], "Fel'd-marshal kniaz' Saken," *RA*, 37 (1900), 1, 179. When Kutuzov took over command of the army in August, 1812 he dispensed with the customary ceremonial parade, saying "on campaign a soldier should not have to think about smartness, but needs to relax after his labors and to prepare for victory." F. N. Glinka, *Pis'ma russkogo ofitsera* . . . (Moscow, 1815–16), iv, 52.

57 J. Tański, *Tableau statistique, politique et moral du système militaire de la Russie* (Paris, 1833), 232; cf. M. D. (contrib.), "Velikii kniaz' Konstantin Pavlovich v somneniiakh i otritsaniiakh sovremennykh emu poriadkov," *RS*, 101 (1900), 123.

58 M. D., "Velikii kniaz'," 95; cf. V. A. Fedorov, *Soldatskoe dvizhenie v gody dekabristov, 1816–1825 gg.* (Moscow, 1963), 18–20.

59 Murav'ev-Karskii, "Zapiski," *RA* (1886), 11, 249. I am grateful to Professor Allen McConnell for this reference.

60 N. Dubrovin, ed., "Pis'ma kniazia P. M. Volkonskogo k A. A. . . . Zakrevskomu, 1815–1825 gg.," *SIRIO*, 1xxiii (1890), 3.

which I can no longer contemplate with equanimity. Everyone is obsessed with these matters and forgets their sacred duty. They prepare for parades in such a way that the Sovereign will take notice of them. Drill goes on day and night, even by candlelight. The soldiers don't have a minute's rest. Hence the desertions [and high] mortality, which explains why no one serves out his full term.[61]

The *mushtrovka*, as it was contemptuously called, was a powerful factor in stimulating disaffection among the more intelligent officers. The senior men protected those who joined clandestine societies and eventually rose in revolt in 1825, during the interregnum that followed Alexander's death. The Decembrists are usually (and correctly) seen as advocates of constitutional reform and serf emancipation, but they also stood for far-reaching changes in the military, notably a shorter service term and humane disciplinary methods. Beyond that, influenced by events in revolutionary Europe, they looked forward to a "citizen army" in which soldiers would obey orders from conviction, not just from fear. This implied spreading literacy among the troops and changing the recruitment system—indeed, a thorough transformation of the society whence army manpower was drawn.[62]

IV

Nothing came of these ideas until after Nicholas I's death. Each of our three tsars by and large adhered to tradition in regard to military law. This was of course the formal basis on which discipline rested, and "paradomania" cannot be understood without some attention to this neglected subject. Peter I's statute of 1716 remained in effect until 1839, and even then many of its provisions were carried over into the new code which replaced it. In 1812 Alexander I introduced regulations for the armies in the field, but this led to an ambiguous juridical situation, since the two statutes coexisted.[63] In practice commanders enjoyed great latitude throughout the period in determining their own procedures, fixing sentences and applying penalties. No records of Russian courts martial have yet been published, so that one can gain only a rough impression of what went on. It appears that although outward forms were scrupulously followed there was ample scope for arbitrariness—even more so than in the civil judiciary at this time. It should be noted that some civil offences were tried by military courts.[64]

In favor of Paul it must be said that he tried to introduce a clearer distinction between military and civilian functionaries, an essential step towards legality. For

---

61 Idem, "Pis'ma . . . I. V. Sabaneeva k A. A. Zakrevskomu," ibid., 577–8.

62 For a thorough discussion see E. A. Prokof'ev, *Bor'ba dekabristov za peredovoe russkoe voennoe iskusstvo* (Moscow, 1953).

63 L. Klugen, "Neskol'ko slov o telesnom v russkikh voiskakh nakazanii po pravilam voennoi distsipliny," *VS*, 9 (1859), 9–10, 193.

64 J. P. LeDonne, "The Administration of Military Justice under Nicholas I," *CMRS*, 13 (1972), 180–91; *idem*, "Civilians under Military Justice during the Reign of Nicholas I," *CASS*, 7 (1973), 171–87; see now Bibliography, items nos. 53, 56, 59.

instance, army officers who held civilian jobs were given civil rank and had to wear civilian uniforms.[65] To some extent such measures offset the steps which the tsar took towards militarization of the bureaucracy, such as appointment in certain cities of military governors with broad police powers.[66] Within the army Paul strengthened the judicial machinery by establishing the office of Auditor-General, who had some civilian officials on his staff. Their job was to put down corruption among the military, supervise courts martial, and investigate complaints by civilians against the troops— which were frequent.[67] One is left wondering how effective these functionaries could be, but the government did at least try to make them do their job properly. For instance, when a private in the Prince Dolgorukii regiment was discovered stealing from the Mint, Paul turned the case over to the Auditor-General and thanked those who had brought it to his notice.[68] On another occasion the emperor declared himself powerless to restore lieutenant-general's rank to an officer named Brazhnikov who had been deprived of it by a military court.[69]

On the other hand Paul subverted these regular procedures by abusing his Imperial prerogative. Not only did he order the demotion or discharge of officers who incurred his personal displeasure; they were frequently subjected to administrative penalties without any proper legal investigation. He even commanded a retired colonel named Alenin (or Olenin?) to be sent to an asylum "for his impertinence and madness,"[70] so anticipating the celebrated measure which Nicholas I took against the philosopher Chaadaev. A Captain Borozdin is said to have been sent to a fortress for six weeks, on a diet of bread and water, for boasting that he was to be appointed one of the emperor's adjutants.[71] Far more serious was the infliction of corporal punishment (which in the Russian army was administered in the most fearsome manner and often resulted in death) on officers, although they had been exempted from it in 1785; Paul got round the ban by simply depriving offenders of their noble status first.[72] In 1800

65 PSZ, xxiv. 17723, 17777, 17817 (January 11, February 1 and 19, 1797).

66 Ibid., xxiv. 17805 (February 1797); xxv. 18296, 18663 (December 28, 1797, September 12, 1798); cf. E. Amburger, Geschichte der Behördenorganisation Russlands von Peter dem Grossen bis 1917 (Leyden, 1966), 375.

67 PSZ, xxiv. 17757, 17719 (January 9 and 24, 1797); xxvi. 18853 (February 11, 1799); Russia. Army. Voenno-iuridicheskaia akademiia, Piatdesiat' let spetsial'noi shkoly dlia obrazovaniia voennykh zakonovedov v Rossii, 1832–1882 (St. Petersburg, [1882]), 7.

68 Shil'der, Aleksandr, 294; cf. also 317, 321, 324 and "Pis'ma imperatora Pavla Petrovicha k moskovskomu glavnokomanduiushchemu," RA (1876), 1, 22.

69 Shil'der, Aleksandr, 304.

70 Ibid., 298 (July 7, 1799).

71 Iskander [A. I. Herzen, pseud.], ed., Istoricheskii sbornik Volnoi Russkoi Tipografii v Londone (London, 1861 reprinted Moscow, 1971), ii. 16.

72 The first instance occurred early in 1797, when Sub-Lieutenant I. Fedoseev, charged with seditious propaganda, was ordered to be knouted in public in St. Petersburg and then sent into exile with forced labor at the Nerchinsk mines in eastern Siberia. PSZ, xxiv, 17776 (January 31, 1797); cf. N. Vish, "Telesnye nakazaniia v voiskakh i ikh otmena," VS (1904), 10, 140.

a Captain Kirpichnikov, serving in a garrison regiment, was demoted to the rank of private and sentenced to run the gauntlet (the normal penalty for common soldiers) once through 1,000 men; there was a certain rough justice here, since he was charged with having illegally beaten an NCO.[73] But there were no mitigating circumstances in the case of P. I. Miliukov, a lieutenant in the Horse Guards, who was to be given 100 (or 500, according to another account) blows with the cane (*palka*) for mishearing a command on the parade ground; he was saved by Constantine, who fell to his knees dramatically before the tsar and won him a pardon.[74] Even worse was the treatment meted out to two brothers in a cossack guards unit, evidently suspected of autonomist sentiment, who were literally beaten to death, although conceivably this action may have been taken by local authorities acting on their own.[75]

Men in the ranks suffered more than officers. Paul ordered an NCO at Khar'kov, who had allegedly displayed a scurrilous caricature of the ruler, to be knouted and sent into exile "without conducting any [judicial] investigation."[76] The regulations of 1796 made the gauntlet a *discretionary* penalty, which meant that a unit commander could legally order it to be inflicted on, say, soldiers charged with disorderly conduct on the march. Some writers state that this now became the principal penalty meted out to privates. The change did not attract public attention at the time.[77]

Paul would on occasion revise upwards courts martial sentences submitted to him for confirmation, although hitherto it had been the convention for all reviewing instances to mitigate them. An NCO found guilty of forgery was sentenced to discharge from his unit; Paul had him flogged with the knout.[78] He would reprimand tribunal members for what he considered excessive leniency.[79] Some soldiers complained through the "proper channels" about a miscarriage of justice but were themselves whipped and sent into Siberian exile, evidently because their action was deemed *ipso facto* subversive.[80] All this made nonsense of the system, which for all its faults was based on the assumption that military judicial institutions reached their decisions after careful examination of the evidence; under Paul "all written documents served simply as material on which the Sovereign based his own personal opinions."[81]

The conventional view is that Paul's "tyranny" stands in total contrast to the

---

73 Shil'der, *Pavel*, 432; M. Sokolovskii, "Iz russkoi voenno-ugolovnoi stariny: vysochaishie konfirmatsii imp. Pavla I po voenno-sudnym delam," *RS*, 123 (1904), 360.

74 Shil'der, *Pavel*, 436, citing a later memoir by A. P. Evreinov, who may have embroidered the story; it is, however, repeated by Vish, "Telesnye nakazaniia," 140, and Lincoln, "Konstantin," 173.

75 This is not the interpretation given by a recent Soviet student of this melancholy affair: O. [S.] Gvinchidze, *Brat'ia Gruzinovy* (Tbilisi, 1965).

76 F. N. Kishenskii, "Odin iz ukazov imp. Pavla 1801 g.," *RS*, 16 (1876), 193–4.

77 Vish, "Telesnye nakazaniia," 139.

78 Sokolovskii, "Vysochaishie konfirmatsii," 361.

79 Ibid., 366.

80 Ibid., 361.

81 Ibid., 366.

"enlightened" rule of his successor, at least until 1815. Alas, so far as the armed forces were concerned, the watchword was continuity. The few changes made were of style rather than substance. Alexander I avoided his father's provocative excesses, and there was a new mood of confidence among his officers (who got a pay raise and other material concessions), but the record of legislative reform is thin. The military continued to play a major role in local government. The balance may even have shifted in favor of them as against civilian officials (at least at senior level), in part due to wartime pressures. On his accession the tsar decreed a general amnesty; in one list of 115 people who were quietly freed, 58 were former or serving officers.[82] He seldom issued personal orders for punishment, although in addition to those noted above he placed under arrest for some trivial fault a guards lieutenant-colonel, A. N. Muravev, an action which pushed him into political radicalism.[83] Deprivation of rank was no longer, as under Paul, a prelude to Siberian exile for officers; instead they might find themselves posted to the Caucasus, where an anti-guerilla war was in progress, and if they survived and performed well could earn a return to favor.[84] Others were sent to the far south of European Russia. Among these were many officers of the Semenovskii guards regiment, who were collectively penalized for a legitimate protest by their men against grave abuses (October, 1820). This act of obvious injustice caused resentment throughout the officer corps, which had now become more conscious of its honor than before.[85]

Alexander's practise in regard to court martial reviews was probably more benevolent than that of Paul, although the sole study of this, published in a rare provincial journal, has not been available. Some attention was given to the quality of auditors, who (as in Prussia) were usually NCOs; their low rank deterred them from standing up to the terrifying court martial presidents. In 1804 Lieutenant-General S. I. Salagov suggested: "we need people with feeling, a sense of honor and knowledge of the law."[86] Measures were taken to upgrade their status[87] and to train them, but it was not until 1832 that an educational qualification was required of holders of this office.[88] Thus the reform produced men who could locate the text of a law but not interpret it. In 1805–6 the Auditor-General's office was reformed, but the change was primarily one of procedure. Cases involving underprivileged soldiers were no longer referred

---

82 *PSZ*, xxvi. 19784, 19814 (March 15, April 2, 1801).

83 N. M. Druzhinin, *Dekabrist Nikita Murav'ev* (Moscow, 1933), 95.

84 As was the Decembrist Peter Kakhovskii, "the Russian Carl Sand": N. M. Novitskii (contrib.), "Iz zapisok veterana," *RS*, 11 (1874), 180. For the appellation see A. G. Mazour, *The First Russian Revolution, 1825: the Decembrist Movement* . . . (Stanford, 1937, reprinted 1965), 129.

85 For a sketch of the "Semenovskii affair" (it was not really a mutiny) in English see J. L. Wieczynski, "The Mutiny of the Semenovskii Regiment in 1820," *RR*, 29 (1970), 167–80.

86 *PSZ*, xxviii. 21134 (January 22, 1804).

87 Ibid., 21904 (September 8, 1805).

88 *Piatdesiat' let* (see note 67), 7–9.

to this functionary or to the tsar, even if the man were sentenced to death; divisional commanders, when prescribing the number of blows to be dealt to men running the gauntlet, could fix it as high as 3,000 and the commander-in-chief at 5,000: a classic case of "overkill," since 500 blows might well finish a man off for good.[89] "Cruel" and "merciless" penalties were prohibited,[90] but the gauntlet evidently did not count as cruel! Imperial ambivalence about reform in this sphere is best demonstrated by a ruling that a doctor had to be present, who could order the punishment to cease if he thought the victim was likely to expire.[91] But as soon as the man recovered the beating recommenced. This was a doubtful relief for the victim—and compromised the doctor, whose official function was scarcely compatible with his Hippocratic oath. Figures from 1819 show that of 52 "rebellious" military colonists at Chuguev in the Ukraine who were compelled to run the gauntlet (up to 12,000 blows), 25 died within ten days.[92] Arakcheev took charge of this judicial massacre; the tsar expressed "warm approval" of his action and concern lest his favorite's delicate health might have been harmed by the experience.

On the other hand some groups of alleged mutineers were granted a full pardon.[93] The tsar accorded wide latitude to individual commanders: Field-Marshal M. F. Kamenskii and his son, a general, both had a reputation for severity, whereas M. S. Vorontsov, who was in charge of the Russian occupation force in France after 1815, was allowed to minimize the imposition of corporal punishment—partly, it seems, out of concern for Russia's international image.[94] The example of the more enlightened chiefs might then be emulated by their juniors. One colonel who announced such a policy was greeted with "roars of satisfaction" by his men.[95] The trouble with this latitudinarianism, from the regime's point of view, was that the beneficiaries naturally expected *all* their superiors to adopt similarly "advanced" practises, and those who held to the old ways found their authority undermined. This division in the upper echelons helps to explain the rapid spread of opposition in the army between 1815

---

89 *PSZ*, xxix, 22322 (October 18, 1806): i.e. six or ten times through a battalion, which normally consisted of 500 men.

90 *PSZ*, xxvii. 20115 (January 18, 1802).

91 *PSZ*, xxvi. 20070 (December 8, 1801).

92 G. A. Vereshchagin, "Materialy po istorii buntov v voennykh poseleniiakh pri Alekšandre I," *Dela i dni*, 3 (Petrograd, 1922), 158–60. On the revolt see the full study by Fedorov (note 58), 43–71.

93 For documents on the protest by militiamen at Insar and Penza in 1812, see P. I. Shchukin (comp. and ed.), *Bumagi otnosiashchikh do Otechestvennoi voiny 1812 g.* (Moscow, 1897–1905), i, 156–76. All but two men convicted of mutiny in the settlements on the river Bug in 1817 were freed with a warning: Bogdanovich, *Istoriia*, v. 358–64; but cf. Fedorov, *Soldatskoe dvizhenie*, 29 for a different version.

94 A. N. Petrov, ed., *Russkaia voennaia sila. Istoriia razvitiia voennogo dela ot nachala Rusi do nashego vremeni. . .* , 2nd ed. (Moscow, 1892), ii, 272; *RBS*, viii, 422, 442. On Voronstov: D. I. Zavalishin, *Zapiski dekabrista*, 2nd ed. (St. Petersburg, [1906]), 109; for the text of his regulations: *VS*, 5 (1859), 2, 495–502; 5, 75–8.

95 S. I. Maevskii, "Moi vek ili istoriia generala Maevskogo, 1779–1848," *RS*, 8 (1873), 298.

and 1825.

Alarmed at the threat, Nicholas I brought the forces under his close personal control, with his celebrated aides-de-camp as the principal executants of his monarchical will. Regulations requiring civilian officials to wear uniform were tightened, as if this external symbol of discipline would of itself instill in them the martial virtues.[96] Those who committed some offence might, if they were not handed over to a military tribunal, be sent to cool their heels in the nearest guardhouse—a fate that befell the diarist A. V. Nikitenko, who left a memorable account of his mishap.[97]

Officers were sometimes humiliated, as under Paul, by being reduced to the ranks or punished in the same way as soldiers. A contemporary French writer observed: "an officer, even if of senior rank, is often sent to prison for some minor fault or else made to march unarmed at the rear of his regiment."[98] Tański (who may be this author's source) states that "I saw with my own eyes a guards general who was six minutes late for a rendezvous between [two] units deprived of his sword and made to march on foot behind his brigade, flanked by two soldier medical orderlies."[99] Authoritarian regimes foster a kind of "disciplinary reflex" which makes those subjected to such treatment all the readier to act likewise against their own subordinates; and brutality became systematized under the rule of the "iron tsar."

> Corporal punishments were the order of the day [noted an officer of Baltic extraction who later rose to general's rank]. Since no limits were set to this rough handling, even educated and decent officers showed indifference and severity towards their men. A slight mistake at drill . . . or indeed any trivial fault in the service was often enough cause for a beating, which varied in severity according to the officer's temperament. The soldier had no protection against the arbitrariness of his superiors, from the most senior to the lowest section commander.[100]

They might receive 100 blows with a cane for an offense which in France would be punished by detention.[101] Senior NCOs seem to have been the most ruthless:

> One such fel'dvebel' moved along a company in formation, and halted before a young soldier. "What are you frowning for? How many times must I teach you that you must look your superiors in the eye cheerfully?" The fel'dvebel' accompanied this shout with a hard slap. The soldier somehow screwed up his eyes in an effort to look cheerful, but without satisfying his tormentor. "Look more cheerful! More cheerful, I tell you,

---

96 Schiemann, *Geschichte*, ii (1908), 107.

97 A. V. Nikitenko, *Diary of a Russian Censor*, abridged, ed. and tr. H. S. Jacobson (Amherst, Ma., 1975), 54–8.

98 C. A. Haillot, *Statistique militaire et recherches sur l'organisation et les institutions militaires des armées étrangères* (Paris, 1846), i, 319.

99 Tański, *Tableau*, 189.

100 H. von Hansen, *Zwei Kriegsjahre. Erinnerungen eines alten Soldaten an den Feldzug gegen die Türken 1828 und den polnischen Aufstand 1831* (Berlin, 1881), 21. (Hansen's work, published abroad, avoided the strict Russian censorship.)

101 Tański, *Tableau*, 189.

you blockhead!" continued the *fel'dvebel'*, raining blows on the man . . . An old veteran standing beside the young soldier tried to console him with words: "That's what real service means, brother: they beat you and won't let you cry."[102]

Commanders were notoriously arbitrary in determining the number of blows administered. One ordered 100 given to a drunken man but 500 to a drummer who missed his beat.[103] A Prussian officer who witnessed a curious "fraternization ceremony" with Russian troops at Kalisz in 1835 saw penalties of 500 blows administered to several men for quite trivial errors; ambulances were kept behind the lines.[104]

The important point here is that such punishment had been explicitly *forbidden* by the 1716 statute, but in practise had always been tolerated as lying within a commander's informal "disciplinary" power. In the last months of his reign Alexander decreed that when a sentence came up for review the whip should be replaced by the gauntlet "as it has a greater exemplary effect."[105] In 1834 Nicholas reduced the upper limit of blows from 6,000 to 3,000 by an instruction which was kept secret lest it weaken the law's "deterrent effect," but the earlier escape clause was retained. The statute which he issued five years later (in lieu of Peter's) brought back the whip as an alternative penalty and defined the number of strokes for the first time; but, as one authority stated later, "in practise, as is known, the number depended wholly on the commander's discretion."[106] In short, nothing had really changed. In 1843 a sensitive twenty-year-old ensign in the Moscow regiment, N. A. Mombelli, witnessed the "execution" of a sergeant-major in the guards, sentenced for striking an officer who had insulted him. In his diary he jotted down a vivid and horrifying description of the scene.[107] Not surprisingly, perhaps, Mombelli joined a circle of progressive minded individuals, known to history as the "Petrashevtsy"; even more significantly, however, he had his own batman given 50 strokes of the birch a few months afterwards![108] Only with great difficulty did more civilized standards become accepted, the landmark in this process being the judicial reform of 1864.

Nicholas I shrank from such fundamental measures. As the final arbiter of military justice in his empire he followed precedent by generally mitigating penalties. Thus some privates as Kishinev sentenced to be birched for drunkenness in 1833 were ordered to be caned instead, and a major in a St. Petersburg fortress, who negligently allowed prisoners confined there to communicate between their cells, was himself sent to a fortress in European Russia, instead of being despatched to forced

---

102 ["Neizvestnyi," pseud.], "Za mnogo let: vospominaniia neizvestnogo, 1844–1884," *RA*, 82 (1894), 111; cited by J. S. Curtiss, *The Russian Army under Nicholas I* (Durham, N. C., 1965), 243.

103 I. V. Sabaneev to M. L. Vorontsov (1826), cited by Vish, "Telesnye nakazaniia," 115.

104 Schiemann, *Geschichte*, iii (1913), 267 (his report is reproduced in ibid., 437–42).

105 *PSZ*, xl. 30324 (April 20, 1825).

106 A. Kudriavtsev, "O distsiplinarnom ustave 1875 g.," *VS*, 167 (1886), 91.

107 "Dokumenty sledstviia po delu N. A. Mombelli," V. Desnitskii, ed., *Delo Petrashevtsev*, i (Moscow and Leningrad, 1937), 251–2.

108 Ibid., 258.

labor in Siberia, as the Auditor-General had recommended.[109] On other occasions
he would simply confirm this official's verdict.[110] Sometimes the tsar would order
a case to be tried summarily within 24 hours and fix the penalty in advance, which
of course made the court martial proceedings a mere formality; and in one case he had
a private guilty of loose talk about dynastic matters sent to a detention company without trial.[111]

The penalties which Nicholas authorized were disproportionately severe. Complaints at cruel or irregular treatment, even if made through proper channels, were
usually treated as instances of insubordination, and the alleged "ringleaders" would
face the gauntlet.[112] Out of a party of 40 recaptured deserters so punished in 1832
on the orders of their corps commander eight men died; Nicholas commented that
this had been a "necessary measure" that had achieved its object.[113] Sometimes he
followed his father's practise of increasing penalties on review. This may seem de-
fensible where the case involved cruelty by an officer toward his men; but on another
occasion he ordered imprisonment of an officer who had deserted, overruling three
subordinates who favored a simple transfer.[114] By reprimanding those who advocated
leniency, Nicholas encouraged military judges to match their decisions to what they
took to be the will of the All-Highest. In making such rulings the monarch acted as
a complete autocrat, without reference either to precedents or to current legislation.
In such matters Nicholas was more consistent than Paul had been; and he was also
anxious to promote a sense of legality among his officials.[115] But in the last resort the
brutal militarism which his reign epitomized severely limited such progress as Russia
made towards developing the modern judicial order which it so desperately needed.

By pretending that all was well in his empire and suppressing every expression
of critical thought, the tsar made the task of eventual reformers more difficult than
it was bound to be. The "Romanov military style" was not a casual foreign import.
It was an authentic native product which corresponded to these rulers' perceptions of
their task. This view coincided with that of the more conservative elements in élite
opinion, not least among the military. It pervaded contemporary Russian society, and
it cast its shadow forward into the later nineteenth and early twentieth centuries. It
helps to explain, for instance, why in 1915 Nicholas II felt it to be his duty to assume

---

109 M. Sokolovskii, "Imperator Nikolai I v voenno-sudnykh konfirmatsiiakh," *RS*, 124 (1905),
    404, 413; cf. V. G. Verzhbitskii, *Revoliutsionnoe dvizhenie v russkoi armii s 1826 po 1859
    gg.* (Moscow, 1964), 94.
110 Verzhbitskii, *Revoliutsionnoe dvizhenie*, 127, 171, 248.
111 Ibid., 31, 102, 268.
112 Ibid., 183.
113 Ibid., 143.
114 Sokolovskii, "Imperator Nikolai," 405, 412, 415.
115 R. S. Wortman, *The Development of a Russian Legal Consciousness* (Chicago and London,
    Univ. of Chicago Press, 1976), develops this argument eloquently; cf. now also W. B. Lin-
    coln, *In the Vanguard of Reform*. The adherents of the revisionist school sometimes press
    their case too far.

the office of Supreme Commander-in-Chief, an act which spelled the doom of the monarchy and empire. In the postrevolutionary society militarism has become a much more pervasive and complex phenomenon, but that is another story.

CHAPTER 9

The Russian Army's Response
to the French Revolution

I

We shall be concerned here with the Russian army as a sociopolitical (and to a lesser extent economic) organization rather than as a fighting force. It is for the specialist in military history to assess the changes in tactics, armament and administration which *ancien régime* armies had to adopt in order to meet the challenge of revolutionary and Napoleonic France. So far as Russia is concerned, the Soviet historian L. G. Beskrovnyi has shown that her army moved from line to column and extended order formation, developed infantry weapons of standardized caliber and artillery comparable to that of its opponents, improved arrangements for supplying troops in the field, and streamlined the central apparatus while conferring more power on divisional chiefs.[1] This is not the place to examine the significance of these changes (or the degree to which they reflected contemporary practise abroad: Soviet historians insist that the new tactics were evolved contemporaneously with or prior to those in the West, not as a reaction to them); instead we may offer some remarks on the nontechnical aspects of the problem.

That the problem exists need no longer be doubted. The army was tsarist Russia's most important institution after the autocracy itself, the principal material embodiment of state power. It could not be insulated from the shocks administered to the old order throughout Europe by events in France after 1789. Yet its response to this challenge has been strangely neglected by historians, although they have written at length about the diplomatic and intellectual aspects of the Russo-French encounter.[2] In recent years Paul Dukes has put forward the hypothesis that Russia should be seen as an integral part of the zone affected by the "Atlantic revolution."[3] His views have not, however,

---

1 L. G. Beskrovnyi, *Russkaia armiia i flot v XVIII v.: ocherki* (Moscow, 1958), 102, 196–97, 277, 330, 456.

2 See, for example, A. A. Lobanov-Rostovskii, *Russia and Europe, 1789–1825* (Durham, N. C., 1947); M. M. Shtrange, *Russkoe obshchestvo i frantsuzskaia revoliutsiia, 1789–1794 gg.* (Moscow, 1956).

3 P. Dukes, "Russia and the Eighteenth-Century Revolution," *History*, 56 (1971), 371–86;

found general acceptance. Dukes seems to exaggerate the direct connections and parallels between events in western Europe and Russia at this time, and overlooks the fundamental point that these influences occurred indirectly and with a considerable time-lag—as much as 35 years after the original stimulus. This long span, one must frankly acknowledge, makes it hard to determine which changes were linked to the French revolution by a meaningful causal relationship rather than one with so many intermediate links that the last seems to have little to do with the first. Yet the risk must be run if we are to close a major gap in our appreciation of the history of the period.

Let us take one example by way of illustration. Between 1797 and 1799 many Russian officers resigned voluntarily from the service. This was the first such act of collective protest in the army's history, and a landmark in its political development. The immediate reason for their step was the Prussian-style reorganization program launched by Paul I (1796–1801). This involved dismissal of a large number of officers whom the monarch deemed inefficient, wrong-headed or old-fashioned, and those who resigned wished to demonstrate their solidarity with these victims of imperial arbitrariness. Paul's purge was in part motivated by his strong personal prejudices, yet it also reflected his desire to forge an instrument totally loyal to himself as Sovereign Autocrat, and thus immune from the subversive pro-French influences which, he believed, had been allowed to permeate the armed forces during the era of Potemkin and Zubov. Granted, Paul exaggerated and misinterpreted the nature of the threat to his power; but he did not invent it. Russia's participation in the Second Coalition war, which took Suvorov across the Alps, had an ideological as well as a strategic purpose.

Before considering the political connections further, let us examine the economic dimension of the problem. French revolutionary expansion led Russia to augment greatly the size of her armed forces, which in the last year of Catherine II's reign (according to official establishment figures) totaled over half a million, excluding 100,000 irregulars.[4] This number has to be deflated to bring it closer to reality—but by how much? A near-contemporary French writer, Damaze de Raymond, offers a guess of 447,000, i.e. 10 percent less than the official figure for regulars,[5] and a modern Soviet demographer, who has studied the data for the 1795 census (*reviziia*), comes up with a figure very close to that: 449,076.[6] However, the well-known

idem. *October and the World: Perspectives on the Russian Revolution* (London, 1979), 42–49.

4 D. P. Zhuravskii, "Statisticheskoe obozrenie raskhodov na voennye potrebnosti," *VS*, 10 (1859), 11, 309; 12, 4; A. N. Petrov, ed., *Russkaia voennaia sila: istoriia razvitiia voennogo dela ot nachala Rusi do nashego vremeni*[2] (Moscow, 1892), vol. 2, 163; F. von Stein, *Geschichte des russischen Heeres vom Ursprunge desselben bis zur Thronbesteigung des Kaisers Nikolai I. Pawlowitsch* (Hanover, 1885; rpt. Krefeld, 1975), 204.

5 Damaze de Raymond, *Tableau historique, géographique, militaire et moral de l'empire de Russie* (Paris, 1812), vol. 1, 516.

6 V. M. Kabuzan, *Izmeneniia v razmeshchenii naseleniia Rossii x XVIII—I-oi polovine XIX v.: po materialam revizii* (Moscow, 1971), 107–18.

prerevolutionary Russian military historian D. F. Maslovskii states that in 1795 there was a deficiency of 93,000 men, so that we should deduct at least 20 percent to arrive at a realistic estimate.[7] Whatever the true figure may be, Paul I, after first reducing troop strengths, later increased them by a fifth. His successor Alexander I went on to launch a major military buildup. No less than 28 recruit levies were raised during his reign. Those effected between 1802 and 1812 would have brought in a theoretical maximum (calculated from the number of "revision souls" in 1806) of 2,158,591 men or 41 percent of men aged between 15 and 35 who were liable to such service.[8] Enrollment reached its peak in 1812, when no less than 21 men were taken from each 500-soul conscription unit, yielding a theoretical maximum of about 600,000 men—roughly equivalent to the *Grande Armée*. It has been said that all in all as many as 1.3 million of the tsar's subjects were in military uniform at this time, including 300,000 in the militia (*opolchenie*)—"a mass of troops such as the world had not yet seen," as one awestruck early historian puts it.[9] These figures may, however, be inflated. A contemporary, C. F. von Toll, claims that this is so and puts the forces' strength at no more than 600,000.[10] Another nineteenth-century authority, General Heinrich Leer, perhaps anxious to minimize Russian strength to make the victory over Napoleon seem more glorious, states that the active army was less than half a million strong.[11] V. I. Babkin, a Soviet student of the militia, on the other hand, comes to a higher figure for this force of 420,000.[12]

One can appreciate the reasons for this enormous effort; it is harder to see why so many men were kept on in service once the war had been brought to a victori-

---

7 D. F. Maslovskii, *Zapiski po istorii voennogo iskusstva v Rossii*, fasc. 2: *Tsarstvovanie Ekateriny II* (St. Petersburg, 1894), pt. 3, 19. Another document from 101–3 of this work, reproduced in L. G. Beskrovnyi, *Khrestomatiia po russkoi voennoi istorii* (Moscow, 1947), 202–3, gives a figure of approximately 267,000 excluding special troops and cossacks, or 53 percent of the establishment total. The disparity awaits satisfactory explanation.

8 Zhuravskii, "Stat. obozrenie," 12, 308–9. He includes those who joined the 1806–7 militia, since many of these men, contrary to the government's original promise, were not returned to civilian life after the Tilsit peace.

9 Stein, *Geschichte*, 271.

10 *Denkwürdigkeiten aus dem Leben des kaiserlichen russischen Generals von der Infanterie Carl Friedrich Grafen von Toll*, ed. T. von Bernhardi, 4 vols. (Leipzig, 1856–8) [hereafter von Toll, *Denkwürdigkeiten*], vol. 1, 231.

11 480,000 men. He excludes 12 newly formed regiments (say 24,000 men) as well as training units and garrison troops, which would have added some 50,000 men. G. A. Leer, ed., *Obzor voin Rossii ot Petra Velikogo do nashikh dnei, sostavlennyi Dubrovinym: posobie dlia izucheniia voennoi istorii v voennykh uchilishchakh*, 4 vols. (St. Petersburg, 1885–96), vol. 1, 345–51.

12 V. I. Babkin, "Organizatsiia i voennye deistviia narodnogo opolcheniia v Otechestvennoi voine 1812 g.," in L. G. Beskrovnyi et al., eds., *1812 god: k 150-letiiu Otechestvennoi voiny: sbornik statei* (Moscow, 1962), 134–63, here 145. He includes some 89,000 men from cossack areas and 97,000 others from territories where the levy was not imposed. Cf. also L. G. Beskrovnyi, ed., *Narodnoe opolchenie v Otechestvennoi voine 1812 g.: sbornik dokumentov* (Moscow, 1962).

ous conclusion—unless one assumes that Alexander was carried away by dreams of military grandeur and now looked upon his army not just as a fighting force but as an instrument for policing his domains and even (through the military colonies) for facilitating its economic development, so containing potential revolutionary subversion. In any case in 1824 his troops numbered well over 800,000 and perhaps more than 900,000[13]—more than could be justified by foreign policy considerations. "As there was one soldier to every 25 inhabitants, one can see what a heavy burden this enormous army imposed on the population," wrote one critic in the 1890s when, he assured his readers, it was only one-fifth as great.[14]

This burden was felt in two ways during Alexander I's reign: in the cost to life and limb, and in the cost to the nation's backward economy. At Austerlitz 21,000 Russians were killed, wounded or taken prisoner out of 75,000 committed; at Preussisch-Eylau the figures were 26,000 killed and wounded out of 65,000.[15] The slaughter at Borodino was long thought to have cost the Russians 57,000–58,000 men, but a recent Soviet researcher has amended this to 42,438, of whom about one-third were killed.[16] A British historian notes that "the Russians probably lost more men in a single span of eleven hours than any modern army before . . . the first day of the battle of the Somme."[17] M. S. Vorontsov's composite grenadier division was reduced from 4,000 men to 300; the Siberian dragoons were left with only 125 men and 3 officers out of a complement of 1,062; on the retreat to Moscow colonels found themselves commanding divisions and lieutenants regiments.[18]

To the victims of enemy action must be added those who died of sickness or starvation. According to A. B. Chicherin, a lieutenant whose invaluable memoirs have only

---

13 Leer, ed., *Obzor*, vol. 2, 408; Zhuravskii, "Stat. obozrenie," 12, 354; V. M–v, "Sostoianie vooruzhennykh sil Rossii v tsarstvovanie Aleksandra I," in Petrov, ed., *Russkaia voennaia sila*, vol. 2, 317.

14 M–v, "Sostoianie."

15 A. A. Kersnovskii, *Istoriia russkoi armii*, pt. 1: *Ot Narvy do Parizha, 1700–1814* (Belgrade, 1933), 189, 193. Casualty statistics in this period are notoriously unreliable, since they do not distinguish clearly between fatalities, injuries, desertions etc. Kersnovskii does not give his sources, but the former figure is confirmed by B. Ts. Urlanis, "Liudskie poteri vooruzhennykh sil v evropeiskikh voinakh," in idem, *Narodonaselenie: issledovaniia, publitsistika: sbornik statei* (Moscow, 1976), 150–216, here 160, and the latter one by B. L. Modzalevskii, ed., *Arkhiv Raevskikh*, vol. 1 (St. Petersburg, 1908), 59.

16 B. Ts. Urlanis, *Voiny i narodonaselenie Evropy: liudskie poteri vooruzhennykh sil evropeiskikh stran v voinakh XVII–XX vv.: istoriko-statisticheskoe issledovanie* (Moscow, 1960), 84. The figure is accepted by C. Duffy, *Borodino: Napoleon Against Russia, 1812* (London, 1972), 138. Cf. Kersnovskii, *Istoriia*, pt. 1, 224.

17 Duffy, *Borodino*, 142.

18 "Zapiska neizvestnogo o sdache Moskvy," in K. Voenskii, ed., "Otechestvennaia voina v vospominaniiakh sovremennikov," *VS*, 316 (1910), 12, 21–42, here 36; M. P. Shcherbinin, comp., *Biografiia generala-fel'dmarshala kniazia M. S. Vorontsova* (St. Petersburg, 1858), 64; cf. his memoirs in V. I. Kharkevich, ed., *1812 god v dnevnikakh, zapiskakh i vospominaniiakh sovremennikov: materialy Voenno-uchenogo arkhiva Glavnogo shtaba*, fasc. 1, Vil'no [Vil'nius] (1900), 204, and the memoirs of K. A. Kreits in ibid., 74.

recently been published, the ratio of the latter to the former was roughly ten to one.[19] The Soviet demographer B. Ts. Urlanis, who deserves credit for a courageous attempt to tackle this tricky subject even if his statistical methods are not beyond reproach, reckons total battle casualties (killed and died of wounds) during the 1812 campaign at 110,000 and "sanitary losses" (wounded and deaths from sickness) at 140,000, making $1/4$ million altogether.[20] Elsewhere he estimates total Russian military casualties between 1805 and 1814 at 420,000, of whom 90,000 were either killed or died of wounds.[21] The two figures are difficult to reconcile; but they are in a range that probably comes nearer the truth than the wild guesses of some earlier writers: F. von Stein, for example, states that "during these terrible years (1802–1815) nearly two million men bled for the Fatherland."[22] The actual figure may have been only one-quarter as great. Beskrovnyi has estimated total military fatalities from battle and disease between 1789 and 1814 at approximately 660,000.[23] Even so, this was roughly one-quarter of all those inducted during this period. Soldiers fell fighting Asians (Turks, Persians and Caucasian tribesmen) as well as Europeans; others perished from disease and exhaustion in camp or barracks, while others again succumbed *en route* to the recruiting depot. The establishment of these latter installations in 1808[24] was designed to cut down on the appalling mortality rate—up to one-third according to some accounts—incurred by the traditional method of despatching untrained recruits on foot directly from the point of enlistment to divisional headquarters, which might be hundreds of miles away.

Turning to military expenditure during this period, we face a dearth of scholarly investigation into this matter. Most early writers were content to reproduce budgetary estimates, which were not always kept to. Fortunately, from 1802 or 1803 onward we have tables giving both estimated and actual expenditure.[25] For some years these are broken down in detail, from which it would appear that they cover not only "ordinary" expenditure on pay and allowances, arms and equipment (as laid down in the *shtaty*, or establishment), but also extraordinary items. No doubt a proportion of military-related expenditure is concealed under other heads, and the determined reader's attention is directed to note 2 in the accompanying Table, which gives our estimates based on A. N. Kulomzin's data (see 236–8).

---

19 *Dnevnik Aleksandra Chicherina, 1812–1813* (Moscow, 1966), 63. This approximates the ratio in the French army of twelve to one: B. Abrahamsson, *Military Professionalization and Political Power* (Göteborg, 1971), 25.

20 Urlanis, "Liudskie poteri," 161–2; cf. E. A. Prokof'ev, *Bor'ba dekabristov za peredovoe russkoe voennoe iskusstvo* (Moscow, 1953), 62: "not less than 200,000"; G. H. N. Seton-Watson, *The Russian Empire, 1801–1917* (Oxford, 1967), 142: "hardly less than $1/4$ million."

21 Urlanis, *Voiny*, 86–7; idem, "Liudskie poteri," 161–3.

22 Stein, *Geschichte*, 327.

23 L. G. Beskrovnyi, V. M. Kabuzan, V. K. Iatsunskii, "Bilan démographique de la Russie en 1789–1815," *Annales de démographie historique*, 2 (1965), 134.

24 Stein, *Geschichte*, 272; M–v, "Sostoianie," 318; [*PSZ*, XXX, no. 23297 (Oct. 10, 1808).]

25 A. N. Kulomzin, ed., *Finansovye dokumenty tsarstvovaniia imperatora Aleksandra I, SIRIO*, vol. 45 (St. Petersburg, 1885).

One has to remember that many goods and services—food and fodder, transport and accommodation—were provided by the population either free of charge or at rates that did not always cover their cost. Damaze de Raymond observed that "le pays soit tenu de fournir aux magasins impériaux les objets de première nécessité à très bas prix," and that the irregular troops received no pay during peacetime but had to equip themselves at their own expense.[26] A. S. Pishchevich, in his useful memoirs, describes how, when serving with the Narva cuirassiers at Usman' in 1794, officers would obtain supplies without payment from the local peasants by first making their elders drunk and then pocketing the sums allocated for purchase of the produce.[27] During the 1812 campaign foodstuffs were paid for by IOUs (*kvitantsii*) which were later redeemed at rates that even some officials considered too low.[28] The hard-pressed Mogilev province alone furnished no less than 3 million kilograms of flour and 300,000 kg of meat in 1812.[29] The militia had to be equipped and supported from nongovernmental funds; the cost of the ¼ million men raised in 1806–7 has been put at 8,671,000 roubles (no estimate is available for its more substantial successor).[30]

In 1767 "ordinary" military and naval expenditure accounted for 47.6 percent of total central government outlays;[31] despite the subsequent expansion of the armed forces, the proportion fell to an estimated 34.3 percent in 1781, rising again to 38.7 percent in 1796.[32] Our data show that the government never succeeded in bringing the proportion back below 40 percent, although it came close to doing so in 1802 and in 1825. At its peak military and naval expenditure accounted for over two-thirds of total outlays. This was the main reason for the collapse of Russia's state finances during Alexander I's reign. The government was obliged to raise an internal loan of 100 million roubles, which it met by inflating the currency, and by 1825 faced a public debt of 1,345 million roubles.[33] This deficit gave the authorities a plausible excuse, in so far as they needed one, for not undertaking the costly reform measures which a large section of the educated public—and not least of the military—were now insistently demanding.

---

26 Damaze de Raymond, *Tableau*, 531.

27 *Zhizn' A. S. Pishchevicha, im samim opisannaia, 1764–1805* (Moscow, 1885), 193.

28 Zhuravskii, "Stat. obozrenie," 12, 313.

29 Prokof'ev, *Bor'ba*, 53, citing archival source.

30 Zhuravskii, "Stat. obozrenie," 12, 294; Stein, *Geschichte*, 266.

31 S. M. Troitskii, *Finansovaia politika russkogo absoliutizma v XVIII v.* (Moscow, 1966), 244.

32 N. D. Chechulin, *Ocherki po istorii russkikh finansov v tsarstvovanie Ekateriny II* (St. Petersburg, 1906), 307, 313: an error in the arithmetic of the latter table has been corrected. He estimates the overall proportion for 1781–96 at 40.7 percent, exclusive of extraordinary expenditure incurred during the second Russo-Turkish war, put at 68 million rubles. [Chechulin's [uncorrected] figures are reproduced by D. Beyrau, *Militär und Gesellschaft im vorrevolutionären Russland* [Cologne and Vienna, 1984], 59.]

33 Prokof'ev, *Bor'ba*, 62; cf. *Ministerstyo finansov, 1802–1902* (St. Petersburg, 1902), vol. 1, 60: 1,323 million rubles.

II

The growth of dissent during Alexander I's reign is usually seen outside the military context, despite the fact that a great many *dvoriane* continued to serve in the armed forces, at least for part of their careers, and even those who did not preserved a "service mentality." As one recent student of the Decembrist movement correctly emphasizes, "the Decembrists came from backgrounds where service to the state was an important tradition."[34] The origins of this dissent go back further than is generally supposed—to the 1790s, when some Russian army officers appear already to have been attracted to French revolutionary ideas. Foreign influences were of course not the prime cause of their disaffection, as some reactionaries held, but served as a means of rationalizing discontents that were rooted in their onerous service conditions. To understand how these sentiments came to be articulated, three points need to be borne in mind.

First, men in the army's upper echelons had long been used to the notion, however heretical it might be in principle, that the military had a part to play in the political process. In the first part of the eighteenth century the guards regiments had been instrumental on at least five occasions in changing the ruler by means of a *coup d'état*. They had acted at the behest of individuals or factions at court, not autonomously, but always with an eye to their own advantage; these actions were invariably presented by the protagonists as taken in the national interest, with which they thus came to identify themselves.

Second, the self-esteem of the military had been greatly fortified by the successful campaigns which they had fought in Catherine's reign, and also by the development in the élite military schools of a western-style educational fare which stressed ethical values and civilized "gentlemanly" pursuits. The generation of officers who came to maturity in the late 1780s and early 1790s not only had broader intellectual horizons than their predecessors but also shared something of the European nobleman's sense of honor—a development assisted by the charter of privileges granted to the *dvorianstvo* in 1785. S. N. Glinka, who studied at the First Cadet Corps under its liberal director von Anhalt (d. 1794), was taught French by a major of Greek descent who admired Jean-Jacques Rousseau and urged his charges to seek inner freedom by scorning material gain; in 1789 Glinka and his fellow-cadets were able to read about events in France from western periodicals, which were made freely available to them.[35] Around 1793 S. A. Tuchkov, then a junior officer in Moscow, joined a "Free Russian Society for Propagation of the Sciences," a literary and cultural association, and when posted to the capital was admitted to a similar group.[36]

Third, in the latter half of her reign Catherine had deliberately devolved decision-making power, in the military as well as in the civil administration. Individual

---

34 W. B. Lincoln, "A Re-examination of Some Historical Stereotypes: an Analysis of the Career Patterns and Backgrounds of the Decembrists," *JGOE*, 24 (1976), 357–68, here 359.

35 S. N. Glinka, *Zapiski* (St. Petersburg, 1895), 46, 67.

36 *Zapiski S. A. Tuchkova, 1766–1808*, ed. K. A. Voenskii (St. Petersburg, 1908), 19–20, 43.

commanders like Rumiantsev or Potemkin ("the northern Lucullus," as Tuchkov called him) enjoyed an authority comparable to that of an oriental satrap. The example of this laxity at the top proved infectious. In eighteenth-century Russia an all-important role was played by "clans" comprising kinsmen and clients of highly-placed patrons, and it was only natural that these dependents should have aped the *mores* of their betters. Middle-ranking officers (*shtab-ofitsery*) and subalterns (*ober-ofitsery*) readily identified with successful senior commanders, particularly if they affected a bluff openhearted manner—as did, for instance, A. V. Suvorov, who became the object of a veritable hero cult even in his own lifetime. In this sentiment there was a blend of nationalism (or at least national consciousness), militarism and male chauvinism— the latter trait stemming from the contempt felt by "men of action" for the effete atmosphere of Catherine's court.

The succession in 1796 of a male ruler with a keen interest in the military *métier*, who made no secret of his loathing for many of his mother's accomplishments, might have been expected to produce a favorable response among these tough-minded legionaries. However, Paul's limited intelligence, brusque manners and tyrannical disposition—to say nothing of his ostentatious predilection for Prussian ways—earned him the hatred of many officers, particularly at the upper level. There is ample contemporary testimony to the growth of disaffection within the military during his brief reign, which had the effect of catalyzing tendencies that up to this point had only been latent. Already in the early 1790s more military men were detained for political offenses than any other class of Russian subject.[37] Now jails and guardrooms across the country began to fill with men in uniform who for some reason earned the emperor's disfavor.

Paul's suspicions were from the start directed against the *protégés* of Potemkin, Rumiantsev, Suvorov and Zubov, whom he held responsible—not entirely without foundation—for the "slackness" he detected in the army, faults which his Prussian-model statute was designed to eradicate. There was, as we have argued elsewhere, an element of misguided rationality in his policies;[38] however, the means employed to attain these objectives nullified whatever good might otherwise have resulted from them. Particularly obnoxious were the summary administration of harsh penalties for trivial offenses and the encouragement of internal espionage.[39] The latter led officers,

37 K. E. Dzhedzhula, *Rossiia i Velikaia frantsuzskaia burzhuaznaia revoliutsiia kontsa XVIII v.* (Kiev, 1972), 171, citing archival source. About 200 people are said to have been involved. One cannot make a direct association between these men and French revolutionary influences, as do Dzhedzhula and, following him, Dukes. Many of these prisoners will have been cossacks protesting against the loss of their privileges, as will be shown below. In 1794 no less than 3,000 rebellious Don cossacks were sent to the Caucasus for holding "dubious gatherings and conclaves": TsGVIA, fond 801, opis' 62/3, ed. khr. 304 (petition by I. Korotkov et al., July 1798).

38 See above 178–9, 187.

39 Paul sanctioned the widespread use of flogging, even against noblemen, and systematically revised *upwards* court-martial sentences, which was a departure from previous policy. M. Sokolovskii, "Iz russkoi voenno-ugolovnoi stariny: vysochaishiia konfirmatsii imp. Pavla

who as a group were highly rank- and status-conscious, to try to settle personal scores with their rivals and to seek preferment by intrigue and delation. In at least one case that has been documented Paul took action on the denunciation of a captain by a private.[40] In less than four months during the summer of 1797 117 officers were discharged, while others were sent for trial.[41] In all 340 generals and 2,261 other officers are said to have been purged.[42] This was a sizeable proportion of an officer corps that numbered only 12,000 (in 1803),[43] and included a large number of men in leadership positions with sufficient wealth, experience and independence of mind to refuse to accept such treatment with the passive spirit characteristic of earlier times. By 1798–9 a French agent in St. Petersburg could report to his government that "on a de la peine à figurer le mécontentement qui règne dans les troupes depuis le feld-maréchal jusqu'au simple soldat" and to prophesy—correctly—that the detestation felt for the monarchy in the guards regiments would sooner or later burst forth in violence.[44]

The army's reaction to the emperor's neurotic security complex took several forms. Apart from the wave of resignations already alluded to, in which no fewer than 3,500 men are said to have been involved,[45] there was much sullen grumbling. Critics poked fun at the ruler's foibles[46] or, more seriously, invoked the law's protection against arbitrary infringement of their rights. This step was taken by a certain Captain Hoffmann (it is no doubt significant that he bore a German name), menaced with discharge because he had been kept in detention, which in his superiors' eyes "dishonored" him and rendered him unfit for further service. Hoffmann requested

---

I-go po voenno-sudnym delam," *RS*, 119 (1904), 7–9, 353–68; N. Vish, "Telesnye nakazaniia v voiskakh i ikh otmena," *VS*, 279 (1904), 10, 133–42; 280 (1904), 11, 113–24, 12, 151–62, here 10, 140.

40 D. A. Tolstoi, contrib., "Arkhiv grafa Igel'stroma," pt. 2, "Ukazy Pavla Petrovicha," *RA*, 24 (1886), 12, 480–96, here 485.

41 "Imperator Pavel Petrovich: prikazy po voiskam, 1797 g.," *RS*, 8 (1873), 959–74. [For a survey of the General-Auditoriat's repressive actions, see now N. Ia. Eydel'man, *Gran' vekov: politicheskaia bor'ba v Rossii, konets XVIII—nachalo XIX stoletiia* (Moscow, 1982), 101–6.]

42 P. S. Lebedev, "Preobrazovateli russkoi armii v tsarstvovanie imperatora Pavla Petrovicha, 1796–1801," *RS*, 18 (1877), 227–60, 577–608, here 247; cf. A. I. Andogskii, "Pavel I," in *VE*. XVII, 241.

43 L. G. Beskrovnyi, *Russkaia armiia i flot v XIX v.: voenno-ekonomicheskii potentsial Rossii* (Moscow, 1973), 81.

44 P. Grouvelle, *Précis anecdotique sur l'état actuel de Pétersbourg* . . . [1798–9]. Ministère des Affaires Etrangères, Paris, Mémoires et Documents, Russie 35 (1778–1828), f. 210.

45 Beskrovnyi, *Russkaia armiia* . . . *v XVIII v.*, 433.

46 An officer named Kop'ev is said to have painted his carriage like a sentry-box and to have driven about the capital dressed in an outlandish uniform. F. F. Vigel', *Vospominaniia*, vol. 2, pt. 3 (Moscow, 1864), 158–9 and Lebedev, "Preobrazovateli," 583, who relate the story, say that he was demoted to soldier's rank but later became a major-general. The record of the case is extant (see Dzhedzhula, *Rossiia*, 183), but the Soviet historian does not refer to the earlier sources. [See also Eydel'man, *Gran' vekov*, 78.]

an inquiry "according to the laws" (*po zakonam*) and was vindicated by the Military Commission. Paul, however, overruled the commissioners' decision and reprimanded them.[47] Such measures demonstrated his contempt for legality and doubtless helped to alienate a class of men who had begun to develop an awareness of their rights.

Another course open to dissidents was to desert. Even the emperor had to admit that "to [Our] extreme sorrow, desertions are on the increase"; typically, he attributed the problem to abuses by commanding officers, who in future were to have their salaries docked by the amount of each deserter's pay, plus the value of his uniform and ammunition.[48] Rewards were offered to those who seized and turned in deserters—reviving an ancient practice.[49] For obvious reasons flight from the colors was more prevalent among ordinary soldiers, whom Philippe Grouvelle speaks of as deserting by entire platoons, but it was not confined to them.[50] In May 1799, A. Mitkov, a noncommissioned officer (NCO) of noble extraction serving in a cuirassier regiment, fled to Austria by way of Brest-Litovsk; Paul ordered the fact to be publicly advertised "because desertion by a nobleman is so unusual."[51] In April 1800 another cuirassier named Sokolov was executed in Moscow for deserting to the French; he held the honored post of standard-bearer (*shtandart-iunker*), which may have aggravated his offense in the Russian authorities' eyes once he again found himself within their jurisdiction.[52] There is evidence in British archives of political disaffection among Russian troops quartered in the Channel Islands after the disastrous Dutch expedition.[53] However, these men did not remain in the West long enough to become a major source of "revolutionary contagion."

Far more important than any direct French influence was that which spread indirectly through Poland to the Ukraine and Don region, where the local *szlachta* and cossack *starshiny* were by no means wholly reconciled to their loss of rights upon assimilation into the empire. This sentiment may help to explain the conduct of Major Vasilii Passek, from the Slobidśka Ukraïna, who when stationed at Kremenchug in the early 1790s is said to have written poems calling upon his compatriots to resist tyranny and emulate the French. When some of his associates were arrested, Passek tried to escape to the Danubian principalities in the company of a Frenchman, but was

---

47 Vish, "Telesnye nakazaniia," 141.

48 Voinskii ustav (Nov. 29, 1796), *PSZ*, XXIV, no. 17588, pt. 9, ch. 6, § 1; cf. XXV, no. 18913 (Mar. 1799); XXVI, nos. 19270 (Feb. 9, 1800), 19645 (Nov. 29, 1800), 20098 (Dec. 31, 1801).

49 *PSZ*, XXIV, no. 18244 (Nov. 15, 1797).

50 Grouvelle, *Précis*; Viazmitinov to Rimskii-Korsakov, Feb. 16, 1798, in P. I. Shchukin, ed., *Sbornik starinnykh bumag, khraniashchikhsia v Muzee P. I. Shchukina*, vol. 1 (Moscow, 1896), 155; TsGVIA, fond 801, opis' 62/3, delo no. 168; fond 11, opis' 6, ed. khr. 33, passim.

51 "Dvorianin—dezertir: ukaz pravitel'stvuiushchago Senata 1-go iiunia 1799 g.," *RS*, 83 (1895), 132.

52 "Pis'ma I. V. Strakhova k grafu A. R. Vorontsovu," *AKV*, 14 (1879), 507; cf. the case of Private Eliakov of the Riazhsk musketeers (1797): TsGVIA, fond 801, opis' 62/3, ed. khr. 26.

53 Great Britain, Public Records Office, Foreign Office, 371.

caught and taken in fetters to St. Petersburg. The Secret Expedition acquitted him and he was posted in the same rank to another unit and kept under surveillance. He was less fortunate under the empress's militaristic successors: as he continued to make trouble, he was again arrested and for four years incarcerated in atrocious conditions at Dünamünde in the Baltic. Freed after Paul's assassination, he soon found himself back in jail under sentence of death; this was commuted to a term of exile in Siberia, where he remained for twenty years. The Soviet historian K. E. Dzhedzhula has recently provided a detailed account of this affair in which he stresses, in conformity with current ideological assumptions, Passek's intellectual debt to Radishchev—but strikingly fails to mention, even as a hypothesis, the possibility that Passek may simply have been the victim of a vendetta waged by his uncle, governor-general of White Russia.[54] This is the reason given by Passek in his own account,[55] where he alleges that his uncle (and guardian) persecuted him for many years in order to deprive him of his rightful inheritance. This story is endorsed by his daughter-in-law, T. P. Passek, a well-known liberal memoirist and friend of Alexander Herzen, who would have had no reason to conceal any revolutionary sympathies on the part of her father-in-law, had she known of them.[56] While in prison V. V. Passek did write some memoranda advocating administrative and social reforms, but these have unfortunately not survived.

While it is difficult to determine Passek's motives, cossack rights seem to have been at the heart of the tragedy of the brothers Evgraf and Petr Gruzinov, respectively a colonel and a lieutenant-colonel of Georgian ancestry serving in the emperor's cossack guard, who were arrested in 1798, sent back to the Don, kept there under close guard, and in 1800 put to death in the most brutal fashion. The Soviet Georgian historian O. Gvinchidze has discovered the records of their court martial, as well as some (unidentified) family papers, which add a lot to our knowledge of this affair.[57] He argues that the Gruzinovs were foes of serfdom and autocracy and that they shared the views of Radishchev. Such an interpretation is less plausible than the simple explanation that they were cossack officers and proud of the fact: it was this that led Evgraf Gruzinov to give an "insolent" reply when reprimanded by Paul I, which the emperor interpreted as evidence of "jacobin" tendencies. There was a streak of utopian fantasy in Gruzinov's views—while under arrest he sketched a future order in which men of all nations would live as brothers—but it would surely be wrong to read too much into this. More pertinent is Gruzinov's desire to win back more rights

54 Dzhedzhula, *Rossiia*, 177–80.

55 "Otryvok zhizni Vasiliia Passeka, im samin sochinenyi v Sankt-Peterburgskoi gradskoi tiur'me v 1803 g.," *RA*, 1 (1863), cols. 627–776.

56 T. P. Passek, *Iz davnykh let: vospominaniia*, 2 vols. (Moscow, 1963), vol. 1, 370–3, vol. 2, 204–17; cf. also V. Korsakova, "V. V. Passek," *RBS*, XIII, 352–5; M. V. Nechkina, *Dvizhenie dekabristov*, 2 vols. (Moscow, 1955), vol. 1, 88. The V. Passek who joined the Union of Welfare (ibid., 265) must be a different individual.

57 O. [S.] Gvinchidze, *Brat'ia Gruznovy* (Tbilisi, 1965).

for the Don cossacks, who were in a state of turbulence at this time.[58] He may also have objected to Russian policies in his original Georgian homeland, which led to its annexation to the empire in 1801.

In 1797 the opposition movement began to acquire a more organized character. Several dozen officers, all of intermediate rank (captain to colonel), came together in an informal circle in which the central figure was A. M. Kakhovskii, a colonel who had been dismissed from a senior position in the military bureaucracy and was living on his estate in Smolensk province.[59] The gentry of this region had a certain tradition of autonomy and were particularly closely interlinked by family and service ties; they may also have been more exposed to Polish influences than servitors in Great Russia. Many officers in Kakhovskii's circle belonged to the St. Petersburg dragoon regiment, which was stationed in the area; its "chief" (*shef*), Major-General D. Tarakhanov, and his successor, General P. Belukha, gave their subordinates what protection they could, as did the local gentry marshal, N. B. Potemkin. Kakhovskii's half-brother was A. P. Ermolov, then a mere lieutenant-colonel in an artillery unit, who already demonstrated the independence of spirit and willfullness for which he would later become celebrated. Members of the group discussed the works of Voltaire and other Enlightenment thinkers and ventilated freely their disgust at Paul's tyrannical regime. Some of them even spoke of regicide. Informants brought the circle's existence to the authorities' notice and in January 1799, after a lengthy investigation, at least 17 men were sentenced to terms of prison or exile. The inquiry was impeded in various ways by highly-placed sympathizers, among them an official of the Secret Expedition, but these patrons could not save the offenders from punishment.

One of the most pertinent features of this affair was that Kakhovskii had at one time served on Suvorov's staff. Involuntarily the respected field-marshal, who in February 1797 had been retired and placed under house arrest, became a potential focus for disaffection within the army.[60] According to Ermolov, Kakhovskii first tried to persuade Suvorov to attempt a *coup*, but he immediately rejected the suggestion, saying that he could not shed "the blood of [my] fellow-citizens"; the wording seems uncharacteristic, and the story cannot be corroborated.[61] But Suvorov made no secret of his opposition to many of the emperor's measures, such as the changes in uniform, the renaming of regiments after their new "chiefs," and the privileges accorded to the *Gatchintsy*—as well as, less justifiably, the appointment of inspectors who were designed to oversee the fractious generals and to put down corruption. This stand was enough to bring him the adulation of all those who, for whatever reason, now looked back nostalgically to Catherine's relaxed style of administration and contrasted it with the militaristic excesses of the present régime. In 1799 many of these men welcomed

---

58 Cf. note 37.

59 T. G. Snytko, "Novye materialy po istorii obshchestvennogo dvizheniia kontsa XVIII v.," *VI* (1952), no. 9, 111–22; cf. Dzhedzhula, *Rossiia*, 184–5.

60 Eighteen officers who resigned and accompanied their fallen leader to his estate were arrested, evidently on suspicion that they presented a security risk: *RBS*, XX, 59.

61 Snytko, "Novye materialy," 112. Ermolov's memoir has not been published in full.

war with France as an opportunity to leave the suffocating barrack-like atmosphere of their native land for the plains of northern Italy, where they could hope to win laurels on the battlefield.

Suvorov's successes in this campaign further raised his personal prestige, although he was now too weak physically to provide leadership for the dissidents. There was a deepening division between the men of action and the desk generals who had remained in comfort in St. Petersburg and whose practical qualifications were scarcely beyond reproach. Unhappy experiences with Russia's Austrian ally helped to fortify existing prejudices against the Germanic powers. Suvorov's style of command was coming to be seen as characteristically "Russian" in opposition to the "Prussian" principles that inspired Paul's unpopular military statute.

The most significant aspect of this development was that the schism at the top of the military hierarchy, which by this time was common knowledge, presented officers of middle (staff) rank, notably regimental colonels, with a loyalty problem. They had to choose between their Sovereign, who in Russia was generally endowed with a sacral aura, and honored senior commanders who were identified with the national military tradition. This unusual situation acted as a stimulus to independent thought. In normal times such men had no reason to reflect on the validity of the orders they received, and their universe was circumscribed by the simple concept of a natural ladder of established authorities. Now the picture had become confused, and perhaps for the first time in their lives they had to make up their own minds on matters of public policy.

Unfortunately the sources do not permit us to trace this growth of political consciousness with any precision. The memoir literature on Paul's reign suffers particularly from bias,[62] since everyone who wrote about this "dark period" was anxious to show his sympathies for the winning side. Very few were sufficiently sincere and courageous to admit that they had been sympathetic or complaisant to Paul.[63]

The emperor's assassination on March 11, 1801, was carried out by a relatively small group of conspirators, whose number is put by one memorialist at 188.[64] Sixty-eight have been positively identified; 50 were in the armed forces and 44 in the guards.[65] Most of them (34 of the 61 whose age is known) were young men in their late teens or twenties; at least 20 are thought to have had some personal grievance

---

62 See below, 243

63 One of the few who did so was Tuchkov, which explains why his memoirs (see note 36) did not appear until 1908. Although a cultured individual and something of a "democrat," Tuchkov made a good career under Paul but failed to do so under his successor, whom he describes as dictatorial, deceitful, suspicious and vengeful towards the military: *Zapiski*, 260, 268.

64 "Zapiski N. A. Sablukova," in *Tsareubiistvo 11 marta 1801 g.: zapiski uchastnikov i sovremennikov* (St. Petersburg, 1907), 1–105, here 87.

65 J. J. Kenney, Jr., "The Politics of Assassination," in H. Ragsdale, ed., *Paul I: a Reassessment of his Life and Reign* (Pittsburgh, 1979), 128–31. Kenney's analysis is preferable to that offered by R. H. Warner, "The Political Opposition to Tsar Paul I," unpub. PhD thesis (New York Univ., 1977).

against the tsar.[66] The successful *coup* had greater public resonance than any that
had preceded it, since by 1801 Paul's rule had lost much legitimacy in the eyes of
élite servitors, not least in the military branch.

Alexander's accession was followed by a number of short-term measures designed
to heal the breach between the autocracy and the army. Apart from the new tsar's
well-publicized return to his grandmother's political style or his other pseudo-
liberal gestures,[67] certain specific steps were taken in the military domain. Some of
Paul's uniforms, for example, disappeared, as did the ridiculous ringlets (although
the tricorne lasted until 1805 and the pigtail until 1806–7).[68] Something was done
to regularize the supply system.[69] More important, new pay scales were announced
already on June 24, 1801. A full colonel in the active army now got 1,040 to 1,250
roubles a year, according to his branch of service, as against 900 roubles in 1798, at
which time he had already received an 111-rouble raise. A captain now received 400
to 495 as against 340 roubles, and an ensign 236 to 325 as against 200 roubles.[70] In
percentage terms the minimum increases amounted to 15.6 percent, 17.7 percent and
18.0 percent respectively—and over the three years the value of the assignat rouble
had appreciated by 10.2 percent![71] Typically, nothing seems to have been done for
the wretched enlisted men, whose cash pay was apparently much the same as it had
been in 1711.[72] Their discontents were evidently not perceived as a threat to the
régime.

Official benevolence extended to the officers' future as well as present material
state. A decree of February 23, 1803, brought in a pay-related pension scheme for
all military officers, who were classified according to their length of service; the
terms were improved a few months later.[73] Finally, the expansion of troop strength,
which added at least 50,000 men between 1802 and 1805, provided extra vacancies

---

66 Kenney, "Politics"; we have added L. L. Bennigsen to his list.

67 On these see A. McConnell, "Alexander I's Hundred Days: the Politics of a Paternalist
Reformer," *SR*, 28 (1969), 373–93—who does not, however, mention military affairs.

68 Stein, *Geschichte*, 253, 261; Petrov, ed., *Russkaia voennaia sila*, 271. The sociopsycholog-
ical aspects of the armed forces' dress still await their historian.

69 *PSZ*, XXVII, no. 20224 (Apr. 9, 1802).

70 *PSZ*, XXVI, no. 19926 (June 24, 1801); Stein, *Geschichte*, 244; Petrov, ed., *Russkaia voennaia sila*, 262; C. von Plotho, *Über die Entstehung, die Fortschritte und die gegenwärtige
Verfassung der russischen Armee, doch insbesondere von der Infanterie* (Berlin, 1811), 42.

71 From 1.77 to 1.51 assignat roubles per 1 silver rouble: P. Shtorkh, "Materialy dlia istorii
gosudarstvennykh denezhnykh znakov v Rossii s 1653 po 1840 g.," *ZhMNP*, 137 (1868), 3,
772–847, here 819.

72 The last pay raise had been in 1794, when they had received an extra 2 roubles: *PSZ*, XXIII,
no. 17229 (June 28, 1794). For the 1711 establishment: *PSZ*, IV, no. 2319 (Feb. 19). [The
statement "nothing seems to have been done" is incorrect: see *PSZ*, XLIII, no. 23603 (Apr.
22, 1809), 125, relating to the cavalry, and our *Soldiers of the Tsar*, 182.]

73 *PSZ*, XXVII, nos. 20631 (Feb. 23, 1803), 20770 (May 21, 1803); cf. N. Solov'ev, "O
pensiiakh za voennuiu sluzhbu v Rossii v XVIII i XIX st.," *VS*, 210 (1893), 2, 302–12, here
304.

for officers and did something to ease the discontents of unemployed supernumeraries (*sverkhkomplektnye*)—a considerable problem for the authorities at this time. Thus when Russia entered the Third Coalition war her officers seem to have responded with relish; at any rate, no evidence of dissension has yet come to light. If they objected to the way the campaigns of 1805–7 were fought, their commanders could with some plausibility divert their anger against the empire's allies, for Austria, Prussia and Britain each in their several ways failed to live up to the hard-pressed Russians' legitimate expectations. Some may have accepted the Holy Synod's rationalization of the conflict as one between Orthodox Rus' and godless atheism.

The treaty of Tilsit was of course very unpopular in educated society generally and has rightly been seen as creating something of a noble *fronde*.[74] There was a sense of moral outrage and humiliation at the enforced compromise with the Corsican "upstart" which merged with economic grievances over the effects of Russia's adherence to the Continental System and with distrust of the centralizing reforms associated with that model but unpopular civil servant, M. M. Speranskii.

How much of this spirit carried over into the armed forces? Not a great deal, so far as one can gather from the published sources. Several reasons may be adduced to explain this. First, the troops were kept busy fighting Turks, Persians and Swedes (and in 1809 had to march about in a mock war with the Austrians). F. F. Vigel' states that in 1809, when four campaigns were under way simultaneously, no one in St. Petersburg society took any interest in these distant events.[75] No doubt the same attitude was true in reverse among the military. Second, there will have been a high rate of officer intake to make up for heavy losses and to command newly formed units. For instance, the engineer officers' corps, set up in October 1809, had a staff of 813, including 102 civilian "military officials."[76] In 1811 came the formation of an "internal guard" (*vnutrenniaia strazha*), a security force that anticipated the better-known *gendarmerie* of Nicholas I, which comprised 20 brigades, or approximately 2,500 to 3,000 officers' vacancies. In neither case, admittedly, were all these *new* jobs; but one doubts whether very many willing supernumerairies were still left out in the cold. Some of the younger men were channeled into one or other of the rapidly expanding military schools. The so-called Noblemen's Regiment dates from March 1807. It was a training unit which took boys aged sixteen and over who would otherwise have had to serve as NCOs in line regiments; its graduates automatically received ensign's rank. On the announcement of its establishment gentry servitors, we are told, hastened to the capital; among them were "many who were enfeebled and sick, and even one who was dumb"—and most were illiterate into the bargain. By 1812 the regiment had two thousand cadets and by 1815 three thousand.[77] Military

74 Cf. A. V. Predtechenskii, *Ocherki obshchestvenno-politicheskoi istorii Rossii v pervoi chetverti XIX v.* (Moscow and Leningrad, 1957), 217–22.

75 Vigel', *Vospominaniia*, vol. 2, pt. 3, 61.

76 Stein, *Geschichte*, 275.

77 G. M. Gol'mdorf, "Dvorianskii polk, 1807–1859: prazdnovanie 75-oi godovshchiny dnia ego osnovaniia," *RS*, 34 (1882), 797–802, here 797–8.

schools were also opened in provincial towns such as Tambov and Tula.[78] Life in these "stick academies" was very tough and left no time for political speculation or scheming.

The situation was a little more favorable in this respect for guards officers in the capital, where a training institution called the Column-leaders' corps (*Korpus kolonnovozhatykh*) came into being in 1811. M. A. Fonvizin, a guards lieutenant and brother of the well-known writer (and later a Decembrist), formed a circle of fellow-officers to study military history. The group included A. A. Veliaminov and Major P. A. Rakhmanov, the latter a remarkable mathematician who founded, at his own expense, the first professional military periodical, *Voennyi zhurnal.*[79] According to M. M. Muromtsev, another subaltern who took part in these gatherings, he and some comrades discussed the democracy of ancient Athens rather too freely for the taste of their commander, who packed them off to Finland.[80] These officers were doubtless animated principally by a desire to better their professional qualifications and thus serve their country more effectively; it was the "top brass" who saw potentially subversive implications in their studies and, by harassing them, accelerated their drift towards political opposition.

An important aspect of this development, still to be studied, is the role of patronage exercised by certain senior officers—particularly those who held to the national tradition and resented the influence exerted on the tsar and in the the army by colleagues whom they held (rightly or wrongly) to be of foreign background or to have first risen to prominence, like Arakcheev, as members of the Gatchina clique. The expression "court general" (*pridvornyi general*) seems to have been employed at this time[81] as a contemptuous epithet for those who, although possessing high rank, did not generally share the hardships of true warriors. Vigel', our informant, adds that some of them "did gallop off to the Moldavian army in search of easy victories and rewards," but that the commander-in-chief, S. M. Kamenskii, refused to give them preference over officers who had served their way up at the front; they intrigued against him, and ultimately he was relieved of his command. Doubtless there was also ill feeling among field-army men at the privileges enjoyed by those in the (now rapidly expanding) guards corps, which was not committed to action until 1812.

III

The "Patriotic War" and the ensuing counteroffensive into central and western Europe transformed entirely the atmosphere in Russia's armed forces. Some of these changes are obvious and have been amply commented on; others are still far less clear. It scarcely needs to be pointed out that the 1812 campaign differed in nature from any that had gone before. Fighting men saw themselves as defending "the sacred soil of

---

78 Beskrovnyi, *Russkaia armiia . . . v XIX v.*, 124.

79 N. V. Bobynin, "P. A. Rakhmanov," *RBS*, XV, 512–17.

80 "Vospominaniia M. M. Muromtseva," *RA*, 26 (1890), 1, 59–81, here 71–2.

81 Vigel', *Vospominaniia*, vol. 2, pt. 3, 107.

the Fatherland"; the war was "popular" in the sense that millions of civilians were caught up in the fray as combatants, voluntarily or (in most cases) involuntarily; some were active partisans, whose deeds gave a new dimension to the horrors of war; many lost their lives or property. Among the social élite there was a rush back to the colors, especially to the hastily remustered militia units where service conditions were generally less onerous.[82] For both regulars and temporary service men the war, with its sudden swings of fortune from humiliating defeat to total victory, had an epic quality. The experience not only stirred up patriotic sentiments that had hitherto lain largely dormant; it also encouraged the growth of independent thought. The rights and wrongs of strategic decisions and the merits of individual commanders were quite freely discussed. Lieutenant Chicherin confided to his diary many observations on the quality of the army's leadership, his reactions to atrocities, his aspirations for the future, and his impressions of those foreign lands he passed through before he met his death in action in 1813.[83]

From memoirs and other historical and literary sources (notably, of course, Tolstoi's *War and Peace*) one can reconstruct with some confidence the *mentalité* of the better educated Russian officer of this period. Even medium-ranking men and subalterns had often acquired a taste for cultural pursuits and were developing a new awareness of their social function.[84] However, it is a mistake to imagine, as many writers have implied, that the "Decembrist generation" possessed a political consciousness in the modern sense. Only a handful of Russian officers had as yet more than the most superficial familiarity with the political theories current at the time in the rest of Europe. Even the most articulate were vague as to the institutional changes necessary to realize their ideals, drawn largely from belletristic sources. This ought not to surprise us, since they had been brought up in the state service milieu, where obedience, loyalty and honor were regarded as the paramount virtues. What occurred was not so much political enlightenment as a heightening of moral sensitivity. More introspective than their fathers, these young men sought to understand the reasons for their presence in camp or on the battlefield, and to analyze their emotions at the sight of hardship or suffering.

Their greater measure of selfrespect went hand in hand with a feeling that men of other classes or nations should be treated with proper consideration for their worth as individuals. This rather elementary humanistic sentiment is well expressed by Chicherin's simple but moving thoughts that "man is born to live among people like himself" or that one had a duty "to make others happy," "to try to be useful," "to serve others."[85] There was nothing revolutionary or subversive in such ideas, which were

---

82 The term "militia" is a little misleading, since the *opolchenie* was not primarily a local defense force but an additional levy which acted as a reserve; several units saw action in Germany in 1813, notably at the siege of Glogau: Babkin, "Organizatsiia," 142; K. A. Voenskii, *Istoricheskie ocherki i stat'i, otnosiashchiesia k 1812 g.* (St. Petersburg, [1912]), 322–3.

83 See note 19.

84 See below, 255–65.

85 *Dnevnik A. Chicherina*, 35–6.

quite compatible with cliché-like expressions of personal loyalty to the Sovereign, love of country, professional zeal, admiration for courage on the battlefield and so on. (The religious note is relatively subdued, and regimental *esprit de corps* was less in evidence in the Russian army than in most others.)

The notion of fraternity among fighting men of equal or near-equal rank was part of the traditional military ethos. Comradeship was bound to seem more important at a time of danger than it did in normal conditions. After all, very little aid was forthcoming from official sources for men who were wounded, fell sick, or lost contact with their units, so that one's life might often quite literally depend on the generosity of one's fellows. The virtues of personal friendship were also much stressed in the Romantic literature of the period, which many officers had read. A. I. Antonovskii, a subaltern in the 26th chasseurs, notes that on campaign officers from different units not previously acquainted with one another found it easy to strike up contact, and that they would sometimes share their last crumbs with a stranger; after experiencing one such act of charity, he vowed that he would never forget "this most noble trait."[86] (Normally, of course, social relationships among members of the élite were governed by a multiplicity of formal conventions.) Expressed in the cold language of modern social science, the war of 1812 produced a strengthening of horizontal affective ties at the expense of vertical hierarchical bonds; or, to put the point somewhat more imaginatively, a man might seek to pattern his conduct on associates rather than superiors.

The spread of dissent within the army after 1814 was rooted in this new spirit. There was a perfectly natural sense of pride in the army's achievements. Officers' self-esteem was bolstered by the new responsibilities they had shouldered. Men who had led others under fire or had successfully carried out orders at personal risk naturally sought new outlets for their energies that would be commensurate with their talents. When the troops returned and the militia units were stood down officers were able to resume contact with civilian society—a contact which for many had of course never been wholly sundered.[87] It was not just that members of élite guards regiments circulated in aristocratic salons; at a lower level the subaltern stationed in some small country town could enjoy the companionship of the local gentry. The war raised the army's prestige to an even higher plane than usual among civilians who, it should be remembered, were themselves for the most part in uniform of one kind or another. Almost unconsciously the military came to assume a leadership role in the general drift of public opinion in a direction unfavorable to the government of the day. Few civilians actually joined secret societies, yet their moral support was important in building up the self-confidence and determination of the military activists.

---

86 A. I. Antonovskii, "Zapiski," in Kharkevich, ed., *1812 god*, fasc. 3, (Vil'no, 1904), 45.

87 General Komarovskii, sent on mission to Zhitomir as Napoleon entered Moscow, was lavishly entertained by aristocratic friends and fellow-officials in that province. "Iz zapisok general-ad'iutanta grafa E. F. Komarovskogo," *RA*, 5 (1867), cols. 748–88, 1276–1330, here cols. 783, 1279.

The abundant literature on the Decembrist movement[88] treats it almost wholly as a civilian phenomenon, which in our view has led to grave distortion. In the first place the very term "Decembrist," although it is too convenient to discard, is misleading, because it conveys the impression that the secret society members were insurrectionists implicated in the events of December 1825. As W. B. Lincoln has shown, this is not the case: " . . . of the eighty-one Northern Society members sentenced by the Supreme Criminal Court, only twenty-nine (35.8 percent) actually took part in the events on the Senate Square."[89] Of the 20 men convicted for their part in the Chernigov regiment's uprising near Belaia Tserkov', only eight had been members of any secret society.[90] We are therefore confronted with two discrete phenomena: the growth of dissent among the military after 1814, and the efforts by some of them to put their ideas into practise during the interregnum of 1825.

Lincoln writes that "the final word has yet to be written about the Decembrists and . . . there still is a need for more intensive study [of] the mass of those who took part in the Russian revolutionary movement during the second decade of the nineteenth century."[91] To take up this challenge would necessitate a book; here we may simply point to two particular problems that deserve investigation.

One of these is the development of ideas on army reform among participants in the secret societies, which was an integral part of their general *Weltanschauung*. We do not wish to imply that the Decembrists—or as they should be called, the "military intelligentsia"—were indifferent to wider concerns, such as constitutional rights or the emancipation of serfs, for this would fly in the face of the evidence, but rather to indicate that their general views were inevitably colored to some extent by their service background and experience. Their broader reform program grew naturally out of the desire for changes within the military environment. E. A. Prokof'ev has examined these ideas in some detail and argues—convincingly, in our view—that they looked forward to a citizen army in which the entire able-bodied male population would share the obligation to defend the state.[92] This was of course an essential element of the French revolutionary legacy.

So, too, was the belief that military force might be used to effect changes in the political and social order. The Decembrists differed among themselves, as everyone knows, about the nature of these changes: Colonel Nikita M. Murav'ev's draft constitution provided for an American-style devolution of political power, whereas

---

88 The liberal approach taken by such late nineteenth-century and early twentieth-century historians as A. N. Pypin, V. I. Semevskii or M. V. Dovnar-Zapol'skii has in large measure been continued by Soviet Marxists, who however insist on the "bourgeois" character of the movement. The military angle is discussed by Prokof'ev, *Bor'ba* (see note 20), V. A. Fedorov, *Soldatskoe dvizhenie v gody dekabristov, 1816–1825 gg.* (Moscow, 1963) and G. S. Gabaev, "Gvardiia v dekabr'skie dni 1825 g.," in A. E. Presniakov, ed., *14-go dekabria 1825 g.* (Moscow and Leningrad, 1926), 155–206.

89 Lincoln, "Re-examination," 363.

90 Ibid., 362.

91 Ibid., 365.

92 Prokof'ev, *Bor'ba*, 109–28.

Colonel P. I. Pestel' wanted to establish a provisional dictatorship and evidently saw himself as potential dictator. (We deliberately refer to these men by their military rank, although a curious convention dictates that it should be omitted.) But both agreed that the initiating role should fall to a relatively restricted group of professional army officers, who should try to win over their troops by humane treatment but should not share with them their thoughts about the purposes or means of the action contemplated. Their attitude had something in common with that of Spanish or Latin American *pronunciados*.[93] In the Russian case the relative stability of the dynasty and the religious awe with which the Sovereign was regarded inhibited the development of Praetorian tendencies.[94]

The organizational ideas and practises of the early nineteenth-century Russian military intelligentsia constitute a second line of inquiry worth pursuing. It is important to bear in mind that " technical" military considerations often vitally affected the fate of the secret societies. Officers might, for example, be posted to other units, and have to break off personal ties; others (like S. P. Trubetskoi) might be granted leave. Army life offered malcontents a chance to contact like-minded spirits, but also heightened the risk of exposure, for discipline was extremely strict and the least insubordination might result in punishment. Alexander revived Paul's system of internal espionage among the military, which had been allowed to lapse at the beginning of his reign. In January 1821 the tsar agreed to a proposal by General I. V. Vasil'chikov, commander of the guards corps, that a secret military police be established to exercise surveillance over troops stationed in and around the capital. It was to have staff of only fifteen and a modest budget of 40,000 roubles;[95] but its real strength lay in the *ad hoc* informer, who could be rewarded for his services as and when they were rendered. In May 1821 the authorities received valuable information from M. K. Gribovskii, librarian to the guards general staff and a key member of the Union of Welfare, who under psychological pressure betrayed his comrades and even helped to organize the surveillance system.[96] Two other such informers, I. V. Shervud and A. I. Maiboroda, reported on Pestel''s activities and enabled the authorities to arrest him on December 12, 1825, so preventing coordinated action by the Northern and Southern societies.

Some dissident officers of the post-1814 period were linked by family and service ties to men who had been active politically in the 1790s. P. G. Kakhovskii, who played a leading role in the events on Senate Square and was one of the five Decembrists to

93 E. Christiansen, *The Origins of Military Power in Spain, 1800–1854* (London, 1967), esp. 18–22, 40–1; [I. de Madariaga, "Spain and the Decembrists," *European Studies Review*, 3 [1973], 141–56.]

94 On Praetorianism see now A. Perlmutter, *The Military and Politics in Modern Times: on Professionals, Praetorians and Revolutionary Soldiers* (New Haven and London: Yale Univ. Press, 1977), esp. 90–92.

95 "Proekt ob ustroistve voennoi politsii pri gvardeiskom korpuse, 1821 g.," *RS*, 33 (1882), 217–19; N. K. Shil'der, *Imperator Aleksandr I: ego zhizn' i tsarstvovanie*, vol. 4 (St. Petersburg, 1898), 203–15.

96 Iu. G. Oksman et al., comps., *Dekabristy: otryvki iz istochnikov* (Moscow and Leningrad, 1926), 109–16; Nechkina, *Dvizhenie*, vol. 2, 348–50.

be executed, was related to the organizer of the Smolensk network.[97] V. P. Ivashev, a prominent associate of Pestel' at Tul'chin, was the son of P. N. Ivashev, a former aide-de-camp (ADC) to Suvorov who was involved in Paul I's assassination.[98] Another participant in this conspiracy (although as a civilian) was Senator Nikolai M. Murav'ev, whose three sons in or after 1814 set up an informal *artel'* of 14 members, otensibly to make common messing arrangements.[99] Such *arteli* offered a convenient cover for political activity. Another, involving some 15 to 20 officers, existed from 1815 in the Semenovskii regiment, and a third among the Izmailovtsy: its founders, the brothers M. N. and N. N. Semenov, are known to have had a well-stocked library of French classics.[100] The first of these three groups had masonic connections, and it was from this source that Colonel Aleksandr N. Murav'ev took many of his ideas on clandestine organizational technique.[101] (Freemasonry does not, however, seem to have been very important generally.)

Two of the Murav'ev brothers were moving spirits behind another organization in the general staff which ostensibly set itself much the same educational objectives as Fonvizin's earlier group and resumed publication of *Voennyi zhurnal*.[102] Once again patronage seems to have been an important factor, for General N. M. Sipiagin (1785–1828), the chief of staff, gave the enterprise his blessing. One interesting fact that emerges from his little known biography[103] is that he was promoted with extraordinary speed: a captain in 1811, he found himself a major-general two years later. The son of a lieutenant-general, he was a professional soldier who took an interest in education for its own sake: when posted away from the general staff in 1819 owing to his "liberal" views, he founded a school for junior officers at his own expense.

Another patron was Ia. A. Potemkin (1778–1831), a distant relative of the field-marshal, who was both an adjutant-general to the tsar and commanding officer of the Semenovskii guards regiment until his dismissal in 1819 (and eventual replacement by the notorious Colonel F. E. Shvarts); as his political reliability came under sus-

97 Nechkina, *Dvizhenie*, vol. 1, 90; vol. 2, 28.

98 Kenney, "Politics," 133; Nechkina, *Dvizhenie*, vol. 2, 219–20, 333, 348.

99 M. V. Nechkina, "Sviashchennaia artel': kruzhok Aleksandra Murav'eva i Ivana Burtseva, 1814–1817 gg. . . ." in M. P. Alekseev and B. S. Meilakh, eds., *Dekabristy i ikh vremia: materialy i soobshcheniia* (Moscow and Leningrad, 1951), 155–88; [M. V. Nechkina, ed., *Iz epistoliarnogo nasledstva dekabristov: pis'ma k N. N. Murav'ev-Karskomu*, vol. 1 (Moscow, 1975), 76, 80, 289–90.]

100 "Vospominaniia A. S. Gangeblova: kak ia popal v dekabristy i chto za tem posledovalo," *RA*, 24 (1886), 6, 181–268, here 190; *Zapiski, stat'i, pis'ma I. D. Iakushkina*, ed. S. Ia. Shtraikh (Moscow and Leningrad, 1951), 9.

101 A. N. Murav'ev, "Avtobiograficheskie zapiski," ed. Iu. I. Gerasimova, in M. K. Azadovskii, ed., *Dekabristy: novye materialy* (Moscow, 1955), 137–230, here 164, 214–15; for the names of some other military members: A. N. Pypin, *Russkoe masonstvo XVIII i I-aia chetvert' XIX v.*, ed. G. V. Vernadskii (Petrograd, 1916), 386–7, 396.

102 Beskrovnyi, *Russkaia armiia . . . v XIX v.*, 217.

103 M. Kochergin, "N. M. Sipiagin," *RBS*, XVIII, 508–10.

picion, he was sent off to command first a guards and then an army division in the provinces—and so escaped implication in the insurrection. Potemkin, like Sipiagin, made a good career under Nicholas I.[104] General A. A. Zakrevskii, also a member of the general staff, was at this time close to the *frondeur* and proconsul of the Caucasus, General A. I. Ermolov.[105] As commander of the Caucasian corps, Ermolov was powerful enough to turn a blind eye to political activity by liberal-minded subordinates, some of whom had been sent to serve in this frontier area as a punishment. When passing through Moscow in September 1821, Ermolov warned his former adjutant, M. A. Fonvizin, that the tsar knew of his secret society's existence.[106] Lieutenant-general M. S. Vorontsov, when commander of the 12th infantry division in France (1815), issued an order that soldiers should be treated in humane fashion.[107] No doubt there were many other senior officers whose protection enabled the young dissidents to operate more easily that they otherwise could have done.

In 1816–17 Colonel A. N. Murav'ev helped to set up a more expressly political association, known as the "Union of True and Loyal Sons of the Fatherland," which at its peak had about 30 members. (The organization is usually referred to as "the Union of Salvation," which though simpler understates its leaders' nationalistic inclinations.)[108] All of them were guards officers. When the guards corps accompanied the court to Moscow for several months in 1817, conspiratorial meetings were held in Murav'ev's quarters. Murav'ev himself favored a military *coup*, but neither this course nor the assassination of the tsar, which was also mooted, won general support. The leaders decided to disband the society and to set up a new body, the Union of Welfare, which on the surface had less overtly political aims but was really intended as a cover organization under which adherents of all tendencies could continue their conspiratorial activities. This act of deception suggests that the leaders had profited from their tactical training and experience, in which *ruses de guerre* were routine.

Another such bogus dissolution was arranged in 1821, when the Union of Welfare gave way to two regional bodies which endeavored to carry on its propaganda work. The Southern society was based on Tul'chin (Bessarabia province), headquarters of the Second Army, where Pestel' held a staff position as well as command of the Viatka infantry regiment. An energetic leader, who reminded at least one associate of Napoleon,[109] he sought to establish a centralized organization with outer and inner rings of members and, at the core, a board (*uprava*) which actually consisted only

104 P. N. Pavlov-Sil'vanskii, "Ia. A. Potemkin," *RBS*, XIV, 686–8.

105 S. N. Chernov, "Iz istorii soldatskikh nastroenii v nachale 20-kh gg.," in Iu. G. Oksman and P. E. Shchegolev, eds., *Bunt dekabristov: iubileinyi sbornik, 1825–1925* (Leningrad, 1926), 56–128, here 60.

106 *Zapiski . . . Iakushkina*, 65; Nechkina, *Dvizhenie*, vol. 1, 353; vol. 2, 110–12, 148.

107 "Pravila dlia obkhozhdeniia s nizhnymi chinami 12-oi pekhotnoi divizii: prikaz nachal'nika 12-oi divizii, general-leitenanta grafa M. S. Vorontsova," *VS*, 5 (1859), 2, 495–502.

108 M. V. Nechkina, "Soiuz spaseniia," *IZ*, 23 (1947), 137–84; idem, *Dvizhenie*, vol. 1, 141–84.

109 *Zapiski dekabrista N. I. Lorera*, ed. M. N. Pokrovskii (Moscow, 1931), 70.

of two men: himself and General A. P. Iushnevskii, the Second Army's chief supply officer (*general-intendant*), who seems to have been something of a "front man" for Pestel'.

The Southerners were in contact from August 1825 onward with another secret organization, the Society of United Slavs, which drew on Polish revolutionary experience and took a more activist line. Its nucleus consisted almost entirely of subaltern officers (the only exception was a major);[110] unlike the two Russian regional groups, its members attempted (with some success) to propagandize rank-and-file soldiers. Relations between the two organizations were rendered difficult not only by programmatic differences but also by their leaders' disparity in rank; neither wished to accept subordination to the other, and so the unity they achieved was merely formal.[111]

One reason why the Northern society was slower to take shape than its counterpart was that in 1821–2 the guards corps was sent off to Lithuania for several months, partly in order to keep potential trouble-makers out of the capital. The members of this organization held high military rank; 69 percent had served at one time or another in the guards, as against 46.5 percent of Southern society members.[112] (There were of course far more guards officers in St. Petersburg than on the southern perimeter of the empire.) Like the Southern society, the organization had an inner core and two outer rings,[113] but discipline within it was less strict.

In 1821, shortly after the celebrated Semenovskii affair, several officers of the Lithuanian guards regiment were reduced to the ranks for protesting against service conditions.[114] In 1822 a similar incident occurred in the Chasseurs guards regiment, when about 20 officers held that Grand Duke Nicholas had insulted one of their comrades, Captain V. S. Norov, and agreed to resign their commissions; six of them actually did so.[115] These were pointers to what would come about in 1825. By that year the Northern society had consolidated its position in a number of guards units: the Moscow, Horse, Finland and First Grenadier regiments, as well as the naval infantry (*morskoi ekipazh*). Nevertheless this was only a fraction of the total guards corps, which consisted of four divisions—that is to say, thirteen regiments (each of about 3,000 men) and a few smaller detachments.[116] All the units just listed, of which

---

110 *VD*, 5 (1926); cf. also M. V. Nechkina, *Obshchestvo Soedinennykh slavian* (Moscow and Leningrad, 1927); [G. Luciani, *Panslavisme et solidarité slave: la Société des Slaves Réunis* (Bordeaux, 1963).]

111 I. I. Gorbachevskii, *Zapiski. Pis'ma*, ed. B. E. Syroechkovskii et al. (Moscow, 1963), 280; Nechkina, *Dvizhenie*, vol. 2, 180.

112 Lincoln, "Re-examination," 362–3.

113 A. M. Murav'ev, *Zapiski*, ed. S. Ia. Shtraykh (Petrograd, 1922), 15, 33.

114 Beskrovnyi, *Russkaia armiia . . . v XIX v.*, 223, citing archival source. (One of those concerned, Captain P. A. Gabbe, was demoted to soldier's rank, rehabilitated in 1823, but then retired; he later went insane: *RBS*, IV, 6.) In October 1820 a number of Izmailovskii guards officers had resigned their commissions in protest: Chernov, "Iz istorii," 95.

115 Nechkina, *Dvizhenie*, vol. 1, 374. Norov had belonged to the Union of Welfare; he was later transferred to a line regiment and was among those punished after the Decembrist revolt.

116 Gabaev, "Gvardiia," 164–72.

elements participated in the insurrection of December 14, were in *one* of the two infantry divisions, which was under the nominal command (*shefstvo*) of Grand Duke
Michael; those units of which Nicholas was *shef* remained loyal to him. (The guards
corps as a whole was headed by Constantine.) In a situation where personal loyalties
counted for so much, and the dynastic succession was unclear, this fact should not be
lost sight of.

The insurrection in St. Petersburg caused thirteen known fatalities among the
rebels, whose total casualties have been estimated at 70–80.[117] This was a relatively
small proportion of the 30 officers (all but one of them subalterns) and 2,850 men
involved in the affair. Altogether some two thousand persons (including civilians) are
thought to have been associated with one or other of the clandestine organizations.
Of the 570 persons considered by the authorities to have been directly involved in
the movement and sent for trial, 78.8 percent were serving officers.[118]

The breakdown by rank is as follows: (a) 17 generals, of whom seven were later
sentenced; (b) 115 "staff" officers, including 68 colonels, of whom 52 (including
28 colonels) were sentenced; (c) 315 subalterns (*ober-ofitsery*), of whom 192 were
sentenced. Of the military men committed, age data are available for 254, and of
those charged, for 179. They indicate that of the former 40.2 percent were 25 or
under; 30.0 percent aged 26–30; 19.3 percent 31–35; 11.4 percent 36–40; and 2.8
percent over 40.[119] Nearly one-third of the total had seen action and had won medals
or awards; 125 (27.4 percent) had completed a military education. Prokof'ev points
out that "many officers found to be involved were sons of the most eminent and
progressive-minded Russian generals and admirals . . . [They] had had direct contact
with senior commanders of the Russian army during the 1812 Patriotic War or had
grown up in the families of generals or [other] officers who had known Suvorov and
Kutuzov well. . . ."[120] This fact can be interpreted a little differently: they enjoyed
the patronage of those who stood in the tradition of the "national school" and resented
the cosmopolitan veneer of court and aristocratic society.

The Decembrists stood for a revival of the service ethos, redirected towards the
people rather than the autocracy. They wanted, not to overthrow the state, but to help
it reform itself so that it might become more efficient and better able to withstand
its internal and external foes. The rationalism of the old century blended with the
romanticism of the new[121] in encouraging a belief that conscious action by a trained

---

117 Ibid., 191–2. Beskrovnyi, *Russkaia armiia . . . v XIX v.*, 229, gives the figure of 80 (without
    indication of source), but states that all of them were killed.

118 To be precise, 456 out of 579 (for nine men were not officially listed). *VD*, 8 (1925), 14;
    Prokof'ev, *Bor'ba*, 98.

119 Prokof'ev, *Bor'ba*, 100 (arithmetic corrected). Lincoln, "Re-examination," 360, gives a
    table of age data for those sentenced, but the age cohorts are not quite the same; they bear
    out the picture of men predominantly in their twenties. Curiously, Lincoln does not mention
    the earlier statistical effort.

120 Prokof'ev, *Bor'ba*, 105.

121 M. Raeff, *The Decembrist Movement* (Englewood Cliffs, N. J.: Prentice Hall, 1966), 16.

élite was essential in order to improve society's physical and moral condition, and that armed force might be used to accomplish these worthwhile ends. The impact of revolutionary France on their ideas, although delayed and indirect, was considerable. In only a few cases was the reading of western books or first-hand experience of conditions abroad fundamental in shaping their attitudes. Dissent grew out of the internal situation of the army itself. It led to a protest movement that was broader than anything the empire had hitherto known—or would see again until the 1870s. It was not a total failure. The reform era that followed the Crimean War brought, if not constitutional government, the freeing of the serfs and the introduction of a system of general (if selective) conscription. A citizen army on the French revolutionary model did not come into being until 1918. The total mobilization of society for warlike ends, which has become so familiar a feature of the twentieth century, would probably have appalled the first representatives of the Russian military intelligentsia—although it might be said that this was implicit in the goals they sought.

1980

Table

Appropriations and Expenditure on the Russian Armed Forces, 1789–1825
(in thousand roubles)[122]

	Appropriations				Expenditure				
	Army	Navy	Total Armed Forces	Total Expenditure	Army	Navy	Total Armed Forces	Total Expenditure	Armed Forces Expenditure as Percentage of Total Expenditure
	(1)	(2)	(3)	(4)	(5)	(6)	(7)	(8)	(9)
1789	(20169) a(16000)	5305	(41474)	(79568)					(52.12)
1790	(21621) a(16000)	5475	(43096)	(82706)					(52.11)
1791	(24590) a(15000)	5470	(45060)	(84870)					(53.09)
1792	(24117)	6188	(30305)	(73225)					(41.39)
1793	23623	5418	29041	(76731)					(37.84)
1794	(21572)	5676	(27248)	(72288)					(37.69)
1795	(22199)	7009	(29208)	(79158)					(36.90)
1796	(22003)	6683	(28686)	(79166)					(36.24)
1797	(20000)	(5000)	(25000)	(63234)				65822	(37.98)
1798	(27000)	(8000)	(35000)	(72076)					(48.56)
1799	(31300)	(8200)	(39300)	(77913)					(50.44)
1800	31718	8892	40610	78211					(51.92)
1801	33630	9016	42646	78214	34435	12000	46435[123]	91730	50.62
1802	33705	9040	42745	79304	31820	9008	40828	90097	45.32
1803	35563	10672	46235	95651	b33522	b10479	b44001	109412[125]	40.22
1804	40579	9200	49779	98980	41942	10742	52684	122164	43.13
1805	41305	12420	53725	112341	43184	14058	57242	125449	45.63
1806	40206	12736	52942	108529	44303	14836	59139	122459	48.29
1807	42665	14645	57310	123842	63402	17155	80557	159021	50.66
1808	53378	16547	69925	134405	118525	20824	139349	248213	56.14
1809	66568	11230	77798	145170	112279	23757	136036	278455	
					11244	251	11495	15309	48.07
1810	91978	15930	107908	184717	127937	19614	147551	278983	
					8566	109	8675	13893	51.23
1811	113782	15214	128996	274037	122414	14490	136904	272155	
					5003	83	5086	6855	50.76
1812	153612	18583	172195	287704	160842	23001	183843[124]	342193	
					2732	63	2795	6007	52.50
1813	130024	17666	147690	276057	264702	20140	284842	423381	
					5852	30	5882	6886	67.07
1814	154392	17733	172125	298229	278775	22278	301053	457214	
					6685	28	6713	7726	65.79
1815	(120000)	(15000)	(135000)	(316032)	213966	16868	230834	391276	
					3368	11	3379	4131	59.14

122 Assignat roubles. From 1809 onwards that part of actual expenditure (top line) disbursed in silver roubles is indicated separately (lower line). The percentages in col. 9 are calculated on the basis of the silver value, using the bourse rate of conversion for each year as given by Shtorkh, "Materialy dlia istorii gosudarstvennykh denezhnykh znakov" (see note 71), 812.

	(1)	(2)	(3)	(4)	(5)	(6)	(7)	(8)	(9)
1816	c167675	16000	183675	344719	c234380	19590	c253970	428105	
					1536	3	1539	6889	56.73
1817	d155834	21247	177081	362996	d178979	23220	d202199	438424	
					1069	105	1174	9111	43.33
1818	171251	22676	193927	406919	188851	23151	212002	443286	
					1480	30	1510	3446	47.38
1819	170740	23255	193995	438486	188430	26188	214618	475950	
					1729	248	1977	3681	46.75
1820	179939	23117	203056	458068	197771	25837	223608	499804	
					1549	22	1571	3386	44.47
1821	182339	23287	205626	454567	204404	27281	231685	482319	
					1678	109	1787	4773	47.30
1822	186489	26786	213275	452203	185889	25216	211105	456471	
					1595	115	1710	5098	45.38
1823	178019	23634	201653	443567	195556	26717	222273	479148	
					1938	80	2018	5952	45.43
1824	161880	23121	185001	419412	157236	23013	180249	417027	
					1356	59	1415	6662	41.48
1825	151834	21951	173785	392998	155202	24225	179427	413460	
					1405	28	1433	9628	40.80

Sources:

1789–1796: Chechulin, *Ocherki*, 307, 314–315 (recalculated). These are properly speaking not appropriations but estimates based on tax receipts and other revenue.

1797–1825: Kulomzin, ed., *Finansovye dokumenty*, passim; cf. *Ministerstvo Finansov, 1802–1902*, Vol. 1, 620–621.

The sums listed under Appropriations are those initially projected in the budget estimates [*rospis'*]; those for Expenditure are the figures reported for actual fulfilment [*vypolnenie*] of these estimates. Sums unspent and carried over into the following year have been disregarded. Figures in brackets are rough approximations only.

---

123 To the figures for total armed forces expenditure should be added a proportion of Interior ministry disbursements on State contruction works, supplies for certain magazines and "established military commands." In 1806–1811, when (partial) figures for this expenditure are given, it totaled respectively 3, 2, 1, 2.1, 1.22, and 2.1 percent of total armed forces expenditure. This has not been taken into account when calculating the figure in col. 9. Prior to 1799 pensions paid to military personnel were not included in the military budget; at that time they appear to have amounted to about 1.8 million roubles per annum.

124 In March 1815 General Barclay de Tolly reported military expenditure incurred by the war in Europe in 1812–1814 at 155.5 million (assignat) roubles: "Chego stoila voina s frantsuzami 1812, 1813 i 1814 gg.", in: *RA* (1874) pt. 2, col. 735. This evidently excluded "ordinary" military expenditure. The figure was later amended slightly to 157.5 million roubles. A. Ia. Pecherin, *Istoricheskii obzor rospisei gosudarstvennykh dokhodov i raskhodov s 1803 po 1843 god vkliuchitel'no* (St. Petersburg, 1896), 54 ff., offers the following data for the period 1812–May 1814 inclusive:

a   Special war allocations.

b   "No exact figures available for distribution of expenditure between government departments":
Ministerstvo Finansov, 1802–1902, Vol. 1, 620–621; cf. ibid., 167, for different estimates.

c   Excludes (also in subsequent years) appropriations for the army of the Kingdom of Poland,
which in priciple were covered from local revenue. This expense was put at 17.5 million roubles
in 1816.

d   Includes appropriations for the military colonies, which in 1820–1825 were running at about
3 million roubles per annum.

	Army	*Navy*
according to estimates	438 028	53 982
surplus to estimates	221 411	8 213

| total expenditure | 659 439 | 62 195 |
| *grand total* | 721 634 million (assignat) roubles | |

P. I. Liashchenko, *Istoriia narodnogo khoziaistva SSSR*, Vol. 1 (Moscow, 1956) 449, states
that if ordinary expenditure is added to de Tolly's figures the total would amount to 884
million (assignat) roubles or 25.5 percent more than our figures. He also offers the following
data, without indication of source:

1810   col. 4   282 m. r., equivalent to 71 m. r. (silver)
1812   col. 5   172 m. r.

125 A. Ia. Pecherin curiously makes no reference to Kulomzin's work, although his own study is
     based on the same official papers. He offers (92) different figures for total actual expenditure
     (but without substantiation or details of the armed forces component), as follows (variations
     from our col. 8 in brackets):

1803	114 302	(+ 4.47%)	1813	444 062	(+ 4.88%)
1804	123 227	(+ 0.87%)	1814	482 824	(+ 5.60%)
1805	129 329	(+ 3.09%)	1815	406 022	(+ 3.77%)
1806	125 468	(+ 2.46%)	1816	379 462	(-11.36%)
1807	162 020	(+ 1.89%)	1817	397 070	(- 9.43%)
1808	250 542	(+ 0.94%)	1818	426 761	(- 3.73%)
1809	279 713	(+ 0.45%)	1819	489 209	(+ 2.79%)
1810	282 453	(+ 1.24%)	1820	504 214	(+ 0.88%)
1811	321 253	(+18.04%)	1821	498 652	(+ 3.39%)
1812	385 979	(+12.80%)	1822	474 405	(+ 3.93%)
			1823	449 837	(- 6.12%)

The substantial differences for 1811–1812 and 1816 remain to be explained.

CHAPTER 10

From the Pistol to the Pen:
The Military Memoir as a Source on
the Social History of Pre-Reform Russia

I

Although state service was the chief factor in the lives of male members of the élite in early Imperial Russia, as it had been also in the Muscovite era, we still know remarkably little about it. Recent studies have enlarged our understanding of the *dvoriane's* role as landowners, officials and incipient intellectuals,[1] but their service in the armed forces has been comparatively neglected, and as regards that of commoners, as soldiers and noncommissioned officers (NCOs), we are even more in the dark. In Europe generally military sociology, as a branch of historical study, is still relatively undeveloped and attempts to apply its insights to Russia are only just beginning.[2] Soviet work on military history has hitherto been rather conventional in scope and approach, but there are some signs of change in this respect.[3]

One source which can throw light on the Russian officer's service experience and

---

1 M. Confino, *Domaines et seigneurs en Russie vers la fin du XVIIIᵉ siècle* (Paris, 1963); R. E. Jones, *The Emancipation of the Russian Nobility* (Princeton, 1973); R. Rexhauser, *Besitzverhältnisse des russischen Adels im 18. Jhd.: historische Fragen, methodische Probleme* (Erlangen, 1971); H.-J. Torke, "Das russische Beamtentum in der I. Hälfte des 19. Jhd.," *FOEG,* 13 (1967), 7–345; W. M. Pintner and D. K. Rowney, eds., *Russian Officialdom: the Bureaucratization of Russian Society from the Seventeenth to the Twentieth Century* (Chapel Hill, 1980); S. M. Troitskii, *Russkii absoliutizm i dvorianstvo v XVIII v.: formirovanie biurokratii* (Moscow, 1974); M. Raeff, *The Origins of the Russian Intelligentsia: the Eighteenth-Century Nobility* (New York, 1966).

2 F. König *et al.*, eds., *Beiträge zur Militärsoziologie* (Cologne-Opladen, 1968); B. Abrahamsson, *Military Professionalization and Political Power* (Göteborg, 1971); R. Hellie, *Enserfment and Military Change in Muscovy* (Chicago, 1971); J. S. Curtiss, *The Russian Army under Nicholas I, 1825–1855* (Durham, N. C., 1965). On developments in Europe generally see A. Corvisier, *Armées et sociétés en Europe de 1494 à 1789* (Paris, 1976).

3 L. G. Beskrovnyi, *Russkaia armiia i flot v XVIII v.: ocherki* (Moscow, 1958); idem, *Russkaia armiia i flot v XIX v.: voenno-ekonomicheskii potentsial Rossii* (Moscow, 1973); M. D. Rabinovich, "Sotsial'noe proiskhozhdenie i imushchestvennoe polozhenie ofitserov reguliarnoi

outlook is the military memoir. The present article is based in part upon more than sixty such autobiographical works. Most of them are journal articles rather than book-length monographs and were published in the late Imperial period, although some appeared earlier and one saw the light of day as recently as 1966. In his very valuable bibliography of Russian memoir literature P. A. Zaionchkovskii lists no fewer than 240 items relating to the land forces in the eighteenth and early nineteenth centuries.[4] This may make our selection seem rather limited. However, the vast majority of military autobiographers wrote only about their campaign experiences and the more professional aspects of their careers and had little or nothing to say of broader interest; moreover, some of our sources were omitted from Zaionchkovskii's list, probably because they were not thought sufficiently important. Since state service was not sharply differentiated between the military and civil branches until the early nineteenth century, any selection is bound to be somewhat arbitrary. We have excluded accounts by foreigners who were not in regular service and by well-known personalities such as C. H. von Manstein, A. T. Bolotov, G. R. Derzhavin, L. N. Engel'gardt, F. F. Vigel', I. I. Lazhechnikov or N. I. Pirogov, whose careers were not primarily in the military, but whose memoirs sometimes have a bearing upon our subject.

It should be made plain at the outset that this type of material suffers from serious deficiencies. It ought to be treated only as an auxiliary source to flesh out the dry bones of official histories and legislative compendia. Its quantity does not make up for its qualitative shortcomings. In the Reform era in particular the writing of reminiscences seems to have become a regular pastime for retired officers with ample leisure and some pretension to literary talent. Their object was to instruct or entertain readers from their own social milieu. Few authors consulted documents or attempted to produce works of scholarship, and so their accounts tend to be anecdotal and superficial. Moreover, they dealt gingerly, if at all, with matters likely to discredit the army or the political establishment. These writers were, almost by definition, men who had been professionally successful; most of them had attained senior rank.[5] They and their publishers had to be ever mindful of censorship requirements, which were unreasonably strict: as late as the 1890s passages were excised from the work of

russkoi armii v kontse Severnoi voiny," in N. I. Pavlenko *et al.*, eds., *Rossiia v period re-form Petra I* (Moscow, 1973), 133–71; idem, *Sud'ba sluzhilykh liudei "starykh sluzhb" i odnodvortsev v period formirovaniia reguliarnoi russkoi armii v nachale XVIII st. Avtoreferat dissertatsii* (Moscow, 1953).

4 P. A. Zaionchkovskii, *Istoriia dorevoliutsionnoi Rossii v dnevnikakh i vospominaniiakh. An-notirovannyi ukazatel' knig i publikatsii v zhurnalakh*, I: *XV–XVIII vv.*, II, part I: *1801–1856* (Moscow, 1976–1977). Few manuscripts have remained unpublished: see S. V. Zhito-mirskii, ed., *Vospominaniia i dnevniki XVIII–XX vv.: ukazatel' rukopisei* (Moscow, 1976).

5 They have disappointingly little to say about their men, and only three pieces were writ-ten by nonofficers: I. M. Minaev, "Vospominaniia Ivana Men'shogo, 1806–1849," *RS*, 10 (1874), 46–59, who is revealing on recruitment procedure; P. N. Nazarov, "Zapiski sol-data Pamfilova Nazarova, v inochestve Mitrofana, 1792–1839 gg.," *RS*, 22 (1878), 529–56; [I. Zagorodnikov], "Dnevnik russkogo soldata, vziatogo v plen pri Bomarzunde v 1854 g.," *RS*, 80 (1893), 185–212, who describes his captivity in England.

one officer who described critically conditions in the army a whole century earlier.[6] Indeed, military autobiographers may be said to have internalized these controls in their desire to avoid crossing the boundary of the permissible. The limits were relaxed during the early years of Alexander II's reign, when there was a flurry of *oblichitel'naia literatura*, and again after the 1905 revolution; but in the latter period writers were of course chiefly concerned with the post-Reform era.

For all these reasons military memoirs tend to reflect official thinking and to adhere to a stereotyped pattern both in subject matter and in the way it is treated. To be sure, criticism of the regime could be ventilated indirectly by attributing defects to a single discredited individual, such as A. A. Arakcheev, and some authors published their works abroad, which gave them a greater measure of freedom.[7] But all in all Beskrovnyi's severe judgement on the value of this type of source material for conventional military history holds good also for Ruddian social history:

> Memoir literature is characterized by a high degree of subjectivism. As a rule historical facts and events are treated . . . in a subjective and clearly tendentious fashion. Their accuracy is greater where the author describes matters that were important to himself. Diaries are not as a rule intended for publication, and therefore judgements and characterizations in them are more expressive and sincere, revealing directly the author's sympathies and antipathies. But memoirs designed to appear in print have generally been toned down. Writers refrain from giving their personal views and aspire to an "official objectivism." They often appeared many years after the events described, and so contain errors in regard to dates and figures; or else the writer changed his mind in the interim and judged events from his new standpoint. Nevertheless memoirs are of extremely great value, since they give the military historian additional material.[8]

II

We may first give a general idea of the chronological scope of this material and of the principal authors involved. In our view the first Russian military memorialist was V. A. Nashchokin (1707–61) whose reminiscences, written in 1758–59, cover the period from 1719, when the author enrolled as a soldier in the Belgorod infantry regiment, to the date of writing, by which time he held the rank of lieutenant-general.[9] Much of his service was in the élite Izmailovskii guards regiment.

6 See our "L'élitisme militaire en Russie à la fin du XVIIIe siècle: le témoignage du comte de Langeron," *Slovo* [Paris], 3 (1980), 165–76.

7 H. von Hansen, *Zwei Kriegsjahre. Erinnerungen eines alten Soldaten an den Feldzug gegen die Türken 1828 und den polnischen Aufstand 1831* (Berlin, 1881); *Mémoires du général-major russe baron de Löwenstern (1776–1858)*, publiés d'après le manuscrit original et annotés par M.-H. Weil, 2 vols. (Paris, 1903) (cited as Löwenstern, *Mémoires*).

8 L. G. Beskrovnyi, *Ocherki po istochnikovedeniiu voennoi istorii Rossii* (Moscow, 1957), 212; cf. V. S. Ikonnikov, *Opyt russkoi istoriografii* (Kiev, 1891), I, part i, 58–63 (for Russian memoirs in general).

9 D. I. Iazykov, ed., "Zapiski Vasiliia Aleksandrovicha Nashchokina, generala vremen elizav-

Two early Ukrainian diarists were M. Khanenko (1693–1760) and Iu. A. Markovych (1696–1770), whose writings cover the periods 1727–53 and 1717–34 respectively.[10] A Baltic German author whose work deserves to be better known is G. E. von Shtrandman (1742–1803); from his manuscript—based on a diary and therefore more reliable—extracts have been published covering the period from 1769, when as a subaltern he served in the first of Catherine's Turkish wars, to 1780, when he was campaigning on the Kuban' in the rank of colonel.[11]

Three other men of non-Russian extraction whose reminiscences deal with the eighteenth-century army may be singled out. One was an anonymous Pole of French descent who entered Russian service in 1736 as a lieutenant, saw service on the Ukrainian line and had been appointed second major by 1752, when the extant portion of his manuscript breaks off; from internal evidence it was written some time before 1792.[12] S. S. Pishchevich (Piščević, 1731–?), a Hungarian Serb, describes graphically, if ungrammatically, the difficulties facing immigrant colonists in the upper Donets valley in the 1750s: at first, he says, they lived "like shipwrecked sailors on a desert island"; subsequently conditions improved slightly, but remained rough at least until the reforms of 1764, at which point his account breaks off.[13] A sequel is provided by his son, A. S. Pishchevich (1764–1805), who, as his literary style testifies, assimilated more successfully into the Russian environment. He describes his experiences in the Crimean campaign of 1783 and later in the Caucasus, as well as in the second Russo-Turkish war. While serving in the Caucasus Pishchevich junior was charged with corruption, court-martialed and deprived of his command over a squadron; this circumstance—which did not prevent him from later serving on such a tribunal himself!—enabled him to provide the first unofficial account of Russian military justice in action.[14] Despite its self-serving tone and stress on the more adventurous episodes in his career, his memoir has an unselfconscious directness lacking in many later works. It can stand comparison with that of his better known contemporary S. A. Tuchkov (1766–1839), who reached higher rank—that of lieutenant-general—and was one of the first Russian officers to develop broad cultural interests. Curiously, he too fell foul of the law (in 1812), but the episode is not

etinskikh," *RA*, 21 (1883), 2, 243–352 (cited as V. A. Nashchokin, "Zapiski"). Some would claim this honor for I. A. Zheliabuzhskii, whose *Dnevnye zapiski*, first published in 1840, cover the period 1682 to 1709; but his duties were as much civil as military.

10 D. Doroshenko, *Study of Ukrainian Historiography* (New York, 1957), 62.

11 N. K. von Shtrandman (contrib.), "Zapiski Gustava fon-Shtrandmana, 1724–1803," *RS*, 34 (1882), 289–318; 43 (1884), 55–86, 271–88 (cited as von Shtrandman, "Zapiski").

12 "Prevratnosti sud'by . . . Vospominaniia poliaka na russkoi sluzhbe v tsarstvovaniiakh Anny Ioannovny i Elizavety Petrovny. Perevod s neizdannoi rukopisi" (annotated by A. A. Chumikov), *RA* (1898), 4, 479–508.

13 N. A. Popov, ed., *Izvestie o pokhozhdenii Simeona Stepanovicha Pishchevicha, 1731–1785* (Moscow, 1884).

14 *Zhizn' A. S. Pishchevicha, im samim opisannaia, 1764–1805* (with a preface by N. Popov) (Moscow, 1885) (cited as Pishchevich, *Zhizn'*).

discussed in his memoirs, which reach only to 1808.[15] Tuchkov served against the Swedes and Poles and later in the Caucasus. Having prospered under Paul I, he was highly critical of his successor. This viewpoint was most unusual at the time and no doubt accounts for the hundred-year delay in publication of his manuscript.

At the turn of the century the spread of education among the Russian gentry led to the emergence of what has aptly been called a "military intelligentsia." The immediate stimulus to this development was the traumatic effect which Paul's brief but turbulent reign had on the officer corps. A fair number of those who suffered personally from his arbitrary rule, or were at least acquainted with its victims, have left impressions of this period; but the value of these records is limited by their obvious tendentiousness.[16] After 1801 the trickle of memoir literature swells considerably. Writers naturally concentrated their attention upon the great conflicts with the armies of Napoleon. For the 1812 campaign the personal accounts by such prominent figures as A. P. Ermolov or K. F. von Toll are of less interest for our purposes than those written by humbler participants. The memoirs of D. V. Davydov (1784–1839), the partisan leader (and poet),[17] and S. N. Glinka (1776–1847),[18] who served in the militia, are fairly well known; much can also be gleaned from the reminiscences of A. B. Chicherin (1793–1813) and A. B. Antonovskii, both of whom were only subalterns. The former text (written in French) came to light quite recently and has been well edited by L. G. Beskrovnyi;[19] the latter appeared in a collection of autobiographical accounts published at the beginning of this century.[20]

Several officers who took part in the campaigns into central and western Europe have left impressions of their experiences. The first to be published, a rambling account in twelve parts, was by F. N. Glinka, younger brother of the man just mentioned; his account of the Habsburg domains in 1805 is fresher and more informative than that of Germany or France several years later.[21] So far as the army's inner state during the latter campaigns is concerned, perhaps the most revealing autobiography is that by N. N. Murav'ev (-Karskii), who went on to fame in the Crimean War.[22] He

---

15 K. A. Voenskii, ed., *Zapiski Sergeia Alekseevicha Tuchkova, 1766–1808* (St. Petersburg, 1908) (cited as Tuchkov, *Zapiski.*) Tuchkov was acquitted of the charge, laid by Prince Radziwill, of permitting his troops to loot (*ibid.*, vii).

16 For an evaluation of memoirs on this period, see M. V. Klochkov, *Ocherki pravitel'stvennoi deiatel'nosti vremen Pavla I* (Petrograd, 1916), 1–46. Among the best: N. A. Sablukov, "Zapiski," in *Tsareubiistvo 11 marta 1801 g. Zapiski uchastnikov i sovremennikov* (St. Petersburg, 1908), 1–105.

17 The Soviet edition by V. Orlov, *Voennye zapiski* (Moscow, 1940), is to be preferred to earlier texts, which were emended and curtailed.

18 S. N. Glinka, *Zapiski* (St. Petersburg, 1908).

19 *Dnevnik Aleksandra Chicherina, 1812–1813* (Moscow, 1966) (cited as Chicherin, *Dnevnik*).

20 A. B. Antonovskii, "Zapiski," in V. Kharkevich, ed., *1812 g. v dnevnikakh, zapiskakh i vospominaniiakh sovremennikov* . . . (Vilna, 1900–1904), 3, 1–207.

21 F. N. Glinka, *Pis'ma russkogo ofitsera o Pol'she, Avstriiskikh vladeniiakh, Prussii i Frantsii* . . . (Moscow, 1815–16).

22 N. N. Murav'ev (-Karskii), "Zapiski," *RA*, 1885–1889, 1891, 1894–1895; for a full biblio-

shared, up to a point, the critical frame of mind which became common at this time among the more intelligent officers and found expression in the formation of secret societies after 1816. Almost automatically one refers to these men as "Decembrists," although this label conveys revolutionary associations that are not always warranted since there was a great range of opinions among them on all questions of the day. The memoirs by serving officers that throw light on the growth of political opposition include those by I. D. Iakushkin, A. S. Gangeblov, I. I. Gorbachevskii, N. I. Lorer (Lohrer) and—despite its extreme brevity—A. M. Murav'ev.[23] These are best considered as a separate category within the "military memoir" genre. Published long after the events they describe, their standard of accuracy may often be faulted, but in this case there is ample information from other sources against which details can be checked.

This is not the case with those memorialists who, writing in the Reform era, gave more or less critical accounts of their experiences during Nicholas I's reign. For these writers it became almost obligatory, if they were to retain their self-respect, to dissociate themselves from the excesses that had characterized military life under the "iron tsar." One man who went considerably further than any of his comrades used an as yet undeciphered pseudonym, "Neizvestnyi" (Unknown); his account did not appear until 1894.[24] Others who adopted a critical stance were G. D. Shcherbachev and I. I. Venediktov,[25] both of whom developed liberal views that led them to transfer to the civil service, in 1856 and 1847 respectively, where they could eventually promote progressive causes. Their accounts are objective and credible, if less than complete; the same may be said of that of M. Ia. Ol'shevskii, which covers only his experiences in an élite military school.[26] Another record of such an upbringing which is much less plausible is that of M. A. Markov,[27] while a favorable view of Nicholas's militaristic system is given by D. G. Kolokol'tsov;[28] all these three men eventually reached general's rank.

---

graphical reference see Zaionchkovskii, *op. cit.*, 145.

23 S. Ia. Shtraykh, ed., *Zapiski, stat'i, pis'ma dekabrista I. D. Iakushkina* (Moscow-Leningrad, 1951); A. S. Gangeblov, "Kak ia popal v dekabristy i chto za tem posledoval," *RA*, 6 (1886), 181–280; I. I. Gorbachevskii, *Zapiski. Pis'ma*, ed. B. E. Syroechkovskii *et al.* (Moscow, 1963); *Zapiski dekabrista N. I. Lorera*, ed. M. N. Pokrovskii (Moscow, 1931) (with commentary by M. V. Nechkina; cited as N. I. Lorer, *Zapiski*; A. M. Murav'ev, *Zapiski*, tr. S. Ia. Shtraykh (Petrograd, 1922).

24 "Za mnogo let: vospominaniia neizvestnogo, 1844–1884," *RS*, 81 (1894), 172–90; 82 (1894), 109–34; 83 (1894), 67–80. (Cited as Neizvestnyi, "Za mnogo let").

25 G. D. Shcherbachev, "Dvenadtsat' let molodosti: vospominaniia," *RA* (1890), 1, 87–130; (1890), 2, 215–284; (1891), 1, 29–76 (under title "Iz vospominanii," indicating censor's cuts); I. I. Venediktov, "Za 60 let: vospominaniia, 1820–1894," *RS*, 127 (1905), 253–85, 580–605; 128 (1905), 39–79, 332–50.

26 M. Ia. Ol'shevskii, "Pervyi Kadetskii Korpus v 1826–1833 gg.: vospominaniia," *RS*, 49 (1886), 63–95.

27 M. A. Markov, "Vospominaniia starogo invalida o sluzhbe leib-gvardii v Pavlovskom polku, 1828–1835," *RS*, 68 (1890), 81–135.

28 D. G. Kolokol'tsov, "Leib-gvardii Preobrazhenskii polk v vospominaniiakh ego starogo

Apart from the military schools and regimental service in peace and war there were two other subjects which attracted many of these writers: the prolonged struggle in the Caucasus and the military colonies. The former involved only a tiny segment of the Russian army but brought these men into contact with an unfamiliar Oriental milieu and one in which the usual rigid service relationships were somewhat relaxed. Prince A. I. Gagarin, a divisional commander, gives a vivid picture of the administrative abuses that characterized this colonial war in an account which for obvious reasons could not appear until after the 1905 revolution.[29] Writers were freer to express themselves critically about the military colonies since this unfortunate experiment was abandoned in 1856–8.[30]

Surveying the genre, it must be said that even the most outspoken military memorialists were far from adopting a radical position; the Decembrist generation does not really constitute an exception.[31] They were "establishment figures" whose outlook was traditional, nationalistic and above all service-oriented. Their loyalty to the monarchy (or perhaps one should say to the monarch, since they thought in personal rather than institutional terms) was rooted not only in their privileged social position but also in their cultural isolation. The pre-Reform Russian army officer belonged to a militarized caste cut off from the rest of the population by a way of life in which violence and brutality were the norm, where discipline was maintained by barbarous means, and where the wider society was visualized in terms of the mechanical subordination that obtained within the military hierarchy itself.

III

Even after the celebrated edict of February 18, 1762, which exempted the *dvoriane* from obligatory State service a large proportion of them—just how large it is difficult to ascertain[32]—continued to enlist in the armed forces. Tuchkov noted that in the 1780s "few gentry served in junior civil service positions, whereas almost all of

---

ofitsera s 1831-go po 1846 g." *RS*, 38 (1883), 273–310, 593–622; 40 (1883), 329–54; 69 (1891), 635–74; also 143 (1910) (cited as Kolokol'tsov, "Vospominaniia").

29 A. I. Gagarin, "Zapiski o Kavkaze," *VS*, 287 (1906): 2, 25–38; 288 (1906), 3, 15–32; 4, 13–32; cf.the section of Murav'ev-Karskii's memoirs in *RA* (1895), 3, 313–56.

30 Cf. A. F. Ushakov, "Kholernyi bunt v Staroi Rusi," *RS*, 9 (1874), 145–62; A. K. Gribbe, "Kholernyi bunt v Novgorodskikh voennykh poseleniiakh," *RS*, 17 (1876), 513–36; N. E. Matveev (contrib.), "Bunt v Staroi Rusi v 1831 g.: rasskaz ochevidtsa," *RS*, 25 (1879), 389–98 and other materials in M. I. Semevskii, ed., *Materialy k noveishei otechestvennoi istorii: graf Arakcheev i voennye poseleniia* (Moscow, 1871).

31 Colonel P. I. Pestel', who paid for his views with his life, was untypical. Admittedly radicals would have been less able or willing to write memoirs, even "for the drawer'"; however, the exception that proves the rule is N. A. Mombelli, one of the "Petrashevtsy," whose diary for May-November 1847 shows him to be mentally unbalanced: cf. his "Zapiski" in V. Desnitskii, ed., *Delo petrashevtsev* (Moscow-Leningrad, 1937), I, 287–315.

32 For a discussion of these difficulties see Jones, *Emancipation*, 43; and W. M. Pintner, "Russia as a Great Power, 1709–1856," Kennan Institute Occasional paper, no. 33 (Washington, 1976), 34.

them were in the army."[33] An observer of Nicolaevan Russia noted that "the gentry joined the service very willingly since it was more attractive in many respects: a military uniform, especially if one were in the guards, and a military rank gave one a social status unattainable in any other way."[34] Shcherbachev confirms this testimony: "in the 1840s all young nobles sought to serve in the army, because it was almost exclusively in the forces that one could make a service career, for all the higher offices of state . . . were given to military men who were more in the Sovereign's eye than civil officials."[35] Yet it was precisely at this time that the civil bureaucracy was emancipating itself from the military influences that had shrouded it since the age of Peter the Great![36]

The decision to join the army was taken for a variety of reasons: family tradition, personal preference, state of health and sheer economic necessity. But above all it depended on opportunity: one needed a vacancy—and a patron. S. N. Glinka probably reflected a widespread opinion when he wrote scathingly of the "spoiled mothers' sons" who in the 1790s, although holding officer's rank, did not serve because there was no room for them in their regiments and chose to remain at home: "without having smelled powder, they hastened off to hunt hare . . . and were afraid to stick their heads out from their rustic retreats to fight for the Fatherland."[37] He was referring to the supernumeraries (*sverkhkomplektnye*) who, it should be added in fairness, were not to blame for their equivocal situation; Glinka admits that they did not draw pay and that the army at that time had more than enough officers for its needs. Moreover, despite his patriotic effusions Glinka himself chose to retire from the service in 1800, aged only 24, when he discovered that he had "an inborn distaste for blood," and thereafter directed his talents to the field of journalism.[38]

H. von Hansen, who came from a relatively poor Baltic German family, joined the army in 1821 as a volunteer aged only 14, but found promotion to officer's rank slow for one of his condition; he would willingly have transferred to the civil service, but realized that "without a fortune or patronage (*Protektion*) such a decision could have had the most sorry consequences for me";[39] he had no choice but to soldier on in a chasseur regiment in dismal provincial Poltava until war against the Turks set him on the upward course that ultimately earned him general's epaulettes.

Most officers must have been obliged to begin service in the ranks, as von Hansen did—and as had been Peter I's original intention. That this was so is stated by von

33 Tuchkov, *Zapiski*, 14.

34 M., "Neskol'ko myslei otnositel'no proizvodstva v ofitsery nizhnikh chinov," *VS*, 30 (1863), 405.

35 Shcherbachev, "Dvenadtsat' let," 87, 123; for an analysis of this phenomenon see W. B. Lincoln, "The Composition of the Imperial Russian State Council under Nicholas I," *CASS*, 10 (1976), 369–81, and "The Ministers of Nicholas I," *RR*, 34 (1975), 308–23.

36 Pintner and Rowney, *Russian Officialdom, passim.*

37 Glinka, *Zapiski*, 136–37.

38 *Ibid.*, 184.

39 Von Hansen, *Zwei Kriegsjahre*, 32.

Toll, whose father commenced his career in this way; his more famous son, however, took a different route. He was enrolled in the Cadet Corps at the age of five, and on graduation was singled out by Paul I for competence in draftsmanship; the tsar appointed him a lieutenant in the so-called "Quartermaster's section," which then did duty for a general staff.[40] Many other writers took a privileged path to officer status. Such individuals would typically either attend one of the military schools or else be educated at home; if they served in the ranks at all, they did so only nominally or for a short term; appointment as adjutant would bring them to the notice of some august personage and assure them almost automatically of a "brilliant" career.

The all-important role of patronage is discussed quite frankly in some of these accounts, especially the earlier ones. When the Crimean War broke out, the future historian S. M. Zagoskin, then aged 20, decided not to enlist because he had no "influential uncle" (*diadushka*) whose orderly he might become.[41] Much earlier A. S. Pishchevich began his education in a school for engineering cadets; in 1783, when the boy had reached the age of 18, Potemkin, who knew his father, found him a place in a dragoon regiment of which he was chief (*shef*); Potemkin wanted to make him one of his numerous adjutants but—a characteristic detail—Pishchevich could not afford to take up the post and to his dismay another lad was appointed in his place.[42] More fortunate were the twenty-year-old A. K. Denisov, who became Potemkin's adjutant in the same year,[43] and S. I. Mosolov, a captain's son who around 1765 was introduced to Field-Marshal P. S. Saltykov, under whom his father had served; he was sent as a soldier to the Arkhangel'sk regiment and after a mere four weeks promoted to junior ensign; his widowed mother thereupon promptly took him back to express his gratitude to Saltykov in person.[44] His subsequent progress seems to have been fairly slow, however: he served as adjutant in 1770 and became a lieutenant in 1773; the ranks of captain followed in 1774, second major in 1780, first major in 1786, lieutenant-colonel in 1793, colonel in 1794, and major-general in 1797. (He seems to have written his memoirs with his *formuliarnyi spisok* set proudly before him.)

A practise which, though familiar, still awaits thorough study is that of juvenile enlistment, notably in privileged guards regiments. Although Catherine II ruled that it should be permitted only with her express authorization in each case, it was still sufficiently widespread to pose a problem as late as 1817.[45] It developed in Elizabeth's

---

40 *Denkwürdigkeiten aus dem Leben des kaiserlichen russischen Generals von der Infanterie Carl Friedrich Grafen von Toll*, ed. T. von Bernhardi (Leipzig, 1856–1858), I, 3, 14.

41 S. M. Zagoskin, "Vospominaniia," *IV*, 80 (1900), 60; he later served in the militia.

42 Pishchevich, *Zhizn'*, 22–6.

43 A. K. Denisov, "Zapiski Donskogo atamana Denisova, 1763–1841," *RS*, 10 (1874), 22.

44 "Zapiski otstavnogo general-maiora Sergeia Ivanovicha Mosolova. Istoriia moei zhizni" (hereafter cited as Mosolov, "Zapiski"), *RA* (1905), 1, 125–6.

45 *PSZ*, XVI, no. 11771 (8 Mar. 1763); N. Dubrovin, *A. V. Suvorov sredi preobrazovatelei Ekaterininskoi armii* (St. Petersburg, 1886), 13; D. F. Maslovskii, *Materialy po istorii voennogo iskusstva v Rossii*, 2: *Tsarstvovanie Ekateriny II* (St. Petersburg, 1894), 43; M. Sokolovskii

reign. In 1749 her favorite K. G. Razumovskii celebrated an occasion in Nashchokin's family by promoting his three sons, aged 14, 7 and 6, to the rank of *fur'er* and corporal; four years later the youngest children had become sergeants, and when 16 or 17 years old entered service in their father's regiment as ensigns.[46] Tuchkov's observations on this practise, cited in several general works, appear to be exaggerated: if he was indeed, as he says, dressed up in an NCO's uniform at the tender age of four and so "turned into a little Prussian."[47] this was probably some whim of his father's. P. M. Volkonskii states that he was enrolled as a sergeant in the Preobrazhenskii regiment on the day of his baptism (in 1776), at the request of an uncle in the service, and given a document entitling him to "home leave" until he had finished his studies;[48] at the age of 16 he wanted to see actual service, got himself posted to another regiment, and within a matter of months was an ensign; two years later he was an adjutant in his original regiment.

Such laxity was, however, characteristic of Catherine's last years;[49] it would be much less usual under her militaristic successors. In 1807 M. M. Muromtsev, on leaving the family "nest," had to take a stiff examination at the Cadet Corps and instead of studying there was sent straight off to the front as an NCO; he was obliged "to carry the standard and to march on foot" because his commander thought him a spoiled noble boy, and two years passed before he became an officer.[50]

Promotion was more rapid in the army than in the civil service, for obvious reasons: it was the correlate of the greater physical risk one ran. How long on average did one remain in each rank: was Mosolov's progress (referred to above) typical? What criteria were employed when filling vacancies? These questions could be answered definitively only after undertaking a thorough examination of service records, but the general picture is fairly clear from the published sources. To use the contemporary jargon, under Catherine *vysluga* mattered more than *zasluga*: that is to say, seniority rather than merit was the normal criterion. The routine procedure was that each army division (a purely administrative unit at this time) prepared a single list of all subaltern officers who had served for the specified term in their present rank, and the divisional commander allocated vacancies to those who were at the head of the queue; for "staff" officers (major and above) and other senior men a similar list was compiled, on an army-wide basis, in the War College and appointments were made by the Sovereign. For each individual concerned a testimonial (*attestat*) was required, in a stereotyped form, confirming his worthiness for promotion; this was

(contrib.), "Iz materialov po istorii russkoi konnitsy, II: Proekt o proizvodstve v ofitsery za otlichie a ne za vyslugu (1817 g.)," *VS*, 280 (1904), 12, 179.

46 Nashchokin, "Zapiski," 304, 309, 323, 346.

47 Tuchkov, *Zapiski*, 3.

48 "Rasskazy kniazia P. M. Volkonskogo, zapisannye s ego slov A. V. Viskovatovym v ianvare 1845 g.," *RS*, 16 (1876), 177.

49 Cf. the similar case of Löwenstern, *Mémoires*, I, 22–26.

50 "Vospominaniia Matveia Matveevicha Muromtseva," *RA*, 1 (1890), 66–9. (Cited as Muromtsev, "Vospominaniia").

supposed to be signed by all officers of the same rank in his unit and then by his superiors.[51] Those who were passed over, but knew of some vacancy for which they considered themselves qualified, might submit petitions, mentioning cases known to them where less senior men had been promoted—a practise which shows that the Muscovite tradition of *mestnichestvo* was not quite dead![52]

The literature suggests that the system did not work well. S. M. Rzhevskii, author of a brief but frank memorandum, complained that the attestation procedure was a mere formality, since officers would sign whatever their colonel wanted for fear of receiving a bad testimonial themselves.[53] The selection procedure was also distorted by social prejudice. A well-informed foreign observer noted in 1810 that talented officers of modest means were aggrieved that their promotion was blocked by aristocratic young generals, so that it took 15 years to reach captain's rank.[54] Certainly the well-connected could reach high rank with remarkable speed. Paskevich was a major-general at 28. Of two sons of Field-Marshal M. F. Kamenskii (1738–1809) the elder became a major-general when aged 26 and the younger when only 22—both appointments being made under Paul I.[55] M. A. Katenin is said to have risen from lieutenant to major-general within a few years by securing appointment as adjutant to a grand duke and then marrying the sister of the emperor's ADC.[56] Cadet Corps graduates posted to units as subalterns "took away promotion chances from ensigns," and when guardsmen joined line regiments they might rise by as many as three grades.[57]

Nevertheless the root of the "promotion problem" seems to have been not social discrimination but natural irregularities in the availability of jobs. The casualty rate fluctuated, of course; so did the size of the "reserve army" of supernumeraries, and thus the labor market was volatile. Unfortunately no military writer seems to have recorded his experiences as a supernumerary, although von Shtrandman does note the death in action of one of them (1770), from which it is clear that some supernumeraries would accompany their units into the combat zone, no doubt in hope of winning quick

51 "Zapiska grafa S. R. Vorontsova o russkoi voiske, predstavlennaia imp. Aleksandru Pavlovichu v 1802 g.," *AKV*, 10 (*Bumagi grafa S. R. Vorontsova*, III) (Moscow, 1876), 487; D. F. Maslovskii, *Materialy*, 3, 10; *PSZ*, XVI, no. 11770 (3 Mar. 1763); A. W. von Hupel, *Beschreibung der Russisch-Kaiserlichen Armee nebst andern kürzern Aufsätzen . . .* (Riga, 1782; rpt. Hanover-Döhren, 1972), 58, 95; L. I. Sazonov, "Attestat," *VE*, vol. 3, 247–9.

52 TsGVIA, fond Voenno-uchenogo arkhiva 1349, delo 300 (Raporty gen. Levanidova o sostoianii voisk, 1796 g.), ll. 19–20 (petition by Capt. D. R. Kossovskii), 23 (Capt. V. A. Kuzmin).

53 M. Rzhevskii (contrib.), "O russkoi armii vo vtoroi polovine Ekaterininskogo tsarstvovaniia," *RA* (1879), 3, 361.

54 C. von Plotho, *Über die Entstehung, die Fortschritte und die gegenwärtige Verfassung der russischen Armee, doch insbesondere von der Infanterie* (Berlin, 1811), 75.

55 Stcherbatow, *Le feld-maréchal prince Paskévitsch: sa vie politique et militaire, d'après des documents inédits* (St. Petersburg, 1888–1890), I, 81; *RBS*, vol. VIII, 423, 439.

56 Kolokol'tsov, "Vospominaniia," 618, 620.

57 Tuchkov, *Zapiski*, 124. Officially there was a *two*-grade difference at this time between the guards and the army.

preferment, instead of staying at home or seeking alternative employment.[58]

Those who had served in a given rank for a certain term were automatically promoted by one grade on discharge.[59] This created problems if they subsequently returned to active duty, for their comrades would resent the unfair advantage they had gained; if they had earned further promotion in the interim, the sense of grievance would be enhanced. Mosolov complains that one of his superiors, a Pole named Szenbek who was allegedly very corrupt, retired in 1799 as a major-general to avoid active service and returned as a lieutenant-general when the war was over; but his information is not corroborated.[60] In 1812, when many retired officers came back to the colors, they were generously treated: F. N. Glinka got his old rank of lieutenant (after some inconvenience as his testimonial had been lost through enemy action); L. A. Naryshkin, who had spent the intervening years at court, was promoted from lieutenant to captain; and even Löwenstern, who had seen service with the French and whose loyalty was suspect, received his former rank of major—which did not prevent him complaining of discrimination for years thereafter.[61] Under Nicholas I the rule was that on reentering the forces one lost any seniority gained elsewhere,[62] so that this particular grievance seems to have been eliminated.

Temporary leave was provided for in Peter I's military statute (1716), and in the period of retrenchment after his death as many as two-thirds of serving officers were sent home.[63] At first furlough was granted by the central authorities, but by mid-century controls had been relaxed: in the 1750s the elder Pishchevich obtained four months' leave from his divisional commander, and in 1783 his son was given three months' leave by his colonel.[64] Our anonymous Pole was twice denied leave (1740, 1752), but this may have been because he wanted to go abroad.[65] Were leave applications in peacetime systematically denied, or was it just a matter of officers not applying because they could not afford to go? A number appear to have never received leave. Lieutenant Vasil'ev, the first Russian military diarist, who served in Poland, was able to visit relatives in Moscow only when he was sent there on an

58 Von Shtrandman, "Zapiski," 405; cf. von Hupel, *Beschreibung*, 130; *PSZ*, XXIII, no. 17149 (12 Sept. 1793), §7. Löwenstern was once a supernumerary (*Mémoires*, I, 73), but says nothing about the fact.

59 *PSZ*, XVII, no. 12552 (27 Jan. 1766) specified three years but this was later shortened to one: XXVII, no. 20358 (3 Aug. 1802).

60 Mosolov, "Zapiski," 148.

61 F. N. Glinka, *Pis'ma*, part IV, 102; "Vospominaniia L. A. Naryshkina," in V. Kharkevich, ed., *1812 god*, 2, 151; Löwenstern, *Mémoires*, I, 177; cf. S. I. Maevskii, "Moi vek, ili istoriia gen. Maevskogo, 1779–1848," *RS*, 8 (1873), 254.

62 C. A. Haillot, *Statistique militaire et recherches sur l'organisation et les institutions militaires des armées étrangères* (Paris, 1846), I, 342.

63 *PSZ*, VII, no. 5016.

64 N. A. Popov, ed., *Izvestie*, 484; Pishchevich, *Zhizn'*, 32. In the latter case this may have been because he was supernumerary; no clear distinction was drawn between the two types of absence.

65 "Prevratnosti sud'by," 493, 504.

official errand.[66] The well-informed von Hupel says that commanders would evade the formalities by entrusting subordinates with such welcome commissions.[67] During the Potemkin era it was relatively easy to absent oneself without permission,[68] and in 1806 E. F. Komarovskii, then deputy military governor of St. Petersburg, was allowed to go abroad by an informal arrangement with his superior without the fact being published in army orders;[69] but probably only the most favored could get away with this. There were frequent official complaints about officers overstaying leave terms by pretending to be ill,[70] but none of our informants, not surprisingly, admits to having done so.

Although from 1762 onward officers were in principle free to quit the armed forces whenever they wished in peacetime, in practise the state managed to protect its interests by keeping discharges under central control. Archival evidence from the 1790s suggests that it was not too difficult for senior officers to obtain discharge to attend to their private affairs, a reason commonly given in petitions;[71] but retirement was seen as a privilege rather than a right, and applicants had to surmount numerous administrative hurdles.[72] Again, it is not clear how often requests for discharge were refused. In 1795 Denisov, then a thirty-one-year-old lieutenant-colonel in a Don cossack regiment, came to the capital intending to apply for discharge, but on being introduced to the empress changed his mind; four years later he found himself a major-general.[73] Demobilizations seem to have occurred in waves, especially at the conclusion of campaigns; this was certainly the case after the Seven Years' War (when they were accelerated by the 1762 edict) and after the Crimean War, when the army's size was substantially reduced; however, no corresponding major movement (except for the militia) seems to have taken place after 1814, which leaves one wondering how far this may have contributed to the disaffection of the future Decembrists. A wave of voluntary resignations occurred during Paul I's reign, on a scale so considerable that it may be regarded as a manifestation of protest against his brutal and arbitrary reinforcement of disciplinary controls.

Only the relatively prosperous and well educated could envisage retirement before expiry of their service term, which (after 1793) in principle was the same as for other

66 E. Shchepkina, foreword to *Dnevnik poruchika Vasil'eva* (St. Petersburg, 1896), v. This memoir is unfortunately of next to no value.
67 Von Hupel, *Beschreibung*, 108, 127.
68 Dubrovin, *Suvorov*, 133.
69 "Iz zapisok general-adiutanta grafa E. F. Komarovskogo," *RA* (1867), col. 760. (Komarovskii's memoirs were published in monograph form in St. Petersburg in 1914).
70 E.g. *PSZ*, XXIV, no. 17570 (20 Nov. 1796).
71 TsGVIA, fond II, op. VIII, ed. khr. 1 (War College reports on personnel matters), l. 24 (case of Lieutenant-General V. Dolgorukov, 6 Feb. 1795); most of these requests for discharge were on grounds of wounds or old age.
72 There was an obligatory minimum service term; requests had to be submitted through a multiplicity of instances, and only during a limited season. Cf. *PSZ*, XXIII, no. 17119 (Apr. 1793).
73 Denisov, "Zapiski," *RS*, 11 (1874), 607; 12 (1875), 35.

ranks. The rest, so long as they remained physically fit, had no choice but to stay on since they were ill equipped for alternative employment. For many poorer gentry the prospect of retirement must have been unwelcome both on material and moral grounds. Löwenstern, who put in for discharge to take up farming at the age of 28 (1804), was sorry to part from the company of his brother officers,[74] and for older men the psychological wrench will have been greater. Many preferred a garrison posting, despite the much reduced pay scale, to return to some bleak rural homestead.

The memoirs are not particularly helpful on this matter. Murav'ev (-Karskii) gives a frank description of the frustration and tedium of life as a *pomeshchik*, for which he had "no desire at all"; as one domestic catastrophe followed another he eagerly grasped each passing rumor that he might be taken back into military service.[75] To be sure, his case was unusual in that he had been relegated on suspicion of disloyalty. Most writers seem to have felt it dishonorable to discuss discharge or transfer to civilian service. One man who did so was Venediktov, a graduate of the Moscow Cadet Corps in the 1830s, where he acquired what he refers to cautiously as "new sentiments" that made the prospect of life in a guards regiment unattractive and led him to "look for a place." He provides no details of the bureaucratic procedure involved, but relates how some friends introduced him to a functionary of the Committee of Ministers, who offered him a position as deputy section head (*pomoshchnik stolonachal'nika*) in the road construction department, which he gratefully accepted. This branch was run on semimilitary lines; on the office wall hung birch rods (*rozgi*) for chastising the clerks, so that his new milieu was painfully familiar.[76]

For many retired officers civil employment was essential to supplement their meager pension. In the late eighteenth century such persons were assigned to live in specified towns, which had to provide for their support. Personal pensions were awarded only to the most meritorious, and only if they had no private means. Individual application had to be made to the Sovereign, who found the resources at her disposal far from adequate to satisfy all approved claims.[77] In 1803 Alexander I introduced a system of payments graduated according to length of service. There were three main classes: those who had served for 40 years were to receive the equivalent of full pay; those with over 30 years' service that of half pay; and those with 20 years' service were to be fully maintained at state expense. Mosolov provides confirmation that this

---

74 Löwenstern, *Mémoires*, I, 85.

75 N. N. Murav'ev (-Karskii), "Iz zapisok N. N. Murav'eva," *RA* (1895), 1, 36; (1895), 2, 180–3; (1895), 3, 315.

76 Venediktov, "Za 60 let," 274, 590, 40–52.

77 "It is impossible to make grants to these officers from the State Treasury": TsGVIA, fond 11, op. VIII, ed. khr. 1, l. 29 (Catherine II—War College, 29 Oct. 1795); l. 36 (Statement of accounts of the order of St. George). For a survey of the relevant legislation see N. Solov'ev, "O pensiiakh za voennuiu sluzhbu v Rossii v XVIII i XIX st.," *VS*, 210 (1893), 302–12; cf. also D. Berezhkov, "Istoricheskii ocherk prizreniia ranenykh," *VS*, 137 (1881), pt.2, 36–58; 138 (1881), pt. 2, 37–55. On personal pensions: A. Lebedev, ed., *Russkaia armiia v nachale tsarstvovaniia imp. Ekateriny II: materialy dlia russkoi voennoi istorii* (Moscow, 1898), 83–90.

decree was indeed implemented, for he had served for 32 years and was pensioned off on half pay.[78] He adds the significant detail that he was permitted to go on owning his house, but that the rent from it had to be handed over to the authorities, who held it on trust for him; however, the fact that he also possessed an estate (which he had won by gambling) suggests that no thorough attempt was made to relate pensions to alternative sources of income. Other memorialists note the existence of semi-official or private pension schemes.[79] These were apparently discontinued after the reform of 1827, which introduced far more comprehensive arrangements.[80] None of our sources refer to them, so that they probably worked satisfactorily; in any case retired officers fared better under Nicholas I than later in the century.

In general military writers were loath to discuss such mundane matters as pay and allowances. One of the few to mention his financial situation was S. I. Maevskii, who was of Polish extraction. He boasts that, whereas his widowed mother in the 1780s had possessed a mere thirty peasant souls (which would have brought her an income of about 200 roubles per annum), by the end of Alexander I's reign he drew a major-general's salary of 8,000 roubles[81]—albeit in paper *assignats*. At the beginning of the century another general, Denisov, bought an estate in Voronezh province for 75,000 roubles; he borrowed two-thirds of the purchase price and soon landed in financial difficulties, from which he was rescued by two wealthy comrades. One can scarcely credit his complaints that his salary was inadequate to pay the expenses of his position, so that he "went short even of necessities."[82]

Some less senior officers present a far more plausible picture of economic hardship. Pishchevich junior's inability to take up a lucrative appointment has already been alluded to; six years later he was still dependent on periodical gifts from his tight-fisted father.[83] In 1778 Colonel von Shtrandman had to finance a journey from Riga to Astrakhan', at a cost of 229.50 roubles, which made a large dent in his fortune of 442 roubles (hastily supplemented by a 400-rouble loan).[84] Fifty years later, on the outbreak of war with Turkey, all the (subaltern?) officers in the Pavlovskii guards regiment had to request an advance of pay, since they had no private means. Markov, our informant, received as an ensign a salary of 440 *assignat* roubles. At that time one *funt* (approx. 400 grams) of tea cost 10 roubles. A young officer could not afford to buy a horse—or to get married; and the colonel showed contempt for his impecunious subordinates, exclaiming "when will they stop sending me beggars?"[85] In the 1860s,

---

78 Mosolov, "Zapiski," 154, 173.

79 Glinka, *Zapiski*, 24 (Kutuzov's widow); N. N. Murav'ev (-Karskii), "Zapiski," *RA* (1886), 2, 128 (Grand Duke Constantine).

80 "Ustav o pensiiakh i edinovremennykh posobiiakh," in *PSZ*, II, no. 1592 (6 Dec. 1827), 1032–1044.

81 Maevskii, "Moi vek . . . 1779–1848," *RS*, 8 (1873), 8, 129; 10, 447.

82 Denisov, "Zapiski," *RS*, 12 (1875), 244–9.

83 Pishchevich, *Zhizn'*, 22, 108.

84 Von Shtrandman, "Zapiski," 84.

85 Markov, "Vospominaniia," 99.

when the first systematic investigations were undertaken into army officers' material condition, only 16 percent were found to own landed estates.[86]

There existed less legitimate potential sources of income, as we shall see in a moment; but the main beneficiaries of corrupt practices seem to have been regimental commanders (and commissariat officials) rather than the humdrum subaltern.

It is clear that the latter, unless he were from a privileged background, had a hard time making ends meet, even though he enjoyed many amenities denied to the rank and file: better food, clothing and accommodation, an orderly to look after his wants, and a horse (perhaps also a carriage) which might allow him to escape the rigor of long marches. Nevertheless the gap between junior officers and their men was a good deal narrower than it was than it was in civilian life, and it would be false to assume that the gentry-serf relationship was simply carried over into the military milieu.

This is apparent from frequent references in memoirs to lack food, especially when on campaign. One source claims that officers were actually worse off than soldiers as they did not get regular allocations but had to make their own arrangements; since there were so many other claims on their resources (for uniforms, horses and so on), "they could afford only the most frugal diet."[87] This is perhaps overstating the case; but few officers seem to have had sufficient cash reserves to acquire enough supplies to last them through a campaign, and some lacked the means to transport them. In practise several would club together for messing purposes, in a manner not too different from the soldiers' *artel'*. An anonymous writer who took part in the campaign against the Crimean Tatars in 1736 states that "each officer was glad if he got his hat filled with grain when it arrived for distribution among his men" and that he paid no less than six roubles (equivalent to a soldier's pay for six months) to a sutler (*markitant*) for a loaf of bread and a rotten cucumber.[88] One need not feel too sorry for Mosolov, who complains that in 1772 "we suffered much deprivation; there was so little food . . . that even the officers had only boiled beef to eat for two days."[89] Both A. S. Pishchevich and A. I. Viazemskii, however, testify that officers would sometimes have to mess together with their men; when news of such practises reached the empress she expressed concern.[90] Pishchevich adds that his soldiers received him well; his initial embarrassment soon wore off and he learned that "there is much more nobility of thought among simple people than among those who boast of this [noble] title." One can see why Catherine was worried.

---

86 L. Il'iashevich, "Zhenatye ofitsery," *VS*, 34 (1863), 422.

87 E. von Stork, *Denkschrift über die Kaiserlich Russische Kriegsmacht* . . . (Leipzig, 1828), 45.

88 "Turetskaia voina pri imperatritse Anne. Sovremennaia rukopis'," foreword by S. Safonov, *RA* (1877), 3, 262. According to the 1731 *shtaty* a soldier was paid 10.98 roubles per annum plus 72 kopecks "meat money."

89 Mosolov, "Zapiski," 130.

90 Pishchevich, *Zhizn'*, 38; A. I. Viazemskii, "Zapiska voennaia, pisannaia . . . v oktiabre 1774 g.," in *Arkhiv kniazia A. I. Viazemskogo*, ed. S. D. Sheremeteva (St. Petersburg, 1881), 20; Dubrovin, *Suvorov*, 9, citing archival source.

In peacetime, of course, supplies were better assured. S. N. Glinka, stationed in Moscow in 1796, states that "at that time officers in camp lacked nothing": his battalion commander, P. S. Bibikov, held open table daily for all of them with money from the so-called "economic" sums or contingency fund, about which more will be said below.[91] In the Baltic provinces at this time General Numsen, who headed a cuirassier regiment, gave a weekly dinner for his officers, who sat down to table at 2 p.m. and did not rise until midnight: "c'était une véritable orgie. Il fallait boire jusqu'à extinction de force ou de raison," remarks a participant in these feasts.[92] Other nineteenth-century sources corroborate the existence of such practises. They not only gave the impecunious valuable material assistance but served to reinforce regimental loyalties and maintain control. However, once the troops marched off to war the banqueting would suddenly cease. In 1810 Muromtsev in the Balkans was living off horsemeat soup, which he pronounced "not bad," and for Shcherbachev on the Alma in 1854 "dinner consisted of only one course, soldiers' *shchi*"[93]—which would have been a luxury for those besieged in Sevastopol' a few months later.

Curiously, the latter two writers are the only ones to allude to the accommodation which officers disposed of during this period. No doubt military men considered it unethical to show too much concern for bodily comfort. As a young guards officer in St. Petersburg in 1809 Muromtsev shared a three-room apartment in the barracks; one year later he was in a tent, keeping warm by using dried grass as fuel.[94] Shcherbachev, quartered in peacetime among the Chukhontsy (a Finnish people in Ingria), remarked on the primitive squalor of their huts.[95] Normally officers would not have been billeted upon peasants, as were their men, but would have found accommodation on a landowner's estate.

IV

The Russian officer of the 1850s differed from his eighteenth-century forerunner primarily in being better educated. Not only was his attitude to the military craft more professional, but his intellectual horizons had expanded. This process went furthest at the summit of the military hierarchy, so that it is fairly well documented in the memoirs.

The empire was comparatively rich in élite military institutions modelled on those of western Europe. To the Nobles' Land (later First) Cadet Corps, founded in 1731 and much modified by Catherine II, there were successively added specialized "corps" (i.e. schools) for artillerymen and engineers (1762), the Corps of Pages (1802), the Noblemen's Regiment (1807), the Guards Subensigns' school (1823) and several so-called "junker schools" for training army ensigns; a number of other training

---

91 Glinka, *Zapiski*, 169.

92 Löwenstern, *Mémoires*, I, 25.

93 Muromtsev, "Vospominaniia," 76; Shcherbachev, "Dvenadtsat' let," 250.

94 Muromtsev, "Vospominaniia," 70, 76.

95 Shcherbachev, "Dvenadtsat' let," 104.

colleges were set up in the provinces. Although only about one thousand cadets had graduated by 1800, 4,329 did so during Alexander I's reign and 17,653 during that of his successor.[96] Neizvestnyi thought that 40 percent of the officer corps under Nicholas I received some kind of higher or secondary education.[97] In 1831, when there were 4,767 pupils in élite military schools, their annual budget stood at 3.3 million roubles, or 698 roubles per head[98]—an inordinately high figure when one recalls that a soldier was then paid from 3 to 6.60 roubles (silver) a year.

The memorialists tell us in great detail what it felt like to enter such schools (often a traumatic experience!), to study in them and to graduate from them; much can also be learned about their administration, personnel, curricula and general ethos. Only a few points will be singled out here. First, the authorities sought to mould an "officer type" with stereotyped personality traits. These are listed by one writer thus: "patriotic, modest, cultured, comradely, patient, attentive, efficient . . . and with a pure zeal to repay [the state] for one's education by honorable service, an honorable life and an honorable death."[99] Second, much emphasis was placed upon the more formal and trivial aspects of the military *métier*—correct turnout, punctilious drill movements, guard duties and the like—which, as Kolokol'tsov remarks, was designed to enforce respect for hierarchical gradations of rank (*chinopochitanie*) and certainly did not make for efficiency.[100] Third, discipline was very strict. It was maintained by a system of petty regimentation which stifled individuality and was administered in a cruel and arbitrary fashion.

Although *dvoriane* had been exempted from corporal punishment by the charter of 1785, this rule was frequently ignored in practise. Some NCOs and teachers lost no opportunity to humiliate upper-class boys whom they considered "soft," and the older lads emulated them by bullying their juniors.[101] In the First Cadet Corps in 1808, where the younger boys were taught by women, one instructress would occasionally substitute for a recreation period a one-hour-long study session, after which "those who had not learned their lesson in time would be beaten with birches (*rozgi*)— and nanny Ivanovna hit to hurt. Pushes, shoves, bruises, pulling one's hair and ears, striking one's fingers with a ruler—all this was a daily occurrence."[102] Older

---

96 Beskrovnyi, *Russkaia armiia . . . x XVIII v.*, 450; idem, *Russkaia armiia . . . v XIX v.*, 123–9; A. N. Petrov, ed., *Russkaia voennaia sila: istoriia razvitiia voennogo dela ot nachala Rusi do nashego vremeni²* (Moscow, 1892), II, 154–5.

97 Neizvestnyi, "Za mnogo let," 120.

98 J. Tański, *Tableau statistique, politique et moral du système militaire de la Russie* (Paris, 1833), 311–14. Another writer put the *total* cost per pupil in the 1840s at 4,000 roubles: "K istorii voenno-uchebnoi reformy," *RS*, 54 (1887), 347, 352, cited by Curtiss, *Russian Army*, 180; Another estimate for 1838 is in Ministère des Affaires étrangères, Mémoires et documents, Russie, 37 (1831–52), ff. 227–8.

99 G. M. Golmdorf, "Dvorianskii polk, 1807–1859: prazdnovanie 75-oi godovshchiny dnia ego osnovaniia," *RS*, 34 (1882), 799.

100 Kolokol'tsov, "Vospominaniia," 276.

101 Ol'shevskii, "Pervyi korpus," 72–6; Markov, "Vospominaniia," 82.

102 "Rasskazy Nikolaia Alekseevicha Titova," *RS*, 1 (1870), 220.

boys would be taken to the college armory for severer punishment. Venediktov, who entered the Noblemen's Regiment in 1830, remembers "hearing the cries" of a fellow-cadet who was beaten for some trivial prank; another, for breaking a window-latch and replying "insolently" when reprimanded, was sentenced by the sadistic General I. O. Sukhozanet to "the bench and the birch," whereupon 300 blows at once rained down upon him.[103]

These tyrannical measures did not achieve their intended object. The cadets responded by neglecting their studies and engaging in acts of passive or active resistance. The first known instance of rebellion occurred in the Corps of Pages around 1813, when a popular cadet named Arsen'ev, abetted by several comrades, resisted "execution" (the standard term for a military flogging). The matter was thought sufficiently serious to be referred to Alexander I, who decided that the "ringleader" of the revolt should receive 30 blows.[104] A few years later, in the First Corps, cadets made a point of demonstrating their solidarity, at considerable personal risk, with comrades confined without food in the college jail (*kartser*). On one occasion (1823) some who were discovered, in their anxiety to escape retribution, broke down a gate, struck two officers and accidentally killed a watchman. The offenders were publicly flogged "as harshly as soldiers" and then sent off to serve in the ranks.[105]

Alain Besançon has recently noted that during Nicholas I's reign there was "[un] déclin de la vocation militaire" among Russian officers, for which the cadet schools were to blame: "les écoles de cadets sont ainsi pour la noblesse russe une évocation de son cauchemar: la perte de sa sécurité personnelle, la violation des droits et de la dignité, qu'elle a eu tant de peine à acquérir et dont Paul I et Arakčeev ont montré la précarité."[106] This is putting it a little too strongly, in our view: certainly many officers did resent the unnecessary hardships imposed upon them by the tsar's militaristic approach to pedagogy, but others were more pliable. In the early 1830s Kolokol'tsov, then a cadet in the Guards Subensigns' school, was discovered riding in a cab (a privilege denied to cadets, as it was to soldiers); he was sentenced to six days' *kartser*, followed by one month's confinement to barracks and repetition of a year's course of study; it was only thanks to protection by instructors who appreciated his talents that he escaped expulsion. Yet these severe penalties, out of all proportion to the gravity of his offence, did not lead Kolokol'tsov to question such disciplinarian methods; on the contrary he observes meekly that they turned out useful, competent officers.[107] Even the critics seem to have objected more to the way the principles were applied than to the principles themselves. Their opposition was, as we might say today, "nonsystemic."

---

103 Venediktov, "Za 60 let," 260, 270–1.

104 "Eshche iz vospominanii A. S. Gangeblova," *RA* (1886), 10, 188.

105 "Posmertnye zapiski generala ot infanterii Alekseia Alekseevicha Odintsova," *RS*, 64 (1889), 304, 306–9.

106 A. Besançon, *Éducation et société en Russie dans le second tiers du XIXe siécle* (Paris-The Hague, 1974), 31.

107 Kolokol'tsov, "Vospominaniia," 284.

Conformist political attitudes were only to be expected, given the elitist nature of the student body, the character of the instruction, and the general political climate. The emergence of a critical spirit among Russian officers has to be seen as one element in a many-sided and gradual process of intellectual maturation. Too often it is considered simply as an automatic response to experiences gained in central and western Europe in the years after 1813. Foreign influences were indeed important, but their source was not always the countries that one might suppose: Poland, and later Austria, may have been as significant before 1812 as Germany or France were to be thereafter; and their role should not be exaggerated.

In the late eighteenth century Russian officers spent their leisure hours in the traditional manner, much as might be expected: carousing, gambling and pursuing the fair sex. A. S. Pishchevich claims to have avoided the first of these vices, says nothing of the second, but makes much of his gallant exploits.[108] Yet an improvement was already under way: when stationed on the Kuban' in 1787 he attended amateur theatricals in which certain roles were taken by his unit commander's children; three or four years later, in Bessarabia, he went to "routs" (*raduty*) at which officers could play cards and dance either with each other's wives or with Moldavian boiar ladies; these seem to have been very proper entertainments, a modest charge being made for admission.[109] In 1809 Muromtsev went to the Hermitage theatre "almost every Sunday"[110]—something he particularly appreciated since before his promotion to officer rank this privilege had been denied him. The cotenant of his apartment was an aspiring dramatist, S. P. Zhikharev, who introduced him to the artistic milieu, and soon Muromtsev was helping him with his literary work; subsequently he joined an informal circle, organized by M. A. Fonvizin, to study military history. The young officers discussed the merits of ancient Athenian democracy in a manner too free for the taste of their commander and soon found themselves in trouble.[111] The episode was a harbinger of what would become almost commonplace in the capital cities after the war of 1812–14.

During those campaigns some officers at least spent their leisure hours in more cultured fashion than their predecessors. F. N. Glinka mentions that on a winter evening "we go to the colonel's or the general's [Miloradovich] to read, draw, talk and joke. Our commander's kindliness and a pleasing informality distinguish these evening conversations."[112] Chicherin, bent studiously over his diary, was mocked by a brother officer, Okunev, of whom he records that his mind was "closed to the pleasures of existence," namely reading, drawing and good talk.[113] In the postwar years a number of the more cultured and serious-minded young officers arranged to

---

108 Pishchevich, *Zhizn'*, 38, 40, 149.

109 *Ibid.*, 87, 133. At this time officers were often allowed to take their wives and families on campaign, if they could afford to do so.

110 Muromtsev, "Vospominaniia," 78.

111 *Ibid.*, 69, 71, 78. See above, 226.

112 Glinka, *Pis'ma*, pt. IV, 241–2.

113 Chicherin, *Dnevnik*, 66.

share living expenses and to enjoy in this way the pleasure of one another's company. One such *artel'* that has been thoroughly studied was set up by the three Murav'ev brothers and had 14 members;[114] another, involving some 15 to 20 officers, existed from 1815 in the Semenovskii regiment, and a third among the Izmailovtsy. Its founders, the brothers M. N. and N. N. Semenov, possessed a well-stocked library of French classics. It was in their company that around 1821 the future Decembrist A. S. Gangeblov, stationed in what he called a "terribly remote" village (not far from the capital!), came across the works of Rousseau. "I was struck," he records, "by the novelty and daring of his views on the way Man had distorted his nature as he passed through the labyrinth of civilization." A comrade who dropped by for a game of chess had even more advanced opinions: all art, he maintained, was "unnatural," a luxury for a minority of privileged aesthetes, who indulged their fancies while most of mankind was struggling grimly for subsistence.[115] The social conscience had been born, and with it a puritanism that would flower in a later age.

The ultimate sources of this new spirit may be traced back to the literary and philosophical influences to which these officers had been exposed during their education, but they would have remained mere abstractions had it not been for their personal experiences during the Napoleonic wars. The young men of Alexander I's reign were more introspective than their fathers; they sought to understand the reasons for their presence in camp or on the battlefield and to analyze their emotions at the sight of hardship and suffering. No longer willing to accept their lot as naturally befitting servitors of the God-given monarch, they began to probe into the whys and wherefores of their condition.

On October 10, 1812 Chicherin discussed with some friends the moral corruption that seemed to him inescapable in high society. "Man is born to live among people like himself"; one had an obligation "to make others happy," "to try to be useful," "to serve others"—in these unaffected terms the young diarist summed up his philosophy of life.[116] One of his interlocutors was Iakushkin, the later Decembrist, but there is no reason to assume that either man influenced the other; such ideas were in the air at the time, and a casual mention of the social contract suggests their source. Chicherin was naively, pathetically keen to perform his military duties to the best of his ability; several times he refers to his readiness to lay down his life for his country (which he eventually did): "I shall be happy to die defending my motherland, the faith and the just cause."[117] He identified strongly with those commanders or fellow-officers who lived up to his own heroic ideal, and in so doing developed his critical faculties; on the basis of gossip and rumor he distinguished between the successful generals and those who committed errors, including among the latter the commander-in-chief,

114 M. V. Nechkina, "Sviashchennyi artel'," in M. P. Alekseev and B. S. Meilakh, eds., *Dekabristy i ikh vremia. Materialy i soobshcheniia* (Moscow-Leningrad, 1951), 155–88. See above, 231.

115 Gangeblov, *art. cit.*, 190, 193–195; cf. Shtraykh, *Zapiski . . . Iakushkina*, 9.

116 Chicherin, *Dnevnik*, 35–6. See above, 227.

117 *Ibid.*, 18.

Kutuzov.[118]

Of particular interest is Chicherin's attitude toward the horrors of war. At first the sight of seriously wounded men left to die without medical care made him "turn aside, perhaps with a sigh, and seize the least excuse to forget"; but a few weeks later he says that he cannot become accustomed to the heaps of frozen corpses along the route.[119] Other writers too seemed initially content with an aesthetic concern for their own emotions; but as time passed they developed compassion for the innocent victims, respect for those—all too few—individuals who tried to relieve the suffering, and disgust at those on either side who committed deliberate acts of barbarism, such as "finishing off" enemy wounded.[120] Löwenstern was present when a watchmaker of Dorogobuzh led his fellow-partisans in a *pogrom* against a totally demoralized party of invaders, in which the man claimed to have killed twenty with his own hands; the spectacle led Löwenstern "to groan over the calamities inseparable from warfare."[121] After coming upon evidence of a mass killing by cossacks, Antonovskii "first raised [his] eyes to Heaven, revering the inscrutable ways of Providence," but then began "to contemplate the fate of these unfortunates": where, he asked himself, did responsibility for the atrocity lie? Had the victims perhaps been found dead by the cossacks, and not killed by them?[122] Clearly this line of thought could not be pressed too far, at least in print, without raising larger issues of responsibility for the war. In 1812 all the blame could plausibly be laid upon the invader, but when Russian troops misbehaved abroad the question was harder to resolve.

At the war's end there was widespread hope within the officer corps, especially in guards regiments, that Alexander I would undertake major reforms in the armed forces and in society generally. The cruel disappointment of these hopes during the so-called *Arakcheevshchina* led the more adventurous spirits along the path of scheming and eventually conspiracy—with results that are common knowledge. "Decembrism" was not a coherent philosophy but a state of mind; its chief element was a new-found and quite justifiable pride in the army's achievements, of which government and society ought to take adequate account. Only a few extremists, notably P. I. Pestel', wished the army to play a direct part in the country's political life by establishing a Bonapartist-type dictatorship, but all were imbued with respect for the military virtues. Nationalism loomed as large in their thinking as liberalism or humanitarianism, and their condemnation of serfdom was rooted in a desire to preserve the national unity that had been demonstrated so effectively in 1812. As firm believers in maintenance of the Russian empire, they were suspicious of such minority groups as Poles, Germans and Jews: the first because they were inconstant in their loyalty during the war, the second because they were thought to enjoy the ruler's special favor, and the third for reasons that had more to do with traditional religious and cultural prejudice.

---

118 *Ibid.*, 55, 87.

119 *Ibid.*, 48, 67.

120 N. N. Murav'ev (-Karskii), "Zapiski," *RA* (1886), 4, 49; (1886), 5, 97.

121 Löwenstern, *Mémoires*, I, 328–9.

122 Antonovskii, "Zapiski," 200.

The nationalist motif was most pronounced among members of the Murav'ev clan. A. M. Murav'ev's oft-cited remark that after 1812 Alexander I rewarded his Polish subjects with a constitution but his Russian ones with military colonies[123] may reflect views that he developed later in life; but Murav'ev (-Karskii), whose memoirs were written (but not published!) in 1818, makes a similar point: Alexander, he writes, "won the goodwill of the French but so caused his victorious army to complain against him."[124] The same view is expressed by Matvei Murav'ev-Apostol', younger brother of the leader of the Chernigov regiment's abortive revolt.[125]

It is a misapprehension to believe that Russian officers who went abroad to fight were necessarily bowled over by the superior conditions they encountered there. A study of their memoirs suggests a more nuanced interpretation. F. N. Glinka describes enthusiastically the prosperity of the Austrian countryside that he saw for the first time in 1805 and the "free rights" enjoyed by merchants and peasants; on entering Silesia eight years later he is equally outspoken in praise of the social arrangements there; but Paris strikes him unfavorably as "a new Babylon," whose swollen populace, he thinks, should be returned to the villages so that they might devote themselves to useful toil.[126] A similar view is expressed by Murav'ev (-Karskii): in Baden-Württemberg he is struck by "the dense population, the fine villages with gardens all around, and fields worked incomparably better than in any other country"; but on crossing the French border he finds the inhabitants dirty, impoverished and ignorant. "Where is that *douce France* of which our tutors had told us, I wondered." Perhaps it still lay ahead, in the capital? But Paris disappoints him too: life is expensive and the people unfriendly; as a professional soldier Murav'ev is more impressed by the Invalides than the Louvre; dutifully he paces out the full length of the Grande Galerie, commenting: "I was unable to judge the beauty of the pictures and statues, although I couldn't help stopping to admire the best"—and after these brief remarks passes on with evident relief to details of his homeward journey.[127]

Even a young subaltern like Chicherin, who had never been abroad before, realizes that the relative prosperity of German peasants—even the poorest, he comments, had horses fit to draw a carriage—is due to the superiority of the political-administrative system under which they live. At Bunzlau (Silesia) he comes upon a throng of well-dressed, cheerful farmers standing in front of the town hall, and discovers to his surprise that they have come to pay their taxes. And yet

123 A. M. Murav'ev, *Zapiski*, 12 (first published in 1902).

124 Murav'ev (-Karskii), "Zapiski," *RA* (1886), 5, 106.

125 M. Murav'ev-Apostol', "S. I. Murav'ev-Apostol', 1796–1826 gg.: zametka po povodu ego biografii," *RS* (1873), 8, 109.

126 F. N. Glinka, *Pis'ma*, I, 6, 19, 54, 179; IV, 249; V, 15–16, 186–88; VIII, 32.

127 N. N. Murav'ev (-Karskii), "Zapiski," 71, 75, 110–117. For more positive views of French life: Maevskii, "Moi vek . . . 1779–1848," 288–9, 302; Shtraykh, *Zapiski . . . Iakushkina*, 8. Iakushkin's oft-cited remark that "one year's stay in Germany and then several months in Paris could not but change the views of any thinking Russian youth; in such a tremendous environment each of us matured a bit" was written in 1854!

the love I bear my fatherland burns like a pure flame, elevating my heart; it is a source of quiet joy to me . . . and I shall maintain it until I die. . . . We continually see here the achievements of civilization, for they are evident in everything—in the manner of cultivating fields, building homes, and in customs—yet never, not even for a minute, would I wish to settle under an alien sky, in a land other than that where I was born and where my forefathers were laid to rest.[128]

Thus foreign experience augmented the sense of *malaise* that Russian officers felt about the direction of affairs at home. It produced contradictory emotions of admiration mixed with shame and envy, a mood that would later be given a philosophical foundation by the emergent intelligentsia but which in the present generation helped to paralyze their will to act. The history of "Decembrism" is long on good intentions but short on deeds: the *coup d'état* was badly bungled, and even within their own milieu the reformers' stance was ambiguous. Some of the most important measures taken at this time to promote the soldiers' well-being were the work of moderates like M. S. Vorontsov, while the radicals, who looked forward to a citizen army on the French model, had a certain sympathy for tough disciplinary regulations. This helps to explain their irresolution and awkwardness in trying to cultivate good relations with their men.[129]

Russian officers at this time—like the *dvorianstvo* whence they sprang—had as yet only an embryonic political consciousness. As military men, bound by their oath and brought up in a spirit of unquestioning obedience to authority, they remained monarchists by conviction: Pestel' was an obvious exception, but then his republicanism was of a peculiar kind. Most would have been well satisfied even with Alexander I, had he but paid greater heed to army opinion. Their attitude to the ruler was intensely personal and emotional, perhaps even more so than it was among civilians. One catches a glimpse of this in the frank confession which some arrested Decembrists made to Nicholas I, or in the adulation which this upholder of absolutist principles received from many of his officers. Markov, when presented to the tsar, feared he would collapse, for "he appeared before my eyes as the very embodiment of the idea of totality . . . I felt the tears coursing silently down both cheeks."[130] Kolokol'tsov tells the story of a certain major-general, Mikulin, who "worshiped" the Imperial family to the point of fanaticism; on receiving an official report from the tsarevich Alexander, he declared that the precious document should be buried with him in his tomb—as indeed it eventually was, after a funeral ceremony held in the presence of the entire regiment.[131] Another officer, after waiting on parade for four and a half hours in the early morning before the Sovereign appeared, was overawed by Nicholas's physical presence: "what a marvel of a man he is; with what

128 Chicherin, *Dnevnik*, 155, 176–7.

129 For a different interpretation, see the thorough study by E. A. Prokof'ev, *Voennye vzgliady dekabristov* (Moscow, 1953).

130 Markov, "Vospominaniia," 84.

131 Kolokol'tsov, "Vospominaniia," 297, 305.

majesty and yet benevolence he inspects the soldiers."[132] Veneration for the supreme power might well be accompanied by a critical attitude towards his entourage, and high-ranking dignitaries in general. Such rivalries within the élite helped to give the Russian autocracy its extraordinary staying power.

What these officers lacked in political *savoir-faire* they made up for in moral sensitivity and zeal. A number of writers denounce corruption, inefficiency and malfeasance among their superiors; understandably, they were less ready to confess their own misdeeds.[133] The impression one gets is that these vices were most prevalent under Catherine, when controls were feeble; this may, however, be less than just, since the bureaucratic centralization carried through by her successors did not eliminate the evil. Perhaps regimental commanders no longer engaged in such spectacular offenses, but the incidence of petty peculation increased; there is no sure means of knowing.

For the late eighteenth century A. S. Pishchevich is once again an invaluable source. He is very explicit on the manner of passing a bribe. In 1795 he went to St. Petersburg to expedite his promotion to first major; early one morning a secretary in the War College, Tarutin, came to his lodgings unexpectedly and said that he "was willing to serve him if he [Pishchevich] would advise him how to proceed"; a few days later Tarutin told him that his papers were in order and that gifts totaling 800 roubles were expected. Pishchevich refused to pay. (He does not say whether his promotion went through; as he soon transferred to the civil service, he will have qualified for advancement then in any case.)[134] Tuchkov offers a detailed breakdown of the principal illegal ways in which a colonel could accumulate funds:

> savings were obtained from (i) the remains of fabrics used to make soldiers' clothing; (ii) keeping fewer horses than prescribed for the baggage-train and artillery; (iii) the men's food allowance (*proviant*) . . . while they were quartered in the villages; (iv) keeping the pay and allowances of soldiers sent on leave; (v) keeping the pay and allowances of deceased soldiers whose death was not reported for several years (this was the most profitable method); (vi) taking men from the regiment into their own service, training them in various skills, and pocketing their pay; in general [such] soldiers had to give part of their earnings to the regiment.[135]

The last remark shows that both officers and men stood to gain from such an arrangement and that an element of collusion was involved. This point is overlooked

---

132 "Otryvki iz dnevnika rotnogo komandira I. I. Gladilova, 1841 g.," in P. I. Shchukin, *Sobranie starinnykh bumag* (Moscow, 1901), vol. 8, 176.

133 G. I. Vinskii, author of "Moe vremia: zapiski," *RA* (1877) (also published separately St. Petersburg, 1914 and reprinted Newtonville, Mass., 1974 with an introduction by I. de Madariaga), was sent to Orenburg for a scandal in which two guards officers stole 500 roubles from a state institution in Reval': but he gives no details of the incident. [The whole subject of corruption in the military is discussed at length by D. Beyrau, *Militär und Gesellschaft im vorrevolutionären Russland* (Cologne and Vienna, 1984), 23–9, 80–1, 168–70.]

134 Pishchevich, *Zhizn'*, 211. Tarutin was exposed, discharged, and exiled by Paul I.

135 Tuchkov, *Zapiski*, 9.

in historical accounts, where the practise is treated simply as an extension of serfdom into state service. It might equally well be regarded as an outgrowth of the soldiers' *artel'*; to the extent that the men benefitted materially from private employment, it cannot be dismissed as mere exploitation, and even where they received no monetary reward they may have appreciated a temporary escape from the parade ground to a familiar rural environment. In any case climatic conditions made military labor a necessity at harvest time. The chief loser from the practise was not the soldier but the state, which had to go on paying soldiers who were only nominally in its service. One military historian claims (without providing evidence) that some 50,000 men, roughly one-eighth of total effectives, were employed in this way at the end of the eighteenth century.[136] Legislators frequently inveighed against the practise but on occasion were obliged to tolerate it.[137] Such ambivalence could only encourage a hypocritical attitude among those involved.

A colonel's profits were not all personal income. Tuchkov points out that some commanders used their funds to assist poorer officers, and this is attested from other sources; another portion might go to embellishment of the regiment. On handing over his command, the colonel would enter into official and unofficial financial transactions with his successor. If there were a large deficit in the accounts, he might be obliged to make it up before the new appointee would accept his responsibilities. Alternatively, a wealthy commander might buy his *entrée* by taking over his predecessor's debts. *Bona fide* shortages would sometimes be made up by higher authority. At such moments informal patronage relationships were of considerable importance. Sometimes a situation would arise where the officers could make their influence felt collectively, and lobbies would form for and against the departing colonel. In the most favorable circumstances his partisans might raise money on his behalf; in the worst a colonel in debt who died might have his property sold off at auction. It was precisely to guard against such contingencies that unit commanders sought to build up unofficial reserve funds. At first tolerated by the state, this practise was legalized by Nicholas I and the money invested on the regiment's behalf.[138] Even so one may doubt whether more than a small fraction of the funds held back was reported. Estimates of a colonel's "take" are available only for the 1780s: von Hupel puts it at 2,000–6,000 roubles per

---

136 V. M—v, "Sostoianie vooruzhennykh sil Rossii v tsarstvovanii Pavla I-go i v nachale tsarstvovaniia Aleksandra I-go," in A. N. Petrov, ed., *Russkaia voennaia sila*, II, 244.

137 For bans on it: *PSZ*, V, no. 2638 (28 Jan. 1713); XXII, no. 15984 (18 Apr. 1784); XXIV, no. 17576 (22 Nov. 1796); XXXIV, no. 26772 (15 Mar. 1817); for toleration of it: Ustav voinskii (1716 g.), in *Pamiatniki russkogo prava*, ed. K. A. Sofronenko, (Moscow, 1961), vol. 8, 333 (§§54–5); *PSZ*, XXIV, no. 17856 (28 Feb. 1797); XXVII, no. 20865 (25 July 1803).

138 Based on Tuchkov, *Zapiski*, 252; Pishchevich, *Zhizn'*, 117; M. Rzhevskii, "O russkoi armii," 357; Glinka, *Zapiski*, 184; M. Apolev, "Ocherki khoziaistva armeiskogo pekhotnogo polka," *VS*, 8 (1859), 1–40; Tański, *Tableau*, 165; Dubrovin, *Suvorov*, 134; S. N. Chernov, "Iz istorii bor'by za armiiu v nachale 20-kh gg. XIX v." [1929], in S. N. Chernov, *U istokov russkogo osvoboditel'nogo dvizheniia: izbrannye stat'i po istorii dekabrizma* (Saratov, 1960), 203.

annum, and notes that cavalry officers did better than others.[139]

From this it is clear that Russian regiments, and indeed the army as a whole, had an "inner life" of which only faint traces have been left in military memoirs. Yet for all its limitations this source lifts a corner of the veil that still enshrouds the social history of the institution which, after the autocracy itself, was the mightiest in the land.

1980

---

139 Von Hupel, *Beschreibung*, 115; Damaze de Raymond, *Tableau historique, géographique, militaire et moral de l'Empire de Russie* (Paris, 1812), I, 535, also offers an estimate of 2–3,000. Ségur's figure of 20–25,000 roubles (*Mémoires, souvenirs et anecdotes par M. le comte de Ségur*, ed. M. F. Bassière (Paris, 1812), I, 379) is echoed by Citoyen Caillard, "Coup d'œil sur l'état politique de la Russie" [Dec. 1800] in Ministère des Affaires étrangères, Mémoires et documents, Russie, 32 (1800–1813), f. 16; cf. also 35 (1778–1828), f. 32. An estimate of 10,000 roubles a year was given by H. Reimers, a partisan of Paul I, in "Peterburg pri imperatore Pavle Petroviche v 1796–1801 gg.," *RS*, 39 (1883), 448. [Count Langeron offered this figure for an infantry regiment colonel (1796) and considered that an income of 15,000 roubles per annum in the grenadiers and 25,000 roubles in the cavalry was reasonable, since some of the profits went to the soldiers and the state was able to keep officers' salaries lower than would otherwise have been the case. "Russkaia armiia v god smerti Ekateriny II: sostav i ustroistvo russkoi armii," *RS*, 83 (1895), 4, 160–2.]

CHAPTER 11

Chernyshevskii and the "Military Miscellany"

How was it possible that, for several months in 1858, tsarist Russia's leading military journal, *Voennyi sbornik* ("Military Miscellany"), should have been managed by the country's best known radical journalist? This curious episode is of some interest to historians of the intelligentsia, as well as to those concerned with civil-military relations in the Russian empire, but it has generally received only passing attention.[1] A definitive account could be written only on the basis of material in Soviet archives that is difficult of access,[2] so that we shall confine ourselves here to raising some of the more pertinent questions rather than trying to answer them all.

The main key to an understanding of the affair lies in the disarray that afflicted the tsarist censors, as it did other officials, in the wake of Russia's humiliation in the Crimean War. As Peter Scheibert notes, "the old order had not only lost credibility but had failed completely; the year of defeat was seized upon by the best and most responsible elements as a choice opportunity to push through reforms."[3] Administrators were uncertain how far they should go in trying to come to terms with the public, and this allowed personal and institutional rivalries to surface. Certain highly-placed individuals began to circulate memoranda, in what would now be called *samizdat* form, in the hope of influencing policy. Meanwhile the mood in educated "society"

---

1 At the height of the Zhdanovshchina [Colonel] N. Makeev published a brief monograph, *N. G. Chernyshevskii—redaktor "Voennogo sbornika"* (Moscow, 1950), excerpted under the same title in *Voprosy istorii* (1949), no. 4, 65–82. Subsequent Soviet historians, such as E. I. Pokusaev, *N. G. Chernyshevskii: ocherk zhizni i tvorchestva: posobie dlia uchitelei*, 5th ed. (Moscow, 1976), 54, or M. S. Cherepakhov, *N. G. Chernyshevskii* (Moscow, 1977), 40, have been content to echo Makeev's arguments and conclusions. The matter is touched on briefly by two western biographers: W. F. Woehrlin, *Chernyshevskii: the Man and the Journalist* (Cambridge, Mass., 1971), 102 and N. G. O. Pereira, *The Thought and Teachings of N. G. Černyševskij* (The Hague and Paris, 1975), 28.

2 In October 1984 I was told that the main relevant file (TsGVIA, fond 38, opis' 23/278, ed. khr. 17, sv. 796) was "being disinfected." Other documents of interest are held in the Leningrad branch of the military-historical archive (TsGVIAL, f. 450, d. 273; f. 772, op. 7, d. 151675); editorial materials relating to the journal are, or were, in TsGLA, f. 1, ed. khr. 238. References from Makeev, *Chernyshevskii*, 33, 35, 65, 96. One would like to hope that some future researcher might take the matter further.

3 P. Scheibert, *Von Bakunin zu Lenin: Geschichte der russischen revolutionären Ideologien, 1840–1895*, vol. 1: Die Formen des radikalen Denkens in der Auseinandersetzung mit dem deutschen Idealismus und französischen Bürgertum (Studien zur Geschichte Osteuropas Nr. 3) (Leiden, 1956), 13–14.

was one of mingled fear and high expectations. The natural goodwill felt towards the new ruler was counterbalanced by a certain skepticism as to Alexander II's willingness to break free from his father's habit of postponing awkward decisions and ruling by coercion. Once serf emancipation had been clearly placed on the agenda (1857), and a measure of public debate permitted, caution gave way to exaggerated optimism. Liberal and radical ideas were soon articulated in the press, which underwent a rapid expansion, and in the salons of the capital. The specific ideas put forward by journalists and others were probably less important than the existence of an atmosphere that favored speculation on a broad range of matters hitherto taboo. Many people felt ashamed of their earlier conformism and, rather than come to terms with their guilt, engaged in a hunt for scapegoats. The chief victims were the courtiers or bureaucrats, but some were also found in the armed forces. In view of the central place which the military had traditionally occupied in the empire's power structure, it was highly significant that, first in the navy and then in the army, spokesmen for various currents of opinion should begin to make their views known, notwithstanding the restrictions placed on political expression and activity by serving officers.

For such a development the existing military censorship authorities were wholly unprepared. Their duties had first been defined in 1812, when Alexander I established an office of censor under the Military Science Committee (*Voenno-uchenyi komitet*).[4] It was laid down that, when examining works submitted to him, this officer (who was appointed by the War Minister) should be guided by the same rules that applied to the general (civil) censorship, so that the latter had no jurisdiction in the military domain. This demarcation of responsibilities evidently remained unchanged when Nicholas I expanded the censorship apparatus in 1826. His comprehensive statute made no specific mention of the military censor, but prescribed that the military periodical of the day—*Russkii invalid* ("Russian Veteran"), published by the so-called "committee of August 18, 1814," which had charge of veterans' affairs—should be exempt from the general censorship.[5] This act also stated that any government agency wishing to start up a new journal had to solicit the tsar's permission through the ministry of Education, which supervised the main (civil) censorship board (*Glavnoe upravlenie po tsenzurnym delam*, here *GUTs*), and that no periodical might publish articles on current administrative matters until the text had been approved by the ministry concerned.

---

4 *I PSZ*, xxxii. 24971 (27 Jan. 1812), ch. III, §§12–14; cf. xxxiii. 26036 (4 Dec. 1815); [Russia. Ministerstvo narodnogo prosveshcheniia] *Sbornik postanovlenii i rasporiazhenii po tsenzure s 1720 po 1862 g.* (St. Petersburg, 1862), 109, 114. On Russian censorship in general see C. A. Ruud, *Fighting Words: Imperial Censorship and the Russian Press, 1804–1906* (Toronto, 1982); F. B. Kaiser, "Zensur in Rußland von Katharina II. bis zum Ende des 19. Jahrhunderts," *Forschungen zur osteuropäischen Geschichte*, 25 (1978); for this period also D. Balmuth, "Origins of the Russian Press Reform of 1865," *Slavonic and East European Review* 47 (1969), 369–388.

5 Statute (*ustav*) of June 10, 1826, ch. X, §112, reprinted in *Sbornik*, 156; cf. *II PSZ*, iii. 1979 (Apr. 22, 1828), §1: publications of ministries and other official bodies "are printed under the supervision and on the responsibility of these agencies." Ibid., 321–322. This act gave wide powers to the newly established Third Department. Ruud, *Fighting Words*, 52–57.

This gave the military a veto right on the public discussion by civilians of matters falling within its domain (which may have existed implicitly before). The detailed prescriptions on what civil censors were to do presumably applied, *mutatis mutandis*, to their military confrère(s).

Their work was of course enshrouded in secrecy and even today very little is known about it. However, it is fairly clear that information policy was an arena of civil-military jurisdictional conflict. On three occasions (1833, 1835, 1850) the War Minister acted to safeguard *Russian Veteran's* privilege of being the first journal allowed to report military operations,[6] and in 1847 a tedious wrangle began as to who should be allowed to censor articles that criticized the textbooks used in military schools.[7] By this time the military censor had acquired an apparatus of his own, the Military Censorship Committee (here MCC). Alarmed by the 1848 revolutions in western and central Europe, Nicholas I, as is well known, set up two secret committees to supervise the civil censorship.[8] The tsar seems to have detected some laxity among the military censors too, for he ordered a copy of each work submitted to them to be sent to the (civil) censorship committee in the capital so that it might "follow the movement of our military literature."[9] Since each individual ministry still had the right (and duty) to vet anything that touched on its domain—this ruling was repeated on April 6, 1848[10]—and even a former minister such as Uvarov might issue instructions to the censors, the result was chaos: a complex network of instances, all acting in secret and eyeing one another suspiciously. Their activities could not be effectively controlled or coordinated, and even loyalist writers might find themselves the object of arbitrary repressive measures. So too might the censors, which was bad for their morale. Some of them harbored doubts as to the correctness or feasibility of the policies they were supposed to enforce. Morally they were in an unenviable position, caught between the opprobrium of the literary public and the whims of their numerous bosses. The intrigues that went on behind the scenes were acidly catalogued by A. V. Nikitenko—a *littérateur* as well as a censor—in his celebrated diary.[11] Nikitenko was one of several officials who favored a more liberal, or at

---

6 *Sbornik*, 223.

7 *Sbornik*, 239–240, 276.

8 The more important one was the "committee of 2 April 1848," sometimes termed the "Buturlin committee" to distinguish it from the one chaired by A. S. Menshikov. M. K. Lemke, *Ocherki po istorii russkoi tsenzury i zhurnalistiki XIX st.* (St. Petersburg, 1904), 183–308, esp. 192 ff.; A. V. Zapadov, ed., V. G. Berezin et al., comps., *Istoriia russkoi zhurnalistiki XVIII–XIX vv.*, 2nd ed. (Moscow, 1966), 300–1; Ruud, *Fighting Words*, 85–86.

9 *Sbornik*, 257. This move, which became known indirectly in February 1849, may have been prompted by earlier dissatisfaction with *Russian Veteran's* practise of reprinting foreign news items literally—so that, for example, Hungarian patriots were termed "courageous" and the Habsburgs "the enemy." Lemke, *Ocherki*, 210. This negligence earned the Military Science Committee a rebuke from the War Minister.

10 *Sbornik*, 244.

11 A. V. Nikitenko, *Diary of a Russian Censor*, ed., tr. and abridged by H. S. Jacobson (Amherst, Mass., 1975).

least more rational, policy toward the press; but there was little that either he or others could do as long as Nicholas I remained alive. Moreover, the Crimean War strengthened the hand of those who wanted to restrict journalistic activity as far as possible.

It was the shock produced by the fall of Sevastopol' that caused the first movement towards *glasnost'* (literally, publicity, or in modern parlance "freedom of information"). During the summer of 1855 non-official journals were permitted to send reporters to the war zone,[12] and on 6 December the watchdog "committee of April 2" was dissolved. "Once its supervision was terminated," writes Lemke, "the censorship . . . was exposed, spontaneously and involuntarily, to an atmosphere of fresh breezes."[13] More precisely, it entered upon a period of drift that would end only in 1862/1865 with the introduction of the so-called Temporary Regulations (which—ce n'est que le provisoire qui dure—would last until 1905!). Woehrlin calls the censors of this era "inept": "crippled by an unimaginative literalness, [they] carefully deleted sentences and paragraphs without affecting the basic message," so that N. G. Chernyshevskii and other radical journalists were able to state the case for revolution and socialism by making use of "Aesopian language" and other evasive techniques.[14]

This was in no small measure the result of vacillations at the highest level. Overall supervision of censorship was entrusted to a noted poet, (Prince) P. A. Viazemskii, who found himself in an unenviable predicament. He advocated three major reforms: elimination of the excessive restrictions imposed since 1848, abolition of the rule giving governmental agencies a veto right over matters within their purview, and (perhaps less feasibly) the issuance of precise, uniform instructions that should be binding on all censors.[15] But unfortunately neither he nor the new Education minister, A. S. Norov, had the requisite standing or determination to impose their viewpoint. Alexander II took a close personal interest in censorship affairs, just as his father had done, and did not shrink from issuing forthright commands or reprimands whenever he found fault with some decision. Two such orders in the spring of 1857 dealt with alleged laxity in the reporting of financial matters.[16] Other senior personages were thereby emboldened to follow the tsar's example.

Later in the year a row broke out over a satirical story in a St. Petersburg journal which poked fun at some railroad officials. Since the War Ministry had yet to shed its supervisory role over public transport, the MCC become involved. Its chairman,

12 Zapadov, ed., *Istoriia*, 333; cf. Ruud, *Fighting Words*, 94.

13 Lemke, *Ocherki*, 308.

14 Woehrlin, *Chernyshevskii*, 112. Peter Scheibert states that "thanks to the helplessness of the censorship, journals filled the most distant provinces with the slogans of the most reckless materialism" (*Von Bakunin zu Lenin*, 16), but this seems an exaggeration, at any rate for the period after 1862. For a study of Chernyshevskii's use of indirection see B. I. Lazerson, "Publitsistika Chernyshevskogo v gody revoliutsionnoi situatsii: k kharakteristike inoskazatel'nogo masterstva Chernyshevskogo," in: *Revoliutsionnaia situatsiia v Rossii v 1859–61 gg.*, vol. 3 (Moscow, 1962), 62–91.

15 Nikitenko, *Diary*, 161.

16 *Sbornik*, 412.

General (Baron) N. V. Medem, took the view that the article cast ridicule on "all company, squadron and regimental commanders." To his credit the War Minister, I. O. Sukhozanet, took a more lenient view, but Norov decided that the rules had been infringed and early in October warned his subordinates not to allow anything to appear that was disrespectful of officialdom; the press, he complained, was adopting an inquisitorial tone and treating the government as if it were on trial[17]—an argument that soon became a cliché on the far right. A few weeks earlier Norov had expressed concern about press treatment of military affairs—evidently the army's responsibility for the Crimean débâcle—and directed censors to pay particular attention "to journal articles which counterpose the War Ministry to the civilian authorities in an unfavorable light, or vice versa."[18]

Just at this time the government was embarking on the difficult and dangerous task of serf emancipation—it was in November 1857 that the tsar issued his decisive rescript to governor-general V. I. Nazimov. A leading pro-reform journal, *Otechestvennye zapiski* ("Notes of the Fatherland"), published without permission excerpts from earlier decrees on the landless liberation of peasants in the Baltic provinces. According to Nikitenko, Norov allowed himself to be manipulated by one of his senior officials, A. E. Kislovskii, into making an issue of this minor technical lapse, and reprimanded the censor responsible, A. N. Beketov.[19] This is of some relevance to our story, for shortly afterwards none other than Beketov was selected to "sign for the press" most of the first issues of the *Military Miscellany*. He had a reputation in literary circles for being "soft" and may conceivably have been impelled to act mildly towards the new periodical out of resentment at the sanctions taken against him—which would have been more severe had he not received strong backing from his immediate superior in the St. Petersburg censorship committee, (Prince) G. A. Shcherbatov. It was two weeks or so after this incident, on January 16, 1858, that Alexander II issued detailed and highly restrictive orders as to how censors were to handle press discussion of the impending serf emancipation.[20] A few days later (January 23) he tightened up the arrangements for ministerial consultation on censorship matters, especially but not solely in regard to the peasant question. Each of the various official agencies was to appoint a trusted official, called a *doverennyi*, who should remain in constant touch with the St. Petersburg censors; the latter were to supply these officials with relevant material, and the *doverennye's* comments were to form "the main basis" for the regular censor's decisions.[21] In the case of the War Ministry, this made the MCC redundant and it was accordingly liquidated on Feb-

17 Ibid., 416; Lemke, *Ocherki*, 23–24.

18 Ibid., 414.

19 Nikitenko, *Diary*, 165. G. Dzhanshiev, *Epokha velikikh reform: istoricheskie spravki* (Moscow, 1898), 363, erroneously states that Beketov was dismissed.

20 *Sbornik*, 422; also reproduced in T. G. Dinesman, comp., *Sbornik materialov k izucheniiu istorii russkoi zhurnalistiki*, fasc. 2 (Moscow, 1952), 207; Ruud, *Fighting Words*, 106.

21 *Sbornik*, 401 (1st addendum to 1857 *Svod zakonov*, §42), 423; reported in *Russkii vestnik*, xvi (July 1858), 53.

ruary 19, 1858.[22] The implications of this move will be considered presently.

These measures evidently flowed from decisions taken at a meeting of the Council of Ministers in mid-January 1858. Norov submitted a report, prepared by Viazemskii with the assistance of the censor (and novelist) I. A. Goncharov, urging a more conciliatory course in information policy—only to be outvoted by the right-wing members led by the Justice minister, (Count) V. N. Panin.[23] The latter was "obsessed"—at least this was Nikitenko's view—with the notion that literary activity was the cause of revolutions everywhere, and even suggested (presumably informally) that censors should be liable to summary punishment, without any preliminary inquiry, for the least oversight.[24] Fortunately, Panin's opinion did not prevail. When Norov resigned in March 1858, together with his deputy Viazemskii, he was succeeded not by a hard-liner but by the scholarly E. P. Kovalevskii, a political lightweight.

The new Education minister at first followed in the errant footsteps of his predecessor. He authorized his subordinates to draft a new censorship statute, but failed to take a firm stand in favor of reform. Thus the unfortunate censors continued to face the threat of sudden reprimands—a fate that befell Shcherbatov in April 1858 for authorizing publication of an article by Chernyshevskii in *Sovremennik* ("The Contemporary") on the peasant question, despite objections by the ministry of the Interior.[25] Later in the year there was talk of setting up yet another committee to give positive guidance to the press, although for the time being nothing came of this. The situation continued to be one of stalemate between the contending forces within the bureaucracy until April 1859, when Kovalevskii took a modest step forward. He issued a circular endorsing a point of view that had long had currency among his officials, namely that press articles critical of existing administrative "disorders and abuses" could serve a useful purpose since they gave the government independent information that allowed it to control its officials' conduct. Such writings were now to be permitted—provided that they did not touch on important matters currently under consideration (i.e. serf emancipation) and were "in conformity with the legislation safeguarding the inviolability of the autocratic regime and state institutions."[26] The limits to freedom of expression were defined narrowly, but a little more clearly than before, and critics had a loophole which they did their best to exploit. The concession is surprising in light of the fact that, during the 15 months that elapsed between the decisions of January 1858 and the circular of April 1859, the conservatives won a major confrontation over journalistic activity in the armed forces.

Under Nicholas I, who had an abiding interest in the minutiae of military life,

---

22 *II PSZ*, xxxiii. 32819 (March 1, 1858).

23 Nikitenko, *Diary*, 166.

24 Ibid., 167.

25 Ibid., 171; Ruud, *Fighting Words*, 108. It is worth noting that Shcherbatov had infringed Alexander II's instructions of January 23, and so laid himself open to sanctions.

26 Lemke, *Ocherki*, 125.

intellectually-minded officers secured few tangible benefits.[27] The progress that had been registered during the previous reign was not sustained, largely because it seemed to have led to the spread of "subversive" ideas and to the two armed insurrections of December 1825. To limit the political risks to his autocratic regime, Nicholas exercised close control over the cadet corps and other élite educational establishments (which were, however, expanded) and also kept his army busy with parades and maneuvers whenever it was not engaged in warfare against Turks, Persians, Caucasian mountain-dwellers, Poles, Hungarians, or—last but not least—the Allied powers in the Eastern War of 1853–5. In the field of military journalism, which is our concern here, the veterans' paper was supplemented in 1827 by a "solid" periodical, *Voennyi zhurnal* ("Military Journal"), published by the Military Science Committee in the general staff. Edited from 1846 by Colonel Bolotov, it more than trebled its readership by the 1850s—but only from a trifling 150 to a modest 500.[28] Its non-official section contained articles of a historical or narrow technical character, most of them translated from western languages and with a limited appeal. There was little in its pages to stimulate interest among serving officers, whose educational standards were still so low that any serious publication was beyond the reach of all but a favored few in the Guards and Grenadiers Corps or in specialized arms.

The navy, too, was ahead of the bulk of the land forces. In November 1847 Nicholas exempted publications of the Naval Science Committee from general censorship.[29] Foremost among these was a periodical, *Morskoi sbornik* ("Naval Miscellany"), founded in the following year, which enjoyed the personal patronage of the enlightened Grand Duke Constantine Nikolaevich.[30] It published articles on a wide range of current topics, as well as professional ones, and soon earned a reputation, inside and outside the armed forces, as one of the liveliest press organs in the country; its circulation was in excess of 6,000 copies. Goncharov and Ostrovskii were numbered among its contributors. The *Naval Miscellany* ran into trouble in 1852, when one issue was banned and GUTs, the main civilian censorship board, secured control over its content;[31] but despite this setback it shone forth as a veritable beacon of

---

27 See J. S. Curtiss's classic study, *The Russian Army under Nicholas I, 1825–1855* (Durham, N. C., 1965), and ch. 14 of my *Soldiers of the Tsar: Army and Society in Russia, 1462–1874* (Oxford, 1985); in German, D. Beyrau, *Militär und Gesellschaft im vorrevolutionären Russland* (Cologne and Vienna, 1984); in Russian, L. G. Beskrovnyi, *Russkaia armiia i flot v XIX v.: voenno-ekonomicheskii potentsial Rossii* (Moscow, 1973).

28 N. G. Chernyshevskii, *PSS*, vol. 5 (*Stat'i, 1858–59*, ed. V. Ia. Kirpotin et al.) (Moscow, 1950), 939. From 1839 the committee also published a periodical for artillerymen, *Artilleriiskii zhurnal*.

29 *II PSZ*, xxii. 21737 (25 Nov. 1847), §17; *Sbornik*, 322–323.

30 On Constantine and his circle, see W. B. Lincoln, *In the Vanguard of Reform: Russia's Enlightened Bureaucrat, 1825–1861* (DeKalb, Il., 1982), 146–8; and on the periodical, E. D. Dneprov, "'Morskoi sbornik' v obshchestvennom dvizhenii perioda pervoi revoliutsionnoi situatsii v Rossi," in: *Revoliutsionnaia situatsiia v Rossii v 1859–61 gg.*, vol. 4 (Moscow, 1965), 229–58.

31 Zapadov, ed., *Istoriia*, 301.

light through the gloom of Nicholas's last years.

The war was not yet over when General F. V. Ridiger (Friedrich Rüdiger), an officer on the general staff of Baltic German background with an independent cast of mind, recommended to Alexander II that a new professional journal be set up to cater to the army's needs.[32] No doubt with an eye to the *Naval Miscellany*'s problems, he specified that its army counterpart should be free from control by the military censorship. The new venture was particularly close to the heart of D. A. Miliutin, then a professor at the (Nicholas) General Staff Academy and one of the brightest minds in the armed forces. In June 1856 he sent a memorandum to the deputy War Minister, A. A. Katenin, in which he deplored the low standard of literary taste among Russian officers. The forthcoming periodical, he wrote, should accustom them "painlessly" to the habit of reading by combining general educational matter with information of a more limited professional or official kind; and its price should be kept low so as to bring it within the means of aspiring young officers.[33] Shortly thereafter Miliutin was appointed acting chief of staff to the Caucasian Army under his patron General (Count) A. I. Bariatinskii. In his absence from St. Petersburg the idea languished—his reform-minded associates had a lot on their hands and were no doubt anxious to see which way the wind would blow under Sukhozanet, the newly appointed War Minister, who was conservative in outlook and disliked Miliutin.[34] On November 1, 1857 two senior guards commanders, Generals Plautin and (Count) E. T. Baranov, sent him a memorandum couched in the same terms as Miliutin's, a copy of which they enclosed but without identifying its author. A military version of the *Naval Miscellany*, they argued, would "clarify for them [army officers] the importance and meaning of each innovation and demand made by the authorities."[35] The sugar coating on the pill was rich enough for Sukhozanet to swallow it. A special committee was at once set up to look into the matter, and its report was approved by the tsar with unusual haste on January 6, 1858. The *Military Miscellany* was to be a monthly, with two issues to a volume, each in four sections: official, professional, literary and miscellaneous (reviews, bibliography). It would receive a subsidy of 12,000 roubles a year, which meant that an individual subscription would cost only six roubles. Last but not least, it was to be published "at the Sovereign's command" by the staff of the Separate Guards Corps.[36]

This was a compromise solution to a thorny issue. Like Ridiger before him, Sukhozanet wanted the journal to come under civil censorship but, evidently distrusting GUTs, suggested the Third Department.[37] This idea did not commend itself to

---

32 N. A. Danilov, in *Stoletie Voennogo ministerstva* (St. Petersburg, 1902–12), vol. 1, appx. 40.

33 Makeev, *Chernyshevskii*, 30 (*Voprosy istorii* ed. [hereafter *VI*], 65).

34 For a sensitive fresh appreciation of his ministry, see E. Willis Brooks, "Reform in the Russian Army, 1856–1861," *SR*, 43 (1984), 63–82.

35 Makeev, *Chernyshevskii*, 2.

36 Ibid., 33 (*VI*, 66), the committee's report is in TsGIAL, f. 450, d. 293. The Guards Corps's designation was changed at this time.

37 Ibid., 34–35 (*VI*, 66), citing TsGVIAL, f. 722, op. 7, d. 151675. Unfortunately Makeev does not date what he calls Sukhozanet's "original report"—perhaps in order to highlight Miliutin's role, although at this juncture the latter was absent from the capital. The real initiator seems to have been Major-General A. P. Kartsev, Chief Quartermaster of the Separate Guards Corps: see E. W. Brooks's biography of him in *Modern Encyclopedia of Russian and Soviet History* (Gulf Breeze, Fla., xvi, 1980), 44–47.

members of the special committee, who saw this organization, which ran the gendarmerie, as a rival to the army and preferred to keep control of the journal in military hands—yet did not relish the prospect of censorship by the MCC. We do not know why. This may have had something to do with the personality of one of its members, Colonel L. L. Shtiurmer (Stürmer), who was destined to play a key role in the dénouement of this affair. From the limited information available he emerges as an unpleasant individual—narrow-minded, pedantic, touchy, tactless and arrogant: the very type, in short, to evoke antagonism among Russian guards officers, whose sense of social exclusiveness was now rapidly acquiring a chauvinistic flavor. Plautin and Baranov presumably put it to the tsar that they could be entrusted with the responsibility of ensuring that the new journal would take a line supportive of the government.

Why did Alexander agree? Perhaps because he knew that, with the impending restructuring of the procedure for ministerial consultation on censorship matters, the MCC would shortly disappear. He may also have felt that traditional military-civil jurisdictional boundaries should be respected and that the army would be "dishonored" by outright subjection to a civilian agency (regardless of, or even because of, the precedent involving the *Naval Miscellany* in 1852). The decision did indeed provide that the *Military Miscellany* should not be liable to civilian censorship, but only in regard to those items that were not of a military nature. This meant that its role would be just a formality and that the main job of control would fall to the guards staff. In Alexander's eyes the risk element must have seemed slight. After all Plautin took the view that "we cannot permit here [in Russia] freedom of debate on political and civic questions";[38] and this sentiment accorded with the tsar's own deeply conservative instincts. The previous year he had once minuted that any exposure of administrative abuses was harmful since it discredited all governmental authority.[39] He was in for a rude shock.

For, concealed in the fine print, was a provision that empowered the guards staff to choose the editors and allowed them in turn to choose the contributors. Major-General A. P. Kartsev promptly invited Chernyshevskii, the 30-year-old editor of *The Contemporary*, to take on the job of chief editor; Lieutenant-Colonel V. M. Anichkov and Captain N. N. Obruchev, two general staff officers who taught at its Academy, were to be his assistants with responsibility for articles on "military science." On January 7, 1858 Nikolai Gavrilovich wrote to his father in Saratov that his job would involve giving the submissions a decent literary form and deciding whether they contained ideas sufficiently "apposite, interesting and just" to merit publication.[40]

fortunately Makeev does not date what he calls Sukhozanet's "original report"—perhaps in order to highlight Miliutin's role, although at this juncture the latter was absent from the capital. The real initiator seems to have been Major-General A. P. Kartsev, Chief Quartermaster of the Separate Guards Corps: see E. W. Brooks's biography of him in *Modern Encyclopedia of Russian and Soviet History* (Gulf Breeze, Fla., xvi, 1980), 44–47.

38 Makeev, *Chernyshevskii*, 35 (*VI*, 66).

39 Iu. A. Gerasimova, *Iz istorii russkoi pechati v period revoliutsionnoi situatsii kontsa 1850-kh—nachala 1860-kh gg.* (Moscow, 1974), 32.

40 Chernyshevskii, *PSS*, vol. 14 (*Pis'ma, 1838–1876 gg.*, ed. B. P. Koz'min) (Moscow, 1949),

JOHN KEEP

This letter must have been written after a preliminary verbal approach by Kartsev, for the official invitation, signed by Baranov, did not reach him until two days later. This asked him to take charge of the business side of the journal as well. In a second letter home (January 14) Chernyshevskii spelled out the financial implications: if there were to be 1,500 subscribers, the profit after covering costs would be 4,000 roubles, of which half would fall to him.[41] Apart from the political prospects, he had every incentive to make a success of the venture to help satisfy the material needs of his wife in the capital and his impoverished parents in Saratov, from whom he had become somewhat estranged.[42]

But why did Kartsev pick on Chernyshevskii? There are two answers to this question, one more obvious than the other. First, the young journalist had made a great success of *The Contemporary*, boosting its circulation (which doubled between 1855 and 1861)[43] and turning it into "a microcosm of post-bellum Russian intellectual life."[44] Turgenev and Tolstoi had yet to part company with the journal, irritated by its editor's self-righteousness and by the growing influence exercised by the even more intransigent N. A. Dobroliubov. Second, Chernyshevskii—generally considered the epitome of the *intelligent*—actually had a long-standing connection with the military. On two occasions in his early career (1850, 1853) he had held temporary teaching jobs in the Second Cadet Corps to help make ends meet.[45] Neither seems to have been a success pedagogically, but this hardly matters: the experience gave him an opportunity to associate with young officers whose outlook differed little from that of ex-*raznochintsy* university students. Later, in 1858, several of these men formed part of an unstructured discussion circle that met each Thursday at his home.[46] We know the names of some of them: for instance V. A. Obruchev (cousin of N. N. Obruchev), who resigned his commission in 1859, was arrested two years later for revolutionary propaganda and sentenced to exile with hard labor, but ended his life with a major-general's insignia.[47] One need not accept the interpretation placed on these contacts

---

41 Chernyshevskii, *PSS*, vol. 14, 354.

42 Chernyshevskii's actual earnings from the enterprise are not known. According to our calculations, if the maximum number of subscribers (6,000) had all paid their dues in full, he should have made 4,000 roubles over an eight-month term.

43 A. Gleason, *Young Russia: the Genesis of Russian Radicalism in the 1860s* (New York, 1980), 99, 105.

44 Pereira, *Thought and Teachings*, 13.

45 Ibid., 26 and Woehrlin, *Chernyshevskii*, 60 mention only the first of these appointments; for the second see Pokusaev, *Chernyshevskii*, 43.

46 Some of them—according to one participant—were as interested in Chernyshevskii's light-hearted wife Olga as they were in their host's earnest conversation. N. D. Novitskii, "O Vvedenskom, Chernyshevskom i Serakovskom," in: S. Z. Katsenbogen, ed., *N. G. Chernyshevskii, 1828–1928: neizdannye teksty, materialy i stat'i* (Saratov, 1928), 296. Novitskii's memoir has since been published in full in *Literaturnoe nasledstvo*, vol. 67 (1959). Then at the General Staff Academy, he later became a lieutenant-general.

47 On the latter see his (unreliable) memoirs, "Iz perezhitogo," *Vestnik Evropy*, 95 (March

by certain Soviet historians eager to portray Chernyshevskii as a consistent Leninist *avant la lettre*. It is no doubt true that he appreciated intellectually the significance of the troops' morale in any revolutionary confrontation, but at this time he was far more interested in propagating the new social doctrines than in building up cadres for some immediate assault on the autocracy. In this he showed a realistic appraisal of the balance of forces. The Chernyshevskii of 1858 was, as Pereira says, a partisan of "meliorism"; under his control the *Miscellany* "did not become a tocsin of revolution; its editorial policy can only be described as moderately progressive in a vein which would culminate with the military reforms of D. A. Miliutin."[48] It was this promise of moderation, coupled with his professional expertise as a journalist, that doubtless commended him to Kartsev, to whom he had probably been introduced by his associate Obruchev. All these men knew each other socially through the contacts forged at the capital's élite military schools. The nuances of view that quite naturally distinguished these actual or former teachers and cadets mattered less than their common desire to see the Russian army transformed and placed at the service of "the people" instead of the tsar. Their liberal and democratic philosophy would animate the first issues of the *Miscellany* and lead inevitably to a showdown with the censorship.

On February 12 a lengthy notice of the journal's forthcoming appearance, signed by the three editors, was printed in *Russian Veteran*. Contributors were invited to submit material in any form, fictional or non-fictional, so long as it was "to the point and truthful" and displayed "commonsense": Chernyshevskii's hand was plain here. Potential authors should not be embarrassed by any lack of literary expertise—a hint that stylistic imperfections would be silently improved. Did editorial intervention extend to content also? Later, when under attack, Chernyshevskii would stoutly deny that he or his colleagues had set the journal's line: it was the voice of "the whole Russian officer corps."[49] His claim was justified, although it was also true that the editors received more contributions than they could print and so had to make a selection; we do not yet know what kind of material they rejected. The preliminary announcement also promised that the new journal would publish "all objections and comments" on the articles it printed, and several of these did appear, notwithstanding their indifferent quality. Chernyshevskii wanted the *Miscellany* to be a vigorous organ of army opinion, for he was confident that in any such debate the advocates of progress would worst their opponents. It was precisely this prospect that worried senior officers with more conventional views, who instinctively looked on public controversy as prejudicial to good order and discipline.

As in civilian literary journals, writers in the *Miscellany* adopted various tech-

---

1907), 122–155, esp. 133, continued in the issues for June 1907 and October 1908. For other names see R. A. Taubin, "K voprosu o roli N. G. Chernyshevskogo v sozdanii revoliutsionnoi partii. . . ," *IZ* 39 (1952), 63.

48 Pereira, *Thought and Teachings*, 28.

49 "Zamechaniia na doklad o vrednom napravlenii vsei russkoi literatury voobshche i 'Voennogo sbornika' v osobennosti, sostavlennyi g. voennym tsenzorom polkovnikom Shtiurmerom." *PSS*, vol. 5 (Moscow, 1950), 445. (Hereafter cited as Chernyshevskii, "Zamechaniia.").

niques to express their thoughts in a way that would not unduly alarm the authorities, although the "cover" was often paper-thin. For example, N. I. Glinoetskii (later a leading military historian) wrote that in western Europe the French revolution had furthered "new concepts of state life" (so avoiding the taboo word "constitution") and that the transition from mass armies to a reserve system had yet to be made everywhere (*scilicet*: in Russia) "owing to various political and local circumstances."[50] None of his readers will have had trouble in following his argument that military expenditure and casualty rates needed to be reduced in order not to overstrain the nation's economic and demographic resources. Such a point might seem so elementary as to be redundant, but in 1858 it was still novel and exciting. Russian officers responded with enthusiasm to the new periodical, the first issue of which appeared on May 1; it had to be reprinted to meet demand. Subscriptions quickly rose to the 6,000 mark—three times the number anticipated, and comparable with the number obtained by leading literary journals.[51] More than 40 individuals, most of them officers, are said to have contributed to the journal on a regular basis.[52] Many of them wrote under pseudonyms or initials which even the omniscient I. F. Masanov[53] was unable to decipher. This practise was permitted under the censorship regulations, provided that the author's name was known to the editor and could be passed on if inquiries were made; but it is not known whether Chernyshevskii and his associates kept such a list.

The burden of the *Miscellany*'s message was that Russian officers bore a moral obligation towards their men, not just towards the state. They were urged to behave honestly, with respect for the natural rights inherent in every individual, and to promote the material and intellectual well-being of those entrusted to their charge—educating and improving themselves in the process.

In other words, they were called on to adopt the professional standards current in western armies, which had enabled them to defeat their Russian antagonist in the recent war. Some contributors also raised basic questions about the armed forces' role in the empire's political and social order. All this was nothing less than a programme for a radical transformation of the traditional military structure and ethos, which it is

---

50 N. I. Glinoetskii, "Voennaia statistika i soldatskii byt," *VS*, 1 (1858), 444–5.

51 Katkov's respected *Russkii vestnik* ("Russian Herald") had 5,000 subscribers, the Slavophil *Russkaia beseda* ("Russian Conversation") a mere 1,200, and *The Contemporary* about 4,800 (7,000 at its height): V. A. Alekseev, "Tipologicheskaia kharakteristika zhurnal'noi periodiki 1860-kh gg.," in V. G. Berezina et al., eds., *Ocherki po istorii russkoi zhurnalistiki i kritiki*, vol. II: *Vtoraia polovina XIX v.* (Leningrad, 1965), 19. Makeev, *Chernyshevskii*, 59 (*VI*, 68) notes that some units ordered as many as 20 to 25 copies of the *Miscellany*, leaving one wondering whether all these actually circulated. Chernyshevskii stated later ("Zamechaniia," 446 n.) that 5,800 of its subscriptions were from members of the armed forces.

52 Makeev, *Chernyshevskii*, 59 (no source indicated; not in *VI*).

53 I. F. Masanov, *Slovar' psevdonimov russkikh pisatelei, uchenykh i obshchestvennykh deiatelei*, 3 vols. (Moscow, 1941–49).

worth considering a little more closely.

A contributor who signed himself D. S. (later identified by Chernyshevskii as an officer of the Izmailovskii guards regiment)[54] revealed that in ten years with the colors he had often been struck by the lack of common humanity in relations between officers and their subordinates. Young noblemen joined the army merely in order to gain a livelihood, not from "love of the soldierly calling," and in consequence became disinterested and alienated from their environment. Emotionally immature, they played safe by sticking to routine; they neglected or maltreated their men and made no effort to understand their psychology. Russian soldiers, far from being slow-witted as many of their superiors thought, responded well to training if they were handled as human beings, patiently and sympathetically, instead of as cogs in a machine who had to be taught the drillbook by rote. Their minds had been conditioned by centuries of self-abasement, a condition which their superiors wrongly thought normal. "I believe one must first of all raise the soldier's self-respect, so that he is aware of his own worth; then he'll look differently on his duties instead of finding them burdensome."[55] There should be less emphasis on formal drill or *shchegol'stva* ("spit and polish") and more on tactical exercises to encourage initiative in the field, as well as on marksmanship and physical training. Gymnastics had recently become fashionable, but typically some officers took the new fad to excess and drove their men too hard, instead of explaining why it was important for a soldier to keep fit.[56]

The writer shared to the full the simple faith in the virtues of education common to reformers in this era: one had but to adopt the correct pedagogic approach and the obstacles to mutual understanding would miraculously dissolve. The first essential was to overcome, by concerted action, the illiteracy that was so widespread in the ranks—90–95%, according to two guesses, or less than 50% according to another.[57] Contributors offered an abundance of practical recommendations: coercion should be avoided; zealous pupils should be rewarded with promotion; reading matter should be appropriate (e.g. historical tales); classes should be arranged in two tiers, graded according to difficulty; and so on. Most of this advice was sensible, but some was superficial or wrong-headed. One writer thought that soldiers could soon learn to read and write so long as an officer tested their progress monthly and taught one class a week to show that the drive had the authorities' backing.[58] Another wanted to make sure that pupils learned rifle assembly before they were taught to read—without using textbooks, lest this encourage rote learning.[59] A third saw correctly that the literacy campaign would be viewed by the men as just another formal obligation unless it were

---

54 Chernyshevskii, "Zamechaniia," 460.

55 D. S., "Zametki komandira strelkovoi roty," *VS*, 1 (1858), 112–114.

56 Ibid., 117, 128–132; cf. L. K., "Soldat i ofitser," *VS*, 4 (1858), 333–46.

57 D. S., "Zametki," 122; M., "O pol'ze obucheniia gramote vsei massy russkikh voisk', *VS*, 1 (1858), 354; ***, "Ob ustroistve shkol dlia rasprostraneniia gramotnosti v voiskakh," *VS*, 2 (1858), 192.

58 M., "O pol'ze," 354.

59 ***, "Ob ustroistve," 191, 198, 201.

followed up by a broader educational program to expand their intellectual horizons.[60] But he went on to call the soldier "a primitive man, as yet untouched by education, [whose] moral forces are asleep," implying that progressive-minded officers were ethically superior beings with a natural right to impose their cultural standards on their subordinates. Thus the old paternalistic outlook survived in a new form. "The Russian soldier's heart," D. S. exclaimed with pathos, "knows how to respond to the innermost (*zadushevnyi*) voice of his commander," who ought to enter into details of his men's lives.[61] It does not seem to have occurred to him that such interference might be resented. Lieutenant-Colonel Anichkov wanted the Russian army to emulate the French in which, so he claimed, promotion went strictly by merit so that senior officers were the most moral.[62]

If Russia's officers lagged in this regard, it was because their intellectual and ethical development had been slighted. Kartsev thought that the general indifference to education had spread down from the top gradually during the previous reign: senior commanders were "remote from the life of the troops" while their subordinates "had been carried away by the desire to win their superiors' approval" through excellence in those matters, such as ceremonial, which the latter deemed important.[63] Anyone who had spent his leisure studying military science had been ridiculed by his comrades as a bookish individual divorced from practical concerns. But experience without reflection was a poor guide; as Frederick the Great had once said, "a mule which had gone on Prince Eugene's campaigns did not thereby make a better tactician."[64] Obruchev echoed these sentiments. Entrants to military schools should be at least 15 and have received a general schooling; the academic quality of their studies should be improved so that they graduated as men of sound education and morals, who could be relied on, for instance, to manage their unit's economic affairs honestly.[65] Another writer adduced statistical evidence in support of a devastating critique of current officer selection procedures. It was too easy for ignorant but well-connected candidates to gain exemption from entrance examinations; cadet corps graduates were too few in number and unevenly distributed between different arms of service; and not enough commissions were granted to promising NCOs from the underprivileged. He recommended a drive to expand the training of *iunkery* (that is, men who took a course in basic subjects less demanding than that offered by the élite cadet corps).[66] He did not dare suggest that these institutions be eliminated entirely—as Miliutin

60 S. N., "O gramotnosti v voiskakh," *VS*, 4 (1858), 6.

61 D. S., "Zametki," 119.

62 V. Anichkov, "Sistema proizvodstva v chiny i zameshcheniia dolzhnostei vo Frantsii," *VS*, 2 (1858), 207–8.

63 . . .', "Vzgliad na sostoianie russkikh voisk v minuvshuiu voinu," *VS*, 1 (1858), 11. For the authorial identification: Brooks, "Reform in the Russian Army," 73, n. 1.

64 . . . ', "Vzgliad," 14.

65 N. Obruchev, "O vooruzhennoi sile i ego ustroistvo [sic]," *VS*, 1 (1858), 46.

66 L. K., "Vzgliad na stepen' obrazovaniia russkikh ofitserov v armii," *VS*, 1 (1858), 145–62, esp. 157.

would try to do a few years later once he had become a War minister, with the aim of substituting Russian officers' exclusive caste spirit by a more professional outlook.[67] But contributors to the *Miscellany*'s first issues did broach Miliutin's main concerns in the educational field.

On the other hand their emphasis on moral regeneration led them to neglect the need for judicial reform within the army, to which the reformers of the 1860s would rightly pay great attention. The underlying reason for this relative neglect may be sought in the anti-juridical bias that ran through the Slavophil-narodnik intellectual tradition (in which Chernyshevskii stood); there was also no doubt a natural reluctance to grapple with sensitive issues that touched on the sovereign's prerogatives. A third reason may be that none of the contributors to the *Miscellany* had served as auditors; these were virtually the only officers knowledgeable in the field, and they tended to be narrowly conservative in outlook. The outspoken Izmailovskii guards officer mentioned in passing the need to mitigate the harsh penalties currently in force: "in minor offences the sanctions imposed should not be insulting: corporal punishment and swearing should be eliminated *as far as possible*" (our emphasis)[68], but he did not develop the point except to suggest—quite unrealistically—that serious offences should be heard in comradely courts. To say, as he did here, that military law should be upheld "calmly" and "without excitement" was to sidestep the problem of instilling in men of all ranks a proper respect for their legal responsibilities. Characteristically, D. S. looked on corruption as an *ethical* problem: if soldiers had to grease the palms of their NCOs in order to avoid maltreatment, this showed that "they lack firm moral convictions [impelling them] to act against such injustices; if they had some good qualities that would help them to defend their rights, this [practise] would not last for long."[69] By "moral convictions" and "good qualities" one suspects that the writer really meant an awareness of their interests rather than of their rights.

In a similar vein L. K. began his article with a reference to the 1839 Military Code and the unexceptionable statement that "the most supreme of all authorities is undoubtedly the law"; the existing statutes prohibited arbitrary conduct (*proizvol*) by officers, which was more harmful to discipline than the comradeship-in-arms between men of all ranks that conservatives seemed to be so afraid of. But then he turned aside—"let us not pursue this angle"—and directed his fire against the familiar "unethical" targets: gentry prejudice against commoners, careerism, favor-seeking, covering up of irregularities, concern with externals and so on.[70] His article epitomized that tragic misunderstanding between *vlast'* and *obshchestvo* which would make it so hard for Imperial Russia to develop a modern legal order. All too often nineteenth-century radical critics of autocracy would take refuge in angry fulminations against those guilty of abuses, or calls for moral renewal, instead of considering what concrete institutional arrangements should be made to ensure that fallible men lived up to their

67 F. A. Miller, *Dmitrii Miliutin and the Reform Era in Russia* (Charlotte, N. C., 1968).
68 D. S., "Zametki," 119–120; cf. V. Matveev, "O telesnom nakazanii," *VS*, 2 (1858), 480–2.
69 D. S., "Zametki," 118.
70 L. K., "Soldat i ofitser," 334–8.

social obligations.

The post-Crimean military scene certainly presented plenty of tempting targets for negative *oblichitel'stvo* (literally, "exposure," denunciation) of this kind. Major-General Kartsev attempted a balanced analysis of the factors that had contributed to Russia's defeat. The army, he contended, was not to blame, since it had faced an impossible task: the soldiers had fought well, but the enemy had enjoyed superiority in numbers, equipment and mobility. Yet in fixing responsibility for the débâcle Kartsev blurred the lines of his argument. He minimized the adverse effect of Nicholas I's regimentation and paradomania, on which so many critics focussed attention, and reduced the whole problem to a lack of initiative among commanders, i.e. to their defective education.[71] His case was not entirely convincing and earned a riposte from an anonymous group of officers—who, however, missed the main point of his remarks, which they misinterpreted as an attack on the honor of their innocent comrades. In their view the blame ought properly to be laid on the old statutes, whose bureaucratic spirit had forced commanders to waste time on useless paperwork.[72] This was hardly an edifying exchange of views, since in neither article did the writers look at the wider political and social context in which military decisions were made.

This step forward was taken by deputy editor Obruchev, whose several contributions to the *Miscellany* in 1858 were the most intelligent, logical and telling. With a three-part article entitled "The Seamy Side of the Crimean War" he stirred up a veritable hornet's nest. The first section covered the cost of the campaign to the Allies.[73] Citing official French medical reports, he maintained that until June 1855 their army in the field had suffered a mortality rate of only 3%, despite epidemics of cholera and typhus;[74] the soldiers had been adequately fed, *inter alia* on tinned meat (a delicacy which would not, incidentally, reach the Russian army for another 15 years). In Great Britain a vocal public opinion had played a constructive part in correcting abuses and putting the authorities on their mettle. England could be proud, Obruchev wrote, that she had treated her soldiers as human beings and not as an insensate capital asset.[75] Napoleon III for his part had acted prudently and promptly on remedial measures suggested by his subordinates, even though he bore ultimate responsibility for the loss of so many lives, since he had confused his own dynastic interest with that of the French state and nation. Obruchev compared him unfavorably with Russian rulers such as Peter I, Catherine II "and others"[76]—the omission of Nicholas I's name from the list was of course deliberate.

The shock to conventional patriotic sentiment was all the greater when, in the

71 . . . ', "Vzgliad," 1–15, esp. 5, 8, 10.

72 "Neskol'ko zamechanii po povodu stat'i 'Vzgliad. . . ,' " *VS*, 3 (1858), 271–288, esp. 277, 281.

73 N. Obruchev, "Iznanka Krymskoi voiny," *VS*, 1 (1858), 545–86.

74 However, *total* French fatalities, including deaths among soldiers evacuated from the front, he estimated at 23.3%: Ibid., 585.

75 Ibid., 571.

76 Ibid., 584–5.

second part of his article, Obruchev turned to Russia's own war record.[77] From data collected by the medical authorities (some of it apparently unpublished) he endeavored to estimate the number of casualties. Even the army stationed on the empire's western border, which had not seen action, had lost the equivalent of an entire corps to the ravages of cholera, typhoid fever and other epidemics.[78] He provided a graphic, but by no means exaggerated, account of the grim conditions in the emergency hospital set up at Nikolaev.[79] Here as elsewhere the excessive death rate was due in large part to sheer administrative neglect; this was particularly evident in the maltreatment of recruits, who were obliged to undertake long marches without proper training or care. "If we continue to keep silent as to how and where our men perish, we shall long have to pay for our inadequate sympathy for science."[80] He concluded by making several practical suggestions about the quartering, movement, clothing and equipment of Russian troops.

This was to have been Obruchev's last word on the subject, but his frank criticisms brought a reply from a senior commissariat official, Major-General F. K. Zatler (Sattler).[81] He made some justifiable points in self-defense—the unfortunate Zatler was made a scapegoat by Russian nationalists and had to stand trail for his alleged malpractises—but showed himself to be vain and muddle-headed. He ended his plea with the rhetorical plea that Obruchev "will not continue to mislead the public." At this point the *Miscellany* editors commented rather smugly the "we shall with pleasure print all articles that serve to elucidate the truth," whereupon Obruchev leaped back into the fray with a final blast.[82] His postmortem on the war, he noted, had evoked no less than four responses in the press, two of them published in *Russian Veteran* (nos. 52 and 230), and Zatler had also put out a brochure in an effort to set his record straight. The *Miscellany* had been asked to print this, but had declined on the grounds that Zatler's argument was hard to follow and needed a running commentary. Obruchev proceeded to take it apart in a manner little different from that of the former *general-intendant*. Statistics at the ready, he in effect indicted him as a liar. Yet Obruchev did not produce conclusive evidence of fraud or inefficiency on Zatler's part. Much of his argument was based on interference and the whole piece was redolent of "muck-raking" journalism. Obruchev was not free from anti-Semitism[83] and

---

77 *VS*, 2 (1858), 429–76.

78 *VS*, 2 (1858), 436, 441, 461. His estimates fell far short of the reality, as calculated later by M. I. Bogdanovich, *Istoricheskii ocherk deiatel'nosti voennogo upravleniia v Rossii v pervoe 25-letie . . . imperatora Aleksandra Nikolaevicha, 1855–1880 gg.* (St. Petersburg, 1789–81), vol. 1, 170–4, appx. 15.

79 *VS*, 2 (1858), 442–53. For supporting evidence, see N. I. Pirogov, *Sevastopol'skie pis'ma* (St. Petersburg, 1899).

80 *VS*, 2 (1858), 462, 466.

81 "Iznanka na litso" [literally "The Seamy Side Inside Out"], *VS*, 4 (1858), 219–38.

82 Ibid., 238; N. Obruchev, "Iznanka Krymskoi voiny: drugaia storona," *VS*, 4 (1858), 239–306.

83 For example, Obruchev, "Iznanka," 304.

in his assault on the commissariat gave the impression that its common failings were universal. He could have made his point far more effectively by showing greater restraint; but his indignation had clearly been aroused by the conviction, right or wrong, that his adversary had thousands of innocent lives on his conscience.

The controversy attracted public attention and no doubt helped to account for the *Miscellany*'s high press run. But there is no evidence that it led directly to repressive action by the authorities against the journal. The Crimean postmortem theme served to raise the temperature, to heighten the emotions of those involved as writers or readers; but it was not the most significant issue that the *Miscellany* raised. This was contained in another contribution by Obruchev, presented in a more temperate manner in the first number[84]—a reflective essay that even today has considerable topical interest.

For the first time in the history of Russian journalism, a writer tackled the question what armies were for. Obruchev set out some basic ideas on international and national security and demonstrated that the forces' role ought to be circumscribed by their security function. To militarists of the Nicolaevan school—and one can think of some twentieth-century parallels—the army needed to be large and powerful because its very existence demonstrated the prestige of the autocrat; it was, so to speak, his *Hausmacht*, as much personal or dynastic bodyguard as a national asset. Such a view, characteristic of the *ancien régimes*, had become anachronistic (although it would live on for several generations in the central and eastern European monarchies). Obruchev was struck by the progress of civilization in the western democracies, as so many mid-nineteenth-century intellectuals were, and thought that the development of communications, science, education, international law and public opinion was tilting the balance from war towards peace as the normal condition of mankind. "An awareness that peace is a good thing," he wrote, "flows from the process of development and perfectioning."[85] Yet he was no naive idealist. The twentieth century, he suggested presciently, might know as many wars as the eighteenth.[86] But for the present international conflicts were less likely, since European states stood to gain little by territorial aggrandizement; their leaders realized that the costs outweighed the advantages; and the accumulation of wealth increased men's desire to enjoy their possessions peaceably. The outcome of wars depended not merely on the strength of the contending armed forces but on a whole complex of factors, including the level of economic and social well-being and the condition of popular morale. "The strength of a state lies in its people."[87] Consequently those states which

---

84 "O vooruzhennoi sile . . . [see fn. 65]," 16–56.

85 Ibid., 18; cf. Kh. G. Okerblom: "War, like any breach of human rights, is a definite evil, which armies exist to deter" ("Mysli o khoziaistve voisk," *VS*, 4 (1858), 60). Unfortunately, he undercut the force of this modern-sounding dictum in his ensuing remarks, where he echoed the conventional view that armies were also necessary to instill in the populace a sense of military valor and national pride.

86 "O vooruzhennoi sile . . . ," 17.

87 Ibid., 21.

nurtured their resources and secured greatest popular support would do best in the international competition for power and prestige.

Obruchev was understandably cautious about spelling out the implications of these principles for the Russian empire. He entered no plea for constitutional government, although he certainly favored it, along with other radical political and social changes. (In 1861 he would be a core member of the embryonic revolutionary organization "Land and Liberty.") His admiration for the western democracies was tempered by a realization that Russia's problems were different, if only because of her size and geographical location. She would always need a strong military reserve—and it was now time to establish such a force. (The idea had been in the air for generations, but Nicholas I had taken only a small step towards it.) In place of the traditional massive peacetime army, recruited indiscriminately from the taxpaying population, there ought to be a small, qualitatively superior cadre force capable of training men who would be assigned to the reserve until they were needed.[88] He undertook to consider in a later article the criteria whereby those reaching military age should be selected for service. Unfortunately this sequel did not see the light, but from Obruchev's later career it is clear what he had in mind. As a close aide of the War minister (on the Military Training Committee) in the 1860s and 1870s, he was one of the architects of the great reform which by historiographical convention bears Miliutin's name: the introduction (1874) of a selective conscription system that, in principle at least, extended equally to men in all social classes.[89] The post-reform Russian army was certainly less "democratic" than the Swiss-style people's militia which Obruchev had initially favored[90] and which would come into being temporarily in 1918, but for the Russian empire it represented a considerable advance. For all its deficiencies it proved its worth for nearly half a century.

If these and other sensible ideas were later acted upon by the tsar's government, why did not the *Military Miscellany* prosper under the Chernyshevskii-Obruchev editorial team? To answer this question we have to return to the obscure world of literary controls. Successive issues of the journal were signed for the press by the censor (Beketov, less frequently D. Matskevich) at the beginning of each month until December, when issue no. 8 was delayed for three weeks[91]—a clear indication, then as now, that a crisis was brewing behind the scenes. Although it is still not possible to reconstruct its dénouement with complete assurance, the main outlines are clear.

88 "O vooruzhennoi sile. . . ," 25, 41–43.
89 See Miller, *Miliutin*; P. A. Zaionchkovskii, *Voennye reformy 1860–1870 gg. v Rossii* (Moscow, 1952); idem, "Podgotovka voennoi reformy 1874 g.," *IZ*, 27 (1948), 170–201; R. F. Bauman, *The Debates over Universal Military Service in Russia, 1870–1874*, Ph.D. thesis (Yale, 1982); and our *Soldiers of the Tsar*, ch. 15.
90 Obruchev, "O vooruzhennoi sile," 33.
91 They were passed for the press on May 8, June 10, July 10, August 7, September 1, October 7, November 1—and December 22; in the first months of 1859 authorization was granted at the end of the month.

The frankness with which writers in the *Miscellany* exposed past and present abuses in the armed forces, and perhaps their very success in building up a wide readership among serving officers, caused the journal to be eyed askance by those in the establishment, from Alexander II down, who entertained different ideas as to the proper role of the press. Chernyshevskii himself seems to have expected trouble from the start, for in his letter home of January 14 he had said that not until July, once three numbers had appeared, would it become clear whether the tsar, Baranov and "their yes-man (*otgolosok*) Kartsev" would be satisfied.[92] The reference to his benefactor Kartsev was ungracious and misplaced, for when the blow came it was not dealt by the guards staff but from a different quarter. Nevertheless caution was clearly in order, and that was no doubt why Chernyshevskii refrained from making any personal literary contribution to the *Miscellany*. Leading articles were in any case still taboo; he seems to have confined himself to the occasional editorial footnote[93]— unless perchance he took charge of the unsigned review of the military press, although this was more probably the work of Okerblom (who signed the one in no. 6).[94] It has to be remembered that Chernyshevskii was also editor of the *The Contemporary* and that he naturally gave that job priority. It was just at this time that he wrote three of his most noted essays, "Party Strife in France under Louis XVIII and Charles X," "A Criticism of the Philosophical Objections to Communal Ownership," and a long critical review of Turgenev's *Asia*, "Russian Man at the Rendezvous," which he published in another journal, *Atenei* ("The Athenaeum").[95] Even for someone with his phenomenal capacity for work it must have been a strain to keep so many irons in the fire simultaneously. Curiously enough, it was actually illegal to be editor of two journals at once,[96] although the authorities seem to have overlooked this ruling of 1841 when Chernyshevskii took charge of the *Miscellany*. It would have been a handy weapon for its growing army of critics.

Military leaders and officials were alarmed at the sight of public wrangling between organs of the press, especially those subsidized by the government. It did not take long for the *Miscellany* to grapple with the staid *Military Journal*. The press review in the first issue singled out for criticism a study published in the *Journal* by Major-General N. S. Golitsyn on the historical development of the general staff. After a reluctant tribute to the author's erudition, the critic questioned the soundness and relevance of Golitsyn's treatment of medieval Rus': what, for instance, had really been the functions of a *zaimshchik* under Vladimir Monomakh? Another writer, who compared training methods in France and Russia, was taken to task for

---

92 Chernyshevskii, *PSS*, vol. 14, 353.

93 These comments are carefully analyzed by Makeev, *Chernyshevskii*, 80–84 (*VI*, 75–76).

94 Okerblom, a captain in the guards staff, replaced Anichkov when the latter was appointed deputy director of the Commissariat department. B. P. Koz'min, "N. G. Chernyshevskii v redaktsii 'Voennogo sbornika': iz vospominanii D. A. Miliutina," *Literaturnoe nasledstvo*, 25–26 (1936), 235.

95 Dinesman, comp., *Sbornik materialov*, 17–24.

96 *Sbornik* [see fn. 4], 233.

"failing to understand" his topic and "formulating his views in the seclusion of his study."[97] There was a nasty taste about these critiques, but the *Journal* evidently felt it beneath its dignity to reply: throughout the year it ignored the *Miscellany* in pointed silence. It was in the *Russian Veteran* that General (Count) Sumarokov, an ADC to the tsar, chose to criticize the *Miscellany* for biassed reviewing.[98] Perhaps unwisely, Sumarokov predicted that the new-fangled ways of training troops would lead to "harmful errors." A more powerful blast came from another of the tsar's ADCs, General (Count) A. A. Rzhevusskii (Rżewuski). He took particular exception to N. F. T.'s "A Voice from the Army"—"a voice hoarse and strained from helpless indignation."[99] A scrutiny of the *Miscellany*'s first issue suggests a reason why the general was so annoyed. He had himself submitted a brief "technical" article on the methods of bringing reserve cavalry squadrons up to strength in mounts. The *Miscellany* had duly published it, but with an acid editorial comment: the writer's scheme for a reserve of 40,000 horses would be a burden on the economy and in any case reliance on massive cavalry forces was outdated. "These and many other considerations undoubtedly explain why C[oun]t Rzh[evuss]kii's scheme has not been implemented."[100] This was twisting the knife in the wound.

Did either of the tsar's adjutants, or others who took offence, press for a purge of the *Miscellany*'s editorial board? In January 1859 Kartsev wrote to Miliutin, then still in the Caucasus, that "the affair was set up (*podstroen*) by Likhachev, a fierce foe of all innovations," who was really intriguing against Baranov, chief of the guards staff.[101] Major-General A. F. Likhachev was director of chancellery in the War ministry. The allegation is plausible—relations between the guards and ministry officials were often strained—but cannot be corroborated. Miliutin himself wrote later, in his memoirs, that the journal's "sharp denunciatory tone" had aroused concern among the "old dogs" (*sluzhaki*), aghast at what they regarded as revolutionary propaganda; but he laid most of the blame on Chernyshevskii. His appointment was "extremely unfortunate and, as subsequently became clear, seriously harmed the publication."[102] But this was written many years after the event, when Chernyshevskii had become an idol of the left and a bogyman to the right.

Whoever initiated administrative action against the *Miscellany* found the right person to do the job: Colonel Shtiurmer, the (former?) military censor. He compiled a critical report which, as Makeev says, amounted to a denunciation.[103] Just what

97 N. S. Golitsyn, "Ocherk istorii general'nogo shtaba v Zapadnoi Evrope i v Rossii," *Voennyi zhurnal* (1858), 1, 1–44; *VS* 1 (1858), 255 ff.; cf. 2 (1858), 542–3.

98 No. 122; cited by Makeev, *Chernyshevskii*, 87.

99 *VS*, 1 (1858), 77–85; *Russkii invalid*, no. 281, cited by Makeev, loc. cit. (*VI*, 77).

100 Gr. Rzh—ii, "O sposobe komplektovat' rezervnye eskadrony loshad'mi," *VS*, 1 (1858), 299–304 at 299.

101 Koz'min, "Chernyshevskii," loc. cit., citing from ff. 19–21 of volume 8 of Militin's unpublished memoirs.

102 Koz'min, loc. cit.

103 Makeev, *Chernyshevskii*, 91 (*VI*, 79).

status Shtiurmer had after the dissolution of the MCC in March 1858 is unclear: he was presumably the War Ministry's delegate (*doverennyi*) on GUTs, the main censorship board. He must have been a bitter man, resentful at the loss of his staff if not of his job. He evidently saw himself as a guardian of traditional ideas and practises in the army that were threatened by the partisans of major institutional changes. Hawk-like, he watched the *Miscellany* for the least sign of subversion. As late as 1864, when he had risen to major-general's rank, he made trouble for the journal, although Miliutin had it well in hand;[104] in 1858 he will have been even more vigilant.

Only excerpts from the report which he submitted to Sukhozanet, the War minister, have been published.[105] He confined his remarks to certain articles (in the first issue?)[106] and was not above seriously distorting the text of those he summarized in trying to substantiate the inferences he drew as to the writers' meaning and intentions. He certainly did not offer an objective, balanced analysis. He insinuated that the editors had chosen as contributors young officers whose views were unrepresentative, and that these writers *inter alia* portrayed rare abuses as typical and overlooked the juridical foundation on which harsh disciplinary penalties rested.[107] If soldiers had been as badly treated as N. F. T. alleged, "any regiment would have run away, but fortunately matters never reached such a pass . . . Humanity sometimes leads to grave error, and the latter to sharp, baseless conclusions."[108] Asperity was a particular feature of the review section.[109] Shtiurmer correctly perceived the significance of Obruchev's article on the military's role in society. He contended that his arguments "diminished the army's significance" and were therefore inappropriate in a military periodical; contemptuously he added that they might appeal to clergymen or professors.[110]

The War minister did not act immediately on this report. Instead, through Kartsev, he asked Chernyshevskii to compile a memorandum that could be submitted to the tsar.[111] This weak, non-committal stance was characteristic of Sukhozanet, but at least it gave Chernyshevskii a chance to refute the allegations. Unfortunately he did not make the best use of this opportunity. Instead of a concise factual statement

---

104 *Zapiski Petra Kononovicha Men'kova v 3 tt.* (St. Petersburg, 1898), vol. III: *Dnevnik P. K. Men'kova* [cited as Men'kov, *Dnevnik*], 315; cf. 300.

105 Chernyshevskii, "Zamechaniia," 459–491, where these excerpts are printed parallel to Chernyshevskii's rebuttals.

106 Makeev states that Shtiurmer examined "the first three issues" (*Chernyshevskii*, 91 (*VI*, 79)), but quotes his report from the printed (i.e. excerpted) version, not from the original manuscript.

107 Chernyshevskii, "Zamechaniia," 460, 463, 465.

108 Ibid., 472–3.

109 Ibid., 485.

110 Ibid., 489.

111 Makeev, *Chernyshevskii*, 91 (*VI*, 80). This was actually a routine move, since under the new censorship rules the tsar was supposed to arbitrate disputes between ministerial *doverennye* and GUTs.

he produced a lengthy journalistic diatribe. His sense of intellectual propriety was outraged by the censor's crude textual distortions, and so he set to work to compare in detail what the contributors had actually written with what Shtiurmer claimed they had said, or meant to say—but without, of course, discussing any of the writers' "subtexts." The upshot was an all but unreadable screed,[112] much of it off the point, and abounding in sarcastic jibes at the colonel's moral and intellectual shortcomings. Chernyshevskii delighted in showing that Shtiurmer did not even know the regulations he was supposed to enforce, and turned the charges of subversion back upon their originators: it was they who were defying the sovereign emperor's will by seeking to conceal abuses and "preaching secrecy and darkness."[113] N. F. T.'s article, "A Voice from the Army," to which Shtiurmer had objected so strongly, had actually been vetted by the tsar (who apparently did not read it).[114] The *Miscellany*'s popularity with army readers was in itself proof of the soundness of its approach.

Chernyshevskii's philippic was too strong to be presented to Alexander II and was returned to him for modification. He toned it down, but without making any substantial changes. It was sent back to Sukhozanet, who seems to have pigeonholed it. What happened next is not at all clear. Apparently, in either November or December 1858, Chernyshevskii was asked, or decided, to resign rather than face dismissal. In one letter to his father (November 11) he stated that he had been offered, bt had refused, an editorial job on the guards general staff, and in the second (January 13, 1859) that he had again been invited to join the *Miscellany* but felt unable to accept.[115] Woehrlin thinks that he sought to mislead his family as to the circumstances in which he now found himself.[116] Perhaps he wanted to soften the blow to his dependents' hopes of lavish financial support. He does not seem to have told any of his associates that he regretted having to leave the journal. He may have been resigned to a step that he had long expected to take, and have reckoned that Obruchev (who was still on the editorial board) could carry on the work. At least he would now have more time for *The Contemporary*, which all along had been his major interest. He could take satisfaction in a far from negligible achievement: much had been done to stimulate among Russian officers a mood favorable to radical change, and these ideas would sooner or later bring fruit. It is unlikely that he had ever expected the *Miscellany* to become the nucleus of a conspiratorial organization or revolutionary movement in the armed forces, as Makeev (not doubt with the Leninist model in mind) suggests: "work on the journal was for him a certain tactical manoeuvre."[117] On the other hand, Pereira's interpretation of Chernyshevskii's state of mind seems to exaggerate the importance which he attached to the venture and the impact which his resignation had on him: "[he had] lost all hope in the tsar's resolution and good

112 Chernyshevskii, "Zamechaniia," 441–91.
113 Ibid., 445.
114 Ibid., 454; Makeev, *Chernyshevskii*, 94–95 (*VI*, 80).
115 Chernyshevskii, *PSS*, vol. 14, 367, 370.
116 Woehrlin, *Chernyshevskii*, 102, 368.
117 Makeev, *Chernyshevskii* (*VI*, 79).

faith, not to mention the possibility of working with allegedly progressive forces in high bureaucratic and court circles."[118]

Meanwhile Shtiurmer's denunciation touched off an inquiry, and a brief report was drawn up in the general staff of the army (*not* the guards!). This criticized indirectly the decree of February 19 (which as we know had been issued after pressure by guards officers) and rather unfairly blamed the civilian censors for letting through "articles . . . prejudicial to the honor of our army." The report was submitted to the tsar, who minuted: "I have nothing to add to today's [oral?] explanations, i.e. the *Miscellany* must be submitted for vetting to the military censor."[119] Proofs have survived of an article, heavily marked with red pencil; there is a note on them in Beketov's handwriting, dated 5 December: "Must be seen beforehand by Shtiurmer," and another note by Shtiurmer, written five days later: "Cannot be printed in [its] present form."[120] From now on the journal had to face a more effective system of dual military-civil censorship, and a search was launched for a new editor.

There were few suitably qualified candidates, and it was a surprise to all that the choice should fall on P. K. Men'kov. Apart from his military rank (major-general) and good connections in the War ministry, he had little to commend him: since 1855 he had been in trouble with the authorities for unofficial literary activity. He had written memoranda that had circulated in manuscript and memoirs that had been published abroad. Men'kov maintained that he had not given permission for this material to see the light, but his pleas lacked credibility. An inordinately vain man, he resented bitterly the social ostracism to which his misdemeanors had led: on one occasion Alexander II had pointedly ignored him at a parade. It was while visiting St. Petersburg in an effort to rehabilitate himself that he came to Sukhozanet's notice and was offered the job.[121]

The new editor was of a different stamp from Chernyshevskii, but he was more than an official yes-man. Nor was he a total stranger to the *Miscellany*, for according to his own account he had previously submitted his campaign memoirs for publication in its pages.[122] Shortly after his appointment in January 1859 he wrote another autobiographical piece which Sukhozanet and the tsar decided could not be printed, since "it threw too bright a light on the military practises of the previous reign."[123] Initially Men'kov faced hostility among officers of the Guards Corps, who regarded him as a conservative (and, probably, as an agent of a rival element in the army establishment).[124] The journal's circulation fell by about one thousand; but after a brief interlude the flow of articles by readers resumed.[125] Unfortunately many of

---

118 Pereira, *Thought and Teachings*, 28.

119 Makeev, *Chernyshevskii*, 96 (*VI*, 81; date not given).

120 Ibid., 97.

121 Men'kov, *Dnevnik*, 219, 256–60, 264, 266, 279.

122 Ibid., 227.

123 Ibid., 269; text in ibid., vol. 2, 139–50.

124 Ibid., 269–70.

125 Ibid., 270–71; Taubin, "K voprosu," 63, calculates that over four-fifths of the authors who had submitted articles to the *Miscellany* refused to write for it after the "purge"; but he fails to allow for "normal" turnover.

these submissions were too frank for the censors' taste and could not be printed. Men'kov thought that the bureaucratic controls "lacked any rational principle." As a Russian chauvinist, he was particularly annoyed by the presence among the censors of "foreigners" such as Shtiurmer or Ober (Aubert?). Despite their strict vigilance there were still complaints by senior commanders that the *Miscellany* was undermining discipline; however, Alexander II told Men'kov that he was fully satisfied with the journal's "line" (*napravlenie*).[126] The new editor was still able to publish a lot of worthwhile material, notably a pathbreaking study by D. P. Zhuravskii of the Russian military budget[127] and several articles on the reform of the army's judicial system. When Miliutin took over the War ministry (1861) he lost no time in making the *Miscellany* his personal mouthpiece—a practice in which several other ministers of the day also engaged. In 1863 it was freed from preliminary censorship and four years later absorbed its old rival, *Russian Veteran*; Men'kov stayed on as editor until 1872.[128]

The "purge" of the *Military Miscellany* was followed by the imposition of tighter controls over its sister organ in the navy.[129] These were two setbacks, albeit temporary ones, in the struggle for freedom of expression in the Russian periodical press. Whether Chernyshevskii's radical tendencies provoked this reaction by the authorities is uncertain: similar measures were taken at this time also against a civilian organ of Slavophil persuasion, Ivan Aksakov's *Parus* ("The Snail") for a totally unrelated reason.[130] The ways of the censorship had a logic, or illogic, all their own. Any editor of the *Military Miscellany* faced an almost impossible task, and the problems which Men'kov (and his patron Miliutin, for that matter) encountered in their dealings with the army's "old guard" surely entitle Chernyshevskii to a good deal of sympathy from the historian.

Having said this, it is still possible to hold that there was some substance to Miliutin's strictures and that the journalist underestimated the value of the "legal" (non-clandestine) press. A less intransigent approach on his part might have been more effective in attaining his ends—which were also those of the more "progressive" elements within the officer corps. No inexorable destiny foreordained that the new journal should have had such a brief life-span under his editorship. This brevity was due in large part to the style which Nikolai Gavrilovich adopted. It was a style very much his own, lacking in subtlety and tact. Although gentle and considerate towards his comrades and those stricken by misfortune, he displayed militant harshness towards those he saw as actual or potential foes—a category that included

the authors who had submitted articles to the *Miscellany* refused to write for it after the "purge"; but he fails to allow for "normal" turnover.

126 Men'kov, *Dnevnik*, 272, 278.

127 D. P. Zhuravskii, "Statisticheskoe obozrenie raskhodov na voennye potrebnosti, 1711 po 1825 gg.," *VS*, 10 (1859), 11–12.

128 Men'kov, *Dnevnik*, 311, 319, 327.

129 Chernyshevskii, *PSS*, vol. 5, 939, editorial note.

130 Koz'min, "Chernyshevskii," 235.

vacillating liberal intellectuals as well as tsarist functionaries. A gifted and highly intelligent writer, Chernyshevskii was sadly lacking in human understanding, emotional maturity and balance; he excelled at *oblichitel'stvo*, at exposing the wickedness or wrong-headedness of others, but was an amateur in the arts of persuasion; there was a dogmatic streak in his mind-set which even many of his friends found objectionable. It was no coincidence that in 1858–9 he split from Turgenev and had a well-publicized difference of opinion with Herzen. This open schism in the Russian opposition movement was a major source of weakness at a time when, with serf emancipation in the offing, it needed to present a united front towards the partisans of untrammeled autocracy. To be sure, this division was not wholly Chernyshevskii's doing, but he made a major contribution to it, not only by his literary writings but even more by allowing himself to become something of a cult figure among Russian student youth—for whom, as Gleason has recently reminded us, images mattered more than ideas.

To speculate a little, if the *Military Miscellany* had shown more consideration for the prejudices of its potential opponents; if it had been able to continue its bold advocacy of reform for a few more years; if it could have built up its clientèle within the officer corps—then the forward-looking elements in the Russian army would surely have responded much more readily and effectively than they did to the revolutionary movement in Poland and the western provinces in 1863–4, after the defeat of which the Russian left entered upon a period of eclipse and anarchic disarray. Had there been stronger military participation than there was among the "men of the sixties" (and their role was indeed far from negligible, as V. A. D'iakov's researches have shown)[131] at the expense of less practically-minded civilian intellectuals, the opposition would have made a better showing than it did. In the event Alexander II's government, though seriously split, was in the fortunate position of facing a public that did not know its own mind and could be fobbed off with reforms that did not go far enough to solve the empire's fundamental problems.

1985

---

131 V. A. D'iakov, "Petersburgskie ofitserkie organizatsii kontsa 50-kh—nachala 60-kh gg. XIX v. i ikh rol' v istorii russko-pol'skikh revoliutsionnykh sviazei," in: I. A. Khrenov, ed., *Iz istorii klassovoi bor'by i natsional'no-osvoboditel'nogo dvizheniia v slavianskikh stranakh* (Uchenye zapiski Instituta slavianovedeniia 28) (Moscow, 1964), 268–369; *Revoliutsionnoe dvizhenie v russkoi armii v ego vzaimosviazi s pol'skim osvoboditel'nym dvizheniem 1856–1865 gg.* (Moscow, 1966); *Osvoboditel'noe dvizhenie v Rossii, 1825–1861 gg.* (Moscow, 1979).

PART III:

THE RUSSIAN REVOLUTION

CHAPTER 12

Emancipation by the Ax?

Peasant Revolts in

Russian Thought and Literature

I

Shortly after the emancipation of the serfs in 1861, an estate manager named N. A. Krylov was touring Kazan' province when, as he wrote to his employer, "I heard the peasants talking of stabbing the nobles, hanging them and hacking them to death with axes . . . It is like the time of Pugachev." A peasant leader of the "old faith" was interpreting the tsar's decree freely in his own fashion. He foretold that at the "appointed hour" a youth, wearing a gold medal on one shoulder and a silver medal on the other, would appear and lead the people to the "true" freedom which the tsar had granted but the nobles willfully concealed. Peasants from the surrounding region flocked to the village of Bezdna to hear his exhilarating message. Anton Petrov, as the prophet was called, assured them that if troops were brought in, their bullets would have no effect. Unfortunately the magic did not work; at least 51 men were killed and 77 wounded when a crowd, armed only with sticks, refused to disperse when called upon to do so and was fired on by the soldiers. Petrov was publicly executed; but his name lived on among the peasants as a martyr in the struggle for social justice.[1]

To the authorities the affair was but one of hundreds of such instances of "disloyalty," symptomatic of the gulf that separated Alexander II's "enlightened" government and the educated elite in general from the "dark" rural masses, still sunk in ignorance and superstition. Like the bailiff Krylov, many upper-class people nervously recalled the Pugachev rising some ninety years earlier, the last and most violent of four great insurrections that shook the Russian state in the seventeenth and eighteenth centuries.[2]

---

1 On the Bezdna affair, see now D. Field, *Rebels in the Name of Tsar* (Boston, 1976), esp. 71; documents in *Krest'ianskoe dvizhenie v 1861 g.*, 2 pts. (Moscow-Leningrad, 1949; German translation, 1958).

2 The best introduction to this subject is P. Avrich, *Russian Rebels, 1600–1800* (New York, 1972; paperback ed., 1976).

That was one reason why they believed serfdom had to go. Despite the emancipation and other measures which significantly alleviated rural misery, peasant unrest continued, although episodically, until the Russo-Japanese war of 1904–5, when the peasants rose again en masse. This time their movement took a more organized form. The chief aim was the expropriation, not the physical liquidation, of the landowners. Just 12 years later, in 1917, the communally-minded peasants achieved their age-old dream of a great "black repartition": the land and stock of "non-toilers" was seized and divided up on egalitarian lines, with the sanction of the Bolshevik government. This was the most far-reaching of the many changes that took place during that momentous year. It was more than just a revolution in property relationships, which transferred 97% of the land to some 25 million smallholders: it was also a protest by country folk against urban domination, against modern technologized industrial society as such.[3] It was not the last protest: during the Russian civil war there were hundreds more local outbreaks, led by guerilla chieftains (Makhno, Grigoriev, Antonov) who could stand comparison with the better-known leaders of the earlier rebellions: Bolotnikov, Razin, Bulavin and Pugachev. But the Bolsheviks, skillfully blending repression with promises of reform, consolidated their dictatorship over the countryside and in 1929 attempted a "final solution" of Russia's agrarian problem. Stalin forced the peasants into collective farms and in the so-called "dekulakization" drive decimated their élite. The smallholders responded with passive resistance, slaughtering their livestock in large numbers, but recognized that active opposition to a totalitarian state would have been suicidal: as it was, millions of them found their way into the Gulag Archipelago. Violence returned to rural Russia in World War II, but this was largely a national (and ideological) struggle, not one fought specifically to uphold traditional peasant ideals. The old rural society had been shattered beyond repair.

Most historians and other commentators, being by status and inclination far removed from the simple peasant world, have discerned a fundamental difference between the earlier rebellions and the later revolutions. Curiously, Stalin himself was among these pundits. In 1932, at the height of the anti-kulak terror, he told a rather naive Western journalist that the peasant rebellions had failed for two reasons: first, the insurgents had been "naive monarchists," who while opposing the privileged élite had retained their trust in a "just tsar"; second, their efforts had not been coordinated by an external force, a class-conscious proletariat.[4] The Soviet leader was merely repeating a cliché. In fact, there was a good deal of continuity between the two kinds of uprising, as the more perceptive writers recognize. Even Soviet historians, who as dialectical materialists insist on class conflict as the key factor, have begun to explore the psychological dimensions of the subject.[5] Western scholars now realize that the

---

3 On the 1917 agrarian revolution, see my *The Russian Revolution: a Study in Mass Mobilization* (London, 1976-New York, 1977), pt. III; G. J. Gill, *Peasants and Government in the Russian Revolution* (New York, 1979).

4 Conversation with Emil Ludwig, as cited by L. Yaresh, "The 'Peasant Wars' in Soviet Historiography," *American Slavic and East European Review*, 16 (1957), 241.

5 The works by A. I. Klibanov and K. V. Chistov on peasant social utopias (see below, fn. 12,

great revolts were complex events, each of which had its own peculiar logic; that the rebels' underlying moral and religious outlook powerfully shaped their conduct; and that peasants were but one of several groups involved.[6] The coordinating role allegedly played in the twentieth-century upheavals by the workers (and, one would add, the intelligentsia) was anticipated in the earlier outbreaks by the cossacks. Emerging from their sanctuaries along the turbulent steppe frontier, these spirited freebooters, many of them fugitives from serfdom, could appeal to the hard-pressed workers of the Urals, to natives in the middle Volga region, to lower-class townsmen, and finally to peasants in bondage. These insurgencies were wide-ranging popular movements. It is misleading to call them "peasant wars" (another cliché, borrowed from Engels); in essence they were protests by disaffected groups in recently settled border regions against encroachment by the centralized absolutist state, which then won a measure of support from aggrieved elements within the empire.[7]

The rebels' objective was to replace the existing political and social order, which they saw as illegitimate and "unholy," with one that embodied their own ideals. They called it *volia*, or "liberty": the mighty would be humbled and the righteous elevated; or as we might say, the agents and beneficiaries of power would be changed, but the institutions would remain as before. A "people's tsar" would rule with justice and mercy, and therefore his people would serve him zealously. As in the medieval West, the peasants wanted an easement of their burdens, but did not question the institution of lordship as such.[8] Their mental horizons were narrow; they reacted against specific abuses and dreamed of a utopia that would right all wrongs. They constructed a belief system which brought solace during the long intervals between periodic bouts of violence.

II

We are concerned here not with the course or outcome of Russia's peasant movements but rather with the ways in which they were visualized by those who took part in them or kept the memory of them alive: the protagonists of a very vigorous social myth, held by the underprivileged common folk. Then we shall consider another myth, held by certain members of the élite: that of the romantic peasant rebel; and finally a degenerate form of this myth, or more correctly a fiction,[9] that is to say a

---

22) deserve to be singled out.

6 P. Longworth, "The Last Great Cossack-Peasant Rising," *Journal of European Studies*, 3 (1973), 1–35; idem, "Peasant Leadership and the Pugachev Revolt," *Journal of Peasant Studies*, 2 (1974–5), 183–205; idem, "The Subversive Legend of Sten'ka Razin," in *Russia: studi e ricerche a cura di V. Strada* (Rome, 1975), 17–40; M. Raeff, "Pugachev's Rebellion," in R. Forster and J. P. Greene, eds., *Preconditions of Revolution in Early Modern Europe* (Baltimore-London, 1970), 169–202.

7 Raeff, *op. cit.*, 194.

8 Cf. F. Graus, "From Resistance to Revolt: the Late Medieval Peasant Wars," *Journal of Peasant Studies*, 3 (1975–6), 4.

9 For the distinction, see S. V. Utechin, *Everyman's Concise Encyclopedia of Russia* (London-

false image deliberately propagated and manipulated for political ends. These myths and fictions may not greatly advance our understanding of what actually occurred, but they are important in their own right.

The peasants' illiteracy makes it difficult to reconstruct their thought-world. Little confidence can be placed in the testimony of outsiders, even those sympathetic to peasant aspirations (Haxthausen, Turgenev), who all too often saw only what they wanted. Folklore sources are abundant, but unfortunately they were collected unsystematically, and the more subversive items could not circulate freely. Nor is it clear how widely held the "just tsar" myth was or what relationship it had to other myths.[10]

We have first of all to realize that the peasant outlook was inherently religious, but that this religion had little in common with that of the upper classes. It should not be confused with piety, which was relatively rare, and had a strong mystical quality, which outsiders often wrote off as mere "superstition." It reflected animistic concepts and practises and was blended with Christian ideas in a system of "dual belief" such as existed elsewhere on the fringes of the civilized world. It implied continued respect for, and even worship of, certain natural phenomena, and a Manichaean view of life as a continuous struggle between good and evil, virtue and vice, personified by a plethora of saints and demons.[11] This vision of perpetual conflict between opposing moral forces was easily transposed to the secular world when this violently forced itself upon the peasants' attention with the growth of absolutism and serfdom. Landlords and officials were obvious candidates for the role of "devils." Hating and fearing these immediate foes, standing before them helplessly and uncomprehendingly, conscious of their isolation and weakness, the "Orthodox folk" looked for assistance to more distant and exalted spheres: to Almighty God and to his earthly representative, the Great Sovereign, the sacred ruler. The Russian concept of monarchy was of Byzantine origin and was absolute in a way unknown in the West: the tsar was a patriarchal figure, the *batiushka* or "little father" of his people; his power derived from God alone, unfettered by any human agency; his will was law. Identified with moral absolutes of Truth and Righteousness (*pravda*), he was a sacred being entitled to worship and propitiation—whatever the established Church might say! If there was misery and oppression among those entrusted to his care, this could be explained only by the intervention of the forces of evil: either news of their plight had not reached him, having been obstructed by ambitious self-seeking individuals in high places; or else he had indeed ordered the wrongs to be righted, but his decree had been concealed by such wicked and powerful persons—as at Bezdna.

If petitions brought no result, and grievances persisted, it was tempting to conclude that the tsar had lost his sanctity; and the rightful ruler must then be sought elsewhere, among the people. At the "appointed hour" such an individual would appear among his loyal subjects, display his royal stigmata, tell how he had miraculously escaped

---

New York, 1961), 180, following R. Redlich, ed., *Ocherki bol'shevizmovedeniia* (Frankfurt, 1956).

10 Longworth, "Subversive Legend," 19; Field, *Rebels*, 25.

11 M. Lewin, "The Peasant and Religion" (unpublished lecture).

his assailants and wandered in distant lands, and then lead his people against those who had misappropriated his power; once restored to his throne, he would punish the evildoers and reward his loyal servants.[12] It was taboo to speculate on the nature of the future utopia, whereas the earlier elements of the myth might be freely embroidered. Despite its many variants the myth remained remarkably consistent from its origins in the early 1600s to the 1860s. The "liberator" was conceived of as a male member of the ruling dynasty, the tsar himself or more often his son, the tsarevich. It did not matter whether the subject's real character suited the role here assigned him: disciplinarians like Peter III, Paul I and the Grand Duke Constantine were acceptable, whereas the reformist Alexander I, though an object of legend, was not associated with a social utopia. The peasants usually gave a new ruler several years in which to prove himself before pretenders appeared. One reason why Pugachev failed, it was believed, was that he had revealed himself before his "appointed hour."[13]

This was the moment when the myth probably achieved maximum impact. Back in the seventeenth century Bolotnikov and Razin had portrayed themselves merely as assistants of the just tsar (Dmitrii II and the tsarevich Aleksei respectively), and Bulavin in Peter I's reign had not utilized the Pretender myth at all; but Pugachev claimed that he himself was Peter III, who had miraculously survived his wife's assassins. It seems that most of his followers saw through his play-acting and were attracted rather by his charismatic personality and the promise of material gain. Pugachev was a rough-hewn illiterate, and could not project a credible image of a rightful tsar; moreover, he created a counteradministration in which his associates assumed the names and titles of real personages at court, were granted estates and so on—all of which went against the average rebel's egalitarian instincts. In the long run the Pretender myth was counter-productive, although it would be wrong to say that this was the principal reason why the revolt collapsed.

Pugachev's name lived on: in the 1830s Pushkin was told by one rustic that "for me he is still the emperor Petr Fedorovich";[14] nevertheless his reputation never superseded that of Razin, who embodied much better the popular ideal of the dashing bandit chieftain and was less pretentious, more obviously intent on the vengeance for which the dispossessed so avidly yearned.

Some of the 150 or so songs in the Razin legendary cycle have a critical ring: he is called a rebel (*vor*) or a dog, who takes the advice of his intimates from the poorer cossack strata instead of consulting the whole assembly, and behaves in a cruel, arbitrary fashion.[15] But in other songs, the majority, he is not the *vor* but the *voron*, or raven—a symbolic play on words and part of the secret language that the

---

12 K. V. Chistov, *Russkie narodnye sotsial'no-utopicheskie legendy* (Moscow, 1967), 24–236, esp. 30–32.

13 Raeff, "Pugachev's Rebellion," 196.

14 A. S. Pushkin, *Sobranie sochinenii v 10 tt.* (Moscow, 1962), vol. VII, 154.

15 B. N. Putilov, ed., *Narodnye istoricheskie pesni* (Moscow-Leningrad, 1962), 176; O. D. Sokolova, "Pesni o krest'ianskoi voine pod predvoditel'stvom S. Razina," *Russkie istoricheskie pesni XVI–XVIII vv.* (Moscow, 1960), 161–2, 168–9.

myth's devotees developed. His men, called falcons or eagles, perform miraculous feats; Razin is physically immune to danger ("the bullet does not touch me, the shell does not strike me"), and is lucky in love as well. The bards concentrated on details of his appearance or behavior, saying little about his deeds or program. But here is one hint of it: Razin has been summoned to the assembly to be punished at the tsar's order:

> Now Stenka stands amidst our throng
> To make a speech, not sing a song.
> "Those decrees are not the tsar's!
> They're written by those damned boiars!"
> Quoth he, and hastens forth
> To move against the servile north.[16]

Nothing is said about the peasants as distinct from the cossacks,[17] which suggests how subordinate their role really was. After his death (which few songs mention) his "good work" is carried on by his son. The use (or abuse) of religious imagery is plain here, although many learned commentators have overlooked it. Razin's son, an invented personage sometimes called Vaniusha (Johnny), represents social justice triumphant. He brings to fulfillment Stenka's promise of freedom, and is assisted in his valorous deeds, such as setting prisoners free, by his father, who returns to earth in supernatural form:[18]

> As the spring flowers began to bloom
> His father came back from his doom.
> He pulled down the prison stone by stone
> And sent the convicts safely home.

In his second coming the Messiah brings ultimate redemption to a desolate and desperate world. But in marked contrast to Christian teaching salvation is accompanied by violence and terror against the ungodly. The liberator is not a savior, not a Prince of Peace but an apostle of vengeance. The wicked governor (who stands for earthly authority in general) is put on trial, in a parody of that of Christ, flayed alive, chopped into pieces, or impaled on a bayonet. In some variants Razin's son spares the governor's wife, while in others he shoots her and hangs their little children by the feet—as the historical Razin did to Prozorovskii's family at Astrakhan.[19]

To be sure, there is also a positive side to the liberator's conduct: he hobnobs with the poor, the "passportless ones," calling them "brothers"; he buys them drinks in the tavern (although at times he is shown as an abstainer!), and consults them as

---

16 Putilov, *Narodnye . . . pesni*, 175; O. D. Sokolova, "Pesni," 177. The last line is our addition.

17 There is only the merest hint of them in the "poor people, fugitive soldiers and passportless braves" (Putilov, op. cit., 191) who join Razin's band; we do not hear of acts of vengeance by peasants against landowners.

18 Ibid., 185.

19 Ibid., 180, 185, 195; D. P. Costello and I. P. Foote, eds., *Russian Folk Literature* (Oxford, 1967), 163.

equals in devising his undertakings—exploits which are of course designed to better the people's condition at the expense of their former oppressors.[20] As one authority comments: "the legend is pervaded by a strong sense of fellow-feeling between bandit and peasant; and it promotes a generally favorable image of the robber, reflecting an 'underground' value system at variance with that of the ruling group."[21] To this one should add that the symbolism is pseudo-Christian. It is the peasant religion's equivalent of the Last Judgement: the righting of wrongs by the Messiah leads to universal harmony, but it is bodies, not souls, that are freed. We are offered a desacramentalized, materialistic rendering of the Christian message, whose spiritual character is perverted for secular ends. The allegorical elements in the Christian faith are reinterpreted in literal fashion, and the transcendental gives way to crude earthiness. Not surprisingly, the established Church inveighed against Razin as a fiend in human shape.

It should be stressed that Russian religious dissenters were theologically and politically conservative. The "Old Believers" who rejected Nikon's reforms were from time to time driven by the government's repressive policies into an unwilling cooperation with rebels, but on principle they disapproved of them just as vehemently as they did of the existing authorities. Some of the evangelical sectarians, who professed a more spiritual Christianity, were socialists, who believed that property should be held in common—but they were in no way revolutionary, as secular radicals discovered to their cost when they tried to enlist their aid. Consider the case of the popular prophet F. Podshivalov, a serf who around 1830 called on Tsar Nicholas I to found an earthly paradise in which all men would enjoy material prosperity and be governed according to "spiritual laws." (He landed up in Siberia.) This utopia was to be a theocracy, in which serfdom had been abolished (with compensation) at the emperor's command—not by violence. The monarch, he thought, should certainly put down those lords who resisted his will, but "those who wished to rebel should do so on their own": bloodshed was morally wrong.[22] Whatever the revolutionary implications of Podshivalov's ideas, it is clear that he, like other dissenters, was far removed from the protagonists of the Razin myth, and it is wrong to obscure the difference, as modern interpreters tend to do.

III

We turn now to our second myth, the one nurtured by the radical intelligentsia. Around 1910 a liberal critic, Peter Struve, called this group the spiritual heirs of the cossacks on account of their anarchistic prejudice against the state.[23] Perhaps he exaggerated,

20 Longworth, "Subversive Legend," 25–6.

21 Ibid., 28.

22 A. I. Klibanov, *Narodnaia sotsial'naia utopiia v Rossii XIX v.* (Moscow, 1978), 93. (The second volume in a work that yields much new material; cf. also, by the same author, *Istoriia religioznogo sektanstva v Rossii* (Moscow, 1965).

23 R. Pipes, *Struve, Liberal on the Right, 1905–1944* (Cambridge, Mass., 1979), 84; the remark was made in 1908.

but certainly educated people were not immune to the appeal of popular (or "naive") monarchism. As a recent historian points out, "they were prone to blame official wickedness and folly on an evil genius who exerted a baneful influence on the tsar: Arakcheev or Pobedonostsev, for example."[24] Moreover, many nineteenth-century writers looked on the peasantry as an abstraction by means of which they sought to learn more about themselves. The *muzhik* was in succession an object of pity (Karamzin), an enigma (Uspenskii), and a source of moral inspiration (Dostoevskii, Tolstoi); only with Chekhov and Bunin (and I would add Turgenev) do we have "a thoroughly prosaic image of the peasant, without the pathos of either great expectations or lost illusions."[25] Bunin's story *The Village*, which appeared in 1910, offers a realistically wretched picture of a village called "Durnovka" (literally, "Rotten") during the 1905 revolution, in which peasants attack the hero's small estate, which is spared destruction only by chance.[26]

Before 1906, when Russia belatedly acquired a semiconstitutional order, the censorship prevented writers from treating the peasant as a rebel, even in the past; the theme could be alluded to only indirectly. What we have is rather a romanticization of the rural milieu in general, linked to a concern for social justice, which can be traced back to Radishchev's famous *Journey from St. Petersburg to Moscow* (1790). In 1825, the year of the Decembrist revolt, Pushkin said that Stenka Razin was "the only poetic figure in Russian history." Towards the end of his life the poet, stimulated perhaps by a revolt in Novgorod province by military colonists (1831), embarked on a search for the historical Pugachev. When he submitted his *History of Pugachev* to Nicholas I, who acted as his personal censor, the emperor pedantically amended the title to *History of the Pugachev Rebellion* on the grounds that "a criminal can have no history," but at least permitted the work to appear. Based in part on official papers, it was designed as a counterblast to the history by Karamzin,[27] to show that the people, not just their rulers, made the country's history. The rebel leader was represented as a "terrible troublemaker," who had committed foul atrocities against innocent people. Pushkin blamed the authorities for weakness in allowing the uprising to attain the dimensions that it did.

Yet this was not his last word on the subject. Pushkin was a foe of serfdom and thought the gentry were largely to blame. He went on to write a fictional work on the

---

24 Field, *Rebels*, 14.

25 D. Fanger, "The Peasant in Literature," in W. S. Vucinich, ed., *The Russian Peasant in the Nineteenth Century* (Stanford, 1968), 256.

26 I. A. Bunin, *Sobranie sochinenii v 9 tt.*, III, *Povesti i rasskazy, 1907–1911* (Moscow, 1965), 28–30.

27 Almost the only work on Russian history then available was N. M. Karamzin's *Istoriia gosudarstva rossiiskogo*, of which Pushkin said that it "proved without bias the need for autocracy and the charm of the knout." Iu. Polevoi then brought out a *History of the Russian People*, in another response to this challenge. [Pushkin's *History of Pugachev* has recently been translated into English—twice, for good measure—after 150 years: by E. Sampson (Ann Arbor, 1984), and by P. Debreczeny in *The Other Pushkin: a Study of Alexander Pushkin's Complete Prose Fiction* (Stanford, 1984).]

same theme, *The Captain's Daughter* (1836), in which the revolt serves as background to a romantic intrigue between the bright young officer Petr Grinev and Masha, the lady of the title. As entertainment it succeeds admirably, as generations of readers can testify: the action develops at a swift pace, suspense is maintained, and the characters are believable. Pugachev appears as a Romantic popular hero,[28] rough-mannered but generous and genial; he carries himself with dignity and has an unaffected sense of honor (points calculated to appeal to élite readers). At the end of the story the bandit chieftain repays one good turn with another by freeing Masha from captivity and re-uniting her with her lover, so that Grinev and Pugachev "part as friends." "He was a monster of evil to all but me," the former remarks. The real monster is on the other side: the officer Shvabrin (modeled on a real person, M. A. Shvanvich), who goes over to the rebels and commits atrocities. Even worse misdeeds are perpetrated by the soldiers of Catherine's army, who requisition whatever they need from the villagers whom they "liberate" from rebel control, and chastise the innocent along with the guilty. (This passage was suppressed by the censor.)[29] The author's well-known characterization of the *Pugachevshchina* as "a senseless and merciless rebellion *à la russe*," taken out of context, misrepresents his meaning: the moral is that humanity should prevail over barbarous deeds, whoever commits them.

Pushkin's interest in peasant rebels was more aesthetic than political, and rightly so. He saw them as historical personages in their own right who epitomized the qualities, good and bad, of the still untamed, "natural" Russian people. They were Romantic figures whose stormy lives showed that exceptional individuals could influence events but that their power was limited by circumstances; that man could rise to moral heights but also sink to an abyss of meanness and cruelty. As a tragic subject Pugachev was little different from Boris Godunov: a natural leader, intelligent and even noble, he achieved much against all odds but ultimately failed because of the flaws in his character, which reproduced in an exaggerated form the shortcomings of the popular movement he directed.[30]

Almost at the same time as Pushkin published *The Captain's Daughter*, Lermontov was writing a novel on the same theme. Called *Vadim*, it was left unfinished— without great loss to world literature, for this is a far inferior work, which seeks to squeeze every ounce of melodrama out of the subject. We do not meet the Pretender

---

28 E. J. Simmons, *Pushkin* (Cambridge, Mass., 1937), 401.

29 Peasants, as distinct from cossacks, play only an incidental role in the story, and the picture conveyed of them is patriarchal: the villagers on the estate of Grinev's father, we are told, rise in revolt as one man, but are generously forgiven by their master; his domestic servants, whom he had treated well, do not join them. Pushkin, "The Captain's Daughter," in *The Queen of Spades and Other Stories*, tr. R. Edmonds (Harmondsworth, 1958).

30 This is not, however, the view of a most perceptive critic, the poet M. Tsvetaeva, "Pushkin i Pugachev" (1937), in *Moi Pushkin* (Moscow, 1967), 105–60, who contends that Grinev's relationship with Pugachev, rather than with Masha, is the crucial one. Other commentators have seen this relationship as symbolic of that between the gentry and the people in general: Raeff, "Pugachev's Rebellion," 201, and A. Besançon, *Le tsarévitch immolé* (Paris, 1967), 164–9.

himself, but only some of his associates, who are depicted as bloodthirsty bandits. The common people are little better: at a public hanging they crowd around, "their savage faces expressing joy."[31] Equally gross is the landowner Palitsyn; a selfindulgent and cowardly man, when danger threatens he takes refuge in a cave as sinister as his own character. The main action is played out by two rivals for his daughter's hand: the unusually handsome Iurii and the "antihero" Vadim, a misshapen hunchbacked cossack who had been wronged by Palitsyn and is obsessed by the urge for revenge.[32] As in some lurid novelette, we are treated to rapid swings between contrasting emotions, scenes of romantic passion alternating with brutal murders.

After the 1830s the theme of peasant rebellion all but disappears from the literary scene[33] and is taken over by the political theorists, who probably had a greater impact on the intelligentsia mind. Mikhail Bakunin, the fiery father of Russian and European anarchism, was the first to propound the view that the social problem could be solved by "the ax"—the codeword of the day for insurrection. An incurable fantasist, Bakunin believed that the rising might be instigated by the robbers who lived along the Volga; he was well aware of the historical precedents.[34] Another influential radical, Nikolai Chernyshevskii, told his fiancée (no doubt to her chagrin!) that "I do not fear dirt, nor drunken peasants with sticks, nor massacres."[35] There was much bravado in this, for unlike Bakunin Chernyshevskii wielded the pen better than the sword (or ax), and in his last writings before his arrest (1862) seemed to be moderating his advocacy of rural violence. He warned the emperor that, if there were to be another revolt, the insurgents would "spare neither our science, our poetry nor our arts; they will destroy our civilization."[36] Other radicals of the 1860s openly called for "a bloody and pitiless revolution, which must change everything down to the very roots, utterly overthrowing all the foundations of present-day society." The author of this broadsheet, entitled *Young Russia*, explicitly summoned up the shades of Razin, Pugachev and the late lamented Petrov of Bezdna. "We do not fear this revolution,"

31 M. Iu. Lermontov, "Vadim," in *Sobranie sochinenii v 4 tt.* (Moscow, 1969), IV, 59.

32 His soul is said to be a battleground between the forces of good and evil. Ibid., 54.

33 One exception was an unsuccessful play about Razin by A. A. Novrotskii (pseud.: N. Vrotskii), *Utes S. Razina* (1876).

34 See A. Lehning, ed., *Archives Bakounine* (Leiden, 1971), IV, 113–14 (M. A. Bakunin to S. G. Nechaev, June 2, 1870); cf. III, 174.

35 F. Venturi, *Roots of Revolution. . .*, tr. F. Haskell (London-New York, 1960), 140. This was in 1850, after Chernyshevskii had discussed the matter with the exiled historian Kostomarov, who later wrote the best prerevolutionary study of the Razin revolt. The "men of the sixties" poohpoohed him as a tepid liberal.

36 F. Venturi, *Roots*, 174. W. F. Woehrlin, *Chernyshevskii: the Man and the Journalist* (Cambridge, Mass., 1971), agrees that it is hard to know just what Chernyshevskii's views were, as he deliberately disguised them to outwit the censorship. Conceivably he had his tongue in cheek here, but it seems more likely that he was advocating reform rather than revolution— i.e. taking much the same position as the liberals whom he excoriated. In 1861, in the celebrated manifesto "To the Landlords' Peasants," which led to his arrest and exile, he called for a coordinated, synchronized peasant revolt but under intelligentsia leadership: Venturi, op. cit., 170; Woehrlin, op. cit., 276.

he added, "even though we know that rivers of blood will flow and that perhaps [sic] even innocent victims will perish."[37]

The terrorists of Alexander II's reign achieved little. The peasants ignored them, or even betrayed them to the police; government and society drew together in revulsion at their extremism; and the tsar's assassination (1881) set back the cause of Russian liberty by a crucial twenty years. By 1900 a new generation of radicals had grown up which sought to act more "scientifically," armed with the latest in western sociological doctrines. They "went to the people" with brochures, including short stories which show that the Romantic myth was far from dead. Their titles are evocative: Chirikov's tale *The Mutineers*, Krasheninnikov's *The Pogrom*, or *The Avenger* by one who signed himself V. Nevol'nik ("Forced Laborer"). This literature helped to foment, but did not cause, the agrarian violence of 1905; what is more to the point, propaganda and agitation numbed the minds of the revolutionaries themselves. They came to believe that the Russian peasant or workman was as "conscious" and cultivated as his comrades in the West, and that the destruction of "capitalism" would usher in a world of lasting social peace. This utopian myth was common to the whole left, irrespective of faction, however much squabbling there might be over points of doctrine. In 1905–6 and again in 1917 they summoned up the sleeping demon, little realizing that, once aroused, mass militancy would sweep most of them away as well. It was irrational to believe, as they did, that popular energies could be confined by programmatic formulas, for instance that after the revolution all the land should be nationalized or "municipalized," that is, brought under the control of progressive-minded bureaucrats: the peasants had their own ideas, for a black repartition, and that is what they eventually obtained. True, the intelligentsia won out in the long run, but only by being untrue to its own ideology of social liberation and imposing its will on the masses by force.

IV

And so we come to the last of our myths, or rather to a fiction: that of "Great October," particularly in so far as this relates to the countryside. We shall not discuss how this has been treated by the historians,[38] but rather look at the literary scene. Curiously, the great agrarian overturn has never been properly treated in fiction, probably because it raises too many awkward problems. Sholokhov's *Quiet Don* hardly counts, for the Don cossacks are a special case and the action takes place mainly during the civil war. So too does that of Leonov's novel *The Badgers*, although it does at least portray events in central Russia. Written in 1925, when literary expression was still relatively free, it gives a frank, amusing and ironic portrait of the peasants' response to the demands of the Red requisitioning squads. The villagers of Vori (the name means "Robbers") flee to a forest fastness where they live like the badgers of the title, carrying on an ancient feud against their neighbors from the next village,

---

37 F. Venturi, *Roots*, 292–3; the author was P. G. Zaichnevskii, a 19-year-old student.
38 On this see 425–39.

Gusaki ("the Geese People"), who for reasons of their own have sided with Soviet power.[39] The author's attitude to the "badgers" is ambivalent: he represents the urban emissaries as more forwardlooking but also mocks the agitators' revolutionary rhetoric and attributes the revolt to "the terror of the towns."[40] The peasants, who fly the black flag of anarchism, are shown as ineradicably hostile to urban life and values: they are willing to let the cities crumble into dust or to set them on fire.[41] They remember Pugachev and his associates, one of whom is rumored to have returned to lead their movement, and they dream, as earlier rebels did, of marching out from their forest retreat and taking "all of Russia."[42] The rebels are drawn as primitive and bestial, creatures of their natural environment, "a people of violent impulses, quarrels and gloom"; fatalistic and yet unpredictable, they behave viciously towards their womenfolk and animals and respond to unfamiliar situations in an irrational manner.[43] The picture is of course wildly exaggerated, but Soviet literature has yet to produce a new portrait more in line with contemporary ideological perceptions.

This is not the case, fortunately, with fictional treatment of the earlier peasant rebellions, and the evolution that this has undergone repays study. From the start Soviet writers and artists were encouraged to look to popular culture as a source of inspiration, to take over folk myths and adapt them to their own purposes and so help to legitimize the great revolution of the age in which they lived. The liberator legend was well suited to such a task, although its tsarist and quasi-religious character had to be downplayed and explained away (or simply ignored). S. Roberts, in a pioneering study of Soviet historical drama, has shown how it was used to develop what he calls "a national mythology." He compares the fictional treatment of the Razin revolt in two very early plays (by Kamenskii and Iurin) with the historical reality.[44] The Pugachev insurrection was the theme to two other plays of the 1920s, Esenin's *Pugachev* and Trenev's *Pugachevshchina*,[45] which cannot be considered here.

---

39 The rivalry concerns possession of a piece of land called Zina's Meadow. Such intervillage disputes did occur during the 1917–1918 redistribution and were misrepresented as class struggles, although they seem to have been relatively rare. Cf. our *The Russian Revolution*, 411–12.

40 L. Leonov, *The Badgers*, tr. H. Kazanina (London-New York, 1947), 158, 211.

41 Ibid., 230.

42 Ibid., 177, 193, 220. The agrarian revolution itself is mentioned only casually. When the peasants burned the manor, they used the owner's books to roll cigarettes (ibid., 175)—a frequent historical occurrence. Cf. the realistic description of a similar incident in 1905 (ibid., 84).

43 Ibid., 217, 243, 224. For a brief critical assessment of the novel: E. J. Simmons, *Russian Fiction and Soviet Ideology* (New York, 1958), 192–4.

44 S. Roberts, *Soviet Historical Drama: its Role in the Development of a National Mythology* (The Hague, 1965), 46–75. Roberts's approach is stimulating but he is uncritical in his use of historical sources and exaggerates the element of banditry in the revolt at the expense of its social aspects, relying on the views of the nineteenth-century historians Kostomarov and Solov'ev.

45 S. Esenin, "Pugachev," in *Sobranie sochinenii* (Moscow, 1962), IV, 159–96. I have not

Instead, let us look at two novelists' views of the Razin uprising, by A. P. Chapygin (1870–1937) and S. Zlobin (1903–65) respectively. The first author, a "fellow-traveler," perished during Stalin's purges. In this vigorously written adventure tale (1924–7)[46] the rebel leader and his comrades are portrayed as swashbuckling pirates, brave and honorable but also temperamental, licentious and sadistic; after one mass execution Razin's "face and hands are smeared with blood."[47] Such vindictive treatment of enemies is easily explained by his own experience as the victim of ghastly tortures. Seventeenth-century Russia is depicted in colors of the darkest hues: the people are sunk in poverty and ignorance, sodden with drink and ridden with vermin, and their rulers, from the tsar down to the meanest clerk, are hypocrites to a man; they lie, deceive and extort, and their sexual appetites can only be described as voracious. The boiar lady Morozova (known to history as a pious defender of the Old Faith) is presented as a lascivious lesbian, and some scenes verge on the pornographic. Muscovy is an oriental despotism, as is made plain from parallels with Persia, where the cossacks first go in search of plunder; the worshipers of Allah have a better life in some respects than those who pray to the God of the Orthodox Christians. The novel has a strong anticlerical bias. Razin is a hearty pagan, who on capturing Astrakhan' forces bereaved noblewomen to mate with his cossacks after a mock mass marriage, celebrated in the cathedral, where he ridicules the sacred images before collapsing in a drunken stupor.[48] Chapygin transposes to the seventeenth century the atheism of the Bolsheviks' League of Godless—an anachronism of which present day Soviet critics disapprove.[49] Another fault laid to his charge is his "neglect" of the peasantry. They are shown as afraid to come to the rebels' support because Razin has been excommunicated and they accept the Church's view of the matter. Only the townspeople, as proto-proletarians, have some sympathy for the cossacks, who carry all the action. The novel deals almost wholly with the period up to the storming of Astrakhan', a scene in which use is made of folklore motifs: Razin's men cry, "Our father sails across the seas on a magic carpet and this day will fly in flames into Astrakhan'."[50] Razin's son, here called Vasilii, survives to carry on the cause.

For all its earthiness this novel does convey the rebels' mutinous spirit, and the barbarous flavor of the times; but the picture is drawn unduly dark, and eventually the endless sex and violence pall: after we have been taken for the *n*th time to the brothel, the bathhouse and the torture chamber, we cease to be shocked. Chapygin's *Stepan Razin* mixes romance, treachery and gore into a heady brew too strong for most readers' taste.

---

seen Trenev's work; it is discussed in *Istoriia russkoi sovetskoi literatury* (Moscow, 1967), I, 599.

46 A. P. Chapygin, *Stepan Razin: a Novel*, tr. C. Paul (London-New York, 1946). In 1929 G. Shtrom wrote a novel with Bolotnikov as the subject.

47 Ibid., 217.

48 Ibid., 411–15.

49 *Istoriia. . .* , II, 139.

50 Chapygin, *Stepan Razin*, 366.

Sensationalism is not a charge that can be leveled against a novel with the same title which appeared in 1951.[51] Stepan Zlobin, born in 1903, received a Communist upbringing and commenced his literary career in 1927. During the 1930s he earned his living as a writer of children's stories, but he was also known as a historical novelist. He began work on *Stepan Razin* in the year of Chapygin's death, 1937, but its completion was delayed by the war, in which Zlobin was inducted into the Red Army and captured by the Germans; he returned in 1944 as an invalid. His personal sufferings are not reflected in the novel, which is cast in the heroic mold and stresses courage, comradeship and faith in ultimate victory for the righteous. Zlobin reproduces loyally the official Soviet view of social and political relationships in the seventeenth century, a period of history which he has studied as closely as circumstances allow. His characters speak in the idiom of their time, depicted as accurately as are the details of their physical environment, but they behave like men and women of the twentieth century. Razin himself would not be out of place in the Komsomol or in a Red Army shock battalion: he is a self-confident, calm, knowledgeable, efficient, rational leader, who mixes freely with his subordinates and so wins their trust but is never reluctant to assume a proper responsibility for his actions. His supporters may acclaim him as their *batko* (father) and credit him with having a thousand arms, but he knows better: he realizes that such strength as he possesses derives solely from them.[52] He is neither proud nor selfish, but is single-mindedly devoted to the cause of social liberation and justice. Even drink, he considers, is a gift of God that brings laughter and joy but has no place when important civil and military decisions are being taken.[53] No question of this Stenka Razin, on conquering Astrakhan', starting a drunken orgy like Chapygin's hero; on the contrary, Zlobin's Razin issues orders for the markets to be reopened so that economic life may revive, and under rebel rule the citizens prosper.[54] Vengeance against defeated enemies is indulged in only

---

51 St. Zlobin, *Stepan Razin: istoricheskii roman v 2 kn.* (Moscow, 1960). [This is the "revised" (*ispravlennoe*) edition, first issued in 1958; a "supplemented" (*dopolnennoe*) one appeared in 1952, one year after the original was published. See *Russkie sovetskie pisateli prozaiki: biobibliograficheskii ukazatel'*, vol. 2, *Zadornov-Liashko* (Leningrad, 1964), 57. Zlobin's personal wartime experiences were reflected in the last of his works: *Propavshie bez vesti* (1962). According to one Soviet critic, in the "subtext" of *Stepan Razin* Zlobin conducted a "creative polemic" with Chapygin: G. M. Lenobl', "Epopeia narodnoi bor'by," in idem, *Istoriia i literatura* (Moscow, 1960), 205–26, here 207. Lenobl' also gives some interesting details of the author's work on the novel, including his reactions to some early critics who charged him with exaggerating the degree of organization in Razin's revolt, and so contravening Stalin's teaching on the matter (218). Shortly before his death Zlobin offered a kind of political apologia: in the light of the "historic decisions" taken at the Twentieth Party Congress (i.e. de-Stalinization), he wrote, Soviet writers should "seriously review much of our history which until now, . . . due to reasons well known to everyone, received incorrect treatment in the literature of the previous period." S. Zlobin, "Zadachi romana," *Voprosy literatury* (1965), no. 9, 51.]

52 Ibid., II, 163, 427.

53 Ibid., 375.

54 Ibid., 166, 374.

after severe provocation; it is the foe who breaks his word, schemes, cheats, lies, and engages in cruel or arbitrary acts.

Likewise, it is the foe who spreads, for evil purposes of his own, the rumor about Razin's supposed magic powers; he and his followers have no time for such superstitions. They are indifferent to religion, although ready to use it when clerical supporters suggest that this might be of advantage. Nor do we hear much about the rebels' "monarchist illusions": towards the end of the novel Razin, *en route* to Moscow in chains, shakes off such beliefs entirely and comes to a proto-Marxist realization that the tsar is no more than an agent of an oppressive class system. He also sees that the Don will become free only once it develops its agricultural and mineral resources and farms the land not for the benefit of individuals but of "the whole host"—a kind of justification in advance of Stalinist industrialization and collectivization.[55] The rebels' class-conscious attitude, which pits them against the wealthy cossacks as well as the nobility, is shared by the peasants too, who in Zlobin's novel play a role that accords with that allocated to them by Soviet historians. The serf Mikhail Kharitonov is a natural leader whose physical and moral strength earns him the respectful admiration of his fellow-peasants and the awe of his master. An ex-soldier (shades of 1906 and 1917!), he leads an assault on the estate buildings with all the refinements of contemporary military technology, disposing of captured supplies in an orderly and sensible manner; no needless looting disturbs this smoothly planned operation.[56]

We shall therefore not be surprised to learn that the rebels are advocates of women's liberation—Razin's wife Alena fights bravely and is judged by her comrades fit to hold political office[57]—or that they are fervent patriots, who scorn the Poles and the Turks (or their vassals) who dare to threaten the security of the Russian land. Appropriately, they encourage fellow-feeling between the Russians and all those peoples who will one day be incorporated into the USSR: Volga tribesmen, Ukrainians and Belorussians (but not Germans or Jews). Even the "elder brother" principle is echoed here: the Ukrainian cossacks are brought to recognize that Razin is a superior leader to Bogdan Khmelnytskii.[58]

Zlobin's novel has an obvious propagandist intent. He offers us not myth but fiction: the conscious manipulation of the legendary tradition in order to bolster ideas and values from a different age. However much we admire his skill in weaving so many ideological desiderata into his plot, as a work of art his novel fails through excessive stereotyping. In the post-Stalin thaw, writers were permitted a slightly more flexible approach, in the interest of sustaining credibility in their readers' eyes, but the authorities' purposes have not undergone any substantial change. Not only literary practitioners but scholars too must observe the Marxist-Leninist canon in their work if they want to see it in print. Perhaps it is a fitting commentary on our unromantic

---

55 Ibid., 429.
56 Ibid., 17–19.
57 Ibid., 337, 423.
58 Ibid., 335.

technological age that myth should be thought dangerous enough to deserve controls of this kind, that it should have to be analyzed at length and reproduced under laboratory conditions in a way that distorts its purpose and destroys its intrinsic value.

1982

CHAPTER 13

Russian Social Democracy
and the First State Duma

I

The defeat of the ill-starred Moscow insurrection in December, 1905, which came as a fitting climax to a year of bitter revolutionary conflict, brought about a state of uneasy equilibrium: the opposition had proved too weak and disunited to overthrow the absolutist regime, but the government was not yet strong enough to carry out a policy of general repression. Although sporadic outbreaks of violence were still to occur, it was now clear that the revolutionary movement had passed its peak; during the next 18 months resistance inevitably had to take a more peaceful form. The central position in the Russian political scene was occupied by the State Duma, which remained for the opposition a symbol of the far-reaching promises of reform made by the tsar in the Constitutional Manifesto of October 17/30, 1905. The first Duma, which assembled on April 27/May 10, 1906, was entrusted by an indignant electorate with a task far beyond the limits set by law to its competence. The government, for its part, regarded the Duma as a dangerous enemy and barely tolerated its existence. In such circumstances the assembly and the administration unavoidably found themselves engaged in a mortal struggle, the outcome of which depended above all upon the degree of unity and organization achieved by the opposition. But the Duma, left high and dry upon the shore by the ebbing tide of revolution, provided a tempting prey for its foes and could be dissolved with ease whenever they chose.

At the beginning of 1906 all attention was focussed upon the impending elections. The moderate elements in the opposition, believing that another revolutionary upsurge was both unlikely and undesirable, were in favor of participating in the elections, and in the work of the Duma, in the hope that the government, faced with resolute action by the assembly, would at last be obliged to bow to the will of the country. On the other hand most Populists advocated a boycott of the elections. Romantics at heart, they believed that, by completing a ballot-paper, they were signing a confession that their revolutionary ideals were impossible of fulfillment. The Social Democrats were also split on this issue. In the stormy autumn of 1905 the party had emerged into the open from clandestine existence, and for the first time in its history had succeeded in exercising an appreciable influence upon the course of events. But this period of freedom was too short to give the still predominantly intellectual party a firm mass following, or to modify the uncompromisingly doctrinaire outlook of its leaders. The differences between the two factions into which the party was split were too deep to be papered over for long; as soon as the Moscow rising had been suppressed, a vigorous polemic developed between the Mensheviks, who were generally prepared to take part in the elections, and the Bolsheviks, who were determined to boycott them. This dispute was more heated than the previous discussion in the party on the attitude to be adopted towards the "Bulygin Duma," for the *ukaz* of December 11/24, 1905,[1] had added, to the three *curiae* originally projected, a fourth *curia* for industrial workers. However, as the delegates from this *curia* numbered a mere 236 out of a total of over 8,000, the innovation could not be expected to alter materially the position in the provincial electoral colleges. Measured proportionally, there was only one deputy to every 90,000 workers, as compared with one to every 2,000 landowners.[2] Moreover, the franchise was not extended to workers in factories employing less than 50 men, or to numerous non-industrial categories such as state and public employees, building workers, casual laborers, and artisans—in all, an estimated 63 percent of the urban male working population.[3] According to the law, electoral rallies did not require the attendance of a police representative, and had only to be notified to the authorities in advance; on the other hand, since all opposition parties were still officially proscribed, there was no guaranteed freedom of canvassing, and the radical parties were unable to nominate their leaders as candidates. For many Social Democrats the restrictions and inequalities of the electoral law were in themselves sufficient reason to boycott the elections.[4]

Members of both factions agreed in anticipating a new revolutionary wave in the spring of 1906. The Mensheviks, for their part, envisaged this as a grandiose repetition of the general strike of October, 1905, in which all social classes had united to win concessions from the regime. In this new upsurge, they held, the Duma would occupy a central position; it was the Social Democrats' task to utilize it, and the preceding elections, in order to expand the scope of the nationwide movement for liberation. P. B. Aksel'rod proposed that, when the time came for the electoral colleges to choose deputies to the Duma, those delegates who could be persuaded to do so should seize the initiative and illegally carry out elections to a separate Duma on a basis of universal suffrage; when the two Dumas faced each other, he argued, popular support would rally to the more democratic body and ensure its triumph. The electoral colleges could

1 *III PSZ*, XXV, no. 27029.

2 A. E. Lositskii, "Izbiratel'naia sistema Gosudarstvennoi Dumy," *Temy zhizni*, II, no. 2 (St. Petersburg, 1906), 34.

3 P. Orlovskii, *Gosudarstvennaia Duma i rabochii klass* (1906), 25; *Rabochii ezhegodnik* I (St. Petersburg, 1906), 216.

4 Cf. Orlovskii, *op. cit.*; P. Rumiantsev, "Osvoboditel'noe dvizhenie i Gosudarstvennaia Duma," *Temy zhizni*, II, no. 4.

thus serve as the nuclei of a genuinely democratic government.[5] G. V. Plekhanov pointed to the immense natural obstacles that had to be overcome before the broad masses of the people could play an active role in public life, and maintained that at the present moment their political awareness could best be developed if they took part in the elections and, if it should meet, also in the Duma: people learnt by experience, and the Duma would serve as an object lesson, teaching them the necessity for a completely democratic Constituent Assembly.[6]

Critically reconsidering the events of 1905, the Mensheviks attributed the failure of the revolutionary movement to its lack of unity. It stood in need of "political centers which could attract the attention and confidence of broad sections of the population, centers in which the organized working class could combine and coordinate with bourgeois democracy in a joint struggle against the old regime."[7] The next revolutionary wave must therefore have a central rallying-point, for which role the Duma was ideally suited. Standing like a city upon a hill, visible to the whole surrounding countryside, it would automatically focus the attention of the entire nation upon the fundamental questions of the day. The Duma, in turn, would be emboldened by the interest of millions in its duel with the government.[8]

The Mensheviks were prepared to admit that the government, and perhaps also most of the deputies in the Duma, would seek to avert a revolution; but this, they held, was no valid objection. The decisive factor was not their subjective intentions, but the objective role which might be performed by the Duma under pressure from below. "What does it matter if the Duma *is* moderate, or even reactionary?" exclaimed F. I. Dan. "Let it decide all questions in an ultra-reactionary spirit; the important thing is that these questions are put, and that they attract the attention of the broad mass of the people."[9] The government was bound to come into conflict with the Duma; such clashes would turn even a pseudo-parliamentary assembly from an instrument of counterrevolution into an instrument of revolution. It was the Social Democrats' task "systematically to widen and deepen all conflicts between the government and the Duma, and to seek to connect them with the demands of the masses."[10] By itself the Duma meant nothing; given popular support, it could mean everything. "The role of the Duma is dependent upon the correlation of forces outside it."[11] Addressing a crowd at Tiflis (Tbilisi) railway station before leaving for the capital, the Social

5 P. B. Aksel'rod, *Narodnaia Duma i rabochii s'ezd*[2] (St. Petersburg, 1907); F. I. Dan, "Gosudarstvennaia Duma i proletariat," F. I. Dan and V. I. Lenin, *Gosudarstvennaia Duma i sotsial-demokratiia* (St. Petersburg, 1906), 20 ff.; *Pravda: ezhemesiachnyi zhurnal iskusstva, literatury, obshchestvennoi zhizni*, II (1906), 5.

6 G. V. Plekhanov, *Sochineniia*, 24 vols. (Moscow-Leningrad, 1923–7), XV (1926), 55 ff.

7 Martynov, in *Protokoly ob'edinitel'nogo s'ezda [RSDRP] 1906 g.* (Leningrad, 1926), 137.

8 M. B[alabano]v and F. I. Dan, *Rabochie deputaty v pervoi Gosudarstvennoi Dume* (St. Petersburg, 1907), 110.

9 *Protokoly ob'edinitel'nogo s'ezda*, 206.

10 Ibid., 360.

11 Ibid., 198.

Democratic deputy N. Zhordaniia rhetorically declared: "the last word belongs to
you, because without the people the Duma cannot solve any fundamental problem.
Prepare yourselves constantly and zealously for the coming struggle. Follow every
step of the Duma. And when the time comes, when the violent struggle begins in the
Duma, be ready to fight for freedom."[12]

The Bolsheviks' attitude towards the Duma was based upon the theory, enunciated
by Lenin the preceding year in his pamphlet *The Two Tactics of Social Democracy
in the Bourgeois-Democratic Revolution*, that the liberal opposition, fearing social
revolution, had no interest in helping to overthrow the absolutist order, but was on
the contrary bound to take the earliest opportunity of concluding a bargain with it
at the people's expense; the working class, consequently, should ally itself, not with
the urban middle class, but with the peasantry, now hailed by Lenin as "absolutely
democratic" and "a bulwark of the revolution."[13] The Bolsheviks still held that a
proletarian insurrection, led by a highly-trained élite, was required to deal the death
blow to absolutism. Indeed, they were alone in maintaining, in defiance of the facts,
that the Moscow uprising represented a defeat, not for the revolution, but for the
government.[14] Nevertheless, after the experience gained in December, Lenin was not
prepared to risk an attack by the workers in isolation, and in practise his tactics were
now based upon the optimistic conviction that a mighty wave of discontent among
the peasantry would soon create an environment favorable to action in the cities. In
spring, he reasoned, climatic conditions would permit the peasants again to take an
active part in public affairs; "even if a new explosion does not come this spring,"
he declared confidently, "nevertheless there is definitely one on the way, and in all
probability it is not far off."[15]

In the Bolsheviks' view, the Duma did not lie upon the highway along which
the Russian revolution was advancing. It had been deliberately contrived by the
government to confuse the people and divert their attention from the revolutionary
struggle. The Duma would inevitably be dominated, if not by reactionaries, then by
middle-class liberals who were by definition eager to compromise with absolutism.
For this reason alone the Duma was bound to play a counterrevolutionary role: "a
Kadet Duma cannot help but display the qualities of the Kadet Party," Lenin asserted
categorically.[16] To place the Duma in the vanguard of the forthcoming revolutionary
upsurge would be tantamount to handing over leadership of the entire opposition to
its most treacherous elements. People would be reduced to reading in the press about
petty parliamentary wrangles, instead of waging an active revolutionary struggle of

12 M. B[alabano]v and F. Dan, *Rabochie deputaty*, 59–60.
13 V. I. Lenin, *Sochineniia*[3], 30 vols. (Moscow-Leningrad, 1930–2), VIII (1931), 94–6.
14 Varshavskii in *Protokoly ob'edinitel'nogo s'ezda*, 266; cf. N. A. Rozhkov in *Tekushchii
    moment: sbornik* (Moscow, 1906), 6. For an overdrawn picture of the rising see Vinter's
    account in *Protokoly ob'edinitel'nogo s'ezda*, 269; P. Larionov even referred to it as "the
    Moscow December revolution" (*Tekushchii moment*, 8).
15 Lenin, *Sochineniia*[3], IX, 26.
16 *Protokoly ob'edinitel'nogo s'ezda*, 195.

their own. The Duma resembled, not a city upon a hill, but a spectacle at which the audience passively applauded.[17] If the Duma met, the Social Democrats should exploit the conflicts that would arise between it and the people, rather than those with government.[18] Lenin criticized the Mensheviks' attitude towards the elections as inconsequential and unpractical. The party's candidates would be needlessly exposed to the risk of arrest, or would be tempted to bargain secretly with the Kadets for seats in the Duma.[19] Above all, by participating in the elections the party would encourage people to believe that the crisis could be solved peacefully through the Duma; the Social Democrats should therefore boycott the elections, concentrating instead upon preparations for an armed insurrection, which alone could lead to the establishment of a provisional revolutionary government and the convocation of a Constituent Assembly. The choice before the party was clear:

> we must either decide that the democratic revolution is over, remove from the agenda the question of an insurrection, and embark upon a "constitutional" path; or else we must decide that the democratic revolution is still in progress, put first the task of completing it, develop and apply in practise the slogan of an insurrection, wage a civil war, and mercilessly brand all manner of constitutional illusions.[20]

Most Mensheviks soon came to accept the idea that the party should participate fully in the elections and the Duma itself; but the leaders of the faction, unable to agree upon a common policy, took the short-sighted step of allowing local party committees to participate in the elections or to boycott them as they chose. The result, as they privately admitted, was chaotic,[21] and inmost committees the boycotters carried the day. The plan to "explode" meetings of the electoral colleges failed abysmally in practise: it was carried out only in the Ukrainian port of Mariupol', and half-heartedly attempted in two other towns. In Ekaterinoslav the local Mensheviks' failure was enhanced when the college proceeded to elect as deputy to the Duma a local miner with Social Democratic sympathies, Mikhailichenko, who subsequently became the leader of the "workers' group" in the Duma.[22] The boycott was most effective in areas where revolutionary sentiment ran most strongly. In Warsaw it was almost unanimous; in St. Petersburg, out of a total of 271 factories concerned, 133 boycotted the elections completely, and in the remainder only a few thousand workers participated. On the

17 I. Bikerman, *Rossiiskaia revoliutsiia i Gosudarstvennaia Duma* (St. Petersburg, 1906), 23.

18 Alekseevskii in *Protokoly ob'edinitel'nogo s'ezda*, 214.

19 Lenin, *Sochineniia*³, IX, 9.

20 Ibid., 36.

21 *Pis'ma P. B. Aksel'roda i Iu. O. Martova (Materialy po istorii russkogo revoliutsionnogo dvizheniia*, II) (Berlin, 1924), 148; L. Martov, "Sotsial-demokratiia 1905–1907 gg.," *Obshchestvennoe dvizhenie v Rossii v nachale XX-go veka*, 4 vols. (St. Petersburg, 1909–1914), III (1914), 604. A frank account of the situation in the Menshevik organization in St. Petersburg is given in a letter from I. Volkov to P. B. Aksel'rod of April 2, 1906, in the Aksel'rod Archives.

22 Martov, "Sotsial-demokratiia," 605; B[alabano]v and Dan, *Rabochie deputaty*, 43.

other hand in Tver' only 13 percent, and in Tula only 6 percent, of the factories were affected by the boycott.[23] The peasantry, trusting that the Duma would bring them "land and liberty," remained almost wholly impervious to the boycotters' propaganda. Since there were no revolutionary candidates in the field, they proceeded to elect Kadets and other moderates. Thus the result of the boycott was precisely the reverse of that anticipated by its advocates: it rallied popular support to the liberals. The Social Democrats found themselves virtually isolated from the Duma, upon which the people's aspirations were now focussed. Under the influence of this disconcerting situation the fourth congress of the RSDRP, which met in Stockholm at the end of April, passed by 62 votes to 46 a resolution endorsing the Mensheviks' ideas.[24] The party was to form a "fraction," or parliamentary party, in the Duma, and was to put up candidates in the elections that were still to take place in outlying areas. In these the party scored notable successes, six Social Democratic deputies being returned to the Duma,[25] but the best opportunities had been missed.

Before the Duma assembled, the government took steps to restrict its authority. The decree of February 20/March 5, 1906 made it clear that, despite the promises made in the October Manifesto, the government still envisaged the Duma as a consultative rather than a legislative body. The direct control which the Duma could exercise over the administration was limited to the right to make interpellations; ministers were responsible only to the tsar, who retained supreme executive power. On April 23/May 6, only four days before the session began, the government promulgated the "Fundamental Laws of the Russian Empire" in which use of the word "constitution" was purposely avoided.[26] On the following day a more pliant prime minister, I. L. Goremykin, was appointed in place of Count Sergei Iu. Witte; it appeared as though the latter's statesmanship was at a discount now that he had strengthened the government's hand by negotiating a new large international loan. Seldom can a maiden parliament have assembled in less propitious circumstances.

II

Opinion in the Duma was overwhelmingly hostile to the government, and most deputies were content to follow the lead of the Kadets, who formed the largest party.[27] The Kadets' policy in the Duma was to exert such pressure on the government that it would be forced to resign, enabling the assembly to appoint a ministry responsible to

---

23 D. Kol'tsov, "Rabochie v 1905–1907 gg.," *Obshchestvennoe dvizhenie*, II (1910), 266; B[alabano]v and Dan, *op. cit.*, 32 ff.; Voitinskii, *Gody pobed i porazhenii*, 2 vols. (Berlin, 1923–4), II (1924), 35.

24 *Protokoly obiedinitel'nogo siezda*, 224.

25 Martov, *op. cit.*, 619.

26 *III PSZ*, XXVI, nos. 27423–5, 27805.

27 Of 478 members of the Duma, 38 were moderates, 179 were Kadets and 50 belonged to other "center" parties, 94 were left wing Trudoviks and 18 Social Democrats, the rest being mainly nonparty peasants. Cf. N. Borodin, "Lichnyi sostav Gosudarstvennoi Dumy," in A. A. Mukhanov and V. Nabokov, *Pervaia Gosudarstvennaia Duma*, 3 pts. (St. Petersburg, 1907), I, 23.

itself. In this way they hoped to realize the radical political and social program to which they were committed to purely parliamentary means. The inevitable conflict between the government and the Duma was not long delayed. The first act of the assembly was to draft an address in reply to the tsar's speech of welcome outlining a wide program of reforms, including the introduction of full civil liberties and the compulsory expropriation of privately owned estates. Speaking for the government on May 13/26, Goremykin rejected the Duma's demands, declaring that a solution of the agrarian question on the lines proposed was "absolutely inadmissible." On behalf of the indignant assembly, the Kadet leader V. Nabokov announced that the Duma would accept the government's challenge by preparing a law based on these very principles; he concluded his speech with the cry: "let the executive bow before the legislature." A Trudovik resolution expressing lack of confidence in the government and calling upon it to resign was passed almost unanimously.[28]

The government, however, did not resign and a deadlock ensued. Ministers stayed away from the Duma, displaying their contempt for it by sending it trivial matters for consideration, while the Duma, for its part, determined not to become another Frankfurt Parliament, busied itself with debates upon the burning political and social questions of the day. The discussion of the agrarian question in particular, which revealed the ruinous condition of the peasantry, served to focus popular attention upon the Duma and undermine the security of the regime. The government could not afford to compromise, and resolved to act while it still commanded superior physical force. In reply to provocative insinuations by the government, the Duma prepared a public declaration of its intentions on the agrarian question. On the grounds that the Duma had exceeded its authority, the tsar ordered a dissolution; on their arrival at the Tauride Palace on the morning of July 9/22 the deputies found the doors locked against them.[29] Thus, after the brief spell of 72 days, Russia's first experiment in constitutional government came to an unhappy end.

The Social Democrats did not play an important part in the work of the first Duma. The prevailing spirit in the assembly was one of solidarity in the conflict with the administration; it was only when the Duma passed from criticism of the government to consideration of its own positive proposals that differences between the center and the left came into prominence.

When the Duma assembled few deputies owed firm allegiance to any particular party, and those who came straight from farm or factory were subjected to energetic lobbying by leaders of the various opposition groups. The handful of workers' representatives, elected in the face of apathy or even direct opposition on the part of local Social Democrats, at first joined with the peasant deputies in the Trudovik group. They were soon persuaded by the Menshevik-controlled party Central Committee to assert their independence, and on May 18/31 they issued a formal "Declaration to the Workers of All Russia" calling upon them to support the Duma's struggle by entering into contact with leftwing deputies. When this "Workers' Group" was in due course joined by the members elected with party support, an official Social Democratic "frac-

---

28 *GDSO*, I, 322–5.

29 *III PSZ*, XXVI, nos. 28104–5; cf. A. N. Brianchaninov, *Rospusk Gosudarstvennoi Dumy: ego prichiny i posledstviia* (Pskov, 1906), 58.

tion" was established, which was obliged to operate under the strict control of the Central Committee.[30] On June 16/29, not long before the dissolution, it made its *début* in the Duma with a doctrinaire declaration of Marxist principles which bore little relation to the business under discussion and was not surprisingly accorded a cold reception.[31]

The Social Democratic deputies sought to apply the official Menshevik policy, whereby the Duma was to be turned into the focal point of a nationwide revolutionary movement. They believed that, to forestall dissolution, the Duma must maintain close contact with the forces hostile to the regime that existed in the country at large. Unless this essential condition were fulfilled, they held, the constructive legislative work which the Kadets advocated so earnestly would be devoid of any realistic basis. In order to make the public aware of the need to rally around the Duma, what better platform could they have than the Duma itself, where as deputies they were virtually shielded from the danger of arrest for inflammatory speeches? The Social Democratic deputies consistently acted as though the Duma were a tribune from which they could address the entire people over the heads of their representatives.

Their attitude to each question under discussion was determined by its suitability as material for popular agitation. Thus, whereas the Kadets were grudgingly prepared to assign 15 million roubles to the government for famine relief, the Social Democrats proposed to "refuse the present government any credits and set up a commission at once, the members of which should be despatched to the affected areas to organize, with the aid of *zemstva* and other public bodies, local committees of starving people."[32] All too often the Social Democratic deputies manifested an irresponsible tendency to emphasize their independence, which led them into pointless rhetoric and disrupted that unity of the entire Duma against the government which the moderates sought to preserve. Drawing attention to a few petty omissions, Il'in demonstratively protested "in the name of the whole proletariat" against the address in reply to the tsar's speech, and with his colleagues abstained from the vote on it.[33] After the effective debate on June 9/22, in the course of which Prince K. D. Urusov revealed sensational details of anti-Jewish *pogroms* instigated by the authorities, the Social Democrats would not rest content with a Kadet resolution demanding the immediate resignation of the government, but insisted on tabling a provocative motion of their own calling for the trial of those suspected of organizing *pogroms* and "expressing confidence that the great Russian people will carry such a decree into effect."[34] A debate on a Kadet bill to establish freedom of assembly degenerated into a bitter wrangle between its sponsors and the Social Democrats, during which Zhordaniia was led to exclaim: "you say we need liberal policemen to preserve law and order, but we say we need no policemen at all, whether reactionaries or liberals!"[35] On the other

30 Martov, "Sotsial-demokratiia," 619; B[alabano]v and Dan, *Rabochie deputaty*, 77.

31 *GDSO*, II, 1403–5; B[alabano]v and Dan, *op. cit.*, 88 ff.

32 *GDSO*, II, 1674.

33 Ibid., I, 181.

34 Ibid., II, 1194.

hand, the moderate Kovalevskii joined the Social Democrats in condemning the bill as insufficiently liberal,[36] and on the question of famine relief the subsequent Gurko-Lidval' scandal lent weight to the arguments of the left.

In the country at large the Mensheviks made a sincere attempt to dispel the popular distrust of the Duma that was fostered by the Bolsheviks. In response to their appeal, the Social Democratic deputies received hundreds of mandates (*nakazy*), petitions, resolutions, and messages of greeting. Even some Bolsheviks were carried away by the general enthusiasm.[37] Deputies undertook speechmaking tours in the provinces. In the capital, delegates chosen by workers in many factories attended a series of conferences with members of the Social Democratic "fraction," at the last of which no fewer than 270 delegates were present.[38] Shortly before the dissolution a Menshevik writer declared that "the Duma is becoming the rallying point for the unorganized masses; this is neither a fantasy of opportunists nor a fiction of doctrinaires—it is a fact."[39] But such optimism was premature. All too often, under Bolshevik pressure, meetings called in support of the Duma turned into demonstrations against it. For Lenin had launched a vigorous campaign to discredit the Duma, and the Kadets in particular. At a public meeting on May 9/22 he carried away a large audience by his oratory; the liberal speaker was shouted down and all present, Mensheviks included, voted for a resolution "warning the people against this [Kadet] party, which is wavering between liberty and the old oppressive absolutism" and stressing the need for an extraparliamentary struggle to obtain a Constituent Assembly.[40] Plekhanov thought that the government was deliberately allowing the Bolsheviks to undermine the Duma's prestige, and implored the workers not to yield to such provocation.[41] This stimulated still further the bitter quarrel raging within the party over a Menshevik suggestion that local committees should publicly declare their support for the Duma's efforts to replace the administration by one responsible to itself.[42]

The Kadets' triumph at the polls came as a rude shock to the Bolsheviks. One of their leaders was so taken aback that he claimed it as a victory for the revolution, and—heresy of heresies—acknowledged the Kadets' title to "hegemony" over all the

---

35 Ibid., II, 1351.

36 Ibid., II, 1458 ff.

37 M. Pavlov, *Dumskaia taktika bol'shevikov v revoliutsiiu 1905–1907 gg.* (Leningrad, 1948), 90 ff.

38 Martov, "Sotsial-demokratiia," 620.

39 N. Gilin, "Narod i Duma," *Voprosy momenta: sbornik* (Moscow, 1906), 90; cf. also B[alabano]v and Dan, *Rabochie deputaty*, 85.

40 Lenin, *Sochineniia*³, IX, 251; *Svetoch'* (Moscow, no. 2, May 13/26, 1906); M. Vinaver, *Konflikty v I Gosudarstvennoi Dume* (St. Petersburg, 1907), 57–8; Voitinskii, II, 54–5.

41 Plekhanov, *Sochineniia*, XV, 89. Lenin's reply (*Sochineniia*³, IX, 276) was unconvincing, but Voitinskii (*loc. cit.*) does not consider the government acted deliberately. Cf. also a letter from M. Panin to P. B. Aksel'rod, May 10, 1906, in the Aksel'rod Archives.

42 Lenin, *op. cit.*, IX, 380 ff., 474, 537–8; F. I. Dan. *Sotsial-demokratiia v rezoliutsiiakh Londonskogo s'ezda; mysli i zametki* (St. Petersburg, 1907), 73.

forces opposed to the regime.[43] Lenin argued that the Kadets had won their victory
only by deliberately deceiving the people, who still remained revolutionaries at heart.
The Kadet party had no firm class basis and would soon fade into insignificance;
it was the Social Democrats' task to free from the Kadets' insecure grasp those
elements among the peasantry whose readiness to accept Bolshevik leadership had
been temporarily obscured, and to continue their preparations for an insurrection.
Least of all should they support the Kadets or the Duma, "the living embodiment
of 'constitutional illusions.'" Just as "in time of war compromisers and deserters
can be even more dangerous than the enemy," so "at such a time as this parties of
parliamentary opposition can be more harmful and dangerous than openly reactionary
parties."[44]

Lenin was embarrassed when events did not bear out his prophesies that the Duma
would compromise with the government. His views on the probable outcome of the
situation, which varied with each passing rumor, testified to the weakness of his
analysis. A chance remark by the conservative paper *Molva*, advising the tsar to
appoint a moderate ministry, was interpreted by Lenin as an inspired revelation of
the government's intentions.[45] P. Rumiantsev thought the government would allow
the Duma to talk itself to a standstill, whereupon it could safely be dissolved.[46] Even
after the stormy debate on May 13/26, Lenin managed to persuade himself that the
conflict between the Duma and the government did not really exist.[47] Although not
entirely excluding the possibility of a dissolution, he contended that the Kadets would
surely prevent the Duma from provoking the government to take such drastic action.
Instead, on the strength of an article in *Le Temps* in favor of a Kadet ministry, he
began to speak of "a sudden change in government policy," and of the Kadets as
"sharing power," as though everything were completely settled.[48] In his next articles
he changed his tone, muting his criticism of the Kadets and the Duma in confident
anticipation of an imminent revolutionary outburst;[49] but on June 22/July 5 rumors

43 Cf. P. Orlovskii, *Kadety v Dume; vozniknovenie rabochego klassa* (St. Petersburg, 1906),
   5, 10. "It is not the Kadets who have become leaders of the people, but the revolutionary
   people who have utilized them as an instrument in their struggle against reaction. . . . History
   has given the Kadets a rare opportunity to perform a great public service, to become the
   leaders of the whole liberation movement, and to turn the scales in favor of the people."

44 Lenin, *Sochineniia*[3], IX, 92, 139, 111.

45 Ibid., 102–3.

46 *Vestnik zhizni: ezhenedel'nyi nauchnyi literaturnyi i politicheskii zhurnal* (St. Petersburg,
   no. 5, May 9/22, 1906, 9; no. 6, May 23/June 5, 1906), 8. Incidentally, this did not prevent
   him declaring after the dissolution that "from its very first session the Duma naturally tried
   to become a genuine parliament, and thus a conflict between it and the government was a
   forgone conclusion." Ibid., no. 9 (July 19/Aug. 1, 1906), 2.

47 Lenin, *Sochineniia*[3], IX, 262. Some other Bolsheviks, however, were more realistic:
   cf. Aleksandrovich in *Svetoch'* (Moscow, no. 6, May 18/31, 1906), 1.

48 Lenin, *op. cit.*, 316–17, 319; cf. P. N. Miliukov's reaction to this article in *God bor'by;
   publitsisticheskaia khronika 1905–1906 gg.* (St. Petersburg, 1906), 356–62.

49 Ibid., 330 ff.

that some Kadets were negotiating with government representatives again convinced him that a Kadet ministry was impending. The following day, when the Kadets officially denied the rumors, Lenin, quite nonplussed, could merely challenge them to publish details of these maneuvers, so that all might see their readiness to bargain with reaction.[50] The Bolsheviks were thus guilty of the same "parliamentary illusions" which they attributed to the Kadets. Vorovskii thought that the Kadets could "talk to the government as equals," and expected the latter willingly to cede them half the portfolios in a cabinet.[51] It is true that the Bolsheviks believed in the imminence of a rising, whereas the Kadets did not, but this does not alter the fact that at the time both shared the same estimate of the government's strength and intentions.

Endeavoring to translate into practise his new theory of a proletarian–peasant alliance, Lenin set out in earnest to woo the Trudoviks. He took it for granted that the still embryonic political parties in Russia were completely representative of the interests of particular social classes, and argued that, while the "bourgeois" Kadets were "a treacherous compromise-seeking party consciously preparing to conclude a bargain with absolutism, incapable of waging a resolute struggle. . . , the Trudoviks were "laboring petty-bourgeois dreaming of an equal redistribution of the land, capable of waging a very resolute struggle . . ."[52] The Bolsheviks continually urged the Social Democratic "fraction" to base its policy upon a coalition with the Trudoviks against the Kadets and the right. One enthusiast went so far as to refer to the Trudovik deputies as "the natural ally of the proletariat."[53] They praised their radical agrarian demands and encouraged them to keep in close touch with their constituents by forming local land committees.[54] Lenin scrutinized their conduct closely, scolding them at each sign of agreement with the Kadets and welcoming any independent step they took. At the end of May he was confident that in a few days they would renounce the leadership of the Kadets, but on the eve of the dissolution he was forced to admit that "this time they are following *quite hopelessly* in the wake of the liberal bourgeoisie."[55]

Unfortunately for the Bolsheviks, the Trudoviks were in fact far from being that ideal "party of the revolutionary petty bourgeoisie" which Lenin's theory postulated. Not all peasant deputies in the Duma were Trudoviks, and only 42 of the 107 Trudovik deputies were peasants.[56] They lacked a common program, party discipline, and firm revolutionary convictions[57]—although Lenin may perhaps have reckoned that

50 Lenin, *Sochineniia*[3], IX, 360 ff.

51 Orlovskii, *Kadety v Dume*, 13. [Orlovskii was V. V. Vorovskii's pseudonym.]

52 Lenin, *op. cit.*, 279.

53 P. Rumiantsev in *Vestnik zhizni*, no. 6 (May 23/June 5, 1906), 9.

54 Cf. N. Romanov in ibid., no. 5 (May 9/22, 1906), 35.

55 Lenin, *op. cit.*, 314, 404 (our italics).

56 Of 111 peasant deputies in the Duma, 9 were Kadets, 12 autonomists, and 48 independents (with leanings to the right or center). Cf. N. Borodin, *op. cit.*, 16, 25, 30, 36.

57 To Borodin (*op. cit.*, 25–6), the Trudoviks described themselves variously as Socialist Revolutionaries (2), Social Democrats and sympathizers (10), peasant unionists (9), independent socialists (7), freethinkers (2), radicals (1), autonomists (8), "to the left of the Kadets" (2), "nearer the Kadets" (18), nonparty (21) and 27 others. The official *Dumskii sbornik* (St.

JOHN KEEP

their vagueness would itself serve to increase the effect of Bolshevik influence. The Trudoviks were united in demanding possession of the land and full civil rights, but many of them, to the Bolsheviks' chagrin, retained the Russian peasant's traditional trust in the tsar.[58] Although the Bolsheviks claimed that the Trudoviks came to follow their lead during the course of the session, the Kadets had some justification for regarding them as their "natural allies."[59] One Bolshevik writer, who did not share Lenin's illusions about his new *protégés*, complained that, whereas the Socialist Revolutionaries were "permanent guests" at private meetings of the Trudovik group, "they open their doors only very unwillingly to the Social Democrats."[60] Shortly before the dissolution 40 Trudoviks and 23 nonparty peasants decided to form a new party in the Duma in close tactical alliance with the Kadets.[61] Lenin's preference for the Socialist Revolutionaries to the Trudoviks during the autumn electoral campaign[62] was perhaps an indication of a sense of disappointment at the coolness with which the peasant deputies had reacted to his advances.

III

All the opposition parties assumed that a forcible dissolution of the Duma would evoke a mighty wave of popular indignation. The government also appears to have expected trouble, for it took the precaution of calling out the garrison in the capital. But on July 9/22 St. Petersburg remained calm; there was a certain tension in the atmosphere, but people seemed to feel that resistance, if possible at all, must begin elsewhere.[63] Contrary to popular expectations the government, far from provoking another "Bloody Sunday," acted when the Duma was not sitting, and did not even hinder some 200 opposition deputies from traveling to Vyborg (Viipuri) in the comparative safety of Finland; here they agreed to issue a manifesto protesting against

Petersburg, 1906), 10, and Pavlov, *Dumskaia taktika*, 125, erroneously citing Borodin, give figures more favorable to the Bolshevik point of view: the category "nearer the Kadets" is omitted, and the number of those "to the left of the Kadets" is shown as 18.

58 One Trudovik deputy, Sedel'nikov, subsequently founded an ineffectual "Popular Labor Party" which combined a radical political program with a demand for a democratic monarchy. (*Tovarishch*, October 4, 1906), cited in Appendix to Lenin, *Sochineniia*[3], 477.

59 I. Petrunkevich, "Politicheskaia rol' pervoi Gosudarstvennoi Dumy," Mukhanov and Nabokov, *Pervaia Gos. Duma*, I, 93. P. N. Miliukov commented that each of the left-wing parties was trying to win the sympathies of the Trudoviks, but that the latter "are displaying a good deal of mistrust towards all intellectual influences," *God bor'by*, 345. The same was, indeed, also true of the Kadets, and Miliukov was perhaps superficial in attributing the subsequent coolness between the two parties solely to the influence of "ill-willed intellectuals": *ibid.*, 396.

60 P. Rumiantsev in *Vestnik zhizni*, no. 7 (June 3/16, 1906), 4.

61 Petrunkevich, *op. cit.*, 43; *Tovarishch*, no. 74, cited by Plekhanov, *Sochineniia*, XV, 216; *Sotsial-demokrat: organ RSDRP*, no. 3 (October 13/26, 1906), 1.

62 Lenin, *Sochineniia*[3], X (1930), 151.

63 F. Kriukov, "9–11 iiunia 1906 g.; vospominaniia," *Vyborgskii protsess* (St. Petersburg, 1908), 233.

the dissolution and calling for a nationwide campaign of passive resistance.[64] The radicalism of this appeal could not compensate for the aura of make-believe which characterized the proceedings at Vyborg. No central or local organizations existed to direct the campaign, which met with only sporadic response and soon died a natural death.[65] On July 17/30 a mutiny occurred in the naval base at Sveaborg (Suomenlinna), near Helsingfors (Helsinki); although it was supported by a general strike in the Finnish capital, within two days the government had succeeded in crushing all resistance. Outbreaks in sympathy amongst part of the Kronstadt garrison and aboard the cruiser *Pamiat' Azova* at Reval (Tallinn) were suppressed with equal promptitude and severity. In the capital the chief revolutionary organizations decided, after some hesitation, to call a general political strike. On July 22/August 4 some 80,000 men stopped work, but on the following day the movement already began to flag, and in Moscow and other cities strike calls met with an even weaker response. Peasant disturbances which occurred in many areas were of no more than local significance. It became increasingly obvious that the dissolution of the Duma had not led even to a shadow of that grandiose popular reaction which had been generally anticipated.

It was the Mensheviks, above all others, who had come to take it for granted that the people would support their representatives in their hour of need. The question for them was merely what form the inevitable rising would take, "a single mighty thunder-clap" or "a more or less prolonged series of isolated flashes."[66] Even Trotskii, who was far from being a conventional Menshevik, wrote that, although

the broad masses of the people do not of course consider the Kadets their representatives, . . . nevertheless their revolutionary instinct will tell them that a forcible dissolution of the Duma cannot remain unpunished. . . . The people will doubtless respond with a manifestation of such scope as our revolution has not yet experienced.[67]

Nevertheless, the government's action caught the Mensheviks without any definite plan. They were opposed to the adventurist schemes of the Bolsheviks but shrank from limiting themselves to the purely passive resistance advocated in the Vyborg Manifesto. They wanted the rising to be truly "national," embracing the middle classes as well as the workers and peasants; on the other hand, they were anxious not to delay too long, and thus miss the opportunity of striking while the people were still indignant at the dissolution of the Duma. In their confusion they rapidly substituted one slogan for another;[68] after each of these had failed to evoke any enthusiasm, they

64 Text in ibid., 7.

65 Three Kadets and ten leftwing deputies who made singlehanded attempts to distribute the manifesto were soon arrested and were put on trial. *Ibid.*, 9 ff.; Voitinskii, *Gody pobed*, II, 85–6.

66 N. Iordanskii, in *Mir Bozhii: ezhemesiachnyi politicheskii literaturnyi i nauchno-populiarnyi zhurnal dlia samoobrazovaniia* (Moscow, April 1906), 8.

67 L. D. Trotskii, *Sochineniia* (Moscow-Leningrad, 1925–7), IV (1926), 173.

68 First: "renew the sessions of the Duma!"; then "against the camarilla, in defence of the Duma, for a Constituent Assembly!"; and finally: "fight for the Duma as an organ of power

advocated uncoordinated local demonstrations and strikes as the only way to keep the flame of resistance alive.[69]

The Mensheviks' failure was due to the inconsistency in their attitude towards the Duma: they participated in it solely in the hope of thereby speedily bringing about its overthrow. True, the Kadets shared the same objective of replacing the Duma by a freely and democratically elected Constituent Assembly, and also hoped to achieve it by winning popular support for the Duma.[70] But they took a long-term view of this policy, seeking rather to familiarize the people gradually with the practise of constitutional rule than to organize them for immediate revolutionary action.[71] The Mensheviks were utopian in expecting that Russian workers would rally around the Duma in much the same way as the citizens of Paris had supported the Legislative Assembly in 1792.[72] They grossly underestimated the difficulty of the task which they set themselves: the broad mass of the workers and peasants, as the *nakazy* they sent to the deputies showed, naively regarded the Duma as an omnipotent executive authority, which had merely to sanction their demands for them to be fulfilled. Their frequent promises to support the deputies in their hour of need[73] really amounted to no more than romantic rhetoric, and did not signify a readiness to take up arms in their defense. It is debatable whether the Mensheviks, for all their faith in the possibility of evoking an organized mass revolutionary movement, could have done so by the means they envisaged. A representative institution such as the Duma lacked sufficient power to overcome the peasants' natural inertia and draw them into organized political

to call a Constituent Assembly!"

69 Voitinskii, *Gody pobed*, II, 108; *Protokoly s'ezdov VKP (b): piatyi s'ezd 1907 g.* (Moscow, 1935), 81 ff.; S. Semenov, "Obshchie i chastichnye massovye vystupleniia," *Politicheskoe polozhenie i takticheskie problemy* (Moscow, 1906), 58 ff.

70 At the third congress of the Kadet party, which took place shortly before the Duma assembled, A. A. Kornilov called for the establishment of "a permanent link" between the Duma and the people, and a resolution in this sense was passed by the congress almost unanimously. *Biulleteni III s'ezda Partii Narodnoi Svobody* (St. Petersburg, no. 4, April 24/ May 7, 1906), 4.

71 "We consider it necessary to exert every effort to mobilize and organize all the social forces in the country," wrote Miliukov, "but we want to organize them for and around the parliamentary struggle. . . . We consider it impossible to organize a revolution in the country, and we declare that all attempts in this direction are extremely dangerous, and impede the realization of those aims which we all share equally." Miliukov, *God bor'by*, 365.

72 Cf. P. B. Aksel'rod, *Dve taktiki. Doklad prochitannyi na s'ezde v Stokgol'me* (St. Petersburg, 1907), 48.

73 The villagers of Osherovka, near Samara (Kuybyshev), for example, ended their *nakaz*: "fear not, comrades, lest you be dissolved [*sic*], act boldly against the foe, knowing that behind you there are many millions of working people, who in the last instance will be able to crush the handful of our enemies." *Krest'ianskie nakazy Samarskoi gubernii: opyt sobiraniia materialov russkoi revoliutsii*, ed. A. A. Vasil'ev and V. A. Kudriavtsev (Samara, 1906), 74. Of 458 *nakazy* collected by P. P. Maslov, 133 promised support. *Agrarnyi vopros v Rossii, s istoricheskim obzorom krest'ianskogo dvizheniia*, 2 vols. (St. Petersburg, 1906), II, 284.

activity—a role that eleven years later was to be performed by the army, demoralized by World War I.

Lenin, for his part, was exultant at the dissolution. "All the one-sidedness and short-sightedness of the Kadets has been exposed," he wrote. "Constitutional illusions . . . are seen by all for what they are: illusions, phantoms, mirages. . . . Laws, deputies, and so forth are worth nothing if there is no real power behind them. That is what the people have learnt from the Kadet Duma." As if replying to Campbell-Bannerman's famous words: *la Douma est morte; vive la Douma!* he exclaimed: "let us chant a funeral dirge in memory of the deceased and make good use of its lesson."[74] To many of his hearers the course which Lenin now recommended savored of "Blanquism." He urged the setting up of military organizations to direct the coming struggle; "these should have as their nuclei tiny bands of volunteers, groups of ten, five, perhaps three . . . free associations of men bound together by friendship, party connections, or simply a common place of residence." As far as the timing of the revolt was concerned,

> we recommend that the all-Russian demonstration, strike and insurrection should be fixed for the late summer or the early autumn. It would be important to utilize the season when building work is in progress in the towns, and when summer work in the fields is just ending. . . . It would be a tremendous advantage if the struggle could begin simultaneously all over Russia.[75]

Despite this militant language, in practise the Bolsheviks proved no more successful in bringing about an insurrection than their opponents within the party. In a sense this failure was less of a setback to them, for Lenin had always been opposed on principle to the idea of linking the revolutionary movement with the Duma. He advised the Social Democratic deputies against trying to make contact with the electorate;[76] as the crisis developed, he warned the workers with uncharacteristic caution not to strike until they were fully prepared, urging instead the formation of special committees to mobilize the peasants.[77] When the Duma was dissolved the Bolshevik minority group on the Central Committee, following his advice, proposed "to get ready and await orders, in view of the likelihood of a peasant revolt in the near future."[78] To their dismay, the peasantry failed to launch the expected general offensive, and it was then too late for action by the industrial workers in isolation. Lenin argued that it was sound strategy to bring the rearguard of one's army closer to the vanguard before engaging the enemy.[79] But to send one's "rearguard" into battle

---

74 Lenin, *Sochineniia*[3], X, 6, 9.

75 Ibid., 12, 16, 18.

76 Ibid., IX, 241–2.

77 Ibid., 400.

78 Cited in Appendix to Lenin, *Sochineniia*[3], X, 449. The Bolshevik committee at Kostroma advised local workers "to adopt for the moment a temporizing (*vyzhidatel'nyi*) attitude, and to refrain from mass action." Pavlov, *Dumskaia taktika*, 137.

79 Lenin, *op. cit.*, IX, 400.

before one's "vanguard" was neither sound strategy nor feasible politics.

The Bolsheviks' tactics accentuated the division between the consciously revolutionary minority and the overwhelming majority of workers. The former, encouraged to regard the Duma as an alien "bourgeois" institution, shrugged off its dissolution as an unimportant matter and turned a deaf ear to all appeals for support;[80] the latter, who had slowly become aware of the significance of the Duma's conflict with the government, hesitantly acted in its defense. During the July general strike in St. Petersburg, where the Bolsheviks controlled the local party organization and had conducted an energetic campaign against the Duma, men in the Obukhov and Semiannikov factories, who had taken the lead in the previous autumn, now worked normally, whereas builders' laborers, cabdrivers and others, most of whom had until recently remained loyal to the government, came out on strike.[81] The Bolsheviks were content to ignore the problem of gaining the allegiance of such elements, preferring to act upon the flattering assumption that the entire Russian working class was already prepared to follow their lead. An even more significant consequence of this approach was their disregard for the spontaneous anarchistic sentiment among many politically inexperienced workers which impelled them to adopt a suspicious or hostile attitude towards the Duma. For a large proportion of those who boycotted the elections were motivated less by revolutionary conviction than by sullen resentment at an unfamiliar obligation imposed upon them by the authorities. Ignorant of constitutional practise, they mistook the Duma for some new bureaucratic institution. When V. E. Mandel'berg, the Social Democratic candidate in Irkutsk, canvassed support in his constituency, he was mocked by voters who refused to believe that a body such as the Duma existed.[82] It was significant that, even in the elections to the second Duma, when the revolutionary parties conducted a vigorous campaign, only about one-quarter of the workers eligible went to the polls.[83]

Many Social Democrats failed to take due account of this important factor; consequently, when some workers "elected" their pet animals as deputies, this was hailed by members of both factions as evidence of their revolutionary consciousness.[84] But

---

80 After Lenin's tirades against the Duma, it was hardly to be expected that the Bolsheviks would prove the most enthusiastic supporters of action in protest against its dissolution. A conference was called at Teriioki to discuss means of extending the strike. The speakers droned on throughout the night. Finally, as dawn broke, a certain Chernov spoke up boldly: "we are deluding ourselves. While we have been here discussing how to extend the strike, it has petered out. And a good thing, too! Why should we go on strike for the Duma, a private affair between the Kadets and the Octobrists? Let *them* go on strike; we don't care a fig. . . ." According to Voitinskii (*Gody pobed*, 91–2), Chernov's speech "shattered the depression which had settled over the meeting; everyone started talking noisily, laughing and joking. . . ."

81 B[alabano]v and Dan, *Rabochie deputaty*, 168; Kol'tsov, "Rabochie v 1905–1907 gg.," 293.

82 V. E. Mandel'berg, *Iz perezhitogo* (Davos, 1910), 110.

83 According to figures given by Lenin, *Sochineniia*[3], X, 356.

84 Lenin, *op. cit.*, IX, 90; N. Iordanskii, in *Mir Bozhii* (March 1906), 9.

it was the Bolsheviks who capitalized on this element of spontaneous anarchism in their campaign to discredit the Duma. A number of rank-and-file Bolsheviks inherited from the anarchist wing of the Populist movement an irrational uncompromising hostility towards constitutionalism as such. One writer exclaimed that it was emotionally impossible for men who "but yesterday were fighting on the barricades" to participate in elections;[85] the Bolshevik committee in Odessa warned workers not to enrol as voters, since this would be equivalent to recognizing the legitimacy of the Duma;[86] another writer, who not inappropriately adopted the *nom de plume* of Bazarov, argued on similar lines that, in order not to be "compromised," Social Democratic deputies would have to walk out of the Duma as soon as it had any dealings with the tsar;[87] a Bolshevik provincial newspaper declared that "the sooner the government dissolves the Duma, the better for the cause of popular liberty; marking time merely prolongs the birthpangs of genuine freedom."[88] For many Bolsheviks reform and revolution were mutually exclusive conceptions. In opposing the Duma, they were giving expression to a deep-rooted fear that the "bourgeois" constitutional regime which it symbolized might indeed satisfy popular aspirations, and that the flame of revolution might thus all too easily be snuffed out.

It may of course be argued that such views were held only by relatively unimportant elements in the Bolshevik ranks who had nothing in common with Lenin or his orthodox supporters. Lenin strongly denied that he was opposed to parliamentary institutions on principle, maintaining that in advocating a boycott of the Duma he was simply drawing practical conclusions from an objective analysis of the existing situation.[89] It is true that Lenin had some initial hesitations about the boycott,[90] that at Stockholm he supported a Menshevik resolution to form a Social Democratic "fraction" in the Duma,[91] and that on the eve of the dissolution he admitted that on the whole the Social Democratic deputies "had adopted a correct position."[92] Moreover, a few weeks later he astonished his followers by declaring that the Bolsheviks should participate in the forthcoming elections to the second Duma.[93] But he seemed unsure

85 K. Levin, "Politicheskie partii v Rossii," *Lektsii i referaty po voprosam programmy i taktiki sotsial-demokratii*, no. 10 (Moscow, 1907), 85.

86 Cited by Pavlov, *Dumskaia taktika*, 58.

87 *Vestnik zhizni*, no. 5 (May 9/22, 1906), 9; cf. Shmidt in *Protokoly ob'edinitel'nogo s'ezda*, 205.

88 *Golos Kurska*, no. 11, cited in *Vestnik zhizni*, no. 7 (June 3/16, 1906), 50.

89 Lenin, *Sochineniia*[3], IX, 110.

90 At the Tammerfors (Tampere) Conference in December, 1905, Lenin at first recommended participation in the elections, but later gave way to the boycotters' pressure. *Pis'ma Aksel'roda i Martova*, 148; G. Kramol'nikov in *Trudy I vsesoiuznoi konferentsii istorikov-marksistov* (Moscow, 1927), I, 226.

91 *Protokoly ob'edinitel'nogo s'ezda*, 242.

92 Lenin, *op. cit.*, IX, 392.

93 Ibid., X, 26.

of his position and took refuge in vague contradictory definitions of the new course.[94] Perhaps the most plausible explanation of his change of tactics is that, although he was now aware of the improbability of an uprising in the near future, he dared not admit in public what he recognized in private.[95] Both now and on subsequent occasions he doggedly maintained that the Bolshevik boycott of the elections had been justified, thus leaving his followers with the unenviable task of attempting to prove that the boycott and its renunciation were, to quote a Soviet historian, "component subordinate links in the chain of a consistent Bolshevik strategy."[96] Not until 1920, in an attack upon "left-wing Communism," did he admit publicly that the boycott had been mistaken—and even then he excused it as the result of pardonable overconfidence in assessing the tempo of the revolution.[97]

Lenin has also been represented virtually as a prisoner of the left wing within his faction, compelled to act against his better judgment.[98] This view needs some qualification. Lenin was certainly not one to conceal serious differences on political tactics for the sake of a superficial unity, and it seems likely that he would have aired his views if he had objected strongly to what may for convenience be called the "anarchistic" trends in Bolshevik policy. As was shown by his encouragement of so-called "partisan warfare" by bands of armed terrorists,[99] at this time his optimistic faith in the imminence of a rising made him temperamentally more inclined to spur on his followers than to restrain them from excesses. In practise, the tactical divergences between Lenin and the extremists on this question were of negligible significance. In so far as Lenin's deliberate policy of "exposing" the Kadets helped to alienate popular support from the assembly and facilitate its dissolution, his tactics towards the first State Duma in 1906 may be said to have foreshadowed his own forcible dissolution of the Constituent Assembly in 1918.

1955

---

94 In the same breath he said that "you could, if you like, call it the old boycotting tactics," and then described it as "a consequential development of the old tactics, but not a *repetition* of them." Ibid., 31, author's italics.

95 This view is unwittingly confirmed by Stalin's version of the episode: "as far as the second Duma was concerned, Lenin considered that, *in view of the changed situation and the decline of the revolution* (our italics), the Bolsheviks 'should reexamine the question of the boycott.' . . . From this it followed that one must not only be able to attack, and be the first to do so, when the revolution is on the upgrade, but also be able to retreat, and be the last to do so, when the upgrade is over." *Istoriia VKP (b); kratkii kurs* . . . (Moscow-Leningrad, 1938), 85. This was precisely what Lenin did *not* argue, at least in public. In this very article he called on Social Democrats to "exert every effort . . . to turn *the upgrade which is probable in the near future* (our italics) into a national armed insurrection against the tsarist government." Lenin, *op. cit.*, X, 30, 32.

96 Pavlov, *Dumskaia taktika*, 5.

97 Lenin, *op. cit.*, XXV (1931), 183.

98 B. D. Wolfe, *Three Who Made a Revolution* (New York, 1948), 351.

99 Lenin, *Sochineniia*³, IX, 26, 43 ff., 84.

CHAPTER 14

Russia 1917:
The Tyranny of Paris over Petrograd

I

When the first anniversary of the October revolution was being celebrated in Moscow there could be seen, upon a long white wall that presented an inviting surface for *graffiti*, the scrawled names of various historical personages deemed to have played an important role in mankind's long struggle for progress. Chronologically, they ranged from Spartacus to Plekhanov; geographically, they spanned the globe. But the most significant point was that the list began with the names of two eminent Frenchmen: Victor Hugo and Emile Zola.[1] The choice may at first sight seem rather arbitrary, but the episode illustrates the fascination which France, and more particularly the French revolutionary tradition, had for so many Russians before and after 1917. The Bolsheviks were not alone in the view that they were bringing to fruition a movement that had its roots in 1789, that they were implementing ideals cherished by some of the most advanced thinkers in Europe during the nineteenth century. Saltykov-Shchedrin had once written that every patriotic Russian had two fatherlands, Russia and France. There was of course, as we now see, an underlying ambivalence in this attitude of veneration for the West: even if the typical Russian progressive might be *un Français manqué*, in his heart there lurked an ambition to prove himself a better Frenchman than any Parisian.[2]

In speaking here of "the tyranny of Paris over Petrograd" we have in mind this intellectual and cultural indebtedness, not any problems of foreign or financial policy.[3] In particular we are concerned with the extent to which this sense of participation in

---

1 A. Paquet, *Der Geist der russischen Revolution* (Leipzig, 1919), 69.

2 A French observer in Petrograd in 1917 noted: "Hardly has liberty been born than the Russian people are leaping to the ultimate limit of their demands. . . . A fortnight ago a decent workable constitution would have seemed an impossible ideal. . . . Now they want a social republic. Some of the less well informed say, with a disdainful grimace: 'The French revolution? That was the product of a nation of bourgeois. We shall do it quicker and better'." M. Markovitch (de Néry), *La révolution russe vue par une Française* (Paris, 1918), 86.

3 The phrase is borrowed, with apologies, from E. M. Butler, *The Tyranny of Greece over*

the French revolutionary tradition may have obscured or distorted men's understanding of the realities of the Russian situation in 1917. As David Anin has pointed out, the inability to discern the threat posed to the gains of February by left-wing maximalism "was not an accidental feature but a 'psychological state' that pervaded all parties or, rather, the whole Russian intelligentsia."[4] He rightly noted, as does Thomas Riha in regard to the Kadets, that they were still living under the impression of their experiences in 1905. One may add that neither this experience, nor the attacks of the *Vekhi* group, nor even the holocaust on the Eastern Front seem to have seriously modified the basic *Weltanschauung* of those who set the tone in Russian public life. Nor was this traditional outlook much disturbed by the incessant and inconclusive polemics between Social Democrats and Socialist Revolutionaries, or the various factions and subfactions of these parties, since these debates were concerned less with fundamentals than with questions of tactics and organization (important though these might be in their ultimate implications). By and large the Romantic spirit continued to encourage a preoccupation with abstract verities rather than practical problems—in deciding which the intelligentsia had after all little or no part to play; their ensuing sense of alienation still aroused messianic expectations of total, radical change; idealism went on masquerading in materialist dress; there was as yet more interest in the redistribution of wealth than in its augmentation, or in matters of economic management; the mood was still hostile to individualism or elitism and favorable to "the masses"; even those who now suspected the democratic virtues of the *narod* or the sacred mission of the intelligentsia did not doubt that the two categories existed. The language of discussion was not really very different from that of the 1890s. As one student of the problem puts it, the view that the intellectuals had played an essential role in the political and social life of the country in 1905, and that they were bound to do so again in any future crisis, was shared by everyone, from Nicholas II to Lenin, prior to 1917; for this reason, although the thesis may well be fallacious, it must nevertheless be considered as one of the "real elements" in Russian situation at this time.[5]

Doubtless in conditions of normal evolutionary change the traditional faith would have been fairly rapidly undermined by shifts in the social structure and by the impact of new intellectual trends in Europe; it was the persistence of tsarism and the war that limited the scope of such developments as did occur, so preserving artificially the time-honored outlook—one which had taken shape in the mid-nineteenth century and owed so much to the age of which Marx was at once the symbol and the expression.

Nothing was more typical of this worldview than its high regard for the France of 1789, of which the votaries had but a very inadequate and stereotyped picture, judged by modern standards of historical scholarship. Professor Alfred Cobban has

---

Germany (Cambridge, 1935), a study of the influence of Greek culture on German writers in the eighteenth, nineteenth and twentieth centuries.

4 *Soviet Studies*, 18, no. 4 (April 1967), 445.

5 G. Putman, "P. B. Struve's View of the Russian Revolution of 1905," *SEER*, XLV, no. 107 (July 1967), 472–3.

recently argued that the social interpretation of the French revolution, indulged in by "system-makers" who proceeded from the assumptions of sociological theory rather than objective empirical research, came to play the role of a Sorelian myth:

> As the mother of revolutions to come . . . it was to be treated with filial solicitude. It represented an earlier stage on the road that civilization had to follow. To see it as in any way a diversion, or even a reversal of the one-way traffic dictated by the laws of a great philosophy of history, was too shocking to consider. Even when evidence that might have led to a different interpretation of the revolution was adduced, it was forced into the preconceived pattern.[6]

While the myth had a powerful effect upon French opinion, its impact was nowhere so profound as in Russia. It was by no means confined to the revolutionary underground, but permeated educated society.

To illustrate the approach of Russian scholars in the early twentieth century to the problem of motive forces in the French revolution, we may cite an essay by R. Iu. Vipper (1859–1954), then known as a liberal historian of antiquity, who in later life was to become a veiled apologist for Stalin as a reincarnation of Ivan the Terrible. Discussing Jacques Thierry's work on the *tiers état*, he claimed that "it laid the foundations of social history," since the author "had clearly formulated the main phenomenon of the social-historical process, which goes by the name of 'the class struggle'."[7] If one thing seemed certain to the men of this generation, it was that the revolution had been directed against feudalism and had been led by the *bourgeoisie*. It was around this time that the latter term entered the Russian language, in a rather clumsy rendering (*burzhuaziia*); in 1917 it was to acquire significant emotive and symbolic connotations.[8]

The force of the European, and particularly French, bias in the intellectual fare offered to Russian students of society in the years before 1917 may be gauged from that curious compendium of bibliographic knowledge published by N. A. Rubakin.[9] A man of encyclopedic learning and philanthropic inclinations, Rubakin was in political terms a Populist; intellectually he was a disciple of Auguste Comte, whose majestic but sadly unscientific scheme for the classification of all human wisdom he adapted in his own work; he wrote prolifically on historical subjects ranging from the Albigensian heretics to the antislavery movement in the United States. A glance at *Sredi knig* will indicate vividly, first of all, the vast amount of literature on political and social problems put out at this time—particularly during the years 1905–7, when the censorship regulations were considerably relaxed and new publishing houses sprang up that were prepared to take big risks, politically and commercially, to assuage the

6 *The Social Interpretation of the French Revolution* (Cambridge, 1964), 171.

7 R. Iu. Vipper, "Liberalizm i pervaia istoricheskaia formula bor'by klassov," *Dve intelligentsii i drugie ocherki* (Moscow, 1912), 109.

8 A study of political jargon in the Russian revolution might be rewarding. Were the "negative" words more frequently of non-Russian origin?

9 *Sredi knig*, 3 vols. (Moscow, 1911–15).

pent-up demand for reading matter in this field. The role of *literator* was an honored one, and many an impoverished "professional revolutionary" kept himself alive on the modest fees earned by translating books and pamphlets from Western languages—a task which, though onerous, at least gave the opportunity to familiarize oneself with the works in question.

History was of course a great favorite, and French history in particular. "It has always attracted the special attention of Russian readers," Rubakin observed, "and there is not one branch of Western European history that offers us such an ample choice of fine books as this;"[10] he went on to quote Thomas Buckle's advice that one should emulate the French, since their only vices came from their despotic rulers and their history taught that in the end the People were bound to triumph. While there was, alas, no general history of France in Russian, there was a particularly rich literature on the Great Revolution. Most of the classic accounts from Thiers and Carlyle to Aulard and Sorel had been translated; so too had the work of Taine, here rebuked for "having conceived his history from partisan considerations"; Louis Blanc, on the other hand, is praised for elevating the role of the masses over that of the individual and for comprehending the key part played in events by the class-conscious *bourgeoisie*. Sorel's history was translated into Russian in eight volumes under the editorial supervision of Professor N. I. Kareev, a well-known liberal Populist, himself the author of works on nineteenth-century France and the French peasantry. The first volume of Jaurès's *Histoire Socialiste, 1789–1900* appeared in two simultaneous Russian translations in 1908. All in all Rubakin could list no less than 26 full-length books and 10 brochures on the subject; it was run a close second in the popularity stakes by the Paris Commune of 1871, on which 26 works were available, only one of them critical of the communards. By way of contrast, a Russian ignorant of foreign languages who wished to acquaint himself with modern German history was most inadequately supplied: virtually the only source in Russian which Rubakin can recommend is a translation—by the philosopher V. A. Rudnev ("V. Bazarov"), then a Bolshevik—of a work written in the 1890s by a German Social Democrat, P. Kampffmeyer.[11]

As for literature on the history and politics of Russia itself in the nineteenth century, the ravages of tsarist censorship and the prejudices of the intelligentsia combined to deprive the reading public of any adequate conception of the many complex problems it presented. There was of course a wealth of theorizing in the various *tolstye zhurnaly*, and some attempt at a historical treatment of these intellectual debates as part of the "liberation movement"; there was also a fair amount of literature on the agrarian problem and the zemstvo. But the other reform measures of Alexander II lacked their historian, and Rubakin justly complained that the literature on Alexander III's reign was "extremely thin": no more than four books and one article could be found which gave a general treatment of the period. On Russia's foreign policy there were but five titles for the reign of Alexander II. Information on the minority regions was scarce:

---

10 Ibid., vol. I, 127.

11 Rubakin, *Sredi knig*, vol. I, 114.

for an area of such importance as Transcaucasia the reader had to be referred to a
dozen rare works of very varied scope and quality.[12]

After this sorry tale can one wonder if the democratic politicians were surprised
when the "nationalities question" burst upon them with such force in 1917, or if they
found it difficult to formulate a viable foreign policy? Their intellectual heritage rendered them ill equipped to handle such painful tasks; training as well as temperament
led them to look elsewhere for mental stimulation.

II

Of the various political groupings on the Russian scene between February and October
the conservative and liberal "defensists" were the least affected by the traditional
mythology. This of course is only what one would expect. It is perhaps characteristic
that Miliukov, when referring to the first Provisional Government, in which he played
so prominent a part, should use the term *burzhuaznaia vlast'*, although one may doubt
whether he regarded himself as representative of the entrepreneurial interest; it was
simply that the customary terminology imposed itself upon him. When defensists
evoked historical parallels, they did so largely for rhetorical effect. Thus in February
the right-wing Duma deputy, V. V. Shul'gin, as he heard the citizens of the new
Russia sing the *Marseillaise*, felt some alarm at "the rivers of impure blood" which,
according to the hymn, were to "water the furrows in the soil"; if we may trust
his impressionistic memoirs, he sighed for the machine-guns that alone could tame
"that wild beast, His Majesty the Russian People."[13] This instinctive fearful reaction
testified to the intellectual bankruptcy of the right: Shul'gin would himself eventually
make his peace with that same People's dictatorial overseers.

More moderate elements sympathetic to the war effort sought to turn the revolutionary tradition to their political advantage by recalling the unity of the French
nation in the year of Valmy. Albert Thomas struck this note in his address to the
Soviet Executive Committee on April 29/May 12: the men of 1792, he averred, had
renounced all ambition for conquest, yet they had aimed to liberate the world; they
had not shrunk from using force to oblige their enemies to recognize the principle
of self-determination.[14] The analogy failed to carry conviction. The internationalists
had historical logic on their side when they replied that the two situations were by
no means comparable, and that the Russian army had yet to undergo the purge which
had made the French capable of resolute resistance to the invader. The defensist
argument was echoed by numerous spokesmen for the Provisional Government, the
army and prowar circles on the left. General Brusilov, for instance, seeking to justify
the restoration of the death penalty for frontline soldiers guilty of serious derelic-
tion of duty, declared that "the lessons of the Great French Revolution insistently call

---

12 Ibid., 66, 74.

13 V. V. Shul'gin, *Dni* (Belgrade, 1925), 165–6.

14 *Discours prononcé par Albert Thomas, ministre de l'armement et des fabrications de guerre,
devant le comité du Conseil des Ouvriers et des Soldats de Pétrograd le 12 mai 1917*, 8. All
dates hereafter O.S.

themselves to mind."[15] The Soviet *Izvestiia* exclaimed sonorously on August 27: "we have faith that revolutionary Russia will be just as invincible as was revolutionary France."[16] The aging Plekhanov, who had had a lifelong romance with the French Enlightenment, now sang paeans of praise to the *tiers état*: it had merged its class interests with those of the French nation as a whole, and for this reason "all that was vital, enlightened and noble in the civilized world at that time followed its movement for liberty, enthusiastically welcoming each least success"; how glaring was the contrast with the narrow egoism of Russia's "fourth estate."[17] There was an element of artificiality and special pleading in these allusions; their authors' sincerity seems in doubt; the operation bears the mark of a public relations exercise. Yet one might argue that at another, deeper level the partisans of national defense drew heavily upon the old intellectual tradition, and we shall return to this point after considering the views of their left-wing opponents.

Among critics of the Provisional Government and the war this legacy made itself felt much more obviously: it was not simply a matter of rhetorical flourishes but a living force that helped to shape their thinking. When Chernov in his memoirs taxes Kerenskii for allegedly believing that Russia was "repeating the story of the French revolution," this is less than fair; rather might it be said that Chernov himself took 1789 as his guiding star. Already in 1906 he had argued, successfully, that the SRs should include in their "maximum program" a provision for a temporary revolutionary dictatorship, on the grounds that the experience of the jacobins and the communards showed this to be necessary.[18] Admittedly, this was a somewhat abstract point, since in Chernov's view full socialization was a matter for the distant future and not immediate practical politics; what concerned him in 1917 was the agrarian revolution. In promoting a fundamental and radical transformation of property relationships in the countryside, he hoped that the popular movement could be kept within institutional bounds by the network of local land committees and soviets. In this he was very conscious of the historical precedents: "for the Russian workers of 1905 and the spring of 1917," he wrote later, "the soviets were in a sense what the revolutionary clubs, particularly the Jacobin Club, had been for the *bourgeoisie* in the French revolution . . . improvised organizations [that existed] due to the absence of stable, well-established and distinct *parties*."[19] That is to say, since political parties and trade unions were much weaker in Russia than in contemporary Western Europe, one had to reach back in time for a different organizational model; the soviets should serve both as rallying points for mass initiative and as organs of popular control.

This doctrine sounded like Leninism, but differed from it in rejecting the concept of "soviet power" on a nationwide scale; for Chernov understood that this implied a

15 L. Trotskii, *History of the Russian Revolution* (London, 1931), vol. II, 131.

16 R. P. Browder and A. F. Kerenskii, eds., *The Russian Provisional Government: Documents and Materials* (Stanford, 1961), vol. III, 1521.

17 G. V. Plekhanov, *God na rodine* (Paris, 1921), vol. II, 120.

18 O. H. Radkey, *The Agrarian Foes of Bolshevism* (New York and London, 1958), 41.

19 V. M. Chernov, *The Great Russian Revolution* (New Haven, 1936), 103.

minority dictatorship, which he thought untimely. He stood for a democratic coalition government, of the conventional type but committed to an uncompromisingly radical social program. This regime was not only to promote agrarian revolution, but also to "democratize" the army, so creating the prerequisites for a successful war of "revolutionary defense." Here too the French analogy was called into service; but whereas for the government's supporters the parallel was already in being, Chernov thought it had to be created. The conflict between officers and men could be ended only in one of two ways: "by granting the old generals unlimited power," which was unthinkable, or "by following that of the French revolution: giving the revolutionized army revolutionary leaders . . . whose intimacy with the soldiers and revolutionary enthusiasm would compensate for their inexperience."[20] The occurrence four times in this sentence of the emotive word "revolution" indicates that we are here deep in the realm of mystique: the harsh reality was that such officers scarcely existed in the Russia of 1917.

With the Mensheviks we encounter the traditional mythology in its dogmatic Marxist form—although the split within the party, which led some of its members into the governmental coalition, was a sign that doctrine was losing its hold. Martov continued to champion the old beliefs: this was the "*bourgeois* revolution" and it was up to the *bourgeoisie* to fulfill its historic role, with the socialists as spokesmen for the proletariat remaining in opposition. In defence of this classic stand he conjured up some familiar imagery. On June 10, addressing the Petrograd soviet at a critical moment, he alleged that "the *bourgeoisie* is recalling its praetorian guard from the front, preparing to play the role of a Cavaignac." In reply Tsereteli, formally his party colleague but now a minister, took up the allusion:

> Comparing our revolutionary army with the soldiers of Cavaignac, you forget that the nineteenth-century revolutionary stereotype is quite inapplicable to our revolution. Then the *bourgeoisie*, relying on a conservative peasantry and an army composed of such peasants, disposed of the proletariat and paved the way for the victorious counterrevolution. But the army of revolutionary Russia is part of the revolutionary peasantry, and is at one with the working class in the soviet . . . in consolidating liberty.

This led the internationalist Sukhanov to hint darkly at the Georgian's supposed political ambitions: "thou art not yet king, Danton," he intoned, quoting the girondin Louvet. Chairman Chkheidze settled the argument with a curious metaphor: "do not trouble historical shades whose position is different from ours."[21]

From this exchange Tsereteli emerges with more credit, but despite his greater sense of realism he was not free from the spell of the mystique. To give Martov his due, after the October *coup* his awareness of the revolutionary tradition enabled him to place Bolshevik rule in an illuminating historical perspective. The jacobins, he recalled, had also exercised power as "a dictatorship of a minority party" and had governed France through a network of institutions which had their contemporary equivalents: "the revolutionary committees of 1794 and 1919 are absolutely identical."

---

20 Ibid., 301

21 I. G. Tsereteli, *Vospominaniia o fevral'skoi revoliutsii* (Paris-The Hague, 1962), vol. II, 214.

While the existence of soviets and other working-class bodies "testifies to the influence of the industrial proletariat, it by no means prevents these purely proletarian class organs . . . from serving as an apparatus whereby a certain minority party implements its dictatorship, just as the jacobins with their different social roots did in 1792–4."[22] All that was lacking in this analysis was a frank recognition that the minority could afford to ignore totally the interests and wishes of the class whence it had sprung, but Martov was writing in the early months of 1919, when few discerned the potentialities in store for Lenin's regime, and he was justifiably more concerned to trace the origins of Bolshevism than to prophesy its future. He went on to sketch the communist strain in European socialism from Babeuf and Buonarroti to his own day.

Lenin himself showed relatively little interest in the European precedents of the Russian revolution—as might be expected of the man whose main achievement, intellectually, was to "russify" Marxism. A check of his *Collected Works* gives the impression that his knowledge of the French revolution was derived wholly from the writings of Marx, Engels and other classic authorities. He referred to it infrequently, and then only to buttress arguments about three political issues of current concern to him. The first of these was the need for an "alliance" between proletariat and peasantry: in Russia, his argument ran, the *bourgeoisie* had little influence in the countryside and the opportunities for Bolshevism were correspondingly great; this situation contrasted sharply with that in 1789, when the *bourgeoisie* had "not even for a moment forsaken its peasant allies."[23] The second point which interested him was the extent to which decentralization had weakened the *bourgeois* state structure and permitted popular self-government.[24] The third point was the Terror, on which his views underwent an evolution. Before 1914 he was content to defend it as necessary and progressive; but by September 1917 he had come to see it as epitomizing the essence of the revolution: "125 years ago the great French *bourgeois* revolutionaries made their revolution great by using terror against all oppressors."[25] It is worth noting that Martov contested the efforts by Bolshevik sympathizers to justify the terror in Russia by referring to earlier precedents.[26]

Lenin's approach to the myth, one might say, was coldly utilitarian and instrumental. Trotskii, on the contrary, had a deep personal involvement in it. His intellectual horizons were broader, and he also knew French well; indeed, he seems to have learned the language when studying the history of the French revolution—an interest

22 L. Martov, *Mirovoi bol'shevizm* (Berlin, 1923), 40.

23 Lenin, *Sochineniia*[3], vol. XVI, 344; cf. vol. VIII, 122, vol. XIV, 50. In 1911–12 he seems to have modified this view slightly in a sense unfavorable to the French *bourgeoisie*: cf. ibid., vol. XV, 342.

24 Ibid., vol. XX, 315; vol. XXI, 387.

25 Ibid., vol. VII, 70; vol. VIII, 64; vol. XIV, 151; vol. XXI, 186. We need not discuss here Lenin's indebtedness to the Paris Commune for the picture of the future soviet democracy drawn in his *State and Revolution*.

26 I. Getzler, *Martov: a Political Biography* (Cambridge, 1967), 193.

stimulated by Plekhanov's taunt that Lenin was a twentieth-century Robespierre.[27] In his essay *Results and Prospects* (1906–7) he warned against drawing facile historical analogies but simultaneously urged the need for Russian Marxists to analyze in depth the "motive forces" involved in European revolutions since 1789. Trotskii's own effort in this direction was little more than a pilot survey, although rather oddly it seems to have frightened other "creative Marxists" off the subject. This is not the place to expound the theory: its substance is perhaps best conveyed by his epigrammatic phrase, "the Russian *bourgeoisie* neglected to supply the country with a French history."[28] This basic assumption, that the Russian *bourgeoisie* was a negligible quantity, led logically to the view that one had to telescope the stages of revolution, and to establish a proletarian dictatorship which would offset Russia's historic lag by actively carrying socialism across national frontiers.[29] It was Trotskii's belief that the Bolsheviks had shaken off their previous narrowness and nationally limited outlook that led him to sink his differences with Lenin in 1917—a decision which by any criterion must be adjudged historic. It might be contended that he would have thrown in his lot with the Bolsheviks in any case, once he saw that they were likely to win, but cynicism can be overdone: intellectual considerations must have played some part, and these were rooted in the mythology of the revolutionary tradition.

Another way—perhaps the most important—in which this tradition affected men's thoughts and actions in 1917, whatever their political position, was through the popular image of "Bonapartism." The *locus classicus* of the widespread belief in the danger of counterrevolution from the right is Kerenskii's reply to Lenin's open challenge at the First Congress of Soviets:

> How did 1792 end in France? It ended in the fall of the republic and the rise of a dictator. . . . The problem of the Russian socialist parties and of Russian democracy is to prevent such an outcome as there was in France—to hold on to the revolutionary conquests already made; to see to it that our comrades who have been released from prison do not return there; that a Lenin, who has been abroad, may have the opportunity to speak here again, and not be obliged to flee back to Switzerland. We must see to it that historic mistakes do not recur. . . .[30]

Kerenskii's recipe for averting such a disaster, as is common knowledge, was to rally the center against its foes on the left as on the right—but with the latter generally receiving the lion's share of his attention.

Despite this is became fashionable on the left, as the year wore on, to charge Kerenskii with Napoleonic ambitions. Sukhanov, for instance, later alleged that his action in accepting ministerial office "was extremely characteristic of the psychology of a certain type of person, who came to be called 'little Bonapartes'. . . . His

---

27 I. Deutscher, *The Prophet Armed: Trotsky, 1879–1921* (Oxford, 1954), 90, 148.

28 Trotskii, *History. . . ,* vol. I, 70.

29 Trotskii's two key pamphlets, *The Permanent Revolution* and *Results and Prospects*, have been translated into English and published jointly by B. Pearce (London, 1962).

30 Browder and Kerenskii, eds., *The Russian Provisional Government*, vol. III, 1305.

'Napoleonic' methods . . . were eventually to prove his ruin."[31]   But Sukhanov also detected such tendencies in Tsereteli and his colleagues in the Soviet Executive Committee, as well as in Lenin, who was said to have invoked simultaneously the ghost of Bonaparte and of Machiavelli—no mean feat.[32] The very fact that such charges could be bandied about so freely is interesting, since it shows how strong a hold the French precedent had upon certain minds.

Lenin made use of the derogatory term *bonapartysh*, no doubt aware of its symbolic efficacy. Trotskii went much further and developed a sociological theory which purported to explain how revolutions could degenerate into Bonapartism. Where opposing class forces were evenly balanced, he argued, it was a likely eventuality—hence the triumph of Napoleon I; by 1848 the proletariat had already become stronger—hence Napoleon III was less successful than his predecessor; by 1917 the proletariat had unquestioningly become the dominant social force—hence the "epigone bonapartism" of Kerenskii had been foredoomed to failure. "There was no equilibrium. The revolution was still full-blooded. No wonder Bonapartism proved anaemic."[33] The symmetry of this theory was rather spoiled by the fact that there appeared to be two potential "epigone Bonapartes" in Russia, Kerenskii and Kornilov; but Trotskii neatly disposed of this difficulty by labeling the former candidate the agent of the "petty bourgeoisie" and the latter the agent of "big capital," working through the army.   Whatever the relation of this theory to historical fact, it was certainly ingenious, and its author long remained enamored of it. After his fall from power he would try to cast Stalin in this historic role; later still he would find yet another "epigone Bonaparte" in the 71-year-old French president, Gaston Doumergue.[34]

What matters here is not the credibility of this intellectual edifice, but the fact that it rested upon certain assumptions that were widely held, although rarely made explicit, by Russian public figures in 1917—especially, but not solely, in the camp of "revolutionary democracy." Perhaps the most influential of these beliefs was that the course of a revolution was governed by some objective law or laws, which could be deduced from historical experience. One did not have to be a Marxist to accept this notion. Many conservatives visualized History as a kind of pendulum, swinging rhythmically between two poles marked "authority" and "anarchy": excesses in either direction were bound to touch off a compensating reaction. After the failure of General Kornilov's "revolt" in August many army officers gave up the struggle against "the forces of dissolution," which seemed to be hopeless, and appeased their consciences with the thought that, as the effects made themselves felt in increased hardship for the masses, "maximalism" would be discredited and the virtues of firm orderly government rediscovered. In a sense of course they were proved right by events—except that it was the Bolsheviks who were to do the governing. Few ap-

31 N. Sukhanov, *Zapiski o revoliutsii* (Berlin, Petrograd and Moscow, 1922), vol. I, 315; cf. vol. II, 285.
32 Ibid., vol. II, 261; vol. III, 61.
33 Trotskii, *History. . .* , vol. II, 163–5.
34 L. Trotskii, *Où va la France* (Paris, 1936), 10.

preciated that they could display the ruthlessness and flexibility necessary to retain and consolidate their dictatorship. As one eminent liberal recalled later: "I never met anyone who doubted that the overthrow of the Bolsheviks was imminent. The only question was how and when."[35] In the case of the socialists this optimism was fortified by an overliteral interpretation of Marxist teaching and an undue addiction to the mythology of revolution.

It was of course quite natural for men faced with an alarming social crisis to search for precedents, and much of this activity was quite harmless. It had happened before: "in the dramatic months leading up to July 1830," a historian of France records, "one finds the press debate dominated by the question: does 1830 bear more resemblance to the France of 1789 or to the England of 1688?"[36] What is surprising is that so many of the men of 1917 seemed ready to forget that Russia was not, and could not be, another France.

A *post mortem* on this historic miscalculation was offered by Tsereteli, whose strictures on orthodox Menshevism are applicable to a wider segment of opinion:

> Social Democracy, which headed the February revolution, had taken shape politically under the influence of the . . . Great French Revolution and its sequels in the nineteenth century. Traditional socialist historiography taught us to revere individuals and parties standing on the extreme left wing of the liberation movement. We were convinced that the working class, even when it succumbed to maximalist illusions . . . was doing the work of the future. . . . *La révolution n'a pas des ennemis à gauche*: this was the intellectual legacy we had inherited from the great popular revolutions of the past. It inspired all our thinking.[37]

Whereas Tsereteli reacted to these excesses by taking his stand upon reformist socialism, other Russian writers adopted a more overtly nationalist position. In 1919 Struve declared: "we were too prone to criticize our country, to besmirch it before foreigners," and called upon his compatriots "to resurrect the shattered temple of the national spirit."[38] The same point was put rather more subtly by Stepun, who criticized the left-wing socialists for idealizing Revolution "as a kind of dazzling archangel, whose sudden appearance had brought happiness to Russia."[39] There is some substance in these arguments, yet they do not go far enough. It would be pointless to substitute a nationalist myth for an internationalist one. Russia needed to be liberated from those who created and sustained myths of all kinds. The alienated intelligentsia, which was so susceptible to messianic longings, had to be replaced by a new elite at once more prosaic and more realistic. This process, already under way before 1914, but

---

35 I. V. Gessen, "V dvukh revoliutsiiakh: zhiznennyi opyt," *Arkhiv russkoi revoliutsii*, vol. XXII (Berlin, 1937), 382.

36 S. Mellon, *The Political Uses of History: a Study of Historians in the French Restoration* (Stanford, 1958), 2.

37 Tsereteli, *op. cit.*, vol. II, 410. This was written in the late 1920s.

38 P. B. Struve, *Razmyshleniia o russkoi revoliutsii* (Sofia, 1921), 6, 16.

39 F. Stepun, *Byvshee i nebyvshee* (New York, 1956), vol. II, 48–9.

interrupted by war and revolution, has regained momentum in our own day.

1968

CHAPTER 15

Lenin as Tactician

Whatever Lenin's merits as a philosopher, historian or literary critic, he was preeminently a politician, and it was as a master of political tactics, who skillfully manipulated men and ideas to achieve power for his party, that he won his greatest success. Indeed, some of his biographers, not only those sympathetic to his views but also severe critics, have seen in this political dexterity the hallmark of genius. If one allows that a genius may occasionally err, the claim is not too sweeping, for it would be wrong to underestimate the importance of his contribution to politics. It might be said that Lenin was an expert in political maneuver rather than an original thinker, still less a statesman.

Before considering his teachings and the contexts in which they were applied, it would be well to identify the two subtle but significant emendations of Marx, at least of the later Marx, which Lenin made in the initial stages of his career. The first is his well-known theory of "consciousness," as set down in *What is to be Done?* and other writings of the *Iskra* period. This theory enabled him to substitute for the proletarian masses, whom Marx had seen as the engine of social progress, a small élite of professional revolutionaries, possessed of superior political insight and practical experience, who for this reason were well fitted to provide leadership for the workers. Lenin held—quite reasonably, as one may think—that ordinary working men would never make the kind of revolution he wanted if they were left to their own resources, but had to be cajoled or coerced into doing so. This discovery led him to a radical interpretation of the fundamental Marxist notion of "combat" or "struggle" (the German *Kampf*, the Russian *bor'ba* are words whose flavor it is difficult to render in English). For Marx this struggle had been primarily a socioeconomic phenomenon, a war of classes for control of the means of production and the transfer of accumulated wealth from private owners to the community at large. For Lenin the struggle was mainly a political phenomenon, a war of organizations which supposedly embodied the will of the classes they represented, and its purpose was to destroy the *bourgeois* state and transfer power to those who could speak for the proletariat. The chief enemy of the working class, in Europe as well as in Russia itself, was tsarism, the symbol of international reaction. The autocratic régime had to be overthrown before the great social transformation could get under way. Not that Lenin ignored the economic struggle between labor and capital; but he subordinated it strictly to political ends, believing that it encouraged potentially dangerous "reformist" notions against which true revolutionaries should be continually on their guard. He adhered to this order of priorities long after his battles with the "economists" in 1901–3, which had originally led him to formulate his ideas explicitly. For Lenin genuine revolutionary consciousness was always immanent in the party, or to be more precise, in that section of the party loyal to himself. This élitist view of the class struggle, with its stress on leadership, organization and control, was, before 1914, the most obvious distinction between the Bolsheviks and their fellow socialists. If the latter thought that these differences were of degree rather than substance, this was largely due to Lenin's skill in obscuring the extent of his departure from Marx. He did not claim to have made any theoretical innovations, but merely to have applied the principles of orthodox revolutionary Social Democracy more consistently than his critics. (It was left to the Stalinists to argue, more plausibly, that Leninism was Marxism brought up to date for "the era of imperialism.")

The second great emendation of Marx which Lenin made likewise remained largely concealed from the eyes of his contemporaries. This was his devaluation of the ethical content of socialism and the revolutionary struggle. It is, of course, true that Marx had advocated a relative morality, adapted to the exigencies of the class war; but he had not taken this doctrine to its logical conclusion. Lenin did. Hitherto Marxists had in practise assumed that there was one code of conduct to be observed in the struggle against the class enemy, but another to be observed within the working class movement itself. Their ethical standards were not radically different from those of their adversaries. But Lenin, drawing upon the traditions of Russian intellectual "nihilism," saw this simply as *bourgeois* softness, and eagerly set about the task of eradicating it. In his view there could be no moral bond between the proletariat (by which he meant, in effect, the party) and its enemies. As one Bolshevik put it with almost embarrassing frankness at a party conclave in 1905: "We social democrats have our own philosophy, our own law, our own ethics. . . . Begone, *bourgeois* ethics! Begone, *bourgeois* justice!"[1] This sense of alienation from their environment enabled Lenin and his followers to act with complete lack of scruple against their opponents, including former comrades in the party who refused to think or behave as Lenin thought fit. With few exceptions, the quality of Lenin's entourage deteriorated as the prerevolutionary years went by, since men of spirit and independence sooner or later rebelled against his intransigence and narrow-minded *Rechthaberei*. After the outbreak of war in 1914 he found himself more isolated than ever. Zinov'ev, his closest confidant at this time, tells us that "he acquired a kind of concentrated hatred of the *bourgeoisie*, as sharp as the keened blade of a dagger."[2] This was the moral dynamite, so to speak, which made October possible.

Some consideration of the Bolshevik leader's psychology is essential if one is to understand his political conduct. This is a line of inquiry which offers promising rewards for those professionally equipped to pursue it.[3] The historian will naturally

---

1 *Tretii s'ezd RSDRP, aprel'-mai 1905 g.: protokoly* (Moscow, 1959), 56–7.

2 G. E. Zinov'ev, *V. I. Lenin: ocherk zhizni i deiatel'nosti* (Leningrad, 1924), 51.

3 The diagnosis offered by S. Possony in *Lenin: the Compulsive Revolutionary* (Chicago and London, 1966), 453–78, though stimulating in many respects, is vitiated by hostile bias.

seek to relate Lenin's character to the circumstances in which he had to operate, the conspiratorial "underground" that shaped the ideas of so many Russian radicals. This highly artificial and emotion-charged atmosphere stimulated may exotic growths. In particular, it encouraged two apparently contradictory yet complementary mental attitudes: on one hand, limitless ambitions, apocalyptic, chiliastic and utopian thinking, often of the crudest kind; on the other, a cramping absorption in pettifogging details, coupled with hysterical fears of weakness and incompetence. The more extreme one's aims, the wider the gulf was likely to be between the ideal and the means available to attain it. The revolutionary lived in continual uncertainty and tension; his mood was alternatively optimistic and pessimistic, according to the rapidly changing situation that confronted him. Opportunities might appear without warning and require prompt imaginative action; yet the ever present risk of "provocation," exposure by undercover police agents, necessitated an attitude of self-restraint, caution and vigilance. Experience taught that reality was seldom, if ever, what it appeared to be; similarly, that for success it was necessary to disguise one's actual intentions. In extreme circumstances it would become impossible to distinguish fact from fiction, and one would fall victim to the delusions of one's own propaganda. Thus, on both sides of the political barrier before 1917, there were men who devised fanciful schemes for extending to the maximum the range of those under their covert control: Nechaev, Sudeikin, Azev, Manasevich-Manuilov—and Lenin.

The important point here is not to denigrate Lenin by placing him in doubtful company, or to prove the existence of a Russian intellectual tradition that led to Bolshevism (a matter that has perhaps attracted more attention than it deserves), but simply to register the fairly obvious fact that, where political repression and socio-economic backwardness go hand in hand, conditions are ripe for the emergence of that ubiquitous figure, the alienated revolutionary intellectual, with all his psychological ambiguities and complexities. It is not difficult to explain Lenin's fanaticism in terms of the milieu from which he sprang.

Intellectually, Lenin's mind was of course shaped paramountly—indeed, almost exclusively—by Marxism. But one non-Marxist thinker who seems to have exercised some influence upon him deserves to be singled out for attention. This was Karl von Clausewitz, with whose writings Lenin became familiar in 1915, while he was living in Switzerland.[4] In the conservative Prussian general Lenin found an exponent of the dialectical mode of thinking made fashionable by Hegel, an acknowledged expert on military strategy whose doctrines he could stand "sideways," as it were, much as Marx had stood Hegel's on their head, and use them to guide the strategy, not of national defense, but of world revolution. Clausewitz taught that struggle was inherent in existence, that the military aspects of war were subordinate to the political, and

Another work of uneven quality is N. Leites, *A Study of Bolshevism* (New York, 1953).

4 The notes which Lenin took on his reading of Clausewitz were published in *Leninskii sbornik*, XII (Moscow-Leningrad, 1930), 387–452. Werner Hahlweg, an authority on both Clausewitz and Lenin, carefully analyzed this document in *Archiv für Kulturgeschichte*, XXXVI (Münster and Cologne, 1954), 35–59, 357–87.

that the successful leader made thorough preparations, taking all relevant factors into account, while at the same time allowing for the element of unpredictability. Lenin reasoned that these precepts were applicable to all kinds of struggle. Where the master observed that generals were obliged "to feel their way in the dark," the pupil commented: "And not only in war."[5] He enjoyed the scorn which Clausewitz poured on those naive or old-fashioned enough to make an absolute distinction between war and peace, offense and defense; these were not logical antitheses but were joined in a dialectical union of opposites; thus in "peace" one prepared for the outbreak of armed combat, and when this occurred consolidated one's forces on chosen ground until, having attained a superiority of power, the moment was ripe to destroy the enemy. Guile and deception were necessary to sow confusion in the adversary's camp. Where Clausewitz remarked that "the conqueror is always peace-loving, since war comes from the resistance which the defender offers to his offensive," Lenin commented: "Ha, ha, that's witty!"[6]

These ideas were not novel for him—like M. Jourdain speaking prose, he had been applying them throughout his political life; but his reading of Clausewitz helped to lend precision and authority to his views. In a public lecture which he delivered shortly after his return to Petrograd, he referred to the general as "one of the most famous writers on the history and philosophy of war," whose ideas "have at the present time been absorbed without qualification by every thinking person."[7] This was useful ammunition in his struggle against the "defensists" who hoped that the World War might be ended by negotiation between the belligerents. Lenin's argument that such a peace could only be a fraudulent temporary compromise, and that the only real solution was to unleash a violent international civil war, had good authority in Clausewitz's belief that future conflicts would have a highly intensive, "absolute" character. The idea was one that had a natural fascination for a man of such extreme and fanatical temperament. He chose to ignore the dialectical qualifications with which the general had carefully hedged his somewhat oracular pronouncements. He did not, for example, consider the reaction which total civil war was likely to produce. Instead, he plunged boldly ahead, harnessing this new authority, along with Marx, to the Bolshevik cause. His attitude remained constant for the rest of his life. In 1922, he remarked to a colleague that "political tactics and military tactics are what the Germans call a *Grenzgebiet*, and party workers would profit by studying thoroughly the works of the great German military theorist Clausewitz."[8]

I Lenin's "Operational Code"

It must be emphasized that Lenin's ideas on tactics did not develop in a vacuum, from pure intellectual effort, but were a logical corollary of the "organizational plan"

---

5 *Leninskii sbornik*, XII, 412.

6 Ibid., 408.

7 *Sochineniia*[3], XXX, 333.

8 *Leninskii sbornik*, XII, 390.

which he outlined as early as 1902, and to which he adhered even when the scale of his operations was incomparably greater. Lenin was remarkably consistent. He seldom modified his basic ideas in the light of experience; on the contrary, as his self-confidence grew, he increasingly referred back to his earlier conduct as a guide to the problems of the present. He sought to apply the same formula towards a handful of *émigré* comrades as he did later towards various segments of the Soviet population or the massed forces of "world imperialism."

Although Lenin's "operational code" is basically very simple and has often been described, it is perhaps worthwhile outlining the principal ideas here. The underlying notion is best conveyed by the phrase *divide et impera*. According to the original model, the active catalyst of change is a body of professional revolutionaries, bound together by close ties of loyalty to their leader, so homogeneous as to reduce to a minimum the likelihood of dissent or indiscipline. This central nucleus has divisions of function, but no formal or institutional barriers within it which could prevent the leader from exercising overall control—for example, by turning to the rank and file for support against errant colleagues at the top. A formal barrier does, however, exist between the members of this "hard core" organization and those in its "soft" peripheral bodies, and the relationship between the two echelons is closely prescribed. The "front organizations" (to use the term that has since entered the language) are to enjoy formal autonomy, so that they may attract the broadest possible membership, but their activities are to be controlled by agents of the parent body, whose identity and purposes may well be concealed from their fellows. Leadership is provided by means of periodical political campaigns, devised by the central organization and embodied in simple slogans that can readily be assimilated. Such campaigns serve a dual purpose: they enable certain limited goals to be attained, thus bringing nearer the achievement of the ultimate ends of the movement; more important, they focus the loyalty of those in the periphery and cause schisms in the opposing forces (which, it is assumed, are organized on a similar pattern). Since the intermediate, provisional objectives seem relatively innocuous, some elements in the adversary's camp can be won over; further campaigns can then be launched to strengthen their new loyalties and win still more adherents, who will naturally tend to rally to the stronger side. Considerations of expediency alone dictate the speed of the process whereby these vacillating elements are successively divorced from their core organization, neutralized, brought under control, and finally absorbed. The object is to bring about a situation in which one's embattled adversary, much reduced in numbers, faces a solid phalanx of loyal troops and either surrenders or is overwhelmed, whereupon the Hegelian synthesis is finally achieved.

The actual tactical doctrines associated with this model of conflict resolution do not amount to much more than a few commonsense rules and precepts.

The first of these rules is that unswerving dedication to the final aim must be combined with extreme flexibility in the choice of means. The tactical line may have to be changed very suddenly when new opportunities appear. The ultimate ends of the movement are certainties that cannot be questioned, but the immediate objectives, which depend partly on the situation of the moment, are open to discussion. In coming to a decision, long-term and short-term goals have to be balanced against each other. Too much emphasis on the former leads to the error of "dogmatism," and on the latter to that of "opportunism." The good Bolshevik takes account of environmental factors, but only up to a certain point, beyond which lies the slough of *khvostizm* (literally, "tail-endism," or lagging behind events). He should not allow his actions to be dominated by external ("objective") circumstances, but should seek to mould reality according to his will. His motto should be "courage, courage, yet more courage"—here Lenin is citing Marx, who in turn is citing Danton. Yet one should not allow one's enthusiasm to run away with one, for this leads to the opposite error of "subjectivism." A leader who becomes isolated from the masses, who confuses his own false image of reality with the actual substance, will lead the party into adventures—actions for which the conditions have not matured and which are therefore foredoomed to failure. The ideal posture is a blend of determinism and voluntarism, with a strong bias towards the latter.

The second rule relates to the different techniques required in offense and defense. When conditions are favorable, the attack must be pressed home relentlessly, with no slackening of impetus; all opportunities must be seized boldly, so that the party's route to its objectives may be as short and direct as possible. On the other hand, when the enemy is attacking, the correct tactic is to retreat in good order, regroup one's forces, and prepare for the inevitable turn of the tide; it is necessary to maneuver and temporize, distract the enemy's attention by feints, giving way neither to panic nor to romantic illusions about the chances of victory. Above all, one should be realistic. "If you can't adjust yourself, if you won't crawl on your belly in the mud, then you're not a revolutionary but a chatterbox," as Lenin put it pithily to the delegates at the Seventh Party Congress in March, 1918.[9] A few weeks later, addressing the All-Russian Central Executive Committee of Soviets, he claimed that from recent experience the Bolsheviks had learned that "one has to follow a tactic of relentless pressure when objective conditions permit this, when . . . the masses are aroused. But we have to resort to wait-and-see tactics, to a slow accumulation of forces, when objective conditions do not allow a summons to general merciless resistance."[10]

From these directives it follows that no single mode of action can be considered valid in all circumstances, and that most situations demand a combination of several. It would be wrong, for example, either to exaggerate or to minimize the value of legal as against clandestine activity or of peaceful propaganda as against violence. These are not antithetical but complementary, and it is up to the decision-maker to opt for the right balance between the various courses of action open to him. In other words, he is faced with the problem of ordering his priorities. "One has to be able at each moment to find that particular link in the chain which, if one grasps it with all one's might, will give one a firm grip upon the whole chain and a solid basis from which to go on to the next link—remembering that the order of the links, their interconnection,

---

9 *Sochineniia*[3], XXII, 324.

10 Ibid., XXIII, 9.

their distinctions, are not so simple and straightforward in a historical setting as they are in the blacksmith's shop."[11] The theory of the "decisive link" was much esteemed by Stalin and was partly responsible for the view, tenaciously held by some Soviet officials, that government should be carried on by a series of offensive campaigns.

The fourth rule, or group of rules, concerns the compromises, agreements and alliances which the party, as one pole in the dialectical contradiction, had to make with the vacillating elements that drift into its orbit during the course of the conflict. As early as 1899 Lenin remarked to a colleague about the Russian liberals: "I think that 'to utilize' is a much more accurate and appropriate word than 'to support' or 'to ally with,' which give the impression of equality, whereas they ought to follow along in the rear with clenched teeth."[12] As he saw it, such partnerships were inherently unstable since they were based upon a transient community of interests. Once the joint adversary had been defeated—indeed, even some time before—the ally would begin to turn away unless forcibly prevented from doing so. For this reason the party must at all costs preserve its separate identity and its cohesion throughout the maneuver, lest it succumb to an act of treachery, and break off contact at exactly the correct moment for an initiative favorable to the party. The extent of the collaboration must depend on the relative strength of those involved: the more powerful and united the core organization, the greater the risks it could take afford to take.

Lenin frequently inveighed against those idealistic but naive Bolsheviks who failed to appreciate the need for such twists and turns of policy, although he did not face up squarely to the essentially moral nature of their criticism, and depicted them simply as "anarchists" deficient in tactical judgement. "The task of a revolutionary party," he explained in September 1917, "is not to renounce compromises altogether but to be able to remain loyal to its principles during all the compromises that may be necessary."[13] Three years later he was preaching the same lesson to foreign sympathizers: "The whole history of Bolshevism, before and after the October revolution, is *full* of instances of maneuvering (*lavirovanie*), agreements and compromises with others." Would one climb a mountain by the direct vertical route in preference to a zigzag path? Changing his metaphor, he went on to misquote Chernyshevskii: "Political activity is not like the Nevskii Prospekt." The error is not without interest; the economic determinist of the 1860s had contrasted the straight St. Petersburg avenue with the deviousness of history, whereas for the voluntarist Lenin it was political activity that mattered most. One had, said Lenin, to ensure that any such detour or compromise "does not lower but raises the general level of proletarian revolutionary consciousness"[14]—i.e. strengthens the party's power position.

On inspection, Lenin's tactical doctrine boils down to little more than a series of injunctions to step forth boldly, stay alert, and keep one's powder dry. While it was sound enough so far as it went, it left a great deal unanswered. The most pertinent

11 Ibid., XXIII, 466.
12 Ibid., XXVIII, 24–5.
13 Ibid., XXI, 132.
14 Ibid., XXV, 210–13

question was how these algebraic formulas were to be expressed in arithmetical terms, how they were to be quantified. How could one know when the moment had come to break an alliance or to pass over to more offensive methods? The stock answer was that this was determined by expediency. But this only left another unsolved question: who decides whether the results justify the action taken or not?

One is thus immediately thrown back to problems of organization. In a party that identified itself with the onward march of History, only the leader could decide how far its actions were "correct." His was the awful responsibility which the Hegelian could conveniently leave to the Godhead. And to make matters more difficult, this function could not be explicitly acknowledged, at least in Lenin's lifetime, since some pretense of collective rational decision-making had to be maintained; it was left to Stalin to claim powers of omniscience. Lenin was of necessity more modest, although even he made some extravagant assertions on behalf of his own proficiency as leader. "The art of the politician. . . ," he wrote in *Leftwing Communism: an Infantile Disorder* (1920), "is to calculate correctly the conditions and moment in which the proletarian vanguard can successfully seize power, when it can subsequently win enough support from sufficiently wide segments of the working class, and when it can subsequently . . . extend and consolidate its rule, educating and teaching and attracting ever broader masses of working people."[15] It is clear from the context that he is referring to his own experience in the revolution. A little later in the same work, discussing the difference between "opportunistic" compromises and those that are permissible, he first says that "every worker understands the difference," but then concedes that it was often as hard to make out as the distinction between murder and homicide, and concludes: "One has to have one's head screwed on straight (*imet' sobstvennuiu golovu na plechakh*) to know what to do in each case. That, by the way, is why we have party organizations and party leaders deserving of the name, [who can] develop the necessary knowledge and experience, the necessary political flair to decide complex political questions quickly and correctly."[16] But this was not very different from the theory propounded by the "idealist" Clausewitz, who affirmed his belief in *der Blitz des Geistes*—that flash of spiritual lightning which illuminated the intellect of a successful commander in the heat of battle, the unconscious impulse which enabled him to surmount unexpected difficulties. When Lenin read this passage, he underlined it three times and noted: "Truth is not in systems." Not book learning but the power of judgement acquired from experience in action—this was the prerequisite of successful leadership. Or, to put it another way, what is today sometimes called "the *x* factor," the unpredictable subjective or chance element, could on occasion make all the difference between victory and defeat.

This was indeed a valuable insight, but it was difficult to reconcile with conventional Marxist determinism, and could not very well be developed at length in public. Instead, a host of devious arguments, and where necessary measures of physical coercion, had to be employed to conceal the fact that the party's supposedly "scientific"

15 Ibid., XXV, 195.
16 Ibid., XXV, 209.

tactics were as often as not decided very arbitrarily, by the spiritual enlightenment of its leader. The most obvious of these devices was to emit a cloud of accusations against those previously identified with the course that it was now found expedient to reject, while simultaneously denying that any significant change had taken place. Thus, in the early months of 1918 the left-wing communists were roundly upbraided as "utopians" and "schismatics" for advocating the revolutionary guerilla war against the invader to which Lenin had committed himself before the Bolshevik seizure of power. Another ruse was to reinterpret earlier statements or formulas in a sense contrary to that given them at the time—a task much eased by the abstract and vague phraseology of Marxism. The term "democratic revolution," for example, did not mean in 1917 what it had signified in 1905. Nor did Lenin find it convenient to spell out in full the implications of his tactical line where to do so might have brought his party into discredit. It is also true that the blinkering effect of Marxist doctrine often hindered him from appreciating all the likely consequences of his actions, and he was liable to ignore whatever did not easily fit into his restricted view of human nature and behavior. When unforeseen effects of his policies obliged him to take remedial action, he seldom acknowledged that the original decision had been at fault, and his first impulse was usually to cast about for a suitable scapegoat. A readiness to employ devious measures of this kind was not original or exclusive to Lenin, and may even be characteristic of the species *homo politicus*; nevertheless, taken in conjunction with his boundless ambitions and addiction to violence, it gave his teaching a markedly sinister quality.

II. The Code in Action

A thorough study of Lenin's successes and failures as leader of the Bolshevik party and Soviet state would require a full-scale biography, since virtually every step he took was motivated at least in part by the hope of tactical gain. We may confine ourselves to examining two episodes from the earlier career and then consider the key period in his life when his skillful handling of affairs stands out in high relief.

The first example seems to show Lenin erring in the direction of excessive voluntarism. At the Second Party Congress of the RSDRP in 1903, evidently overestimating the extent of his support within the party, he pushed through his own scheme for its reorganization with such ruthlessness as to provoke a schism. He had expected that the democratic elements, discredited by his propaganda in *Iskra* as "economists," "opportunists," "revisionists" and the like, would be utterly routed, and that his uneasy colleagues on the editorial board of *Iskra* would bow to his will by helping him build a centralized, disciplined organization under his own active leadership. These calculations proved to be mistaken; his fellow editors revolted against his high-handed methods and within a year he had lost all his positions of authority within the party. The schism had the important effect of paralyzing Russian Social Democracy at the very moment when, with the outbreak of war in the Far East, great revolutionary opportunities were opening up before it. For this reason not only the Mensheviks but also many of Lenin's own associates condemned his line as unduly "sectarian." But he refused to accept any responsibility for the split, laid the blame wholly upon his opponents, and called on the rank and file to assist in building up a "true" party in place of the existing one, which had been sullied by treachery. Lenin's argument was that "all the organs of the party are conspiring against the party." The implication was that only he and his followers represented its real "consciousness," its revolutionary self, and that all means were justified in ridding it of its temporary heterodox leadership.[17]

One might have expected that this hysterical argument, with its overtones of some medieval religious disputation, would have been treated with contempt; but the intellectual climate in the party was not conducive to precise or rational thought, and extravagant accusations were readily believed. It was widely assumed that the very vehemence with which Lenin presented his grievances indicated that he must have at least some right on his side. In the event, many of his critics were willing to give him the benefit of the doubt and to make concessions in the hope of securing a lasting compromise. This was eventually accomplished in 1906, whereupon Lenin was restored, temporarily at least, to a position of eminence. While in a sense his intransigence had paid dividends, one may doubt whether the struggle was worthwhile even from a narrow Leninist point of view. There is much evidence to suggest that, if the Bolsheviks had adopted a more sophisticated, permissive approach, they might have wielded greater influence in the party and in radical circles generally during the revolution of 1905–7 than they actually did.

In the broader arena, however, Lenin does seem to have become more flexible and venturesome after 1905. This was partly due to the conviction, based on experience, that some "open" organizations could serve a useful purpose as instruments for the mobilization of public opinion. This did not imply any concession to constitutionalism, any willingness to allow himself to be influenced by the ideas which others might express in debate. Rather the reverse: he was less fearful than before of enemy penetration, provided the necessary safeguards were taken, and more confident that Bolshevism could compete effectively in the political marketplace. For this reason he advocated participation in the first Duma. He argued in favor of this course as early as December, 1905, at the Tammerfors (Tampere) conference, but then yielded to the left-wing activists who dominated the proceedings, and whom he could ill afford to affront after the disastrous Moscow uprising. These enthusiasts, strangers to the dialectic, were opposed on principle to participation in a parliamentary-type assembly. Convinced that a new revolutionary upsurge was in the offing, they stood by the old insurrectionary tactics. For the next few months Lenin publicly endorsed this idea, although it is difficult to say how far the wish was father to the thought.

Eventually his sense of realism gained the upper hand. As the summer of 1906 wore on, with only limited manifestations of popular discontent, he changed his line. In July he advocated guerilla action rather than insurgency on the 1905 pattern; in August he startled his colleagues by advising them to participate in the elections to the

---

17 Cf. our *The Rise of Social Democracy in Russia* (Oxford, 1963), 138 ff.

second Duma.[18] Lest his prestige suffer by the sudden shift, he continued to maintain that his earlier tactical line, involving a boycott of the Duma, had been correct, and when recalcitrant leftists charged him with inconsistency, replied with counter-accusations of "dogmatism," "anarchism" and other sins. He also claimed that there was a substantial difference between his own position and that of the Mensheviks, who had advocated participation in the elections to the first Duma as well as in those to the second. The argument was not very plausible, but it was politically astute. Not until fourteen years later, when memories of the affair had dimmed and he was anxious to overcome left-wing extremism in the Comintern, did he admit that the initial boycott of the Duma had been mistaken.[19] Even so, he did not acknowledge that his policy had vacillated under contrary pressures from left and right.

By 1917, we are confronted by a Lenin more self-confident than ever of his manipulative skill, heartened as well as embittered by the war. He is of course greatly helped by the fluidity of Russian politics after the overthrow of the tsar, which ensures that such errors of judgement as he makes are generally outweighed by those of his adversaries. No sooner has he returned to Petrograd than he propounds the startling doctrine that the *bourgeois* phase of revolution, although barely a few weeks old, has already exhausted its potentialities, and that power must pass to the proletariat and its allies. A Soviet regime is to overthrow the *bourgeoisie*, end the war, and set the scene for the international socialist revolution. This is no mere tactical shift but a revision of basic strategy: strong medicine for those party stalwarts who had read Marx but never really understood Lenin. As they listened to his exposition, Sukhanov tells us, "their eyes roved about unseeingly, showing complete confusion."[20] Yet within a month he has brought them round to his point of view, not by convincing them that his opinions are ideologically sound, but by employing "organizational" methods. He communicates directly with the rank and file, who respond readily to the new gospel, and the activists and generals must either rally to him or forfeit their authority.[21]

At the same time Lenin is careful not to identify himself too strongly with the semi-anarchistic masses who flock to his banner and, by trying to force the pace, implicitly challenge his leadership. He preserves his control by giving tacit encouragement to the participants in the demonstrations against Miliukov, but then lightly reprimands them for premature use of the slogan "All Power to the Soviets!"—premature because he had recommended "patient systematic explanatory work" by the Bolsheviks to win a majority in the soviets before they took power. Outwardly he appears to preach restraint to the war-weary masses; but this leaves him wholly free to scourge the government for its pusillanimity in dealing with the urgent issues of the day and

18 *Sochineniia*[3], X, 12 ff., 26.

19 Ibid., XXV, 183.

20 N. N. Sukhanov, *The Russian Revolution 1917: an Eye-witness Account*, tr. and abridged by J. Carmichael (Oxford, 1955), 285.

21 L. Schapiro, *The Communist Party of the Soviet Union* (London and New York, 1960), 164. Cf. also S. W. Page, *Lenin and World Revolution* (New York, 1959), and I. Petrov, *Strategiia i taktika partii bol'shevikov v oktiabr'skoi revoliutsii* (Moscow, 1957).

to build up his party's organizational strength. In the "June Days" his forces pass in review, as it were; while the majority socialists win a formal victory, the events in the streets show that the Bolsheviks are increasing their hold. New slogans are conjured forth from the Kseshinskaia Palace to maintain the momentum of advance. Yet the front is somewhat ragged; it is open to argument whether Lenin really sought to provoke a confrontation with the soviet by his forceful statement on June 3 that his party was willing to take power, or whether it was an ill-judged gesture which turned moderate opinion against him.

It was his good fortune that any effect this might have had was nullified by the controversy aroused by Kerenskii's ill-fated offensive. Lenin is thus able to parry the blow. But events then move too fast for him. In the "July Days" he vacillates, anxious not to exploit the crowds' discontent yet fearful that this is not yet the moment for general insurrection. The fiasco undermines his standing in the party: on the right wing he is regarded as irresponsible, on the left as inconsistent. It is a bad moment for Lenin, and it is not surprising that in the Finnish marshes he should overreact to the Bolshevik setback. He announces that the counterrevolution has triumphed and repudiates the slogan of "All Power to the Soviets!"; the party itself is to carry out the insurrection, but this is seen as a fairly distant objective. The proceedings of the Sixth Congress indicate that, as on so many other occasions, his lieutenants fail to appreciate the finer implications of this tactical shift and continue to regard the soviets as organs of insurrection, adhering to the line which had been set in April. Perhaps the difference between their position and his own might have assumed more importance had he remained in Petrograd, or had the pace of events been less hectic; but as it happened he is saved by the Kornilov affair.

This gives him a chance to outbid the left-wing extremists by adopting an ultra-radical stance and urging immediate preparations for insurrection. As in April, he wins over his party by a combination of pressure from above and from below. Announcing this new "revision of tactics," he is clearly on the defensive against the charge of "opportunism," but argues that this can be avoided by a campaign on two fronts: against Kerenskii as well as Kornilov. This operation the Bolsheviks and their allies now carry out with great dexterity, until the Provisional Government is isolated and discredited—a classic instance of the practical implementation of Lenin's teachings on alliances, since few members of the "Committee for Struggle against Counterrev-olution," created and effectively controlled by the Bolsheviks, fully appreciate the part they are playing in the unfolding of Lenin's plans. His tactics achieve success because they are attuned to the "objective" situation, although not quite in the way that Bolshevik spokesmen maintain. It is less a matter of mobilizing "class-conscious proletarians" than of harnessing elemental energies and hatreds in all segments of so-ciety. In any case, there can be no doubt that the necessary work of "disinformation" by slogan and rumor is adroitly managed, and the very decisiveness of the October victory may be held to settle any argument about the correctness of his tactical line. Nevertheless, in the interests of historical accuracy, it is worth pointing out that Lenin was less astute than Trotskii in his appreciation of the role which various mass bodies could play in the organization of the *coup*. Thus, participation in the "Preparliament" was not the risky venture that Lenin feared it to be, and the Second Congress of Soviets helped him to disguise and legitimize the seizure of power. On these issues Lenin was the prisoner of his own recently adopted ultra-leftism; and if this caused him no serious damage, the credit lay primarily with his adversaries, whose errors of judgement far transcended his own.

The next few months show Lenin at the acme of his tactical skill. His success in consolidating his party's power was due to clever political manipulation rather than to use of the coercive instruments available to the ruling group. The latter were admittedly important, but they could not by themselves have turned the scales. In many of his key decisions at this time Lenin showed a masterly comprehension of political realities: for example, in his handling of the Left Socialist Revolutionaries, who were at first excluded from his government, then admitted to play a decorative role, and finally allowed to depart once they had served their purpose. His treatment of the Constituent Assembly, symbol of the democratic opposition to Bolshevism, showed an almost diabolical finesse: he resisted his initial inclination to prohibit it from convening at all, then progressively curtailed its scope for action, and at the crucial moment dissolved it without giving the deputies the chance of martyrdom or of effective resistance.[22] Similarly, Lenin won over the peasants with the Land Decree, neutralized the national minorities by an apparently contradictory policy of concessions and coercion, and abandoned old slogans and commitments without compunction. At this period he was concerned chiefly with the preservation of his party in power, and for the sake of this he was willing to make virtually any maneuver that expediency might dictate. From his own point of view, which gave primacy to the political struggle, he was of course being perfectly consistent. Only Lenin was capable of such iron logic: certainly not Trotskii, who vacillated at Brest-Litovsk, or Stalin, who vacillated over the confrontation with the Constituent Assembly, and still less the left-wing communists with their high-minded but naive addiction to principle.

In this way Lenin secures his precious "breathing space" and Bolshevism survives. But, as the months pass by, history takes its revenge upon the great tactician; the problems which he has put off by skillful maneuvering come relentlessly to the fore. Henceforth he finds himself increasingly on the defensive against forces whose *raison d'être* he does not understand, because there is no place for them in his narrow world view.

III. History Takes Revenge

The bitter truth was that Lenin knew how to win power but not how to use it. This deficiency became painfully clear as the "international proletarian revolution," whose outbreak he had so confidently anticipated, failed to materialize, and his party faced the task of governing a people largely indifferent, if not hostile, to the ideas that

---

22 L. Schapiro, *The Origin of the Communist Autocracy* (London and Cambridge, Mass., 1955, rpt. New York and Washington, 1965), 80–7.

animated their new rulers. Rather incautiously, perhaps, Lenin had committed to paper his views on the government of a socialist state; but these notions, borrowed by way of Marx from the nineteenth-century utopians, were soon proved totally irrelevant. Although it was possible to abandon them in practise, it was extremely difficult for him to evolve any new formulas to put in their place. Since *State and Revolution* could not be expunged from the Leninist canon, the Bolsheviks had to maintain that its principles were being applied in real life and to make belief in this fiction obligatory upon all Soviet citizens. Thus Lenin's Russia became the world's first, albeit rather imperfect, totalitarian state: that is to say, a country in which the principal feature of public life was a sharp contrast between reality and its official image. The fraudulent element which thereby entered into the Soviet political order stemmed ultimately from Lenin's own manipulative approach, which he carried over mechanically into the postrevolutionary era. He tackled his work as ruler of Soviet Russia, as architect of the new regime, in precisely the same spirit as he had the struggle for power. He could not grasp that a sovereign state was essentially different from a revolutionary party, and that to attempt to run it by the same methods must lead to disaster, by destroying that mutual trust between rulers and ruled which is the basis of civilized government.

Until the day of his retirement from public affairs, Lenin continued to believe that the dictatorship should be above the law, which it should utilize as an instrument of social control; that direct democracy by the working masses was both possible and reconcilable with single-party dictatorship; that the old informal *camaraderie* of the underground could be carried over into a governing party with hundreds of thousands of members; that moral exhortation and a good example at the top would suffice to keep all those in authority loyal, honest, efficient, responsible and humane in their attitude to the toiling poor. When all these ideas were shown to be utopian nonsense, Lenin could not take the necessary dialectical leap to a realm of higher truths; instead, he was left by the wayside of history, clinging pathetically to his timeworn theoretical baggage. On occasion he would utter an intellectual protest at some retrograde phenomenon to which the revolution had given rise; more frequently he would suppress his doubts and assert that all was well. "I hate bureaucracy heartily; it paralyzes and corrupts from above and from below," he says to Klara Zetkin; but the remedies he devises are often worse than the disease. In a regime that cries out for order and legality, his use of his old manipulative techniques merely adds to the prevailing chaos by confusing people's ideas about the purposes of the supreme power.

In November, 1918, for example, Lenin "agitates" for a more conciliatory line towards the *petite bourgeoisie* (by which he understands the smaller property-owning peasants and the professional men). "Now that these people are beginning to turn towards us, we ought not to turn away from them just because we used to have a different slogan in our pamphlets; we ought to rewrite these pamphlets . . . and say that we're not afraid to use conciliation as well as coercion."[23] But in the next breath

---

23 *Sochineniia*[3], XXIII, 317 ff.

he justifies as necessary the violence done to these peasants by the class struggle in the countryside, since "war is war"; he does not suggest any check upon the arbitrariness of the Cheka or other instruments of the dictatorship, the chief obstacle to any sincere collaboration on the part of the elements concerned. It might be argued that this apparent inconsistency on Lenin's part is deliberate, that he is trying to weaken and divide the opposing forces by holding out a carrot while applying the stick. This is partly so, but it would be wrong to go too far in rationalizing his policy, to see in it a logic that is no longer there; rather it might be said that he is groping in the dark but failing to come up with answers to his problems. The same applies to his policy towards the national minorities. On countless occasions he urges his followers not to surrender to chauvinistic tendencies, and to heed the sensitivities of the non-Russian peoples, yet he simultaneously authorizes acts of violence on their part which are bound to stimulate opposition and a desire for genuine national independence. This is not so much Machiavellian tactics as an endeavor to reconcile the irreconcilable, to have both real federal equality and unlimited dictatorship. In effect, the Lenin of 1918–22 has no "nationalities policy" but flounders from one enforced expedient to the next.

Even the transition to the New Economic Policy, which is sometimes viewed almost as an act of statesmanship, seems in retrospect little more than another such expedient, hastily conceived under external pressure, which left open the major questions regarding its scope and duration. Only in one sphere were the decisions of the Tenth Congress clearly the fruit of calculation: in their effect upon the situation within the party itself. Here on this familiar territory Lenin preserves his old competence. He artfully discredits the leaders of the potentially popular Workers' Opposition as "anarcho-syndicalists," saddles Trotskii with the onus of identification with authoritarian policies, pushes through his own ostensibly "centrist" platform, which in effect subordinates the unions to the bureaucracy, and under the impact of the Kronstadt rising wins general support for a resolution making "factionalism" a punishable offense.[24] A similar expertise is evident in his handling of Comintern politics, where he dexterously makes the unpopular Paul Levi the scapegoat for the failure of the attempted *putsch* in Germany of March, 1921, so preserving the Bolsheviks' image relatively untarnished and making it possible to go over to an effective "united front" strategy.

However, it soon emerged that the power-political thinking which Lenin had imposed on his party in Russia could not be transposed automatically to a foreign environment, where Bolshevism was one of several competing currents, and disillusionment with its cynical practises was bound to find expression. In Russia, on the other hand, the problem of widening the regime's popular base could be solved by forceful methods.

The party's problems were greatly eased by Lenin's withdrawal from the scene after 1922 and his eventual replacement by Stalin. No longer did its members need

---

24 Schapiro, *Origin*. . . , 314; the same point is made by A. Ulam, *The Bolsheviks* (New York, 1965), *Lenin and the Bolsheviks* (London, 1966), 470.

Lenin as Tactician

to wrestle with their consciences, as Lenin had done, to reconcile the requirements of practical politics with the overt goals of the revolution; instead they could become straightforward functionaries, executives rather than decision-makers, who received their tactical line ready made from above. They ceased to treat Lenin's ideas as a source of inspiration and were content to render them respectful but meaningless lip service. One of the many paradoxes of the Stalinist era was that, with the elimination of autonomous political forces from Soviet life, the principal sphere in which Lenin's manipulative tactics continued to be employed was within the party leadership itself— until the bizarre and horrific climax was reached with the purges of the late 1930s.

Lenin's talents as a political leader enabled him to seize and hold state power against tremendous odds. But even for Lenin power was but a means to an end, the Marxist millenium, and when he died there seemed little chance that this could be accomplished by following the course he had set. The experience of the revolution suggested rather that his principal theoretical innovations had been false. October had not sparked off the international socialist revolution, and all his subsequent moves had been no more than gifted improvisations. Had Clausewitz been alive to comment on his pupil's handiwork, he might have observed that, where the basic strategic decisions were faulty, even the most brilliant tactics could be of no avail.

1967

CHAPTER 16

Lenin's Letters as an Historical Source

I

The correspondence of the great has always exercised a powerful fascination for the historian or the biographer. Ideally, it ought to reveal the hidden aspects of a man's psyche, his secret motivations and objectives; at least it may cast light upon his personal relationships with others in a way that would not be apparent from more formal documents. In our age, the growth of modern technology and the public relations industry have, alas, all but killed this medium of communication. One may doubt whether any present-day statesman (with the exception, perhaps, of Charles de Gaulle) will bequeath to posterity correspondence which in the nineteenth century would have been deemed worthy of inclusion in one of those elegant tomes of *Letters and Papers* that graced library shelves. Least of all can the epistolary art prosper in an authoritarian society, for the qualities most in demand of the successful letter-writer—above all frankness and modesty—are not conspicuous in public life, which indeed may well be overshadowed by a false image of the Leader, deliberately built up as part of a system of ideological molding.

In this respect Lenin occupies a unique position among twentieth-century dictators. Not only was he personally less vain and less secretive than his successor, but his posthumous near-deification in the USSR has caused a tremendous effort to accumulate and preserve his literary legacy. Every scrap of paper to which he put his pen, no matter how trivial or ephemeral the subject, is of interest to the high priests of the Lenin Cult. The Central Party Archive in Moscow's Institute of Marxism-Leninism is said to have contained 29,800 items in 1953.[1] The basis of the collection was laid in 1923 by a Central Committee appeal calling on all Soviet citizens to surrender to the Institute any Lenin documents in their possession. Trotskii has told us that they were promised photographic copies in exchange, but that this promise was not generally kept. Maybe this is one reason why, in the words of one Soviet historian,

---

1 Iu. A. Akhapkin, "Organizatsiia Leninskogo arkhiva," *Voprosy istorii* (1970), 3, 60; cf. V. A. Liubisheva, "Vossozdanie arkhiva Predsedatelia SNK V. I. Lenina," *Voprosy istorii* (1969), 4, 47. This figure refers to "fond 2," established in 1939 (see below). In 1934 the archive comprised 26,687 documents by Lenin or addressed to him, and in late 1927 there were 34,493 items including 20,905 Lenin documents. Ibid., 46.

"the Lenin documents came in slowly, and often individuals surrendered them only after requests by the directors."[2] The history of the archive was a troubled one. In 1928–29 the Institute was merged with *Istpart*, and its "basic fund" grew so large that it was hard to use; then in 1939 Stalin, as part of his effort to rewrite party history, ordered that the documents actually written by Lenin should be separated from the rest, thus arbitrarily breaking the relationship between them and making things still more difficult for any potential researcher with a disinterested concern for the truth.[3] These obstacles are now to some extent being cleared away. The full story of these pious laborers in the inner sanctum of Soviet historiography, could they tell it, would be an absorbing one.

Equally fascinating, so far as we can reconstruct it, is the tale of the efforts made over the years to publish such selections from Lenin's correspondence as would satisfy the shifting requirements of the party line. These documents comprised most items in the so-called "Lenin miscellanies" (*Leninskie sborniki*) which appeared with decreasing frequency as Stalin got into his stride, until in 1945 the series seemed to have come to a halt. In 1959, three years after the Twentieth Party Congress had exposed some of Stalin's misdeeds, a new volume—the 36th—was issued. It contained a number of documents that hitherto had clearly been suppressed.

From time to time Lenin documents have also appeared in volumes of memoirs, central or local newspapers or journals, or various editions of Lenin's *Collected Works*. Publication has depended not simply upon a document's availability but also upon its "topicality," i.e. its relevance to the current concerns of the Soviet political elite. Each successive leader (or group of leaders) has striven to legitimize their authority in Leninist terms, to present their version of Lenin as the authentic one. This has often meant taking great liberties with the Bolshevik chief's writings. Thus, in the 1930s, Stalin would sometimes select for ostentatious publication in *Pravda* messages which passed between Lenin and his "closest comrade-in-arms" during the dark days of the civil war. The subject matter of the *Leninskie sborniki* was also adjusted to the spirit of the times. Volume 21, which appeared at the height of the collectivization drive, contained materials on the party's peasant policy under "war communism," and the last two volumes of the Stalin era, published during World War II, dealt mainly with military questions. These selections did not, as is sometimes said, suppress all mention of Trotskii. Nevertheless certain documents which must have been in the archivists' possession at the time were omitted, without any public indication of the fact, while others were published in an abbreviated or distorted form. The most

---

2 Liubisheva, "Vossozdanie," 41.

3 Ibid., 48, 49. [The history of Lenin's archive in the 1920s is treated, not very informatively, in *Fond dokumentov V. I. Lenina*, 2nd ed. (Moscow, 1984), 7–9; cf. 48 ff. (The first edition of this work appeared in 1970.) In 1946–8 the Central Party Archive received 1,000 Lenin documents which, for reasons the authors do not explain, but were presumably connected with Stalin's directive of 1939, had until then been kept in the Central Committee (72). We are told (76) that 6,500 Lenin documents were discovered in Soviet state archives between 1923 and 1978, but not how many the Central Party Archive now possesses. In 1953 fond 2 (see note 1 above) held 23,752 units, excluding 29,280 Lenin documents (ibid., 218).]

common ruse was to exclude the names of prominent Oppositionists from the text or from the instructions for dispatch, so that the very fact of these men's existence might vanish down the "memory hole" in the minds of all loyal Soviet citizens.

Stalin's assumption that the popular consciousness was infinitely malleable had the simplicity of genius, but it could not outlast his own mortal frame. In 1956 his successors, or some of them, loudly proclaimed their intention to restore "Leninist norms in party life." Did this mean a total repudiation of Stalinist practises? Or were only those falsifications condemned which the new rulers found inexpedient?

It is now all too plain that the new fashion for veracity was a transient and fragile thing. Khrushchev's approach to politics was more sophisticated than Stalin's, yet in the first years of his rule, when under pressure, he resorted to the old Stalinist technique of selectively publishing Lenin documents which would afford the highest sanction for contentious current policies—for example, "peaceful coexistence" with the capitalist powers.[4] In general, the long-term rather than the short-term interests of the regime were given precedence. To put it differently, genuine scholarship in the fundamentals of the faith has as much scope as is possible in an ideologically determined totalitarian polity.

We may now consider what this means in practise by taking a closer look at Lenin's correspondence as published in the fifth edition of his *Works* (hereafter called the *Works*), concentrating on a limited period: the first three years after the October revolution. This is to be found in volumes 50 and 51 of this edition, which appeared in 1964 and 1965—a time when Khrushchev was still in power or only just out of it, before the chill neo-Stalinist breezes had begun to blow in earnest. We have a total of 1,455 items, nearly two hundred (194) of which are published here for the first time. The two basic questions which a historian must ask of this source, as of any other, are: (1) how reliable is it?, and (2) what value does it have for the student of Lenin and Leninism or of Russian history in the first years of Soviet power?

II

Let us take the question of reliability first. As a historical source the *Works* may be said to bear the hallmarks of their "iconological" function. On one hand, great care has been lavished on certain details in presentation: we are told in each case whether the item is printed from the original manuscript or from a copy, when it was written, and where it was first published. The chronological arrangement is also a great improvement on the thematic one favored in earlier editions of the *Works* and in the *Sborniki*. On the other hand, the documents are presented in isolation from their historical context. The object of the editors is not to encourage critical examination by dispassionate historians or biographers, but rather to provide an authoritative manual for the guidance of the faithful. Lenin has to be portrayed not as a creature of flesh and blood, bound to his fellow men by a complex network of personal and operational relationships, who like all mortals had his moments of doubt and whose actions were

---

4 *Kommunist* (1957), no. 15, 10–14.

often contradictory, but as a lofty genius, serenely selfconfident and consistent. To this end we are offered only the documents of which Lenin was the sole or joint author, but not those which he received, even where these would be highly relevant to an understanding of the problems that beset him and his attitude toward them. What we have is in effect an arbitrarily truncated body, a graven image that speaks but does not listen.

Only by dint of patient labor can we reconstruct the actual context in which a particular action was taken. Our task is not eased by helpful references to secondary sources, as might be expected in an academic enterprise of such magnitude.[5] Certainly the notes (printed at the rear) are far more informative than those in the fourth edition, which appeared in the late Stalin era; on the other hand, they fall far short of the standard attained in the second edition, compiled in 1920s, although the scope of this edition was of course much slighter (a mere 105 letters for the whole Soviet period). In the notes to the fifth edition "incoming" messages are sometimes summarized or quoted in excerpt, with a reference (unnumbered) to the Central Party Archive. This is better than nothing, and whets one's appetite for access to this holy of holies, but is no substitute for a full collection that would enable one to see its subject in the round. The compilers of the apparatus (notes, biographical data, etc.) have clearly had to work under severe limitations. Thus the entry on Nadezhda Allilueva fails to mention the fact that she became Stalin's wife.[6] This can hardly be due to inadequate scholarship.

Politics are also to blame for certain "inaccuracies" (to use a polite euphemism) in the editorial matter accompanying the documents themselves. This, as already mentioned, normally includes a reference to the place of first publication, in one of two variant forms; either "first published in. . . " or "first published incompletely in. . . ." A check on some of these references in the first form shows that they should really be in the second, because the text as printed was in fact distorted, i.e. incomplete. A glaring example of this occurs in a telegram to Dzerzhinskii of August, 1920. The annotation reads: "first published incompletely in 1938 in the journal *Bolshevik*, no. 2. Published in full (facsimile) in 1951 in the book *F. E. Dzerzhinskii, 1877–1936*, Moscow." This latter volume does indeed contain what appears to be a facsimile of this message—but with the names of two of the addressees, Smilga and Radek, blotted out. The present edition enables one to reconstruct the original, but the editors presumably wished to conceal the fact that the document had twice been tampered with.[7]

Turning now to the reliability of the documents themselves, three main questions arise: have the distortions and falsifications of the Stalin era been made good?; do

5 There is one curious exception to this rule. The commentary on those documents in which Lenin expresses his interest in broadcasting refer to a work by A. M. Nikolaev, *Lenin i radio* (Moscow, 1960).

6 Lenin, *PSS*, vols. 50 and 51; here 51, 481. Hereafter cited as *L* (50) or *LI* (51).

7 *LI*, no. 472. Cf. nos. 363, 365, where it is claimed, falsely, that the document was first published in full in the Moscow, 1956 edition of Lenin's *Voennaia perepiska*.

the documents published for the first time add much to our knowledge?; and can the collection now be regarded as complete? On the answers to these questions must depend our estimate of the editors' *bona fides*.

Fortunately we have an invaluable non-Soviet source to assist us here: volume I of *The Trotsky Papers*, edited by Professor Jan Meijer and published in the Netherlands in 1964, almost simultaneously with the *Works*. These papers cover the years 1917–19 and include a number of Lenin documents as well as other Party papers of which Trotskii had copies made in the mid-1920s; these copies he then took abroad when he was expelled from the USSR. A comparison of the texts common to both volumes shows that we can answer the first question affirmatively: i.e. the proper names that were suppressed in earlier editions of the *Works* or the *Sborniki* have been restored. One example among dozens may suffice: Lenin's telegram to Lashevich of June 18, 1919, when first published in *Leninskii sbornik*, omitted the words "from Smilga," which have here been reinserted.[8]

The second question we may also answer affirmatively. The documents published here for the first time include both runs of correspondence with particular individuals, notably Chicherin and Ioffe, which *may* previously have been suppressed, and individual items which *must* have been suppressed, because they form part of a series and the other items in it were published earlier. The former throw some new light on several questions relating to Soviet foreign policy. The latter are of considerable interest for the study of "high politics" during the civil war years, not least the nascent conflict between Trotskii and Stalin. We shall return to this point, and shall indicate by an asterisk in references to the *Works* those messages published for the first time since Stalin's death.

The third question could only be answered with complete assurance if one had free access to the archives. But there are good reasons for answering it in the negative, i.e. for suspecting that a significant number of Lenin documents remain unpublished.

In the first place, some items which appeared in the second and third editions of the *Works* have been excluded, without any explanation, from the present one. As there are only four instances of this, we may itemize and attempt to explain them here:

1. Two messages addressed to Stalin, of January 24 and April 3, 1919, about the Commissariat of State Control—a vexed issue on which the two leaders' views differed significantly—a point which the present editors evidently wish to conceal.[9]
2. One message addressed by Lenin to other members of the Council for Labor and Defense, dated April 1919, ordering emergency measures to cope with the "perfectly catastrophic situation on the railways." There are ample other references to this problem, and the omission of this letter may be due to editorial scruples about reproducing Lenin's unusually brutal, indeed cynical phrase: "let thousands

---

8 *Leninskii sbornik*, XXXIV (1942), 174; *L*, no. 644; J. M. Meijer, ed., *The Trotsky Papers, 1917–1919* (The Hague, 1964), I, no. 314. Hereafter cited as *TP*.

9 V. I. Lenin, *Sochineniia*³, XXIX, nos. 186, 190.

more [workers] perish, but the country will nevertheless be saved."[10]

3. One message to Trotskii and others, dated May 18, 1919, dealing with the mobilization of Donets coalminers to check the White advance.[11] This was originally published with Kamenev as the addressee, but since this error was already corrected in the fourth edition, it is hard to see why the document should be omitted. It may simply be deemed of insufficient importance, in much the same way as a number of items published in the *Sborniki*, mainly of a very ephemeral nature, have likewise been excluded from the *Works*—although some equally trivial ones have been included. More detailed study would be necessary to elucidate this matter further.

But the main evidence for the incompleteness of the *Works* stems from a comparison with the *Trotsky Papers*. The latter contain 172 documents from Lenin's hand, of which 50, or 29 percent, are missing from the *Works*. (A further 17 have been published in other Soviet sources.) Does this mean that the whole collection is about 30 percent short? An intriguing thought—but before we leap to conclusions we should remember that the years 1917–19 may not be typical either of Lenin's correspondence habits or of the papers which Trotskii gathered together. Professor Meijer very plausibly suggests that Trotskii made his selection from the Soviet archives with the express purpose of accumulating material which would testify to his close relationship with the Bolshevik leader, a fact which his Stalinist enemies questioned.[12] If this is so, it would be natural to find an unusually high proportion of Lenin documents in Trotskii's collection from the civil war years, when the collaboration between the two men was at its peak, and when their relationship found expression on paper because Trotskii was usually absent from their capital. We shall have to await publication of the second volume of the *Trotsky Papers* before we can establish whether the new pattern in later years is very difficult from that of 1917–19. All we can say for the present is that a significant (but uncertain) fraction of Lenin's correspondence, which we know to exist, is not to be found in the *Works*.[13]

Does this mean that it has been deliberately suppressed? The omission might be due to simple "technical" rather than political causes. The original documents may have been lost since the mid-1920s, when Trotskii took his copies (he did *not* take away any originals). There is some evidence to support this hypothesis. Meijer prints two messages from Lenin to Trotskii, sent on successive days in May, 1919, only the

---

10 Ibid., no. 191.

11 Ibid., no. 269; *TP*, no. 225.

12 This view is supported by the presence in the *Works* (*L*, no. 640) of a document *not* to be found in the Trotskii archives: a letter to the Central Committee of June 17, 1919 strongly critical of Trotskii.

13 According to Iu. A. Akhapkin, of the Central Party Archive, about 14,000 Lenin documents remain unpublished, most of these being either brief resolutions on incoming reports, etc., or official documents which Lenin helped to compile. Akhapkin does not state that these categories account for all the unpublished items. "Organizatsiia," 65.

second of which occurs in the *Works*.[14] Yet this shows Lenin taking a *more* charitable attitude towards Trotskii than the one which is omitted. The same apparently arbitrary juxtaposition of consecutive messages, this time addressed to Smilga, one printed and the other not, occurs in October, 1919.[15] Unless we assume that the editors are playing a trick on *bourgeois* historians—a pleasing but extravagant notion!—we must conclude that they are here innocent of any political bias.

Does this mean that we can acquit them entirely? Far from it. Of the fifty Lenin documents exclusive to the *Trotsky Papers*, more than half (27) are addressed to Trotskii himself; these often depict him in a positive light, or else add materially to our knowledge of important historical questions. There are too many of these messages, and they fall into too logical a pattern, for their omission from the *Works* to be due to pure chance.

Let us mention a few of these. On August 22, 1918 Lenin wrote to Trotskii that treason at the front made it imperative for him to proceed at once to the Saratov area.[16] The editors must have known of this message, since Trotskii published it in his autobiography, which appeared in Berlin in 1930; yet they have chosen to ignore it. They have acted likewise with a letter sent to Trotskii on December 31, 1918, after the collapse of the Third Army, in which Lenin mentioned that "they" (presumably the *Revvoensovet* of the Eastern Front) wanted Trotskii to undertake an investigation into its causes. In this case Stalin went instead, and later he was to make much of the fact. Yet this document—significantly enough, without the materially relevant phrase *prosiat vas priekhat' tude* ("they ask you to go there")—was published in 1960 in another Soviet work, P. G. Sofinov's study of the Cheka; Trotskii had published it in two of the works he wrote after leaving Russia.[17] Other documents exclusive to the *Trotsky Papers* illuminate the outbreak of the Stalin-Trotskii quarrel in May, 1919, which led to the replacement of the Commander-in-Chief, Vatsetis,[18] or to the aftermath of this affair, when Trotskii tried to recover the ground he had lost.[19] There is also the matter of the famous "blank check" which Lenin gave Trotskii, endorsing in advance any orders he might give because "I am absolutely convinced of [their] correctness, expediency and necessity"; this likewise is omitted from the *Works*.

Now it might be thought that since most (though not all) of these documents were published by Trotskii abroad, Soviet editors would thereby be debarred automatically from infringing the taboo that surrounds them, for the existence of these writings has never been acknowledged in the USSR. However, even in Stalin's day it was found possible to print in a volume of the *Sborniki* a Lenin document which had

---

14 *TP*, nos. 21, 217, May 14 and 15, 1919; *L*, no. 569.

15 *TP*, nos. 377, 378, Oct. 4 and 5, 1919; *LI*, no. 89.

16 *TP*, no. 50.

17 *TP*, no. 128; I am following Meijer's excellent notes here.

18 Ibid., nos. 207, 229, 273, 275, 278, 282; the latter is in *LI*, no. 616, but with Stalin as the addressee.

19 Ibid., no. 330.

first appeared in 1932 in Trotskii's *Stalin School of Falsification*,[20] although naturally enough without any indication of its prior publication. The present editors, however, have had to face a ticklish problem here, since they have made it their rule to give the date and place of first publication of each document printed. Their solution is to ignore Trotskii's work and to cite the *Sbornik* instead.[21] But what are they to do when they decide to publish a document that has *not* appeared previously in the USSR? Here they have simply dropped the customary annotation altogether, leaving a glaring blank upon the page.

There are four instances of this, all connected with disputes over strategy. The details are as follows:

1. Lenin to Trotskii, Serebriakov and Lashevich, September 6, 1919, informing them that the Politburo has overruled their representations and endorsed the strategic plans of the new Commander-in-Chief;
2. Lenin to Trotskii, October 17, 1919, informing him that the Council for Labor and Defense has accepted his (Trotskii's) plan for the defense of Petrograd and instructing him to prepare to evacuate the city if necessary;
3. Lenin to Stalin, February 20, 1920, expressing fear that Denikin's shattered forces might nevertheless counterattack in the Donets;
4. Lenin to Trotskii, April 4, 1920, part of an exchange on Wrangel's intentions, in which Lenin accepts Trotskii's complaint that Stalin has bypassed the proper military channels in communicating directly with him (Lenin), and remarks: "there seems to be some caprice here."[22]

Do Soviet editors of Lenin's *Works* really still need to engage in such simple subterfuges? Now that so much of the correspondence with or about Trotskii has been (or shortly will be) published, could they not risk a more objective approach to the polemics of the Stalin era? One can scarcely imagine that the Communist party's aura of legitimacy would be seriously undermined by a frank recognition of the existence of Trotskii's writings and of his archive.

To sum up: the *Works* contain a selection, rather than a collection, of Lenin documents for the period in question, one which is less comprehensive or reliable than the editors would have us believe. Nevertheless it probably contains a fairly representative sample of the affairs which passed through Lenin's hands during his first years in power. In the absence of minutes of top party and state organs, its value is very considerable. By reading Lenin's letters in conjunction with other sources, such as memoirs and official decrees, as well as the *Trotsky Papers*, we can gain an authentic glimpse from an unfamiliar angle of the inner workings of the Soviet dictatorship in its formative years.

---

20 Lenin to Mezhlauk, Voroshilov and others, June 1, 1919; *Leninskii sbornik*, XXXIV (1942), 158.

21 *L*, no. 605. It was not the case that only previous Soviet publications was deemed to count, for where a Lenin letter had been published in a source as impeccably *bourgeois* as the *Times Literary Supplement* this was stated: *L*, no. *34.

22 *LI*, nos. *75, *101, *241, *370.

III

Let us now try to prove this claim by examining, on the basis of this correspondence, the most important aspects of Lenin's activities during the civil war period. Three questions in particular lend themselves to analysis in this way: his efficacy as the Soviet state's "chief executive"; the role of coercion and terror in his conception of government; and his attitude to socioeconomic questions, above all to the peasant problem.

Two points may be made at the outset. Lenin's absorption in public affairs (perhaps his most salient characteristic) slackened as his health gave way under strains of office. This might be demonstrated diagrammatically, but it will suffice to state here that this diminution of interest is particularly noticeable in November–December, 1919 and again in August–September, 1920: it is on the latter occasion that he complains of feeling tired. When convalescing at Gorki, outside Moscow, he seems to have left the major decisions to others and to have busied himself mainly with relatively trivial matters. (On the other hand, after the attempt on his life in 1918 he recovered remarkably quickly.) Secondly, his interest in particular questions is often very spasmodic: he indulges in a kind of *shturmovshchina*, to use a later term. For example, in the spring and summer of 1918 he is much concerned with the supply problem, but it suddenly drops out of sight in September; his preoccupation with military matters is most intense in the spring and summer of 1919, but is relatively slight in 1920; the transport crisis bursts upon him unawares in December, 1919; and his efforts to remedy individual grievances, while never wholly abandoned, reach a peak in November, 1918 and after a break are suddenly resumed in August, 1919.

Lenin's style of leadership was the product of his unusual ability to combine supreme self-assurance as a politician with great personal modesty. While taking it for granted that the life of the Soviet state would be shaped in conformity with his own ideals and prejudices, he was strangely reluctant to exercise the responsibilities that naturally fell to him as head of the party and government. Characteristically, when in October, 1918, he was asked to complete a questionnaire, he entered his profession as "journalist."[23] The chief reason for this diffidence was ideological— an uncertainty as to the durability of the Soviet regime so long as the international socialist revolution remained in abeyance—a problem that need not be elaborated on here. The consequence was that for all Lenin's preeminence the early Soviet regime lacked a firm guiding center, and individuals and institutions were left fairly free to

---

23 *L*, no. 347, Oct. 1918. [Lenin's activities as chairman of the Council of People's Commissars have been expertly illuminated by T. H. Rigby, *Lenin's Government: Sovnarkom, 1917–1922* (Cambridge, London and New York, 1979). For a Soviet treatment in two volumes which stress respectively the creation of the state apparatus and military affairs, see M. P. Iroshnikov, *Predsedatel' Soveta Narodnykh Komissarov Vl. Ul'ianov (Lenin): ocherki gosudarstvennoi deiatel'nosti v 1917–1918 gg.* (Leningrad, 1974) (reissued in 1976 with the title *Vo glave Sovnarkoma: gosudarstvennaia deiatel'nost'. . .*); idem, *Predsedatel' Sovnarkoma i Soveta Oborony V. I. Ul'ianov (Lenin): ocherki gosudarstvennoi deiatel'nosti v iiule 1918—marte 1920 g.* (Leningrad, 1980).]

work out for themselves, by trial and error, their mutual relationships.

Lenin was not a man of faction—or more accurately, he ceased to be one after the October revolution. That is to say, he remained utterly irreconcilable in his attitude to any group of persons deemed antagonistic to the Bolsheviks, but he did not identify with any particular group of persons within the party or state. On the contrary, he endeavored to preserve a certain distance from all such groups, so reinforcing his natural paramountcy as the architect and symbol of the revolution. He did not, like Stalin later, intrigue to divide his supporters and play them off against each other, but sought rather to rally them behind him in a solid front. He reacted strongly to any action likely to involve him in factional intrigue—*skloka*, as he called it. In July, 1918, he received from Ioffe a dispatch which contained derogatory remarks about his immediate superior, Chicherin. Lenin rebuked Ioffe for placing him in an embarrassing position vis-à-vis the commissar for foreign affairs; he had no wish to become "an instrument of intrigue."[24] Similarly, two years later, when the communists of Tula split into a majority of "hard-liners" and a minority of "liberals," and the former appealed to Lenin for his support, he replied that while he agreed with what they had told him, "if you wish to use my opinion against your 'opposition,' let them have both your letter to me and my reply. Then they will be [properly] informed and will be able to give me their version, and I shall not be informed partially."[25]

This tactful, commonsense attitude towards his associates—one should scarcely exaggerate it into statesmanship—is exemplified by his handling of the celebrated antagonism between Trotskii and Stalin. His correspondence (in the *Works* and the *Trotsky Papers*) suggests that he strove to maintain a balance between the two rivals, whose complementary qualities he doubtless appreciated, but without complete success, for the shifts which took place in this triangular relationship came about spontaneously rather than on Lenin's own initiative.

In May, 1919, when the conflict over military strategy and appointments burst into the open, he accepted most of the arguments put forward by the "military opposition" (with which Stalin was allied), but tried to soften the blow to Trotskii's prestige and self-esteem.[26] Only in June, after Trotskii had insinuated that Lenin and other members of the Central Committee had given way to panic, did he rebut the charge and turn it round against Trotskii and his military chiefs. He appears to have been somewhat appeased by Trotskii's offer to resign (July 5), but relations between the two men remained cool for about a month.[27] By mid-August Lenin was already expressing confidence that he could "work amicably" with Trotskii.[28] However, differences persisted over the employment of ex-officers in the Red Army, and when

---

24 *L*, no. *204, July 1, 1918.

25 *LI*, no. 559, Oct. 20, 1920.

26 *L*, no. 577. For earlier moves, see nos. 390, 418; *TP*, nos. 148, 174. Despite some uneasiness at the turn of the year, Lenin's relations with Trotskii seem to have been generally good until this point.

27 *L*, no. *640; for the repercussions see *TP*, nos. 275, 278, 285.

28 *LI*, no. *55.

catastrophe threatened in the south in the late summer part of the blame naturally stuck to Trotskii.[29] This gave an opening for Ordzhonikidze, an intimate of Stalin, to try to undermine Trotskii's position. Lenin's comments upon this message suggest that he was embarrassed and tried to temporize.[30] He was evidently relieved when Trotskii's successful defense of Petrograd made it possible to restore him to favor. During 1920 Lenin became disenchanted at the Stalinists' handling of the nationalities issue and also of certain strategic problems, but he did not withdraw his confidence from them.[31] Meanwhile Trotskii's standing remained high, especially during the Soviet-Polish War, and it was only at the end of that year, as the "party discussion" got underway, that his relationship with Lenin again deteriorated.[32]

One might add that despite continual friction Lenin also managed to maintain an effective working relationship with his sulky aide in Petrograd, Zinov'ev.[33] There is little evidence in the correspondence on his relations with Kamenev or other leaders who stayed mainly in Moscow, and with whom he could communicate orally.

This political skill in handling individuals was, however, no substitute for a properly functioning network of institutions, and this the young Soviet state conspicuously lacked. The powers of the various administrative organs were ill-defined and conflicts of jurisdiction between them were endemic. From time to time Lenin tried to arbitrate between them, but he does not seem to have acted upon any clear principles. Moreover, his interventions frequently appear to have been disregarded and their effectiveness was thus doubtful; sometimes they actually seem to have made confusion more confounding.

His problems were aggravated by the fact that he deliberately maintained a large number of competing channels of communication, which got clogged. Through these channels he received a great deal of haphazard information of unequal value, which could not readily be checked against that from other sources and was sometimes downright contradictory. Consequently he could seldom be quite certain that he was backing the right side in any controversy.

He was prone to initiate more investigations into alleged shortcomings or abuses than could conveniently be followed up. These were sometimes triggered off quite casually. For instance, on three successive days in January, 1920, he issued an order on fuel supply to a different organization, prompted respectively by a chance letter from a "specialist," an item in a newspaper, and an official report from the provinces.[34] This haphazardness was by no means untypical. Matters were taken up as and when they became urgent, with little regard for their relative importance. All this encouraged in Lenin and in others the illusion that he was exercising overall control, whereas, in fact, the most important decisions were being made elsewhere—

---

29 *LI*, nos. *82, 98.

30 *LI*, no. 115.

31 *LI*, nos. *309, *436, *441.

32 *LI*, nos. 113, 138, *237, *270, *370, *525, *536, 562.

33 *L*, nos. 179, 228, 348, *378, 400; *LI*, nos. 47, 79, 406, *534.

34 *LI*, nos. 201, *203, 206, Jan. 14–16, 1920.

or not at all. The attempt to direct everything from a single center, which flowed logically from the basic precepts of Bolshevism, was extremely naive, particularly in the chaotic conditions of the civil war. Lenin had at his disposal only the most rudimentary secretarial organization, and his communications system was likewise primitive: he was forever complaining about his malfunctioning telephone.[35] Frequently he had to remind his correspondents that they should wire back how long telegraphed instructions had taken to reach them. How, therefore, could he intervene effectively in the jungle of the early Soviet administration?

Let us now look more closely at the effect of Lenin's interventions first upon the central and then upon the local government authorities.

There were, in practice, four main channels of authority in the civil administration at this time (the Red Army was, arguably, more important than any of them). These were: the Communist party, the Cheka (security police), and two of the commissariats, those for Supply and Transport. Each of these four agencies maintained a network of officials scattered throughout the country.

We shall discuss the Cheka and the Supply organization later in their appropriate context. So far as party affairs are concerned, Lenin's correspondence for these years contains less material than one might at first expect. This reflects the fact that the party was slow to assume in practice the "leading role" mapped out for it by Bolshevik doctrine. Not until November, 1918, did Lenin make use of party channels to bypass a bottleneck in the state apparatus,[36] and it was only in 1919, at the Eighth Congress, that the party's functions were formally laid down. Even so the proper relationship between party and state authorities was far from clear even to a man as senior as Kalinin. In May, 1919, he took a liberal view of his responsibilities to the Supply commissariat and was rebuked by Lenin for straying from the party line: "Do not infringe the relationship between state and party."[37] It was not until 1920 that Lenin spelled out for two of his correspondents' benefit what they should do to ensure that state organs complied with party policy: they were to arm themselves with copies of the relevant decisions and complain directly to him, repeating the complaint as often as necessary. On the first occasion he added that "anyone who does not know this is naive," but on the second occasion he implied that he himself had doubts about the efficacy of this procedure: "I shall sign [reminders and requests] in two minutes . . . and *sometimes* they will bring some practical benefit."[38]

As for the inner life of the party, Lenin restricted himself to ordering the occasional investigation of suspected malpractises and ensuring that even the most junior organizations had the right to communicate directly with him, so that he might be fully informed of any lapses at intermediate levels in the hierarchy.[39]

35 *LI*, nos. 231, 405, 549.

36 *L*, no. 368.

37 *L*, no. *566.

38 Our italics. To Chicherin for Karakhan, *LI*, *394, June 24, 1920; to R. E. Klasson, no. 582, Nov. 2, 1920.

39 *LI*, nos. 79, *249, 252, 571.

What, one may ask, of the soviets, nominally the sovereign bodies in the "Soviet state"? These occupy an even more modest place in Lenin's correspondence for these years. The ambiguity of their role was made plain as early as November, 1917, when he sends two messages to the soviet of Moscow (not then the capital): in one it is told that its action in replacing the provincial commissar (a post inherited from the previous regime, soon to become defunct) did not need the central government's approval, whereas in the other message Lenin did so confirm their action in dissolving the municipal Duma.[40] He concurred silently in the whittling away of the soviets' democratic rights. In April, 1919, some villagers in Kursk province sought to exercise their constitutional prerogative of recalling their deputies and holding new elections. When Lenin heard of this, he asked the commissar for Internal Affairs as a matter of course to hold an inquiry, implying that this body's sanction for such a step was now required.[41]

Characteristically, there is no record in the correspondence of Lenin having intervened to define or regulate the provincial soviets' uneasy relationship with the ubiquitous supply commissars or other agents of the center. True, he did once take up the cudgels on behalf of the Moscow soviet against the Education commissariat, which wanted to close down the Maliy Theater; but he may well have done so because this body had previously obstructed his will in similar matters, and in any case his intervention was unsuccessful.[42] On two occasions we find Lenin rebuking local soviets for contravening government policy, but the circumstances are extraordinary: a matter of the Allied landings at Archangel and Murmansk.[43] It is not so much a question of the soviets' power being deliberately curtailed as of their lapsing into impotence without the chief executive even registering the fact. And yet his ambitions to control them are limitless. He would apparently have welcomed the chance to enter into direct contact with each soviet in the land down to *volost'* level—at least he once expressed such a wish in regard to all the *volost'* soviets of Tula province[44]—which was clearly a fanciful notion. In the event he exchanged only a few messages with such local worthies.[45]

As the civil war progresses, so too does the size of the Soviet bureaucracy. It is hard even for Lenin to keep up with its ramifications. *Kto takoe Pravbum?* ("Who on earth is 'Pravbum'?"), he once inquires querulously of Krasin. It turns out to be the Petrograd section of the Main Administration for the Paper Industry.[46] Later he asks Krasin for a copy of the table of accounts for the Transport commissariat, and on receiving it expostulates that it is "worse than the commissariat of State Control

---

40 *L*, nos. 14, 11, 19, Nov. 16, 1917.

41 *L*, no. 496.

42 *LI*, no. 210; cf. *L*. nos. *131, 329, 338; 51, no. 174, on the question of displaying propagandist statuary in the Moscow streets, a matter which Lenin took very seriously.

43 *L*, nos. 118, 197.

44 *L*, no. 320.

45 *L*, no. 497; *LI*, no. 235.

46 *L*, no. 488, March 12, 1919.

. . . a pile of official ranks, Chief So-and-so and Assistant So-and-so."[47] A month later he explodes again, this time to the central trade union organization, which has delayed action on an order to send 10,000 metallurgical workers (no fewer) to repair railway rolling-stock. "I never doubted," he writes, "that there is still a great deal of bureaucracy in our commissariats, but I did not expect to find just as much of it in the trade unions. This is a tremendous scandal."[48]

But what *is* bureaucracy? In Lenin's eyes it seems like some monstrous parasitic growth on an otherwise healthy body politic, and he has no idea how to cure it. In the instances just quoted he touches upon two of its characteristics: inflation of unproductive staff and obstruction of commands from the top. On other occasions he inveighs against officials' old-fashioned leisurely ways, particularly their inability to submit regular reports in a brief, factual and businesslike form.[49] At other times he identifies the evil with corruption, and deplores the low moral standards of those in authority. In the countryside, he remarks to Zinov'ev in April, 1919, "there are few honest men . . . the need for honest men is desperate."[50] Even sharper is the judgement he passes on his officials, perhaps half in jest, in a letter to a leading Bolshevik agent in England: "one has to curse Russians 20 times and check them 30 times before they can do the simplest thing properly."[51]

What never seems to cross Lenin's mind is that these shortcomings are an insepa- rable concomitant of the centralization to which he is so strongly committed in every field, and that he himself is by no means the least of offenders in this respect. In Au- gust, 1918, he reprimands leading officials of the Supply commissariat for indulging in "the devil knows what sort of bureaucratic red tape," in that they had failed to mo- bilize sufficient workers to help gather in the harvest; yet in the same breath he lays down the exact proportion of trade-unionists—20 percent—who should be enrolled in each harvesting team, and is evidently quite oblivious of the contradiction.[52]

Equally harmful to efficient administration was his practice of meddling in petty matters of detail, however benevolent his intention may have been. A Western biogra- pher remarks that he assumed the functions of an "All-Russian Complaints Bureau."[53] One might say that the role he aspired to lay somewhere between that of a public prosecutor and chairman of a supreme administrative tribunal. His efforts to set- tle countless individual grievances took up time and energy which would have been better expended in deciding basic questions of state policy. They also demoralized

---

47 *LI*, no. 165. The Russian is more expressive: *t'ma i kucha chinov, pod-, nad-, ot-, dlia i proch.!!*

48 *LI*, no. 205, Jan. 16, 1920.

49 Not until January, 1919, did he receive one which measured up to his expectations, as he remarked with pleasure to his secretary. The author, a minor functionary in Tula province, nevertheless failed to make much of a career in the world of Soviet officialdom. (*L*, no. 432).

50 *L*, no. 544.

51 *LI*, no. *424, July 15, 1920.

52 *L*, no. 254.

53 A. Ulam, *Lenin and the Bolsheviks* (New York, 1966), 528.

ordinary Soviet functionaries, who never knew where they stood—as perhaps was partly Lenin's intention. These men naturally tried to guard against his interventions from on high by bringing all vertical channels of communication under their control; meanwhile the stream of petitioners, encouraged by the success of the fortunate few, grew even larger. This phenomenon, by the way, had been a familiar feature of tsarist administrative practise before the "great reforms" of the 1860s. Old traditions die hard, and the village emissaries (*mirskie khodoki*) who in former times had made their way to petition the divinely appointed autocrat now stood patiently outside the doors of the Predsovnarkom.[54]

One cannot but be struck by the triviality of some of the petitions which Lenin feels it his duty to consider and, if possible, grant. As early as December, 1917, he finds himself embroiled in the affairs of one particular steelworks in the Donets.[55] In March, 1918, he asks why the clerks in the Moscow post office are required to work such long hours.[56] Then comes a string of complaints at the arbitrary requisitioning of property. In July, 1918, as the war clouds gather in the east, Lenin writes to one Ivanov, in a village between Kazan' and the Urals: "It is alleged that you have requisitioned some writing materials, including a table, belonging to the stationmaster. Return these objects at once. Telegraph your explanations. . . ."[57] History, alas, does not record the fate of the stationmaster's table, nor that of the bicycle belonging to the pharmacist at Zhlobin, which calls forth two letters from the ever solicitous Vladimir Il'ich.[58] These are situations with comic possibilities worthy of a Chekhov. Yet there are others where it is a matter of life or death for the unfortunate petitioner, which bring us face to face with the grim realities of totalitarian dictatorship. It is to this aspect of Lenin's activities that we may now turn.

IV

Implicit in the foregoing is the self-evident point that a revolutionary state, as much as any other, needs sound laws, based upon popularly accepted notions of justice, if is is not to degenerate into an arbitrary tyranny. Yet Lenin's concept of "revolutionary legality" always remained valid, and was extended to justify any action, however reprehensible, deemed expedient by those in power. This development certainly had the leader's personal sanction, for as a trained jurist he was fully aware of the issues, yet deliberately chose to make as complete a breach as possible with *bourgeois* concepts of law. As he himself put it succinctly, "dictatorship is precisely the exercise of power unfettered by any law."

The correspondence not unexpectedly contains very little material on legal ques-

---

54 Cf., for example, *LI*, no. 193, Jan. 5, 1920: a touching appeal by a *khodok* from a distant factory for increased rations so that the men might work harder "for our revolutionary Russia."

55 *L*, no. 33.

56 *L*, no. 99.

57 *L*, no. 237.

58 *L*, nos. 524, 580, April 21 and May 20, 1919.

tions. In April 1918 Lenin called together senior members of the Justice commissariat, which until recently had been headed by a Left SR, and pressed them to step up their efforts "to take quicker and more merciless proceedings against the *bourgeoisie*, embezzlers, etc."[59] A few weeks later he made the same point in a letter to Kurskii, the new Bolshevik commissar, and such a law was indeed passed.[60] But shortly thereafter, on the evidence before us, Lenin seems to have lost interest in such matters. The only practical step he took was to have a pamphlet printed, and distributed to officials in all commissariats, in which they were enjoined to observe "revolutionary legality."[61] Instead Lenin came to take the view that judicial cases were best handled by extralegal procedure, i.e. by the Cheka. Early in 1919, when the public prosecutor, Krylenko, opposed a Cheka move to have proceedings against a group of common criminals transferred to its jurisdiction, and the matter was referred to Lenin, he sided with Dzerzhinskii: "Krylenko," he observed dryly, "is fussing to no purpose."[62]

Dzerzhinskii, the Cheka chief, was one of two persons (the other was Sverdlov) who had the right to enter Lenin's Kremlin apartment by a special door.[63] This close personal contact no doubt helps to explain why relatively few messages between the two men have been preserved. The possibility of using physical coercion on a massive scale against actual or potential enemies of the new order can never have been wholly absent from Lenin's mind, but in the first weeks of Soviet power he proceeded circumspectly, confining himself to threats of court proceedings against recalcitrant *bourgeois*, and recommending that some of those arrested be sentenced to a limited term of forced labor in the coal mines.[64] By the following June, however, the situation had changed considerably, and he could insist on much harsher measures. It was now a question of threatening capital punishment or encouraging indiscriminate killings by the mob. After the assassination of Volodarskii he sent a notorious message to Zinov'ev instructing him not to obstruct "mass terror" by Petrograd workers against (unspecified) "counterrevolutionaries"; this he considered "perfectly correct."[65] It is interesting to note that he was still cautious enough to advise restraint in dealing with foreigners who aided the enemy, since he feared that this might provoke reprisals; such persons were to be done away with only if they offered resistance, whereas Russians in the same category were to be shot out of hand.[66]

59 *L*, no. 111, April 15, 1918.

60 *L*, no. 134.

61 *L*, no. 385; cf. *LI*, no. 167.

62 *L*, no. 449. [Much useful material on this question has since been published by S. K. Tsvigun et al., eds., *V. I. Lenin i VChK: sbornik dokumentov, 1917–1922 gg.* (Moscow, 1975). This contains 374 documents relevant to our period, some of which (for example, excerpts from proceedings of the Sovnarkom) had not previously appeared in print. The notes to items of Lenin's correspondence are fuller that those given in the fifth edition of the *Works*.]

63 P. Malkov, *Zapiski komendanta moskovskogo kremlia* (Moscow, 1959), 148.

64 *L*, nos. 26, *30, 36.

65 *L*, no. 196, June 26, 1918; cf. no. 202.

66 *L*, no. 213, July 7.

The "Red terror" began in earnest on August 9, 1918—not, as is often stated, after the attempt on Lenin's life on the 30th of that month, and seems to have been prompted less by the Allied intervention than by peasant risings. Three major innovations were now made: first, the shooting of innocent hostages received Lenin's sanction;[67] second, specific groups of the population were earmarked by him for the supreme penalty (including—rather curiously—"hundreds of prostitutes who made [our] soldiers drunk, ex-officers, etc." in Nizhnii Novgorod);[68] third, execution by hanging, as distinct from shooting, was recommended for the first time[69]—a measure calculated to produce a particularly horrifying effect upon morally sensitive and historically conscious Russians. On August 22 lenin also advised his agent in Samara on the Volga that "vacillating elements" were to be shot out of hand, "without asking anyone or permitting idiotic red tape," whereas as recently as the ninth of that month he had ordered such people to be confined to a concentration camp.[70] By August 30 he was suggesting to Trotskii that even top-flight military commanders on the Red side, such as Vatsetis, should be shot if the military operations outside Kazan' should be delayed or prove unsuccessful.[71] Fate then took a hand: on the very day the author of these bloodthirsty epistles himself fell victim to a terrorist's bullet.

It would be nice to think that the experience sobered him: certainly there is a gap of several months in the correspondence before the next outburst of ferocity. However this may be, by May, 1919, Lenin is calling for "the most merciless repression, cost what it may" of rebellious Don cossacks or suspected White sympathizers in the Saratov area,[72] and for a further toughening of the hostage system: those taken are now to include officers' families, not just the officers themselves.[73] He has now forfeited his earlier respect for public opinion abroad, for he entertains the rather crazy notion that all foreigners living in Petrograd should be incarcerated in a concentration camp, to form a kind of pool of hostages.[74]

By this time a much larger proportion of his threats is directed "inwards," i.e. against people who could not by any reasonable criterion be considered opponents of the regime. Summary execution is recommended of anyone living in a frontline area who conceals the fact that he has a rifle, or of Red Army soldiers guilty of theft or acts of violence.[75] By 1920 he is naming even wider groups of potential victims: for example, civilian functionaries in the Moscow soviet who could not bring about an immediate improvement in the fuel supply, and Ukrainian peasants who were unable

---

67 *L*, nos. 255, 261.

68 itl L, no. 257, 259, Aug. 9.

69 *L*, no. 292, Aug. 20, 1918.

70 *L*, no. 302, cf. no. 259. The term used is *kontsentratsionnyi lager*.

71 *TP*, no. 61; not printed in the *Works*.

72 *L*, no. 573; *LI*, no. 4.

73 *L*, no. 625.

74 *L*, no. 609.

75 *L*, no. 624; *LI*, no. *57; June 6 and Aug. 29, 1919.

to meet their targets for deliveries of produce.[76] When Kamenev and others warn him that the Cheka's depredations in the Ukraine "had brought a mass of evil," he takes the line that this is simply due to the inferior quality of the personnel employed in the organization and orders a purge (*chistka*)[77]—incidentally, the first occasion when this term appears in the correspondence.

This dismal catalogue shows plainly the truth of the old adage that "absolute power corrupts absolutely": the scope of the terror becomes steadily wider and its impact more arbitrary. Lenin remained creditably modest in his private life but behaved with increasing arrogance in the exercise of his police functions. In a fit of temper or pique he would order the punishment of men who caused him displeasure on some matter in which he happened to take a close personal interest. For example, as a journalist he was keen to maintain certain standards in the production of printed works. In October, 1919, the State Publishing House brought the minutes of the first Comintern congress, and Lenin discovered to his disgust that on page 99 of the pamphlet there were numerous misprints. He thundered to Vorovskii: "put those guilty in jail and make them paste correction slips into all copies."[78] A few months later, vacationing at Gorki, he noted that someone had felled an elm tree in the park which he considered quite healthy. He put the blame on the manager of the sanatorium, a certain E. Ia. Veber, and sentenced him to one month's imprisonment. Nor was this just a passing whim which he regretted on reflection; one week later the order was confirmed.[79]

It is in this context that one should consider Lenin's interventions to secure the release of individuals arrested without due cause by the Cheka or other organs of authority, and whose fate was somehow brought to his attention—often by an old comrade, or by a female relative or acquaintance.[80] The importance of these actions appears to have been exaggerated by sympathetic biographers, although it is difficult to be certain, since such interventions were frequently effected by oral communication and have left no trace in the correspondence. This source yields evidence of no more than 17 such incidents, nearly all of them concerning intellectuals. Of these pleas one was refused[81] and sixteen were granted. Of these, two yielded no result because of opposition by the Cheka;[82] in six cases the subsequent fate of the individual concerned

---

76 *LI*, nos. 383, 433; June 16 and July, 1920.

77 *L*, no. 615, June 4, 1919.

78 *LI*, no. 118, Oct. 24, 1919.

79 *LI*, no. 393, June 22, 1920.

80 E.g. by Krupskaia, *LI*, no. 61, or Kollontai, *LI*, no. *148.

81 *L*, no. 335; cf. *L*, no. *94, a similar case of refusal of permission to visit political prisoners. [For other cases see Tsvigun, *Lenin i VChK*, nos. 85, 88; and for a study of the whole problem G. Leggett, *The Cheka: Lenin's Political Police* (London and New York, 1981).]

82 *L*, no. 460; *LI*, no. 211.

is unknown;[83] and in the remaining eight cases the individuals were freed.[84] How representative this breakdown is remains uncertain.

The humanitarian role of Maksim Gor'kii in securing these favors is well known,[85] and here one need add merely that two cases in the last category were due to his persistence (Vol'nyi, Sapozhnikov). Gor'kii also won other material concessions for hard-pressed intellectuals,[86] and persuaded Lenin to countermand a terroristic order that had been issued by an irascible supply official.[87] In April 1920 Lenin gave Gor'kii a useful document instructing the Petrograd authorities to render him every assistance.[88] But he did not always deal with his old friend in a straightforward manner on this issue. In September, 1919, he agreed to set up a commission to review the cases of arrested "*bourgeois* intellectuals of the Kadet type" and to free them where possible, but in informing Gor'kii of this he mentioned the names of only two of its three members; the third was none other than Dzerzhinskii. It was in this letter, one of the most revealing in the collection, that he attempted to rationalize the terror on the following grounds: first, it was essential for the regime's survival; second, the number of victims was far fewer than those resulting from the "imperialist war"; third, many intellectuals were not persecuted but were actively serving the new state; lastly, in any case such persons had a highly inflated view of their own importance, for in reality they were worth no more than a (four-letter word, suppressed for decency's sake in the original).[89]

Fortunately for the future of the Soviet state, he was not entirely consistent in maintaining this brutal position, but somewhat belatedly came to recognize the valuable role played by "specialists" of various kinds in the construction of the new order.

V

In the social and economic sphere, as in the political, Lenin's correspondence suggests that vital decisions were often delayed, or not taken at all, because basic ideological assumptions impeded clarity of thought and firmness of action. Yet in comparison with some of his colleagues the party leader was an exemplar of rationality and commonsense. As is well known, he long resisted the temptation to socialize industry wholesale; he also endeavored to check the excesses of anarchistic "workers' control"

---

83 *L*, nos. 278, 358, 374, 382; *LI*, nos. *148, 261 (in the latter case the victim was not jailed but "molested by the mob").

84 Palinskii (Perm'), *L*, no. 223; Palchinskii (Petrograd), *L*, no. 379; Rizenkampf (Samara), *L*, no. 381; Kurdinskii (Petrograd), *LI*, no. 61; Pervushin (Kazan'), *LI*, no. 268; Volnyi (Orel), *L*, no. 514; Shorin (Nizhnii Novgorod), *LI*, no. 244; Sapozhnikov (Petrograd), *LI*, no. 287.

85 B. D. Wolfe, *The Bridge and the Abyss: the Troubled Friendship of Maxim Gorky and V. I. Lenin* (New York-London, 1967), 95–8.

86 *LI*, nos. 389, 466, 561.

87 *LI*, no. 233.

88 *LI*, no. 324.

89 *LI*, no. *80; cf. no. 84 to M. F. Andreeva.

and to inculcate notions of labor discipline. Furthermore, he was prepared to tolerate a range of income differentials that many of his colleagues found shocking.

The left-wingers' citadel was Petrograd, where they enjoyed Zinov'ev's protection. They regarded as potentially disastrous any relaxation of the centralized system of economic controls. Lenin was firmly committed to the maintenance of the state monopoly on internal trade—the fundamental principle of what later came to be called "war communism"—but was anxious to utilize the resources of the cooperative movement in distributing rations, because he was confident that it could without much trouble be integrated into the general state economic administration. In November, 1918, a government decision was reached to this effect but it met with opposition from the "Northern Commune," as the Petrograd Bolsheviks were pleased to call their organization. Lenin wrote to Zinov'ev reassuring him that no harm would result from this step: "I ask you," he said mildly, "to give the cooperators a chance to work."[90] This plea had little effect. Cooperatives in Petrograd were forcibly closed down and their stocks requisitioned. These acts earned their tormentors a reprimand from Lenin.[91] Shortly afterwards a dispute broke out on this matter within the central Supply commissariat which called forth another intervention on his part in favor of the "liberals."[92] In May 1919 the Petrograd "supply commissar," the former Bolshevik Duma deputy Badaev, submitted his resignation in protest at the decision of his superiors in Moscow to allow a group of Ukrainian refugees resident in the former capital to retain in their possession some food supplies they had brought with them. Badaev argued that this would give them a privileged status vis-à-vis their less fortunate fellow-citizens. Lenin amicably but firmly rejected his request, saying: "don't indulge in caprices. You're not a fine lady. . . . Get on with your work . . . and in future carry out all orders from the center."[93] The controversy was not stilled, but continued into the NEP era, when it became a leitmotif of Soviet politics.[94]

The reverse side of the medal was that Lenin took a tough realistic line towards the aspirations of the common people for some early alleviation of their hardships. So far as the industrial workers are concerned, ostensibly the backbone of the new order, it is remarkable how rarely they figure in Lenin's correspondence of these years. He had neither time nor inclination for exchanges of stereotyped messages with "the toiling masses," such as became a prominent feature of public life in the Stalin era.[95] The little he had to say on labor matters was concerned less with the workers' welfare

---

90 *LI*, no. *378, Nov. 30, 1918.

91 *LI*, no. 400, Dec. 25, 1918.

92 *LI*, no. *477, Feb. 27, 1919.

93 *L*, no. *552, May 4, 1919.

94 *LI*, nos. 47, 216, *534; Aug. 7, 1919, Jan. 26, 1920, Oct. 6, 1920.

95 There are only two of these, both relatively early, to the workers of Rybinsk and Vytsa respectively: *L*, nos. 112, 161, April 15 and May 31, 1918. When a party official in western Siberia sent a formal message of greeting to the leadership, Lenin not only refused to accept it but ordered proceedings to be taken against the offending functionary for wasting state funds (*LI*, no. 254, Feb. 27, 1920). He did, however, accept a rather similar communication from some miners in eastern Siberia: *LI*, no. 504, Sept. 15, 1920. A number of goodwill

than with industrial discipline, and in particular with the mobilization of workers for various military or semimilitary tasks. Thus early in 1919 he ordered five thousand Petrograd employees to be resettled in Izhevsk Zavod, and in the following winter dispatched some workers from this isolated place in the approaches to the Urals— conceivably the same men—to the railway repair shops at Omsk, where subsequently sabotage was suspected.[96]

This was the moment when Trotskii and others had the unhappy idea of forming surplus Red Army soldiers into "labor armies" and employing them on civilian tasks. Lenin welcomed this scheme warmly and took steps to enforce it with a minimum of delay.[97] A few weeks later, however, he wrote to Trotskii: "I fear that we were in too much of a hurry over the labor armies, unless they can be used wholly to rush supplies to the Western Front."[98] These second thoughts implied only that the scheme was inexpedient, not that it was wrong in principle.

Towards the countless peasant millions Lenin's attitude was sterner still. They alone could provide the grain and other produce essential for the physical survival of the Red Army and the dwindling urban population. This basic task was given precedence over the implementation of general revolutionary strategy, which dictated that special care be taken to preserve the so-called *smychka*, or proletarian–peasant alliance. Industrial chaos, along with the effects of war and the Allied blockade, had put a virtual stop to normal market relationships, and massive coercion was seen as the only alternative. The shock troops in the battle for grain were armed gangs of desperate and hungry men from the cities, dignified by the name of "supply detachments." They were empowered to seize, for a nominal return, such produce as they considered surplus to the peasants' own requirements. From the countryman's point of view this system was an abomination, and it certainly acted as a strong disincentive to producing any "surplus" whatsoever.

The first reference to the supply detachments in Lenin's correspondence occurs as early as January 13, 1918.[99] They were still seen as an auxiliary weapon, the main emphasis being laid upon efforts to transport to the hungry cities what remained of the previous year's crop. But once the Brest-Litovsk treaty had deprived Soviet Russia of her Ukrainian breadbasket, the problem suddenly assumed catastrophic proportions. On May 10 Lenin urged Tsiurupa, his Supply commissar, to send "20,000 men on a disciplined and merciless military campaign against the village *bourgeoisie* and

---

messages also reached him from the "lower depths" of Soviet society, to which he sometimes replied, but these are not considered "canonical writings" and are to be found in a volume edited by V. V. Anikeev *et al.*, entitled *Tovarishchu Leninu. Pis'ma trudiashchikhsia Leninu, 1917–1924²* (Moscow, 1969). [In the anniversary year 1970 no fewer than 60 such volumes were published, and by 1980 their total number, including reprints, had reached 90. *Fond*, 84–5.]

96 *L*, no. 448, Jan. 31, 1919; *LI*, no. 219, Jan. 29, 1920.

97 *LI*, nos. 196, 227.

98 *LI*, no. 254, Feb. 27, 1920.

99 *L*, no. 51.

speculators."[100] Ten days later he suggested that each provincial supply organization should have a leavening of up to 50 stalwart proletarians. When Tsiurupa pointed out that this would make these bodies top-heavy, Lenin rather weakly replied that these men's function should be to agitate rather than to organize.[101] This remark showed how inadequately he had grasped the problem.

Not that he was entirely blind to the importance of giving the peasant producers some material incentives. Three weeks later he stated that "it is extremely important to make use of experienced honest practical men" (presumably merchants) to organize the collection of grain.[102] But he failed to appreciate that this idea was incompatible with wholesale coercion and lawlessness. Similarly, early in August, 1918, he authorized Tsiurupa to spend 30 million roubles on providing machinery and welfare facilities for the peasants, but in the same breath recommended that "a harvest drive upon Elets province" be carried out by the starving populace of the surrounding countryside.[103] Another idea which he pressed strongly at this time was that the supply detachments should cleanse each area of its entire surplus before moving on to the next,[104] although there could scarcely have been a better way of alerting the potential victims as to what lay in store for them. It was only when some railwaymen protested at the depredations of these squads, and Transport commissar Nevskii boldly brought their protest to the government's notice, that Lenin gained an inkling of the true situation and ordered measures to be taken to restrain the wrongdoers.[105]

With the harvest, such as it was, gathered in and the Ukraine shortly afterwards opened up to Bolshevik reconquest, the supply crisis lost some of its urgency. During the winter of 1918–19, and again in the following spring, Kamenev suggested that the state trading monopoly might be relaxed. On both occasions, however, he met stubborn resistance to the idea from his chief: it would mean, Lenin said, "a concession to the alien [class]," "a rotten compromise."[106] Kalinin, as we have seen, ran into trouble on the same score.[107] Lenin produced figures to show that the monthly rate of grain procurements by the state was rising rapidly[108] —and convinced himself that there was no need for any radical change of policy. The matter slipped from his attention until January, 1920, when the Politburo examined a recent government decision to allow greater flexibility in determining the price of forage procured for state purposes. Lenin voted against the measure.[109]

Thereafter he is again silent until September, 1920, when the peasants' plight is

100 *L*, no. 139.

101 *L*, no. 147, May 20, 1918.

102 *L*, no. 180, May 11, 1918; cf. no. 130, April, 1918.

103 *L*, no. 249.

104 *L*, nos. 275, 294.

105 *L*, no. 203, July 1; for an example, cf. no. 248.

106 *L*, nos. 384, 546, Dec. 10, 1918, Apr. 1919.

107 Cf. supra, n. 36.

108 *L*, no. *607; *LI*, no. *5.

109 *LI*, no. *94, Jan. 1920.

suddenly brought home to him in almost melodramatic circumstances. The tired and ailing leader goes hunting in the forests near Moscow. Passing through Bogdanovo, he is presented with a petition by the villagers, who complain that the local soviet, in order to meet its tax liabilities, has taken from the inhabitants, rich and poor alike, their entire crop, including the seed grain. To the local authority Lenin dispatches a letter that might have been penned by some eighteenth-century *grand seigneur*: "I can confirm the difficult supply position of the village of Bogdanovo, commonly known as Bogdanikha." Would they kindly investigate the matter and adjust its tax assessment?[110]

But were there not many thousands of Bogdanovos, scattered across the length and breadth of Russia, whose plight remained outside the dictator's ken? For them nothing was done until the strategic retreat of NEP, the inception of which in March, 1921, owed much to multiplying signs of peasant unrest. The party leader had been caught off balance by those "forces of spontaneity" he so distrusted, and which the Soviet state as yet found difficult to control.

VI

The material examined here also contains some interesting data on Lenin's handling of military and foreign policy matters, but perhaps enough has been said to demonstrate the value of this source. Whatever its inadequacies from an editorial standpoint, Lenin's correspondence affords the historian a unique means of penetrating the Bolshevik leader's mind and analyzing his approach to the myriad problems that beset him. It shows us that behind the facade of perfection presented to the world by the practitioners of the Lenin cult there was a fallible human being, a man of many parts, who was becoming increasingly frustrated at the imperfections of the new order. Within a few years he would also realize that the sickness went too deep to be cured by any remedy of which he knew.

1971

---

110 *LI*, no. 490, Sept. 6, 1920; cf. no. 562, Oct. 31, 1920.

PART IV:

SOVIET HISTORIOGRAPHY

CHAPTER 17

The Rehabilitation of M. N. Pokrovskii

Some years ago a Soviet historical journal published an article with the somewhat sensational title "Who Killed Rasputin and How?"[1] It was the sequel to a documentary series on the court of Nicholas II introduced by the late A. L. Sidorov, a leading Soviet historian. Although the article contained little that would have surprised those familiar with relevant sources published in the West, the choice of theme and the manner of its presentation constituted a sharp break with a tradition that dominated historical writing under Stalin, and to some extent survives today. Soviet historians have responded to recent changes in the political climate, although more reluctantly than their colleagues in fields such as economics, or creative intellectuals outside the academic world. Progress was slow until the Twenty-second Party Congress in 1961. Since then there has been vigorous activity, although the pace has diminished markedly since 1966. Today, despite the limitations that have been reimposed upon the choice and treatment of sensitive themes, several schools or trends of thought can be identified, all operating within a common ideological framework, but competing with one another for the allegiance of professional historians and the interested public.[2]

One significant aspect of these changes has been the rehabilitation of Mikhail Nikolaevich Pokrovskii (1868–1932), the leading Marxist historian in the early years of the Soviet regime. The purpose of this article is to examine the way in which this reform was carried through and to assess its significance for the evolution of Soviet historical thought. The problem is as much political as historiographical, for reasons that will be clarified below.

I

Pokrovskii, who was of middle-class background, studied history at Moscow University under Pavel Vinogradov and Vasilii Kliuchevskii, and took up a teaching career. His first works were influenced by the "legal Marxist" ideas much in vogue at the turn of the century, but his political affiliation was to the liberal constitutionalists. In 1904 he turned to the Social Democrats, largely, it seems, under the influence of the

---

1 *Voprosy istorii* (1965), no. 3, 211–17.

2 For appreciations of the state of Soviet historiography in the 1960s see John Keep and L. Brisby, eds., *Contemporary History in the Soviet Mirror* (London-New York, 1964); H. Rogger, "Politics, Ideology and History in the USSR: the Search for Coexistence," *Soviet Studies*, 16, no. 3 (January, 1965), 253–75.

errant Bolshevik A. A. Bogdanov, with whom he collaborated on the non-party legal journal *Pravda*. He was drawn to Bolshevism because it seemed to him the most activist of the many left-wing groups then competing for the support of progressive-minded intellectuals. In 1905 he engaged in propaganda work under the aegis of the Bolshevik-oriented Moscow committee of the RSDRP and made a trip to Geneva, where he met Lenin; later he played a modest and nonviolent part in the Moscow insurrection. He was able to continue his journalistic activities, although a pamphlet which he wrote on *Economic Materialism* was impounded by the censor. In December, 1907, after the collapse of the first Russian revolution, he moved to the relative security of Finland, and in 1909 to Paris, where he lived until 1917. He joined Bogdanov and Lunacharskii in the *Vpered* group which opposed Lenin's leadership of the Bolshevik faction, and he later associated with the Trotskyists. When World War I broke out he became an Internationalist and in 1915, as a member of Trotskii's *Nashe slovo* group, attempted without success to bring together those Mensheviks and Bolsheviks who shared this point of view. Like Bukharin, Pokrovskii believed that the nation-state had outlived its day and that the coming revolution would be international in scope. This view led him to oppose Lenin over national self-determination.[3]

Although an *émigré*, he could still publish his work legally in prewar Russia, and it was at this time that he established his reputation as an historian. His four-volume *History of Russia from Ancient Times* (published between 1910 and 1912) was not well received by the critics. It was an obvious effort to produce a Marxist alternative to the work of Kliuchevskii, then at the height of his fame. Whereas his former master had illuminated Russia's social and economic history with erudition and profound knowledge of the primary sources, Pokrovskii operated with schematic sociological formulas and displayed a militant partisanship. The political aim of his work was painfully clear: to discredit both Russia's "ruling class" in all phases of its history, and the state which, he believed, acted merely in the interests of that class. He selected his facts to "prove" the theses, commonly accepted by Russian Marxists of the day, that economic causes were "basic" and all others derivative; that the class struggle was the motive force of history; that progress resulted, not from the will of individuals, but from "objective" socio-economic forces, operating in accordance with scientifically determinable "regularities" (*zakonomernosti, Gesetzmässigkeiten*); and that the regular succession of "formations" which Marx had identified in Western European history was equally valid for Russia. In common with nearly all his party colleagues at this time, Pokrovskii was first and foremost a European. It was to the West that he looked for capitalist progress and proletarian revolution, which would bring emancipation to backward agrarian Russia. In Russia modern social classes were still in the process of development; feudal relics in economic life went hand in hand with an autocratic political system disguised in quasi-constitutional forms. He criticized without equivocation the aggressive imperialist foreign and colonial

---

3 On Pokrovskii's attitude during World War I, see O. Gankin and H. H. Fisher, *The Bolsheviks and the World War: the Origins of the Third International* (Stanford, 1940), 162 ff.; L. D. Trotskii, *Permanentnaia revoliutsiia* (Berlin, 1930), 52.

policies of the tsarist regime. Despite his obvious bias, superficiality and intellectual arrogance, his writing at this time gave evidence of sincerity and an independent questing spirit. He was sympathetic to the long-suffering Russian masses and applied the Marxist historical method in an original way: although he treated factual evidence arbitrarily, he did not distort it beyond all recognition. A fruitful dialogue between a historian of his ilk and non-Marxist scholars was still possible.

The February revolution surprised him at his studies in the Bibliothèque Nationale. It was some months before arrangements could be made for the return of Russian political *émigrés* in France. When Pokrovskii got back to Moscow in August Trotskii's *mezhraiontsy* group, with which he had most in common, had just joined the Bolsheviks. Pokrovskii does not seem to have followed their example. In his unpublished memoirs he states vaguely that he "formulated his relations" with the Bolsheviks in September;[4] his position at this time can best be described as that of an enthusiastic sympathizer whom the local Bolshevik committee found very useful but did not completely trust. He joined the Moscow Soviet and represented it at the Democratic Conference, in which the Bolsheviks participated contrary to Lenin's express wishes. In October he wrote first-hand reports for the Moscow Committee on the fierce fighting that took place in the city. Pokrovskii believed, somewhat naively, that the Bolshevik revolution would establish a more democratic system of government, resting on autonomous local soviets. It was in this idealistic spirit that he assumed the title of "People's Commissar for Foreign Affairs" in the Moscow soviet, an office which, had it carried any power, would have directly challenged the authority of the new government in Petrograd. As the dictatorial nature of the "Soviet" regime became apparent, however, he had to modify his views. At Brest-Litovsk, where he participated in the peace negotiations, he did his best to resist German pretensions and, when his efforts failed, joined Bukharin and other leading Bolsheviks in calling for a "revolutionary war" against the invader. But Lenin overruled this "leftist" opposition; Pokrovskii lost his post on the Moscow Soviet (he had in the meantime become its chairman) and was transferred to the cultural field, where his deviant political opinions could do the party less harm.

As deputy to his old friend and associate Lunacharskii, the first People's Commissar for Education, and head of the State Council on Scholarship (GUS), Pokrovskii was entrusted with wide supervisory powers over the country's academic life, in so far as it continued at all at this time. The civil war and economic chaos almost totally disrupted the working of universities and other institutions of learning; scholars and teachers fled, were arrested, or eked out a precarious existence under the constant threat of denunciation. Pokrovskii brought the handful that were sympathetic to the new regime together in a Socialist (later Communist) Academy of Social Sciences, visualized as a body that would rival and supplant the prestigious Academy of Sciences. Other institutions of learning were reformed in such a way as to transfer effective

---

4 ORF IIAN, f. Pokrovskii, d. 42, cited by E. A. Lutskii, "Razvitie istoricheskoi kontseptsii M. N. Pokrovskogo," *Istoriia i istoriki: istoriografiia istorii SSSR. Sbornik statei* (Moscow, 1965), 348.

power from the established administrative or academic authorities to the more militant elements of the student body, loosely supervised by the local party committee.

In few fields of learning were the changes more fundamental than in history, a subject to which the new regime, for obvious ideological reasons, attached the utmost importance. It was no coincidence that Pokrovskii, an historian, should have been given such broad responsibilities over all the social sciences, or that the borderline between history (and politics) and other subjects should have been deliberately blurred. Pokrovskii's inadequate understanding of historical materialism or Leninist doctrine was overlooked. He was virtually the only pro-Bolshevik scholar of any standing, as well as a man of immense energy, able and willing to impose his views. He saw it as his duty to permeate Russian intellectual life with Marxist ideas, and to ensure that all institutions of learning complied with the party's requirements. Lenin appreciated the practical value of his services and gave him more or less a free hand. Soon he acquired an impressive variety of functions which taxed even his tremendous strength.

The transition to NEP brought a change of perspective. The class struggle against *bourgeois* tendencies, in the cultural as in the economic sphere, was now seen as extending over a more prolonged, but indeterminate, period of time. In February, 1921, Pokrovskii formed the Institute of Red Professors (IKP) to train cadres of Marxist teachers and research workers in social science subjects, and became director of this institute, at first situated incongruously in a former Moscow monastery. Most of the entrants were men of middle-class origin who had been educated under the old regime, so that their training consisted largely of political indoctrination. Until newly trained Marxists could take over key posts, teaching and research were carried on by *bourgeois* elements under Pokrovskii's watchful eye. At first they continued to work at the universities to which they belonged and supervision was fairly lax. In 1924 six local bodies were brought together to form the Russian Association of Institutes for Scholarly Research in the Social Sciences (RANION). Pokrovskii was the most prominent member of its directing board, which was nominally headed by a leading non-Marxist scholar, the medievalist D. M. Petrushevskii. By the following year the IKP's cadres had grown sufficiently to permit an organization to be created specifically devoted to historical studies, the Society of Marxist Historians (OIM). This, too, was naturally headed by Pokrovskii. He edited its organ, *Istorik-marksist*, as well as other well-known journals, notably *Krasnyi arkhiv*. This was published by the Central Archive Administration of the People's Commissariat for Education, a body which had as its chief none other than the ubiquitous Mikhail Nikolaevich. Somehow Pokrovskii also found time to preside over seminars and give lectures at the IKP, the Sverdlov University and elsewhere, as well as to write books and articles.

Although he could now draw upon archival sources which had been denied him before revolution, the quality of his scholarly work deteriorated in the Soviet period. He saw himself chiefly as a propagandist and a popularizer. His condensation of his four-volume work, *Russian History in Very Brief Outline*, first published in 1920, went through no less than ten editions in the author's lifetime. It was based on lectures and retained an enviable freshness, laced as it was with rhetorical flourishes; but it was also superficial. Complex problems were grossly simplified or evaded; it did not give a comprehensive Marxist evaluation of all Russian history. Pokrovskii could plead in extenuation that his purpose was to awaken among the semieducated an interest in history, and more especially a proper positive attitude toward the revolution. To this end he struck a strong moral note and presented the whole of Russia's prerevolutionary history as a logical build-up to October (although chronologically his work stopped in 1910). Emphasis was laid upon the succession of historical "formations" and on the masses' just and heroic struggle against wicked or incompetent rulers. Characteristically Pokrovskii gave a graphic picture of the cruelty and corruption inherent in Russia's administrative and judicial system prior to the "great reforms" of the 1860s; equally characteristically, he went on to say that matters had been no better in the conservative monarchies of central Europe.[5] For he still saw Russia's development as closely bound up with the international revolutionary process. She had lagged in her development because her *bourgeoisie* had been weaker and less radical than in the more advanced countries; as a result her revolution had been carried out by the proletariat, and had gone beyond "*bourgeois* democracy" to socialism. The impression he left was that this had been something of a distortion of the proper historical process, and that further proletarian revolutions in the West were essential to rescue Soviet Russia from her dangerous isolation. This could be interpreted—and was—as indicating a lack of faith in Russia's capacity to build socialism by her own unaided efforts. Although Pokrovskii dutifully accepted Stalin's thesis of "socialism in one country," and as early as 1922 joined in the chorus against Trotskii,[6] he retained ideological affinities with his one-time associate. Indeed, it could hardly be otherwise: he belonged to the "Old Bolshevik" generation, idealistic romantic, and increasingly out of touch with the harsh practical necessities of power which Stalin understood so well. He could not accept the cynical argument that, to ensure the survival of the dictatorship, "politics must command," and that the economic interpretation of history he held dear would have to be stood on its head.

For the moment these differences remained latent. Pokrovskii's career reached its zenith in December, 1928, when he presided over the first All-Union Conference of Marxist Historians. It was a decisive turning-point in Soviet historiography, as it was in the history of the USSR in general. Stalin was about to launch his all-out drive for industrialization and collectivization of agriculture, which would bring in its train the full panoply of totalitarian rule. In the intellectual field this meant a campaign to eliminate the last remnants of *bourgeois* influence and the creation of a monolithic *apparat* able to control every expression of opinion. The time for "coexistence" and makeshift devices had passed. Pokrovskii was no longer indispensable. Although he was appointed director of the newly founded Institute of History in the Communist Academy and elected to the governing body of the USSR Academy of Sciences (now brought under party control), his ramshackle empire was in danger.

Hitherto one major sector of the "historical front" had remained outside his com-

---

5 *Russkaia istoriia v samom szhatom ocherke* (Moscow, 1920), 143.

6 M. N. Pokrovskii, *Istoricheskaia nauka i bor'ba klassov* (Moscow, 1933), 1, 152–66.

mand: the history of the VKP(b) itself, for which he lacked the the necessary political qualifications. Stalin's choice of commanding general—until he was ready to take on the job himself—was E. E. Iaroslavskii, an Old Bolshevik of considerable seniority, who had rendered him valuable support in his struggle for power. Iaroslavskii's *Istpart* machine was between 1922 and 1928 a department of the Central Committee; it took its line directly from the source of power, and had its own arrangements as regards finance, publication outlets, and the like. After 1928 institutional and personal rivalries developed which Stalin exploited with his customary skill. There is an ironic element in the developments that ensued. Pokrovskii was put in charge of the struggle against *bourgeois* historiography; but the more he attacked his old enemies, the more he himself came under fire as insufficiently "party-minded." Some of the cadres he had trained joined in the criticism. It has been stated that a "deliberate persecution" of Pokrovskii was organized by L. M. Kaganovich, secretary of the Central Committee.[7] Whatever the truth of this, the operation must surely have been masterminded by Stalin himself.

A major point of criticism concerned Pokrovskii's ideas on commercial capitalism, which he saw as the dominant force in the Russian economy, and the power behind the throne, from the mid-sixteenth to the nineteenth century. This chronology had enabled him to depict Russia as a relatively advanced European state, and therefore as less immature for socialism than the Mensheviks (and Trotskii) implied. But in 1931 he was obliged to admit that Russia had known only "commercial capital," not "commercial capital*ism*"; that "feudal" elements had survived longer than he had previously thought; and that the autocratic state had rested upon an alliance of landlords and capitalists rather than simply upon the latter. "In the first editions of my scheme," he confessed, "insufficient attention was paid to the relative independence of the political superstructure from the economic basis." But he still held to his general scheme, and contended that in nineteenth-century Russia the main conflict had been between commercial and industrial capital—more specifically, between small-scale merchant producers and large-scale manufacturers. The final picture was confused and contradictory, the more so since Pokrovskii did not adjust his views on tsarist foreign or colonial policy.

These revisions were due to political pressure. The reasons for the change in the party's ideological line at this time are fairly familiar.[8] Stalin's desperate attempt to construct "socialism" at a dizzying pace, relying on mass enthusiasm and terror,

7 *Vsesoiuznaia soveshchanie istorikov o merakh uluchsheniia podgotovki nauchno-pedago-gicheskikh kadrov po istoricheskim naukam 18–21 dek. 1962 g.* (Moscow, 1964), 262. D. Dorotich, in his article "The Disgrace and Rehabilitation of M. N. Pokrovskii," *CSP*, 8 (1966), 169–81, accepts this charge as valid. He does not ask himself whether the ultimate responsibility for this campaign should not rather be ascribed to Stalin.

8 See C. E. Black, ed., *Rewriting Russian History: Soviet Interpretations of Russia's Past* (New York, 1956), 12–16; K. F. Shteppa, *Russian Historians and the Soviet State* (New Brunswick, 1962), 94 ff.; A. G. Mazour, *Modern Russian Historiography* (Princeton, 1958), 196 ff.; P. N. Miliukov, "Velichie i padenie M. N. Pokrovskogo," *Sovremennye zapiski*, 65 (Paris, 1937), 379, for an interesting contemporary view.

required that historians should stress Russia's uniqueness, her backwardness vis-à-vis the West; in this way the achievements of the Five-Year Plan would stand out in a still more glorious light. Related to this was the need to cultivate feelings of patriotism among the *apparatchiki* and the broad mass of the population, now that proletarian revolution abroad would clearly be postponed to the Roman kalends (or, to put it more precisely, that indigenous communist forces would have to be helped to power artificially by intervention on the part of a strong socialist state). Stalin realized that in totalitarian conditions national sentiment could serve as a useful means of binding the masses to their rulers. The internationalism of the Old Bolsheviks had become an archaic embarrassment. Equally awkward was their "objectivism"—i.e. their stress on the need to shape policy in accordance with environmental factors—which could only hinder the regime in its efforts to mobilize the masses for its purposes.

Pokrovskii never really grasped the measure of the men and forces that opposed him. Although he put up a valiant rearguard action, his days were clearly numbered. With some of his critics he dealt harshly, banishing them to minor provincial posts by administrative fiat. S. M. Dubrovskii, one of his pupils, was charged with "right-wing opportunism" on the grounds that he had presented the transition from feudalism to serfdom as a peaceful, gradual change. The actual cause of Dubrovskii's fall, however, seems to have been a work disputing the relevance of the Asiatic mode of production, which may have been written at Stalin's behest to aid the latter in his struggle against Trotskii over policy in China.[9] On the other hand, Pokrovskii was willing to adjust his views where he felt his opponents had a case. In 1929 only certain aspects of his work, such as the commercial capitalism theory, were under attack; by the winter of 1930–1 it was being said that his entire "historical conception" was un-Marxist. Thereupon, we are now told, "after careful preparation, on February 5, 1931, he sent a letter to the secretaries of the Central Committee of the VKP(b), in which he dissected and refuted the charges leveled against him."[10] The rather elementary exposition of his views which he gave makes painful reading today. The response which this petition evoked has not been revealed. It may be that at this moment Stalin was angry with Iaroslavskii for having mentioned in his party history Stalin's tactical errors in 1917, and that he took Pokrovskii's part. In any case in November, 1931, he dispatched his celebrated letters to the editors of *Proletarskaia revoliutsiia*, the main *Istpart* organ, condemning then for tolerating Trotskyist tendencies. This was the signal for a violent press campaign in which, however, Pokrovskii was spared; instead he "was singled out as the one Bolshevik historian correctly applying the Marxist conception of history."[11] But he could draw little comfort from this praise.

---

9 Shteppa, *Russian Historians*, 67–80.

10 TsPA IML, f. 147, op. 1, d. 42, 1. 35, cited by Lutskii, "Razvitie," 364.

11 P. H. Aron, "M. N. Pokrovskii and the Impact of the First Five-Year Plan on Soviet Historiography," *Essays in Russian and Soviet History in Honor of Geroid Tanquary Robinson* (Leiden, 1963), 301. Aron argues that Pokrovskii was saved by his eminence, but this had not prevented criticism before, and a personal decision by Stalin seems more plausible. For evidence of Stalin's attitude, see Sidorov's memoir quoted below, n. 31. [See

Stricken with cancer, he had entered the Kremlin hospital in the summer of 1931. Bravely he continued writing to the last, but his strength was ebbing and on April 10, 1932, he died. He was buried with full honors, Stalin himself acting as one of the pallbearers.

Hardly had his ashes been laid to rest in the Kremlin wall than the attack on his legacy began. Already on March 15 the Central Committee had ordered a reorganization of scholarly work that would "place first the elaboration of key concrete problems connected with the party's current tasks and the class struggle of the world proletariat at the present stage." *Istorik-marksist*, the OIM organ, had to suspend publication for several months while organizational changes were carried through. In August, 1932, an official pronouncement criticized inadequacies in the teaching of history and other social sciences and ordered the preparation of new textbooks. In May, 1934, a decree set up a special commission to produce more acceptable versions, in which there should be "due emphasis . . . on important historical facts, the names of historical persons, and chronological dates," in place of the "abstract sociological schemes" that had hitherto prevailed. Several of Pokrovskii's works were published in posthumous editions, but in 1934 the body charged with this task, headed by the party historian A. S. Bubnov, unobtrusively ceased its labors. The universities reverted to what seemed to be a more conventional administrative structure; faculties of history, compulsory attendance at lectures, and regular curricula were restored; the earlier periods of history again became respectable. In 1936 Stalin demanded that historians shake off "the erroneous views characteristic of the so-called Pokrovskii 'school'" and portray the Russian past in a way that reflected credit on its national traditions; a new textbook compiled in conformity with these instructions finally received official sanction. Some of Pokrovskii's old associates, such as N. M. Lukin, P. O. Gorin and S. A. Piontkovskii, were liquidated in the purges.[12] A few historians whom Pokrovskii had discredited as *bourgeois*, notably E. V. Tarle[13] and R. Iu. Vipper, returned to positions of authority; other leading posts were filled by former RANION graduates such as M. V. Nechkina, N. M. Druzhinin and V. M. Khvostov.

The nadir was reached in 1939 when a *Pravda* article by Iaroslavskii, one of the few Old Bolsheviks to survive the holocaust, inaugurated a further campaign against Pokrovskii's memory. The Institute of History rallied its leading collaborators to help compile a two-volume collection of essays, which exposed his erroneous treatment of various historical themes and put the worst construction on his early political

also J. Barber, *Soviet Historians in Crisis, 1928–1932* (London and New York, 1981), and G. M. Enteen, *The Soviet Scholar-Bureaucrat: M. N. Pokrovskii and the Society of Marxist Historians* (University Park, Pa., 1978).]

12 Lutskii, "Razvitie," 337.

13 For a valuable biography of Tarle, see E. Hösch, *Evgenii Viktorovic Tarle, 1875–1955 und seine Stellung in der sowjetischen Geschichtswissenschaft* (Wiesbaden, 1964). [Tarle's career is discussed by H. Hecker, *Russische Universalgeschichtsschreibung: von den "Vierziger Jahren" des 19. Jahrhunderts bis zur sowjetischen "Weltgeschichte" (1955–65)* (Munich and Vienna, 1983), 159–65.]

The Rehabilitation of M. N. Pokrovskii 391

deviations.[14] These outpourings reflected Stalin's paranoid fears for the security of the party leadership which he purged into trembling docility. "It is with a heavy heart," writes the Soviet historian E. A. Lutskii, "that the author of this article now recalls this collection."[15] During World War II exponents of official "Soviet patriotism" such as Tarle attacked Pokrovskii for his cosmopolitan opinions, which he said had contributed to "the moral disarmament of the Russian people."[16] In the years that followed Pokrovskii's name was mentioned rarely, and then as a term of abuse. His works had long since been withdrawn from libraries and bookshops, and to the postwar generation of Soviet scholars he was less familiar than certain conservative historians of the nineteenth century. To all intents and purposes he had become "unpersoned."

II

The partial demolition of the Stalin myth at the Twentieth Party Congress in 1956 unleashed a ferment in Soviet intellectual life and created conditions in which Pokrovskii's ideas and achievements could be reassessed. Before discussing this matter one important point needs to be made. The drive for his rehabilitation was not the work of those younger historians who objected most strongly to the frauds and injustices perpetrated under the shield of the "personality cult," but of older men who had begun their careers in the 1920s and had in many cases suffered hardship on account of their association with Pokrovskii. Politically, these scholars identified themselves with the mild revisionism of Khrushchev; they welcomed such relaxations as the party permitted, but did not actively press for further concessions which might imperil the regime's stability. As thoroughly loyal elements, they cannot be regarded as sympathetic to *bourgeois* Western liberal values or modes of thought. Yet it is an elementary lesson of history that reforms often lead to results neither anticipated nor desired by those who initiate them. By casting doubt on previously accepted assumptions, the revisionists stimulate critical thought, which may become more radical as it meets resistance from conservative elements. This pattern could be illustrated from many aspects of Soviet intellectual life since Stalin's death.

One should perhaps enter a *caveat* here against the tendency to personalize intellectual conflicts of this kind, and say that the struggle is as much one within men's minds as one between individuals. For Soviet historians the tension is between their professional interest in elucidating the truth and their political interest in bolstering the official ideology, with its immutable and sanctified precepts.

---

14 *Protiv istoricheskikh kontseptsii M. N. Pokrovskogo* (Moscow, 1939), 9. (The second volume of this work, published in 1940, substituted the word "anti-Marxist" for "historical.") A. M. Pankratova, for example, alleged that in 1918 Pokrovskii had prepared the ground for treacherous anti-party activities by Bukharin and Trotskii, and hailed "our great security workers" for having "cleaned out this nest of counterrevolutionaries." The very fact that Pokrovskii had later recanted his errors enhanced his appeal for the unwary, and thus made him more dangerous.

15 Lutskii, "Razvitie," 337–8.

16 Cited in ibid., 338.

The first indications of impending changes came in January, 1956, when Pokrovskii's name received favorable mention in an official statement: he was credited with important services in the struggle against *bourgeois* historiography, although he had also been guilty of "vulgarizing errors" which had been justly condemned.[17] The authorities seem to have planned a gradual revision of their line, carried out under close party control, but events moved too fast for them. E. N. Burdzhalov, editor of *Voprosy istorii*, provoked a crisis by questioning the legitimacy of the October revolution. Not until this affair had been settled by his dismissal and a reconstitution of the journal's editorial board was it safe to take further steps towards Pokrovskii's rehabilitation. The revisionists (as we may call them) hoped that, by presenting him as a loyal Leninist who had been unjustly victimized by Stalin, they could improve their own image in the eyes of younger and more skeptically-minded historians. But it was not easy to overcome the conservatism of those brought up in the Stalin mold, who feared, not unreasonably, that any rethinking would encourage heretical ideas. Late in 1957 M. E. Naidenov could write that, although Pokrovskii had played a positive role in Soviet historiography during the 1920s, "his views upon a whole number of important questions concerning the October revolution differed radically from the precepts of Lenin. He understood neither Lenin's teaching on imperialism nor his theory that the revolution could grow over from the *bourgeois*-democratic to the proletarian-socialist phase."[18]

The nettle was not grasped firmly until the following summer, when, apparently without any preliminary announcement in the press, a meeting was held at the Museum of the Revolution in Moscow to celebrate the 90th anniversary of Pokrovskii's birth. The main report was delivered by S. M. Dubrovskii, who thirty years earlier had been one of his fledglings. Later he had suffered under Stalin: an acknowledged authority on prerevolutionary agrarian conditions, he published little or nothing between the late 1920s and 1956. The text of his report appears to have been circulated *na pravakh rukopisi*, as is the usual practise with politically sensitive documents, but its tenor can be reconstructed fairly well from materials published subsequently. In the autumn of 1958 a conference was held in the editorial offices of *Voprosy istorii*, the record of which likewise remained in manuscript. Among those present was a lady who had once attended Pokrovskii's seminar in the IKP and now recalled sympathetically his efforts to correct his mistakes.[19]

The next phase in Pokrovskii's rehabilitation came in 1960–1, when the journal *Istoriia SSSR* began a lethargic and scholastic discussion on "the periodization of Soviet historiography." The participants labored under the hindrance of being unable to mention explicitly the role played by individual historians or politicians. The revisionists, led by the formidable M. V. Nechkina, drew heavily upon Pokrovskii's published writings as well as other materials of the 1920s, which had now evidently been made available again, at least to approved scholars. They also used some

17 *Voprosy istorii* (1956), no. 1, 4.

18 Ibid. (1957), no. 10, 171.

19 Cited from the MS. by Lutskii, "Razvitie," 364.

unpublished material, notably from Pokrovskii's personal archive, preserved in the Institute of History.

Their arguments can be summarized as follows. First, Pokrovskii had made a notable contribution to the struggle against *bourgeois* historians and deviant communists (e.g. Trotskii) in difficult conditions. Secondly, he deserved credit for his endeavors to acquire a wholly orthodox Leninist *Weltanschauung*; it was necessary to view his work "dialectically," in its process of development, rather than "statically" and dogmatically. Third, it was implied—but not clearly stated—that his political vacillations were not really relevant to his work as a historian, and that they were in some way offset by the political "mistakes" committed by his Stalinist critics. Finally, Pokrovskii's best known work, his *Brief History*, had been approved by Lenin in a letter of 1920,[20] and indeed actually "commissioned" by him. (This letter had been frequently referred to when Pokrovskii's career was at its height, but had since either been passed over in silence or else cited selectively—a procedure that aroused much indignation.) An element of special pleading was involved here, since the relationship between party leader and scholar in Lenin's day was very different from what it was to become later, and the Bolshevik leader's attitude to Pokrovskii had actually been equivocal. But the maneuver was necessary because it at once indicated to potential critics that they should move cautiously.[21]

Had logic been given its due in this discussion, the conservatives might well have pointed to the inconsistencies in the revisionist position: it was still said that Pokrovskii's methodology and his erroneous views on periodization had "caused tremendous harm to historical science," yet the overall evaluation was positive. But they preferred more devious tactics. They argued, for example, that the early period of Soviet historiography ought rightfully to be named after Lenin rather than Pokrovskii, and that the real turning point in its development had come in the mid-1930s.[22] Naidenov now admitted that Pokrovskii's role had been "indubitably progressive," but complained that Nechkina was divorcing the development of Soviet historiography from the political struggle in the country at large (which, however, neither of them could discuss frankly), and drew attention to Pokrovskii's sympathies for "Bogdanovism" and his "national nihilism."[23] The debate was inconclusive, and had to be settled at a higher level. In the summer of 1961 a hint was given in *Kommunist* that the Central Committee was about to intervene.[24]

At the Twenty-Second Party Congress in October, 1961, L. F. Il'ichev, the chief ideologist, stated authoritatively:

In the period of the personality cult some quite inexplicable things occurred, such as

---

20 V. I. Lenin, *PSS*, XXXII, 348.

21 V. M. Nechkina, *Istoriia SSSR* (1960), no. 1, 83–5; she was supported by G. D. Alekseeva and E. N. Lutskii's article in ibid. (1961), no. 2, 102–15.

22 V. F. Inkin and A. G. Chernykh in ibid. (1960), no. 5, 75–81.

23 Ibid. (1961), no. 1, 81–97.

24 Ibid. (1961), no. 9, 58.

suppressing the names of leading scholars. This was the fate of the eminent Marxist historian and Old Bolshevik M. N. Pokrovskii. In his scholarly and political activity there were no few mistakes. This is true and account should be taken of it. But it is well known that he defended Marxism and made a great contribution to the writing of Russian history.[25]

He proceeded to quote (in full) Lenin's familiar letter and to contrast his gentle paternalism with the brutal attitude of Stalin. So began the third phase in the rehabilitation process. The leading historians now fell into line, although some of them put up a kind of smokescreen to cover their retreat. At a meeting held in December, 1961, to discuss the implications of the party congress decisions, the man chosen to deliver the report was, significantly, Dubrovskii. He ended on a note of self-vindiction:

> The decisions of the Twentieth and Twenty-Second Congresses, the exposure of the personality cult, . . . the crushing of the anti-party group of Molotov, Kaganovich, Malenkov and co. have created favorable conditions for . . . an objective assessment of our historiographical legacy, including Pokrovskii's work.[26]

I. I. Mints, whose position was somewhat delicate since he had succeeded Pokrovskii as head of the IKP, made the point that Dubrovskii had been the first to criticize Pokrovskii's entire conception of history in the 1920s—a remark which might be thought to imply that Dubrovskii was something of a weathercock.[27] M. P. Kim repeated the Stalinist argument that Pokrovskii had tried to build up for himself a monopoly position in the field of historical studies. On the other hand, A. L. Sidorov broke new ground by making the first public criticism of the two-volume critique of Pokrovskii, which he had helped to edit. Summing up the discussion, the chairman held out the prospect of a thorough investigation into Pokrovskii's work. One of the questions that needed to be answered was: "what were the consequences for Soviet historical scholarship of the struggle against Pokrovskii during the period of the cult?"[28]

One year later another conference was held to discuss the general subject of history teaching.[29] The debate had now broadened out into a general indictment of Stalinist methods—something of much greater significance than the question of Pokrovskii's merits or demerits, which were scarcely discussed at all. One of the few references to him was by Burdzhalov, the *enfant terrible* of 1956, who made a strong attack on

25 *XXII s'ezd KPSS: stenograficheskii otchet* (Moscow, 1962), vol. 2, 185.

26 *Voprosy istorii* (1962), no. 3, 30 (text of report, 3–31).

27 Ibid., 34. It is interesting that A. I. Gukovskii should have come to Pokrovskii's defense against Mints's charge that he did not know Lenin's works: cf. *Istoriia SSSR* (1965), no. 6, 89.

28 Ibid., 40.

29 The proceedings were published under the title given in note 7. It is instructive to compare this record of the lively debates with the dry and abbreviated version initially given in *Voprosy istorii* (1963), no. 2, 3–75, which *inter alia* omitted the exchange discussed below.

Sidorov for having criticized Pokrovskii as late as 1955.[30] One might think that this was scarcely fair: after all, at that time such articles were quite in order, and in the last few years Sidorov had changed his line as fast as anyone else. But the radicals were playing the game by different rules; their main objection was precisely to what they felt was a hypocritical readiness on the part of leading historians to adjust their views to the political *koniunktura*. Burdzhalov was probably paying off an old personal score as well. In any case Sidorov did his best to make amends. In March, 1964, he published a revealing memoir in which he recalled his experiences as a member of Pokrovskii's seminar in the 1920s.[31] He mentioned that in 1929, "with the best of intentions and a clear conscience," he had rashly suggested to the great man that he make certain alterations in his *Brief History*, whereupon he had been sent to do practical work in Nizhnii Novgorod (now Gor'kii).[32] He had taken it in good heart and did not hold Pokrovskii himself responsible so much as his associates Gorin and Fridliand. He had now been asked to give some advice to young scholars. "I should prefer that young people, reading my story, should draw from it the conclusions they think useful."[33] He ended by warning his colleagues against concentrating too heavily on collective works, which could inhibit them from expressing individual ideas; they should study the technique and methodology of *bourgeois* writers—as Pokrovskii had recommended.

Since 1962 Soviet historians have indeed tried to grapple with the legacy of the 1930s, although a thoroughgoing *Bewältigung der Vergangenheit* remains to be accomplished. A valuable but brief sketch of Pokrovskii's career has been given by E. A. Lutskii, and L. V. Danilova has discussed the contribution which he and other early Soviet scholars made to the study of feudalism.[34] O. L. Vainshtein has described, a little drily for one of his experience, the general historiographical scene in the 1920s.[35] Pokrovskii's selected works have appeared in a four-volume edition.[36] The first three volumes comprise his two major historical works; the last contains a rather uninspiring choice of his articles and book reviews, devoted mainly to such topics as Lenin, the Russian revolutionary movement, historiography, archive administration, and academic organization. Volume IV of the new official history of Russian historiography, published in 1966 under the chief editorship of M. V. Nechkina, contains an authoritative assessment, by L. V. Cherepnin, of Pokrovskii's position in Soviet scholarship as the revisionists see it. It is not calculated to stimulate any intellectual interest in the Old Bolshevik's ideas. Cherepnin states unequivocally:

---

30 *Vsesoiuznoe soveshchanie istorikov*, 368–9.

31 *Istoriia SSSR* (1964), no. 3, 118–38.

32 Ibid., 136.

33 Ibid., 138.

34 Lutskii, "Razvitie," 334–70; L. V. Danilova, "Stanovlenie marksistsogo napravleniia v sovetskoi istoriografii epokhi feodalizma," *Istoricheskie zapiski*, 76 (1965), 62–119.

35 *Voprosy istorii* (1966), no. 7, 32–47.

36 *Izbrannye proizvedeniia M. N. Pokrovskogo* (Moscow, 1965–7).

Pokrovskii belongs to history. It is not a matter of restoring his conclusions, or idealizing his works or conceptions, but of establishing in an objective scientific way his role in the establishment and development of science.[37]

No comprehensive systematic study has been made, or is in present circumstances likely to be made, of Pokrovskii's thought and its implications for the contemporary Soviet historian.

In what ways, then, if at all, one may ask, is his rehabilitation likely to change such historians' image of the world?

III

At first sight it may seem that the positive developments in Soviet historical writing during recent years represent a return to the relative freedom of the 1920s. Such a conclusion would, however, be superficial.[38] There are a number of common features between the Pokrovskii era and the present: greater variety in the institutional pattern, a more tolerant intellectual climate, increased contact with other countries and greater attention to combating "*bourgeois* ideology." But the historian's function today is still basically what it was in the Stalin era: to provide an intellectual legitimation for the existing regime and the order of society it has established. A great deal of scholarly effort is devoted to expounding fictions which substantiate the party's claims to be the authoritative interpreter of "the logical process of mankind's movement toward communism" (N. E. Fedoseev). The Soviet historian is not simply required to eulogize his political masters: he must adopt enthusiastically a *Weltanschauung* centered upon the collective experience of party and people in the "building of socialism and communism." When assessing any historical event, idea, or problem, however remote in time or space, he is to take as his criterion its "progressiveness"—meaning in effect the contribution it made to the events that led to the current might of the USSR and world communism. This creed governs his perception of historical facts, as well as his manner of interpreting them.

The spirit of official thinking is thus closer to that of the 1930s than the 1920s. Stalin's arbitrary despotism has gone, but the substance of his system remains. The party still sees itself as engaged upon a worldwide struggle which necessitates the consolidation and extension of its power at home and abroad. The revolutionary internationalism of the early Bolsheviks, to which Pokrovskii and even Lenin were committed, has little relevance to the position of post-Stalin Russia.

There is thus an artificial quality about the rehabilitation of Pokrovskii: it is his reputation that is being salvaged rather than his ideas. The prime motive of the

---

37 *Ocherki istorii russkoi istoriografii*, vol. 4 (Moscow, 1966), 198.

38 Dorotich, in the article cited in n. 7, claims (181) that "[Pokrovskii's] rehabilitation is certainly not forced from above. In the final analysis it is historical truth that is being rehabilitated, together with M. N. Pokrovskii." This judgment is perhaps a little too sweeping. Certainly a natural professional desire to tell more of the truth, if not all of it, is one of the motives behind the campaign; but Soviet historians are still far from able to present the truth as they see it. "Politics commands," as it always has done in the USSR.

revisionists is to present a politically acceptable image of Soviet historiography, from Lenin to the present, as monolithically united in a relentless struggle against hostile ideas. But some Soviet historians with strong professional loyalties pursue a rather different aim: to right a tragic injustice, and so to arrive at a closer approximation to actual truth. The tension between these two purposes may be illustrated by reference to several specific problems.

The first is that of methodology. It is not surprising that the official revisionists should have said little favorable about Pokrovskii's historiographical technique, although this aspect of his work is probably of the greatest interest to the professionals. Stalin had indicted him in the first instance for methodological errors: for making broad generalizations unsupported by facts, for disregarding or confusing chronological details, and for a naive understanding of Marxism. But Stalin's own disciples had then substituted even crasser simplifications, had been even more selective in their choice of factual evidence, and had forbidden creative Marxist thought altogether. With almost diabolical cunning they accused Pokrovskii of the very sins that they were themselves committing on a far grander scale. He was said to have preached the necessity of "projecting politics into the past,"[39] although they themselves molded the historical record unashamedly in accordance with political expediency.

Two charges were fundamental in the Stalinist indictment. The first was that Pokrovskii retained, as the legacy of his early academic upbringing, a nonpartisan respect for factual evidence. Wherever possible, he had based his more specialized work upon research in the primary sources; he set high standards for his pupils in this regard; and the collections of documents which he edited by and large conformed to normal scholarly standards. Naturally this respect for observed fact had its limits: he was not prepared to question the fundamental dogmas of Marx or Lenin, but he sincerely believed that scholarly analysis of objective evidence would validate the Marxian scheme. Such faith his Stalinist successors conspicuously lacked.

The second major point of criticism was that he made no secret of his political bias. He took the crude but intellectually honest view that all historical interpretation was politically motivated. The class struggle, which determined men's political beliefs, made nonpartisan historiography impossible; one had to take one's stand on one side of the barricades or the other. This simple formula was inappropriate to totalitarian conditions. Intellectuals were now required to pretend that their *Weltanschauung* was truly scientific, while at the same time suspending all critical judgement in regard to the central core of their beliefs, loyalty to the party (*partiinost'*). Various formulas have been evolved in an attempt to reconcile the contradictory strains, one scientific and

---

39 This charge rested formally upon a remark of Pokrovskii's taken out of context: "History is the most political of all sciences, it is the politics of the past without which it is impossible to understand the politics of the present." Mazour, *Modern Russian Historiography*, 193, and Aron, "Pokrovskii," 294, erroneously repeat this Stalinist allegation, which has been corrected by the revisionists. See *Voprosy istorii* (1963), no. 8, 39, and R. Szporluk, "Pokrovsky and Russian History," *Survey*, 53 (October, 1964), 107–18.

the other fideistic,[40] in Stalinist and post-Stalinist thought. It is argued, for instance, that true objectivity (as distinct from *"bourgeois* objectivism") can be attained only by partisanship, the two principles being allegedly "related dialectically": the party, intervening in the historical process, influences its objective regularities, to which its own actions naturally conform.[41]

The valiant efforts recently made by Soviet philosophers and historians to enrich their stock of theory have not brought its inherent contradictions any nearer solution, but have helped crystallize two points of view. The conservatives take a classic utilitarian stand. In effect they see it as the historian's job to provide evidence that will substantiate the current official analysis of the speed and direction of the historical process. They emphasize the general at the expense of the particular and are suspicious of mere "factography." The revisionists are more interested in the way that general regularities work themselves out in specific concrete conditions, and are more willing to let the facts speak for themselves. They would like to refine the concept of regularity in such a way as to distinguish between those laws that are applicable to broad sociological processes, e.g. the succession of socioeconomic formations, and those laws that govern their implementation within a narrower frame of reference.[42] The revisionists emphasize the distinction between the social and natural sciences and come close to recognizing history's claims as an autonomous discipline, in which factual description and narrative have an important part to play. Thus the philosopher A. V. Gulyga argues:

> In branches of learning which pursue descriptive aims as well as that of generalization, factual material plays a special role, different from that in purely theoretical disciplines. The latter utilize factual data simply as an aid to generalization. These sciences go through the stage of accumulating empirical material, but their aim is always to establish a law, and when this has been done the empirical material loses its importance. Historical research also begins with the collection of facts. Here, too, facts are to an even greater degree the air which the scholar breathes. . . . Without a firm, assured groundwork of fact no historical generalization is possible. At the same time the historical fact is not simply material for generalization; it is not just an example which can be dropped or replaced, to illustrate the operation of a social law. Historical generalization is no substitute for fact. To a certain extent facts in history have a value in themselves.[43]

---

40 Stalin himself recognized the nature of his creed. He is said to have refused to allow the study of the history of Western philosophy in Soviet universities after World War II on the grounds that "we have to strengthen the faith before we can expose heresies" (*snachala nado ukrepit'sia v verouchenii a potom izoblichat' eresi*). M. T. Iovchuk of the Institute of Philosophy in *Istoriia i sotsiologiia* (Moscow, 1964), 203.

41 See, for example, N. E. Zatsenker, "Marks i Engel's ob istorii," *Voprosy istorii* (1964), no. 6, 23.

42 Cf. Rogger, "Politics," 267. When Rogger wrote he had at his disposal only the abbreviated report of the important conference on methodology held in January, 1964, the full proceedings of which have since been published (see note 39).

43 *Istoriia i sotsiologiia*, 83. Gulyga's views were sharply criticized by B. M. Kedrov,

A provincial historian from Kalinin, A. Iu. Gurevich, has pleaded for a more sophisticated interpretation of the concept of regularity in the historical as distinct from the sociological context; quoting Sir Isaiah Berlin (although in a critical sense), he suggests that the laws of social development should be seen merely as trends (*zakony-tendentsii*).[44] Gurevich, in common with several other writers, also points to the role of probability and chance in interrupting or diverting the logical flow of events: a number of options are available to the decision-maker, and a given situation may have several possible outcomes. This new flexibility seems to reflect recent trends in mathematics. It certainly shows that some Soviet historians are dissatisfied with conventional doctrine, which asserts that "historical necessity makes its way through an endless multiplicity of fortuitous events," but does not explain *how* it does so.

Other revisionist writers have stressed the aesthetic aspects of the historian's craft, and held up for emulation the more sensitive approach of literary and other cultural historians. Excessive concentration on the typical, they point out, is liable to bore the reader, who is naturally interested in whatever is individual and unique. Such study is perfectly permissible, they maintain, since even the unique is socially conditioned and derives ultimately from the operation of general laws; the typical and the individual are not diametrically opposed categories, but are dialectically linked.

Truly the conservatives face an unenviable task in trying to stop all the loopholes in the official philosophy of history, which can be readily exploited by ingenious critics. Pokrovskii's legacy in this field could strengthen the revisionists' hand, by giving them an officially sanctioned example of creative Marxist thought. In a speech of 1928, for example, he too distinguished between sociological and historical interpretations of events.[45] This was not directly quoted by any participant in the recent discussion on methodology, but it is not surprising to find one leading historian complaining that his colleagues were still thrashing out the problems of thirty-five years ago.

Another fruitful field which they may wish to explore is Pokrovskii's concept of the role of the individual in history. Although he is usually regarded, not without reason, as a crass economic determinist, his attitude was really much more subtle. It is true that Pokrovskii minimized the role of Russian rulers, generals and saints, some of whom Stalin later resurrected and even glorified. But he was also willing to recognize that revolutionary leaders and elites could decisively alter the shape of events, and he regarded the October Revolution as a supreme example of this. We shall come back to this point in a moment.

Turning now from methodology to particular problems of Russian history, one may identify three fields in which, if and when the political climate again improves, Pokrovskii's rehabilitation may serve to accelerate the movement of opinion away from Stalinist traditions.

G. E. Glezerman and other speakers, who accused him of empiricism (ibid., 105, 130). For a favorable comment on Gulyga's view by a historian, see A. M. Sakharov, *Istoriia SSSR* (1965), no. 4, 8.

44 *Voprosy istorii* (1965), no. 8, 21.

45 M. N. Pokrovskii, *Leninizm i russkaia istoriia* (Moscow, 1930), 7.

The first is the problem of prerevolutionary Russian colonial and foreign policy. As a consistent internationalist, Pokrovskii emphasized the imperialist nature of tsarist diplomacy, particularly in regard to the Balkans and Near East; he even exaggerated the aggressiveness of Russia's drive for control of the Straits. In a popular sketch of 1926 he suggested—on the basis of very dubious evidence—that the Entente, not the Central Powers, was responsible for the outbreak of World War I.[46] In his *Brief History* he argued that the Russian state had been built up by the conquest of successive native peoples, from the Finns of the northern forests in Kievan days to the Moslems of Central Asia in the nineteenth century. Stalin, of course, changed all this and introduced into Soviet historiography a strident patriotic note. Emphasis was laid upon the positive effects of absorption into the Russian empire for the minorities concerned. Parallels were drawn between the German invasion of 1941 and Napoleon's campaign of 1812, a subject which Pokrovskii had neglected: looking at it in a European perspective, he had roundly condemned the Russian role as reactionary and shown more sympathy for the relics of the Grande Armée than for the peasant guerillas.

In recent years some of the worst nationalistic distortions have been discarded. Among the keenest advocates of revision, of course, are historians from the non-Russian (and especially non-Slavic) republics. The conservatives have their principal stronghold among military historians, who currently occupy an almost privileged semi-autonomous position.

The ramifications of this argument cannot be discussed in detail here.[47] In general it may be said that any thoroughgoing revision of historical doctrine on this issue is exceedingly unlikely. Characteristically, in the new edition of Pokrovskii's history virtually the only passages selected for editorial comment are those in which the author expressed his internationalist viewpoint. For example, where he criticizes Alexander II's government for seeking to liberate "brother Slavs" (the author's inverted commas!) in the Balkans, a discreet footnote refers the reader to a remark by the Bulgarian communist leader Dimitrov on the "liberation" of Bulgaria by "the Russian people" in the war of 1877–8.[48]

The party leaders know that national feeling, in its guise of Soviet patriotism, is a more important prop than ever. If spokesmen for the minorities go too far, they can easily be discredited as "*bourgeois* nationalists." They cannot look to Pokrovskii for support, since he took little direct interest in minority problems, but they may benefit if some other historians of the 1920s again become respectable. Russian revisionist historians have little incentive to recall Pokrovskii's views. Dubrovskii has pointed out in his defense that Pokrovskii had to combat the chauvinistic and nationalistic sentiments so widespread under the old regime. But Fedoseev, warning that Pokrovskii's

---

46 M. N. Pokrovskii, *Vneshniaia politika Rossii v XX veke: populiarnyi ocherk* (Moscow, 1926).

47 One interesting example is the effort of I. S. Braginskii and others to rehabilitate some leaders of the prerevolutionary Jadidist movement in Central Asia, which strove for national progress and cultural advance. See *Istoriia SSSR* (1965), no. 6, 26–38.

48 *Izbrannye proizvedeniia*, vol. 1, 325.

rehabilitation should not be pressed too far, specifically mentioned his error in "not always indicating the significance of national traditions and permitting wrong evaluations in this regard."[49] To illustrate his point he referred to Pokrovskii's positive assessment of the thirteenth-century Tatar invaders of Rus'—which his percipient audience will have construed as a blow against certain pro-Chinese historians who have endeavored to rehabilitate Genghis Khan. The present is scarcely an opportune time for anyone to probe deeply into this aspect of Pokrovskii's legacy.

A related problem is that of the Russian revolutionary tradition. For Pokrovskii—as indeed for Lenin—Bolshevism was intimately linked with international left-wing socialism and "revolutionary Marxism." In the Stalin era, when the Comintern and all that it stood for lost importance, these connections were played down. Instead, emphasis was laid upon antecedents of Bolshevism in the Russian past—in the "men of the 1860s," the Decembrists, and even the peasant rebels of the seventeenth and eighteenth centuries. One link in the chain, however, was conspicuously missing: the revolutionary populists, who were influenced either by Bakunin's anarchism or the "Blanquist" Jacobinism of Zaichnevskii, Nechaev and Tkachev. The populists were presented as reactionary and anti-Marxist. One reason for this was that during the 1920s a number of writers, some of them former Mensheviks, had sought the antecedents of Leninism among these radical populists, and for this had been sharply condemned. For example, in 1925 the journal *Katorga i ssylka* published an article by S. Mitskevich on "the roots of Bolshevism" which had been rejected by the more orthodox *Proletarskaia revoliutsiia*; six years later, after Stalin reproved the latter journal for its laxity, the editors of *Katorga i ssylka* apologized for having "granted a rostrum to those who had no right to it."[50] Pokrovskii did not go quite so far as Mitskevich. But in a course of lectures delivered in 1923–4 he stated that Tkachev "undoubtedly had a Marxist concept of history" and, referring to Nechaev, went on:

> . . . already at the end of the 1860s there was formed in Russian revolutionary circles a plan which the Mensheviks later mocked so greatly and which was put into effect almost literally on October 25, 1917—the plan for an *appointed* revolution.[51]

Pokrovskii considered the populist Jacobins both naive and *petit bourgeois*, but saw a continuity between them and the Bolsheviks in that both had built up a conspiratorial party with the deliberate object of seizing power.

In recent years Soviet historians, following the initiative of the late B. P. Kozmin, a distinguished authority on the period, have sought to present populism in a truer perspective. The artificial and illogical distinction between the radicals of the 1860s and of the 1870s has been discarded. V. A. Tvardovskaia has criticized those historians,

---

49 *Istoriia i sotsiologiia*, 45–6.

50 This episode is fully discussed by V. Varlamov in Black, ed., *Rewriting Russian History*, 318 ff. *Katorga i ssylka*, the organ of the Society of Former Political Prisoners and Exiles, most members of which were non-Bolshevik socialists, was suppressed in 1935.

51 M. N. Pokrovskii, *Ocherki russkogo revoliutsionnogo dvizheniia XIX–XX vv.* (Moscow, 1924), 63–4.

of whom Nechkina was the *doyenne*, who exaggerated the revolutionary role of the peasantry in post-reform Russia.[52] A noteworthy feature of this rehabilitation is that it concentrates on the *narodovol'tsy* at the expense of those identified with anarchism or Jacobinism.[53] One party historian has angrily rebutted the suggestion of a link between Tkachev and Lenin.[54] The specific problem of Bolshevik antecedents has been gingerly taken up by V. V. Shirokova,[55] but her article seems to have evoked no response.

Future writers on this theme will welcome the access now granted to the historical literature of the 1920s. But they will have to go carefully in citing such sources on later stages of revolutionary history, where a conflict is likely with the Leninist canon. Pokrovskii, discussing the events of 1905, minimized the role of the peasants as an active and "conscious" revolutionary force; in his treatment of 1917 he maintained that the February revolution had already brought the working class to power *de facto*, and that the Bolsheviks did no more than establish the proletarian dictatorship *de jure*.[56] These assertions reflected the Trotskyist affiliations which he had shared at one time. Yet despite the obvious difficulties involved, Soviet historians *are* today revising their views on the revolution itself, partly as a natural consequence of destalinization, partly in response to recent developments in world politics.

The significance of this will become clear if we turn to our third specific problem, Russia's social and economic development in the prerevolutionary period. Pokrovskii, as we have seen, was forced by the Stalinists to modify his views on the chronological dating of Russia's transition from feudalism to capitalism, and a new doctrine on this point became established in the 1930s. It was somewhat closer to the facts than Pokrovskii's scheme, and was probably accepted with relief by specialists on this period. They could now give the landowning nobility its due in an epoch when it was dominant, and recognize, at least in part, the achievements of those monarchs, officials or capitalists who had promoted Russia's economic advance. But some historians still considered that less than justice was being done to business enterprise among the peasants prior to the Great Reforms, and once discussion again became possible they pressed for the onset of capitalism to be backdated. A long and arid debate ensued, in which the weight of opinion came down in favor of the accepted late dating, approximately in the mid-nineteenth century. If the issue is raised again, the revisionists will be able to draw upon Pokrovskii's arguments in support—with their implication that imperial Russian society was closer to that of Western countries

---

52 *Obshchestvennoe dvizhenie v poreformennoi Rossii: sbornik statei k 80-letiiu so dnia rozhdeniia B. P. Koz'mina* (Moscow, 1965), 78, 81.

53 Of more than thirty papers read between 1961 and 1965 to the Study Group on Social Movements in Postreform Russia, only one, by G. S. Ul'man of L'vov, treated such a theme: Tkachev's views on state and revolution. It has not been published. Ibid., 367.

54 *Voprosy istorii KPSS* (1963), no. 4, 51 n.

55 *Istoriia SSSR* (1962), no. 3, 72–8.

56 Pokrovskii, *Ocherki russkogo revoliutsionnogo dvizheniia*, 150, 229.

than the Stalinists cared to admit.

The same issue is raised by the attempt to fix chronological limits for the supposed "imperialist" phase in Russian history. Pokrovskii first took the view that this could be dated only from 1914, when Russia had entered the "imperialist war," but later pushed it back to 1890. In his view the main criteria involved were protective tariffs and an expansionist foreign policy; and in the 1890s Russia had had both. The existence of trusts and syndicates he considered a less important characteristic, for these had been much weaker in Russia than in more advanced countries such as Germany or the United States. It was only in the immediate prewar years that Russia had developed a "finance capital" of her own, since previously she had depended heavily upon foreign investment. An economic satellite could hardly be imperialist in the economic sense. Pokrovskii's views were quite reasonable and in the 1920s the question was debated fairly on the basis of objective evidence. Some of his pupils emphasized the role of native capital more than Pokrovskii did. Others were more inclined to portray Russia as a colony of foreign investors. Pokrovskii had greater sympathy for the latter view, which carried the implication that the revolution had been as much a national anti-imperialist movement as a social one, and which cast doubt upon the existence of any objective basis for socialist construction in the USSR.

Stalin first beat all these historians into silence with the stick of orthodox Leninism, pointing out dogmatically that Lenin had dated imperialism from 1900, and then appropriated their opinions himself. In 1934 he stated that prerevolutionary Russia had been a "semicolony" of Western capital. This theme was much stressed in the post-World War II years, when the anticosmopolitan drive was at its height.

Destalinization in this field got under way shortly before the Twenty-Second Party Congress, when a conference for this purpose was held in Leningrad; its sponsor was a body known rather grandly as the Section on Regularities and Particularities of the Development of Russia under Imperialism, a subgroup of the Council on the History of the Russian Revolution.[57] The "semicolonial" theory was explicitly discarded, freeing the way for a rehabilitation of native Russian capital.

It seems that there emerged two schools of thought, each of which sought to provide a more up to date and credible historical legitimation for the October Revolution. This was no academic issue, for as one historian observes:

> . . . the rise and development of the world socialist system after the Great Patriotic War has made particularly topical the problem of the regularity of the transition from capitalism to socialism, which began in October 1917.[58]

One tendency, represented by A. V. Pogrebinskii and Ia. I. Livshin, emphasizes the dominant position of monopolistic trusts and syndicates in Russia's economic and political life prior to 1917, and especially their responsibility for the outbreak and prolongation of the war. The reader is left with the impression that Russia's privileged

---

57 *Ob osobennostiakh imperializma v Rossi* (Moscow, 1963), 7.

58 E. D. Chermenskii, *Istoriia SSSR: period imperializma (90-kh gg. XIX v.—mart 1917 g.): posobie dlia uchitelei i studentov pedvuzov* (Moscow, 1965), 10.

groups formed a powerful and united reactionary bloc, which could be overthrown only by a still mightier union of the popular masses, and that such a national union came about in opposition to the war, into which the people were dragged by domestic and foreign business interests. Seen in this perspective, 1917 appears as the forerunner of the "anticolonial" revolutions in China and other developing countries. The political implication is that Russia's historical experience entitles her to a vanguard role in the emergent peoples' struggle against "Western imperialism," from which she was the first to emancipate herself.

The second tendency views the revolution in a European rather than an Asian perspective, and is closer to the Western standpoint than to the Chinese. Spokesmen for this tendency are of course totally opposed to the evaluation of Bolshevism given by *bourgeois* scholars. But they do not contest too strongly the argument that the Bolsheviks' victory was largely a matter of superior leadership and organization. They conceal this de-emphasis of the role of the masses behind loud endorsement of the current extravagant cult of Lenin. The implication of this line of thinking is that, but for Lenin and his party, Russia would have had to develop along the road of Western *"bourgeois* democracy." The alternative to Bolshevik rule is thus seen as limited progress rather than outright reaction. It is further suggested that Russia had been prepared for such progress by her previous history: her industrial growth prior to 1914 was quite significant; monopolistic restrictions were not all-important; the role of foreign investment was not exclusively negative; the ruling groups were divided among themselves. The chief obstacle to Russia's advance, it is implied, was not so much the capitalists, native or alien, as the court camarilla and other archaic "feudal" survivals within the privileged elite. Hence Sidorov's interest in Rasputin. In short, this school inclines toward a more sophisticated—and in Western eyes realistic—understanding of the causes of the Russian revolution, even though the explanation given might not satisfy non-Marxists.

Among those who have intervened on this side of the debate are the late A. L. Sidorov, I. F. Gindin and V. K. Iatsunskii,[59] who worked with Pokrovskii in the 1920s. The latter's rehabilitation should reinforce their position, and may encourage younger, more questing spirits to urge greater frankness in discussing this key problem. How far can the pendulum swing toward a less standardized interpretation of October? Will Soviet historians be able to refine the concept of *zakonomernost'* to a point where they can accept Pokrovskii's view (which many early Bolsheviks would have shared) that it was an "appointed" revolution, carried out in contravention of "narrow economic laws"?

The answer to these questions cannot be given by the historians alone. In the last resort their evaluation of the past depends upon the politicians. In the decade 1956–66 the party permitted a notable advance both in methods of research and in quality of analysis. If and when the present "freeze" is over, these progressive trends may reassert themselves.

1972

---

59 *Istoriia SSSR* (1964), no. 5, 74–91; (1964), no. 6, 156–9.

CHAPTER 18

Soviet Historians on "Great October"

I

Nowhere is the "mythogenetic" function of Soviet historiography more pronounced than in the literature on the "Great October Socialist Revolution." The Bolshevik seizure of power in October, 1917, which led to the establishment of the world's first Communist dictatorship, is officially regarded as the single most significant turning point in human history. For many years in the USSR all writing on the events of 1917, whether on the academic or on the popular level, has been subject to the most severe political constraints. The guardians of ideological orthodoxy have consistently maintained a close watch over everything published in this sensitive field, for they are anxious to prevent opinions being expressed which might conceivably cast doubt on the CPSU's right to govern.

Historians of the Russian Revolution are required to magnify the achievements of the victors and to minimize the role played by their opponents, even if this involves manipulation of the facts in the most partisan manner. In trying to understand and pass judgement on the past they face obstacles much more formidable than any confronted by their colleagues in other countries, for the political authorities claim nothing less than to be in step with History itself. They see it as the historians' job to demonstrate, by reference to a limited and officially sanctioned body of evidence, the supposedly "correct," "scientific" and "law-governed" character of their ideas and policies.

In the world view of the believing Communist, "Great October" plays much the same role as the Gospel story once did for pious Christians. Any writing on this subject, or on other subjects related to it, impinges to some degree upon matters that have been invested with a sacramental character. That is to say, they are deemed to be beyond criticism; their veracity has allegedly been established for all time, and the record may consequently not be revised, even on the basis of new evidence or insights. Differences of opinion are permitted only in regard to relatively minor details which do not raise doubts as to the authenticity of the received dogma, which has to be taken on trust.

It is important to emphasize the underlying consistency of the Soviet approach to the history of the Revolution in order to set in proper perspective the changes that have occurred over the past twenty years or so. Significant as these are in many ways, their impact should not be exaggerated. Recent Soviet scholarship in this field still has much more in common with that that of the Stalin era than with that of the pretotalitarian 1920s. The style of discourse is scholastic, formal and repetitious. From time to time some new concept may be introduced (for example, "the political army of the socialist revolution," in reference to the radicalized masses of 1917); but it must be of impeccable Leninist ancestry and cannot but degenerate into a mere cliché, for scholasticism does not permit intellectual development from within but requires instead the constant reiteration of stereotyped assertions.

This essentially unhistorical approach to the subject naturally arouses some dissatisfaction among the interested public. Evidence of this may be found in a brief report of a conference held in 1974 between the editors of the journal *Istoriia SSSR* and some of its readers. One of those present (I. A. Kirianov) called for more discussion articles; another (V. S. Lel'chuk) urged writers to leap boldly across the barriers between successive socioeconomic formations, for instance comparing the condition of the working class before and after the Revolution; a third (V. G. Sirotkin) suggested that more attention be paid to Russia's place in world history; and a fourth (V. A. Cheremisskii) was anxious to see more memoirs published.[1]

Partly in response to such pressures from below and partly in order to give an impression of intellectual vitality, discussions on approved topics are held both at conferences and in the columns of scholarly journals. In either case the limits are drawn so narrowly that the exchanges do not often contribute much to clarification of substantial issues. The conferences may even serve as a kind of professional tribunal at which the party historians (and their allies among the military) seek to mobilize opinion against individual deviants. At least two such heresy-hunting meetings have been held since 1971, both of them on matters relating to the historiography of the Russian Revolution; their implications will be examined below. In March, 1973, a general conference of Soviet historians was held with the explicit purpose of reaffirming support for the official line.[2] As a result of these maneuvers in March, 1974, P. V. Volobuev, a leading specialist on the revolutionary period, was dismissed from his post as director of the Institute of USSR History in the Academy of Sciences; he has been replaced by A. L. Narochnitskii. An authoritative *History of the Three Russian Revolutions*, under the editorship of a collective chaired by S. P. Trapeznikov, is scheduled, the aim of which is to provide formal guidance on all matters under

---

1 *Istoriia SSSR* (1974), no. 4, 234 ff.

2 The volumes in question were: *Istoricheskaia nauka i nekotorye problemy sovremennosti* (Moscow, 1969); *Rossiiskii proletariat: oblik, bor'ba, gegemoniia* (Moscow, 1970); *Sverzhenie samoderzhaviia* (Moscow, 1970). Another volume which has incurred criticism but has not been made the subject of a formal discussion and condemnation is *Voprosy istorii kapitalisticheskoi Rossii: problema mnogoukladnosti* (Sverdlovsk, 1972). For the criticisms, see *Voprosy istorii* (1971), no. 10, 159–66; (1972), no. 8, 141–5; *Istoriia SSSR* (1973), no. 1, 211–18; I. A. Aluf, "V. I. Lenin o stikhiinosti i soznatel'nosti v revoliutsionnom dvizhenii," *Voprosy istorii KPSS* (1973), no. 5, 110–20. For the March, 1973, conference see *Istoriia SSSR* (1973), no. 5, 3–16. A general review of these discussions in English is given by George M. Enteen, "A Recent Trend on the Historical Front," *Survey*, 93 (1974), 122–31.

dispute.

Thus the present climate of official Soviet historical scholarship, at least in this politically sensitive field, may be characterized as "neo-Stalinist." A counteroffensive is under way against those who have attempted, not without success, to broaden the scope of discussion, to raise interesting and sometimes even provocative issues, and to interpret the historical record with greater respect for the facts. Another target of this campaign are the so-called "*bourgeois* falsifiers" outside the USSR, that is, non-Communist historians generally and specifically those concerned with Russian or Soviet affairs. Their work, which under Stalin was more or less passed over in silence, is now scrutinized with almost excessive thoroughness; indeed, whole volumes are devoted to refuting the arguments of certain Western critics and to reasserting the canonical interpretation.[3]

II

Before examining the monograph literature on 1917, a few words are in order with regard to the sources upon which these studies are based. Since Stalin died Soviet historians have been encouraged both to use archival materials and to acquaint themselves more thoroughly with earlier literature on their subject, including the writings of non-Soviet authors. For those concerned with the Revolution, one significant implication of this reform has been the access granted to works produced under the aegis of M. N. Pokrovskii in the 1920s, which has allowed contemporary historians to situate their work in the context of the Marxist historiographical tradition. Still more important in the long run is the opening up of the archives, since at many points the documentary evidence is bound to conflict with the official interpretation, thereby placing the conscientious researcher in something of a quandary. If he takes the evidence before him as his guide, he will soon find himself in political difficulties, and the fruits of his research may well not be approved for publication. He must therefore learn the delicate art of squeezing as much as possible of the evidence into the approved conceptual structure. Those pieces of information that he knows to be true, but which cannot be fitted in, may be kept in reserve for possible use on some future occasion, if and when the political climate improves.

One other difficulty confronts the historian of the revolution in particular, and that is the profusion of published documentary collections (or more accurately, selections) in this field. Since 1956 many hundreds of such volumes have appeared, some of them topical but most of them geographical in scope. In normal conditions such compilations would be of considerable value to the scholar, since they would save him much tedious searching in manuscript repositories. In the USSR, however, the reverse is the case, for the documents concerned have been thoroughly vetted according to political criteria; moreover, these selections of documents are regarded as authoritative

3 See, for example, I. I. Mints, ed., *Zarubezhnaia literatura ob Oktiabr'skoi revoliutsii* (Moscow, 1961); G. Z. Ioffe, *Fevral'skaia revoliutsiia 1917 g. v anglo-amerikanskoi burzhuaznoi istoriografii* (Moscow, 1970); K. V. Gusev and V. P. Naumov, eds., *Velikii Oktiabr' v rabotakh sovetskikh i zarubezhnykh istorikov* (Moscow, 1971).

manuals, so that anyone conscientious enough to verify this "filtered" evidence against the original materials (or even, say, newspaper files) lays himself open to the charge of "factography," or excessive concern with facts at the expense of proper Marxist-Leninist analysis. Human nature being what it is, the majority of Soviet scholars will probably be content to rely upon this published evidence and to supplement it, largely for form's sake, with an occasional glance at archival sources. In this subtle way, without resorting to any direct constraints, the ideological controllers are able to influence the historian's perception of his subject.

It should be made clear that in Soviet conditions only those sources are considered valid which have been duly processed, or to use the technical term "exposed" (*vyiavlenyi*). This means that they have undergone classification according to their class and party-political character. If they are thought suitable for publication they are then prepared in accordance with certain strict rules, the object of which is to produce a volume that reflects as closely as possible the official view of what occurred.[4] The screening process is so thorough that none of the countless documentary volumes on the revolutionary period published in the last twenty years seems to have been criticized as containing ideologically reprehensible material.

In the mid-1960s the principles underlying this manipulation of historical evidence came in for criticism by some of the more responsible Soviet historians. One of them openly condemned what he called "the illustrative method of selection" and called for a return to the normal procedure, followed in the USSR before the Stalin era. This procedure is based upon the archival group to which a document belongs and the historical significance of its contents; anything omitted is summarized where necessary.[5] Interestingly enough, this procedure does seem to have been followed in at least one instance: the minutes of the Petrograd Military Revolutionary Committee (MRC), published in three volumes in 1966–7. (The minutes of its counterpart in Moscow, which appeared in 1968, were *not* treated in this way, and a comparison with an earlier partial edition shows that some silent cuts have been made on political grounds.)[6] What is the reason for the exception? Apparently the motive was not aca-

---

4 In antifalsification literature Western historians are sometimes accused of acting improperly by failing to apply such criteria themselves. For example, some years ago Richard Pipes was taken to task for having quoted, in his *Formation of the Soviet Union*, sources that had been "dredged up" (*vyiskivany*) rather than "exposed": the works in question had been published in the USSR in the 1920s but are no longer deemed ideologically respectable (R. G. Simonenko, in *Zarubezhnaia literatura*, 274 ff.). For the whole question of the treatment of sources, see George Katkov, "Soviet Historical Sources in the Post-Stalin Era," John Keep and Liliana Brisby, eds., *Contemporary History in the Soviet Mirror* (London-New York, 1964), 130–44.

5 A. I. Gukovskii, "Spornye voprosy sovetskoi arkheografii," *Voprosy istorii* (1966), no. 8, 75. Cf. also the strictures of M. S. Seleznev, "Voprosy metodiki publikatsii istochnikov po istorii Velikogo Oktiabria," ibid. (1967), no. 8, 146–55. More recently B. D. Gal'perina has carefully distinguished between *pofondovye* and *povidovye* publications, both of which she considers superior to the normal kind produced in conformity with the 1960 rules ("Vidovye publikatsii po istorii Velikoi Oktiabr'skoi revoliutsii," ibid. (1973), no. 11, 135–41).

6 V. A. Kondrat'ev, comp., *Moskovskii voenno-revoliutsionnyi komitet, oktiabr'—noiabr' 1917*

demic objectivity but political expediency, for publication *in extenso* of the Petrograd MRC minutes could be expected to show that it ran its affairs as a collective and that Trotskii's role in it was less prominent than Trotskii contended or is generally thought.[7]

Another research aid capable of serving the purposes of the ideological controllers is the "revolutionary chronicle," an essential tool when dealing with the complex and chaotic events of 1917. Any chronology must be selective and therefore contain an element of bias; but few can be so tendentious as the four-volume work entitled *The Great October Socialist Revolution: Chronicle of Events*, published between 1957 and 1961.[8] This is designed to supersede the six-volume chronicle begun in 1922 by N. Avdeev and completed in 1930 by I. N. Liubimov, which deteriorated in quality as Stalin tightened his grip on the historical profession. In the new work the principle of selection is blatantly political. The entries for each successive day are arranged according to a scheme which gives pride of place to statements and actions by Lenin, then to the affairs of the Bolshevik party, and after that of Bolshevik-controlled organizations; the affairs of other bodies are mentioned, but on a much less generous scale, the dosage generally decreasing as one moves toward the right. Characteristically, votes in soviet plenums and executive committees are given in numerical form when these organizations passed pro-Bolshevik resolutions, but in a more generalized form (if at all) where they passed resolutions in a contrary sense. For all its defects, the new chronicle is a useful tool of reference, provided that one uses it with due caution.

Similarly, the new editions of memoirs first published in the 1920s are generally less reliable, since sentiments no longer considered acceptable have been excluded. A case in point is the reminiscences of N. I. Podvoiskii, re-edited in 1958, which lack much of the lively detail that characterized his writing after the Revolution.[9] One wonders how many readers will be perturbed by such treatment, and how many will simply be glad that at least some forgotten revolutionary heroes have been permitted

---

g. (Moscow, 1968). The record of the minutes of the committee's meeting on November 4, 1917 (193 ff.) omits, without the obligatory *mnogotochie*, the interesting discussion on the problem of censorship which was included in the first edition, printed in *Krasnyi arkhiv*, 23 (1927), 99.

7 J.-J. Marie, "Le Comité Militaire Révolutionnaire du Sovet de Petrograd et son président," *Cahiers du monde russe et slave*, 8 (1967), no. 2, 189–204. The work in question appeared as D. A. Chugaev *et al.*, eds., *Petrogradskii voenno-revoliutsionnyi komitet*, 3 vols. (Moscow, 1966–7). Gal'perina lists further *povidovye* publications which "with difficulty conquered their right to existence," notably the proceedings of Tsentrobal't and of the Petrograd district soviets; a three-volume edition of the proceedings of the Petrograd soviet has been heralded.

8 *Velikaia Oktiabr'skaia sotsialisticheskaia revoliutsiia: khronika sobytii*, 4 vols. (Moscow, 1957–61). The chief editors of the four volumes are respectively: V. V. Kutuzov, G. P. Makarova, S. L. Dmitrenko and S. S. Tarasova. A sequel volume covering the period October 26, 1917–January 10, 1918, is L. M. Gavrilov et al., comps., 1. G. Dykov et al., eds., *Bor'ba za ustanovlenie i uprochenie sovetskoi vlasti: khronika sobytii* (Moscow, 1962).

9 N. I. Podvoiskii, *God 1917* (Moscow, 1958); cf. his *Krasnaia gvardiia v Oktiabr'skie dni* (Moscow-Leningrad, 1927). Such volumes as M. F. Komarova *et al.*, comps., *Rasskazyvaiut uchastniki Velikogo Oktiabria* (Moscow, 1957), are so thoroughly screened as to be worthless as historical sources; they include new material evidently written for the occasion.

to return from the limbo whither they were consigned by Stalin.

III

Turning from historical sources to the monographs based upon them, one should first of all pay tribute to the industry of those involved. Scarcely a month passes without some worthwhile new addition to the historical literature on the Russian revolution. Indeed, so much has been published in the last two decades, all of it rooted in the same Marxist-Leninist *Weltanschauung*, that the Western student is likely to feel somewhat overwhelmed by the sheer mass of material, and to find himself following the same well-charted tracks as his Soviet counterpart or asking himself the same kind of question.[10] Notwithstanding this caveat, it is worthwhile looking at the discussion among Soviet historians on the causes of 1917, or, in the language of determinism, "the prerequisites of the socialist revolution." Its object is to demonstrate that the establishment of the Soviet regime was a "law-governed" event and not merely the result of chance factors.[11]

Let us first recall some basic facts. During the revolutionary period most Marxists, in Russia as elsewhere, considered that the country was much too backward, both economically and politically, to engage in socialist experiments. Socialism, they believed, could only be achieved in Russia as part of a worldwide proletarian upheaval. A premature seizure of power by the working class, or by a party acting in its name, would be self-defeating. Even if the revolutionaries succeeded in maintaining their control of the state machinery, they could not build a genuinely socialist society, since the prerequisites were lacking; instead, they prophesied, they would be forced to resort to increasingly repressive measures which would discredit the socialist cause.

Marxist historians of the 1920s, faced with the problem of providing a plausible interpretation of the revolutionary events in terms of their own theory, might have argued, as Lenin did in one of his last writings, that in 1917 the Bolshevik party had simply taken a calculated risk, and that its task was now to create the prerequisites of socialism. However, this view was too voluntaristic to command general assent. Nor

---

10 For example, D. N. Collins, "A Note on the Numerical Strength of the Russian Red Guard in October 1917," *Soviet Studies*, 24 (1972–3), 270–8, fails to note that what matters is not the absolute but the relative strength of these paramilitary forces, especially vis-à-vis the soldiers, whose role in the October events is consistently minimized by Soviet historians for ideological reasons.

11 The following section is based mainly on the following: S. M. Dubrovskii *et al.*, eds., *Osobennosti agrarnogo stroia Rossii v period imperializma: materialy sessii Nauchnogo Soveta po probleme "Istoricheskie predposylki Velikoi Oktiabr'skoi sotsialisticheskoi revoliutsii," mai 1960 g.* (Moscow, 1962); A. L. Sidorov, "Ekonomicheskie predposylki Velikoi Oktiabr'skoi sotsialisticheskoi revoliutsii," *Istoricheskie predposylki Velikoi Oktiabr'skoi sotsialisticheskoi revoliutsii* (Moscow, 1970), 58 ff. (a report delivered in 1957 and not previously published); K. N. Tarnovskii, "Problemy agrarnoi istorii Rossii perioda imperializma v sovetskoi istoriografii (konets 1930-kh gg.—I-aia polovina 1950-kh gg.)," *Istoricheskie zapiski*, 83 (1969), 196–221; A. L. Sidorov et al., eds., *Ob osobennostiakh imperializma v Rossii* (Moscow, 1963).

could they rest content with the ultradeterministic interpretation that the revolution was the result of the war, which had created an extraordinary situation in Russia and had forced "the masses" to take power in self-defense. Instead Soviet historians sought to prove that the prerequisites for a socialist revolution *did* exist in 1917, and indeed had existed for some time prior to this; and that the Bolsheviks had correctly perceived this "maturity," which other Marxists had denied, and had drawn the appropriate inferences in their successful revolutionary strategy. The socioeconomic order of tsarist Russia was accordingly characterized in Leninist terms as one of "monopoly capitalism," the implication being that there was no *substantive* difference between her level of development than that of, say, Germany (where a socialist revolution was still expected).

Marxist historians in the USSR were still elaborating and refining this interpretation when in 1929 Stalin imposed totalitarian controls upon the country's intellectual life. Discussion of these issues abruptly ceased. For the next quarter-century those historians who survived the purges could do little more than echo the formulas contained in the official handbook of party history, the *Short Course*, which ruled ex cathedra that only fainthearts or saboteurs could doubt Russia's readiness for socialism in 1917. Contradictorily, however, Stalin also laid it down that tsarist Russia had been a semicolony of foreign imperialism. This latter proposition owed more to propagandist considerations than to scholarship: it was expedient to blacken the prerevolutionary past in order to exalt the socialist present, and to foment nationalistic emotions in the face of the new threat from the West. It also implied that Russia's revolution should serve as a model for the colonial and semi-colonial countries of the East, where the prospects of revolution now seemed brighter.

It goes without saying that, so long as the dictator lived, no one could even hint at the inconsistencies in his theory. Debate became possible only in the mid-1950s, when de-Stalinization allowed historical thought to revive and it was renewed at the point where it had been interrupted. To supervise it there was established under the aegis of the Academy of Sciences a grandiosely titled Scientific Council on the Prerequisites of the Great October Socialist Revolution. From 1958 onward this body arranged a series of conferences, attended by large numbers of professional historians as well as ideologists. As was only to be expected, differences of view soon began to make themselves felt. Broadly speaking, a distinction may be made between those whom one might term "mainstream revisionists," who were chiefly interested in arriving at a viable consensus, and the critics or innovators, who were more concerned with establishing the truth within the framework of Marxist doctrine. The latter included such prestigious "establishment" historians as A. L. Sidorov and I. F. Gindin as well as a host of younger men, among whom one may mention P. V. Volobuev, A. M. Anfimov and K. N. Tarnovskii. It would, however, be misleading to see these groups as clearly divided along factional lines; moreover, the critics differ profoundly among themselves.

The chief line of investigation pursued by the "mainstream revisionists" was into the growth and operation of the industrial cartels and trusts which, in their view, had dominated the Russian economy before 1917, and which they took as an indicator of the country's maturity for a socialist revolution. One may note that they tended to examine these matters in isolation and did not venture far into the field of comparative economic history; had they done so, they would have had to admit that Russia's "monopoly capitalism" was a good deal less developed than that of the other European Great Powers. They laid much emphasis upon the relative strength of native as against foreign elements within the entrepreneurial milieu—here expressly disassociating themselves from Stalin's views on Russia's semicolonial status—and also upon the close collaboration that had existed between these business interests and the bureaucracy. The image they conjured up was of a powerful and firmly entrenched politico-economic establishment, a worthy antagonist for the Russian proletariat, which was cast as the hero in the revolutionary saga.

The second major preoccupation of this school was with the struggles of the labor movement under Bolshevik direction against its formidable foes. This, too, was regarded in isolation from contemporary developments abroad. L. S. Gaponenko, a leading labor historian, is at pains to inflate the size of Russia's working class before and during 1917. To this end he includes such doubtful elements as domestic servants, construction workers and agricultural laborers, and arrives at an estimate of 15 million persons,[12] whereas previously historians had reckoned with a figure only about one-fifth as large. Even so this is a mere one-tenth of the total population, now put at 142 million.

Perhaps aware that they are on weak ground here, the historians of this school fall back on the argument that quality makes up for quantity. The high degree of concentration of workers in large enterprises in such important centers as Petrograd, as they see it, helped to develop among them a spirit of militant class consciousness. There is something to this, of course, for no one denies that many of Russia's workers were in an angry and desperate mood by 1917. But several comments are in order. First, it has yet to be shown that these workers, taken as a body, were *more* revolutionary than those in other European countries at a higher level of industrial development; second, there can be no doubt that Russia's workers lagged behind their comrades elsewhere in experience of industrial and political organization; third, this argument fails to show that the revolutionary agitators moved the workers to action *because* of their objections to the accumulation of economic power by "monopoly capitalists." The evidence available points in a different direction. Russian workers of the 1914–17 era were aggrieved at their low wages, poor living conditions, and lack of basic civil and political rights. If they disliked the tsarist state, it was because they associated it with reactionary policies in general rather than with concentration of ownership under monopoly capitalism; their objectives were as much anarchist as communist.

The historians of the critical school are conscious of shortcomings in the interpre-

12 L. S. Gaponenko, *Rabochii klass Rossii v 1917 g.* (Moscow, 1970), who here elaborates on the data he first discussed in "Rabochii klass nakanune Oktiabria," *Istoricheskie zapiski*, 63 (1958), 75–89.

tation advanced by their colleagues. Proceeding from certain remarks made by the ailing and disillusioned Lenin toward the end of his life, some of them argue that the socioeconomic order of prerevolutionary Russia may best be described by the term "multiformity" (*mnogoukladnost'*). This puts the accent less on class composition and conflict than on economic structure, in particular on the coexistence of several different types of economic organization, ranging from advanced capitalist monopolies at one extreme to self-sufficient family farms at the other. The exact meaning of the term *uklad* is rather unclear, as is its relationship to the concept of a socioeconomic formation (for example, capitalism); one suspects that this obscurity is not unwelcome to the innovators. They argue that the traditionalists have exaggerated the importance of the large monopolies and thus have given too rosy a picture of the country's economic maturity. In agriculture, too, much emphasis has been placed upon the role of the large estates, whereas in reality both artisans and agricultural petty producers were not only numerically strong but also played a constructive economic role.

Although the critics do not question basic Leninist assumptions about the structure of Russian rural society (in which class actually played at best a subordinate role), their thinking on such matters is a good deal more sophisticated than has hitherto been customary. Instead of a straightforward struggle between forces of "progress" and forces of "reaction," they see a complex web of interactions; no longer is white ranged neatly against black, but everything appears in some intermediate shade of gray, and issues that once were thought to be quite clear are now regarded as complex and contradictory. No longer are socioeconomic formations visualized as integral wholes, locked in remorseless combat; they are rather seen as interrelated in a variety of subtle ways. Likewise social conflict is treated with greater refinement, since it is recognized that these struggles are of varying intensity, both geographically and chronologically, and that common cultural traits may often bridge the class divide.

Of particular interest is the willingness of these critical historians to acknowledge that regional differences played an important role in determining the revolutionary pattern. This insight seems to be a byproduct of the encouragement given to research in local archives. Many of the innovators are themselves "provincials" who have made their professional careers by studying the materials lying most readily at hand. Their task was to substantiate the official interpretation by working up concrete data relating to their own region, but in the process they were often tempted to go further in the direction of "particularism" (that is, emphasis on local peculiarities) than some of their senior colleagues in the metropolitan centers evidently think desirable. In the national republics this tendency raises the specter of "*bourgeois* nationalism," in the form of a more positive reassessment of those national groups that at one time or another collaborated with the Bolsheviks but have since been repudiated as "counterrevolutionary," but it is also noticeable within the RSFSR, particularly in Siberia and the Urals. In 1972 V. V. Adamov, a history professor at Sverdlovsk, and others brought out a volume of essays devoted to the question of "multiformity" in prerevolutionary Russian society,[13] which has since been criticized *inter alia* for

---

13 See note 2 above.

overestimating the importance of those features specific to the Urals region. Indeed, some of its contributors do come near to claiming that the Urals, with its geographical position on the divide between Europe and Asia, its backward but potentially important heavy industry, and its militant radical tradition, offers a specific revolutionary model for the developing world.

This argument takes to an extreme a suggestive hypothesis which in a more general form is to be found in the writings of other contributors to the debate on the prerequisites of 1917. Precisely because they are aware of the relative "underdevelopment" of prerevolutionary Russia, the critical historians are inclined to see the revolution in terms of a "national liberation struggle" for emancipation from Western imperialism. Here Stalin's theory of the country's semicolonial nature comes in: it is one point where they find themselves in agreement with the former dictator (and they can use this fact as a shield against criticism by the "mainstream revisionists"). They argue that the Russian revolution was the prototype for all subsequent revolutions in what we today call the Third World, and that the CPSU's victorious strategy should commend itself to all aspiring Afro-Asian revolutionaries. Such an argument is of course calculated to counteract the natural appeal of the alternative model of revolutionary development projected from Peking, and for this reason, if for no other, commends itself up to a point to the ideologists. Unfortunately it suffers from a basic flaw which prevents it from being taken to its logical conclusion. For how can this notion be squared with the fact that at the time the Bolsheviks saw their revolution as keyed primarily to the industrialized countries of the West? If the Russian model is declared apposite to the Third World, can it simultaneously be presented as relevant to Europe also? If the Bolsheviks succeeded because of Russia's backwardness, does it not follow that the industrially advanced West is territory lost to the Social Democrats and other "revisionists?"

Such a conclusion is of course unpalatable. When the fiftieth anniversary of the revolution was celebrated with great pomp in 1967, official ideologues such as P. N. Fedoseev proclaimed that its message was of global import, and to bolster this claim turned to the theory of "multiformity." On one hand, the country's agrarian backwardness had given rise to a vigorous peasant movement, which had attained its aims with help from a working class led by the Bolsheviks; here was a lesson for the developing countries. On the other hand, the Russian proletariat had risen in revolt against "monopoly capitalism" with a zeal worthy of emulation by the Western workers of today, whose problems were allegedly of the same order. In sum, 1917 had given everyone something to learn, and its centrality in human history was therefore self-evident.

It will be interesting to see whether this view will be modified now that the concept of "multiformity" has come under attack. Its principal defect in the eyes of the ideological controllers is that it errs too far in the direction of specificity and so casts doubt upon such basic propositions as the homogeneity of the "all-Russian proletariat" and the primacy of the class struggle. There is a risk that the critics, with their more nuanced and relativized interpretation of the Russian revolution, might go over to a semi-Menshevik position which assigns to the Russian working class "general democratic" rather than socialist tasks or might argue that October was above all else a result of World War I and not of any inner contradictions in Russian society.

The official doctrine has always been that the war only *accelerated* a crisis that was already manifest in 1914 or earlier, since it derived from the nature of "monopoly capitalism" itself. Although this theory cannot be publicly controverted, in their specialized studies Sidorov and others have undermined it. They argue, in common with many Western historians, that the crisis of the *ancien régime* did not become acute until the summer of 1915. In their analysis the key factor in the causation of the 1917 revolution is external rather than internal, namely, Russia's subordination to her allies in the Entente, which first of all acquired a strong position in the economy and then interfered extensively in domestic politics, making it impossible for Russia's leaders to conclude the democratic peace which the country so desperately needed. This was why the moderates lost popular support so rapidly and the Bolsheviks were hoisted to power by the masses—forced to take control by pressure from below.

Admittedly, this interpretation does strain the historical evidence at certain points; however, it also contains a good deal of commonsense and is immeasurably superior to that offered by the "mainstream revisionists," for whom everything that happened turned out for the best, and was in any case foreordained by History (embodied in Lenin). It provides the basis for a genuine Marxist revision of Russia's recent historical experience, should political conditions ever allow this. We may now turn to some specific issues in the history of the Russian Revolution.

IV

One might have expected the Soviet historical profession would by now have provided us with a detailed and plausible picture of the breakdown of the Russian economy during World War I and of its consequences for the working class. This is, however, not the case. Ideology demands that labor's struggle to protect and improve its living standards be fitted into a political framework in which the masses do not act autonomously on any issue but are led forward by the Bolshevik party.

This narrow and distorted perspective prevents Soviet historians from asking themselves such logical and worthwhile questions as the following: (1) How far was industrial action in 1917 politically inspired and how far a spontaneous response to adversity? (2) How far did the strikes and unrest contribute to the deterioration of the economy and thus indirectly to the worsening plight of labor itself? (3) How did real earnings and employment opportunities fluctuate in different branches of industry and in different regions over the period? On such questions as these we are still almost as much in the dark as we were in the early 1920s, when the first monographs on the subject appeared.[14]

---

14 The author of one of the best of them, S. G. Strumilin, became the doyen of Soviet economic historians. In the 1950s he revised some of his earlier judgements. His selected works have been republished (*Izbrannye trudy v 5 tomakh* [Moscow, 1963–64]), but they omit some of the articles he wrote in 1918, when he was still a Menshevik.

416   JOHN KEEP

Even as sophisticated a writer as Volobuev is constrained to assert that inflation was not an objective phenomenon, rooted in excessive government spending on wartime needs, but was deliberately encouraged by "the *bourgeoisie*" to lower mass living standards and to maximize profits; similarly, he argues that industrialists sabotaged their own plants by closing them down without due cause.[15]

No attempt has been made in recent years to construct a more accurate consumer price index to replace the rather amateur (and little known) one compiled by M. P. Kokhn in 1925.[16] Yet the establishment of basic data on prices and incomes (using 1913 as base year) is essential for any serious work on labor history during the revolutionary period. The obsession with industrial and political strife distorts the perspective of virtually all writers on the subject, so that economic (and specifically labor) history, contrary to what one might expect, is among the weakest sectors of research.

On the credit side one may note that the prewar tradition of compiling histories of individual enterprises has recently been resumed,[17] although business history in the Western sense is still unknown. Some pioneer work has been done on public finance during the last years of tsarism,[18] and there is also some interest in the activities of the War Industries Committees—largely as a byproduct of the investigations into the workings of "monopoly capitalism."[19]

One curious consequence of the neglect of economic history is that, while we are told continually that "it is the masses who make history," and *bourgeois* historians are reprimanded (not always unjustly) for concentrating on the powers that be, it is very difficult to reconstruct the actual lives and thoughts of ordinary folk during this period, since the sources are so deficient and so tainted. Impressionistic memoir accounts by outsiders, usually revolutionary activists, are no substitute for authentic records; and the resolutions passed at mass meetings or village assemblies (of which only the most radical, needless to say, find their way into recent documentary volumes) cannot be taken as representative of mass opinion. Instead of real flesh-and-blood individuals, with all their human frailties and ambiguities, we are offered the "dark masses" of contemporary publicists in a new heroic guise, a faceless crowd pulled hither and thither by revolutionary activists and class enemies.

One encouraging move away from this stereotyped approach is the attempt by the

15 P. V. Volobuev, *Proletariat i burzhuaziia Rossii v 1917 g.* (Moscow, 1964), passim (especially 219).

16 M. P. Kokhn, *Russkie indeksy tsen* (Moscow, 1926); the work is referred to by Volobuev (loc. cit.), but this author has been unable to trace a copy.

17 For bibliographical details see L. S. Rogachevskaia, *Voprosy istorii* (1967), no. 8, 155–62; also Z. K. Zvezdin in ibid. (1968), no. 11, 167–9 and *Istoriia SSSR* (1973), no. 2, 3–20. Most such historians cover the whole pre-Soviet of Soviet periods and do not concentrate on the revolutionary years.

18 A. L. Sidorov, *Finansovoe polozhenie Rossii v gody pervoi mirovoi voiny, 1914–1917* (Moscow, 1960).

19 E.g. in I. Maevskii, *Ekonomika russkoi promyshlennosti v usloviiakh pervoi mirovoi voiny* (Moscow, 1957).

sociologist O. I. Shkaratan to study the social structure of the working class in 1917–1918.[20] Shkaratan has run into trouble for his unorthodox terminology—establishment historians objected to his use of the term "social structure" without mentioning which class he was referring to—but so far their verdict has been guardedly positive.[21] Less successful in obtaining a clean bill of ideological health was Iu. I. Kirianov, author of a valuable work on the Ukrainian proletariat during World War I in which some attention was paid to the social (in the Western sense) and cultural aspects of the theme.[22] Kirianov also contributed to the ill-fated volume of essays on the Russian working class, in the title of which there appeared the term *oblik* ("physiognomy"). This alerted the conservatives to the risk of heresy, for it suggested that psychological characteristics were at least as important as, if not more important than, class affiliation in determining a working man's conduct during a revolutionary crisis. Kirianov has been charged with "depoliticizing" the role of the proletariat by trying to study, in his words, "its most essential elements and aspects."[23]

Such efforts to see either workers or peasants "in the round" can only be welcomed. It should not be forgotten that "Great October" took place amidst mass hunger and unemployment, or that it accelerated one of the most significant demographic movements in modern Russian history, as hundreds of thousands of city dwellers left for the countryside in search of food and security. This phenomenon is touched on incidentally in M. I. Davydov's study of "the struggle for grain" (that is, the institution of the supply dictatorship) and in V. M. Selunskaia's work on proletarian-peasant relations;[24] but it is no exaggeration to say that the social history of the Russian revolution remains to be written. One need but consider the vast amount of solid work that has been done on the changes in French society during the decade after 1789 to appreciate the extent of the lag.

If there is ever to be a change in this regard, it will probably come about as a byproduct of a reassessment of the peasant world on the eve of revolution. This, too, is a sensitive area, since relations between town and country continue to be troubled. Since the ideological logjam was loosened in the mid-1950s, contending schools of thought have begun to appear among the agrarian historians. Up to a point the authorities have welcomed this development, since they realize that the intellectual stagnation under Stalin had detrimental effects upon the economy. Narrow limits have been set to this revitalization, however, and the impetus seems to have flagged

---

20 O. I. Shkaratan, *Problemy sotsial'noi struktury rabochego klassa SSSR* (Moscow, 1970); V. Z. Drobizhev and A. V. Sokolov, "Rabochie Petrograda v 1918 g.: opyt strukturnogo analiza po materialam professional'noi perepisi 1918 g.," *Istoriia SSSR* (1973), no. 1, 32–54.

21 Iu. V. Vosresenskii *et al.*, "Aktual'nye zadachi izucheniia istorii sovetskogo rabochego klassa," *Istoriia SSSR* (1973), no. 4, 3–33.

22 Iu. I. Kirianov, *Rabochie iuga Rossii, 1914—fevral' 1917 g.* (Moscow, 1971).

23 *Istoriia SSSR* (1973), no. 1, 215.

24 M. I. Davydov, *Bor'ba za khleb: prodovol'stvennaia politika Kommunisticheskoi partii i sovetskogo gosudarstva v gody grazhdanskoi voiny 1917–1920 gg.* (Moscow, 1971); V. M. Selunskaia, *Rabochii klass i Oktiabr' v derevne* (Moscow, 1968).

in recent years.

The main breakthrough came in May, 1960, when the Scientific Council called a conference to discuss "The Peculiarities of Russia's Agrarian Structure in the Age of Imperialism." (The council's responsibility did not extend to the revolution itself, which would have raised still more delicate problems.) The object of the conference was to reach a consensus on the degree of capitalist development, but it soon emerged that no agreed criteria existed for measuring either the extent or the characteristics of capitalism in agriculture prior to 1917. One of the participants, Tarnovskii, proceeding from the unexceptionably Leninist assumption that the technically modernized and market-oriented estates had played a "progressive" role, went on to suggest cautiously that the same might be true of some independent peasant farms as well. This was close to heresy, for such farms had always been categorized as *kulak*, a term which carries strong pejorative associations. Tarnovskii argued that the exploitative aspects in the relationship between the wealthier peasants and their fellows had lessened as capitalism had advanced, and that the beneficiaries of the Stolypin reform had played a useful role by providing employment for the surplus rural population.[25]

These debates were published in 1962, a year which saw the first public reference, in Alexander Solzhenitsyn's *One Day in the Life of Ivan Denisovich*, to the ultimate fate of so many of Russia's former yeomen farmers. The history of collectivization was also being discussed with considerable frankness, and there was an upsurge of interest in the flexible agrarian policies associated with the NEP. To the unreconstructed Stalinists it must have seemed as though everything were in a dangerous state of flux.

Disregarding these "establishment scholars" (most of whom are specialists in party history) we may distinguish two main schools of thought among the agrarian historians. The "mainstream revisionists" are represented by P. N. Pershin and E. A. Lutskii, whose scholarship is characterized by exceptional thoroughness. Lutskii's contributions lie scattered in various journals or collections of articles; Pershin is the author of a comprehensive two-volume study of the agrarian revolution, published in 1966, which is perhaps less well known abroad than it deserves to be.[26] It is based upon an intensive study of the records of many local soviets and land committees, preserved in dozens of provincial archives—and these sources are conscientiously detailed in an appendix, which is a rare virtue since Soviet scholars are normally lax about identifying the archival documents to which they refer. Pershin's monograph acquires a special poignancy in view of the fact that he himself, as an official of the land resettlement agency, participated in the events he describes, and in the early 1920s actually came out as a protagonist of individual peasant proprietorship.[27]

25 K. N. Tarnovskii, "Problema sotsial'no-ekonomicheskikh ukladov imperialisticheskoi Rossii na sovremennom etape razvitiia sovetskoi istoricheskoi nauki"; V. V. Adamov et al., eds., *Voprosy istorii kapitalisticheskoi Rossii* (see note 2 above), 20.

26 P. N. Pershin, *Agrarnaia revoliutsiia v Rossii: istoriko-ekonomicheskoe issledovanie* (Moscow, 1966).

27 P. N. Pershin, *Uchastkovoe zemlepol'zovanie v Rossii: khutora i otruby, ikh rasprostranenie za desiatiletie 1907–1916 gg. i sud'by vo vremia revoliutsii 1917–1920 gg.* (Moscow, 1922).

Characteristically, he does not even refer to his former views, which have long since ceased to be ideologically respectable.

Despite these far-reaching concessions to current orthodoxy, Pershin's work contains an abundance of material which cannot but encourage critical thought about agrarian problems during the revolutionary period. Among such "critical scholars" are Anfimov and Tarnovskii. The former is the author of a valuable history of the peasantry during World War I and has edited a documentary volume on agrarian conditions in 1917, in which he displays as much objectivity as present circumstances allow.[28]

If one may generalize and overlook the many qualifications with which they hedge their arguments, we may say that this school proceeds from four major assumptions, each of which departs in significant ways from the Stalinist stereotype. First, they see the peasant movement as a spontaneous popular phenomenon which owed relatively little to any political directing agency. Second, they point out that insofar as revolutionary activists from outside the rural milieu were important, these were more often soldiers than workers and were affiliated politically to the Left Socialist Revolutionaries rather than to the Bolsheviks. Third, they regard the peasant movement as autonomous, pursuing objectives of its own which in some degree coincided with those of the urban workers but were nevertheless distinct. Fourth, they seek to distinguish between two main phases in the development of the agrarian revolution, with the break occurring in the spring of 1918. This enables them to adopt a more realistic and sophisticated standpoint on the vexed question of peasant sociology. During the first phase, in their view, class differentiation in the village was of relatively minor account, and practically the entire rural population in effect sympathized with the movement for "soviet power." In the second phase class became more important, but less as a result of organic processes than through the external stimulation of the "supply detachments" of armed workers and soldiers sent to requisition the peasants' grain. The critical historians are fully aware of the negative effect the detachments' excesses had upon agricultural output and consequently upon relations between town and country—a fact which the establishment historians for obvious reasons prefer to play down.

The critics are now under attack for showing too much sympathy with the peasants —for "Neo-neo-Populism," so to speak. There is a natural affinity between their ideas and those in vogue among a segment of the literary intelligentsia, who look for moral inspiration to the traditions of the Russian countryside. The conservatives see the agrarian revolution as a major step forward to collectivization. They exaggerate the role of the first producers' cooperatives and argue that the peasants were from the start irreconcilably split into antagonistic classes, with the *kulak* as the embodiment of "reaction" and only the "poor" and "landless" (*bedniaki, batraki*) as reliable allies of the proletariat. Each side seeks—and finds—authority for its views in Lenin's

28 A. M. Anfimov, *Rossiiskaia derevnia vo vremia pervoi mirvoi voiny* (Moscow, 1962); *Ekonomicheskoe polozhenie Rossii nakanune Velikoi Oktiabr'skoi sotsialisticheskoi revoliutsii*, vol. III (Moscow, 1968).

writings. The conservatives cite those of 1917, when the Bolshevik leader made
much of the alleged tripartite differentiation among the peasants; the critics prefer the
Lenin of 1919, who had learned from experience how perilous it was to offend the
"middle peasant." As in medieval religious disputations, such "battles of texts" tends
to produce more heat than light. What we have here is less a scholarly argument than
a competition between typologies. The symbolic value of the charges and counter-
charges is of greater account than the proximity of either camp to actual historical
truth. Nevertheless, whatever the motives of those involved, such debates may help
to encourage a more pluralistic approach to historical investigation.

Another forum in which such ideas may be expressed is the literature on the role
of the mass organizations during the revolutionary period. Since Stalin's death a large
amount of attention has been paid to this hitherto largely neglected subject. The object
of this current concern with "popular creativity"[29] is to emphasize the basic continuity
of the revolutionary process. To this end the present-day concept of "the unity of
party and people" in a society moving from socialism to communism is retrojected
into the past, and the Bolsheviks portrayed as solidly rooted in the masses from the
very beginning. In accordance with these ideological guidelines the Bolshevization of
the soviets and other mass organizations in 1917 is represented as a natural process,
as a synthesis between a spontaneously revolutionary populace and its conscious
"vanguard." This is a different approach from that adopted under Stalin, which put the
emphasis on the party and on the skill displayed by the Bolsheviks in outmaneuvering
their rivals, while the rank-and-file members of the mass organizations were cast
somewhat in the role of a Greek chorus.

Despite the obvious element of partisan distortion involved, the new trend has
had positive results. It is now almost respectable to study the mass organizations for
their own sake instead of simply as transmission belts of party influence and control.
The most tangible benefit has been the appearance of a welter of monographs on the
soviets, factory committees, trade unions, and so forth, in which the accent is placed
less on the political struggle for domination over these bodies than upon their role
as articulators of mass opinion.[30] These works contain much valuable new information. Their principal defect (apart from the congenital insistence on minimizing
the non-Bolsheviks' role) is the tendency toward schematization. That is to say, the
historians concerned (who usually work as a team on collective projects) overlook
the natural differences that existed between the various types of mass organization,
each of which after all had its own functions and objectives, and treat them as if
they were analogues. Similarly, the very real regional differences are minimized, and
events which occurred in the most diverse local situations are pressed willy-nilly into

---

29 Iu. S. Tokarev, *Narodnoe pravotvorchestvo nakanune Velikoi Oktiabr'skoi sotsialisticheskoi
revoliutsii* (Leningrad, 1966), seems to have introduced this concept into the literature.

30 See especially *Sovety v period oktiabr'skoi revoliutsii i grazhdanskoi voiny*, 3 vols. (Moscow,
1967–8); M. N. Potekhin, *Pervyi sovet proletarskoi diktatury: ocherki po istorii Petrograd-
skogo soveta* (Leningrad, 1966); V. I. Startsev, *Ocherki po istorii Petrogradskoi krasnoi
gvardii i rabochei militsii, mart 1917–aprel' 1918* (Moscow-Leningrad, 1965).

conformity with the approved pattern. The pit committees of the anarchistic Donets miners, the guerilla bands of the southern Urals, and the councils of workers' control in the textile mills around Moscow—all are considered as though they were identical units in a homogeneous proletarian army (this is where the now popular cliché of "the popular army of the socialist revolution" lies readily to hand).

Many of the younger historians would argue that the regional distinctions are significant enough to require revision of the stereotyped notion of the "all-Russian proletariat" as a single entity. They try to take more account of the gradual spread of revolutionary impulses outward from Petrograd and the front, as well as of differences in the social and occupational composition of the local populace. They would probably admit privately that in many regions of the former Russian Empire the idea of proletarian class solidarity was extremely weak—not least in view of the fact that ethnic loyalties were now rapidly developing; but this aspect of the subject cannot be pursued here.

A similar schematizing pressure exists upon historians of the CPSU. Since this is a more familiar topic, it need be touched upon only briefly. The current fashion, which once again imposes a reflection of present ideals upon the past, emphasizes the "monolithic unity" which supposedly obtained throughout the country among party members, regardless of their ethnic or social affiliation or the positions they held within the party apparatus.[31] Through the mechanical elimination of its socialist rivals the Bolshevik party can be made to appear an all-national as much as a class organization. The image presented is one of party and people rallying around the larger-than-life figure of its Leader.

The Lenin cult is partly a matter of filling the void left by the disappearance of his once omnipotent successor; it is also a consequence of the general revival of interest in the role of personality in history, which was suppressed during the Stalin era (except, of course, in regard to Iosif Vissarionovich himself). The drive to reperson party history, launched at the Twentieth Congress in 1956, is sometimes taken to ridiculous lengths, as when historians dutifully list the complete (or near complete: we have not yet got rid of those meaningful " . . . and others"!) membership of relatively trivial committees or commissions. Apart from those yet to be rehabilitated, such as Zinoviev or Bukharin, the lesser leaders are sometimes made the subject of biographies in which, as Nancy Heer has pointed out, they are treated as pale shadows of their chief rather than as personalities in their own right.

Vladimir Il'ich himself, the object of so much adulation, stands as a synthetic monument rather than as a real historical figure.[32] Lenin seen by Soviet historians today is an almost superhuman creature (the term *ispolinskii*, "giant," is encountered).

---

31 The significance of the latter factor is correctly emphasized by Alexander Rabinowitch, *Prelude to October* (Bloomington, Ind., 1967).

32 Volobuev stated (*Sverzhenie samoderzhaviia*, 32) that "from a socioeconomic standpoint and from that of its political development any revolution is the result of a spontaneous objective process independent of the will of individual classes, parties, leaders, etc." This is probably the phrase that most aroused the irritation of his critics, although they chose to pick on others that were less objectionable—a characteristic device in such controversies.

Like some fairy-tale magician, he has but to issue a command for it to be immediately realized by his obedient and efficient helpmates. The actual historical relationship between the leader and his associates during the revolutionary period, which was in truth quite subtle and complex, a commingling of comradeship and command, remains hidden behind a veil of sickly platitudes. Similarly, the institutions of the early Soviet state are presented as functioning with the smooth rationality of a modern bureaucracy, whereas in fact the tension between the ultrademocratic ideals of the revolutionized masses on one hand and the imperatives of the dictatorship on the other led to near total administrative confusion, in which it was extremely difficult for those in power to translate their will into action.

The mythology demands that the party be shown at all times as fully in control of events—even as early as February, 1917, when it was just emerging from clandestinity. The perfectly reasonable suggestion by Volobuev that the general strike in Petrograd began in a spontaneous fashion on February 23, and that it took some days before the local party organization found its feet, led to charges that he was denying the principle of "proletarian hegemony" over all the revolutionary forces. Volobuev's estimate of the balance between spontaneity and conscious direction in the February revolution is much the same as that arrived at by E. N. Burdzhalov, who was written a two-volume work on the subject,[33] and recalls Trotskii's *History of the Russian Revolution* (1931–2).

The intraparty opposition plays a less prominent part in accounts of 1917 than it used to: the right-wingers (Zinoviev, Kamenev, Miliutin, Riazanov) are more or less passed over in silence. The Left Communists of 1918 have recently been returned to the rogues' gallery, but only in the context of foreign affairs, apparently as a reflection of Moscow's current preoccupation with Peking.[34]

To sum up, Soviet historians of the Russian revolution, although more restricted than their colleagues in their ability to reason deductively on the basis of their research, have advanced from time to time since Stalin's death a number of propositions which apparently reflect a more objective understanding of historical reality. It would, however, be naive to assume that these critical tendencies are bound to triumph over the more straitlaced views held to by other members of the historical establishment. For in a totalitarian polity such as the USSR the social sciences remain subject to the dictates of political expediency. The acceptance of a particular point of view depends not on its intrinsic merit, its credibility, but on its usefulness to the ideological controllers.

The tightening of the screw in Soviet intellectual life generally since 1968 has adversely affected those historians concerned with politically sensitive issues such as the Russian revolution. Nor is it just a matter of repression. The notion of an

---

33 E. N. Burdzhalov, *Vtoraia russkaia revoliutsiia* (Moscow, 1968, 1970). (Vol. 2 deals with Moscow and the provinces.)

34 For a further discussion of this point, see Nancy W. Heer, "The Non-Bolshevik Left and the Idea of Political Opposition," in S. H. Baron and N. W. Heer, eds., *Windows on the Russian Past: Essays on Soviet Historiography Since Stalin* (Columbus, Ohio, 1977), 157–69.

irresistible and all-conquering bolshevism, identified with Progress, exerts a powerful influence on many Soviet intellectuals. There is as yet no sign that the CPSU leaders and the Soviet political élite have lost the will to place their country's vast resources at the service of their messianic ambitions. On the contrary, the present world situation encourages them to persist in this way of thinking. It is therefore conceivable that the official Soviet interpretation of the history of the Russian revolution, for all its inconsistencies and implausibilities, will one day become a self-fulfilling prophecy. But other scenarios are also possible.

1977

CHAPTER 19

The Agrarian Revolution of 1917–1918 in Soviet Historiography

I

Some years after the Russian agrarian revolution K. D. Brutskus, the eminent Russian liberal economist, described it as "a mass movement of an elemental fury, the like of which the world has never seen."[1] He did not exaggerate. This violent upheaval led to the redistribution on the most egalitarian principles of a vast area of land. Some of this land had previously been owned by members of the privileged classes, by the state, or by peasant beneficiaries of the Stolypin legislation; some of it had been held as allotment land by members of village communes. The "black repartition" long awaited by generations of serfs and their descendants was more than a simple act of "social justice." Seen from today's perspective, it was also a revolt of the village against the towns, one of the last attempts by humble country folk to halt the process, a seemingly inevitable concomitant of "modernization," whereby authority comes to be wielded by an urban élite unsympathetic to the needs and values of poor farmers. The agrarian revolution led to a temporary "rusticization" of Russian society which in turn helped to shape the nature of the Soviet political order. The Russian peasants' example has not been without its emulators in other less developed parts of the world over the last seven decades.

One would expect such a significant phenomenon to have been the object of intensive historical study, but this is not the case. Even specialists in Russian or Soviet affairs customarily dismiss the agrarian overturn as a mere appendage to "Great October."[2] There are several reasons for this neglect: the traditional western bias among students of general European history, the paucity of reliable source material,

---

1 "Die russische Agrarrevolution," *Zeitschrift für die gesammte Staatswissenschaft*, 78 (1924), 301–45.

2 L. A. Owen, *The Russian Peasant Movement, 1906–1917* (London, 1937; reprinted New York, 1963), 132–247, was for long the only comprehensive treatment of the subject in English. Oliver H. Radkey's probing and provocative history of the SRs in 1917–18 (*The Agrarian Foes of Bolshevism* [New York, 1958], and *The Sickle under the Hammer* [New York, 1963]) has little to say about the agrarian disturbances. I have endeavored to fill the gap in *The Russian Revolution. A Study in Mass Mobilization* (London, 1976; New York,

and the absence of good interpretive studies by our Soviet colleagues, hamstrung as they are by the limitations of official Marxist-Leninist ideology. It is the last of these factors that will concern us here.

Before examining the way in which Soviet writers have treated the subject, let us first summarize the principal features of the agrarian revolution as they appear to most non-Soviet historians. Five main points may be noted:

1) This was no orderly government-controlled land reform, such as has been attempted in several Third World countries. It was a violent challenge to all existing legal norms, designed to destroy the traditional social structure in the Russian countryside and to transfer power to the peasant smallholders. It is thought that at least 96 percent of the former estates were liquidated and redistributed (the rest being turned into state or collective farms). The dispossessed landowners were eliminated from the rural milieu, some of them perishing in the civil war and others emigrating to the towns or foreign countries; many succumbed to famine or disease. Proportionately the peasant "separators" probably suffered more hardship than former members of the élite.

2) The agrarian revolution was by and large carried out by the peasants themselves, with some aid from low-level "cadres" or activists (more usually soldiers or sailors rather than workmen), who might or might not be strangers to the community concerned. The actual redistribution was effected by the traditional communal authorities, but the impetus was often provided by district (*volost'*) committees or rural soviet executives, staffed mainly by peasants in and out of uniform. Redistributions on an all-county (*uezd*) basis were relatively rare. The element of central government direction was slight, although local activists often took as their guide the provisions of the land socialization law of February 19, 1918. The Bolsheviks (and their Left Socialist Revolutionary allies, so long as they were in the government) had no alternative but to let the peasants have their way. Lenin hoped to neutralize the so-called "middle peasants": so long as they were busy carving up the land, they would be less likely to interfere in the power struggle that was being decided in the towns; later, he believed, they could be won over without great difficulty to socialist cooperative farming.

3) The peasants' aim was *par excellence* egalitarian: to level out socioeconomic differences so far as possible. Available resources were parceled out according to "need," i.e. the number of mouths to be fed. This did not necessarily make them collectivists or socialists as these terms were then understood by intellectuals. They were wedded to the idea of the smallholding or family farm, although voluntary cooperation was not excluded and communal values were still strong. Social differentiation within the village, never very marked (particularly in Great Russia), was reduced by the land redistribution and the general poverty which reigned during the civil war. A "*kulak* class" existed only in the Marxist imagination, although no doubt speculators were to be found in many rural communities, just

---

1977), 153–247, 383–463, where the story is taken up to the fall of 1918. [See also G. J. Gill, *Peasants and Government in the Russian Revolution* (New York, 1979).]

as they were in the towns.
4) Peasant aspirations were articulated by the Socialist Revolutionaries (SRs), especially those of the left, who founded their own party in November, 1917. However, the latter were inexperienced in politics and easily worsted by the Bolsheviks. They did not have time to establish an organizational base among the rural masses before the Communists, in the course of 1918, made it all but impossible to oppose their regime in overt fashion. Peasants who objected to forced requisitioning of alleged agricultural "surpluses," or to enrollment in the Red Army, could engage in passive resistance or take to the countryside as guerillas, but the so-called "Green" movement was limited to certain areas and had only an indirect impact on the policy of the self-styled "proletarian dictatorship."
5) Economically, the immediate (and arguably also long-term) effects of the upheaval were retrograde. The few additional parcels of land (one half-*desiatina*, or about one-fifth of an acre, per head) merely spread existing misery more widely. Agricultural production declined (although not only for this reason) and the peasants became more self-sufficient and inward-looking than before. The civil war accentuated the schism between town and country that had been growing since 1914, and which was to confront the Soviet government with its most serious domestic problem. Lenin's provisional answer to it was the New Economic Policy (1921). Stalin's, eight years later, was forced collectivization. This, however, led to a new catastrophe from which the USSR has yet to recover—morally, if perhaps no longer economically.

II

From this bald summary it will be apparent that historians loyal to the Soviet regime—and from the 1920s they alone have been allowed a voice—were bound to find the record embarrassing. Marxist-Leninist theory, at best a clumsy tool for the explication of historical phenomena, was likely to prove an actual impediment to understanding of a matter so crucial to the Bolshevik's self-image. Yet the problem could not simply be sidestepped. On the contrary, a picture had to be painted which would gild historical reality without becoming implausible. One could of course take Lenin's writings as a guide, but unfortunately his statements were often contradictory, and (since they) could not be examined in their historical context) various interpretations of them were possible. This did not matter too much so long as a certain variety of scholarly opinion was still tolerated and even non-Marxists permitted to express their views. After 1929, when Stalin established a full-blown totalitarian regime, the dissenters could simply be suppressed. But in the last 30 years, when the party has sought to revitalize the historical profession without jeopardizing political controls, the lack of an authoritative consensus on this issue has troubled the ideological watchdogs. After all, the agrarian revolution cannot be separated from the Bolshevik conquest of power, a sacramental topic on which an obligatory "line" has long since been established. It also raises questions about the merits of the "soft" policies towards the peasantry pursued under the NEP by Bukharin, who has yet to be rehabilitated—

and by implication the wisdom of Stalinist and post-Stalinist agrarian measures. Any contestation in this field cannot but strike a sensitive nerve in official quarters.

In the early 1920s, when M. N. Pokrovskii and his followers spoke in the party's name, history as a discipline was ideologically suspect: it was taught and studied, if at all, as a branch of political sociology. Yet the lessons of the Russian revolution had to be brought home to the masses, at home and abroad. To this end a number of academic institutions were set up under Pokrovskii's aegis which published documentary materials, notably excerpts from the militia records of 1917,[3] and monographs which may still be consulted with profit today.[4] These writers' approach, needless to say, was highly partisan. The agrarian movement of 1917–18 was studied far less for its own sake than for its topical relevance to Comintern policy abroad or to the party's current concerns with the countryside under NEP. It was viewed not as an exceptional phenomenon but as a climactic point in a long chain of events reaching back to the 1861 peasant reform and forward to the future of collectivized agriculture. In this way it could be fitted into the appropriate ideological slot as a *"bourgeois* democratic" development, occurring parallel to the "proletarian" revolution in the towns, which had swept away the relics of "feudal" landlordism and so prepared the ground for a further advance. No one claimed that the agrarian upheaval as such had been socialist, although those elements in the village which had collaborated with the Bolsheviks, for instance by establishing committees of poor peasants (*kombedy*) or collective farms, were thought to deserve such a label. Those aspects of the peasants' behavior which Marxists found objectionable, such as burning down manor-houses on advanced estates, or refusing to part with surplus grain, were automatically ascribed to influence by the *bourgeois* class enemy. In accordance with Lenin's views the peasants were seen as divided into three distinct groups of *kulaki, seredniaki* and *bedniaki*. Despite all the energy expended it was far from clear how these supposedly antagonistic classes were to be distinguished or how they were interrelated, either during the revolution or since. In fact the term *kulak* soon became a pejorative epithet affixed to any villager deemed insufficiently obedient to the country's new rulers.

One may add that this view was influenced not only by the writers' political convictions as Marxists but also by their social status. They were intellectuals of urban background, and to nearly all educated Russians the city was an embodiment

---

3 K. G. Kotel'nikov and V. L. Meller, *Krest'ianskoe dvizhenie v 1917 g.* (Moscow, 1927). Although useful, these records suffer from serious defects as source material which not all historians who have utilized them have sufficiently heeded. On this point see S. G. Pushkarev, in his edition of S. P. Mel'gunov, *The Bolshevik Seizure of Power*, trans. J. S. Beaver (Santa Barbara, Calif., 1972), 198–204.

4 For example, the statistical data were analyzed by B. N. Knipovich, A. I. Khriashcheva, N. P. Oganovskii, V. Kachinskii and others. Interpretive studies were provided by S. M. Dubrovskii, *Ocherki russkoi revoliutsii*, fasc. I. *Sel'skoe khoziaistvo* (Moscow, 1922; 2nd ed. 1923); G. S. Gordeev, *Sel'skoe khoziaistvo v voine i revoliutsii* (Moscow, 1925); A. V. Shestakov, *Ocherki po sel'skomu khoziaistvu i krest'ianskomu dvizheniiu v gody voiny i pered Oktiabrem 1917 g.* (Leningrad, 1927); while V. P. Miliutin edited a four-volume compilation entitled *Agrarnaia revoliutsiia* (Moscow, 1928).

of Progress. It would have seemed to them obscurantist to have described the agrarian movement as it appeared to the "dark" peasant masses themselves,[5] who were conceived of as recipients of impulses generated outside the rural milieu.

For all this the degree of distortion involved was not yet excessive, judged by later standards. For example, no one questioned the key role which World War I had played in catalyzing rural discontent, or denied that soldiers returning to their villages had been a prime stimulus to radicalism. The Left SRs were criticized for errors, but their historical role was mentioned, as was the anarchic and violent character of the expropriations in many regions. In 1920 Iurii Larin, an ex-Menshevik and senior planner, could still write that the chief consequence of the agrarian revolution had been "a social and economic leveling of the rural population," that the additional land had made little practical difference, and that forced requisitioning had led "to a whole number of insurrections among a certain part of the peasantry in all parts of Soviet Russia, among those who had previously welcomed the proletariat's victory."[6] He did not blame these revolts on *kulaki* and quite reasonably treated the peasants as a more or less homogeneous social group.

In this view he was on common ground with the Populists, or more correctly Neo-Populists, whose expertise on agrarian matters made them valued collaborators in the People's Commissariat of Agriculture and other key institutions under NEP. These writers had to be careful in expressing themselves, but they could put forward the claim that the agrarian revolution had justified the theories which they had developed in 1917 in controversy with the Marxists. They argued that peasant smallholding should not be categorized as *petit bourgeois* or "capitalistic" but that it had its own structure and dynamic.[7] It was in these difficult years that A. V. Chaianov, the most original of these thinkers, perfected his concept of the family farm as an enterprise which sought, not to maximize profits, but to maintain a balance between the number of "eaters" and "workers" in the household. Despite the awkward policy implications of this theory, Chaianov could still publish legally in Moscow as late as 1927.[8]

---

5 In 1929 I. V. Igritskii compiled a collection of interviews with peasant survivors of the revolution (*1917 g. v derevne. Vospominaniia krest'ian*, ed. Ia. A. Iakovleva, Moscow), in which the interpellees expressed strong anti-*kulak* sentiments, in conformity with current party policy. In 1960 Dubrovskii revealed that only 50 out of 431 interviews were printed in this volume and the the questions were "angled": "K voprosu ob urovne razvitiia kapitalizma v sel'skom khoziaistve Rossii. . . ," *Osobennosti agrarnogo stroia Rossii v period imperializma. Materialy sessii Nauchnogo soveta po probleme "Istoricheskie predposylki Velikoi Oktiabr'skoi sotsialisticheskoi revoliutsii," mai 1960 g.* (Moscow, 1962), 15.

6 I. [=Iu.] Larin and L. Kritsman, *Wirtschaftsleben und wirtschaftlicher Aufbau in Sowjet-Russland, 1917–1920* (Berlin, 1921), 13–34. This report was compiled for a foreign audience, but Larin expressed similar views in the Russian press.

7 J. R. Millar, "A Reformulation of A. V. Chaianov's Theory of the Peasant Economy," *Economic Development and Social Change*, 18 (1970), 219–29. Chaianov's principal works have been translated into English: *The Theory of Peasant Economy*, trans. R. E. F. Smith (South Holland, Ill., 1966); *Peasant Cooperation: Basic Concepts and Organizational Forms*, trans. I. Guelfat (London, 1973).

8 K. N. Tarnovskii, "Problemy agrarnoi istorii Rossii perioda imperializma v sovetskoi isto-

The Neo-Populists could be faulted for cavalier handling of statistical evidence, for *a priori* reasoning, and for paying insufficient heed to the changes that were occurring in agriculture under NEP. Their ideas were based on observation of subsistence farming in backward areas, and they overlooked the resurgence of the market economy and the growing power of the single-party state. (In the former error they were following an old tradition on the Russian Left; in the latter they had the company of many western socialists and liberals.) These weaknesses gave the Marxists an opportunity they were quick to exploit, both intellectually and politically. Sympathy for Neo-Populism was not uncommon among rural cadres, who naturally took a more flexible line than their superiors in Moscow. The threat of ideological infiltration was regarded seriously. Some Neo-Populist writers were won over to Marxism. Chaianov was pressed into a partial recantation of his views in 1928, but was arrested a year or so afterwards.[9]

Meanwhile a more rigid treatment of agrarian history was being demanded of the Marxist historians, who by now formed a recognizable school led by Pokrovskii's young protégé S. M. Dubrovskii.[10] The chief organ of the Marxist *agrarniki* was the journal *Na agrarnom fronte*, founded in 1922, whose very title betokened its combative spirit. In 1927, in time for the decennial revolutionary celebrations, Dubrovskii wrote the first monograph on the agrarian disturbances of 1917; it was later translated into German.[11] The pressures of the "great turn" were evident from the title of an article he wrote in 1931, "The Struggle for the Peasantry and its Leadership by the Bolsheviks." This contained in capsule form one of the major propositions of the 1930s and 1940s, namely that the agrarian movement had really been "Leninist" from the start, in much the same way as disaffected industrial workers had (purportedly, but less contentiously) looked to the Bolsheviks for guidance. In this perspective the 16 million votes cast, mainly by peasants, for the SRs in 1917 could be reduced to the dimensions of an unfortunate historical accident.

The impact of Stalinism was as baneful upon the writing of agrarian history as it was in other fields of intellectual life. In the words of a later Soviet critic, K. N. Tarnovskii, it led "to stagnation and in some respects actually to a return to views and concepts which had already been superseded."[12] One cannot, however, agree

riografii, 1917—nachalo 1930–kh gg.," *Istoricheskie zapiski*, 78 (1965), 54. The sequel to this article, covering the 1940s and early 1950s (ibid., 83 (1969), 196–221), is predictably much less informative.

9 E. H. Carr and R. W. Davies, *Foundations of a Planned Economy, 1926–1929*, vol. I (*A History of Soviet Russia*) (London, 1969), 21 n. For his later fate see A. I. Solzhenitsyn, *The Gulag Archipelago, 1918–1956. An Experiment in Literary Investigation*, vol. 1 (New York, 1973), 50 n.

10 Other prominent members of the group were A. V. Shestakov and O. N. Chaadaeva. For a full account see Tarnovskii's first article (fn. 8) and his contribution to *Ocherki istorii istoricheskoi nauki v SSSR*, vol. 4 (Moscow, 1966), 381–98.

11 S. M. Dubrovskii, *Krest'ianstvo v 1917 g.* (Moscow, 1927); *Die Bauernbewegung in Russland im Jahre 1917* (Berlin, 1928).

12 Tarnovskii, in *Ocherki* (fn. 10), 394.

with Tarnovskii's appreciation of the phenomenon. Stalin, he avers, put forward an erroneous and un-Leninist evaluation of the stage of capitalist development which Russia had reached in 1917; he saw the revolution as emancipating Russia from the yoke of foreign capital (that is, placed it in an antiimperialist context) rather than arising inexorably out of the development of native class antagonisms. However this may be, on agrarian matters in 1917 Stalin's views seem to have been unexceptionally orthodox and unoriginal: the peasant revolt was said to have completed the *bourgeois-democratic* revolution and taken a step forward to socialism.[13] To be sure, a non-Marxist reader of the celebrated *Short Course* might question his logic, for having stated that on the eve of October the middle peasantry "whole-heartedly swing over to the revolution and join forces with the poor peasantry" he goes on to describe them as still vacillating between rich and poor in 1918–19;[14] but such inconsistencies are unavoidable when history is pressed into a dogmatic mould, and almost any Marxist-Leninist writer could be faulted for them.

Where Stalin and the Stalinists sinned was not in preaching false doctrine but in presenting complete fabrications as commonplace truths and obliging the populace to repeat them *ad nauseam*, like mindless robots—in short, for creating an intellectual climate in which genuine scholarly inquiry became impossible and heresy-hunting was substituted for civilized discourse. Like other historians, the *agrarniki* were driven to take account of the "political equivalent"[15] of whatever they wrote. They had to emphasize the allegedly socialist features of the agrarian revolution of 1917–18 lest, by failing to do so, they lay themselves open to suspicion of *bourgeois* sympathies. It was not that Stalin himself had overstressed the role of the collective farms in this period: if anything, the reverse was the case.[16] It was rather that the agrarian historians responded to the titanic collectivization struggle by seeking its logical antecedents in the past, so that they could rationalize and propagandize it as a supposedly "law-governed" (*zakonomernyi*) phenomenon.

Thus at a time when millions of villagers were, in Solzhenitsyn's words, "being rounded up with their families, stripped of their possessions, and driven naked into the tundra and the taiga,"[17] they maintained that Lenin's benign concept of unbreakable alliance (*smychka*) between workers and peasants was still valid—and projected it backwards into the past, claiming that it had existed right from the beginning of 1917. For even one hint at some past imperfection was to suggest that one harbored secret sympathies for it. Ideological rectitude demanded that the "popular masses" be shown as at all times militantly revolutionary and wedded to their party as it struggled to expose its covert foes—and that the historical evidence be molded accordingly.

---

13 J. V. Stalin, *Problems of Leninism* (New York, 1946) 309.

14 *History of the Communist Party of the Soviet Union (Bolsheviks). Short Course* (Toronto, 1939), 213, 234.

15 K. Shteppa, *Russian Historians and the Soviet State* (New Brunswick, N. J., 1963), 47.

16 They are not even mentioned in the relevant chapter of the *Short Course*. I. Laptev, *Sovet-skoe krest'ianstvo* (Moscow, 1939), 46, wrote that they were "minimal in number."

17 Solzhenitsyn, *Gulag Archipelago*, 56.

This approach to history had its roots in the Leninist heritage of intellectual intransigence, although it went beyond it. It engendered a whole complex of fallacies, or fictions, that even today have not been wholly discredited: for example, that the *kulaki* were invariably both reactionary and powerful; that every Russian village had been polarized on class lines; that the peasant masses had always acted in a defensive, and never in an aggressive, spirit; that the entire upheaval had not been spontaneous and chaotic, as customarily supposed, but had been consciously directed and controlled by "the party of Lenin and Stalin"; and that this party had been infallible, for any errors had been the fault of subordinates (or traitors) and had been quickly set right before harm could ensue.

In this way the mythmakers could construct an idealized image of the past to legitimate the dictator's power. In public utterances absolute conformity to the official scheme was insisted upon. Creative thought and discussion all but ceased; the flow of documentary publications dried up.[18] A popular history of 1939 (no longer referred to today) was studded with imprecations against "Judas Trotskii" and the "Trotskyite-Bukharinite traitors" who had allegedly sought to subvert Bolshevik agrarian policy as early as April 1917.[19] During this intellectual ice age most agrarian historians had to rest content with work on collective textbooks, such as the *History of the Civil War in the USSR* or A. A. Arutunian and B. L. Markus's *Development of the Soviet Economy* (1940), which were designed as authoritative embodiments of the official truths. Historians were permitted to illustrate these truths by adducing new material, for instance with regard to developments in specific regions, although here too they had to guard against excessive emphasis on local "particularities" which might cast doubt on the veracity of established general laws. Partly for this reason, it seems, a number of dissertations on agrarian history written in the 1940s and early 1950s were never published.[20]

III

A new era dawned in Soviet agrarian historiography, as in so much else, with the "de-Stalinization" that followed the marshal's death in March, 1953. It was not long before the Soviet academics began to explore the bounds of their new freedom—only to discover that they were closely circumscribed. In the Khrushchev era the function of historical research continued to be viewed in a narrowly instrumental manner, as a means of justifying the party's current policies. No change occurred in basic principles; nevertheless, once the floodgates had been opened for information to flow more freely it was no longer possible to maintain a single "line" on contentious issues or to prevent the emergence of competing schools of thought. Up to a point this

---

18 Such volumes were confined to "village poor" committees, e.g. *Komitety bednoty*, 2 vols. (Moscow, 1933).

19 Laptev, *Sovetskoe krestianstvo*, 28, 34.

20 M. L. Bogdenko, "Nekotorye voprosy istoriografii sovkhoznogo stroitel'stva v SSSR," *Problemy agrarnoi istorii Sovetskogo obshchestva. Materialy nauchnoi konferentsii 9–12 iiunia 1969 g.* (Moscow, 1971), 266.

development was welcomed by the ideological authorities, who wanted scholarly life to revive, if only because intellectual stagnation harmed the economy and the USSR's standing abroad. Historical investigators were now encouraged to treat matters in greater depth, on the basis of archive material, and to exchange views in journal articles or at conferences.

In the field of agrarian history the result has been an enormous expansion in the quality of the literature, as well as a considerable improvement in its quality. We now have a two-volume monograph by P. N. Pershin[21] on the antecedents, course and consequences of the 1917–18 rural revolution. It is based upon a mass of unpublished sources, many of them in provincial archives. (These sources are identified and conscientiously listed in an appendix—a rare virtue in Soviet scholarship.) As a young man the author served as an official in the Stolypin land administration, and in the early 1920s he came out as an advocate of individual smallholding,[22] but his present views on the matter could scarcely be more orthodox; characteristically he makes no mention of these youthful peccadilloes. Pershin's work deserves to be as well known in the West as that of his more familiar colleague, A. M. Anfimov, who has, among other things, written a valuable study of the peasantry during World War I[23] and edited some documents on agrarian history under the Provisional Government.[24]

The early history of the state farms, formerly the subject of much ideological mystification, has been expertly surveyed by I. E. Zelenin,[25] who has also pioneered Soviet investigations into Stalin's collectivization drive. There are now a fair number of regional studies of the agrarian revolution, notably on the Ukraine, White Russia, the Petrograd area and the Volga provinces;[26] as yet there is no equivalent for the Central Agricultural region, which was then the SRs' principal stronghold, nor for

21 *Agrarnaia revoliutsiia v Rossii: istoriko-ekonomicheskoe issledovanie* (Moscow, 1966); the work had previously appeared in Ukrainian. More limited in scope is N. A. Kravchuk, *Massovoe krest'ianskoe dvizhenie v Rossii nakanune Oktiabria, mart—oktiabr' 1917 g.* (Moscow, 1971).

22 P. N. Pershin, "Formy zemlepol'zovaniia," *O zemle* (Moscow, 1921–22); *Uchastkovoe zemlepol'zovanie v Rossii. Khutora i otruba* . . . (Moscow, 1922). See above, 418–19.

23 A. M. Anfimov, *Rossiiskaia derevnia vo vremia Pervoi mirovoi voiny, 1914–fevral' 1917 g.* (Moscow, 1962).

24 *Ekonomicheskoe polozhenie Rossii nakanune Velikoi Oktiabr'skoi sotsialisticheskoi revoliutsii. Dokumenty i materialy*, vol. 3 (Leningrad, 1967).

25 I. E. Zelenin, *Sovkhozy v pervoe desiatiletie Sovetskoi vlasti, 1917–1927* (Moscow, 1972); this work supersedes V. N. Lavrent'ev, *Stroitel'stvo sovkhozov v pervye gody Sovetskoi vlasti, 1917–1920* (Moscow, 1957).

26 M. A. Rubach, *Ocherki po istorii revoliutsionnogo preobrazovaniia agrarnykh otnoshenii na Ukraine v period provedeniia Oktiabr'skoi revoliutsii* (Kiev, 1957); B. M. Fikh, *Agrarnaia revoliutsiia v Belorussii* (Minsk, 1966); V. M. Gubareva, *Razvertyvanie sotsialisticheskoi revoliutsii v derevne v 1918 g. Po materialam Petrogradskoi gubernii* (Moscow, 1957); N. Sautin, *Velikii Oktiabr' v derevne na severo-zapade Rossii, oktiabr' 1917–1918 gg.* (Leningrad, 1959); A. L. Litvin, *Krest'ianstvo Srednego Povolzh'ia v gody grazhdanskoi voiny* (Kazan', 1972); E. I. Medvedev, *Krest'ianstvo Srednego Povolzh'ia v Oktiabr'skoi revoliutsii* (Kuibyshev, 1970).

the area around Moscow. In general regional disparities are touched on very gingerly lest they discredit the class approach which ideology requires.

The more political questions are involved, the less valuable is the recent literature. Peasant organizations, once almost wholly neglected, are now the subject of several works which, however, suffer from a doctrinaire tendency to equate these bodies with their urban soviet counterparts.[27] Least successful of such studies are those on the village poor committees, for no one can admit the harm these did to relations between town and country. Socialist-Revolutionaries of various hues are now once again thought worthy of mention, but writers on this theme are under compulsion to stress the Populists' alleged *bourgeois* leanings and to minimize their popular support.[28] As for Bolshevik agrarian policy, this suffers most of all from dogmatic treatment. E. A. Lutskii, a senior scholar who in 1956 made so bold as to imply that the egalitarian land redistribution had been inherently socialist, and that this was why Lenin had endorsed it,[29] was promptly jumped upon by several critics,[30] who charged him with blurring the differences between Bolshevism and Populism. Lutskii has, however, published (usually in less conspicuous places) some useful detailed studies of party policy.

Several hundred Soviet scholars are today engaged in research on agrarian history. They do not have a journal of their own, since this would evidently be regarded as "particularism" and a threat to ideological controls. The work of these *agrarniki* is coordinated by various topical scientific councils (*nauchnye sovety*) in the Institute of USSR History (formerly Institute of History) in the Academy of Sciences. Two that are of immediate concern to us here are the councils on Socialist and Communist Construction in the USSR and on the Prerequisites of the Great October Socialist Revolution. Shortly after the Twenty-first party Congress (1959), which called for a reinvigoration of ideological work,[31] three all-Union historical conferences were held. At the first of these, in March, 1960, papers were read on developments in each of the national republics during the Soviet period. Curiously, the volume containing these reports, published in 1962,[32] includes a contribution on the history of the working class but nothing on the peasantry; it later emerged that such a report had indeed been given (by V. P. Danilov), and that it had been printed separately, without identification

27 O. I. Moiseeva, *Sovety krest'ianskikh deputatov v 1917 g.* (Moscow, 1967); V. I. Kostrikin, *Zemel'nye komitety v 1917 g.* (Moscow, 1975).

28 K. V. Gusev and Kh. A. Eritsian, *Ot soglashatel'stva k kontr-revoliutsii. Ocherk istorii politicheskogo bankrotstva i gibeli partii Sotsialistov-Revoliutsionerov* (Moscow, 1968); P. I. Soboleva, *Oktiabr'skaia revoliutsiia i krakh sotsial-soglashatelei* (Moscow, 1968); L. M. Spirin, *Klassy i partii v grazhdanskoi voine v Rossii, 1917–1920 gg.* (Moscow, 1968).

29 *Voprosy istorii* (1956), no. 9, 59–70.

30 Ibid. (1957), no. 3, 113–20; no. 4, 43–58.

31 "O zadachakh partiinoi propagandy v sovremennykh usloviiakh. Postanovlenie TsK KPSS," *Kommunist* (1960), no. 1, 10–24.

32 *Istoriografiia sotsialisticheskogo i kommunisticheskogo stroitel'stva v SSSR. Sbornik statei po materialam sessii Nauchnogo soveta* (Moscow, 1962).

of its nature, in the journal *Voprosy istorii*.[33] This was presumably connected with the decision taken at the conference, which was likewise not revealed at the time, to hold a meeting wholly devoted to Soviet agrarian history.[34] Meanwhile, as a preliminary to this, a conference had been held in May, 1960 on "Particularities of the Agrarian Order in the Imperialist Epoch." All this represented something of a breakthrough for the hard-pressed *agrarniki*, who made the most of their new opportunities.

At the May, 1960, conference the *rapporteur* was none other than Dubrovskii, who had now reemerged after some years in the shadows. Initiating the discussion, V. K. Iatsunskii observed that the participants were resuming a debate which Stalin had arbitrarily truncated. Dubrovskii came under fire for being insufficiently factual and for neglecting regional differences. Danilov, without going so far as Lutskii had done a few years earlier, stressed the progressive role of the 1917–18 land redistribution and deplored its neglect by Soviet historians. Anfimov attempted a more sophisticated definition of the *kulak*; and another scholar, K. N. Tarnovskii, suggested that it was un-Marxist to approach social differentiation in the village statically: "*kulak* exploitation" had been most characteristic of the *early* phases of capitalism, but with time these better-off peasants had actually done some good, e.g. by helping to absorb surplus rural manpower.[35]

If the organizers had hoped that these exchanges would lead to uniformity of views on the extent of capitalist development in the prerevolutionary Russian village, they must have been disappointed, for what emerged was a verdict worthy of the Delphic oracle: it should indeed not be overestimated (witness the survival of crop-sharing and similar "feudal" practises), but on the other hand it should not be minimized either (*vide* the advanced latifundia of the Ukraine). In brief, no agreed criteria existed for resolving this somewhat metaphysical question.

The third conference met almost a year later, in April, 1961. Its theme was the history of the peasantry in the Soviet period. No less than 96 scholars offered to read papers, and 27 of them were invited to do so.[36] Of six papers on the precollectivization era published in the official proceedings no less than four dealt with developments in the eastern regions of the USSR—perhaps a sop to the critics. The other two speakers were Iu. A. Poliakov, who provided a useful analysis of the social changes that resulted from the agrarian revolution, and Danilov, who argued that capitalist and socialist elements were closely intertwined in the village under NEP. Since both these *rapporteurs* adopted a flexible "reformist" stance the discussion was less acrimonious

33 *Voprosy istorii* (1960), no. 8, 34–64; attribution from the work cited in fn. 20, 219.

34 *Istoriia Sovetskogo krest'ianstva i kolkhoznogo stroitel'stva v SSSR. Materialy nauchnoi sessii sostoiavsheisia 18–21 aprelia 1961 g. v Moskve* (Moscow, 1963), 4.

35 *Osobennosti* (see fn. 5), 268–320. Tarnovskii later developed his arguments in *Voprosy istorii kapitalisticheskoi Rossii. Problema mnogoukladnosti* (Sverdlovsk, 1972), a volume which was later criticized and withdrawn; cf. also his article in *Problemy sotsial'no-ekonomicheskoi Istorii Rossii. Sbornik statei k 85-letiiu so dnia rozhdeniia akademika N. M. Druzhinina* (Moscow, 1971), 265–9.

36 *Istoriografiia* (see n. 32), 4–5.

than at the earlier meeting. Most of the criticism came from conservatives who reiterated the familiar Manichean view. One participant went so far as to deny that the *kulaki* of the 1920s might properly be referred to as peasants, rather than *bourgeois*; another questioned Danilov's use of the term "precollectivization village" on the grounds that Lenin had not used it, but received a devastating reply (Lenin had used any number of descriptive adjectives).[37] All this scholastic logic-chopping over the vexed question of "periodization" achieved little, for official quarters now favored the moderate reformism espoused by the *rapporteurs*.

But for how long would this mood continue? The publication of these proceedings coincided with that of Solzhenitsyn's *One Day in the Life of Ivan Denisovich*, which first revealed to ordinary Soviet citizens the ultimate fate of so many millions of former peasant proprietors. It was a high-water mark in the country's intellectual life. To some members of the political establishment it seemed that the "ideological front" was in a dangerous state of flux. The debate on collectivization in particular had portentous implications for contemporary agricultural policy. Khrushchev's fall from power would soon give the conservatives an opportunity to tighten the vice.

During the past decade or so three tendencies may be observed among agrarian historians on the problems under consideration here.[38] In the center are those whom one might call "mainstream revisionists": men who seek a plausible, well-founded scholarly consensus on all disputed questions except those too delicate to broach, which they prefer to leave in their present obscurity. To their left are the "radicals" who place respect for objective fact higher than mere self-preservation. Finally there are the neo-Stalinists, who would like to reestablish strict orthodoxy.

Broadly speaking, the first group includes most of those whom we have so far considered (Dubrovskii and Pershin, both now deceased, Lutskii, Danilov, Zelenin). They are mainly senior men working in the major centers, whereas those in the second group are their juniors in age and have been associated with provincial institutions, notably in the Urals, Siberia, or one of the national republics, although they may have a Moscow "patron."

Evidence to support this assertion may be found in the proceedings of the follow-up conference to that of April, 1961, held under the same official auspices in June, 1969—not long after the invasion of Czechoslovakia. Of the 60 reports and communications 23 dealt with the early period and 10 with agrarian historiography; of these 12 and 7 respectively were published.[39] Lutskii, Zelenin and Danilov were among the *rapporteurs*. For the conservatives I. M. Volkov ostentatiously praised

---

37 Ibid., 147, 144.

38 This categorization would not be pressed too far in a "kremlinological" sense. In Soviet politics it is rare for any individual to become wholly identified with any consistent intellectual stance, as distinct from expressing shifting nuances of view. We have no more reason to assume the existence of discrete factions among historians than among Central Committee members. This need not rule out linkages based on personal friendship, generational and occupational affinity, career patterns etc., but these cannot be investigated here.

39 *Problemy* (see fn. 20), 3.

the party decision issued after Khrushchev's ouster, while N. Ia. Gushchin called for greater "party-mindedness" and militancy in combating *bourgeois* ideology.[40] Both these men were high academic officials. For the radicals V. I. Pogudin, a publishing-house operative, argued that Lenin had always distinguished *kulaki* from bourgeois and that he had advocated the use of persuasion rather than outright expropriation, unless they physically resisted Soviet power (an interesting argument which no one took up), while G. F. Dakhshleiger, from Kazakhstan, put in a plea for toleration of dissenting opinions: "we should not rely on propositions that have been canonized in scholarship but do not correspond to historical truth. . . . No viewpoint deserves to be 'eliminated'."[41]

Adherents of the latter tendency base their stand on some remarks by Lenin towards the end of his career to the effect that in pre- (and post-)revolutionary Russia several socioeconomic structures coexisted, ranging from highly developed industries at one extreme to primitive peasant family farms at the other. The Russian term for this diversity is *mnogoukladnost'* or multiformity. But what is an *uklad*? Evidently something less than a formation (*formatsiia*), like capitalism or feudalism, but just how to define it was far from clear. The radicals could seize on this doctrinal lacuna and without much difficulty show that in old Russia the more primitive *uklady* had predominated. This implied that the peasantry were far from ripe for socialist experiments; that October was as much the product of fortuitous circumstance as the inevitable outcome of inherent class contradictions; and that the Bolsheviks had been pushed into exercising sole power by mass pressure from below and the failings of the other left-wing parties. While this line of reasoning may not convince all non-Marxists, it is at least incomparably more sophisticated, and closer to historical reality, than the conservative version, according to which everything happened as it had to happen—and turned out for the best. It represents the beginning of an authentic Marxist revision of Russia's recent historical experience, including Stalinism (which these critics would probably term an unfortunate lapse into "military feudal despotism").

So far as the agrarian revolution is concerned, the radicals make four fundamental innovations. (*i*) They view it as an essentially spontaneous movement which owed little to any external stimuli, and in so far as it did so was more influenced by the SRs than by the Bolsheviks, at least until 1918. The Left SRs, whom mainstream revisionists handle with extreme caution, are seen sympathetically, though not uncritically. (*ii*) They regard the peasants as an autonomous force, allied to the workers but having different aims, the soldiers often forming a bridge between them. (*iii*) They consider that class differentiation was of slight importance before the spring of 1918, and that when it did develop it was in large measure a product of external intervention by the food requisitioning squads, a tragic necessity which led to many avoidable excesses. (*iv*) In lieu of the horizontal differences so strongly emphasized in the orthodox interpretation they stress those of a vertical character, i.e. regional particularities.

---

40 Ibid., 320–1, 330–2.

41 Ibid., 323–4, 326.

The specific socioeconomic profile of each area shaped the pattern of the agrarian movement, and such differences must be taken into account if the final picture is to be historically accurate and not merely schematic.

These critics are not dissenters: they do not express, at least in public, that moral concern which is the hallmark of the dissident movement. Only subtle nuances distinguish them from the mainstream revisionists. But this does not mean that their influence is negligible. In Russian intellectual history such "critics from within" have usually been more effective than the alienated and rebellious outsiders. This is probably why the conservatives have moved quickly to suppress them.

The latter faction is strongest among the party and military historians. They, and the ideological controllers, are responsible for staging at least three "book trials" since 1971, at which the editors of and contributors to certain volumes of essays have been publicly condemned.[42] The concept of multiformity has been sharply attacked and at least one prominent historian has lost his job. The main charge against the errant *agrarniki* is that they minimize class differentiation. To cite one recent writer:

> In the early 1970s several historians aroused serious objections from the scholarly community by . . . incorrectly interpreting a number of questions regarding the socialist revolution, in particular the proletariat's allies during the struggle for power. V. V. Adamov, P. V. Volobuev, K. D. Petraev, K. N. Tarnovskii *et al.* failed to analyze the concrete historical material [*sic!*] and, contradicting Lenin and party decisions, maintained that the proletariat had the support of the entire peasantry.[43]

The old stereotypes are being refurbished, and S. P. Trapeznikov, a leader of the conservative trend recently elevated to high office, has even developed a new one: that of the "three revolutions." Its purpose is to underline the logical continuity of all twentieth-century Russian history, not least in the agrarian field. His two-volume work of 1967, *Leninism and the Agrarian-Peasant Question*, an ultradogmatic study which takes as its starting point not historical evidence but Leninist teaching, appeared in a second edition in 1974.[44] In a review, couched in reverential tones, V. M. Selunskaia, one of the mainstream revisionists, remarks that Trapeznikov exaggerates the role of large-scale landowning before 1917 and the peasants' antagonism toward those who left the commune.[45] Thus the battle is not yet over. Whether the conservatives will succeed in imposing their line depends on political factors that cannot be discussed here.

---

42 For further development of this theme see above, 406, 413–14.

43 T. V. Osipova, *Klassovaia bor'ba v derevne v period podgotovki i provedeniia Oktiabr'skoi revoliutsii* (Moscow, 1974), 21. Cf. I. D. Koval'chenko, "Izuchenie istorii Rossii perioda kapitalizma (XIX–nachalo XX v.)," *Razvitie Sovetskoi istoricheskoi nauki, 1970–74* (Moscow, 1975), 47, for another criticism of Tarnovskii.

44 [*Leninism i agrarno-krest'ianskii vopros*, 2 vols. (Moscow, 1967). A third edition appeared in 1983.]

45 *Voprosy istorii* (1976), no. 3, 143. Selunskaia is the author of *Rabochii klass i Oktiabr' v derevne* (Moscow, 1968).

To end on a positive note, there is no doubt that, despite all their ideological limitations, the labors of Soviet agrarian historians in recent years have vastly increased our knowledge of Russia's rural revolution and related topics. One may hope that non-Marxist students will respond to the challenge which their interpretations present.

1977

Bibliography

* (included in this volume)

A. Books

1. *The Rise of Social Democracy in Russia*. Oxford: Clarendon Press, 1963. 305 pp.
2. *The Russian Revolution: a Study in Mass Mobilization*. London: Weidenfeld & Nicolson, 1976; New York: Norton, 1977. 614 pp.
3. *Soldiers of the Tsar: Army and Society in Russia, 1462–1874*. Oxford: Clarendon Press, 1985. 418 pp.
4. *Moscow's Problems of History: a Select Critical Bibliography of the Soviet Journal "Voprosy istorii," 1956–85*, Ottawa: Carleton University, 1986. 209 pp. (Soviet & East European Institute, Bibliography no. 5.)
5. (edited) *Contemporary History in the Soviet Mirror*. London: Allen & Unwin, 1964. 331 pp. (Includes Introduction, 9–18 and "Western Post-war History in the Soviet Mirror," 92–109).
6. (edited) *The Debate on Soviet Power: Minutes of the All-Russian Central Executive Committee of Soviets, Second Convocation, October 1917–January 1918*. Oxford: Clarendon Press, 1979. 465 pp. (Includes Introduction, 1–36 and Notes, 268–421.)

B. Articles

*7. "Russian Social Democracy and the First State Duma." *Slavonic & East European Review*, 34 (1955), 180–99.
*8. "Bandits and the Law in Muscovy," ibid., 35 (1956), 201–22.
*9. "The Decline of the Zemsky Sobor," ibid., 36 (1957), 100–22. Also in *Readings in Russian History*, ed. S. Harcave, New York: Crowell, vol. I, 1962, 195–211.
10. "Recent Soviet Historiography," *Survey* (London), 1957.
11. "Soviet Policy in Eastern Europe," in: *The Absent Countries of Europe*, Berne-Strasbourg: Collège de l'Europe Libre, 1957, 55–73.
12. "Russia, 1861–1907," in: *New Cambridge Modern History*, vol. 11, 1960; 2nd ed. 1975, 352–82.
*13. "The Regime of Filaret, 1619–1633," *SEER*, 38 (1960), 334–60.
14. "Soviet Foreign Policy," *Survey*, 40 (1962), 11–23.
15. "Freedom of Expression," in: *Personal Freedom in the Marxist-Leninist Countries. Conference Report*, London: Amnesty, 1962, 8–20.
16. "The Sickle under the Hammer," *Soviet Studies*, 16 (1964), 63–68.
17. "The Context of Early Soviet Planning: a Comment," ibid., 16 (1965), 467–70.
18. "The Growth of Russia," in: C. M. MacInnes (ed.), *History: Man's March through Time*, London: 1965, 142–7.
19. "Moscow and Belgrade: a Calculating Courtship," *Orbis* (Philadelphia), 40 (1966), 754–81.
*20. "Russia 1917: the Tyranny of Paris over Petrograd," *Soviet Studies*, 20 (1968), 22–35.

21. Postscript (and editing) to: R. H. Bruce Lockhart, *The Two Revolutions*, 2nd ed., London: Background Books; Chester Springs, PA: Dufour, 1968, 123–41.
*22. "Lenin as Tactician," in: L. B. Schapiro & Peter Reddaway (eds.), *Lenin: the Man, the Theorist, the Leader: a Reappraisal*, London: Pall Mall; Stanford: Hoover, 1968, 135–58. Reprinted Boulder CO: Westview, 1987.
23. "October in the Provinces," in: R. Pipes (ed.), *Revolutionary Russia*, Cambridge MA: Harvard University Press, 1968, 229–75. Also New York: Anchor, 1969.
24. "The Soviet Union and the Third World," *Survey*, 72 (1969), 19–38.
*25. "The Muscovite Elite and the Emergence of Pluralism," *SEER*, 48 (1970), 201–32.
26. "Russia and the Soviet Union to 1956," in: G. Schöpflin (ed.), *The Soviet Union and Eastern Europe: a Handbook*, London/New York/Washington, 1970, 127–37. New edition (to 1985), Avon: Muller, Blond and White; New York: Facts on File, 1986, 173–87.
27. "Russia, 1613–1645," in: *New Cambridge Modern History*, vol. 4, 1971; 2nd ed., 1979, 602–19.
*28. "Lenin's Letters as a Historical Source," in: B. W. Eissenstat (ed.), *Lenin and Leninism: State, Law and Society*, Lexington MA: Heath, 1971, 245–68.
29. "Andrei Amalrik and 1984," *Russian Review* (Stanford), 30 (1971), 335–45.
30. "Light and Shade in the History of the Early Russian Bureaucracy," *Canadian-American Slavic Studies*, 6 (1972), 1–9.
*31. "The Rehabilitation of M. N. Pokrovskii," in: A. & J. Rabinowitch (ed.), *Revolution and Politics in Russia: Essays in Memory of B. I. Nicolaevsky*, Bloomington IN: Indiana University Press, 1972, 293–313.
*32. "Paul I and the Militarization of Russian Government," *C-ASS*, 7 (1973), 1–14, reprinted in H. Ragsdale (ed.), *Paul I: a Reassessment of his Life and Reign*, Pittsburgh, 1979, 91–103.
33. "The Current Scene in Soviet Historiography," *Survey*, 86 (1973), 3–20.
34. "Programming the Past: Imperial Russian Government and Society under the Scrutiny of Mr. George Yaney," *C-ASS*, 8 (1974), 569–80.
35. "The Bolshevik Revolution: Prototype or Myth?" in: T. T. Hammond (ed.), *The Anatomy of Communist Takeovers*, New Haven: Yale University Press, 1975, 46–60.
36. "Imperial Russia: from Reform to Revolution," in R. Auty & D. Obolensky (eds.), *Cambridge Companion to Russian Studies*, vol. I: *An Introduction to Russian History*, Cambridge: Cambridge University Press, 1976, 196–271.
*37. "Soviet Historians on 'Great October,' " in: S. H. Baron & N. W. Heer (eds.), *Windows on the Russian Past: Essays in Soviet Historiography since Stalin*, Columbus OH: American Association for the Advancement of Slavic Studies, 1977, 139–56.
38. "The Shadow of St. Petersburg," *Queen's Quarterly*, 48 (1977), 259–66.
39. "MERSH: Flawed Giant?", *C-ASS*, 11 (1977), 419–30.
*40. "The Agrarian Revolution of 1917 in Soviet Historiography," *Russian Review*, 36 (1977), 405–23.
*41. "The Secret Chancellery, the Guards and the Dynastic Crisis of 1740–1741," *Forschungen zur osteuropäischen Geschichte*, 25 (1978), 161–93.
42. "L'élitisme militaire, en Russie, à la fin du XVIIIe siècle," *Slovo* (Paris), 3 (1980), 165–76.
*43. "Catherine's Veterans," *SEER*, 59 (1981), 385–96.
*44. "From the Pistol to the Pen: the Military Memoir as a Source on the Social History of Pre-reform Russia," *Cahiers du Monde russe et soviétique*, 21 (1980), 3–4, 295–320.
*45. "The Russian Army's Response to the French Revolution," *Jahrbücher für Geschichte Osteuropas*, 28 (1980), 500–23. Précis in *Proceedings* of the Consortium on Revolutionary Europe, vol. I, Athens GA, 1980, 231–6.
46. "Mutiny in Moscow, 1682: a Contemporary Account," *Canadian Slavonic Papers*, 23

(1981), 410–42.

*47. "Emancipation by the Axe: Peasant Revolts in Russian Thought and Literature," *CMRS*, 23 (1982), 45–61; also in *Peasants in History and Literature*, Canberra: Australian Academy of the Humanities, 1981, 27–52.

*48. "The Military Style of the Romanov Rulers," *War and Society* (Duntroon, Australia), 1 (1983), 61–84.

49. "Net, my slushaem" [We Are Listening], *Kontinent*, 40 (1984), 231–8.

50. Introduction to Marc Raeff, *Russia under the Old Regime*, New York: Columbia University Press, 1984, ix–xix.

51. "The Origins of Russian Militarism," *CMRS*, 26 (1985), 5–19.

*52. "Chernyshevsky and the *Military Miscellany*," in: G. Schramm et al. (eds.), *Felder und Vorfelder russischer Geschichte: Studien zu Ehren von Peter Scheibert*, Freiburg i. Br.: Rombach, 1985, 111–33.

53. "The Case of the Crippled Cadet: Military Justice under Nicholas I," *Canadian Slavonic Papers*, 28 (1986), 37–51.

54. "The Russian Army in the Seven Years War," in: B. Kroener (ed.), *Krieg, Wirtschaft und Gesellschaft im Zeitalter Friedrich des Grossen*, Freiburg i. Br.: Militärgeschichtliches Forschungsamt, [in German, in press].

55. *Soldiering in Tsarist Russia*. 29th Harmon Lecture. 30 pp. Colorado Springs CO: USAF Academy, 1987.

56. "Justice for the Troops: a Comparative Study of Nicholas I's Russia and the France of Louis-Philippe." *CMRS*, 27 (1986), 31–54.

57. "Feeding the Troops: Russian Army Supply Policies during the Seven Years War," *Canadian Slavonic Papers*, 29 (1987), 24–44.

58. "Lenin's Time Budget: the Smolny Period" [proceedings of conference on the Russian Revolution, Hebrew University of Jerusalem, 1988; in press].

59. "The Sungrov Affair, 1831: a Curious Conspiracy," in: E. Mendelsohn & M. S. Shatz (eds.), *Imperial Russia, 1700–1917: Essays in Honor of Marc Raeff*, DeKalb IL: Northern Illinois University Press, 1988.

60. "Social Aspects of the Russian Revolution (1917–1923) in Recent Anglo-American Historiography," [forthcoming in *East European Quarterly*].

C. Varia

"The USSR." *Annual Register of World Events*, London: Longmans, 1954–63 (annually). English-language contributions to: *Bibliographie zur osteuropäischen Geschichte bis 1945*, ed. K. Meyer, Berlin, 1972.

ditto to: *Bibliographie zur osteuropäischen Geschichte bis 1945 (1965–1974)*, ed. C. J. Schmidt, Berlin, 1984. *The Slavonic & East European Review Index, 1932–1969*, London: SSEES, 1970 (principal compiler).

ca. 35 articles for encyclopedias.